The Dream of
Christian Nagasaki

The Dream of
Christian Nagasaki

*World Trade and the Clash
of Cultures, 1560–1640*

REINIER H. HESSELINK

McFarland & Company, Inc., Publishers

Jefferson, North Carolina

LIBRARY OF CONGRESS CATALOGUING-IN-PUBLICATION DATA

Names: Hesselink, R. H., author.
Title: The dream of Christian Nagasaki : world trade and the clash of
cultures, 1560–1640 / Reinier H. Hesselink.
Description: Jefferson, North Carolina : McFarland & Company, Inc.,
Publishers, 2016. | Includes bibliographical references and index.
Identifiers: LCCN 2015041702 | ISBN 9780786499618 (softcover : acid free paper)
Subjects: LCSH: Nagasaki-shi (Japan)—History—16th century. | Nagasaki-shi
(Japan)—History—17th century. | Christians—Japan—Nagasaki-shi—History—
16th century. | Christians—Japan—Nagasaki-shi—History—17th century. |
Nagasaki-shi (Japan)—Ethnic relations.
Classification: LCC DS897.N2957 H47 2016 | DDC 952/.24402—dc23
LC record available at http://lccn.loc.gov/2015041702

BRITISH LIBRARY CATALOGUING DATA ARE AVAILABLE

ISBN 9781476624747 (ebook)

Front/back cover images: *Ohato landing of Christian Nagasaki
with a view of the Jesuit mission at Morisaki*, detail of a pair
of screens depicting Chinese and Portuguese ships, owned by
Kyushu National Museum. Photographed by Shinichi Yamasaki

Printed in the United States of America

*McFarland & Company, Inc., Publishers
Box 611, Jefferson, North Carolina 28640
www.mcfarlandpub.com*

To Tomie and Klaertje

Table of Contents

Part Three: Forging a Yamato Soul (1614–1629)

Acknowledgments

This book has involved countless trips that took me several times around the world. Wherever I went in Asia, America, or Europe, I have encountered genuine kindness, helpfulness, and all kinds of generous support. People have selflessly received me (a total stranger, usually a foreigner, often a poor linguist, frequently an ignoramus, mostly a mediocre conversationalist, and always an awkward socializer) into their houses, their libraries, their archives, and their universities or research facilities.

They have asked me to sit down, listened to me with patience, answered my questions with forbearance, lodged and fed me generously, and finally showed me their treasures, pulled them out of vaults, carried them to my desk, allowed me time to study them, and explained their meaning to me when I was lost. Living the research for this book provided a powerful antidote to the pessimistic conclusions I draw about mankind when I depend on my written sources only.

The Historiographical Institute of the University of Tokyo is one of the places to which I owe my life as a scholar. Both as an institution for the storage of historical knowledge about Japan as well as a marketplace for new ideas, I do not know of any institution that can equal it in the whole world. The people who make up its personnel are among Japan's most learned historians, and they have a decidedly uncommon tradition of welcoming and helping scholars from all over the world.

At the Institute, I depended on Professors Gonoi Takashi, Komiya Kiyora, Matsui Yōko, Matsukata Fuyuko, Oka Mihoko, Yokoyama Yoshinori, and Yukutake Kazuhiro. There, I also had the opportunity to meet and/or listen to presentations by Professors Kishino Hisashi, Miki Sei'ichirō, Takase Kō'ichirō, and the late Juan Ruiz de Medina. In Kyoto, Professor Gonoi introduced me to Professor Ōtsuka Mitsunobu, the editor of the *Zangeroku* and an expert on the Japanese language of the Momoyama period as recorded by the missionaries.

The Kirishitan Bunko on the eighth floor of Sophia University Library is another place that has been indispensable for this book. This is a little known oasis on a busy campus, where I have had the privilege to meet its former librarian, the formidable Ms. Tsutsui Suna. Here, within a few steps, researchers have available to them most of the Japanese as well as Western source materials on Christianity in Japan, and much of the secondary literature in a great variety of languages. Other friends at the university who have helped me include Michael Cooper, former editor of *Monumenta Nipponica*, and Bettina Gramlich-Oka, one of the journal's present editors.

At the beginning of my research, I spent a year affiliated with Nagasaki University. It was the horrified expression in the eyes of my sponsor Professor Himeno Jun'ichi when he heard me pontificate about my plan to "write a history of Nagasaki," that made me realize I should redefine my project as a history of Christian Nagasaki. Professor Himeno has been a loyal friend and supporter of my research ever since. At Nagasaki University, I also depended on Professors Toyama Mikio, Wakaki Tai'ichi and Yamaguchi Takamasa for their expertise on Nagasaki's history.

Coming to Lisbon in 2008, I was warmly received by Professor João Paulo d'Oliveira e Costa in his Centro de Historia de Alem Mar, another stimulating environment full of scholars dedicated to Portugal's overseas history. At CHAM, I met and was helped by Sophia Diniz, Jessica Hallett, Suzanna Münch Miranda, and Madalena Ribeiro. At Portugal's National Archive Torre de Tombo, I depended on Hugo Crespo and Professor Fernanda Olival of Evora University. Outside of academia, but very relevant for my research, I was fortunate to meet Matilde and Francisco Gago, who opened up their house and family archive to me.

During my visits to Spain in 2005, 2008, and 2009, I depended on Professor Geoffrey Parker for advice on Spanish archives, and on Juan Francisco Torres Arce and Kobayashi Yūko for providing lodging for my family and myself. In Holland, Forum Booksellers under its new management by Laurens R. Hesselink continued the company tradition of giving me access to whatever I needed from their collection of rare and valuable manuscripts and books.

I was invited to present parts of my research to the faculty of Nagasaki University in April 2004, the Center for Asian and Pacific Studies at the University of Iowa in November 2004, the Department of History and Phi Alpha Theta at the University of Northern Iowa in April 2005, the Nagasaki Museum for History and Culture in June 2006, the Department of Chinese and Korean Studies of the Eberhard Karls Universität, Tübingen in October 2008, and the Centro de História de Alem Mar of the Universidade Nova de Lisboa in February 2009. In Canada, I was asked to take part in the research group organized by Guy Poirier, "Textes missionnaires dans l'espace francophone" (2011–13), which forced me to brush up on my French when presenting my ideas on the Jesuit letters from Japan. In March 2014, I was invited by David Howell to give a presentation of my research on Nagasaki to the Edwin O. Reischauer Institute at Harvard University.

At the University of Northern Iowa, I depended on Linda Berneking and Rosemary Meany, who processed my endless Interlibrary Loan requests, and on Professors Kenneth Atkinson, Charles Holcombe, Robert Martin, and Charlotte Wells, who were always ready to help and share their expertise with me. I am grateful, also, to the students of my seminars, "Christianity in Japan" and "European-Asian Connections in the 16th and 17th Centuries" for their forbearance of my hobby horses and their stimulating comments.

For financial support to travel, retrieve documents, study, and write in Alcala de Henares, Belem, El Escorial, Evora, Kobe, Lisbon, Madrid, Nagasaki, Ōmura, Rome, Salamanca, Serpa, Sevilla, Simancas, 't Goy, The Hague, and Tokyo, I am indebted to the University of Northern Iowa Professional Development Assignment Committee (2002), the University of Northern Iowa Summer Fellowship Committee (2004), the Kajima Foundation (2005, 2006), the National Endowment for the Humanities (2008–9), and the Japan Foundation (2009–10).

I also owe a great debt to my colleagues, friends, and relatives, the readers of chapters or parts of this book, who provided me with valuable feedback and much needed encouragement: Beth Berry, Frits Hesselink, Herman Ooms, Geoffrey Tudor, and Stephen Vlastos. Special thanks are due to Kate Wildman Nakai, professor emerita of Sophia

University, who read most of the manuscript while it was first being brought into this world (and was much in need of a midwife), and to Larry Rogers, professor emeritus of the University of Hawai'i at Hilo who proofread the whole manuscript just before it was due to be delivered to the publisher. My daughter Saskia Hesselink not only read through and commented on the manuscript in its various stages, but also contributed her drawing skills to produce the maps. All questionable opinions and/or mistakes remain of course my own responsibility.

For moral and logistical support I am grateful to my parents-in-law Sasaki Ken'ichi and Sasaki Hiroko, and my in-laws Yamaguchi Daizō and Keiko, Yamaguchi Naka, and Yamaguchi Takashi, all of Miyako City, Iwate Prefecture. My most heartfelt thanks, however, go out to my wife, Tomie Sasaki-Hesselink, who was always ready to scoop up our household at a moment's notice to move everyone to some faraway place. I dedicate this book to her and to my daughter Klaertje (Clarita), for they have been with me all the way.

MAP OF HIZEN

CHIKUZEN

CHIKUGO

HIGO

Takaku

Chijiwa

Arima

Fujitsu

Sonogi 山

NAGASAKI

Nishi Sonogi

GOTŌ ARCHIPELAGO

AREA OF ENLARGEMENT

© SASKIA HESSELINK

CASTLES AND STRONGHOLDS △

1. NAGOYA
2. KARATSU
3. HIRADO
4. SAGA
5. TAKEO
6. ŌMURA
7. ISAHAYA
8. HARA
9. HINO'E
10. SHIMABARA

MOUNTAINS 山

1. TARA-DAKE
2. TATEYAMA

BAYS, COASTS, AND STRAITS

A. SOTOME COAST
B. HARI'O STRAIT
C. ŌMURA BAY
D. TACHIBANA BAY
E. YASHIRO BAY

ISLANDS

a. IKITSUKISHIMA
b. TAKUSHIMA
c. KABASHIMA
d. AMAKUSA

VILLAGES ●

1. MATSUURA
2. FUKUOKA
3. YOKOSEURA
4. IKIRIKI
5. NAGAYO
6. TOKITSU
7. TEGUMA
8. FUKUDA
9. SAKURABABA
10. MOGI
11. HIMI
12. YAGAMI
13. KUCHINOTSU
14. KAZUSA
15. ARIE
16. HACHIRAO
17. TAKASE
18. SHIKI
19. SETO

Introduction

This is the story of the birth of the city of Nagasaki, where two very different worlds intersected in a prolonged and intensive manner. The first of these is Japan, an island-empire roughly located between the 30th and 40th degrees latitude off the eastern edge of the Eurasian continent, and, although clearly part of East Asia, always proud to remain separate from it. The second world is represented by late medieval and early modern Iberia, on the western edge of the same landmass. Iberia had started, for better or for worse, to pull away from its traditional center of gravity, the Mediterranean, to cross and systematically explore the Atlantic, the Indian, and the Pacific oceans. We are dealing with the second half of the sixteenth century and the first four decades of the seventeenth century, a period of roughly eighty years.

Already a century and a half of exploration had preceded our starting point of 1560, with the Portuguese sending out ships along the coast of Africa from the beginning of the fifteenth century.[1] First, as a spillover of the medieval Reconquista movement in Iberia, Africa's extreme northwestern corner was colonized by Portugal's military orders under the leadership of the House of Avis, the country's second royal dynasty. Later, the Portuguese Crown continued to explore the coast as part of what it saw as its mission to defeat Islam and bring Christianity to the heathen. Its ships sailed from Lisbon with the large cross of the Order of Christ on their mainsails.

When neighboring Spain had managed to complete its own Reconquista in the 1490s, it followed Portugal's lead across the Atlantic, discovering the Caribbean islands and the Americas. At the very same time, the Portuguese reached the southern tip of Africa and discovered a new route to India. The Portuguese presence in sixteenth century Asia should be understood against this background of their previous exploitation of the West African coasts. Having left behind the crude Viking-type *modus operandi* they had pursued against the Moors and other peoples of Africa in the fourteenth and fifteenth centuries, the Portuguese invented a new system for the littoral of the Indian Ocean.[2]

Here, with far denser populations and stronger social organizations, two elements became crucial to Portuguese success: their artillery advantage at sea and their ability to use this power to play off local rulers against their neighbors. A policy such as had been pursued in Africa would ultimately have proved disastrous in Asia, for the Portuguese were just a tiny minority, which even with their artillery advantage might eventually have been crushed if sufficient local resources had been pooled together. It is to the credit of Portuguese political savvy that this never happened, although there were some close calls. As it was, the Portuguese became known for their artillery to the degree that (loan)

1

words for "cannon" and "European" in different Asian languages became similar to the point of being used interchangeably.[3]

The concept of raiding is helpful to understand the structure and reality of the Portuguese domination of the Asian seas.[4] Raiding often is a private enterprise, done by small armies of closely knit and highly trained groups of warriors. In the Portuguese case, the leadership of these small private armies was usually provided by the second and third sons of Portugal's landed gentry, who equipped their own ships for their expeditions in Asia. At the top of this structure stood the King of Portugal, who, in return for support for his increasingly centralized rule at home, rewarded the nobility of the country with written permissions to go raiding overseas in one capacity or another.

Thus, while the Spanish were building their land-based empire in the Americas, the Portuguese were founding a thalassocracy in Asia, a raiding and trading empire dominating the oceans and stretching for about a century from Africa to the Moluccas. This thalassocracy had three centers, each dominating local trade routes. Trade in Arabia was dominated by the Portuguese fortress at Hurmuz, and that along the coast of the Indian subcontinent was subject to the fortress of Goa, the seat of the Portuguese Viceroy. The most important stronghold at the eastern end of the thalassocracy was the fortress of Malacca.[5] From there, the Portuguese had been exploring the islands that now make up Indonesia since the second decade of the sixteenth century.

Since the third decade, the Portuguese were sailing to the north of Malacca along the coasts of Indochina and China. Early on, they learned that China was a different world altogether from all the nations they had encountered up to that time, whether they were the technologically primitive Africans and Americans, or the squabbling and warring Arabs, Indians and Malay.[6] Not only was China the most populous and best organized state in the world, with a two-thousand-year-old tradition of statecraft, it was also the world's most productive manufacturing center, producing textiles and porcelain of a quality far superior to those produced anywhere else. China was politically, economically, socially, and technologically a most advanced society, and as such it was ready to become the engine that powered the world trading system.[7]

Four Empires Connected by the Global Silver Trade

It was especially China's lack of one specific resource that jumpstarted the motor. The empire craved silver, which was required by its government in payment of the tax burden it had imposed, and demanded by its merchant class as the medium of exchange to circulate goods throughout the empire. It was in China that the Portuguese were finally forced, after more than a century of discoveries and empire building, to make the epochal change from raiders who sometimes traded to traders who would never admit to raiding.[8]

Traditionally, Japan was both inside and outside the Chinese cultural sphere. It had been intellectually inside for over a millennium, benefiting from the accumulated knowledge of China's written tradition. To gain access to this tradition, the islands had adopted the Chinese writing system and much of the vocabulary of Chinese civilization, many of its most basic philosophical ideas, its religion, and literature. Politically and economically, however, Japan's ruling class had striven all these centuries to remain outside of China's reach, at times even competing with it for the status of Central Kingdom. The polity pursuing this agenda, established on the Chinese model during the seventh and eighth centuries, had slowly broken down through internal corruption over the ninth through the fourteenth centuries.

In this way, the government of the three main islands of Honshu, Shikoku, and Kyushu (and countless smaller ones) had slowly disintegrated into a confusing array of hundreds of mutually competing warrior families, large and small, each dominating a small part of the original imperial state. The middle of the sixteenth century in Japan represented the zenith of this state of civil war that had become so endemic that it almost seemed normal.[9] As a matter of course, this warlike character of Japan spilled over its terrestrial boundaries into the seas surrounding the islands. Not only did pirate-warlords dominate the Seto Inland Sea, situated between the three main islands,[10] groups of Japanese pirates roamed across the China Sea and pillaged the coasts of Korea, China, and as far as the Philippines and Southeast Asia.[11]

For this reason, by the middle of the sixteenth century the Chinese empire had forbidden the Japanese to set foot on Chinese shores, even for purposes of peaceful trade, and prohibited its Chinese subjects from engaging in trade with Japan. These prohibitions only exacerbated the situation, forcing many coastal Chinese to join the Japanese as pirates on the high seas. The Portuguese, who first arrived in this environment in the 1520s, could perform a useful function. On the one hand, their well-armed ships did not have to fear the pirate junks they encountered. On the other hand, the very dependability of the Portuguese ships made them the ideal medium to transport Chinese silk to Japan (where demand for it continued to be high) and cheap Japanese silver to China, where the metal was worth twice as much as in some countries in Europe.[12]

Although the big warrior leaders in Japan were steadily absorbing the small fry of independent warrior landholders in their vicinity, the relationships between the more powerful warlords were characterized by a technological stand-off, where the balance of power tipped to the best-organized, the most ferocious or daring among them. Due to increasing warlord exploitation of the mineral resources at their disposal and improvements in the mining techniques employed in the first half of the sixteenth century, by 1550 Japan had acquired a large surplus of silver, the more so because the warriors generally had little use for the soft metal.[13]

The coming of the Portuguese in the waters off East Asia and their introduction of portable firearms into Japan's civil war radically changed the technological stand-off between the warlords.[14] From the Japanese perspective, the second half of the sixteenth century is the story of the political reunification of the country by those who used their resources to buy, copy, adopt, stockpile and improve the new weaponry and its tactics. We will have to keep this process in mind as we see it illustrated in a close-up of the environment in which Nagasaki came into existence.

In the second half of the sixteenth century, China was absorbing silver from three main sources. The first of these was Japan. The other two were the newly discovered mines of the Americas, i.e., the silver mines of Mexico and Peru. Peruvian silver was shipped to Panama and from there to Spain, or clandestinely through Brazil to Portugal. Thence, it was exported again to India, and eventually used to buy Chinese manufactures, either to sell in Japan or to bring back to Goa and Portugal. Mexican silver was used, in part, to pay for the Spanish thrust across the Pacific and ended up in Spain's colony in the Philippines, where the Spanish similarly were using it to buy superior Chinese products.[15]

Four ports came into existence at around the same time with essentially the same function: that of shipping silver to China. These four ports were Macao, Acapulco, Manila and Nagasaki. Macao was founded and built between 1555 and 1557 as the entry point for Japanese silver into China.[16] Around the same time, Acapulco became the usual starting point for Spanish ships crossing the Pacific.[17] Manila was founded in 1571, and the first streets of Nagasaki were also built in that very same year. The only difference between the latter two ports was that silver from the Americas was carried from Manila to China in Chinese junks, while silver from Japan was carried to Macao in Portuguese vessels.[18]

Thus, in the second half of the sixteenth century, silver was connecting four empires: the Chinese empire, the Spanish empire in the Americas, the Portuguese thalassocracy in Asia, and the reemerging Japanese empire. With the exception of China, these empires were still growing or just starting to grow in 1560. And so, while the flow of silver may have linked them together, they were competitors where the accumulation, concentration, and consolidation of power was concerned.

Christian Missionaries Overseas

Power is a reality difficult to analyze without reference to its own system of justification, the discourse that we call ideological today. Both the Portuguese and the Spanish thrusts across the Atlantic justified themselves largely by the perceived necessity of fighting Islam and converting the heathen to Christianity. Both nations were supported in this endeavor by the papacy, still based in its ancient seat of power in the Mediterranean, but anxious not to be left out of the gains from the newly discovered parts of the world. Christianity as brought overseas in the fifteenth and sixteenth centuries, therefore, should be treated as an essentially ideological discourse that helped expand, consolidate, and justify the newly acquired powers of Portugal and Spain.

Although the Franciscan and Dominican orders first started this ideological mission in the Americas, after the Council of Trent it was the Society of Jesus, newly established by Ignatius de Loyola (1491–1556) in 1540, that took the lead in the overseas missions to Asia. The order was well suited for the task, for its outlook was essentially pragmatic. What becomes clear, when we take a global view of the Society, is its great adaptability. In whatever circumstances they found themselves, its members always found ways to accomplish the core program of their mission by allying themselves with and behaving like the local upper class. In the New World, the upper class consisted of great landowners, the descendants of the conquistadores, so the Jesuits behaved like them.[19] In China, the upper class was made up of the literati, the "mandarins" of Western literature, so the Jesuits aspired to acquire the same type of learning.[20]

In Japan, the upper class was made up of warriors, and so (however unlikely it may sound) the Jesuits, at first, behaved in a more warlike manner than in any other place in the world.[21] They became the founders of a military colony, called Nagasaki.[22] Considering the rules of the Society that had been hammered out during the decades of the Council of Trent (forbidding the pursuit of worldly power, church office, and the accumulation of wealth on the part of its members), to be in charge of a military stronghold represented at best a grey area between being in the world and belonging to the world.[23] The only major concern for the pragmatists, however, was to keep their interest in and management of such worldly projects as quiet as possible.

In fact, the problem lay in the contradiction between a Society of Jesus ostensibly dedicated to spiritual goals and its priests in Japan having founded a strategic stronghold dedicated to monopolizing the China trade brought by the Portuguese merchants. Without the China trade, it was impossible for the mission to survive in Japan.[24] The object of Jesuit control of Nagasaki was always that it should be direct only for as long as it took for Japan to adopt Christianity, for after that the believers themselves would, just like in Europe, support the priesthood. Nagasaki, in fact, was one of the few places in Japan where this goal was actually reached. For a few short years after 1614, when all remaining priests had to go underground, the town supported its shepherds until they had all, one by one, been caught in the net of the authorities.

The history of Christian Nagasaki, therefore, is inextricably intertwined with the history of the Jesuit mission, for although not its first worldly effort, Nagasaki certainly represented the Society's greatest investment in time, resources, and energy spent in Japan. To understand the position of Nagasaki within the framework of the Jesuit mission, it is necessary to briefly survey the history of that mission in Japan.

Francisco Xavier (1506–1552), the first Jesuit to arrive in Japan in 1549, originally conceived the Japan mission as a conveniently located training ground that would allow the Jesuits to acquire experience for the great future project of the conversion of China.[25] This is one of the reasons why, during the initial ten years of the mission, great stress was laid to maintain a foothold in Kyoto, the old imperial capital of Japan.

After about ten years, however, continuous physical hardship and lack of success in gaining converts in sufficient numbers forced the Jesuits to change tack. The decision was made to use the knowledge of the Japanese language and customs acquired by the members of the mission up to that time to become intermediaries between Portuguese and Japanese merchants, the former as ignorant of the latter as the latter were of the former. In other words, from the 1560s onwards, the Jesuits became what Philip Curtin in his thesis on merchant diasporas has called "cross-cultural brokers."[26] To better perform this function, and in order to be able to use the trade for the purpose of strengthening the mission, it soon became clear that the order needed a safe harbor for the yearly arrival of the Portuguese carrack, known in Portuguese as the *nao*, or "the Ship," and in Japanese as *kurofune* or the "Black Ship."

If a harbor could be found where the trade between the Portuguese and the Japanese could be conducted safely without interference from the civil war, the Jesuits might be able to steer most of the profits on the Japanese side into the hands of a small and closely knit group of Christian converts. This principle ran into snags, because Japanese Christians, at least in the beginning, tended to be poor and without sufficient capital to buy up large quantities of silk. It took time to accumulate the necessary capital. The profits on the Portuguese side, it goes without saying, would go to those who were willing to follow the lead of the Jesuits. In this way, the Jesuits were able to dominate the trade, because they played an indispensable role in it. The second period of the mission, between 1560 and 1570, was characterized by the search for a safe port.

If there ever was a seminal moment for the Christian mission in Japan, it was the baptism of a small regional warlord, Ōmura Sumitada, on the west coast of Japan's southern island of Kyushu. After fourteen years of missionary work, he was the first from Japan's sixteenth century ruling class to convert. In contrast to Ōtomo Yoshishige, the daimyo of Bungo on the island's east coast, whom the mission's leader Cosme de Torrès had courted for six years between 1556 and 1562 but who had kept the religion at arm's length even while favoring the missionaries, Sumitada converted within less than a year of his first contact with a European; no wonder he was hailed back in Europe as someone particularly touched by the grace of God. It was in his domain that the Jesuits decided the new port was to be established.

After a few failures, an appropriate spot had finally been located by 1571. In the spring of that year a settlement was started at the very end of Nagasaki Bay, one of Kyushu's prime anchorages. For the next sixteen years, between 1571 and 1587, the Jesuits were able, by and large, to put into practice the idea hammered out among their leadership over the previous decade. What emerged was a fortified town, under the leadership of a number of European Jesuits, located on a promontory in the manner of many other Portuguese fortresses in Africa, Arabia, and Asia. The town had its own citizen militia, city walls with cannon on its ramparts, and it had a moat on the landside.

This semi-independent city dominated the bay and its surroundings with a small warship, its influence stretching north along the sea coast of Western Sonogi until the point where the warlord of Hirado could put a check to it. In other words, the Jesuits had become small, but economically significant, territorial lords in Japan. It goes without saying that the success of this change in policy can be measured in the numbers of baptisms the Jesuits were able to perform in Japan.[27] While in the twelve years before 1562 the Jesuits possibly baptized some six thousand Japanese, in the twenty-four years that followed the number of baptized Christians reached an impressive one hundred and seventy thousand.[28] An objective assessment of this fourteen-fold increase in the rate of baptisms, therefore, will need to find its cause in the access to the trade and connected livelihoods that the Jesuits provided.

As we shall see, apart from silk in exchange for silver, the Jesuits provided such opportunities to those dealing in or in need of guns and ammunition, slaves, and gold. This, to be sure, is not to say that the above economic incentives exhausted all the reasons for becoming a Christian, just that the overwhelming majority of conversions were at least partly fueled by such motives. We will, of course, encounter other motives as well, among which faith in the truth of the Jesuit message, as encouraged and reinforced by Western painting techniques, as well as in the effectiveness of Western magic through music, recitation, or incantation (resembling the Buddhist practice) figured prominently.

What may have looked, to an untrained observer around 1586, like the beginning of a Christian empire in Japan, however, was shattered in one blow in 1587. From 1560's onward another small warlord, called Oda Nobunaga (1534–1582), from central Honshu, had made great progress, by force of portable firearms, in carving out a domain that by the early 1580's was starting to look like it would succeed in reunifying the whole archipelago. Nobunaga was assassinated in 1582, and so the country seemed on the verge of relapsing into another protracted round of civil war. Against all expectations, however, one of Nobunaga's lieutenants, called Hideyoshi (1537–1598), a soldier of simple background who had made a lightning career in his lord's service, succeeded in taking over his master's legacy and, within a decade, managed to finish the task of the reunification of Japan.[29]

The Prohibition of Christianity

It was Hideyoshi's invasion of Kyushu that in 1587 sounded the death knell for Nagasaki's independent existence. Even worse, Japan's new ruler was informed about

Christian effrontery in destroying the native religious sanctuaries of Shinto shrines and Buddhist temples wherever it made converts in Japan. As a consequence, he prohibited the religion, told the padres to leave Japan, and annexed Nagasaki into his personal domain, the *tenryō*. This is known as the first prohibition of Christianity.

These edicts ushered in a fourth period for the mission, lasting eleven years, in which the Jesuits decided to remain in Japan, but to go into hiding. We shall see how this great change in their situation affected Jesuit ideas about the meaning of their own efforts in Japan up to that time. Although Hideyoshi sent his own men to administer Nagasaki, it soon became clear that the Jesuits were not so easily dismissed. Hideyoshi realized that if he wanted to expand and enlarge the town's function as Japan's main port of entry for the lucrative foreign trade, he would (for the moment at least) be wise to count on the help of the padres to conduct the trade.

For this reason, he decided not to press his anti–Christian edicts and to allow a small number of padres to live in the city in order to keep the Portuguese in line.[30] In this way, he could use Nagasaki's Christian merchants to deal with the great merchant houses from the rest of Japan, who came to Nagasaki to do their buying. However, the arrival of mendicants from the Philippines a few years later brought a new destabilizing factor into this fragile understanding between Hideyoshi and the Jesuits. Having come to East Asia via Mexico and the Philippines, where they had provided ideological support for Spanish rule, the mendicants were unprepared for the delicate situation in Japan. Soon they were making the same mistakes for which the Jesuits were already being punished, and so enraged Japan's hegemon that he ordered six of them to be crucified in Nagasaki in 1597.

The fifth period of the mission starts with Hideyoshi's death in 1598. It lasted for sixteen years. Again, it was expected that the civil war would resume, but again the country was quickly reunified, this time by Tokugawa Ieyasu (1543–1616). After defeating his opponents in an epic battle on 21 October 1600, Ieyasu struggled with many of the same problems that his predecessor had faced. Where Nagasaki was concerned, the problem was how to uncouple trade from the missionaries and their religion, which Ieyasu clearly recognized for the ideological discourse it was and so rejected as proper for his subjects. Just after his victory on the battlefield, however, there were other, more pressing matters to deal with, i.e., the punishment of his opponents and the rearrangement of the domains for his vassals, that were to take up the better part of the first decade of the seventeenth century.

Thus Nagasaki could wait, the padres could stay for the moment to help with the trade, and even friars were welcome if they brought trade and technological know-how from the Philippines and Mexico. All this flexibility, however, did not mean that Ieyasu was willing to rescind Hideyoshi's ban on the propagation of the Christian faith. At the same time, however, Ieyasu's advisers were quietly experimenting with measures designed to test if the missionaries had outlived their usefulness. By late 1613, they had convinced the hegemon that it was now possible for the officials representing him in Nagasaki to dispense with the padres and to conduct trade on their own terms and with their own interpreters. Therefore, in early 1614, Ieyasu proscribed Christianity throughout Japan. This is known as the second prohibition.

Again, we are reminded of Philip Curtin's general finding that the cultural brokers of the "trade diasporas tend to work themselves out of business."[31] Such trade diasporas begin, Curtin has argued, because cultural differences cause a need for mediation. The longer the mediation lasts, however, the less important these cultural differences become, and the easier it becomes to dispense with the intermediaries. This is exactly what happened in Japan between 1587 and 1614. In these twenty-seven years, enough Japanese traveled abroad to Macao and Manila (and, as we shall see, sometimes further, even all the way to Europe) to become fluent in Portuguese and Spanish and to learn how to do business with Europeans on the home turf of their fortresses. How much easier, then, it would be to conduct trade with these same Europeans in their homeland of Japan.

What is more, other Europeans had appeared on the scene in Japan by this time, for it was no longer Iberia alone that sailed the oceans. Since the last quarter of the sixteenth century, competitors from Europe's northern Atlantic littoral had joined the rush for overseas riches with smaller ships but armament superior to anything the Portuguese and Spanish could muster. If the sixteenth century had been that of the Portuguese and Spanish overseas empires, the seventeenth century was going to be that of the Dutch and the English trading networks. The fact that these two nations were sending ships to do business on the island of Hirado, not far from Nagasaki, without the help from any missionaries is certain to have contributed to the final decision to expel all the padres and their helpers from Japan.

Thus, the sixth period of the mission started in 1614 and lasted until 1639. It basically coincided with the last period that trade was conducted between Macao and Nagasaki in Portuguese vessels. For twenty-five more years, the Portuguese were allowed to prove they could do business in Japan without the support of the padres. They failed the test. In the end, the faith proved to have too strong a hold over the minds of these late medieval adventurers. However much the resident merchants of Macao tried (among whom former Jews or New Christians figured prominently), they were unable to shake off the shackles of the ideology imposed on them by the Portuguese Crown and enforced by those who arrived with the King's permission to be in charge of the trade.

The powerful Jesuit lobby in the city, moreover, resisted abandoning the Japanese mission with all the might at its disposal. In Nagasaki, it had seemed initially, just after 1614, as if the city was going to be allowed to hold on to its Christian belief system. With the appearance of new rulers (Ieyasu's son, Hidetada, and his grandson, Iemitsu), the measures repressing the religion became more severe until, from 1626 on, the whole population of the city was systematically forced to apostatize. This process was mostly accomplished by 1629.

While the greater part of the Jesuit missionaries in Japan came from Portugal, among those in positions of command in the Japanese mission we often find Italians and Spaniards as well. Generally, these were the best educated and one might assume the more cynical, i.e., aware of their function as supporters of the ideology of the Portuguese and Spanish crowns. It would be a mistake, however, to see the Jesuit missionaries in Japan as a monolithic group pursuing the same goals under a cynical leadership that used the vow of obedience extracted from all members to stifle any questioning of their methods. Even among the leaders of the Society, there were different approaches to the problem of how to convert Japan.

At first, under the leadership of the Spaniard Cosme de Torrès, the order made a great effort to adapt itself to Japanese custom. Torrès himself behaved like a great merchant or a small regional lord, traveling around the territory of the mission with a large retinue of followers and supporters, wearing silk clothing, dealing in guns and ammunition, gold and silver, silk and slaves. When news of this behavior reached Goa and the

Portuguese were duly scandalized, a new superior was sent out to put an end to this development. From 1570 on, all the Jesuits in Japan were forced to wear their black cotton *sotanas*, even though many older and more experienced missionaries still felt that this was separating them unnecessarily from their flock.

Mostly, however, the change was cosmetic, for the order continued on the path started by Torrès to perform as cultural brokers. On this fundamental policy point, too, there were Jesuits who opposed the involvement of the order in the trade. The degree of accommodation to Japanese custom and the appropriateness of being involved in the trade continued to be points of internal discussion until the second prohibition of 1614. The main policy also shifted 180 degrees sometimes. After the first prohibition of 1587, for example, wearing the *sotana* was abandoned again, and all the Jesuits went back to wearing Japanese attire in order to be less conspicuous. I have found that, in general, the lower the rank of the members of the Society in Japan, the higher the degree of sincerity and enthusiasm for the mission's stated goal of converting the heathen.

Here we come upon a difference between the European and Japanese members of the Society. In general, it was difficult, sometimes taking years, for a Japanese to rise from *dōjuku* or "fellow traveler," and be allowed to enter the order's two-year novitiate, after which one was accepted as an *irmão* (Jpn *iruman*) or brother in the Society. From there, however, it was almost impossible to rise to the status of *padre* (Jpn *bateren*), or ordained priest.[32] To be a Japanese brother in the Society required not only intellectual ability, commitment, patience, and endurance of prejudice, but also many of the qualities usually associated with fully fledged priests. The Japanese brothers, because of their linguistic versatility, did most of the Society's preaching and proselytizing, and were also indispensable in producing the Society's written texts in Japanese and most of the artwork produced in Japan. A few exceptions notwithstanding, they represented the cream of the Society's recruits in Japan.

By contrast, the average quality of the European brothers in Japan was much lower. One gets the impression that they were often employed mainly for particular skills that the order needed. Some were knowledgeable about the armament or silk trade, others were experienced sailors who could safely ferry other members of the mission by sea to their posts. They might be fluent in spoken Japanese, but were mostly of a much lower educational level than the Japanese brothers. Still, these European brothers would often be ordained priests and so join the elite corps among the Society's members, who alone were empowered to hear the confessions of the faithful. The padres, in fact, employed the Japanese brothers wherever and whenever they themselves lacked the necessary linguistic skills. One can imagine the resentment caused by this set-up, which started to explode with increasing frequency by the end of the sixteenth century. At that time some of the most gifted Japanese brothers began to run out of patience, thus "proving," in the eyes of the European Jesuits, that because of their lack of obedience, indeed, they had not deserved to be entrusted with the priesthood.

A World Steered by God and the Devil

To a degree difficult to understand for us today, the lives of people in the late sixteenth century were still determined by their religious beliefs. Although the Portuguese knew how to use and manipulate their environment to survive, and at times even to become rich and powerful, they did not understand most of the workings of that environment. Modern man is mostly free of the fears that motivated his ancestors of the sixteenth and seventeenth centuries. He no longer sees the hand of God everywhere in his everyday life. It is important to remember that the Jesuits' own particular strength in Japan was of an intangible nature: it consisted mainly of their spiritual and intellectual control over the Portuguese adventurers.

These men were the product of Portuguese (and in a larger context, of Roman Catholic) society, in which a late-medieval worldview still predominated. According to this worldview, God was everywhere, not just in the larger scheme of things, but also in the nitty-gritty detail of daily toil. But if God was omnipresent, so was Beelzebub. The problem everyone faced was to distinguish between those features of everyday life which were clearly part of God's design and those behind which the devil lurked and were known as "sin." For all practical purposes, here lay the task of the church, which had reserved for its representatives the right to be the final arbiter of what constituted God's will and what distinguished God's will from the evil designs of the devil. The church was interpreter of God's will, mediator between God and His flock, and provider of punishment or absolution to those who had "sinned," that is, flouted, transgressed against, or ignored His will.

In Roman Catholic society, this right of the church was universally acknowledged by even the highest worldly authorities. For those who were not experts themselves on making such distinctions between good and evil, there were few options other than to live as if there were no choices to be made, and then to submit to periodic checks, at least once a year, in the confessional by the local representative of the church. It was different, however, for those who left their native village, or their parental property, to seek an uncertain livelihood on the High Seas. At sea, suddenly, God was everywhere, in the waves and in the winds. The weather was considered the most direct manifestation of God's will on earth. Sailors, therefore, considered themselves to be "in God's hand." To arrive at one's destination meant to do so with God's express approval, to meet disaster and drown at sea was to be stopped in one's design by the same higher power.

For medieval Roman Catholics, the church's representative in their midst, the priest, was their direct link with God. He was different from others because of his celibacy, real or presumed. His daily sacrifice of sexual pleasure, of the joy of having offspring, of living a normal life of man and wife, made him, in a very real sense, a *holy* man. Whereas no one could be sure about their own fate after death, heaven or hell, that of the holy man was certain to include a direct one-way passage to Heaven.

How strong this belief was, and how far sailors were willing to go in order to make sure they would get to Heaven, is clear from the following passage from the journal of Afonso de Lucena (1551–1623), a Portuguese Jesuit, who has recorded for us a moment from his own experience when everybody thought that their ship was lost and they were all going to drown in a few moments:

> While the ship was hanging in the water like that, five Portuguese took one of the fathers, two holding onto his legs, two hanging onto his arms, and one clinging to his rump; and they said that we were all six going to go down into the sea together and die together. The one, who was holding onto the father's belt, whispered into his ear that he promised God to enter the Society of Jesus if he were to escape with his life from this storm.[33]

Not all Portuguese ships were lucky enough to have representatives of God on board, so priests never seem to have had much trouble finding free passage wherever they wanted to go. Many Portuguese captains must have welcomed the opportunity to get dispensation for their sins while they were committing them, and the priests, dependent as they were on the goodwill of the captains, did not have a whole lot of leeway to withhold absolution at sea.

To sum up, the main theme of this book is the birth of the modern world through ocean travel, world trade, and the clash of different configurations of power, each with their own pre-modern mindset. We do so by looking, in turn, at around fifty people of a variety of nationalities. About half of them are Japanese, the other half being Portuguese, Spanish, Italian, Chinese, Korean, English, and Dutch. These people have been chosen because their lives may serve to demonstrate some aspect of the history of Christian Nagasaki between 1560 and 1640. Several of the people profiled played important roles on different occasions, as fortunes rose and fell. Where these are included in multiple entries, these are noted with a "1" and "2" in the table of contents and text.

The title of Part One, "Founding Fathers," refers to the Jesuit priests and their Japanese sponsors, who were central to the city's founding and the first years of its existence up to 1587. Part Two, "Brave New World," explores the world of Japanese Christendom and its troubled relationship with the central authorities between 1587 and 1613. Part Three, "Forging a Yamato Soul," tells the story of the last decades of the city's Christian identity after the prohibition of 1614 and how its population was gradually forced into apostasy.

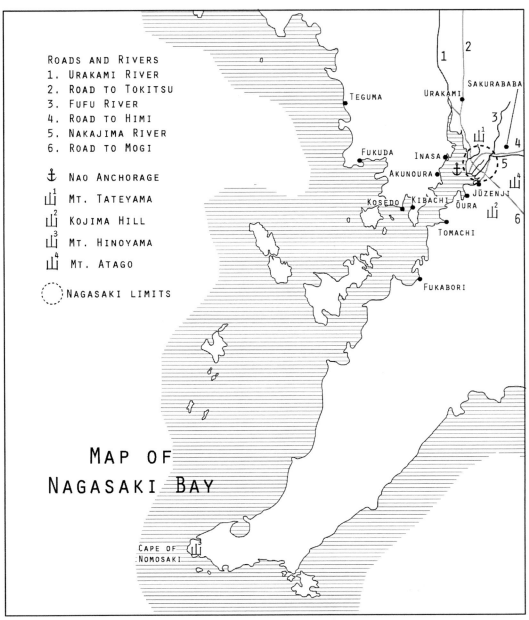

ROADS AND RIVERS
1. URAKAMI RIVER
2. ROAD TO TOKITSU
3. FUFU RIVER
4. ROAD TO HIMI
5. NAKAJIMA RIVER
6. ROAD TO MOGI

⚓ NAO ANCHORAGE
⛰¹ MT. TATEYAMA
⛰² KOJIMA HILL
⛰³ MT. HINOYAMA
⛰⁴ MT. ATAGO
◯ NAGASAKI LIMITS

TEGUMA

URAKAMI
SAKURABABA
1 2
1
3
⛰¹
INASA
4
AKUNOURA
⚓
5
JŪZENJI
KOSEDO KIBACHI ŌURA
⛰⁴
⛰²
FUKUDA
TOMACHI
6

FUKABORI

MAP OF
NAGASAKI BAY

CAPE OF
NOMOSAKI

©SASKIA HESSELINK

Abbreviated Genealogies
of the Arima, Ōmura, Nagasaki
and Chijiwa Houses

[Christian names in brackets]

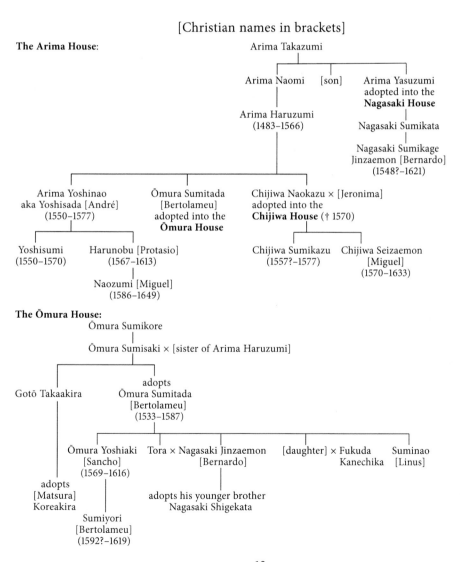

The Arima House:

Arima Takazumi

Arima Naomi   [son]   Arima Yasuzumi
adopted into the
Nagasaki House

Arima Haruzumi
(1483–1566)   Nagasaki Sumikata

Nagasaki Sumikage
Jinzaemon [Bernardo]
(1548?–1621)

Arima Yoshinao   Ōmura Sumitada   Chijiwa Naokazu × [Jeronima]
aka Yoshisada [André]   [Bertolameu]   adopted into the
(1550–1577)   adopted into the   **Chijiwa House** († 1570)
                        Ōmura House

Yoshisumi   Harunobu [Protasio]   Chijiwa Sumikazu   Chijiwa Seizaemon
(1550–1570)   (1567–1613)   (1557?–1577)   [Miguel]
                                                            (1570–1633)
            Naozumi [Miguel]
            (1586–1649)

The Ōmura House:

Ōmura Sumikore

Ōmura Sumisaki × [sister of Arima Haruzumi]

                        adopts
Gotō Takaakira   Ōmura Sumitada
                        [Bertolameu]
                        (1533–1587)

Ōmura Yoshiaki   Tora × Nagasaki Jinzaemon   [daughter] × Fukuda   Suminao
[Sancho]   [Bernardo]   Kanechika   [Linus]
(1569–1616)

adopts
[Matsura]   adopts his younger brother
Koreakira   Nagasaki Shigekata

    Sumiyori
    [Bertolameu]
    (1592?–1619)

13

Timeline for the History of Christian Nagasaki (1549–1640)

1549	**Francisco Xavier** arrives in Japan and begins the Jesuit mission.
1551	Francisco Xavier leaves Japan. **Cosme de Torrès** takes charge of the newly established Japanese mission.
1553	Hirado becomes the preferred port of call for the Portuguese.
1561	In a *mêlée* in Hirado, fourteen Portuguese including the Captain Major **Fernão de Souza** are killed.
1562	Yokoseura in Omura is the first Christian settlement of Japan and becomes the preferred port of call for the Portuguese.
1563	**Ōmura Sumitada** is the first Japanese warlord to accept baptism. Yokoseura is set on fire by merchants from Bungo.
1565	Fukuda becomes the preferred port of call for the Portuguese. A surprise attack from Hirado on the carrack of Captain Major **João Pereira** is unsuccessful.
1567	**Luis d'Almeida** baptizes the first converts in the Nagasaki Bay area.
1570	Captain Major **Manoel Travassos** takes the first Portuguese ship into Nagasaki Bay. **Cosme de Torrès** is replaced by **Francisco Cabral** as superior of the Jesuits in Japan.
1571.03	Work is started on a new Christian settlement at the end of Nagasaki Bay.
1573–1574	The new town of Nagasaki is attacked by men from Fukabori and Isahaya, but fortifies itself and survives.
1580	The Jesuits are offered and accept lordship over Nagasaki by **Ōmura Sumitada**. The town expands and is further fortified into an independent stronghold.
1584.05.04	After the battle of Okitanawade on the Shimabara peninsula, Nagasaki becomes a tributary of the domain of Satsuma.
1587.07.20	After the Kyushu campaign, **Toyotomi Hideyoshi** proscribes Christianity and nullifies Jesuit authority in Nagasaki.
1587	Although ordered to leave Japan, the Jesuits choose to go into hiding instead. **Hideyoshi** sends **Tōdō Takatora** and one other retainer as his representatives to Nagasaki. The bastions of the city are demolished, and its moat is filled in.

1588	**Hideyoshi** sends **Toda Katsutaka** and **Asano Nagayoshi** as his representatives in Nagasaki during the trading season. The city is incorporated into Hideyoshi's personal domain.
1589	**Hideyoshi** appoints **Terazawa Hirotaka** and **Tōdō Takatora** as his representatives for Nagasaki, but as no Portuguese ship arrives they do not come to the city.
1590–1591	**Hideyoshi** sends **Nabeshima Naoshige** and **Mori Yoshinari** as his representatives to Nagasaki.
1591	As a result of an embassy led by **Alessandro Valignano** in the name of the Viceroy of Goa, Hideyoshi allows ten Jesuits to reside in Nagasaki.
1592.07	**Hideyoshi** appoints **Terazawa Hirotaka**, daimyo of Karatsu, as Governor of Nagasaki. Terazawa will hold this position until 1603.
1592.09.01	By order of **Hideyoshi**, Governor **Terazawa** begins the dismantling of the São Paulo church of Nagasaki and the Jesuit compound, both at Morisaki.
1595.05	The Franciscans under **Pedro Blásquez** establish a residence and church in Cruz-machi.
1597.02.05	By order of **Hideyoshi**, six foreign Franciscans and twenty Japanese Christians are crucified in Nagasaki. **Governor Terazawa**'s younger brother **Hanzaburō** is in charge of the executions.
1600	Nagasaki consists of four distinct neighborhoods: Uchimachi, Funazumachi and the right and left bank of the Nakajima River known as Sotomachi (see map on p. 12). **Governor Terazawa** aligns himself with Tokugawa Ieyasu.
1603	**Tokugawa Ieyasu** appoints **Ogasawara Ichi'an** as Governor of Nagasaki. The Dominicans first establish a residence and church in Katsuyama-machi.
1604	The *pancada* system of wholesale purchasing of the silk cargo brought by the Portuguese is adopted. It has the effect of drastically lowering Portuguese profits.
1605	**Ieyasu** forces **Ōmura Yoshiaki** to consent to a forced exchange of Nagasaki's Sotomachi for Urakami.
1607	**Ieyasu** appoints **Hasegawa Sahyōe** as Governor of Nagasaki, a post he will hold until his death in 1617.
1609	Captain Major **André Pessoa** does not want to submit to new harbor rules in Nagasaki.
1610.01.06	Attacked by an army under **Arima Harunobu**, **André Pessoa** blows up his ship near Fukuda Bay.
1610	**João Rodrigues**, fourth ranked among the Jesuits in Nagasaki, is expelled from Japan.
1612	The Augustinians establish a church in Furukawa-machi on the left bank of the Nakajima River. The trade with Macao is restored on condition that it will be conducted under the new rules.
1614.01.31	**Ieyasu** proscribes Christianity and orders the expulsion of all missionaries as well as the destruction of all the churches of Nagasaki.
1617	**Tokugawa Hidetada** appoints **Hasegawa Gonroku** as Governor of Nagasaki. Gonroku will hold the position until 1626.

1622.09.10	Great martyrdom of Nagasaki: fifty-five people are executed, among them twenty-five religious figures, who are burned alive.
1624	A Spanish embassy from the Philippines is refused.
1626	**Tokugawa Iemitsu** appoints **Mizuno Morinobu** as Governor of Nagasaki.
1628	**Iemitsu** appoints **Takenaka Shigeyoshi** as Governor of Nagasaki.
1629	Governor **Takenaka** forces mass apostasy in Nagasaki through torture. All citizens are registered in newly built Buddhist temples.
1633	Governor **Takenaka** is indicted and forced to turn to Edo. **Iemitsu** appoints **Imamura Masanaga** and **Soga Hisasuke** as *daikan* of Nagasaki.
1634.03.20	Governor **Takenaka** is found guilty and ordered to commit *seppuku*.
1637–8	A rebellion of Christian farmers starts in Amakusa and spreads to the Shimabara peninsula. The inhabitants of Nagasaki are careful to remain on the sidelines.
1639	The Portuguese are expelled from Japan.
1640	Sixty-one men of a Portuguese delegation from Macao are beheaded in Nagasaki.
1641	As reward for its neutrality during the Shimabara Rebellion, Nagasaki is awarded the trade brought to Japan by the Dutch, who are forced to move from Hirado to Deshima, an artificial island in Nagasaki Bay.

A Note on Currencies,
Weights and Dates

Currencies

In this book, generally, the following equivalencies for the currencies in use in Christian Nagasaki are employed: 1 [Portuguese] cruzado = 1 [Spanish] ducat = 1 [Chinese] tael = 1 [Japanese] *koku* (the value of around five bushels of rice).

More precise are the following monetary equivalencies:

1 *tael* (1 *ryō* in Japan) = 10 *mas* (*mon* or *momme*) = 100 *conderins* (*bu*) = 1000 *cash* (*sen*) (cf. Carletti 1966, pp. 144, 188–9; Himeno 1986, p. 43).

1 *kan* or = 3.75 kg of silver = 100 *taels* = 1000 *mon*

1 bar (*ichimai*) of silver = 4 *taels*, 3 *mas* in Japanese currency = 4 *cruzados*, 6 *vintis* in Portuguese currency (Shimizu 2001a, p. 345).

1 coin *(ichimai)* of gold = 43 bars of silver = 43 cruzados (Shimizu 2001a, p. 345).

Weights

1 picul = 100 catties = 60 kgs

Dates

All Japanese dates have been recalculated into the Gregorian calendar, except where it is explicitly stated that they are in the Japanese calendar.

PART ONE. FOUNDING FATHERS
(1561–1586)

From Hirado to Yokoseura:
Luis d'Almeida (1)

In trying to assemble the strands that come together to make up the background to the founding of Nagasaki, the first key person we encounter is Luis d'Almeida. It is proper, therefore, that we start with him. One of the earliest notices about Almeida, dating from 1560, tells us that he was a rich surgeon who had been received into the Society in 1556. He brought five thousand cruzados with him. Apart from working in the hospital he had established, he also made sure the fathers and brothers in Japan were getting what they needed. "He orders from the Portuguese, who sail from Japan to China, what they need to bring back to Japan, and does all the negotiating with them, thus freeing the fathers from such temporal matters."[1] We shall see shortly many examples of the things included among these "temporal matters."

Luis d'Almeida was born into a Jewish, or New Christian, family in Lisbon in 1525. On 3 March 1546, he was awarded a surgeon's certificate by the Secretariat of the King of Portugal.[2] Two years later, he left for the Indies. On 14 August 1552, we find him in Japan for the first time, arriving in Tanegashima, from where he traveled via Satsuma to Hirado and then on to Yamaguchi. In 1555, he was again in Japan and joined the Jesuits in Funai (Oita). The next year, Viceprovincial Cosme de Torrès accepted him into the Society as a brother.[3] In 1560, Almeida was forced to give up leading the hospital, because a new confirmation of the rule that members of the Society should concentrate on missionary work and not provide medical services had reached Japan.[4] The Society was still in its formative years. From this time on, Almeida was officially an accountant. In that function, he visited each year the places where the Portuguese ships came to anchor. Because of Torrès' ill health, also, Almeida fulfilled some of the duties of his superior, visiting the churches of each locality, transmitting messages between the different missionaries, and representing Torrès in the negotiations with the different rulers of Kyushu. Because of his incessant travels and ceaseless proselytizing he was nicknamed the *perpetuum mobile* of the Society.[5]

In these early years, after largely abandoning Tanegashima, Kagoshima, and Usuki as their ports of call, the Portuguese were trading in Hirado. Here, however, just as in Kagoshima, the missionaries soon outlived their welcome because of their implacable animosity towards the Buddhist religious establishment. By 1559, the lord of Hirado Matsura Takanobu (1529–1599) had already ordered Padre Gaspar Vilela (1526–1572) out of his domain.[6] The church and the Jesuit residence were burned, even though there were ninety Portuguese (merchants and sailors) in the port at the time.[7] Almeida, as trader turned missionary, continued to be able to blend in with the Portuguese in town, but he had been advised to make sure the authorities did not get wind of his presence.[8] So, on 10 August 1561, we find him back in Hirado, and, for lack of a church on shore, celebrating the Sunday mass on the Portugese trading carrack, baptizing no less than fifty Japanese, and discussing the change of port with the Captain Major.[9]

Later that same month, a dispute over the silk price escalated into a *mêlée* in front of the Shichirō shrine in Kagamigawa-machi, in which fourteen Portuguese, including Captain Major Fernão de Souza, were slain before the daimyo gave orders to stop the killing. Here was a golden opportunity for the Jesuits, the more so because the Japanese involved were not punished severely. Now there was no reason any longer to hesitate and cut the link between the Portuguese traders and Matsura Takanobu, who had not wanted to accommodate the Jesuits.[10]

A plan for just such an emergency was already in place.[11] Luís Fróis, the historian of the Jesuit mission, writes with surprising candor how Torrès had secretly sent Almeida "to Takushima, which belonged to Dom Antonio [Koteda Yasutsune] and is two miles distant from Hirado. The father wanted to see if it was not possible to convert one of the daimyo of Kyushu by giving him hope that the *nao* from China would come to a harbor in his domain, in case he possessed any appropriate anchorages. To fix these kinds of things, Brother Luis de Almeida was extraordinarily able and talented."[12]

Thus, Dom Antonio, a Matsura vassal and Christian convert, may have been the first to suggest the port of Yokoseura as an alternative to the anchorage before Hirado. Now, plotting with Domingos Riveira, the Portuguese pilot, Bartolomeu Konoe, a convert from the capital region,[13] went with the pilot to sound the harbor of Yokoseura, located in the neighboring domain of Ōmura at the very tip of the Sonogi peninsula. With the right wind, it was less than six hours away by boat.[14] To hide the presence of the foreigner on the boat, they went in one that was roofed over like a house-boat, of the kind that local fishermen used to sail along the coast accompanied by their wives and children.[15] If the harbor proved deep enough, the plan was to obtain permission from the nearby warlord, Ōmura Sumitada (1533–1587), to use his domain for trade and missionary work.[16]

Finding the harbor usable, the two men went on to Ōmura and managed to contact Sumitada's senior retainer Tomonaga Ise no kami Sumitoshi.[17] The answer they brought back was positive. Sumitada said that he would be happy to receive the Portuguese ship in his domain. When the good news reached Cosme de Torrès, he sent his own emissary and one of his oldest converts, Uchida Tomé, to the warlord to make sure there were no misunderstandings. Again, Sumitada answered that his decision had not changed and that Torrès should send a missionary, so he could support the building of a church. He would give them some rice fields to pay for its upkeep, tax-free status for ten years for the Portuguese, and the assurance that, without permission from the Jesuits, gentiles would not be allowed to live in Yokoseura.[18] All this took time, of course, and it is doubtful that the decision not to come back to Hirado could have been made before the Portuguese left that year.

The next year, therefore, although Pedro Barreto Rolim, the Captain Major of the carrack of 1562, had been planning to return to Hirado, a message from the Jesuits reached him at sea.[19] He was told a new and safer harbor had been prepared and to continue sailing along the West and North coast of the Sonogi peninsula. We do not know the exact date of Barreto's arrival, but it must have been in the first half of July. On the fifteenth of that month, Luis d'Almeida, accompanied by a Japanese we only know by his

Christian name of Melchior, also arrived in the port.[20] The next day, Almeida and some representatives of the Captain Major, whose names have not been preserved, left Yokoseura by boat to sail through the Hariʾo channel into Ōmura Bay, the large inlet around which the domain of the same name was situated.

The Portuguese arrived in Sumitada's stronghold on 17 July. They were the first group of Europeans he had met. During their interview, Sumitada deeded the hamlet of Yokoseura and two miles of land around it, including its inhabitants, to the church. In this area, Buddhists would not be not allowed to live, unless specifically authorized to do so by the church. As announced before, Portuguese merchants who came to Yokoseura would be able to do business tax-free for ten years.[21] Their negotiations concluded, Almeida and his companions returned to Yokoseura two days later.[22] Next, Torrès himself also suddenly came to the new port and spent the summer there, bringing a number of Christians from Funai.[23] The Jesuits and their Japanese converts must have been busy. They built a church and a residence on the spot where formerly a Buddhist temple had stood. It was a secluded place surrounded by tall trees. As the Jesuits write, it was the Good Lord himself who had determined that He and His servants were to dwell in the best spot of the hamlet.[24]

*   *   *

Becoming a Christian: Ōmura Sumitada (1)

Right away, Japanese Christians, encouraged by the establishment of the first exclusively Christian community in Japan, started to converge upon Yokoseura. On 24 February 1563, Ash Wednesday and the first day of Lent, the settlement already counted people from Bungo, Hakata, Yamaguchi, and even from Miyako, the ancient capital of Japan, who all came to receive the ash mark on their foreheads.[1] The majority of these Christians, of course, were mobile merchants, who realized that the surest way to obtain access to Chinese silk and the other foreign merchandise brought by the Portuguese was to follow the directions of the padres. In March, an enormous cross, eighteen feet tall and nine feet wide, made of lumber more than a foot thick, was erected on a hill in front of the church.[2] In spite of having sprained his ankle, the Superior walked between the church and the cross in a procession. A thousand people are said to have participated, with the Portuguese children of the town dancing in the van.[3]

In the second half of March,[4] Sumitada himself visited Yokoseura, bringing half a dozen casks of sake, a large quantity of fish, a good-sized boar, and some silver as presents for Torrès.[5] This was the first time in almost two years that he showed personal interest in the joint venture that was taking shape in his domain.[6] He was accompanied by all his principal retainers. Padre Torrès "was happy to see his good will, and returned it by going to visit him in his lodgings with five worthy Portuguese [*Portugueses honrados*], who had wintered in Yokoseura, inviting him to dinner in our residence on the following day."[7] The Japanese warlord accepted the invitation and he arrived the next day with some of his relatives. They were given the best lunch the Jesuits were able to prepare for them, while Portuguese merchants served at the table as if Sumitada were a European prince.

After the meal, the father took him apart and

told him that for many reasons he was much "consoled" by his arrival, among which one of the most important was the opportunity to show him the law that we preach. For it behooved him, just as the farmer, who sows his field and looks for the best seed, to search out the best law to plant in his heart and those of his vassals, and that this was the seed of peace and eternal life. And then he took him to the altar, which had been prepared in advance as if for a holy day, with a painting of Our Lady of Grace, which the Japanese lord was very happy to see.[8]

We clearly see here the method of the Jesuits to start a Japanese nobleman without any background in Christian doctrine on his way to conversion. An exotic meal had been served with richly dressed Portuguese merchants at the beck and call of the padre and his guests, illustrating the primacy of religious over secular power. Then, the novice was led to the sacred space of the altar and shown a portrait of the Virgin Mary. We know that, from their very first arrival in Japan, the Jesuits used oil paintings they had brought all the way from Europe to get their ideas across.[9] Later, in the seventeenth and eighteenth centuries, there existed a whole industry in Italy producing oil paintings on copper (easier to transport and more sturdy than paintings done on canvas) for the sole purpose of equipping missionaries traveling to out-of-the-way places in the newly discovered parts of the world.

We should not underestimate the effect such paintings had on those, such as Sumitada, unfamiliar with them. In contrast to the rather formulaic representations of people in Japanese secular and Buddhist painting on silk and paper, religious oil paintings on canvas in the Flemish style (in vogue in mid-sixteenth-century Portugal) had reached great heights of realism.[10] In general, European artists of the time had learned to paint human faces so life-like that it seems as if they are alive themselves. Eyes on the canvas may stare back at the viewer from whatever angle they are perceived. Walking past the painting, it is as if such eyes are following us.[11]

When one is not used to this degree of realism (and even if one is), there is powerful magic in this kind of painting. Their approximation of reality itself is so close that, after viewing such a painting, it must seem but a small step to conclude that people who are able to achieve this type of truth in painting also must be privy to other religious truths. Oil painting thus bypasses rational discourse to appeal directly to the emotion of recognition. We will have to come back later to the function of paintings in the efforts of the Jesuit missionaries, but for the moment it is enough to signal the artificial epiphany induced by Cosme de Torrès in Ōmura Sumitada. Of course, a painting like the one Sumitada had viewed was hard to come by. It would have been awkward if the warlord had asked for it, so another painting of the cross "very well done" by a Japanese Christian artist from Miyako had been prepared to head off any inopportune requests.

Fróis continues:

The father told him that he had no other gift for him than a golden fan with a calligraphy of the letters Jesus and a cross with three nails on top which had been sent to him from Miyako by Father Gaspar Vilela. Sumitada asked Brother Juan Fernandez what the writing on the fan meant. The brother answered him that it was the father's great desire that he should carry that name imprinted on his heart and he was giving him this fan for that reason, but that more time was needed to understand such lofty matters and that he should prepare himself to listen to these things in more detail in other sermons. Sumitada answered that he had decided to do so without fail.[12]

Brother Fernandez (1526–1567) hailed from a rich merchant family in Cordoba, Spain. In May of 1547, while working for his father's business in Lisbon, he had applied to join the Jesuits, was accepted, and in 1548 he was one of the first Jesuits to be sent to the Indies.[13] It is likely that he traveled to India on the same ship as Luis d'Almeida and Luís Fróis.[14] In Goa, he joined the founder of the Jesuit mission in Asia, his fellow countryman Francisco Xavier, with whom he came to Japan in 1549. By the spring of 1563, he was a veteran of the Japan mission, having been in the country for almost fourteen years. Fróis mentions that Fernandez was in the habit of speaking nothing but Japanese, even to the Portuguese traders and his newly arrived fellow Jesuits, and did not care whether he was understood by them or not.[15] At the time of Sumitada's first visit to Yokoseura, he was in all likelihood the best speaker of Japanese among the European members of the order.

The next day, Father Torrès went with his Portuguese companions to thank Sumitada for having come to the residence on the previous day. That same night, the warlord came again to the residence with many of his followers, all of whom he left in the courtyard, taking with him only Tomonaga Shinsuke, the younger brother of his senior retainer.[16]

> Father Torrès came outside to receive him in the church and told him that, as he had come to listen to a sermon, Brother Fernandez would stay with him, and that he asked to be excused so he might go to bed because his sprained ankle was still troubling him. The brother stayed with him and spoke at length about the things that were the most necessary to know, such as the creation of the world, the mystery of the Holy Trinity, the downfall of Lucifer and those who fell from grace with him, about Adam's sin, and the manner in which mankind is redeemed as well as the last judgment.[17]

Sumitada then asked the brother "to tell him about the wondrous merits of the name Jesus, and the mysteries of the cross. Therefore, the brother told him the story of the Emperor Constantine and how he came to recognize the great excellence of the cross, which Sumitada rejoiced to hear. He asked for the words *per signum crucis*, the Pater Noster, and Ave Maria prayers to be written down for him."[18] He inquired why it was Lent, how Christians did penance, and why such a season had been adopted? He also asked for a paper with the names of the days of the week, on which days Christians did not eat meat, the days of the saints, and the other holy days of the year. In order to remember all of this, he wrote it down in his own script. This kept him occupied "from the time of Ave Maria until two o'clock in the morning when Father Torrès went to say goodbye to him and he returned to his lodgings."[19]

Sumitada displayed commendable humility by coming again to learn more about the new religion. He is most likely to have chosen to come after sunset. Although the text does not say so, he may even have been in time for the Angelus prayer, which is traditionally said half an hour after sunset. As the sun in the second half of March sets in Nagasaki prefecture around 6.30 p.m. this all-night jam session on Christian doctrine is likely to have started sometime after seven in the evening and to have lasted between six and seven hours. Although Brother Fernandez spoke Japanese quite well, it seems as if Sumitada had understood very little of the doctrine that had been explained to him.

All of the topics touched upon are, of course, far from being easily intelligible to anyone without any knowledge of the scripture on which they are based. Sumitada's question afterwards shows, moreover, that he was more interested in the benefits of the incantation of Jesus' name and the magic charms of the cross, in the fashion of Japanese beliefs known as *gense riyaku* or "divine favors received in this world." To answer his query about the magic merits of the cross, Brother Fernandez told him the story of the Emperor Constantine, who in AD 312 before the battle of the Milvian bridge near Rome had seen a cross with the words "Under this sign you will conquer!" As a result of this vision, Constantine had had his soldiers paint crosses on their shields, and then led them to a decisive victory over his rival Maxentius.[20] Now, here was a story that Sumitada understood and to which he seems to have paid close attention.

The great question about Sumitada has always been whether he converted wholeheartedly to Christianity or whether he became a Christian out of expedience. Each historian who has written about him has marked off a different space for the degree of his involvement with Christianity.[21] Here I will try to bring out the tension that exists in our sources between Sumitada as a survivor of Japan's Civil War period (*sengoku jidai*) and the Jesuit idea of a sincere Christian. We will continue to follow the process of his conversion as closely as our sources allow.

The next day Sumitada sent Tomonaga Shinsuke to tell Torrès

> that with the sermons he had heard he had been sufficiently instructed in the tenets of our holy faith and that he had decided to become a Christian as soon as the Lord would give him a son, for having an heir to his domain he would be able to do and order more freely what Father Torrès might ask of him. And even though he was not yet baptized for the moment, he was already a Christian at heart and would like, if Father Torrès permitted him to do so, to wear a cross and entrust himself to Our Lord Jesus Christ.[22]

Torrès answered him that if he could not become a Christian just yet, but intended to do so, he would allow him to wear a cross. He hoped he would persuade his followers to obey God's Law, "because he understood the good results that would necessarily follow if such a holy law were to be practiced in his domain. He further let him know that if he did so, this would lead him to his baptism, because he would be doing such good works, and he hoped that the Lord would grant him the son he asked for and wanted so much, as well as many other sons."[23]

After this, Sumitada went back to Ōmura, where he ordered a golden cross to be made "which he wore in public around his neck in front of all his dependents. And when he went to visit his brother, the king of Arima,[24] the latter asked him upon seeing the cross around his neck if he had become a Christian. He answered yes and when his brother showed that he did not mind at all, the lord of Ōmura was extremely satisfied and happy about this."[25]Thus we see that family considerations may have been the true reason why Sumitada had not been able to receive baptism the first time when he came to Yokoseura. He needed to make sure that his older brother would not object.

For Sumitada, whose position as an adopted heir in the Ōmura domain had always been weak, the military support his brother could give him was a *sine qua non* for holding on to power. Receiving Yoshisada's consent to become a Christian, then, opened the way for adding another pillar to shore up his shaky hold over the domain. His conversion would not only assure the powerful support of the Jesuits for the arrival of the Portuguese carrack in his domain, making it the most important center for foreign trade in Japan, but it would, more specifically, greatly facilitate the acquisition of firearms, gunpowder, and ammunition for both Sumitada and his brother. Therefore, Sumitada's future suddenly looked much brighter than it had been for a long time. No wonder he was, in Fróis' words, "satisfied and happy."

Sumitada's brother, Arima Yoshisada, was also negotiating with Torrès to have him come and reside in his domain.[26] The daimyo of Shimabara sent the padre a present which was brought by the "governor" of Kuchinotsu, the port that could be used by the Portuguese in his domain.[27] So it was possibly to head off his own brother that on Monday,

5 April 1563, Sumitada went back to Yokoseura to celebrate Easter. He announced he was going to build himself a house next to the church, because he expected he was going to spend much time in the new port. The house was erected with the usual speed during Easter week, but Sumitada left again on Holy Saturday, embarking from a stone stairway of twenty-five steps leading down from the church to the water.[28] He promised to return the next month.

Juan Fernandez writes: "[Before he left,] he gave us a number of sign boards with his signature, containing seven or eight laws, which Father Torrès had asked him to write down for the sake of the good government of the port. The first of these was that anyone who wished to live in this settlement should obey the law of God, and if he did not he could not reside here."[29] To this Fróis' account of this occasion adds that Sumitada also ordered some of his men to remain behind to back up Torrès and make sure that the people living in the port would all "listen to the sermons and the matters of our holy faith, and if they did not, they would be thrown out of the settlement. And he returned to Ōmura on Holy Saturday, for he had important matters of war and peace to attend to."[30]

Sign boards were the usual form of public announcement of new laws in Japan. These rules established the precedent for the exercise of power by the Jesuits that remained in force at least until 1587, the year of Sumitada's death as well as of Hideyoshi's take-over of Nagasaki. Attendance at mass, then, was compulsory in Yokoseura for those who made the port their home. It seems that Sumitada had originally intended to stay in Yokoseura until after Easter Sunday, but he must have gotten word on Good Friday that while he was gone trouble was brewing back home. Fróis, as usual never giving us facts, but only a glimpse of what might have been going on, writes: "In Ōmura, Sumitada's[31] principal town, a sudden quarrel between two knights left one of them injured, and all his relatives were gathering to avenge the injury, while those of the offender prepared to defend themselves, so that the whole domain began to stir and everyone came running to him."[32]

Subsequently, the news from Ōmura must have continued to be bad. Two weeks after Easter, on 26 April, Torrès decided to send Luis d'Almeida with orders that if Sumitada was not in any personal danger he was to stay by his side and send reports about what was going on. The distance from Yokoseura to Ōmura by boat was "five or six of our leagues."[33] The wind was favorable, for Almeida arrived on the same day as he had left. He found the whole domain in an uproar. "He took lodgings in the house of a brother of the man who had injured the other, for he was a great friend of the church and about to become a Christian."[34] That night and the following day, everyone was up in arms and ready to fight, but eventually Sumitada's decision to exile the offender calmed down the anger of the injured party and left everyone else with a sense of relief.

The next day,[35] Sumitada sent word to Almeida that he wanted to hear more about his religion, but asked him to come at night when he was less busy. Moreover, he said, the women of his household also wanted to hear him. The brother came that same night and held a long sermon to which his audience listened with great attention. Afterwards, Sumitada had many questions and he seemed very pleased with what he had heard.

On 21 May 1563, Cosme de Torrès decided to go and pay Sumitada a visit in his castle town. The padre brought with him three "worthy" Portuguese traders who had spent the winter in Yokoseura.[36] We are reminded of the five "worthy" Portuguese who had originally accompanied Torrès when he first had gone to see Sumitada on his first visit to Yokoseura in March, as well as those who had served Sumitada during the guest meal at the Jesuit residence. But again the historian remains annoyed with the Jesuit letter writer of the *Cartas* and the mission's historian Luís Fróis, who used the same letter in his voluminous *Historia de Japam* and only adds that these were "highly ranked persons."[37] But, however worthy or highly ranked these Portuguese may have been, they were not worthy enough to be included by name.

The delegation from Yokoseura was received with great warmth in the castle town. Sumitada first invited all of them to an elaborate banquet. Later he spoke in private with the padre, who proposed that he build a church in the town. The warlord's answer was that this was exactly what he wanted to do, because he was sure that there would be no one of account in his domain who would not become Christian. Before a church could be build, however, it would be necessary to destroy the great Buddhist monastery in town. Regrettably, the bonzes were well-connected in Ōmura and he feared another uprising over this issue, so, with the padre's consent, he preferred to wait for an opportunity that would allow him to do as he wanted. Torrès could see the reasonableness of this plan and thanked him for the reception he had received before returning to Yokoseura.

This is the way Torrès' visit is presented in the Jesuit sources.[38] We are left with an uneasy feeling that something has been left out here. Was the plan to construct a church in Ōmura really a compelling reason for Torrès, who still had trouble walking, to go all the way to Ōmura? Was it not a little premature to ask of Sumitada that he build a church in his castle town before he had been baptized himself? The importance of Torrès' mission, of course, lay precisely here. The padre needed to forge the iron while it was still hot. The longer he waited, it must have seemed to him, the greater the chance that Sumitada would become distracted by other concerns. Torrès, of course, had no intention to let the affairs of this world, *i.e.*, trouble in Ōmura, stand in the way of God's design. Most likely, then, his intention in visiting Ōmura was to nudge Sumitada a step further towards his intended baptism.

This is why it was important that the three "worthy" or "highly-ranked" Portuguese came with the padre. What Torrès was doing with this visit was, in fact, to introduce Sumitada to three potential *padrinhos* or godfathers, there being no Japanese Christian of sufficient rank available to lead Sumitada to the altar to be married to the Good Lord until the end of time. The problem was, of course, that the Portuguese available were not likely to have been of sufficient eminence for the task either. That must be the reason why their names were omitted from the record. Whoever they may have been,[39] the stage was now set for the morality play of a warlord's baptism.

Two or three days after Torrès' departure from Ōmura, Sumitada sent him a message that he would like the padre to send him one of the Japanese converts from his household who knew enough about his religion to explain it to him. Torrès sent back a message that the person he had in mind had been sent to Hirado and that he had no one else who would serve. Instead five or six days later,[40] Sumitada came to Yokoseura again with "twenty or thirty of his retainers, for his desire to receive baptism was growing by the day."[41] He sent word to Torrès that he very much wanted to talk to him, but that before coming to see him he wanted to know how he should dress, and for that reason he asked to be sent someone who spoke Japanese well, so he could tell him what the padre desired.

Torrès sent a knowledgeable Japanese Christian and Sumitada spent half the night with him. The man returned to tell the padre that Sumitada was ready to receive baptism if Torrès would be willing to allow it. However, although he was lord of his domain and his vassals, he still had to be mindful of his oldest brother, the "King of Arima," who would not "allow him to burn all the Buddhist temples or tear down the monasteries of the bonzes. But he promised and gave his word that he would not have anything to do with them, and that if he did not support them they would wither away by themselves."[42] Thus, Torrès seems at least to have hinted to Sumitada that his conversion would necessarily entail the destruction of the work of the Devil in his domain, as represented by the Buddhist establishment.[43]

At this junction, however, the good padre chose to refrain from insisting on this point. The conversion of a territorial ruler (the first in Japan!) was enough of a success by itself. The destruction of Buddhism in Ōmura could wait. His answer, however, left no doubt about what he expected would be their common goal from now on, saying that: "with this promise and the intent he had to rid himself and to destroy everything in his power when the moment for it had come, he would baptize him, for he had already achieved a good understanding of the Christian religion."[44]

Later that night, a happy Sumitada came with all his retainers to hear sermons until the early morning. Finding him sufficiently instructed because of all the sermons he had heard so far, Torrès proposed to call together all the Portuguese so that the baptism might be celebrated in an appropriately festive manner. Sumitada, however, did not seem interested in publicity of the event. Just one Portuguese, he said, who was staying in the house of the father would suffice as godfather. And so he was baptized the next morning together with all the retainers who were accompanying him, "and before they received the baptismal water, Dom Bartolomeu [Sumitada] ordered them to recite the Christian doctrine in a loud voice, which they all knew, and to tell Father Torrès that none of the men who were being baptized there was unworthy to receive baptism."[45]

Again the historian is dissatisfied with this account of Sumitada's baptism. Why are we not given a firm date for this event?[46] Why don't we have a letter written by the principal actor in this morality play, Cosme de Torrès himself? Jesuit historians are in agreement that such a letter has existed, but that it did not survive.[47] We have already seen how Fróis has made use of this letter in his *Historia*, but he, too, refrains from giving the exact date, and, what is more, he only makes the most cursory mention of the baptism itself.[48]

In view of the fact that the baptism of a warlord was a major event in the history of the Jesuit mission in Japan, and that Sumitada's baptism was to have endless consequences and ramifications, this general Jesuit reticence is exceedingly suspect. The solution to the problem must lie in the rather hurried and premature nature of the affair, which was, already at the time it had occurred, a rather shameful way to do things.

A more detailed description, of course, would have had to include, apart from the date, at least the name of Sumitada's godfather. As we have seen, the social background of the most likely candidate, here described flatly as "one Portuguese who was staying in the house of the father," was totally inappropriate for the occasion, at least in the opinion of the readership of the Jesuit letters back in Europe. And what about the godfathers of Sumitada's twenty-five samurai retainers? These men must have been the *fudai* or hereditary retainers of the Ōmura House, and possibly the former *jizamurai* or *jitō* or landowning samurai of the Ōmura domain. They are likely to have included men from the Ichinose, Imamichi, Kosasa, Nagasaki, Nishi, Shō, Tomachi, Tomonaga, and other families.

It is doubtful that they really knew what they were doing, apart from what they had been told by Sumitada, namely that their conversion would bring sizeable profits to the Ōmura domain. It would certainly stretch the truth to assume that, apart from Sumitada's own, most of these other conversions were anything else but acts of obedience to Sumitada's will. We have the Christian name of at least one these men, Nagasaki Jinzaemon Sumikage (1548–1621), who, fifteen years old, is likely to have received the baptismal name of Bernardo at this time.[49] If he had a godfather, it would probably have been another non-descript Portuguese wintering in Yokoseura. Where the lack of a clear date in the record is concerned, such an unequivocal date might show that this seminal baptism had not taken place on an auspicious day at all.[50]

Almeida, who had started it all, was not present,[51] and he too mentions his learning of the event only once or twice, and then in the shortest of possible ways.[52] Surely, Sumitada and his retainers would have been disappointed, and maybe even indignant, to learn that their baptism generated so little enthusiasm on the part of the Jesuit who had first introduced them to the benefits of Christian dogma. Four centuries later, all we can do is conclude that the Jesuits in Japan must have decided together that, for all practical purposes, it was better to play down this event.[53]

But there was, of course, in contrast to hard facts like dates and names, always room in the Jesuit letters for more evidence of genuine piety on the part of Sumitada. So our account of the baptism in the *Cartas* or Jesuit Letters ends with his request that, as soon as a new and larger painting arrived from India, he would be given the painting of Nossa Senhora da Graça, standing on the altar of the church at Yokoseura, which he had admired so much on his first visit. "This one is but small," the new convert argued, "and therefore perfect to be carried around on his campaigns so he could worship it every day." The next morning he left the port in a hurry, because he had received word from his brother that he should come to his aid with his men. Before he departed he sent word to the padre "to ask God to be on his side and that of his men and of his pregnant wife, so that He might grant her an easy childbirth."[54]

Somewhere along the way to the battlefield, Sumitada made sure that God saw that, from now on, he would be fighting "under the sign of the cross," just like the Emperor Constantine. Passing by a large temple complex dedicated to Marishiten, the bodhisattva of war in the Buddhist pantheon in Japan,[55] he ordered his men to dismount and hold back the people. The pagoda of the temple had a bird at the top,[56] which the Japanese of the time could not pass without doing it reverence and consulting it for their problems. Sumitada,

> with great daring, ordered his men to pull down the pagoda and burn it, and after that the rest of the temple too. He took the bird and slashed it with his sword, saying "Oh, how many times have you deceived me!" When the fire had burned itself out completely, he ordered a beautiful cross to be erected on the same spot. After going on his knees with all his men in front of it, they rode off into battle.[57]

What lessons can be learned from this baptism and how it is reported? First, the lack of appropriate godfathers, its hurried nature, and the lack of a firm date indicate that, for Torrès, his chosen strategy to establish a stable and safe haven for the trade was more important than any consideration of the readiness of these candidates to receive baptism, all stories of Sumitada's great piety notwithstanding. This must have been clear to anyone familiar with the usual church practice in establishing the eligibility for baptism of an adult. Although eminently understandable from the point of view of the survival of the Japanese mission, in this way Torrès nonetheless opened himself up to criticism from more doctrinally inclined fellow Jesuits outside Japan.

* * *

The Mission's Superior: Cosme de Torrès

Torrès was a special case inside the Society. Born in Valencia in 1510, he had left for Mexico in 1538, already an ordained priest.[1] This was two years before the Society of Jesus was established. In 1542, over the protests of his parishioners at the court of the viceroy of Mexico City, who "loved him more than if he were their own flesh and blood,"[2] Torrès left for the Moluccas, where, in Ambon, he met one of Loyola's initial companions, Francisco Xavier (1506–1552), who had been chosen to found the Jesuit mission in Asia.[3] In 1548, the two priests travelled back to Goa together, where Torrès was admitted into the Society.[4] Xavier must have liked Torrès, just as his parishioners in Mexico City had, for they traveled again together to Japan in 1549, and shared the initial hardships of setting up the mission. When Xavier left Japan in November of 1551, he left Torrès in charge. In view of Xavier's sacrosanct stature in the Society, which he acquired immediately upon his death in 1552, Torrès' position in Japan may have been virtually untouchable at first, even though his familiarity with Jesuit custom and practice as it grew over the Society's first decades during the Council of Trent must have been sketchy at best.

To the Jesuits who had joined the Society after Torrès, then, his handling of Sumitada's baptism may have highlighted his lack of training in what was rapidly becoming the traditional Jesuit mold. Torrès, in fact, did not really fit into any of the official categories of the Society, the professed, the spiritual coadjutors, the temporal coadjutors, etc.[5] By 1563, Torrès had been a Jesuit for fifteen years, and Superior of the Japanese mission for twelve. Still, at the time of Sumitada's baptism, he had not even professed the required first three vows of poverty, chastity, and obedience. There was a fourth vow as well, that of special obedience to the pope himself, which was reserved for the elite among the Society's members and becoming *de rigueur* for any leader of a mission field.[6] The problem with professing the vows was, however, that this could only be done before someone who had already professed them himself, and that would have entailed a trip for Torrès to Macao, or even further afield, and the Superior may have felt he could not be missed in Japan, or that, in case he went, he might not be able to get back.

Three ships from Macao arrived in Yokoseura on or around Tuesday, 6 July 1563. The Captain Major was Dom Pedro d'Almeida da Gueira. He was accompanied by a galleon of Francisco Castão and a large junk from Siam under Gonzalo Vaz.[7] They brought two more Jesuits to Japan: Padre Giovanni Battista di Monte (1528–1578) from Ferrara in northern Italy and Padre Luís Fróis (1532–1597) from Lisbon. Two more Portuguese, Jacome Gonçalves and Michael Vaz, born in India, arrived on the same fleet. Both applied for admission to the Society upon arrival in Japan, and were permitted to do so the following year.[8] On Friday, 9 July, that same week, Luis d'Almeida arrived to join the other Jesuits in Yokoseura.[9] Altogether there were now three padres, two brothers, two novices, and several Japanese live-in helpers (*dōjuku*) in the new town.[10]

On Saturday, Almeida left again to go and bring the news of the arrival of the

Portuguese to Sumitada, who was now, a little over one month after his baptism, at his field headquarters somewhere in Ōmura.[11] They met on Sunday, and again on Monday 12 July. When the brother called, Sumitada paid him the honor of coming outside to greet him. Later, Almeida reported:

> He was dressed in completely new armor and over everything else he wore a garment of hemp, with a little below each shoulder a white sphere with the word JESUS in green letters inside it and from their middle arising a very pious cross with its usual INRI inscription, and in the white of the sphere around it the three nails all put in their right places, and in the same way he had another one on his back with other freshly painted images on the same fabric. He wore a rich cross around his neck from a chain of beads.... He was surrounded by many knights, his retainers, who were dressed in the same manner with golden crosses around their necks and almost all had well-made beads."[12]

The warlord and his retainers put on a good Christian show. The fan, with its design of the cross, the letters JESUS, and the three nails which Torrès had given to Sumitada on his first visit to Yokoseura, had evidently been put to good use to design a new *mon* or crest for Sumitada. This is indicated by the spots on Sumitada's over-garment, below the shoulders in the front and below the nape of the neck in the back, which correspond exactly with the places reserved for *kamon* or family crests on traditional Japanese dress.

After a meal of freshly caught trout, there was time for more piety. Sumitada had been able to lay his hands on a booklet containing questions on Christian doctrine asked by some educated people from Miyako and answered by Padre Gaspar Vilela, who had been stationed in the capital since 1559. The warlord now asked Almeida to answer the same questions for him. In this manner they again spent a few hours elucidating the religion to which Sumitada had converted. The warlord invited his retainers to sit in and listen to their conversation, so that it "was wondrous to behold such devotion in someone of such high rank and so recently converted."[13] Several days later, on Thursday, 15 July, Almeida returned to Yokoseura and the next Sunday it was decided that he would bring Padre di Monte to Bungo.[14] They probably left on Monday 18 July.

There is a gap in the record until the beginning of August, when Sumitada visited Yokoseura for the fourth time that year. He came to see Cosme de Torrès and the Portuguese merchants. An anonymous Portuguese merchant has left an account preserved in the *Cartas* reporting how happy Sumitada was with his reception by the Captain Major aboard the carrack ("to judge from the expression on his face he appreciated our efforts more than anyone on earth. Strangely, he seemed to like all the Portuguese"), and how impressed the Portuguese were with the warlord's "devotion and humility."[15]

What happened next is unclear. Sumitada does not seem to have stayed in Yokoseura very long. We know that, also in the beginning of August, he gave another proof of the sincerity of his conversion to Christianity (one that may have been demanded by Torrès himself) namely the burning of his adopted father's votive tablet.[16] It was and is the custom in Japan for the deceased to be given a posthumous Buddhist name to be carved on his gravestone and on a votive tablet which is kept on the family altar in the home of his surviving wife and children. There upon occasion rites are offered before it and it is kept supplied with symbolic food and drink.

The arrangements for Sumitada's adoption into the household of Ōmura Sumisaki had been made in 1538, when Sumitada was five years old, but he had not actually moved from Arima to Ōmura until he was seventeen or eighteen.[17] Thus he had grown up as a member of the Arima family (and he must have felt himself a real son only of Arima

Haruzumi, 1483–1566). Why was this second son of Arima Haruzumi destined to become the successor of Ōmura Sumisaki, in spite of the fact that the latter had a son of his own? First of all, Sumisaki himself had succeeded his father Sumikore, in spite of the fact that he had an older brother, Yoshizumi, by a different mother. So by-passing the oldest son had happened once before in the Ōmura family.[18]

Next, although in 1538 the rival houses of Arima and Ōmura had set their differences aside and concluded a firm alliance,[19] they had been rivals until that time. The adoption of Sumitada as heir to the Ōmura family likely cemented the alliance and is proof of the stronger position of the Arima House.[20] Sumisaki's real son, Taka'akira, was later adopted into the Ōmura vassal house of Gotō of Takeo, while eighteen of the traditional Ōmura retainers moved with him to his new family. Later, Taka'akira took a wife from the Saigō family of Isahaya, the strategic crossroads of Hizen, and adopted Kore'akira, the younger brother of Matsura Shigenobu (1549–1614) of Hirado, as his heir.[21]

Thus, an anti–Sumitada alliance was being forged inside Ōmura even before Sumitada had entered the domain's ruling family. Upon his succession to the headship of the Ōmura House in 1550, its retainers split into three groups: those who were willing to follow Sumitada, those who refused to consider anyone else but Sumisaki's older brother, the priest Sei'a, and those who had followed Suzuta's grandson Taka'akira to Gotō.[22] For all of these retainers, with the possible exception of some of the younger members of the first group, who had been baptized with Sumitada, the burning of his father-by-adoption Sumisaki's votive tablet was an extremely unfilial as well as a sacrilegious act which provided additional ammunition to his rivals inside the domain.

We look in vain, however, in the Jesuit reports for a description of this act that may have been designed by Torrès as a real test of the sincerity of Sumitada's conversion. Again, we cannot help noticing how the Jesuit letters withhold from us the most crucial details for understanding what happened. Descriptions of trouble in Ōmura at this time, yes, we have plenty, but almost nothing about the reason for the tumult. On Wednesday, 8 August 1563, at seven in the morning, Yokoseura was in a sudden uproar. Japanese merchants who had come to buy the silk from the Portuguese were embarking to go to Hirado. The Christians of the settlement came to warn Cosme de Torrès and the other Jesuits that the situation had turned serious and to embark on one of the Portuguese ships. Although he was sick with fever, Torrès did as he was told, and so did everyone else, so that the whole new town remained deserted. In the end, however, it turned out to have been a false alarm, for the enemy never materialized.

Torrès was told that "the population of the domain was going to rise up against their king [Sumitada] for being a Christian and for wishing so much that a father would reside in his castle town. It would be easy for them to come that night to the settlement to kill Father Torrès together with the king."[23] The phrase about Sumitada's wish that Torrès or another Jesuit would come and take up residence in Ōmura may be read as a tacit admission that the tumult was indirectly caused by the Jesuits, for a padre inside Sumitada's castle could not be expected to tolerate the idol worship of the votive tablet for the soul of the dead Sumisaki.

Good news reached Yokoseura on 13 August. It was brought by Dom Luis [Tomonaga Shinsuke], Almeida's first convert in Ōmura. Gotō Taka'akira, Sumitada's rival, had sent word that he wanted to hear a sermon and was ready to convert to Christianity. He therefore required the presence of a priest in Takeo. Cosme de Torrès, because of his fever, was in no condition to travel, so it was Luís Fróis who would have to go. Having arrived just one month earlier, and not yet knowing any Japanese, Torrès decided that Brother Juan Fernandez should accompany him. Suddenly, there were not enough hands in Yokoseura to make all the preparations. For one thing, the two missionaries decided to take with them the best ornaments for celebrating mass that had just arrived from China.[24] The padres and brothers must have realized that there was danger involved in this trip, but the chance to have another powerful man in the area convert to Christianity was too important to pass up.

There was another task, however, that needed to be taken care of before Fróis could leave. Torrès' condition had not yet allowed him to obey a special order that Fróis had brought for him from Antonio de Quadros, the Provincial of India (in office 1559–1572). This was to profess the three vows of the spiritual coadjutor in front of his newly arrived colleague. When it was announced, on 14 August, that Cosme de Torrès was going to profess his vows the next day, the inhabitants of Yokoseura had no idea what this meant and jumped to the conclusion that Torrès was going to be sworn in as Bishop of Japan. Calls went out for a celebration like they had had that year at Easter. Streets and doorways were decorated with branches, flags put up, and everybody dressed up. The Portuguese in the port also decorated their ships with flags, loaded their artillery, and changed clothes as well.[25]

Thus, on 15 August, Cosme de Torrès finally professed his three solemn vows.[26] The superior was so sick he had to be carried into the church, but not too sick to refrain from a little manipulation of the emotions of his congregation:

> prostrated on the ground, with his face on the floor and his arms raised up before the altar, Father Torrès held, before professing his vows, a colloquy and made several exclamations, with so much tenderness and feeling interrupted by bursting into so many tears and sighs, that neither the Japanese Christians nor the Portuguese, men as well as women, who filled the church to capacity, could contain themselves. And there arose among everyone in the church a lamentation of weeping and sobbing in loud voices that it seemed a completely spontaneous stirring of the people.[27]

By the end of the day of Torrès' vows, both Torrès and Fróis were clearly too sick to travel. Dom Luis, Sumitada's retainer, had already been waiting in Yokoseura for three days to take Fróis and Fernandes to Takeo, and because he could not wait any longer he left after sunset without taking any of the missionaries with him. That same night, he was ambushed by Taka'akira's men in the Hari'o strait and killed, together with every man in his party. The next morning, believing they had succeeded in killing the missionaries, the attackers sent a smoke signal to Taka'akira, who gave orders to attack Sumitada in his own castle to punish him for his unfiliality towards his adoptive and Taka'akira's real father.[28] This smoke signal could be seen from Yokoseura as well, and it dawned on its inhabitants that this time it was no false alarm. Soon, confirmation of the death of Dom Luis and his companions reached the port accompanied by rumors of all kinds: "Some said that Dom Bartolomeo was already dead, others that the rebels would come for the *nao* and other ships lying in the harbor."[29]

With the population of Ōmura in turmoil, the merchants from the rival domain of Bungo saw their chance to destroy the town.[30] In the six years between 1556 and 1562, Torrès had invested much energy in trying to convert the daimyo of a domain in that general area, Ōtomo Yoshishige (1530–1587), but he had not succeeded. Although Yoshishige (who, from 1562 on, was also known as Sōrin) had been gracious and accommodating to the Jesuits, allowing them to build churches and to proselytize freely in his domain, his failure to convert must have irked Torrès and made him all the readier not to be fussy about Sumitada's all too easy acceptance of the faith. With the latter's conversion, the Bungo merchants must have understood that the Portuguese carrack would no longer be coming to their side of Kyushu. According to Fróis, they started a quarrel with the Portuguese and set fire to the town in a fit of malice and jealousy.[31]

While this was going on, Torrès and Fróis were both sick in bed, and so they were among the last to try to get to the safety of the Portuguese ship. When they were about to embark, the Bungo merchants took them hostage and put them in a storehouse with men to guard them both inside and outside. "The reason why they detained the fathers was that they [the merchants] had already handed over more than seventy thousand cruzados worth of silver before all this had started, and feared that with all the offense they had given they would not be able to recover this sum or use it for the trade."[32] This meant that the Portuguese would have to do business with their enemies from Bungo or forfeit the lives of the padres. Sick and hungry in this dark and gloomy space, the two Jesuits spent three or four awful days until their release could be negotiated. They were freed on 20 August.[33]

When they left their jail, the town lay in ashes. Its spacious and pretty church had been burned and razed to the ground. "The Japanese Christians, who had come to live under its protection were once more strangers and exiles, and had scattered and left with their wives and children, without knowing where to go, for everything was in turmoil everywhere."[34] At least Torrès and Fróis, sick as they were, could go and stay on the Portuguese ships, the former on the junk of Gonçalo Vaz and the latter on the *nao* or carrack. This is where they spent the next three months, for the carrack left in the second half of November that year.[35]

For the missionaries there was no longer any point in staying, so Torrès sent Fróis and Fernandez to Takushima, an island not far from Hirado, where most of the population had been converted. Michael Vaz was sent back to Macao as a special envoy from Torrès to report on the events at Yokoseura.[36] Torrès himself went to Shimabara and from there to Takase in Higo,[37] taking with him Luis d'Almeida and Jacome Gonçalves.[38] After the Portuguese ships had left, the large crosses the settlement had erected on Hachinokoshima and on the hill overlooking the town were cut down by men from Hirado.[39] When the Portuguese came back to Japan in July of the next year, 1564, they put into Yokoseura bay, just to make sure, but finding the town still in ruins, they left again and went to Hirado to trade.[40] That meant that the Jesuits were back at square one.

*   *   *

A New Anchorage:
Luis d'Almeida (2)

Sumitada had been converted in the late spring of 1563. For a while, however, after the events at Yokoseura that summer, Torrès did not know whether the ruler of Ōmura had survived the revolt of his own retainers and the direct attack on his stronghold, and if he had, what his whereabouts were. Sumitada, at thirty still young and nimble, had in fact managed to escape into the mountains of Taradake, where he was forced to hide for three months at the Hōenji temple. It is possible that it was at this time that he was forced to take the tonsure by its head priest Hō'in Ashun and took the Buddhist name of Risen, or possibly he did so at the urging of the head priest of the Kinsenji temple Hō'in Agon.[1] We should not take either Sumitada's conversion to Christianity nor this possible reconversion to Buddhism too seriously. If he was anything, Sumitada was a survivor who did whatever was expedient to make the best of any bad situation he found himself in.

As we have seen, after the carrack of that year had left, Torrès had traveled with Luis d'Almeida to Shimabara, where they stayed eight days and whence they crossed over to Takase in Higo.[2] It seemed the safest place to go for the moment, for it was still unclear if Sumitada could get his domain under control again and the troubles in Ōmura had also caused a similar anti–Christian reaction started by the Buddhists in Arima.[3] The loss of Yokoseura must have been a brutal shock to Torrès and the other Jesuits. It took them more than a year to recover from it.

Again, it probably was Luis d'Almeida who came to Torrès with a plan for a new Christian settlement, even more ambitious than the first. It is not surprising, of course, that Almeida initially played the key role in these projects. He was, after all, the most energetic of all the Kyushu Jesuits, and, as a former soldier, sailor, and medic, the horizon of his practical experience was larger than that of any other member of the mission. Having been a layman himself, he also may have been more keenly aware than most of the other missionaries that their most precious asset was their religious leverage over the Portuguese traders.

On his incessant travels throughout Kyushu during 1564, we know of at least one time that Almeida is sure to have passed the future anchorage of the Portuguese ships. On 9 November of that year, he left Hirado, probably very early in the morning, to arrive in Kuchinotsu on the Shimabara peninsula the night of the next day.[4] This means that, on the first day of that trip, he had sailed almost continuously along the Sotome coast of the West Sonogi peninsula. For a sailor like Almeida, it would be second nature to check for inlets and possible anchorages. We can be virtually certain, also, that the men on whose boat he traveled were Japanese Christians eager to quench his thirst for information. It is inconceivable, therefore, that they would not have told him on this occasion (or even on previous ones of which we have no record) about the most famous anchorage of Kyushu, i.e., Nagasaki Bay, even if they did not take the time (or were afraid) to enter the bay and explore it for themselves on that November morning.

The next piece of the reality puzzle that we are trying to put together is the first document directly related to the history of Nagasaki to come from the Japanese side.[5] It consists of a letter written by Sumitada dated the second day of the fifth month of what is, from its context, most likely the year 1565. Although this particular letter lacks a formal addressee, it is part of a number of letters written by Sumitada to Fukuda Kanetsugu, the local strongman of the area along the bay that carried his family name, just north of the entrance to Nagasaki Bay. Sumitada's tone is respectful, even though Kanetsugu was nothing but a small local samurai with only two villages to his name on a bay facing the China Sea. Up to this time, Kanetsugu had been able to preserve a measure of independence between the two regional lords of Arima and Ōmura. It would only be later, from the time of his son Tadakane onwards, that the Fukuda would become more closely linked to the Ōmura house with Tadakane's son Kanechika marrying one of Sumitada's later born daughters.[6]

Also, Sumitada needed Kanetsugu at this moment more than Kanetsugu needed Sumitada, for Sumitada had proof that Yokoseura was not a good place to rebuild the port for the Portuguese. It was too far from his new stronghold of Sanjō Castle, which he had finished against all odds the year before, in 1564.[7] For the Portuguese ships to come further into Ōmura Bay also was not an option. The Hari'o strait leading into the bay was too narrow and dangerous for the large carracks.[8] It was, therefore, futile to hope to get the Portuguese nearer to Ōmura via the large body of water that should, more appropriately, be called the Ōmura Inland Sea. For the Portuguese to keep coming to the Ōmura domain, the only solution was the Sotome coast of West Sonogi, the part of the domain that faced the ocean.

Even today, Nagasaki Bay is still one of Kyushu's best anchorages, but there were several contenders to deal with there, and Sumitada, at this point, was not sure he could dominate them all at the same time. Furthest along the long cape, from which the whole Nagasaki (Jpn *naga* = long, *saki* = cape) area takes its name, and sticking out into the sea, was the lair of the pirate clan of the Fukabori. Always aligned with the powers in Kyushu the furthest away from its home base, the Fukabori were allied with Ryūzōji Takanobu (1529–1584), the powerful adversary of both Ōmura Sumitada and his older brother Arima Yoshinao. Then, dominating roughly the middle of the cape, was the Tomachi family. Originally part of Tajihi family of the medieval Sonogi estate, the Tomachi were now allied to the house of Ōmura.[9]

At the very bottom of the long cape and Nagasaki Bay—a place also known as the Deep Inlet [Fukae-ura]—there was another local *jitō* (originally a shogunal agent of Kamakura), the Nagasaki House, with a stronghold a little over a mile inland on a hill at Sakurababa. As we have seen, Jesuit authors usually assume Nagasaki Jinzaemon to have been one of the twenty-five retainers who were baptized at the same time as Sumitada. Jinzaemon was around fifteen years old at the time, so it is certainly possible, even likely, that he was serving some sort of apprenticeship under Sumitada, who at twenty-nine was almost twice the boy's age. Later (we don't know exactly when), Jinzaemon would marry Tora, Sumitada's third daughter, a fervent Christian, who was born in the year of the Tiger 1554, of a concubine from an old and faithful retainer family of the Ōmura House, the Ichinose.[10] At this time, Jinzaemon's father Nagasaki Samadayū Sumikata[11] was still heading his ancestral charge and he had his own ideas about how to utilize Nagasaki's harbor.[12]

In any case, at least when he wrote his letter to Kanetsugu in 1565 (and, as we shall see, until well after), Sumitada was not yet really thinking of the interior of Nagasaki Bay as the final calling point for the Portuguese carrack, although he did not rule it out:

> Shortly, it will be the time for the ship of the southern barbarians to arrive. If that ship anchors near Hirado or Yokoseura, Buzen, Isahaya and Gotō will be sure to try and take advantage and in particular our enemies will be supplied with too many armaments such as cannon and handguns. That will not be good for the House of Arima in Takaku, nor for myself, so it would be better to be smart and devise a way to have this ship come to Fukuda, Tomachi, or Kuchinotsu in Shimabara.[13]

The next thing we know is that the carrack of 1565, under the command of Dom João Pereira, was warned at sea not to return to Hirado, like the one the year before had done, but to anchor in the bay of Fukuda, just outside the entrance to Nagasaki Bay.[14] It was late June or the beginning of July 1565. We do not have the exact date of the carrack's arrival this year. The first Jesuit to arrive in Fukuda to greet and confess the Portuguese traders was, again, Luis d'Almeida. He had come from Kuchinotsu in Shimabara, where he had just reported on his mission to Bungo to Cosme de Torrès. While in Fukuda, he received word from Ōmura that Sumitada wanted him to come so that he might nurse his daughter, who had fallen sick.[15]

The fastest way from Fukuda to Ōmura was to travel the length of the Nagasaki Bay, next to go ashore near Urakami, and then to continue overland to Nagayo, from where it was easy, at Tokitsu or another port, to find a boat to Sumitada's stronghold on the other side of Ōmura Bay. It is likely that Almeida traveled this route (both coming and going) in July of 1565. This may have been the first time a Jesuit traveled from the mouth of Nagasaki Bay to its far end, and it must have been an eye-opener for Almeida.

In Ōmura, Almeida again preached to Sumitada and his retainers (the first time in two years) after a meal at which Sumitada placed Almeida above himself. During the sermon, Sumitada sat at Almeida's feet in the midst of his retainers of far lower status than himself. It was behavior such as this that convinced the Jesuits of Sumitada's Christian humility, or so they professed. Almeida faithfully recorded his amazement.[16] Back in Fukuda, after the condition of Sumitada's daughter had stabilized, Almeida found a letter from Torrès waiting for him, ordering him to return forthwith to Kuchinotsu to receive instructions for another trip to Bungo. Evidently Torrès still had not quite given up hope that Ōtomo Sōrin might convert, especially now that he had seen that Sumitada had beaten him to the right to receive the Portuguese traders.

After Almeida had left, the Portuguese flock at Fukuda was not left bereft of a sheppard, however, for Torrès now ordered Belchior de Figueiredo (1528–1597) to go there. Like the Jesuit stationed at Hirado at this time, Balthasar da Costa (1538–1577?), Figueiredo was a Portuguese born in India and therefore most likely had an Indian mother.[17] He had arrived in Japan on the carrack of 1564. He came to Fukuda sometime in August 1565, and immediately started to build a church. Later, on 22 October, he wrote a letter in which he reported that Dom Bartholomeo [i.e., Sumitada] had come to visit him in Fukuda many times over the past two months, and so had many other Christian gentlemen holding the strongholds along the coast, who "all came to tell me how glad they were that we had come to their lands."[18]

By August of 1565, however, things were heating up again in northwestern Kyushu, although the Portuguese were still unaware of it. First, another letter from Sumitada written on the 24th day of the month arrived, again addressed to Fukuda Kanetsugu.[19] It warned him about a possible attack on Fukuda Bay by the men from Hirado, and contained an urgent warning to make sure his artillery was in good condition. Second, there was a letter from Padre Balthasar da Costa, stationed at Hirado, warning the men in Fukuda of the same thing, i.e., that an attack by Hirado on Fukuda Bay was imminent.[20]

The padre had seen the preparations with his own eyes:

All the gentiles [of Hirado] took great pleasure in this enterprise because of the great profits they hoped to obtain from it. They prepared in great unity and with singular diligence. The gang planks were of such size that they came up almost as high as the shipboards. In this way, eight or ten large vessels and seventy small ones set out with the best soldiers that the ruler had at his disposal and well supplied with munitions and other necessary gear for this engagement.[21]

The Portuguese, however, did not believe what they heard on the beach of Fukuda from Fukuda Kanetsugu's men, nor did they believe what they read, black on white, what Padre Baltasar da Costa had written to the Captain Major personally. The fact is, Captain Major Dom João Pereira felt on top of the world, and so he was not prepared for what was in store for him. He may also have been dismissive of Baltasar da Costa personally, because of the latter's mixed blood heritage.

* * *

A Knight in Superior Armor: Dom João Pereira

The Portuguese who came to Japan were led by those who owned and commanded the carracks on which the merchandise was transported. These men are known as the *capitães mores*.[1] These Captains Major received, because of their service to the crown and often just because of their birth, "mercies" from the Portuguese kings. Their family backgrounds tended to be similar, the majority being second, third, or bastard sons of medium-ranked nobility. First sons of these families would stay at home to inherit the family title and property.

The common denominator that brings these men together in the sources is a royal letter of appointment, the so-called *alvará*.[2] To be more precise, the captains of the Japan voyage constitute a sub-group of a larger group of Captains Major, who held royal appointments as outbound or inbound commanders of Portuguese fleets, overseas settlements, and other trade routes in Asia. It is impossible to study the captains of the Japan voyage apart from this larger group, for the appointment to the lucrative Japan voyage was usually the result of years of service in the other capacities.

When we check the background of Dom João Pereira, the Captain Major who came to Japan in 1565, we find that he was one of the few captains who came from northern Portugal. He was born the second of fifteen children that the third Count of Feira, Dom Manuel Pereira, sired with three women.[3] The Count of Feira was the head of one of Portugal's great families, owning the famous castle of Santa Maria da Feira, just south of Porto, which was an ancient stronghold in the battle against the Moors dating from before the time that Portugal had a royal family.

Diogo do Couto (1542?–1616), the contemporary historian of Portugal's thalassocracy in Asia, mentions Dom João Pereira several times as an active participant in several raids by the Portuguese in India.[4] Ostensibly in reward for these "services," he was given an *alvará* for the captaincy of Malacca on 10 March 1546.[5] He was also admitted into the Order of Christ, on 18 January 1547.[6] Back in India, Governor Francisco Barreto, a fellow member of the Order of Christ,[7] finally sent him to Malacca in March of 1556 to replace Antonio de Noronha, who had died.[8] The captaincy of Malacca was a real test of a person's abilities, and it is likely that Pereira failed here, for he never finished the three-year period allotted to him, but was replaced after one year by João de Mendonça, who would become Governor of India in 1564.

It is unclear what happened. Diogo do Couto must have known, but he does not tell us. At any rate, Dom João continued to be protected by Francisco Barreto with whom he returned to Portugal, leaving Goa on 20 December 1560 on the governor's carrack *S. Gião*.[9] They arrived in Lisbon on 13 June 1561.[10] He must have gone to India a third time, with the next fleet leaving Lisbon 15 March 1562, for he commanded a ship in the great armada prepared by the Viceroy Dom Francisco Coutinho, another member in the Order of Christ, in December of 1562.[11] In 1564, we find him in Macao, where he refused to support his fellow–Portuguese in attacking Chinese "pirates," and the next year he came to Fukuda.[12]

Here, in the fall of 1565, Portuguese traders and Japanese samurai from Hirado, dismayed that their island was no longer the port of call for the Portuguese carrack, came to blows. Fróis' description of the battle shows Dom João in a rather un-heroic light. The Jesuit chronicles: "The battle lasted for almost two hours. Both sides fought with a strange fierceness, the Portuguese to defend themselves and the Japanese in order to carry away in their claws their victory and prize. They shot with a powerful musket at the Captain Major Dom João Pereira and hit him in the head, but as he was wearing a demonstration helmet, it did not nothing but make a dent into it."[13]

It is likely that Dom João was carried into his cabin at this point. Not dead, it is true, but at least with a violent headache. Fróis continues:

> When the battle was at its most fierce on the deck and along the railing of the *nao*, the Japanese with their usual audacity and courage were entering the vessel through the open passageways of the poop until they entered the cabin of the Captain Major, where they held him and took his writing desk. Quickly, those who were defending the quarterdeck came to the rescue and killed some of these men on the spot, while others fell into the sea.[14]

Dom João's mistakes, as listed by Fróis, were: he refused to heed the good advice of the Jesuits and their Japanese allies. When he was anywhere near the battle, it was only to get shot in the helmet, and then to be carried away, presumably to his cabin, only to be taken by surprise a second time, when bold Japanese warriors penetrated the poop deck of the carrack. He ended up in his cabin and, *en passant*, was taken hostage. In the end, he needed to be rescued a second time, probably only surviving because nobody in the *mêlée* was paying him any attention.

By now, however, we have come to know the Captain Major as a typically arrogant Portuguese nobleman and member of the Order of Christ, whose career was built on connections but whose abilities did not live up to the challenges of East Asia. What happened in Fukuda nicely fits into this pattern, except for the fact that he survived the engagement. The historian, however, remains dissatisfied with Padre Fróis' account, until he finds another letter from Sumitada addressed to Kanetsugu, in which the former congratulates the latter on his victory over the men from Hirado.[15]

This letter is dated the twenty-sixth day of the ninth month, which corresponds with 19 October 1565. Assuming that it took a day for news to travel from Fukuda to Ōmura, this must mean that the battle took place on the day before, in the morning of 18 October.[16] After three large Japanese attacking vessels had been disabled, the men from Hirado called it quits and returned home with their wounded. Eight Portuguese were dead and many others were hurt, but they had proven that even with an inept commander they could withstand a surprise attack from a large force of professional Japanese warriors.

The latter had retired with seventy dead and more than two hundred wounded. It suddenly changed the perception in Japan about the Portuguese "merchants."[17] The incident illustrates also how deadly accurate Portuguese fire could be in a close engagement. And although João Pereira was exceptional in being the most exalted Captain Major ever to reach Japan (he was both high nobility and a professed Knight of Christ), his career in Asia is in general pretty typical in showing the importance of connections, both in getting royal permits as well as in actually being appointed and sent to one's post by the Viceroy. Connections were important on all levels, even historiographically.

Fróis, for example, who must have known about Dom João's unheroic behavior in Macao in 1564 and possibly also of his failure in Malacca, never made any allusion to it in his account of his poor showing in Fukuda in 1565. And even the punch of that account was pulled by the omission of the date on which the incident had taken place. This made it—for all practical purposes—essentially a non-event, a mercy and a bounty to the Captain Major's place in history, and more especially in the annals of the House of Feira. In our context here, the account of Dom João's character and career serves to establish some parameters for Portuguese greed and arrogance. Not all Captains Major coming to Japan were as close to the caricature of the Portuguese *fidalgo* that Dom João represents, but they all shared some of his characteristics.

* * *

The Chinese in Nagasaki Bay: Nagasaki Sumikata

That year of 1565 Padre Figueiredo was joined in Fukuda by Luis d'Almeida sometime in October. We have a letter written by Almeida from Fukuda on 25 October, or one week after the engagement with Hirado.[1] It would be interesting to know if Almeida had arrived before the attack on the 18th of that month, and if so, if he, an ex-soldier, participated in the battle on the Portuguese side. Of course, the Jesuit correspondence does not provide us with such suggestive dates or such compromising information. Both Almeida and Figueiredo left Fukuda after the Portuguese embarked to return to Macao, the former for Kuchinotsu, Cosme de Torrès' new base, and the latter for nearby Teguma.[2]

We may be pretty sure, however, that both missionaries already had had ample opportunity to take a close look at Nagasaki Bay. Fróis in his *Historia* pretends that before the Jesuit "discovery" of the bay nobody had been aware that this was Kyushu's prime anchorage. This is at best wishful thinking, but probably proof of more deviousness than Fróis is usually credited with. We have already noted, however, how, with Fróis, we always have to be alert when we notice that something, like a crucial name or date, is missing. How much more so, when we notice that Fróis studiously avoids writing anything at all about the situation in Nagasaki Bay before the founding of Nagasaki.

But in the absence of Fróis' testimony there is very little left to go on. The reader will have to be patient and give the historian a chance to make his case for an alternative explanation of the founding of Nagasaki than the Jesuits have supplied so far.[3] Here it will be assumed that Nagasaki Bay was, in fact, being used for intensive, but clandestine, trade between China and Japan, mostly carried in Chinese vessels. Even though the Ming had forbidden its subjects to engage in illegal overseas trade outside the tally-trade system, there existed before the arrival of the Europeans "a chain of port communities of Chinese traders" all the way from Java to Japan.[4]

The last tribute-trade ship to reach China from Japan had been sent by the Ōuchi House of Western Honshu in 1547. After that the Ming Court had halted the exchange because the competition for access to Chinese ports by the different houses of Western Japan, such as the Hosokawa, Ōuchi, Ōtomo, and Shimazu, had led the court to conclude that it was impossible to determine who was Japan's legitimate ruler, worthy of investiture by the Ming and deserving to be the recipient of legal opportunities for trade.[5]

When Ming officials tried to enforce the laws forbidding trade outside the official tribute system, they met with widespread Chinese and Japanese resistance that crystallized in combined Chinese-Japanese organized attacks on the Chinese coastal provinces, especially in the years between 1552 and 1565.[6] Most of these Chinese pirate-traders were from Fujian, the mainland's coastal province that faces Taiwan. Its special position is due to its mountainous character and the salinization of its coastal areas, which meant that agriculture could not feed the population of the whole province.

It therefore needed to import food. This led to monocultures of crops used to pay for the import of rice, sugar, fruits, tea, and indigo.[7] Trade was the natural result of this situation. Fujian had large wood reserves that lent themselves to shipbuilding. The Fujianese were familiar with the sea, used to contact with foreigners, and forced to trade even if the laws of the rest of China forbade it. This gave them the name of lawless marauders. Nine out of ten people in the province were said to have been involved in maritime pursuits. Almost all ships reaching Japan between 1550 and 1567 came from harbors in Fujian.[8]

The official interdiction of overseas trade by the Ming resulted in a transfer of the private trade from the large cities (Canton, Fuzhou, Ningbo, where the official tribute trade was located) to less easily patrolled and controlled smaller harbors along the long coastline, to out-of-the-way inlets and bays, or even to the numerous small islands lying off the coast.[9] This led to a separation of anchorages and markets, which in its turn resulted in the building of numerous small craft transporting the imported goods from the anchorage to the markets where they were to be sold. The market places, also, were not located at cross-roads of major transportation arteries, but in rather out-of-the-way places seen from a Chinese perspective.

The fact that such market places were nevertheless frequented by merchants from all parts of China speaks eloquently of the degree to which the maritime prohibitions hindered the normal development of overseas trade and resulted in outrageous prices.[10] In other words, the maritime prohibitions pursued by the Ming became a windfall for Fujian Province as a whole.[11] It is useful, therefore, to distinguish markets from harbors and anchorages. The first served for the distribution of goods, the second for the building and maintenance of shipping, and the third for entering the country unnoticed from overseas.[12]

The prohibitions also caused a wide-spread involvement of bureaucratic officials in the forbidden trade. Overseas trade with Japan, for example, could only be pursued with large ocean-going ships that could not remain unnoticed by the local authorities, who needed to be paid off in return for their silence and protection against the state itself.[13] Political power was always linked to economic resources among the Chinese gentry, and it was here, also, that the financial resources were available for large scale trading enterprises requiring a high initial outlay. Most of the trade was in their hands, not only as ship owners or money lenders but also as organizers of overseas voyages, hiring the necessary manpower to man their ships while staying home themselves.[14]

Chinese products brought to Japan could be sold there for ten times the buying price.[15] With such profit margins, it becomes understandable that the local gentry in China never tried to undo the maritime prohibitions. They were simply too advantageous to be abolished.[16] The illegality of the whole enterprise, however, made everyone engaged in sailing the high seas automatically into "pirates." Violence, perpetrated by such "pirates," was usually an answer to broken promises and greed on the part of the officials on shore. Escape to the high seas was, in such cases, the only way out, and armed existence became a necessity. With the decline of the Ming such independent groups of traders on the high seas achieved great riches through their trading connections raging from Manila, Taiwan and Japan to Southeast Asia and Insulinde.[17]

We have already met several collaborators of the Fujian traders on the Japanese side: the Matsura of Hirado, for example, were deeply involved in supplying both manpower and connections to sell the merchandise for the Chinese. Between 1540 and 1544, the Chinese merchant Wang Zhi settled in Fukue on the Gotō islands. He became the chief of the overseas Chinese in Japan.[18] Later, at the invitation of Matsura Takanobu (in the Jesuit correspondence known by his Japanese title "Hisho"), he moved to Hirado.[19]

That the Nagasaki area, too, was involved in this trade is clear from a notice that "A certain no-good called Lieh Feng-chi said that, from 1557 on, about 20 to 30 Ming merchants went to Nagasaki, but that now this has increased, in less than ten years' time, to 2,000 or even 3,000 people, and if you add all the islands (to which merchants go, like the Ryūkyū islands) approximately 20,000 to 30,000 people."[20]Others, such as the Fukabori family of the extreme tip of the long cape that gives access to Nagasaki Bay were known to prey upon these Chinese merchants.

Fróis gives us a rare glimpse of this in his *Historia*

> This heathen [Fukabori Sumimasa] is an inveterate enemy of God's Law, strangely greedy, and known by everyone to be a pirate and a great corsair, who not only takes the vessels of his fellow-countrymen at sea, but even those of the poor Chinese merchants who come to Japan in their *somas* to fulfill their contracts. And although these foreigners are allowed to take their trade freely to any port in Japan, this [unbeliever] deceitfully and greedily waits for them at sea and there kills them and takes their vessels.[21]

Thus, Fróis seems to be familiar with the contractual nature of this trade, and the extreme powerlessness and poverty of those engaged in the actual sailing to Japan.

Lin Renchuan quotes from Chinese source materials: "...sometimes they [the rich and powerful families of the coastal region of Fujian] obtain children abandoned by poor people and raise them as their own flesh and blood. When these children have grown up, they let them go overseas for trading and no one needs to worry whether they remain alive or not."[22] These adopted sons "travel through many kinds of dangers, some will disappear in enormous storms or fight for one fleeting moment of life with the wind and waves. Their real sons, however, can enjoy the profits without physical danger."[23] Lin quotes Ming legislation that shows that the social position of such adopted sons was very low and was the same as that of household bondservants or slaves. "Their lords did not only possess extra-economical physical control over them, but even wielded the right to kill them at mercy. Thus the slaves who traded overseas were treated with extreme cruelty."[24]

For the year 1558, we have another intriguing notice. If clandestine trade was going on in Kyushu, it was robbing Shogun Ashikaga Yoshiteru (1536–1565) of tax income. An Edo period account of the Nagasaki area has this shogun send a certain Kojima Bizen no kami to Nagasaki "to inspect the Chinese ships in the harbor." According to the same source, he was assassinated at the order of Nagasaki Jinzaemon, but as Jinzaemon was only ten years old at the time, this order, if true, must have come from his father Sumikata.[25] The hill where the gallant tax collector had made his camp is still called Kojima (or Koshima) in present day Nagasaki.

According to another Edo period source, from the hand of the amateur historian

Nishikawa Joken (1648–1724), the first Chinese ship to visit Nagasaki Bay did so in 1562, when it anchored at Tomachi. Later a sort of Chinatown (Tōjinmachi) seems to have existed there, where Chinese merchants such as Wu Sanguan and his brother Wu Wuguan were active and were later buried.[26] The community was located on the shore at the spot where the domains of Tomachi and Fukabori met, a typical no-man's land, where it was easier for foreign traders to settle.[27]

Each account by itself does not amount to much, but all of them taken together are starting to make a case for a sizeable, if seasonal, presence of Chinese smugglers in Nagasaki, allied to the local *jitō* Nagasaki Sumikata. As we have seen, the Nagasaki had their stronghold at Sakurababa, a little over a mile inland from where the Nakajima river now flows into Nagasaki Bay. Today this site of the old Nagasaki stronghold is an overgrown jungle on Todozan, a steep hill behind the graveyard belonging to the Shuntoku temple,[28] but from some of its highest points, it is still possible to see the bay, as well as most of the surrounding countryside. This peak had served as the base for the Nagasaki family since 1333, when Nagasaki Kageyuzaemon no Jō Taira no Tamemoto is said to have first built a stronghold there.[29]

In the early sixteenth century the Nagasaki House was allied with the House of Arima. Jinzaemon's grandfather was Samadayu Yasuzumi, the third son of Arima Takazumi, the Warring States daimyo and patriarch of the Arima family who, as we have seen, was engaged in a competition for territory with the House of Ōmura in the late fifteenth and early sixteenth centuries. While Ōmura was extending its influence into Western Sonogi,[30] the Shimabara-based Arima managed to cross the mountains on the other side of Tachibana Bay and take most of the land on the long cape (except the very tip), from which Nagasaki takes its name.

Samadayu Yasuzumi's adoption into the Nagasaki family, therefore, can be seen as the recognition of this fact. Arima's influence in the Nagasaki area reached as far as Urakami, beyond which it bordered on the lands of the village of Nagayo, which had been an Ōmura possession since the Meiō period (1492–1500).[31] As we have seen, in 1538, Arima and Ōmura decided to cooperate instead of compete, and Haruzumi's second son, Sumitada, was adopted as the official heir into the House of Ōmura, in the same manner as Samadayu Yasuzumi had been adopted into the Nagasaki family a generation earlier, expanding and assuring Arima's influence throughout the western seaboard.

It is likely that Nagasaki Sumikata was among the Arima retainers transferring their allegiance from Arima to Ōmura at that time. This was advantageous for the Nagasaki, because Sumitada was clearly going to be a weaker overlord than his brother Arima Yoshinao. The relationship between Sumitada and Sumikata must have been an uneasy one: both were related to the House of Arima, but Sumikata was senior in age while Sumitada was paramount in social standing. More specifically, in Nagasaki Bay, Sumikata may have received extra strength from the profits brought by the Chinese ships, a trade he would not be willing to give up without good reason.

We do not know exactly at which point Jinzaemon started to serve Sumitada, but it is likely to have been after his *gempuku*, or "coming-of-age," ceremony, usually held for samurai boys between the ages of twelve and fifteen. For Jinzaemon, who was born in 1548, this would mean that he may have started to serve under Sumitada between 1560 and 1563. These dates, too, make it likely that Jinzaemon was among the twenty-five or so samurai retainers who were baptized at the same time as Sumitada, as we have seen above. Of necessity, then, Jinzaemon was more closely linked to Sumitada than his father was.

If Sumikata was committed to the Chinese smuggling trade in Nagasaki Bay, we have, at last, come upon a good reason why neither Fróis nor Almeida, nor any of the other Jesuits ever mention his existence, although they must have come to know him very well in the years after the change from Yokoseura to Fukuda.

*   *   *

A Man for the Jesuits: Ōmura Sumitada (2)

From the events of October 1565 it was clear that if Yokoseura had been too exposed to attack from the outside, Fukuda was not much better. But whatever the Jesuits may have argued with Sumitada, at first he does not seem to have been willing to put pressure on Sumikata to allow the Portuguese into Nagasaki Bay. Thus, the Captain Major of the next year, Simão de Mendonça, again took his carrack to Fukuda, where he arrived in July of 1566.[1] Almost at the same time, Gotō Taka'akira of Takeo, whom we have already met wreaking havoc inside Ōmura in 1563, invaded Nodake in East Sonogi.

This was very close to Sumitada's home base. What is more, the invader received again support from inside the domain: from Sumitada's relatives by adoption, the *ichizoku* of the Ōmura House.[2] Having been supplied with a large number of small arms by the Portuguese at Fukuda, however, Sumitada this time took the offensive and managed to defeat the invading force.[3] The Portuguese at Fukuda were not molested, for Hirado was still licking its wounds and did not participate in the attack on Sumitada. When the Portuguese left in November, Sumitada went to Fukuda to express his gratitude for the arms received and say goodbye to the Captain Major in person.[4]

On 24 October, Cosme de Torrès wrote his last surviving letter from Kuchinotsu.[5] This is worth noting because it is unlikely that the mission's superior really stopped writing.[6] His own uncertain status as a full-fledged Jesuit must have compelled him to write detailed reports to the general of the Society Francisco de Borja (in office: 1565–1572) or to the Provincial in Goa, Antonio de Quadros.[7] And the project on which the Jesuit mission in Japan was about to embark certainly was something that needed to be explained to higher authority and approved, especially in the case of a man like Torrès.

By now, we are starting to see evidence that Almeida had convinced his superior that the Jesuits should try to push the Chinese out of Nagasaki Bay, for although Almeida was still maintaining the connection with Bungo and he was also sent to the Gotō islands that year, he still managed to make two appearances in Fukuda, just like the year before, one visit at the beginning and one visit at the end of the trading season.[8]

What is more, in April of 1566, Torrès had sent for Gaspar Vilela, who was, after the superior himself, the second most senior member of the mission. Vilela had been stationed in the Kinai for the previous seven years. After the debacle of Yokoseura, however, it had become doubly important for Torrès to make sure that everyone who counted among the missionaries was informed and agreed with the new effort. In his letter of 24 October, half a year later, Torrès explains: "I ordered Father Vilela to come from Miyako, which he did last May, *in order that we might agree on how to proceed*" (italics added).[9]

Although Torrès does not specify what the urgent matter was that required Vilela to make the long trip from the Kinai down to Kyushu, the next thing we know is that the superior sent Vilela to Fukuda to take a look at its bay and, it goes without saying, at Nagasaki Bay as well.[10] In other words, Torrès wanted Vilela to make up his own mind about God's new plan.

Vilela and his companion João Cabral (?–1575)[11] stayed in Fukuda from May until the Portuguese left that year in November.[12] Although he had spent most of the year dodging his enemies, when Sumitada heard that Vilela and Cabral had arrived in Fukuda, he came to see them with a following of fifty retainers. As soon as they reached the port, the whole train made straight for the church without stopping at the lodgings that had been prepared for them. First things first: a prayer in the church and a salutation to the padres. "All this with so much humility and devotion, that all the Portuguese remained much edified by him."[13] We have to give it to Sumitada: his ability to become the man the missionaries wanted him to be made him truly a worthy ally.

The next step was to make clear to Sumitada that it was God's new plan to build a new Christian settlement somewhere along Nagasaki Bay. For this it would be convenient if Torrès had the backing of the Portuguese authorities in Lisbon, Goa, and Macao. The carrack of Simão de Mendonça had taken care of the first problem, for it had brought a letter from the King of Portugal Dom Sebastião, dated 22 February 1565, expressing the king's satisfaction about Sumitada's conversion to Christianity.[14] Somebody had been whispering in the boy-king's ear.[15]

Sumitada must have realized that he needed to take a step towards satisfying Torrès. At least, that is my explanation for an event that took place the next year of 1567, i.e., the succession of Jinzaemon to the headship of the Nagasaki House.[16] We do not know in what month this succession took place, before or after the summer, but it can only have been accomplished through heavy pressure from Sumitada, possibly even applied through his older brother Arima Yoshinao. As Jinzaemon was still only nineteen years old, there was probably no good reason for Sumikata to retire other than that he was forced to do so.[17]

Moreover, in 1567, there occurred one of those coincidences that almost forces one to believe that Heaven steers affairs on earth: the Great Ming revised its laws proscribing overseas trade. Non-tributary overseas trade was now allowed, except with Japan.[18] This meant that from that year onwards the great bulk of Chinese shipping concentrated on reaching Southeast Asia, Insulinde, and the Philippines. Very few ships came to Japan this year, and it is likely that suddenly none arrived in Nagasaki Bay at all. This is certain to have weakened the reliance of the Nagasaki House on the Chinese and may have weakened their resistance to allowing the Portuguese into the bay. With a similar dearth of Chinese shipping continuing in 1568 and 1569, the problem of the incompatibility of Portuguese and Chinese shipping in the same bay may have solved itself seamlessly.

Meanwhile, Sumitada was upset that the carrack of 1567 had not come to Fukuda, but had been directed to Kuchinotsu in Arima instead. To do penance, he visited Kuchinotsu in person to see Torrès and to promise his cooperation in founding a new Christian settlement along Nagasaki Bay.[19] These were the years that Sumitada's conversion was still provoking a backlash among his retainers, and so we can understand Sumitada's desire to go slow. But the advantages of being a Christian, in terms of his access to fire arms, had already been so tangible that there really was no going back for him any longer.

Moreover, the new Chinese regulations meant that, with fewer Chinese ships reaching Japan, the Ōmura domain stood to become the most important entry point for the

China trade if Sumitada were able to hold on to the trade with the Portuguese. All Sumitada had to do, therefore, was to hang in there and make the best of his assets, sometimes using force if he had to (but sparsely because of his severely limited manpower), but mostly through the art of dissimulation.

We have already seen, upon several occasions, how Sumitada was able to set aside his samurai pride to sit at the feet of the padres. This was really most unusual and something that was never reported about, for example, Ōtomo Sōrin, whom Cosme de Torrès had courted for so long. Sumitada must have had a natural feeling for what it was that the Jesuits craved most. In this connection, there exists an interesting remark in one of Torrès' letters, where he refers to Sumitada as "the first Christian prince of Japan, who, because the gentiles have destroyed him after he was baptized, *has to dissimulate in some way with the gentiles* at least until he has his domain in hand again, *although he really is a very good Christian.*"[20]

In other words, Torrès admits here that he knew about Sumitada's tactic of downplaying his conversion to Christianity in front of his Japanese retainers. This was even true for Sumitada's relations with his closest adviser in the years 1561–1568, his *karō* or senior retainer Tomonaga Ise no kami Sumitoshi. The latter seems to have been able to see the advantages of having direct access to Western weaponry, but never could understand the attraction of the Christian religion itself. Fróis pays him the compliment of calling him "the stubborn heathen."[21]

It is in this same light that we have to see the notices, dug up by Professor Toyama, that Sumitada was in 1567 still making donations for the upkeep of the Ise shrine.[22] Not to have done so would have highlighted Sumitada's conversion to Christianity at a time he was still anxious to downplay it. We can see, therefore, that Sumitada was surviving by telling both sides exactly what they wanted to hear: to the Jesuits he played the humble believer, praying with them, and sitting at their feet. To his fellow samurai, he extolled his access to weaponry through his connections with the Jesuits and he may have downplayed his baptism as nothing but a few drops of water on his head.

If it is necessary to ask the question "Who was the real Sumitada?," the answer would probably boil down to something like "a member of the Arima family, committed to creatively surviving in a hostile environment." In the sense that Sumitada was willing to give conversion to Christianity a try, to really learn (as he must have) about the new religion he had adopted, he was, also, a typical child of his time. Decades of civil war in Japan had brought to an end any automatic reliance on tradition. This was the age, after all, that saw such unusually meteoric careers as that of, for example, Toyotomi Hideyoshi.

In showing genuine interest in the Christian religion, moreover, Sumitada was not alone. He was just the most exalted of all the converts the Jesuits had made so far. But the founding of Nagasaki would within a few short years lead to the existence of a whole city full of people similar to him. Although their motives were, like Sumitada's, mixed, they all shared a common willingness to try something new, to venture outside of traditional Japan while remaining, mostly, physically inside. If the Portuguese and the Jesuits were adventurers in the physical sense, their Christian converts in Japan were not inferior in a spiritual and intellectual sense.

Without the Portuguese carrack in their bay, the Christian community of Fukuda did not warrant the presence of a padre in 1567. But Sumitada, who was regaining confidence in his ability to control his domain, irrespective of the presence of the missionaries, requested Torrès to send Luis d'Almeida to come and see him. And so in October of that year, the brother left from Kuchinotsu to travel via Kabashima, an island off the very tip of Nagasaki Cape, to Fukuda.[23] Again, Almeida traveled the same route to Ōmura as he had taken in 1564. This time we have no account of the purpose why he had to visit Ōmura (apart, of course, from the indispensable sermonizing), but on his way back to Fukuda, he is said to have stopped "in Nagasaki" and to have baptized five hundred people there.[24]

Because Christian Nagasaki had not yet been founded, it is clear that Nagasaki Jinzaemon's stronghold at Sakurababa is meant here. There now reigned a completely different atmosphere around the stronghold of the Nagasaki House. By this time, surely, the succession ceremony of Jinzaemon to the headship of the Nagasaki family had taken place. His father is no longer mentioned anywhere. The Portuguese had not come to Fukuda this year; and of the Chinese traders none or very few had come. Sumitada had forced the retirement of Sumikata and Jinzaemon must have realized that, for better or for worse, he had thrown in his lot with Sumitada and the Jesuits. Word must have gone out, before Almeida's arrival in the village, that the new master would not oppose any baptisms the missionary might want to perform. About a third of the village, or about five hundred people, took the hint. Almeida is said to have left Nagasaki for Fukuda on Christmas day 1567.[25]

*   *   *

Nagasaki Bay in 1568: Gaspar Vilela

On 26 June 1568, the carrack of Dom Antonio de Sousa entered Fukuda Bay. By this time, we may assume, it was guided by the large cross erected on the shore that later featured in the description of the access to Nagasaki Bay by the Dutchman Jan Huygen van Linschoten in his *Itinerario*: "Thus steering for land, you will see a cross standing on a point of land and opposite this cross is the anchorage. Eastward of this cross is a very good harbor, this is the harbor of Facunda."[1] Everyone in the village was relieved to see the Portuguese back in their domain (instead of in Kuchinotsu in Arima) and an impressive number of people rowed out to the carrack or came to welcome the Portuguese on the beach singing *Te Deum Laudamus*.[2]

A little later some "Christian gentlemen" came to see the Italian Padre Alessandro Valla-Reggio (1530–1580), who had arrived on this ship. Among them was the local strongman, called Dom Ioachim. This is our first indication that Fukuda Kanetsugu had, sometime between 1563 and 1568, also been baptized. Again, we note that this key baptism, too, is not described anywhere in Fróis' *Historia* or any of the *Cartas* editions. Kanetsugu made the padre "many offerings, with which he showed his happiness to see me." Two days later (a round-trip to Ōmura and back), Sumitada sent a retainer to tell the padre that he wanted very much to come and greet him in person but that he was too busy to be able to do so, for "a son had been born to him."[3]

This year Torrès was at Shiki in Amakusa, where he called together all the Kyushu Jesuits for a *consulta* in July. Vilela was there, having come back from the Gotō islands, west of Hirado.[4] Almeida had been in Shiki since May.[5] Belchior de Figueiredo was also present,[6] and so was Giovanni Battista di Monte.[7] The discussion centered, of course, on the progress and the subsequent steps to be taken to bring the Nagasaki project to fruition. The failure at Yokoseura may have been analyzed, as well as the providential non-appearance of the Chinese traders in Japan and the successful removal of Nagasaki Sumikata from the headship over Nagasaki Bay. It was decided that a padre should be stationed permanently in Sakurababa, who could, in the summer while the Portuguese carrack lay at anchor, easily go to Fukuda as long as the new settlement had not yet been built.

Gaspar Vilela, after Torrès the most senior member of the mission, was chosen for the important task of preparing the ground for the future settlement, something that had not been done thoroughly at Yokoseura. The indifference of the local population around Yokoseura bay to the mayhem caused by the merchants from Bungo must certainly be considered one of the causes for the failure of the first Jesuit settlement. The choice of Vilela, the second most senior padre of the mission, indicates that the *consulta* had fully endorsed Almeida's plan to settle along Nagasaki Bay, by now possibly already four years old. Afterwards, in September,[8] Torrès felt he needed to go and see Fukuda and Nagasaki Bay for himself.

If we thought the superior of the Jesuit mission in Japan would travel modestly, accompanied by just one or two brothers, we are mistaken. On his way to Fukuda, Torrès was accompanied by Baltesar Gamboa and Bertolameu de Gouvea, in addition to Francisco Ferreira, the Portuguese business manager of the daimyo of Bungo, Ōtomo Sōrin, and two Japanese merchants, called "Suete and Betodono."[9] These laymen must have added a considerable number of people to the train of the superior. It is, therefore, possible that Torrès arrived in Fukuda surrounded by about fifty people. This number may even be a conservative estimate when we remember that the merchants accompanying him were about to make their yearly purchases of silk in bulk and may have come in their own vessels, bringing their own personnel and trains of coolies.

After Torrès had been in Fukuda for ten days, Sumitada came to see him and hear mass. Torrès then made a counter-visit accompanied by seventy Portuguese. They decided after two days of mutual visits and negotiations that Torrès should travel on to Ōmura. Sumitada stayed only a few days longer, but managed to surprise the Portuguese with his faithful attendance of the early morning mass.[10] It is clear, however, that Sumitada's visit to Fukuda was not about hearing mass, but about determining a site for the new Christian settlement to be founded along Nagasaki Bay: "In Fukuda, Father Cosme de Torrès heard from the Japanese about [the situation in] that bay of Nagasaki. He went there with the following Portuguese: Fernão de Lemos, Baltasar de Gamboa, Bertolameu de Gouvea, António da Costa Famiboa, and Baltasar Gentil. They went to [the spot of the later] Nagasaki, which was [still covered in] brushwood of tall trees."[11]

This was the first time Torrès traveled the whole length of Nagasaki Bay, going ashore at the village of Funazu,[12] on the north side of the overgrown land tongue between the Urakami and Nakajima rivers, that apparently had already been chosen as the site for the future Jesuit settlement. The Portuguese who accompanied the padre may have advised him on the appropriateness of the chosen location. Together they inspected the spot, then descended down to the bank of the Nakajima river, which they followed upstream until they found a place to cross it and continue their way to Sakurababa, where they were received by Dom Bernardo, i.e., Nagasaki Jinzaemon.[13]

At Sakurababa, they also found Gaspar Vilela, who had preceded Torrès to Fukuda[14] and was already on the spot known later on as Todos os Santos (All Saints).[15] It is likely that he was living in a former Buddhist temple that Jinzaemon had given him to use as a church.[16] We remember that, the year before, Almeida had baptized five hundred people in this village, a labor force that could be employed to accommodate the party of padres. From Sakurababa, Torrès continued overland to Ōmura on 5 October,[17] via the road through the mountains passing by the village of Tarami.

Officially (that is: as professed in the Jesuit letters), the superior went to baptize Sumitada's wife and son,[18] but in reality he came to finalize the arrangements for the founding of the Jesuit settlement.[19] After Torrès' arrival in Ōmura, Sumitada visited him first, bringing his newly born son and legitimate heir Shinhachirō.[20] He then consulted with his senior retainers and informed them of Torrès' presence and his intention to ask him not to leave his domain immediately, but to stay to take care of the building of a church for which he himself would donate the land.[21]

By this time Sumitada's senior retainer Tomonaga Ise no kami had been dismissed, and among the remaining retainers no one dared any longer to disagree with this proposal. Work on the new church was started on 17 October on the grounds of Sumitada's Sanjō Castle, and on 8 December 1568 the first mass was said there by Torrès himself.[22] Two weeks later, on Christmas eve, Sumitada organized in his new church a grand enactment of the life of Joseph and the scene of the birth of Christ complete with a stable, the shepherds, etc. Next to the church, he erected a stage surrounded by numerous tribunes. Apart from Sumitada and his family, Torrès, and the two brothers Luis d'Almeida[23] and Giacome Gonçalves, about two thousand people attended.[24]

Vilela, meanwhile, did his best in Sakurababa. Later, in a letter written from Cochin on 4 February 1571,[25] he would commemorate his work during the two years he was in Nagasaki. In this letter, he describes his stay between 1568 and 1570, conflating them into one narrative:

> I lodged in a pagoda, which is a temple of idol worship, given to me by this lord to establish a church there, but as there were no other Christians around, I just play-acted and gathered the heathen of that place there to listen to my sermons.[26] The first time, they were not very pleased, but the second time they had already started to grasp much of the true knowledge, so that after some requests and answers, and many questions asked, they came to understand and receive holy baptism, once two hundred at one time, and another time four hundred, so that after one year everyone in the village, that is, fifteen hundred people, had been baptized.[27]

In the summer of 1569, Vilela decided

> to take the pagoda apart and rebuild it as a pretty little church, which I called All Saints.[28] This much increased the devotion of all the Christians, who praised the Lord for the great mercy He had shown them by saving them from the darkness in which they had been wandering. And to show their devotion and happiness, and the love they bore their creator, they destroyed some houses with heathen deities, which stood around where they lived.[29]

Vilela is referring here to the destruction of a number of small Shinto shrines, such as may have been dedicated to Ebisu, and Suwa or Sumiyoshi Daimyōjin.[30] This missionary had been expelled once before, in 1559, by Matsura Takanobu from Hirado for inciting similar behavior of the people he had converted there, but in Ōmura he could do as he pleased.

"On Fridays," Vilela continues, "I preached about the passion, and because they are naturally inclined towards self-chastisement, they practiced it inside the church after the sermon was over, shedding many tears. They did this with so much fervor that often it became necessary to put up signs on the doors forbidding them to chastise themselves more, for I feared they might do themselves permanent harm because of their devotion."[31] During Lent and Easter, Vilela organized more flagellations and processions, the first taking place on Palm Sunday. The second occurred on the evening of Maundy Thursday. The third was a procession of flagellants on Good Friday, and the fourth took place at midnight on Easter Sunday.

There can be no doubt that walking in procession during Easter week became part of the later town of Nagasaki's Christian identity, as is the case with so many other Roman Catholic communities all over the world. We will have occasion to come back to these processions later, but for the moment it is necessary to draw attention to the one that occurred on Good Friday in Vilela's description: "Next, still whipping themselves, they left the church until they arrived at a faraway cross."[32] Apparently, then, just like at Yokoseura, a great cross had been erected somewhere "faraway" from Todos os Santos. If we think of Yokoseura, a similar cross had been erected on a hill away from the settlement. It had also served as the turning point for an Easter procession.[33] But, at Yokoseura, there was another large, gold-colored cross, which had been erected on Hachinokoshima and served as a mark which could be seen from sea.

If the mistakes of Yokoseura were not going to be repeated at Nagasaki, it would have been prudent to have one cross perform both functions at the same time, that is to place it on a hill from where it could be clearly seen by ships entering the bay, while at the same time serving as the furthest point for a procession to reach. In the neighborhood of Sakurababa, there is such a point: the foot of Mt. Tateyama facing the bay. This point would have had the flagellants traverse the distance between Todos os Santos and Mt. Tateyama, i.e., along the old road that is now known as Shin Daiku-machi. What is more, as crosses were also often used as boundary markers, the foot of Mt. Tateyama facing the bay would also have been the logical boundary of Nagasaki Jinzaemon's domain. In this way, a large cross placed some place in the general area where recently the new Nagasaki Museum for History and Culture was built in the shape of the *bugyōsho* of the Edo period, would have served these three purposes very well.

*   *   *

The Busy Scribbler: Luís Fróis (1)

Twice more, in 1569 and 1570, did the Portuguese carrack anchor in Fukuda. Both times it was commanded by Manoel Travassos, another professed Knight of Christ.[1] It is not entirely clear why the Portuguese had to wait two more years before they could do business in Nagasaki Bay. It is likely that the carrack had entered the bay at the end of the trading season of 1570. For on 20 November 1571, Gaspar Vilela wrote from India: "I resided there [Nagasaki] for two years and I embarked for India from there."[2] The fact that Vilela clearly states that he left from Nagasaki (i.e., Sakurababa) and not from Fukuda must mean that the carrack was lying, at the time of his embarcation, in Nagasaki Bay.[3] The new settlement, however, had not yet been started. Maybe Fukuda was somehow more attractive to the Portuguese than the far end of Nagasaki Bay. Possibly, also, Nagasaki Jinzaemon kept on hoping for the return of the Chinese ships and resisted the idea of becoming dependent on the Jesuits for income from the trade.

It is also true that, in the summer of 1569, Sumitada had been preoccupied with another rebellion by one of his relatives and so simply may not have had the manpower to put at the disposal of the Jesuits to clear the site and build the settlement.[4] Larger powers in Kyushu also worried Sumitada, who had allied himself with the Mori of Western Honshu. When their home base was threatened that year, the Mori withdrew from Kyushu, leaving Sumitada helpless in the face of the forces of Ōtomo Sōrin.[5] However, the Ryūzōji, led by the house's retainer Nabeshima Naoshige (1538–1618), inflicted a decisive defeat on Sōrin's army, which had to refrain from the conquest of Hizen.[6] So Sumitada again squeaked by.

By this time, however, all the pieces for the founding of Nagasaki were in place. Let us see, therefore, how this seminal event is reported in the Jesuit sources. The most important account can be found in Luís Fróis' voluminous work *Historia de Japam*,[7] which is based upon the letters written by the various missionaries until the 1590s (especially those written by Fróis himself). Thus, his work shows all the characteristics of these letters, such as their didactic and their propagandistic purposes. The most difficult problem with this author, however, is his deceptively simple style, so charming, so open that it seems as if he is holding nothing back. We should expect to be forced to read closely:

> Four or five years had passed since the conversion of Dom Bartolomeo, when Father Cosme de Torrès ordered Father Belchior de Figueiredo to go and live in a port by the name of Fukuda. He did this for two reasons: first to preach to and confess the Portuguese who came there in the *nao* of China, and second to take care and develop the Christian community there which followed the *nao* wherever it went and had grown to a sizeable population in that port. This harbor of Fukuda being unbecoming, however, and the *nao* there at risk of various dangers, the father wished to find it a safe haven so that it might continue to come to the domain of Dom Bartholomeo and favor and help him and the Christian cause.[8]

Although this introduction seems unproblematic, we note that at the very beginning Fróis is waffling. Four or five years? Which was it? The year, if not the date, of Sumitada's baptism is clear, and so four years later would put us in 1567. But in 1567, Figueiredo was not in Fukuda at all, for as we have seen the Portuguese carrack was directed to Kuchinotsu in Arima that year and no padre came to Fukuda.[9] Five years after Sumitada's baptism, 1568, also does not work. In that year Figueiredo attended a *consulta* called by Torrès in Shiki, and after the meeting he returned to Bungo,[10] where he had been stationed since 1566.[11] So, neither four nor five years after Sumitada's baptism was Belchior de Figueiredo anywhere near Fukuda.

He had been in Fukuda in 1565, of course, and was there again in 1570. The length of time between those two visits was indeed five years. So, was Fróis getting old when he wrote this, or did he have another reason for confusing the dates and people involved in the founding of Nagasaki? The next thing that strikes us as strange in the original Portuguese text is the way Fukuda is described. The port is called "indecente," which I have translated as "unbecoming," the least offensive English word I could find within the range of meanings associated with the Portuguese term.[12] "Indecent" or "obscene" seem too strong for what has, in the previous sentence, just been described as a place with a sizeable Christian population. What was so indecent about that?

Was it, possibly, because the local strongman of the place, Fukuda Kanetsugu, although baptized Dom Ioachim, did not behave like a true Christian at all? Was it, maybe, because he provided the same type of amenities to the sex-starved Portuguese traders that Hirado was famous for? Fróis writes clearly that there were two problems with the port: Fukuda was "indecente" *and* the Portuguese ships were exposed to danger there. The latter was true, of course, as we have seen in the section on Dom João Pereira, but now we also know about the former.

The third point I want to raise about this passage is another phrase: "the father wished to find it a safe haven." After having thoroughly confused his reader about the time and place that Figueiredo was in Nagasaki, Fróis says that Torrès wanted "to search for a safe haven for it." With this he clearly implies that the "search for a safe haven" for the Portuguese carrack began "four or five years" after Sumitada's baptism.

Strictly speaking, as we have seen, this is an untruth, for that search is likely to have started already one year after Sumitada's baptism and the subsequent destruction of Yokoseura. To say it is a lie, however, would be going too far, for there are too many elements in this mixture that are true, and, after all, it is nothing but a conclusion on the part of the close reader of Fróis' text. Therefore, let us once again give the mission's historian the benefit of the doubt and continue to pay close attention to what he writes. We're back, presumably, with Figueiredo as the subject of the sentence:

> And taking a pilot and some other companions, the father went sailing along that coast for the purpose of sounding the entrances [of its bays] to discover the one that seemed the best. In this way, he found Nagasaki Bay to be suitable and convenient, and after first having made the necessary arrangements with Dom Bartholomeo, the father started with the Christians, who traveled with their families along the coasts and lived in the shadow of the *nao*, to organize a basic settlement there and a secure place to dwell.[13]

The reader may recall that Fróis had arrived in Japan in 1563 and had been present at the destruction of Yokoseura. After the Portuguese had left that year, Torrès had sent him with Juan Fernandez to Takushima. It was the quietest and safest place for a year of language study with the knowledgeable but stubborn brother, who refused to speak anything else but Japanese. Exactly one year later, on 9 November 1564, Luis d'Almeida came to Hirado[14] to take Fróis via Shimabara[15] to Bungo on the other side of Kyushu,[16] and from there through the Inland Sea to the Kinai, where they arrived in Sakai on 27 January 1565.[17] In other words, Fróis made that same trip with Almeida when he is sure to have passed by the entrance of Nagasaki Bay.

About the later stages of the project to found a new Christian settlement, however, Fróis seems singularly badly informed. In the passage quoted above, he writes that it was Figueiredo who did all the exploring and not Almeida. Or is the Jesuit historian giving us a glimpse of a trip about which we have not encountered any information before? In other words, did Belchior de Figueiredo indeed scout the Sotome coast of the West Sonogi peninsula? There was indeed an occasion on which such a trip may have taken place. When Figueiredo left Fukuda, in the last week of November 1565, he is said to have gone to Teguma, which lies further north along the Sotome coast from Fukuda, although there was no Christian community there as yet. The next thing we know is that in December of the same year Figueiredo returned from Teguma to Kuchinotsu, where he met Torrès, before going on to Bungo.[18]

It is definitely possible that the trip described by Fróis took place between these dates. Figueiredo may have been charged by Torrès with this task, so that he would have another independent opinion on the problem of which bay along the Sotome coast would be the most appropriate for the Portuguese carrack to frequent. This conclusion is all the more attractive because the alternative (i.e., Figueiredo's trip not having taken place at all) would make Fróis into a liar.

So far so good. But it is the second half of the quoted passage that is troublesome, especially the question of the grammatical subject of "after first having made the necessary arrangements with Dom Bartholomeo, the father started…."[19] It had certainly not been Figueiredo who conducted all the necessary discussions with Sumitada, but the superior of the mission Torrès himself. As we have seen, Torrès was in Ōmura from October 1568. He stayed until August of the next year, and then went on to Amakusa.[20] Later that year, Torrès was back in Ōmura, where he spent another winter until, in April of 1570, Sumitada judged his castle town too dangerous because of the imminent threat from Ōtomo Sōrin, and advised Torrès to go and stay with Vilela at Sakurababa, which the superior did until July of that year.[21]

Here, then, we see Fróis definitely slipping on the slope of vagueness into untruth. He is saved (or he may have considered himself saved) by his use of the vague term "the father" which, of course, may refer to any padre, in this case either Torrès or Figueiredo. Where things are really tricky, however, is that we know that it was indeed Figueiredo, who was involved in the lay-out and building of the new settlement in the spring of 1571. On the one hand, then, there is enough factual truth in Fróis' account to satisfy formal standards of veracity, and on the other hand he leaves his reader with the (completely mistaken) impression that the founding of Nagasaki was nothing more than some half-baked plan of Figueiredo, cooked up in the few months before the carrack came to Japan in 1571.

The best we can say is that Fróis is disingenious in this passage, for he must have known very well that it had taken more than five years (possibly as long as seven years) to get all the pieces for the founding of the new town into place, even if he was in the Kinai for most of that time. With that conclusion we end our close reading of Fróis' description:

> These Christians were joined by many others who were displaced from various domains, some because they had been exiled by their lords or had exiled themselves because they did not want to abandon their beliefs, and others who wandered far from their home lands which had been destroyed in the civil wars. Some came from Shimabara, others from Shiki, Gotō, Hirado, Yama-guchi, Hakata and other kingdoms. And to take care of all these people the father, who was all by himself at that time, spent almost the whole year listening to confessions, making of the days and months one continuous season of Lent to be able to better help their souls…."[22]

This is all. Fróis says nothing more about the greatest single project the Jesuits ever undertook and brought to fruition in Japan.

Everyone who has tried to tell the same story after him has always had to face the wall that Fróis, in the passages quoted above, has built around the topic. It is clear that Fróis' rendering is so unhelpful as to force us to restart from scratch, but, as usual, without Fróis there is not much else to go on. Key letters by those involved (such as Torrès and Figueiredo) are all missing.[23] It takes a soul really trusting in the sincerity of the Jesuits to believe that all this is accidental and not a deliberate conspiracy to erase the early history of Nagasaki, and especially the crucial involvement of the Jesuits in the making of the town.[24] We will analyze the reasons for this in Part Two below.

*   *   *

The Founding of Nagasaki:
Francisco Cabral

For now, all we can do is follow the snippets connected with Nagasaki that are left (overlooked?) in the Jesuit correspondence. We know for example that, on 18 June 1570, a new superior by the name of Francisco Cabral (1533–1609) arrived in Japan to take over the leadership of the mission from Cosme de Torrès. In many ways, Cabral was similar to Almeida: also a man of action, more than—in spite of his vocation—of the spirit, but he was better connected in and outside the Society, and so came to Japan as the new superior.

Cabral's arrival and his announcement of a new mission policy more in line with the decrees of the Council of Trent must have come as a great shock to Torrès. Cabral also brought the news that Torrès and Vilela were being recalled to Goa.[1] Both men, having entered as fully ordained priests during the initial stage of the Society's formation, were obviously considered responsible for having led the Japan mission astray.[2] Having been physically weak for years, the Superior died a few months after Cabral's arrival on 2 October 1570. Gaspar Vilela, was sent off to India with the first ship that left Japan.[3]

Being the conquistador he essentially was,[4] however, Cabral was immediately taken with Almeida's idea for a Jesuit settlement on the land tongue near Sakurababa. Although he conspicuously removed Almeida from the actual ground-breaking scene of the new town in 1571,[5] Cabral relied on Almeida a great deal just after his arrival in Japan, so that the brother might show him all of Kyushu. The record of their travels together runs from August through October 1570, starting from Shiki, visiting Kabashima, Fukuda, Sakura - baba, Ōmura, Suzuta, Kuchinotsu, Arima, Shimabara, Bungo, Akizuki, Hakata, Hirado, Gotō, and again Hirado.[6]

It was Figueiredo, however, to whom Cabral gave the responsibility for the new town in its infancy between 1571 and 1574. Torrès, Vilela, and Almeida may have been the pioneers of the Japan mission working with the general rules set by Xavier, but they were not yet Jesuits in what would later become the "traditional" mold.[7] Cabral, on the other hand, had entered the Society in 1554 in Goa at the age of twenty-one, after having spent four years in the service of the Viceroy of the Indies, Dom Afonso de Noronha.[8] He had been born on the island of San Miguel of the Azores group into the well-known Portuguese family of Ayres Pirez Cabral.[9]

After studies at Lisbon and Coimbra, Cabral had left for the Indies in 1550, and in 1552 had seen action during the Portuguese expedition against the Turkish fleet at Hurmuz.[10] In the Society, he was known for his maturity, his knowledge, and his leadership qualities. He seems to have been ordained in 1558, or only four years after starting his novitiate. According to his fellow Jesuit Melchior Barreto, there was no one who entered the Society in the Indies able to compete with Cabral.[11]

In the four years he spent in training in Goa, he acquired the new mindset of the Jesuits. On 20 November 1559, his superior Melchior Carneiro wrote in his evaluation:

Father Francisco Cabral has been in the Society for five years, he is noble, firm in his vocation, and has made great progress in the virtues in this short period. He likes public speaking, has much aptitude for the written word, has taken the liberal arts course and the most difficult course in theology. When he preaches he satisfies those of high positions, but he is badly thought of by the common people. I don't know of any other fault in him than that he is somewhat irascible and has issues with his will power, but he works hard to correct this and therefore I believe that it will not last long. He is 26 years old.[12]

Cabral spent the next ten years teaching philosophy and theology[13] in Goa, Bassein, and Cochin.[14] Once, in 1559, he traveled for the Provincial Antonio de Quadros all the way to Malacca and Macao.[15] At an early stage, he was destined for the Japan mission, but he must have refused to go until he was finally appointed its superior in April of

1568.[16] In August of the same year, Cabral arrived in Macao, and although he tried to get to Japan in 1569, the carrack that year left too late and was forced to return to port, so Cabral's stay in China was prolonged by another year.[17]

In Macao, meanwhile, Cabral was allowed to profess the fourth vow in 1569.[18] This assured that his authority in Japan would be unchallengeable. It is likely that the news of his appointment had reached Japan as early as 1569, and this may have been another reason why Torrès had held off on pressing forward with the Nagasaki project. Immediately upon his arrival in Japan, in June of 1570, Cabral called all the Jesuits in and around Kyushu together for a *consulta*. Cosme de Torrès and Gaspar Vilela came to Shiki (Amakusa) from Sakurababa (Nagasaki), Baltasar da Costa from Hirado, Alessandro Valla-Reggio from Gotō, Belchior de Figuereido from Kuchinotsu, and Giovanni Battista di Monte from Bungo. Brothers Luis d'Almeida and Jacome Gonçalves also participated. Padres Organtino and Baltasar Lopes had arrived together with the new superior in Shiki.[19]

The missionaries consulted with each other for thirty days, mainly, of course, to inform Cabral of the state of the mission. It must have been a difficult month for Torrès, made even more difficult by Cabral's announcement of the decisions that had been made in Goa. In the name of the Visitor Gonzalo Alvarez and the Provincial Antonio de Quadros, Cabral issued a prohibition against the missionaries wearing silk clothing. Everyone had to promise from now on to wear in public the black cotton *sotana* or cassock.[20]

Portuguese merchants seem to have complained in Goa about the life style of the Jesuits in Japan. Since Almeida had entered the Society with his five thousand *cruzados*, that money had been invested in the Macao-Japan trade, and the Jesuits were no longer the poor, struggling missionaries they had been before. Now they lived, dressed, and acted rather like nobility.[21] The prohibition of silk clothing was only the beginning of a controversy in the Japan mission on the issue whether to adapt to Japanese customs or whether to adhere to the strict rules of behavior the Jesuits observed elsewhere and try to change Japan instead. Only two of the old Japan hands at the *consulta* seem to have agreed with Cabral's new stress on frugality and austerity and his unwillingness to adapt to Japan.[22] One of them must have been Belchior de Figueiredo, who knew a good politic move when he saw one. It earned him the honor of being chosen to assist Cabral in Nagasaki and to be stationed there from 1571.

In that year, Cabral spent much effort on the conversion of Tomachi Sōhei Shigekata and his wife.[23] Shigekata was the younger brother of Nagasaki Jinzaemon, who had been adopted into the Tomachi family.[24] The hamlet of Tomachi, about halfway along Nagasaki Bay, was of strategic importance for the safety of the new settlement. From this effort we know that Cabral was in the area, at least in the first half of the year until the carrack of Tristão Vaz da Vega came to the area in July.[25] Also, on 13 September 1571, Cabral wrote in a letter from Kuchinotsu: "concerning the domain of Dom Bartholome, where Father Figueiredo is stationed, many have converted so far and are still converting, among them several belonging to the nobility,[26] which I will not describe in detail because Your Reverence will be able read about this in the general letter written by Father Figueiredo."[27]

The general letter referred to here has not survived. Rather more helpful is a letter written by Brother Miguel Vaz from Shiki on 8 October 1571: "The *nao* came around the usual time, accompanied by a junk, to a new port in the domain of Dom Bertholameu, which is called Nagasaki.[28] This year a large settlement was built in this port, to provide a place for the Christians wandering without home or roof over their head. I was called by Father Francisco Cabral to go and help with the division of the house lots."[29]

Interestingly, the last sentence was edited out of the printed version of this letter, an act which effectively limited the number of Jesuits involved in all accounts of the founding of Nagasaki until now.[30] Michael Vaz continues with a story about a family of emigré exiles from Shiki who had been persecuted for their faith, but remained steadfast, emigrated to Nagasaki, and paid with their lives for their defiance of their lord. In his letter written from Ōmura on 16 October 1571, Belchior de Figueiredo reports the same story about these Christians from Shiki.[31]

Thus, in contrast to Fróis' account, we may conclude that the following three Jesuits were directly involved in the founding of Nagasaki: Francisco Cabral, Belchior de Figueiredo, and Miguel Vaz. If such a crucial task as the division of the house lots in the first streets of the new settlement was left to the lowest ranking member of the three Jesuits, Miguel Vaz, the tasks of the two others must have been even more important and prestigious. Cabral being as yet completely dependent upon the other Jesuits because of his ignorance of Japanese, it is likely that he and Figueiredo collaborated where the crucial contacts with the leaders of the labor crews from Ōmura and Arima were concerned.

The site of the future town had, as we have seen, already been determined when Torrès had visited the area in 1568. It was a land tongue known as Morisaki (literally: "wooded cape"), which stretched from the foot of Mt. Tateyama into the far end of Nagasaki Bay, among the tide lands of the area. It was a high ground consisting of sediments brought together over the ages by the confluence of the Urakami and Nakajima rivers, which flow through different valleys separated by a low mountain chain. The forces of erosion had extended and heightened a sandbank until it was almost a promontory sticking out into the deep end of the bay, about three miles away from the ocean. Lying in between the jurisdictions of the domains of Ōmura (Nagasaki Jinzaemon) and Arima (the village of Urakami), it was a no man's land that had seen no official claimants until 1568.

It was overgrown and needed clearing. On its northwestern side, it was flanked by a small beach and the hamlet of Funazu ("Landing"), while on its northeastern side it was not far from the hamlet of Fufugawa and the village of Sakurababa. Once cleared, however, it was an ideal spot to build a settlement designed for trade.[32] It was as close to the deep water of the bay as one could get. Its high ground formed a natural defense against attackers and provided a splendid view of the bay stretching several miles out to sea. The soil, however, was poor, mostly sandy, and so food would have to be imported, while only wells for brackish water could be dug. Bishop Cerqueira would later write that the peninsula contained no "fields for rice, no land for pasture or gardens, no wells for drinking water, no river for washing clothes, no forest for firewood, no place to get rock and earth to be used for [the town's] buildings."[33]

Japanese historians have spent great efforts in trying to unravel the details of the building of the first six streets from Japanese sources.[34] It is likely that the site was cleared during the summer of 1570, for from 15 March 1571, the original six *machi* may have been laid out.[35] Work was started on building the dwellings on 9 April.[36] Six machi were planned,[37] and from their names we see that the bulk of Nagasaki's early population did not consist of the poor exiled Christians of the Jesuit correspondence, the "desterrados" of Miguel Vaz' and Figueiredo's letters, but of Christian merchants from Hirado, Yoko-seura, Ōmura and Shimabara.[38]

Hokaura-machi was populated by people from the Sotome coast of West Sonogi. It may originally not have been a very Christian machi at all,[39] or it may have been populated by people who moved to Nagasaki from Fukuda.[40] Bunchi-machi seems to have been named after the residence of the merchant Hiradoya Bunchibō,[41] a Chinese merchant who had befriended Ōmura Sumitada and at whose house in Ōmura Torres and his following had stayed for fifteen days in 1568.[42] This is likely to be the same merchant (or his son) about whom João Cabral wrote in 1566: "although he himself remained gentile, he nevertheless rejoiced to make his son a Christian."[43]

Of the six streets, Shimabara-machi was the first to be built. In charge of the building site was Arima Shuridayu Yoshizumi (1550–1571), a son of Arima Yoshinao and Sumitada's nephew.[44] Ōmura-machi was built by Tomonaga Tsushima, a retainer of Ōmura Sumitada. Hirado-machi was led by Hiura Yozaemon,[45] while Yokoseura-machi and Hokaura-machi were both headed by Yokoseura Yogozaemon.[46] The involvement of merchants from Arima seems to have been crucial to the survival of Nagasaki in its early stages. Later, during the Edo period, the chief official or *otona* (originally *tōjin*) of Shimabara-machi would still take precedence over all the other street elders of Nagasaki at the Hassaku ceremony (1st day of the 8th month, a national holiday commemorating Ieyasu's entrance into Edo).[47]

Conspicuously absent among all these leaders is Nagasaki Jinzaemon, the local strongman. The reason why it was Tomonaga Tsushima, and not Jinzaemon, who was the most powerful layman involved in the project, may have been the fact that the lord-vassal relationship between the Ōmura and Nagasaki families was still too recent, while the Tomonaga family was one of the oldest and most trusted family of retainers of the Ōmura House.[48]

The six "streets," or *machi*, of the new settlement consisted of two blocks along three roads running parallel to each other. Shimabara-machi consisted of a road running the length of the land tongue between two rows of houses facing each other, with the flood lands of the mouth of the Nakajima river, down below to the back of the row of houses on the outside of the land tongue. Bunchi-machi was its extension towards Morisaki, the tip of the land tongue sticking out into the bay. Parallel to Shimabara-machi ran Ōmura-machi, also two rows of houses facing each other along a road that occupied roughly the middle of the land tongue. Its extension towards Morisaki was Hokaura-machi. In size, the two largest machi were Ōmura-machi and Shimabara-machi, possibly because both Sumitada and his brother, Arima Yoshinao, needed space for barracks to house the troops they had sent to help with the building of the town.

On the Funazu side of the land tongue stood Hirado-machi with its extension Yokoseura-machi. It seems there was not enough surface space left over (or maybe the number of people from these two places was much smaller than those from Arima and Ōmura), so these two streets consisted of only a single row of houses along a road running beside the edge of the land tongue. These houses looked out over the bay where it met the mouth of the Urakami river and provided a good view of the Portuguese carrack and other ships at anchor. From the beginning of the city until the mid–1630s, these two machi housed the Portuguese traders during the three to six months that they stayed in Nagasaki. Innkeepers and householders, originally from Hirado and Yokoseura, traditionally dominated the respective machi organizations because of their experience dealing with the foreign Portuguese.[49]

The population of the new settlement is said to have been around one thousand people, divided over 200 households.[50] The bulk of the population is likely to have come from Ōmura, for three of the six machi (Ōmura, Hokaura, Bunchi) were essentially populated by people from this domain.[51] That the vast majority of people involved in the founding of Nagasaki had been baptized as Christians, however, and recognized the authority of the Jesuit padres involved in the project, is proven by the central location of the church of this small community.[52] The prime spot of the place, the very tip of the land tongue, was reserved for the Jesuits. The first thing built there may have been a chapel, which would later be enlarged four or five times over four decades to become eventually the largest church of premodern Japan.

At first the chapel blended, in Japanese fashion, through covered walkways with the other buildings in the compound. Some gnarled, old and venerable fir trees from among the ancient groundcover had been preserved.[53] They proclaimed age-old sagacity, provided decoration, and the encouragement that comes from recognition. The air is fresh and cool in that spot where air currents from two different valleys meet. Moreover, the heady view one has from there of Nagasaki Bay may lead to heights of spiritual, as well as temporal, audacity. Likely to have been picked in 1565 by Luis d'Almeida, during the subsequent six years all the details necessary for the realization of the vision he had seen there had slowly come into place.

*   *   *

No Place for the Fainthearted: Belchior de Figueiredo

Like Cabral, Belchior de Figueiredo had started his career in the Society in the Indies. He had joined the same year as Cabral, 1554, in Ternate of the Moluccan Spice Islands, that is: the very source of the wealth of the Portuguese trading empire.[1] Six years later, he was ordained in Goa and then served, again like Cabral, as a master of novices. He was rector of the same college[2] where Cabral taught philosophy.[3] Thus, Cabral and Figueiredo knew each other and had much in common, and it is not surprising that Cabral chose Figueiredo to be his right-hand man at first. Figueiredo had been in Japan since 1564, not long enough to belong to the old guard that Cabral had come to replace, but with enough experience to know the language passably well and with first-hand knowledge of the Kyushu missions in Ōmura, Arima, as well as Bungo.[4] He was someone on whose judgment Cabral could depend and who could be expected to be loyal to him.

Cabral was back in Nagasaki in June of 1572.[5] From the dates of his correspondence, again, we may surmise that he spent the three summer months with Figueiredo in the new settlement, before going on, once more, to Kuchinotsu in the last week of September.[6] That year Captain Major Dom João de Almeida had sailed his carrack to Nagasaki and brought the missionaries Sebastião Gonçalves (1533–1597) and Gaspar Coelho (1529?–1590) to Japan.[7] Cabral first sent Coelho to the Gotō islands, west of Hirado, to learn Japanese.[8] Although we are less well informed about the superior's movements during the next year, 1573, we know that, during the summer months, he was again waiting at Nagasaki for the carrack's arrival.

In 1573, however, Cabral waited in vain for the Portuguese to arrive. Captain Major Dom Antonio de Vilhena perished in a storm off the coast of Satsuma.[9] This was a major setback for everybody: the Portuguese, the Jesuits, Sumitada, and the people of Nagasaki. There were 5 Jesuits on board,[10] who all drowned, while 16,000 ducats worth of cargo belonging to the Society was lost.[11] Sumitada's financial situation, also, was so precarious that he could not resist the forces of an invader. Aware of Sumitada's weakness, his neighbor Saigō Sumitaka of Isahaya attacked, and so did Sumitaka's brother Fukabori Sumimasa.[12]

We have seen how the Fukabori occupied the very tip of the long cape, from which the Nagasaki family is likely to have taken its name.[13] The older families in the area (such as the Tomachi, Nagasaki, Ōgushi, and Tokitsu houses) were originally all local branches of the Tajihi family, which, since the late ancient and early medieval periods, had been the most prominent family in Sonogi-*shō*, a tax-exempt estate, which had included both Ōmura and Nagasaki bays.

During the late Heian period, the Tajihi had functioned as Heike vassals, which of course made them suspect in the eyes of the Kamakura *bakufu*, even though they had been quick to switch loyalties after the fall of the Taira in the Gempei war (1180–1185). When, in 1255, the Eastern warrior house of Fukabori was sent as local *jitō* to the Nagasaki peninsula, they found themselves opposed by the Tajihi. Thus, the antagonism between the Fukabori and the Nagasaki-Tomachi families went back a very long time.[14] The main point of contention between these warrior houses was, of course, about who was to dominate the access to and the use of Nagasaki Bay.

The arrival of the Jesuits in the area only exacerbated these local tensions. Fukabori Sumimasa was, like his ally from Isahaya, an older brother of Ōmura Sumitada's wife. Sumimasa himself had been adopted into the Fukabori family, and was married to a daughter of Nabeshima Naoshige, a retainer of Ryūzōji Takanobu, and so he was also allied to Sumitada's worst enemy. Based in Tawaraishi castle, he was the *kokujin ryōshu*, or landed samurai, of a large part of the Nagasaki peninsula. He had always deemed himself to have the right to demand toll from all merchant shipping entering Nagasaki harbor.[15] When the news of the shipwreck of Vilhena's carrack spread, Fukabori Sumimasa knew he had a chance to take back control over the entrance to Nagasaki Bay, which had gradually slipped away from him since the Portuguese had begun to come to Fukuda in 1565.

Here Fróis gives us a rare glimpse of the situation in Nagasaki Bay, as well as of the character of Francisco Cabral. The superior, writes Fróis, needed to leave Nagasaki to go to Bungo, but the state of war with the Fukabori made the narrow strait out of the bay dangerous. Still, Cabral tried to pass through in the early morning: "The Christians [of Nagasaki] prepared seven vessels well equipped with munitions that would allow them to resist the enemy who wanted to waylay them."[16] Fukabori, however, was on the alert and waiting for the Superior in vessels armed with muskets. "They came with so much fury at the boats accompanying the father, that they killed five or six men right off and took one of his vessels. The other six, when they managed to escape by the force of their oars, believed that this was no small benefice from God. Thus, they returned with the father to Nagasaki as best they could."[17]

Clearly, this adventure was an unnecessary one. In spite of what Fróis says about there being no other route, this really means there was no other *comfortable* route, for there were three other land routes out of Nagasaki: via Urakami (to Ōmura), or over the Himi pass via Yagami (to Chijiwa), or again via Mogi (and then by boat to Kuchinotsu and Kazusa on the Shimabara peninsula).[18] But land travel was hard, while travel by boat was easy, especially if one, like the Superior, did not have to do any rowing oneself. The episode is, therefore, a measure of Cabral's confidence in the fire power of his ships. The force of the attack he had faced, however, must have come as a rude awakening to our conquistador and missionary. This event occurred during the summer, likely August of 1573, after Cabral had heard the news of the carrack's shipwreck (or had simply given up on its arrival) and was preparing to leave Nagasaki.

But Vilhena's shipwreck presented a danger to Sumitada greater than to any other party, and if Sumitada was destroyed the settlement of Nagasaki was surely doomed as well. It was likely after Cabral's departure that worse news reached Nagasaki. Fróis, as always willing to spill ink over an edifying tale of Christian hardship and steadfastness in the face of adversity, suddenly and uncharacteristically inserts in his narrative the only extensive report on early Nagasaki of the *Historia*.[19] It is as if the mission's historian felt guilty about having shortchanged Nagasaki so much in his account of its founding and saw himself compelled to record at least something of its early existence.

The rumor reaching Nagasaki that summer was that Saigō Sumitaka of Isahaya had invaded the Ōmura domain and that Dom Bartholomeo [Sumitada] had been given up for dead. The men from Isahaya seemed to be in control of the domain. Hearing this, the leaders of Nagasaki came to Padre Figueiredo to consult with him about what course to take. They found the padre in the church getting hoarse from consoling women convinced that the hour of their destruction was at hand and that within a short time everyone in Nagasaki would be dead or sold as slaves. He counseled the Christians to abandon the settlement, which was without ammunition, and flee "among the brambles and brushwood of the mountains in which that area is particularly rich. They also took with them the tabernacle in which they had packed the painting of Our Lady that stood on top of the altar, and they carried this on their backs."[20]

The people of Nagasaki remained hidden in the mountains for two days without any further news from Ōmura. They did hear that the men from Isahaya were rounding up the sons of Sumitada's principal vassals as hostages. The nearest of these vassals was, of course, Nagasaki Jinzaemon of Sakurababa, who was ordered to submit to Isahaya. Jinzaemon, reports Fróis, was just as scared and at a loss about what to do as everyone else around him. He seemed ready to submit, but only held off because he did not have any certainty yet about what had become of his liege lord Sumitada. Meanwhile, he refused to open his fort to give shelter to Figueiredo and the few Portuguese who lived in Nagasaki.

Only Jinzaemon's wife, the nineteen-year old Tora, Sumitada's third daughter, remained steadfast in her loyalty to the Christians, scorning "her husband for the friendship he had shown them in times of peace and his abandonment of them now in times of need. But her husband did not pay the least attention to her entreaties, so that he would not be suspected by the enemy of aiding them, for fear that he might lose his income and estate for this reason."[21] We already knew that, when he wants to, Fróis can be devastatingly precise in naming names. We have also already had occasion to note Jinzaemon's ambivalent attitude towards the alliance with the Portuguese and the Jesuits that Sumitada had thrust upon him. It is not surprising that now, in this time of great insecurity, he would not want to stick his neck out for them, no matter what his own wife might think of him.

Also, Fróis lets slip here another piece of information that we did not know before, namely that, apparently, there were already a handful of Portuguese, i.e., non–Jesuit laymen and traders, living in Nagasaki, just as there had been in Yokoseura. Regrettably, their names have not been preserved, but possibly they belonged to the group we have seen travel in Torrès' company to the future site of Nagasaki in 1568, such as Bertholameu de Gouvea and Baltasar de Gamboa.

On the night of the second day, a man reached Nagasaki from Ōmura with the following news: "Dom Bartholomeo is alive with a few men who at that very hour are with him in his stronghold. Everything else is under the sway of the enemy. Dom Bartholomeo has sent me through all this danger to give you this news and he asks you to hold out in Nagasaki and sustain all the lords of its surrounding countryside, for if this place holds, that news alone will strengthen every other place and enable the domain to recover."[22] These were, indeed, encouraging tidings which caused the people of Nagasaki to take heart and prepare to defend themselves. It was decided to build a wooden palisade around the town and to dig a moat through the land tongue on the mountain side of the settlement, turning Nagasaki into a virtual fortress.[23]

These defenses enraged Isahaya, who sent men to lay waste to the outskirts of the town. One night, they burned the hamlet of the fishermen along the Nakajima river.[24] On another day, they came up close to the wall in boats with the tide and attacked the town with muskets and arrows. With each successful foray, the enemy became more and more confident while the Christians became more disheartened. Because there had been no trade this year, the town's supplies were soon exhausted that winter, and the people of Nagasaki had to scavenge for herbs and roots, "which they went to pick in secret in the bush every day, but never the same group. During the day they would dig [the moat] and build the walls around the settlement and at night they would continually stand guard."[25]

Fukabori went to Ōmura and saw with his own eyes how far his brother from Isahaya had come to dominate the domain. Returning to Nagasaki Bay, he sent a message to the town that it was better to surrender than to be conquered. The town decided to play for time and sent him a message back that he was probably right and that they would soon be forced to give up. Meanwhile they continued to fortify their stronghold as best they could. When, however, a man from Isahaya was spotted inside the town, he was killed by some hotheads among the Christian youths. With that killing, it was clear that fighting had become inevitable. "Fukabori, puffed up with arrogance and confident in his forces and the little resistance the fortress of Nagasaki could offer him, decided to gather his men and make an assault by sea and over land."[26]

Fróis mentions that this final assault took place during Easter week, and so this must be Easter of 1574, when the winter had left the population of Nagasaki weak as well as poor. Also, an attack during one of the new settlement's most important holy days of the year made, from the point of view of the attackers, good tactical sense. Here the voice of Fróis' narrative switches over to an eyewitness account, which is most likely to come from one of the "lost" letters of Belchior de Figueiredo:

> They finally came after midnight with the high tide that thrashed around our fortress with seventy vessels over the water of the bay and many men overland along the shore. They burned everything up to the foot of Lord Nagasaki's stronghold and they even burned the houses that were standing there right under his walls as well as the Church of All Saints that we had there. There was nothing anyone could do to stop them. The mountains were lit up with the light of all the fires they had set which illuminated our fortress as if it were a lamp in the midst of the flames.[27]

This incited the Christians of Nagasaki, the more so because they heard the enemy taunting and mocking them from the ships that had come over the water. "Someone's voice imitated and distorted the singing, with which we teach the doctrine to the children in our churches."[28]Figueiredo, however, tried his hardest to calm everyone down, telling them: "My sons, the enemy is numerous and you are few, even if you kill many of them you will gain nothing, but when they kill one of you we will lose much and put our fort at risk, and with that the whole domain of Dom Bartholomeo and all its Christendom."[29]

Such were the intrepid words of the padre. Happily for Nagasaki, however, he was disobeyed by some of his own flock endowed with more sense of how to carry the day against this particular enemy. For to wait inside the palisade for the attackers to spend themselves on the settlement's defenses was a sure recipe for an eventual assault large enough to storm the citadel, burn the settlement, and kill or enslave all its inhabitants. Four men recently arrived from Shiki were the first to disregard the orders of the padre and dashed out of the fort. Evidently, they had decided to sell their lives as dear as possible.

> They saw that the principal leaders and officers of the enemy were standing together in one group, whom they knew by their rich clothing and their shining weapons, for their swords and daggers were garnished and decorated with gold. Notwithstanding that these men were surrounded by the greater part of their soldiers and the spot was the most dangerous for the Christians, they were oblivious of any terror born from the immediacy of danger, and charged them with great force.[30]

Such was the fury of their attack with arrows and muskets while still at a distance, and with lances after they had closed in, that even these high-ranking samurai, who could not afford to behave cowardly before their own men, had no response. Nine of them were dead before the four brave Christians themselves were slain.[31] When the rest of Nagasaki's defenders saw their valor and success, they also jumped over the wall and ran after them to grapple with the enemy, who "with their officers dead and their heads already cut off"[32] were fleeing to their ships and did not dare approach Nagasaki again.

Now it was the turn of the Christians to follow up and pursue the enemy into his own lands "abusing and hurting them more than they had been hurt by them in the first place, taking away booty, burning houses, and wreaking other destruction on their islands."[33] This is Fróis at his very best, describing miracles of Christian valor. The principal actor of his account is, of course, God Himself, who is interfering personally for the continued existence of the Christian town. How bitter it must have been for the Jesuits that God did not interfere thirteen years later when Hideyoshi took Nagasaki away from them! Or after 1614, when all Jesuits left in Japan were doomed to die horrible and pointless deaths, and Japanese Christendom was, for all practical purposes, extinguished.

Still, we must again ask ourselves the question why "the father" in this account remains unidentified. Why did Fróis have to hide away this name? As always, when crucial names are lacking, we must assume there was some compelling reason to do so. One of the common denominators for missing names in Fróis' *Historia* is mission policy. Wherever naming would reveal aspects of mission policy, Fróis systematically omits names, for, in his opinion, mission policy is nobody's but the mission's business. As I have described, the padre involved must have been Figueiredo, whom Cabral had chosen to be his right hand man. When the superior heard the detailed report of what had happened in Nagasaki, he, the conquistador, likely was severely displeased with Figueiredo's cowardly leadership of Nagasaki's warriors.

Figueiredo's lack of spirit showed Cabral he was unfit to be stationed in Nagasaki, at the forefront of the mission's expansionist policy. The citizens of Nagasaki themselves may even have requested his transfer. It is possible, also, that racial prejudice played a role. As we have seen, Figueiredo is likely to have been of mixed Portuguese and Indian blood and darker-skinned than most European Jesuits. Although Cabral had not held this against him when he had first arrived, his Japanese flock may have had their own thoughts on the subject, and Cabral was later easily convinced that the blood of the true *fidalgo* had been dangerously thinned in Figueiredo's case. In any case, Figueiredo was transferred to Gotō in 1574,[34] where he stayed only a short time, and the next year to Hakata.[35]

* * *

Christian Champion:
Gaspar Coelho (1)

Gaspar Coelho, who followed Figueiredo as Nagasaki's main priest, was born in Porto, probably in 1529. This is the port city at the mouth of the river Douro in northern Portugal and exports the country's most famous product, port wine.[1] In December of 1579, when Coelho was fifty years old and had reached the position of superior of the Kyushu Jesuits, he was described as "professed of the three vows, of good physical and mental health, although small of posture, thin, and weak of stomach. He has been a member of the Society for twenty years, nine of which were spent in Japan, but he does not speak the language, although he understands many things."[2]

What is surprising here is that Coelho had reached this high ranking among the members of the Japan mission in spite of the fact of his rather late (at age 27) entry into the Society and after having spent only five years in Japan.[3] What did Coelho have in the eyes of Cabral that the others did not have? I think the answer is: both good connections and singular chutzpah. Only four years after he had joined the Society in Goa in 1556, Coelho was given the exceptional honor of accompanying the highest official of the Society in Asia, the Provincial Antonio de Quadros, on his inspection tour of the mission establishments in India.[4] This was, it will be remembered, the same provincial who had sent Cabral to Japan as the new superior, replacing Torrès.

In the fall of 1574, only a few months after having replaced Figueiredo, Coelho already showed his gumption when he started pushing for the complete extinction of Buddhism in the Ōmura domain.[5] This was just after Sumitada had escaped annihilation at the hands of Saigō Sumitaka of Isahaya, and had received "blessings from the Lord" in the form of a shipment of firearms. To see how important the Jesuits had become to Sumitada over the previous decade, all we need to do is follow their footsteps, which sometimes speak in a clearer voice than their letters.

We know, for example, that Miguel Vaz was back in Nagasaki during the summer of 1574, for he reported he was with Coelho in the Christian settlement when the Captain Major of that year, Simão de Mendonça, arrived. According to Vaz, the Captain Major had come with his carrack and three other ships in order to help Dom Bartolomeo, which "was a great service rendered to the Lord and help for the Christians, and simultaneously put fear into the gentiles. In the end, everyone who heard of this could not help but be amazed at the love that Christians have for each other, even though they had never met."[6]

It is clear what this "great service rendered to the Lord" was, for only a sizeable shipment of arms and ammunition could "put fear into the gentiles." It is not surprising that a letter with such unedifying content was not included in the printed Evora edition of the *Cartas*. It is a wonder it has survived at all, but it can be found in a Spanish manuscript of the letters from Japan, which was used to be read aloud during meals to the novices of the Jesuit seminary at Alcala de Henares.[7] Now we understand how Sumitada was able to get rid of the occupation of his domain by Saigō Sumitaka.

As always, though, there was a price to pay. Vaz goes on to explain that one should "forge iron while it is hot," and this was, therefore, the right time for "some things of great importance."[8] Vaz does not specify what these "things" were, but anyone with experience reading between the lines of these letters understands that an arms shipment like the one Sumitada had received was well worth the destruction of some property dedicated to the service of the Devil. Thus, it was time for some serious demolition of Buddhist temples. We have seen how hesitant Sumitada had been about such a drastic confirmation of where he stood. Now it seemed, however, that there was no way back for him any longer. At one time he may have grumbled about "how troublesome" the Jesuits were[9]; now he complied with Coelho's demands, as transmitted to him by Michael Vaz, as much as he could.[10]

After this was "accomplished," Vaz reports that Coelho went to Ōmura to show his appreciation of what had been done and force the reconversion of all those who had gone back to Buddhism at the time of the occupation of the domain by Isahaya. Fróis gives a candid example of Coelho's methods in Ōmura:

> A Christian happened to visit Padre Gaspar Coelho. Because it was just a time of fasting, and he wanted to do something to make up for the sins he had committed, he requested the father to give him a penance. The father answered him that one thing that would please God and would count to make up for his sins, would be if he found a good opportunity along the roads he travelled and be the first to set fire to a pagoda.[11]

The Omura record *Gōsonki* mentions the names of eight temple complexes that were destroyed at this time,[12] as well as the fact, not mentioned in any Jesuit account, how the grave of Sumitada's adopted father Sumisaki at the Hakusui Temple was opened, the bones taken out and thrown by the frenzied Christians into the Kōrigawa river.[13] All of Sumitada's vassals, that is 60,000 souls, were converted to Christianity.[14] Those who did not want to become Christians were forced to leave the domain. The Buddhist clergy, in so far as they refused to convert, was killed.[15] Between 18,000 and 20,000 people were baptized, including about two hundred Buddhist monks.[16] Buddhist statues were destroyed and new churches and crucifixes erected. Even little children took part in the destruction and desecration of Buddhist property.[17]

The point has been made that, for Sumitada, the destruction of the Buddhist temples and the forced conversion of the domain's population served to reinforce his hold over both his retainers and the population of Ōmura.[18] There may have been some short-term truth in this, but the fact remains that it was such wholesale destruction of Buddhist property and forced mass conversions to Christianity that ultimately brought on the strong reaction by Japan's new central authority which proscribed the new religion in 1587. The strategy pursued by Coelho and Cabral was therefore, essentially, a shortsighted and self-defeating one.

The arrival in August of the carrack of 1575 under Vasco Pereira further strengthened Sumitada's defenses and those of Nagasaki. Miguel Vaz writes that the arrival represented "no small help for Don Bartolomeu's war."[19] In late August, Sumitada came to Nagasaki to thank the Captain Major in person for the arms he had brought. By now, Nagasaki was a well-fortified town with a citizen militia of about four hundred men, eager to defend their religion and newly won independence.[20] As each household was required to provide one man for this militia, we have some idea of the size of the town which may have counted some 2000 inhabitants by this time. Some *rōnin* mercenaries from the surrounding areas are likely to have given its militia some samurai expertise as well.

It is no wonder that the newly found strength and confidence of the Christians gave the surrounding gentiles pause. Miguel Vaz writes in the same letter that many of the town's former enemies now were coming to be converted.[21] The next year, 1576, however, Sumitada's fortunes changed again radically for the worse. His rivals to the north, Ryūzōji Takanobu of Saga and Matsura Shigenobu of Hirado had formed an alliance, and an attack was pressed on the Ōmura domain from three sides. Takanobu himself made camp inside Ōmura with a force of no less than 8000 men at Kaize, about five kilometers away from Sumitada's stronghold.[22]

After losing the ensuing battle, Sumitada surrendered, and on 12 July he signed an oath, with his Buddhist name Risen (but simultaneously pledging "the grace of God" as guarantee for his Christian sincerity), that he would no longer oppose Takanobu and his son Shigemasa.[23] To seal their new lord-vassal relationship, Sumitada was forced give a daughter in marriage to Takanobu's fourth son Egami Iegusa.[24] Next, Takanobu also required the presence of one of Sumitada's sons as "a witness to the wedding," or, in other words, as a hostage, and although Sumitada was extremely angry at this new humiliation, he was forced to send his second son Suminobu to Saga.[25]

Nagasaki, meanwhile, was left to fend for itself. The second half of the 1570s is the least documented part of its poorly documented early history.[26] If we may believe the testimony of the padres the town was becoming an agreeable place to live for newly arrived missionaries. The climate was not too extreme, of course, and every permanent resident was a Christian.[27] The proximity of the Portuguese carrack during the second half of the year provided safety as well as supplies of the things the European padres appreciated. Nagasaki, for example, was the only place in Japan where red wine, bread, and beef were always available. Every year, also, the Portuguese brought a new shipment of arms and ammunition. On the other hand, daily quarrels of the Japanese with the Portuguese merchants over merchandise seem to have marred the town's existence.[28]

* * *

The "Donation" of Nagasaki: Alessandro Valignano

After his "success" in Ōmura, Coelho had been concentrating his efforts on the conversion of Arima Yoshisada (1521–1577). We have, again, to thank Fróis for a candid assessment of how Coelho proceeded: "In order to happily reach this goal, it was a great advantage and a special help of our Lord that Brother Louis d'Almeida was charged with this business, for by God's special grace and favor he had been given the ability to win the hearts of the Japanese princes and lords."[1] Of course, Fróis does not mention it in so many words, but it should be clear that Almeida, as usual, was charged with the dirty work that the padres did not want to do themselves. The special lubricant used by Almeida in his dealings with Japanese princes were timely shipments of arms and ammunition.

Yoshisada was finally baptized by Coelho on 15 April 1576.[2] He died, however, the next year leaving a ten-year old son, Shigezumi.[3] Although initially pro–Buddhist and anti–Christian, Shigezumi was hard-pressed by Ryūzōji Takanobu of Saga who continued to expand his power at the expense of the Ōmura and Arima houses. He decided, therefore, to ally himself more closely with his uncle Sumitada by marrying the latter's daughter Luzia. He approached Padre Coelho to help arrange this marriage, and promised to convert to Christianity for the occasion. Sumitada, although he was initially willing to cooperate, later reneged on this promise when he realized that his daughter did not want Shigezumi for a husband.

This left Coelho severely displeased with Sumitada who had broken his word in spite of "how important this was for the well-being of so many souls [in Arima]."[4] With Takanobu breathing down their necks, however, something was needed to break the impasse. As if by magic, the carrack arrived, on 25 July 1579, not in Nagasaki, but in Kuchinotsu.[5] It brought not only the mission's Visitor Alessandro Valignano (1539–1606), who had personally intervened with its Captain Major, Leonel de Brito, to change the port of his destination,[6] but it also carried 600 ducats worth of military supplies, mostly lead and saltpeter, for the Arima cause.[7]

Valignano was born in Theatina (Abruzzi), in Italy. He entered the Society in 1566 at the age of twenty-seven. His education included a doctorate in law. His connections must have been exemplary, for in August of 1573, he was called to Rome, where on 8 September he professed the four vows in front of the Society's General, Everard Mercurian (1514–1580). Two weeks later, Mercurian appointed him Visitor (i.e., Inspector General) of all the Jesuit missions between the Cape and Japan.[8] As such, he was to represent the long arm of Rome in Asia. Subsequently, Valignano's influence on the Jesuit mission in Asia would reach all the way into the eighteenth century.[9]

He left Lisbon on 21 March 1574 and six months later arrived in Goa.[10] For three years, he occupied himself with the different missions in India, but in September of 1577, he set off for Japan.[11] When he arrived there, almost two years later, it was again through an arms deal that God's designs were furthered: the lord of Arima, now called Harunobu, presented himself to Valignano and expressed his desire to be baptized. Not to make unseemly haste, however, the baptism was set for the next Lent of 1580.

That the carrack had arrived in Kuchinotsu, however, is likely to have had more reasons than just to nudge along the conversion of the Arima family. It clearly was also a rebuke to Sumitada for breaking his word to Coelho and to remind him that such uncalled-for independence and respect for his daughter's opinions might cost him his own head at the hands of his nemesis Ryūzōji Takanobu. Sumitada got the message loud and clear. In the fall of 1579, he went to Shimabara to meet with the Visitor in person,[12] just as he had done in 1567 when the Portuguese carrack had also been directed to Kuchinotsu and he had visited Torrès there.

The next thing we hear is that, poker-player that he was, Sumitada had upped the ante again. He now proposed to Valignano to cede Nagasaki to the Jesuits, whom he would allow to take over the administration and jurisdiction of the town. Because of its sensational nature, this is the first fact of the existence of Nagasaki to have received a measure of scholarly attention over the years, in Japanese as well as in Western literature.[13]

It goes without saying that Japanese writers are generally indignant about Sumitada's cession (to foreigners!) of his sovereignty over Nagasaki.

Edo period accounts report, for example, the story that either Ōmura Sumitada or Nagasaki Jinzaemon had borrowed from the Jesuits (i.e., Cabral and Coelho) for purposes of the defense of their respective holdings, either money or, more likely, such articles of trade as cannon, guns, ammunition and/or gunpowder, and that either (or both) of these men had used the newly built town of Nagasaki as security for their loans. The *Nagasaki Engiryaku*, the *Kiyōki*, and the *Nagasaki Yuraiki* say it was Nagasaki Jinzaemon who pledged the town, while the *Ōmura hiroku* says it was Ōmura Sumitada himself.[14]

Most Catholic historians have tried to dispose of this story by demonstrating the untrustworthiness of the Edo period materials and then pointing out that the story does not even appear in the secret correspondence of the Jesuits themselves.[15] On the one hand, it should be admitted that such Edo period materials are marred by their essentially anti–Christian bias. On the other hand, the latter part of the Catholic reasoning is widely off the mark, for (assuming, for the sake of argument, the allegation to be true) this was just the kind of thing that no Jesuit in his right mind would ever write down on any account.

We have seen above ample evidence of the essential truth that the Jesuits manipulated the arrival of the carrack for their own purposes, either to favor or to rebuke the local rulers of Kyushu, and the arrival of the Portuguese always was especially important for the access it provided to Western arms and ammunition. Thus, it is a matter of semantics to assert or deny that the Jesuits were involved in the arms trade. For all practical purposes, again, we have seen ample evidence that they were, although they did their very best to hide it.

There is no need to suppose, however, as the Edo period Japanese sources do, that they would be so crude as requiring the town of Nagasaki to be given as collateral for their cooperation so that it might fall into their hands if their "debtors" were unable to repay their loan. Such a scenario is more like a description of early modern capitalism, as might have been practiced by Japanese bankers of the eighteenth century, than a reflection of the fluidity of power relations which characterized the *sengoku* period of civil wars.

We may be fairly sure, therefore, that donating Nagasaki was indeed Sumitada's own idea. In the first place, the arrival of the carrack in Kuchinotsu that year meant, of course, that Sumitada had lost his income of the harbor tax, which could amount up to 3000 ducats a year,[16] a sizeable sum for such a small warlord.[17] In the second place, Arima Harunobu's impending baptism was another powerful stimulus for Sumitada. If, from the missionaries' point of view, Arima replaced Ōmura as the most docile domain of Kyushu, and Kuchinotsu became the usual port of call for Portuguese ships, it was clear that Nagasaki would be doomed to fall back into oblivion.[18] Safeguarding his income and his access to munitions were powerful motives for Sumitada to make concessions to the Jesuits.[19]

Also to the point is the argument that, by donating Nagasaki to the Jesuits, Sumitada secured an escape route from his stronghold in Ōmura, across Ōmura Bay, via Tokitsu and Urakami to Nagasaki, and from there across the mountains to Mogi, a hamlet facing the Shimabara peninsula. Mogi is situated on Tachibana Bay on the other side of the "long cape" and, as we have seen, was the point of departure for boats to Shimabara. To throw in Mogi in the Nagasaki deal seems to have been part of Sumitada's proposal from the very beginning. This indicates that concern for his personal safety may also have been important for Sumitada, for adding Mogi would mean to safe-guarding this most important access and escape road to and from the city.[20]

Some historians think that Sumitada's proposal was not totally unexpected for Valignano, for the subject may have been debated between Sumitada and Cabral, who put off taking this important decision until Valignano's arrival.[21] Valignano, for his part, knew better than to accept Sumitada's proposal immediately. There were three main objections: 1. the Order was forbidden to acquire real estate; 2. the Order could not administer justice to criminals; 3. the rumor that the Order's real ambition was to acquire political power would be confirmed.[22] The first of these, as we have seen in the introduction, was a rule mainly prominent in its non-observance by the members of the Society.

The second objection could be easily solved by appointing trustworthy lay officials who would not make any independent decisions. The third objection, however, prevented any unseemly haste in accepting Sumitada's offer.[23] Accordingly, Jesuit documents have that it was only on 9 June 1580, that Sumitada officially extended his offer that Nagasaki and Mogi be administered by the Jesuits. They would also receive the income from the anchorage tax, while Sumitada retained the right to levy customs duties for himself. These amounted to more than one thousand cruzados a year.[24]

Thus, the cession of Nagasaki may have been Sumitada's master move. With it, he eliminated any threats, real or imaginary, posed by the imminent confiscation of Nagasaki by Takanobu. He could write off his debts to the Jesuits. He secured the fiscal advantage of the trade tax for as long as the Portuguese would come to Japan. Finally, by magnanimously adding the harbor-hamlet of Mogi to the deal, he assured himself of a permanent escape route in case he was about to be routed.

After holding a *consulta* in Nagasaki in July,[25] Valignano called another meeting in Bungo in October. Its resolutions have been preserved. The donation of Nagasaki, the acceptance of which had clearly long since been decided, featured only as point 14 on the agenda.[26] Among the five reasons adduced why "it would be wise to take and hold these two places of Nagasaki and Mogi" the most interesting is the last: "The fifth reason is because every time we think it would be better not to own these places, we have already come to understand, in this first year that we are holding it, how much our reputation has changed among the non–Christian gentlemen who live around this port of Nagasaki and who are now coming to visit us with presents and other proofs of friendship to try and ingratiate themselves with us, quite the contrary of what they used to do."[27]

Whatever the details about the exact date on which Sumitada's offer had been formally "accepted" by Valignano,[28] in this document we find that by October of 1580, for all practical purposes, Nagasaki had already been "owned" by the Society for one year. This means that the experience of the Jesuits as territorial lords goes back to the fall of 1579, or exactly the time when Sumitada had come to see Valignano in Shimabara to make sure that the Portuguese would come back to Nagasaki. Thus, even if Valignano and the other Jesuits were pretending, on paper, that they were "still thinking about it" and "had not made a decision on the matter," in practice they had already been pleased to receive the homage of local strongmen from around Nagasaki Bay and along the Sotome coast of West Sonogi who had not yet converted to Christianity.

Revealing, also, are the expressions used in this document for Nagasaki: in Portuguese *forte* and in Spanish *lugar fuerte*, i.e., "stronghold" or "fortress," which is, in Portuguese *de sua natureza muy forte*, or in Spanish *natural monte situado en lugar fuerte*, or "located in an elevated and easily defensible spot." In this respect, Nagasaki shared some important characteristics with other spots chosen by Portuguese adventurers to establish their colonies, such as Diu in India or Macao in China. It too was fortified and located on an easily defensible promontory. It dominated a bay particularly well suited for the anchorage of the Portuguese carracks.

Most importantly, foreigners and Japanese alike, while in Nagasaki, were not subject to Japanese law, although what law they were subject to and who was to dispense it remained a problem. With the acceptance of the donation of Nagasaki, the Jesuits became responsible for the administration of justice in the town. Valignano, a trained doctor of law himself, naturally was concerned with this conflict between the spiritual goals of the Society and its now very real temporal powers. He also was the one who came up with a solution which combined Japanese custom with Christian spirit and Church law.

First, he separated criminal law from civil law in Nagasaki, and distinguished between civil law and canonical law. In criminal cases, the Portuguese in Nagasaki were subject to the authority of the Captain Major. The Japanese of the city were subject to courts, the judges of which had been appointed by the Jesuits, but who derived their judicial powers from Ōmura Sumitada, for he remained "overlord" of the area.[29] In this way, the Church did not need to take responsibility for the punishments meted out. This was a typical Jesuit sleight of hand to avoid the impression that they were engaged in activities that did not conform to their priestly status.

On the other hand, according to the contract made with the Jesuits, Sumitada continued to receive a sales tax from the Japanese merchants coming to do business in Nagasaki and in that sense also retained some measure of real influence. Nagasaki, therefore, was a hybrid anomaly: it was neither a Portuguese colony nor a Japanese domain, but something in between, a creation which, like any hybrid or hermaphrodite, seemed destined to die an early death. The miracle is that the city survived.

Valignano made sure that it did. Only two weeks after Sumitada signed over Nagasaki to the Jesuits, the Visitor composed his *Regimen for the Japan Superior*, dated 24 June 1580, in which he instructed that the two towns, Nagasaki and Mogi,

> should be protected with forts and equipped with munitions, weapons, and artillery for defence.... Both fortresses are to be armed in a manner to withstand any attack..., and as many married Portuguese are to be settled there as will be able to find a way to make a living in the town. In case of a siege, these men will be taken into the fort and will reinforce it. The Superiors are to take care that the inhabitants increase, and that they are equipped with all necessary weaponry.[30]

Also, from this time on, money was set aside to replace the temporary defenses which had been erected during the city's early years by more durable stone ramparts. By Valignano's orders, of the seven hundred ducats that the Portuguese paid yearly for the right to anchor in Nagasaki Bay, one hundred and fifty were to be spent every year on the fortification of Nagasaki "so that the city might be stronger every year and better supplied with artillery and other necessary things."[31]

Later, both the Visitor and Coelho would give glowing descriptions of Nagasaki's strength. Valignano wrote that the fortress was "surrounded by water on almost all sides, and on the side where it is connected with the land it is well fortified with its bulwarks and moat. On the highest point of this site is our headquarters, which is like a fortress set aside from the rest of the settlement."[32] This description was originally accompanied by a drawing of the bulwarks, but the drawing does not seem to have survived. Coelho extolled the safety of the Jesuit headquarters at Nagasaki with its new rock wall,[33] "which was built this year around a very strong rampart which surrounds the whole fortress of Nagasaki. This wall includes several bastions.... We also built into one of the bulwarks several beautiful apartments equipped to receive guests."[34]

In the absence of any pictorial representation of Nagasaki at this time, it is difficult to visualize from this description the exact nature of this "wall around a very strong wall."[35] The description may indicate fortifications, modern at the time, of the *trace italienne* type, which were the answer to the new power of siege artillery and made taking cities by assault virtually impossible.[36] An actual siege of Nagasaki, then, would have required starving the city into submission through a complicated combination of naval and land-based blockades, something quite out of reach for any local power such as Fukabori or Isahaya, and because of its costliness not really an option for the Ryūzōji of Saga or the Shimazu of Satsuma either.

In October of 1580, Valignano consulted with his fellow Jesuits in Bungo. It was during this *consulta* that the differences in style of the mission's management between the Visitor and Cabral came to the fore,[37] but these differences did not concern the militant attitude taken by the mission's superior. They were initially mainly about the internal management of the mission, and especially concerned the treatment and training of its Japanese members.[38] In June or July of the following year, 1581, Cabral was relieved from his position as the superior of Japan and was sent to Bungo to become head of the mission there. Next, in September of 1581, Gaspar Coelho was appointed the new superior of the Japan mission.[39]

It is, therefore, wrong to think that Cabral was relieved of his post because of his militant attitude. As we have seen, Valignano was just as ready to use military hardware as a means to spread the faith as Cabral and Coelho were. What is more, in spite of misgivings,[40] Valignano left Coelho in charge of the mission after his departure in February of 1582, while Cabral was appointed rector of the Collegio de São Paulo in Macao.[41] Coelho's appointment is another indication that, if Valignano has gone down in history as the advocate for non-interference with Japan's internal politics,[42] the principles of this stance were only formulated after 1588, when Valignano first learned of the failure of Coelho's management of the mission.

*   *   *

The King-Sized Admiral: Ambrósio Fernandes

Ever since 1573, when Cabral had been prevented by the Fukabori to leave Nagasaki by boat, the Jesuits had been trying to assure their control over Nagasaki Bay. During the time that the Portuguese carrack was not in port, i.e., between February and August, there was no other solution to this problem than the acquisition of an armed vessel. This assured that indispensable supplies would be delivered regularly to the settlement and it could be used in other armed conflicts of the town with the Fukabori. The first ship is likely to have been of one of local design. It is said to have been captured for a short time by the town's enemies in 1579.[1]

After he had been appointed superior of the mission in 1582, however, the first thing

Coelho did was to have a new, Portuguese-style warship, a *fusta* (or foist) built at Nagasaki. A *fusta* was a long and flat ship in the Mediterranean tradition, usually propelled by oars and sometimes by means of a lateen type sail on a mast in the middle. It was generally able to carry 300 tons. In Asia, *fustas* were often used for war expeditions. They had ten to twenty oars on each of its two boards, but had no deck. Water was stored under the net, and the provisions in the movable store rooms at the waist. They were small ships built for speed and short-distance travel, armed with several light caliber cannon. Some are on record, however, as having sailed all the way from India to Portugal.[2]

The *fusta* of the Jesuits was financed by the Portuguese merchants living in Nagasaki, who stipulated that it be designed larger than strictly necessary for its use in Nagasaki Bay. This way, it could also be used to tow the Portuguese carracks into the bay. It was rumored to be the fastest vessel in Japan.[3] Coelho's *fusta*, fully manned, had room for 300 men,[4] a crew consisting mostly of Japanese Christians, with the exception of the captain and passengers. If the *fusta* had fifteen oars on each side and each oar was pulled by two or three men, that would mean a regular crew of oarsmen of sixty to ninety men.[5] For longer trips, there might be two or three crews, taking turns pulling the oars, so that the vessel could make good time even if the winds were not cooperating. If the wind was right, the crews would have an easier time of it for the ship also had a large triangular sail.

The captain of the *fusta* in the 1580s was Brother Ambrósio Fernandes (1553?–1620).[6] We have already met this Jesuit as the anonymous sailor who in the extremity of a storm at sea "holding onto the father's belt, whispered into his ear that he promised God to enter the Society of Jesus if he were to escape with his life from this storm."[7] The information that he later became the *fusta*'s captain is, of course, not found in the Jesuit archives, but originates in the testimony of the Franciscan Marcelo de Ribadeneira (1560?–1610), who writes blandly: "I got to know Brother Ambrosius, a Jesuit, who was the captain of a small ship like a trireme which guarded the city and the port."[8]

Fernandes was born in Aldea de Sisto, diocese of Oporto. He grew to be a large man. Even shortly before Fernandes' death in a Japanese prison at age sixty-seven, his companion at the time Padre Carlo Spinola, still described him, somewhat illogically, as "more robust than any of us."[9] Fernandes had come to India as a soldier in 1570 or 1571 and had once been taken prisoner by the Arabs. Upon being freed, he had entered the service of a rich merchant of Goa, who made him his secretary. After some years, he left for Macao with permission of his patron, and found employment there with another Portuguese merchant, who sent him on different trips throughout East Asia.[10]

It was on his second trip to Japan that Fernandes made his vow to enter the Society, into which he was officially admitted by Cabral in January of 1579. Clearly, he was a man of the same mold as Luis d'Almeida and Cabral himself: a man of action and a product of the Portuguese empire of his time. A summary of Fernandes' career up to 1614 gives him thirty-six years as a member of the Society in Japan, of which he spent the last four as an assistant to the mission's *procurador* or chief financial officer, Carlo Spinola, and the twenty-one years before that as the steward of the Nagasaki Colegio.[11]

That leaves the first eleven years after he joined the Society unaccounted for. We know that Fernandes was stationed in Nagasaki until 1589,[12] and that he entered the Society in 1578. The time span in between is exactly eleven years. I conclude, therefore, that it was during these first eleven years that he served as the captain of the Society's *fusta*. It was, of course, not expedient to call him the Society's admiral. In contemporary Jesuit records, therefore, Fernandes only appears as the man in charge of the daily necessities of the Nagasaki residence.

This was true, of course. It is certainly not stretching the imagination if we surmise that, while on patrol around Nagasaki Bay and along the Sotome coast of the Sonogi peninsula, the *fusta* also served as a means to bring fresh supplies of water, food, and firewood into the citadel. In this connection, it is interesting to remember that at around the same time the *fusta* was built, the Jesuits also built a pier on the beach below their stronghold, a spot now only known as the Ōhato stop of Nagasaki's tramway system. A stone staircase led up from the beach to the Jesuit headquarters.[13]

There are different accounts of Fernandes' command of Japanese. In 1593, he is said to have spoken Japanese well,[14] but ten years later, in 1603, his knowledge is said to have been "average."[15] One reason for these different evaluations may be due to the general improvement of the ability to speak Japanese among the European members of the mission. It may also be due, in part, to Fernandes' lack of knowledge of the written language and its extensive vocabulary derived from Chinese. It is likely, therefore, that he had mastered the language of the common sailors and coolies, the fishermen and the farmers, the workmen and the artisans of the Nagasaki region. With a well-armed warship such as this "fastest vessel in Japan" (its name has unfortunately not come down to us) commanded by an experienced soldier and sailor like Ambrósio Fernandes, there was no longer any doubt as to who was in charge in Nagasaki Bay and its surroundings.

* * *

Militant Missionaries: Gaspar Coelho (2)

In this manner, under the leadership of Gaspar Coelho, the Jesuits were now small players in the game of Kyushu power politics, dominating a part of the coastline of Western Kyushu as well as, to varying degrees, its hinterland. If they had realized that it was only an endgame, they might have been more careful about getting involved. To do so under a leader who did not even know how to speak Japanese was folly of the highest order and proof of an incurable misconception about their own superior knowledge, power, divine support, and ability to come out on top.

Again, we have to point the finger at Valignano, who seems to have been aware that Coelho was not really an adequate choice for the position he occupied. In an appraisal of the new superior, Valignano wrote on 12 December 1584: "I don't think he is someone capable of being in charge of the whole mission, for learning he has none or very little, and, although he is prudent, he does not have the capacity or authority to manage such a great undertaking ... for he lacks the vigor and knowledge for this, but with the instructions that I have left him he may be all right for a while, because he is obedient, and I believe that we don't have to remove him."[1]

One of the things that had bothered Valignano, when the Visitor had just left Japan was that Coelho "neither knows the language nor is there any hope he will be able to learn it."[2] What seems to have escaped Valignano, however, is Coelho's pride. Maybe, the Visitor was blind to the danger of having Coelho lead the mission at this time precisely because he himself would have made the same mistakes, and thought those who might have done better as particularly unsuitable for the position.

By 1582, Arima Harunobu was again so hard pressed by Ryūzōji Takanobu that he saw no other way out than to try to ally himself with the Shimazu of Satsuma, rulers of the largest domain of southern Kyushu. Harunobu must have come to the conclusion that he needed more help than the Jesuits could provide. In 1583, he broke off his alliance with Takanobu and attacked one of his vassals, Antoku Sumiyasu.[3] When the Ryūzōji counterattacked, Daimyo Shimazu Yoshihisa (1533–1611) sent Niiro Tadakata who defeated the Ryūzōji army.

Later that year, the Shimazu and the Ryūzōji made peace, but Harunobu's fate was still hanging in the balance. Early the next year, 1584, Takanobu announced his intention to deal with the Arima once and for all. Frois writes: "And the first thing which he would do for fun after returning victoriously from the battlefield, was to order the crucifixion of the Padre Viceprovincial [Coelho] and to give the port of Nagasaki to his soldiers to be sacked and destroyed as a reward for their trouble."[4]

The fortune of war turned out otherwise, however. When it was announced that Shimazu Yoshihisa would personally lead his troops into the Shimabara peninsula, Takanobu also came in person to Arima with 25,000 men.[5] Once more, Harunobu turned to the Jesuits, promising temple lands in Unzen if they came to his aid. Coelho sent a supply of guns and mortars by land and the *fusta* by sea. Together the confederates only had 13,000 men in the field. On 4 May, at eight o'clock in the morning, an engagement started at Okitanawade in Shimabara.[6] Takanobu had five hundred muskets which he all ordered to be fired at the same time. The men from Arima, however, possessed two field cannon.

Too fat to sit on a horse, Takanobu went about in a palanquin carried by six men. The commander of the contingent from Satsuma on the battlefield was Kawakami Sakyō-no-suke Tadakata, who was advancing at the head of a number of his men to near the palanquin. Mistaking the Satsuma warriors, who had pushed into the ranks of his soldiers, for troublemakers among his own men, Takanobu yelled out to them to stop fighting among themselves and did they not know how close they were to their own commander? Thereupon, Sakyō-no-suke jumped forward to cut down the palanquin carriers, and yelled out: "It is you we all came to get!"[7]

With these words, he ran Takanobu through with his sword. While the wounded man was chanting the mantra "Namu Amida Butsu," the warrior from Satsuma cut off his head.[8] With the death of Takanobu, the Ryūzōji forces broke. After the defeat, all of Arima as well as Nagasaki celebrated.[9] Harunobu considered himself saved by God Himself, and, not being able to wrest Unzen from its monks, deeded in gratitude the village of Urakami to the Society of Jesus.[10] These were the last lands that the Arima controlled in the Nagasaki area, and the donation considerably expanded the area controlled by the Jesuits around their fortress.[11]

One lucky victory, however, was not enough for Coelho, who spent the summer of 1584 trying to put together an alliance of Christian samurai to confront both the Ryūzōji and, eventually, the Shimazu. Both Ōmura Sumitada and Arima Harunobu were advised to join forces in order to oppose the Ryūzōji.[12] On 11 September, moreover, Coelho wrote a letter to the Governor of the Philippines and the religious orders there, in which he asked for "four ships laden with men, artillery, and food ... to come to the aid of the Christians of Japan who are pressed by the heathen."[13]

Two months later, on 11 November, he wrote once more to the Manila Governor repeating this request for military assistance.[14] The request was repeated once more, on 24 January of 1585.[15] Most revealing is a letter Coelho wrote on 3 March 1585 to his counterpart in Manila, Antonio Sedeño, advocating the dispatch of a Spanish fleet to Japan to subdue the coasts of Kyushu, to assist his coalition of Christian warlords with artillery and gunpowder, and to make war upon the heathen in order to eventually convert all of Japan to Christianity, and so win soldiers with which to conquer China.[16]

These letters with their dreams of power and conquest become more poignant if they are seen in the context of the harsh reality that the proud Coelho had to face in Nagasaki. After their victory over the Ryūzōji, after all, the Shimazu of Satsuma considered themselves the new overlords of both Arima Harunobu and Ōmura Sumitada. In the eyes of the Shimazu, therefore, the Jesuits were nothing but foreign-born vassals of Sumitada, and thus owed their new overlords in Satsuma a formal act of obeisance.

Although Coelho had moved quickly after the victory to strengthen the Jesuit hold on Nagasaki Bay and the Sotome coast, he seems to have been slow to submit to Satsuma. This is the moment that the Jesuit fief of Nagasaki is mentioned in a Japanese source for the first time. It occurs as a short entry for 9 June 1584, just one month after the battle of Okitanawade, in the diary of a senior Satsuma retainer (*karō*) by name of Uwai Kakken (1545–1589). Kakken represented Shimazu Yoshihisa as one of his field commanders and as such could write letters in his lord's name: "From the Southern Barbarian priests we heard that they had taken hostages from twenty places along the western seacoast [of the Sonogi peninsula] and that these had been brought under guard [to Nagasaki], and that, from now on, they wanted to be on good terms with us and they had given [our envoys] a list with the names of all the hostages they had taken."[17]

To inform Satsuma of having taken hostage every Ryūzōji supporter along Nagasaki Bay and the Sotome coast and to provide a name list of those detained in Nagasaki was a beginning, of course, but certainly did not suffice as an act of formal submission. Jesuit sources do not give much insight into the dilemma of who it was the Jesuits recognized as their overlord at this time.[18]

Happily there is testimony from a rival, the Franciscan Juan Pobre de Zamora (?–1615?), who reports:

> When the King of Satsuma [Shimazu Yoshihisa, 1533–1611] saw that only Nagasaki, where the fathers were, did not recognize him, he sent a messenger who threatened them with the words "that they should tell him the reason why they did not come and submit to him. Now, I command you (said the tyrant) that you come immediately in my presence and that each padre brings a spear in each hand." The fathers became very afraid. They wanted to send one of them who lived in Ōmura, but this father did not dare to go.[19]

Juan Pobre's essentially corroborates information in Kakken's diary that "local officials from Nagasaki" had asked for the incorporation of the town into the Satsuma domain.[20] The Franciscan continues:

> Then they took counsel together and decided to send the *otonas* of the village, who are the officials and most important citizens of Nagasaki, telling them that they should say to the King of Satsuma that the fathers did not come themselves because they were not soldiers [*gente de guerra*], but that they remained at his service. This is what they told the King of Satsuma on behalf of the fathers, and with this message they also gave him an expensive present, with which and the submission and obedience they had professed he was satisfied.[21]

There is another entry in Kakken's diary for 1 December of 1585 that confirms the position of dependency upon Satsuma that the Jesuits had acquired after 1584: "Today … I received a letter from the priest at Nagasaki saying that he had planned to travel to Kyoto this year, which we have forbidden. He thought this was a shame because Lord Hashiba had given him permission to build a church in Ōsaka and he just wanted to travel to Kyoto to thank him. We have sent him word to abandon the idea, for we will not allow it."[22]

Here we clearly have Coelho asking permission from his overlords in Satsuma to travel to the Kinai. Fróis tells essentially the same story: how Coelho was preparing to leave for the Kinai, but was held back in Nagasaki by two emissaries from Satsuma, who carried letters in the name of Shimazu Yoshihisa forbidding his departure. According to Fróis, Yoshihisa feared that it was Coelho's intention to plead with Hideyoshi [Lord Hashiba] on behalf of the Ōtomo who were being pressed by the Shimazu.[23] Coelho submitted his dilemma, to go or not to go, to a *consulta* with his fellow Jesuits. They decided together that it was better to postpone his departure until the beginning of the next year, for if he started at that time he would not have gone against the letter of the Satsuma brief commanding him to stay put in the old year.[24]

How much Coelho must have resented the Satsuma presence in Nagasaki, we can also read in a remark of the Satsuma men in Nagasaki quoted by Fróis that "we [the Jesuits] were all their [the Shimazu family's] servants and slaves, and they held as much jurisdiction over the people of Nagasaki as over those of their own castle town of Kago-shima."[25] Later, in the *Anua* or annual letter of 1588, Fróis would write that these men and soldiers from Satsuma in Nagasaki "insulted the fathers and committed many outrages against the crosses and the churches without there being anything we could do about it."[26]

In the end Coelho left for the Kinai on 6 March, a date which corresponds with the 16th day of the first month of the Japanese calendar. This was truly the first day Coelho could decently leave if he wanted to pretend to "obey" the orders from Satsuma, for the first half of the first month of the Japanese New Year was traditionally the time to make visits to one's superiors and receive visits from one's inferiors.[27]

As part of his own New Year's ceremony, Yoshihisa announced his intention to wage a definitive campaign against Ōtomo Sōrin this year.[28] This may have provided a window of opportunity for Coelho, who gambled that with the Shimazu forces engaged on the other side of Kyushu, no one would take the trouble to pursue and kill him, as the Satsuma emissaries of November 1585 had been ordered to do if they had found that Coelho had already left Nagasaki before they arrived in the city.[29]

PART TWO: BRAVE NEW WORLD
(1587–1613)

The Conqueror of Kyushu:
Toyotomi Hideyoshi (1)

The China trade was a seasonal business. The trading season started with the arrival of the Portuguese in Nagasaki Bay in July or August of each year and lasted until their departure some six to eight months later. The dependability of the Portuguese ships in seaworthiness, their ability to take on any adversary, their nautical science and, of course, their access to the markets of South China had given the carracks of the 1550s through the 1580s a virtual monopoly over Japan's trade with China, a monopoly which the Portuguese tried to reinforce or protect by aggressive military action whenever necessary. Even Jesuits were liable to get shot at in Macao if they were suspected of smuggling goods to Japan.[1] For a while, until 1587, the profits on this trade route were among the largest the Portuguese made anywhere in Asia, and to be the Captain Major of one year's China voyage often sufficed to set up a man for the rest of his life.[2]

It was a situation too good to be true. To have foreigners make such profits was only possible in a country embroiled in civil war, where many longed to participate in the trade and there was no central authority strong enough to regulate it. By the beginning of the 1580s, however, the civil war was finally coming to an end. Since the late 1560s, the rise of Oda Nobunaga (1534–1582) and his string of successes on the battlefields of the Tōkai, Tōsan, Kinai, Hokuriku, San'in and Sanyō regions had thrown its long shadow over the whole country.

Nobunaga's assassination in 1582 did not really represent a serious set-back for his armies, for one of his generals by the name of Hideyoshi quickly avenged his master's death and managed to step into his shoes to continue the reunification of the country. In 1585 he sent a large expedition of more than one hundred thousand men to conquer Shikoku. In the same year he brought Etchū under his dominion. In 1586 he started preparations for a campaign on an even greater scale than those he had just successfully concluded. Approximately 250,000 men were mobilized for the conquest of Kyushu in 1587.[3] As a result, the island's rulers submitted to Hideyoshi's authority in just six months. For our purposes here, the most important outcome of the campaign were the proscription of Christianity, an order for the Jesuits to leave Japan, and the incorporation of Nagasaki into Hideyoshi's personal domain, the *tenryō*. From the conquest of Kyushu until just after the start of the Korean campaign, Hideyoshi provided a new foundation for the administration of the city and its surroundings.[4]

It is clear from Hideyoshi's actions in the years after the Kyushu campaign that his main concern in Nagasaki, like that of his successor Tokugawa Ieyasu after him, was with curbing the exorbitant profits of the Portuguese and taking a greater share of these for himself, as well as bringing the city of Nagasaki under his firm personal control. To achieve the latter he aimed at first separating the traders from the missionaries, allowing the former to continue to come to Japan, but expelling the latter. As he was grappling with unprecedented problems, Hideyoshi's approach was, of necessity perhaps, characterized by happenstance and *ad hoc* solutions that sometimes contradicted his earlier orders and conflicted with other concerns. It was only after his death, under Tokugawa Ieyasu and his successors, that they were slowly solved to the satisfaction of the rulers of the *tenryō*. It goes without saying that the problem in implementing these changes was how to do so without killing the proverbial goose that laid the golden eggs.

It was to meet with Hideyoshi himself that Gaspar Coelho had left Nagasaki on 6 March 1586.[5] His dilemma was whether or not to obey the orders he had received from his masters in Satsuma. In the end, as we have seen, he decided to gamble that Satsuma would be too preoccupied to bother with him. In this he was mistaken, for when, after a journey of fifty days, he finally arrived in Sakai on or just after 25 April,[6] an emissary from Satsuma was waiting for him, probably to warn him to return to Nagasaki immediately. Coelho refused to see the man or deal with him in any way.[7] On the contrary, he met with Satsuma's enemy Ōtomo Sōrin, who had specifically come to the Kinai to ask Hideyoshi for military assistance.[8]

From a message sent by Satsuma to Nagasaki later that year, it is clear that had things turned out differently and had Satsuma emerged the winner, Coelho would have been executed and the Jesuits would have been expelled from Kyushu.[9] As luck would have it, things turned out worse. Within ten days after his arrival, on 4 May 1586, Coelho had an audience with Hideyoshi at Osaka Castle, accompanied by more than thirty Jesuit padres, brothers, *dōjuku*, and other boys serving the Jesuits.[10] The meeting seemed to go off splendidly. After the initital ceremonial, Hideyoshi came and sat next to Coelho and Fróis, who served as interpreter, so that "not more than half a tatami mat" separated Coelho from Hideyoshi.

Japan's ruler started off with praise for the intentions of the padres who had come, it was clear to him, all the way to Japan just to spread their doctrine.[11] This he repeated several times. Next, he explained that now that he had conquered most of Japan, he wished for nothing else than to leave a great name and fame after he died. After he had reorganized Japan "in a way so that the country would be at peace,"[12] he intended to turn the realm over to his brother, while he would occupy himself with the conquest of Korea and China.

He had already ordered enough wood to be cut to build two thousand ships to ferry his army across to the continent. For this project, he wished for no other help from the padres than that they would procure two large and well-equipped Portuguese vessels for him, not for free to be sure, for he would pay silver cash for everything. The Portuguese who would sail the ships would receive land and income from him. After his victory on the continent, he would build churches all over China and order all the Chinese to become Christians, while back home the Jesuits should make Christians of "half or the major part of Japan."[13]

Then, acting as a guide himself, Hideyoshi gave the Jesuit group a grand, three-hour tour of Osaka Castle, during which, from time to time, he came back to business. In Kyushu, he promised with a laugh, he might give Hizen to his Christian retainers, Takayama Ukon and Konishi Ryūsa, while he would definitely leave Nagasaki to the Church.[14] Coelho, on his part, promised the help of his coalition of Christian daimyo in Kyushu against Satsuma and Ryūzōji Masa'ie, the two ships Hideyoshi had asked for, as well as other help from India.[15]

Two things are clear from all the empty promises made during this elaborate charade: Hideyoshi was keenly aware of the Jesuit pretension to have a monopoly on religious truth, and he clearly knew that the ultimate goal of the order was the conversion of all of China and Japan. Just before his planned Kyushu campaign, however, he preferred to have Coelho's Christians on his side. On the other hand, what is difficult to understand is how Coelho could have been so foolish as to believe what Hideyoshi was promising him.

After more than fifteen years in Japan, the Vice-provincial had still not learned enough of the language and customs of the country to be able to see that Hideyoshi actually may have been admonishing him, especially when he stressed, over and over, that he admired the padres for coming to Japan "solely to teach their Law." This meant, of course, that the Jesuits should not engage in anything else in Japan (such as distributing artillery and gunpowder, or monopolizing the trade). Hideyoshi's overblown promise to order all Chinese to become Christians, out of all proportion to the potential merits of the Jesuits for Hideyoshi's cause, also were reminders as well as warnings to be mindful of the Kampaku's supremacy. (Hideyoshi had been awarded the court title *kampaku* [regent of an adult emperor] in the seventh month of Genshō 13 [1585]).

Coelho, however, remained as deaf as a doorknob to all this. On the contrary, after this visit, he became thoroughly convinced of his own intimate relationship with the ruler of Japan. He stayed in the Kansai for almost three months, and left Sakai only on 23 July.[16] There was no need to hurry back home, for with the possibility of the war between the Shimazu and the Ōtomo spilling over into the port, the Portuguese went to Hirado instead of Nagasaki this year. Coelho finally returned to Nagasaki on Christmas Eve, even though he was now considered an enemy by the Shimazu.[17]

Back home in Hizen, in the spring of 1587, Ōmura Sumitada lay on his deathbed. Twice, he sent a messenger requesting Coelho to come and visit him, but both times he was rebuffed.[18] Evidently, the Vice-provincial could not forget that Sumitada had once reneged on his promise to have his daughter marry into the Arima family, and other peccadillos, even though his conversion in 1563 had been so crucial for the survival and success of the mission as well as the founding and continuing existence of Nagasaki.

Blinded by a completely mistaken idea of his own importance, Coelho had also fallen out with Arima Harunobu, who was found to be less than enthusiastic about the necessity to form a common front of Christian warlords against Satsuma. As we have seen, Harunobu had since 1584 thrown in his lot with the Shimazu of Satsuma. In consequence, Coelho ordered the padres and brothers to leave the domain of Arima and that the seminary be transferred to Urakami, a village near Nagasaki, which had been added as a gift of Harunobu to the Jesuits in 1584.[19]

After Hideyoshi's fleet under the command of his Christian retainer Konishi Yukinaga had sailed into Nagasaki Bay in February of 1587,[20] Coelho and his closest advisers Belchior de Mora, Luís Fróis, and Jorge Carvahal embarked to go and visit Hideyoshi once more. Three Portuguese, one of them the *feitor* or chief financial officer of the Portuguese carrack which had wintered in Hirado that year, also went, carrying a present from the Captain Major for Hideyoshi.[21] Next, Satsuma withdrew its forces from the Shimabara peninsula, and Nagasaki was again a free town, although it was a freedom that would only last a couple of months.[22]

The flotilla under Konishi called at Kuchinotsu and then attacked Satsuma positions to the south.[23] On 14 May 1587, it arrived at Yatsushiro in Higo, where Hideyoshi was staying. Two weeks later, on 28 May, Hideyoshi met with Coelho and the sumptuously dressed Portuguese merchants. It was the first time the ruler of Japan laid eyes on the Portuguese. He showed an interest in the weapons they carried and told them he wanted the carrack to come to Sakai or another port near Osaka. When Coelho asked him to spare the Christian prisoners from Yatsushiro Castle, he granted the request.

Hideyoshi told Coelho to come and see him again in Hakata, where he planned to go after Shimazu Yoshihisa had been defeated.[24] And so, in the beginning of July, Coelho, Fróis, and three brothers left Nagasaki for Hakata, along the way stopping over in Hirado for eight days. After their arrival in Hakata, they were waiting for the conqueror of Kyushu,[25] when suddenly on the fifteenth of the month Hideyoshi arrived with several boats alongside the *fusta* that served as Coelho's sleeping quarters. This was an unprecedented honor, and Coelho pulled out the gangway to welcome and give Japan's ruler a tour of the whole ship, which was carrying its full crew of three hundred rowers.

After the tour, Coelho treated Hideyoshi and his entourage to wine and sweetened fruits on deck, and they again had a long conversation. The *fusta* evidently pleased Hideyoshi enormously, and he praised its solid construction. It was clear he wanted it for himself. Instead of immediately offering the vessel, Coelho tried to barter it against the grant of Fukabori Sumimasa's fief.[26] Such effrontery did not deserve an answer: "the ruler angry about this, turned away his face, and did not mention the matter again."[27]

So far Hideyoshi had not yet seen a carrack or any other big Portuguese ship. When he heard that a Portuguese vessel was lying at anchor in Hirado, he ordered Coelho to have it come to Hakata. The moment when he was leaving the *fusta*, he desired some of the wine and fruits he had been served. He told Coelho that he could not trust anyone but the Jesuits, and wanted him to send some, under cover, over to his camp.[28] Coelho was ecstatic about the visit. Hideyoshi's Christian retainers, Takayama Ukon and Konishi Yukinaga, however, knew their master better than that.

When they heard how the visit had gone, they immediately started to fret. Even if the *fusta* was small for a warship, she was well equipped to deal with the emergencies of wartime. Its inspection, therefore, might induce Hideyoshi to rethink his attitude towards the church and the Portuguese. They warned Coelho that it would be better to offer the vessel to Hideyoshi right away, stressing that it had been built especially for him. Coelho, however, preferred to trust his own impression of Hideyoshi's good mood and ignored their warning.

Exactly one week after Hideyoshi's visit, on 22 July, Hideyoshi's Christian retainer Takayama Ukon came to the *fusta* to meet with Coelho in person. He told the head of the mission that "because God's designs are always opposed by the devil, he was sure that some great calamity was about to befall Japanese Christendom."[29] It would be good, therefore, for the padres as well as for the Christians of Japan to prepare for it. Asked by Coelho if he knew of anything in particular that the devil might be planning against them, Ukon denied this, but said that he was "entirely convinced that the devil cannot stand such great successes in converting the Japanese without doing his utmost to put some obstacle in the way."[30] From this entry, Professor Alvarez-Taladriz has concluded that Takayama Ukon was already familiar with the fact that Hideyoshi intended to issue an anti-Christian edict. For fear of being disloyal to his liege lord, however, he was not able to warn the Jesuits in any more explicit manner.[31]

The Slave Trader: Domingos Monteiro

As we have seen, in 1586 the Portuguese carrack had gone to Hirado instead of Nagasaki. This was the first time in 21 years that the Portuguese had chosen to come to this port. However, because of the unsettled situation in Kyushu, where the Shimazu were attacking the Ōtomo along a broad front, no merchants were coming from the Kinai to trade during the summer and fall of 1586. The Portuguese, therefore, were unable to sell their wares and were forced to winter in Hirado.[1] The carrack of that year was captained by the New Christian [i.e., Jewish convert] merchant Domingos Monteiro, who was a great friend and supporter of the Jesuit mission.[2]

Apart from ferrying the members of the Society to and from Japan without charge, he had been careful to donate large sums of money to the mission. But in 1586, he had refused the padres' request to come to Nagasaki. Later, Visitor Valignano would wax indignant, just thinking about the lack of obedience on the part of this merchant: "Receiving the anchorage fees of the carrack strengthens the Matsura, who were on the verge of returning territory previously taken from Sumitada. Now they feel strong enough to refuse to do so. What is more, they threaten Sumitada with the loss of still more land, so that the latter is now forced into a peace agreement that includes the marriage of one of his daughters, who is a Christian, to a pagan son of the Matsura family.... If there were a bishop in Japan, this kind of thing [i.e., Monteiro's refusal to come to Nagasaki] could be punished with excommunication."[3]

Wintering in Hirado, however, was not a wholly unwelcome development, for there may have been more than one reason why the New Christian Portuguese trader had preferred to anchor there. Hirado was an easier place than Nagasaki to buy large numbers of slaves, especially cheap these years because of the wars between the Kyushu daimyo.[4] During the mid–1580s, the price of a Japanese man or woman was far cheaper than that of a cow in Kyushu.[5] In 1588, for example, it was two or three *mon* in Shimabara, although that price was, because of war and famine, particularly low.[6]

Significantly, a Japanese account of Hideyoshi's movements during his Kyushu campaign of 1587 includes a short but telling description about this type of merchandise bought up by the Portuguese, suggesting the testimony of an eyewitness: "The slaves, men and women, were chained hands and feet and loaded by the hundreds like merchandise into the hold of the carrack."[7] Even after Hideyoshi's proscription of the trade, Hirado continued to be the last stop of a smuggling network that collected human beings for sale to foreign traders until the 1620s: the men to be used as soldiers and the women mostly as (sexual) servants. The only difference was that prices went up steadily. By the beginning of the 17th century, prices in Hirado had risen to between 7 and 10 *taels* for a good slave.[8]

Coelho, trying to evade all blame for the trade, wrote on 2 October 1587: "Another evil they [the Portuguese traders] commit, which scandalizes many here, is their willingness to obtain in any manner possible, by force if necessary, Japanese men and women. And because the Japanese are poor, they offer them this opportunity to make some money by selling people. They think up a thousand different ways to trick and deceive, and go about the towns stealing and robbing fathers and mothers of their sons and daughters."[9]

In the same source, however, Coelho admits some Jesuit involvement in this trade:

"And because the fathers give them certificates for the bishop of China that these are slaves obtained in a legal manner, they engage in much deception in cahoots with the Japanese who sell the slaves to them."[10] Constant Jesuit involvement in the slave trade stands here in only the thinnest of disguises: the padres are deceived and tricked by evil merchants into issuing certificates for slaves obtained in an illegal manner.[11]

A short description of the Jesuit compound at Morisaki in Nagasaki in the 1580s, during the time of the year that the Portuguese carrack was at anchor, also illustrates how central the role of the Jesuits was to the whole trade:

> When the carrack arrives in Nagasaki, they [the padres] transfer its whole cargo, not just their own but also the merchandise belonging to others, and bring it to their convent, so that the Jesuit compound of Nagasaki is like the Customs House of Sevilla, where all the merchandise that comes from the Indies is registered. There are so many different things, and such a variety of contracts and agreements is entered into here, not only for the merchandise of the carrack *but also for the slaves who are shipped in the same vessel*, the one as well as the other passing through their hands, that I do not know if there would be more in the Vendution House of Sevilla.[12]

Jesuit involvement in the slave trade went all the way back to the leadership of Cosme de Torrès. In a Jesuit handbook, dating from 1570, on how to handle problems arising from confessions, Japanese girls "robbed from their fathers and mothers" and brought as slaves to Macao are on record as having complained that the Superior had issued the licenses legalizing their sale. The writer of the handbook, taking the position of the haves against the have-nots, concludes that the true merits of such allegations can only be decided in Japan, and that therefore "in dubiis" these sales must be considered "legal."[13]

On the other hand, it should also be noted that it was the same Cosme de Torrès who issued the Jesuit request to King Dom Sebastião to put a stop to the slave trade by the Portuguese in Japan. This prohibition was actually proclaimed on 20 September 1570,[14] although the Portuguese merchants routinely ignored it for another 17 years. It stands to reason, then, that it paid for a Portuguese merchant to have good relations with the padres.

We can also see why one of Hideyoshi's first priorities in dealing with the foreign traders was to put a stop to this traffic. Not, to be sure, out of any moral considerations (as his Korean campaigns would abundantly show),[15] but simply because his pride as the ruler of the realm would not allow his subjects to be sold overseas. Hideyoshi proscribed the slave trade on 23 July 1587, the day after Takayama Ukon had warned Coelho of a calamity about to befall Japanese Christendom, at the very same time and in the very same document prohibiting the Christian religion.[16]

Around the middle of July, however, when Domingos Monteiro was notified by Coelho that he was to come to Hakata and show his carrack to Hideyoshi, he did not yet know that the latter was about to prohibit the sale of human beings. Still, we can imagine the Captain Major's predicament: he was to sail his ship, likely with a hold full of the slaves he had purchased over the past year, from Hirado to Hakata to show it inside out to the man who had just conquered Kyushu. Could the precious cargo be unloaded? No, for there was nowhere (except in the hold of the ship) that so many people could be kept secure and out of sight.

If Domingos Monteiro had been another man, he might have set his cargo free and sailed his ship to Hakata. Such a gesture would have greatly benefited the Portuguese in

Japan. Helped and usually guided by the missionaries, however, the Portuguese had been playing off one daimyo against another in Japan for the past thirty-some years, trading guns and gunpowder against slaves, just as they had been doing along the coast of Africa for more than a century and a half. It was difficult to change such bad, old habits overnight.

Thus, the Portuguese merchant naively tried deception. Preparing gifts to the value of more than five hundred *cruzados*, he traveled to Hakata in person, where he told Hideyoshi, on 24 July, that it would have been too dangerous to sail the carrack to Hakata. During the interview, Hideyoshi seemed to accept the excuse. He offered Monteiro a sword, and treated the Captain Major, the missionaries, and the other Portuguese who were accompanying him in a friendly manner before giving them their leave.[17]

That very same night, however, evaluating the audience with his closest advisers, Hideyoshi decided to take his first concrete step towards challenging the bond between the merchants and the missionaries.[18] The result was a revision of his edict proscribing the slave trade and Christianity. Thus, there are two anti–Christian edicts, with two different, but consecutive dates: one that had been prepared on the night before the reception of the Portuguese, and one composed after their visit.

The first had been concerned with Christianity as a general problem for the realm Hideyoshi ruled, but had not addressed the immediate departure of the missionaries from Japan. The second stipulated clearly that the missionaries had to leave "within twenty days."[19] No other conclusion can be drawn from the fact that Hideyoshi deemed it necessary to redraft the document he had prepared the night before the audience[20] than that he had repressed his anger at being taken for a fool by the Portuguese merchants and their missionary guides on 24 July 1587.[21]

* * *

Rewriting History: Luís Fróis (2)

Hideyoshi's prohibition of Christianity has received almost continuous scrutiny by Western writers since the sixteenth century. Unsurprisingly, at first, the Jesuits did most of the soul searching. Their dilemma was of two kinds. The first was theological: the existence of God being an absolute, He necessarily was pleased with the efforts of the Jesuits in Asia. How, then, was it possible that He could allow such a flagrant denial of His own best interests? The second dilemma, while more prosaic, was more serious: how was it possible that, even with divine help, none of the Jesuits had seen Hideyoshi's prohibition coming?

The fact is, in Hideyoshi the Jesuits had met more than their match. If the Jesuits were adept at manipulating people and events to their own advantage, the conqueror of Kyushu was even more able to do so. If the Jesuits were relentless in pursuing their goals, while at times unscrupulous about the means they employed, the man who had risen from peasant to supreme commander of Japan's warrior class could outdo them on all fronts that counted. Dissimulation and disinformation were among the most innocent of his talents.

Hideyoshi was very clear about the Jesuits and their pretensions. In her biography, simply entitled *Hideyoshi*, Professor Berry has put it in a nutshell: "The target of [his] edict was an evangelical band of priests who sowed disorder, maintained an independent base in Nagasaki, acted as gold and silver brokers for Kyushu generals, trafficked in shares of the Portuguese carracks, and inspired raids on native sanctuaries."[1] This is, from what we have seen above, still a pretty mild assessment, for we could easily add the slave and armaments trade to the list of sins that Hideyoshi himself may have had in mind.

From the point of view of an unbeliever, therefore, Hideyoshi's decision was perfectly rational. As the supreme ruler of Japan himself explained to a Portuguese merchant in the fall of 1588:

> … in as much as the Fathers preached a law so hostile to the *kami* and *hotoke* [deities] of Japan, I was constrained to banish them…. *Kami* and *hotoke* are none other than the Lords of Japan, who, by their victories and exploits deserve to be worshipped as true *kami* by the people. Therefore, the aim of every Lord of Japan is to end his life with illustrious deeds which may inspire the minds of his subjects so that they will give him this cult of honor and reverence. The law preached by the Fathers, being so opposed to the *kami* and *hotoke* of Japan, is for the same reason opposed to the Lords of Japan: although it may be good for other countries, it is not good for Japan. For this reason I have sent the Fathers away. Aiming to deride and to destroy the *kami* and *hotoke*, they are, in consequence, trying to deride me and to belittle my memory and glory after my death: therefore I cannot be friendly and well-disposed towards them, unless I was to be hostile and badly disposed towards myself.[2]

From the point of view of the Christians, however, this same decision could not be anything else but irrational. Therefore, a common theme in Western literature has been a tendency to stress Hideyoshi's irrationality, his hubris, and plain "craziness." The earliest advocates of this position were the Jesuits themselves, of course, for if Hideyoshi was crazy then they could not be held responsible for failing to predict his behavior.[3] Padre Pedro Gómez already wrote on 7 January 1588:

> This man [Hideyoshi], of peasant stock, has become so powerful that he is now the acknowledged master of the whole of Japan. So long as he was engaged in victorious warfare, he showed himself well disposed towards us. We prayed for the successful issue of his military campaigns, and we rejoiced when we should have wept. For after he had completed the conquest of Japan, he became so proud as to covet that one day divine homage would be paid to him. The Evil One, the Prince of Pride, made use of him as a tool to bring about our ruin, and put it into his head that, since he was Japan's overlord, he had to banish a religious teaching, which condemned and threatened to overthrow the worship of the Kamis.[4]

There is another question, however, that has not received much attention in Western literature. This is what effect Hideyoshi's proscription had on the management of the mission and the spirit of the Jesuits? It cannot be doubted that this effect was profound and that the prohibition caused the members of the Japan mission to reflect upon their whole effort up to 1587 in order to try and salvage of it what they could. At first, the years between 1549 and 1587 must have been seen as one great failure. The Jesuits had tried, in the beginning, to work by themselves to spread their message, but had met with very little success.[5]

When they changed direction, in the early 1560s, and became interpreters and agents for, as well as manipulators of, the trade brought by the Portuguese,[6] the numbers of baptisms had begun to rise,[7] but simultaneously the order's involvement in the dangerous game of power politics in the final stage of Japan's civil war brought complications they were unable and unwilling to face. One thing, for example, that the Jesuits in Japan did not foresee was the speed with which Hideyoshi managed to unify the country and impose his will on the whole archipelago. Another was how this unification would affect their mission.

This was such a serious miscalculation that it should have called into question the competence of the whole Jesuit leadership in Asia, not just Padre Coelho, the mission's leader on the scene, but also, and especially, that of his superior Visitor Alessandro Valignano.[8] When one year after Hideyoshi's proscription, upon his return to Macao on 28 July 1588,[9] Valignano finally learned what had happened in Japan, he started a prolonged and concerted effort to clean up the mess. In a way, Coelho was lucky to die on 25 July of 1590, only four days after Valignano had come back to Japan, for he would certainly have received an ignominious punishment, just as posthumously he has been made a scapegoat for the failure of the mission.[10]

From this time on, Valignano pretended that he had always advised the Vice-provincial not to get involved in military adventures or meddle in Japan's internal politics. In view of the instructions Valignano himself had left for making Nagasaki a strong military colony and his concern with the legal and political system of the city, this accusation rings lame and hollow.[11]

It goes without saying, however, that it was of supreme importance for salvaging the mission that the meaning of the efforts made by the Jesuits in the years up to 1587 received a reinterpretation. This reinterpretation was, in turn, informed by the new mission policy of trying to adapt to the changed situation in Japan after the prohibition. Of necessity, therefore, the order would try to conceal or, when concealment was not an option, downplay the militant behavior of the Jesuits before 1587 that from that time onwards contradicted the new goals of the mission.

Of this effort the mission's spin doctors Alessandro Valignano and Luís Fróis were the main brains. Fróis' *Historia de Japam*, for example, has to be examined first and foremost in this light, for, although the author seems to have started the work before Hideyoshi's edict, its final version clearly is the result of Valignano's clean-up effort.[12] Here, we finally come upon the true reason why we found Fróis to be so waffling about the Jesuit involvement in the founding of Nagasaki: Hideyoshi's edict had suddenly made the founding of the city into the order's most important failure, which was therefore most urgently in need of being erased.[13] The effort to rewrite the history of the Jesuits in Japan was, on the whole, extremely successful, but it necessarily involved the willful destruction of a number of important documents.[14]

When Domingos Monteiro finally left Japan at the end of February 1588, he had, in spite of Hideyoshi's expulsion order, only three brothers on board, who had been scheduled to go to Macao to be ordained anyway.[15] Again, the Captain Major and the Jesuits thought they could deceive the ruler of Japan, who was being kept informed of the situation in Kyushu and especially in Nagasaki by numerous spies in his employ. This time, two emissaries from Nagasaki were sent to him after the carrack had left.[16] On 8 March 1588, Francisco Garces and Antonio de Abreu, the first a Portuguese living in Nagasaki and the second a Japanese Christian, likely with a Portuguese (New Christian?) father, visited Hideyoshi to explain why not all the padres had left Japan. The reason they gave was that the ship had been unable to accommodate such a great number of people.[17]

Understandably annoyed (remembering the large number of Japanese slaves who were being taken out of Japan against his express orders), Hideyoshi immediately retaliated. Within a little over half a year, the victor of Kyushu had reason to feel twice deceived by the Portuguese, the merchants as well as the missionaries. Yet he exercised exemplary restraint, for he had his own strategy for dealing with the matter. The Jesuits were punished first, for Hideyoshi now ordered the destruction of all Jesuit establishments in Miyako, Osaka, and Sakai.[18] The Portuguese traders still had a little punishment coming to them later.

* * *

Master of the *Tenka*: Toyotomi Hideyoshi (2)

No new Portuguese carrack had arrived in Nagasaki in 1587. As the carrack of 1586 had not come back and the news from Japan had already been bad before it had left, the merchants of Macao had evidently come to the conclusion that it was better to hold off on investing in a new cargo for Japan until more definite tidings reached them in China. When, in June of 1587, the news arrived in Nagasaki that Shimazu Yoshihisa (1533–1611), his head shaven like a priest and his name changed to Ryūhaku, had begged Hideyoshi's pardon, the town was quiet and relieved to have avoided the war.[1]

Although, subsequently, Hideyoshi's edicts against Christianity did not explicitly provide new rules for the city and its immediate environment, the bad news of the prohibition depressed the population of Nagasaki almost immediately. It was clear that something needed to be done to appease Hideyoshi. The various *tōnin*, or headmen of the town's wards, decided to make a trip to Hakata to see what Hideyoshi intended to do about their city.[2] These men had been educated and appointed by the Jesuits. For 1587, we have the Christian name of the most important of them, a Japanese baptized Bento [i.e., Benedict], but alas no way of knowing what his family name was.[3] In any case, Hideyoshi refused to receive them.

Luís Fróis was living in Nagasaki at the time. He reports that the town's inhabitants were forced to pay "a large fine of more than eight thousand cruzados" to their conqueror while the fortifications of the city were to be destroyed by Hideyoshi's men.[4] When this was announced, a panic in the city ensued: "People carried their belongings on their backs. Men, women, the old and the young, the highly placed as well as those without status, all fled weeping into the mountains. The fathers, fearing the churches would be defiled,[5] took away the paintings and locked the doors of the churches."[6]

Hideyoshi sent two of his men to Nagasaki, of whom only Tōdō Sado no kami Takatora's name has survived.[7] Tōdō Takatora (1556–1630) had been, since 1576, a retainer of Hideyoshi's nephew, Hashiba Hidenaga. During the Kyushu campaign, he received the title of *Sado no kami*, as well as a fief of 20,000 *koku* in Kii. After Hidenaga's death in 1591, he would become a direct retainer of Hideyoshi.[8] The two men arrived in the city by the end of July with four ships full of soldiers. Their task was to execute Hideyoshi's orders, and they started by pulling down the city's defenses. By the time they arrived, the Jesuits had already removed the artillery that went with these fortifications into some secret storage chamber, likely in one of the many caves along the coast line of Nagasaki Bay.[9]

The fine, mentioned above, is confirmed by some later Japanese sources,[10] but not in any contemporary Japanese documents. The size of the fine remains unclear. Fróis mentions a figure of eight thousand *cruzados* in his annual letter, quoted above, but this has become five hundred silver *ichimais* for Hideyoshi and fifty each for Takatora and his colleague in his *Historia*.[11] The people of Nagasaki were too poor to pay their share, Fróis writes, so Portuguese married to Japanese women living in Nagasaki and the Jesuits made up the difference.[12] In the end, Hideyoshi's men, after demolishing the defenses of the city, proved venal and took money to leave the crosses and churches of the city alone.[13] Such matters are likely to have been negotiated by the same *tōnin*, whom Hideyoshi had refused to see because they were rich Christian merchants.

In these emotional months, Nagasaki Jinzaemon's stronghold at Sakurababa was burned.[14] Some say that it was the disgruntled *jitō* himself who set the fire, others that the castle was ordered destroyed by order of Hideyoshi,[15] who blamed Jinzaemon for Nagasaki being a Christian town and required that he leave the Ōmura domain.[16] At the same time, all the padres were ordered by Hideyoshi to go to Hirado in order to be ready to leave the country on the Portuguese ship. At a *consulta*, held there in August of 1587, it was decided that they would stay in Japan under-cover so as not to excite Hideyoshi's anger. The college and novitiate, which had just been transferred to Nagasaki, were moved back to Arima, the college to Chijiwa and the novitiate to Arie.[17]

By September of 1587, Tōdō Takatora had already returned to Osaka.[18] While the *consulta* had provided the Jesuits with a common objective, i.e., to remain in Japan as inconspicuously as they could, privately some of them fired off missives expressing preferences for a different response. Spanish Padre Pedro Ramon (1550–1611), for example, wrote on 15 October 1587 a letter to the General of the Society, in which he proclaimed the need for the King of Spain to send an invasion force to obtain a safe stronghold in Japan ("in Nagasaki or elsewhere") to protect the Christian mission.[19]

Between Hideyoshi's prohibition of Christianity and his appointment of officials to govern Nagasaki more than ten months went by.[20] In the beginning of 1588, Ōmura Yoshiaki (1568–1616), Sumitada's son,[21] and Arima Harunobu seem to have protested to Hideyoshi that Nagasaki/Sakurababa, Mogi, and Urakami had belonged to their respective domains before these lands had been given in trust to the Jesuits to hold as long as they were in Japan. Now that Hideyoshi had ordered them to leave, the two warlords asked him to return the land to their previous owners. According to the Jesuits, Hideyoshi readily assented to this.[22]

Although such requests can be documented, it is most unlikely that Hideyoshi agreed to comply with them.[23] Upon his return to Osaka in the summer of 1587, the conqueror of Kyushu first had to deal with an uprising in the domain of Sasa Narimasa in Higo. He immediately sent Narimasa's brother-in-law, Asano Danjō no Shōhitsu Nagayoshi to deal with it. The appointment of officials may, for that reason, have been delayed and the city of Nagasaki likely became, once again, semi-independent, governed by its own local officials, the *tōnin*.

Before the expected arrival of the carrack of 1588, however, Hideyoshi again turned his attention to the problem presented by the incorporation of Nagasaki into the *tenryō*. We have the texts of three documents issued by him between 27 April and 8 July 1588.[24] The first contains the appointment of Nabeshima Naoshige (1538–1618) to Nagasaki *daikan*, or Hideyoshi's official representative.[25] This able, former retainer of the violently anti–Christian daimyo Ryūzōji Takanobu was at this time still known as Shinsei (or Nobunari).[26] Shinsei had married into his lord's family. After Takanobu's death on the battlefield of Okitanawade in 1584, he became the Nabeshima family's most influential member.

In 1590, with Hideyoshi's backing, he was able to take over the Saga domain, north of Ōmura, and he seems to have actually lobbied Hideyoshi to receive the Nagasaki appointment. He may have wanted to realize the old dream of Ryūzōji Takanobu of taking over Nagasaki.[27] Naoshige, however, was neither present in Nagasaki in 1588 at the time that the Portuguese carrack was in port, nor for the next carrack in 1590. Probably, therefore, Hideyoshi did not mean for him to function as his representative in taking over the foreign trade. Naoshige's task, rather, was to provide the muscle of his military might to keep the peace in the city and keep an eye on its Christians, as well as the Christian warlords of the area.[28]

It has also been suggested that Naoshige's appointment was Hideyoshi's signal to Sumitada's son Ōmura Yoshiaki that Nagasaki, i.e., the original six *machi* of 1571 and twenty other *machi* that had grown up around them, no longer belonged to Ōmura.[29] As we have seen, the key focus of Hideyoshi's policy towards Nagasaki was to try and separate the trade from the activities of the missionaries. To do this, he first needed to clarify the jurisdictions between the different officials he had appointed. Nabeshima Naoshige was responsible for collecting the taxes and corvées. A document from Hideyoshi's cabinet, dated 12 June 1588, appointed Toda Katsutaka and Asano Nagayoshi to act as Nagasaki's administrators if Naoshige was not around.[30]

After the Kyushu campaign, Katsutaka had first worked, with Fukushima Masanori (1561–1624), as Higo *daikan* and *bugyō* of the land survey Hideyoshi conducted in all domains he added to his rule.[31] Both officials, then, were chosen to deal with Nagasaki because of their proximity to Higo, by boat just a day or two away from Nagasaki. This had also been the main reason why Tōdō Takatora and his companion had been chosen to go to Nagasaki the year before. Katsutaka and Nagayoshi seem to have visited Nagasaki together during the summer of 1588 to formally announce the incorporation of Nagasaki into the *tenryō* or Hideyoshi's personal domain and, simultaneously, Hideyoshi's generous remittance of the land tax.[32]

It is likely that Hideyoshi (and others, such as the Shimazu of Satsuma, before him) essentially considered Nagasaki a *jinaichō*, or temple town, such as existed all over Japan. Jinaichō were usually located along major trade routes, often held markets, were tax exempt like the Buddhist temples that formed their center, and were protected by moats and walls.[33] Waiving the land tax, therefore, meant that Hideyoshi was treating Nagasaki as an important center of trade, which he wanted to preserve and if possible increase.

The carrack of Captain Major Jeronimo Pereira reached Nagasaki on 16 or 17 August 1588.[34] Pereira would later write about the Jesuits:

> [Hideyoshi] cast them out of Japan for their possession of firearms and ordered them to destroy their churches while I was present there in that same year of 1588…. The fathers of the Society had in 1588 in Japan a magazine for storing their heavy bronze artillery and arquebuses. While I served as the captain of the ship of 1588 … they put many pieces of artillery inside my ship so that they might be safe there and [Hideyoshi] would not take them when he came to destroy the churches.[35]

It is doubtful that the transport of such a bulky cargo into the carrack could have been kept a secret. It is more likely, then, that Hideyoshi was duly informed about this transport, just as he was kept abreast of everything else. To mention but one other thing, the news that the Jesuit padres were taking the opportunity of the presence of so many Portuguese in town to come back out into the open in Nagasaki may also have been reported, even though the padres refrained from wearing their identifying black robes.

When the public news of the arrival of the Portuguese reached Hideyoshi, he sent Konishi Ryūsa or Joaquin (1533–1592), an early convert to Christianity from Sakai, with silver worth more than 200,000 *cruzados* to buy 900 *piculs* of raw silk for himself. Ryūsa carried orders from Hideyoshi forbidding others to do business with the Portuguese until the sale had been finalized.[36] This order extremely displeased the Portuguese, of course.[37] Although it also interfered with the ability of the Japanese merchants to do business,[38] Ryūsa probably had come to Nagasaki in the company of merchants of his acquaintance from Sakai, Osaka, Kyoto, and Hakata, who must have been briefed about Hideyoshi's orders.[39]

Ryūsa, being a Christian himself and one of two *mandokoro* (or administrators) of Sakai,[40] was therefore a felicitous choice, and eventually with the mediation of the Superior of Kyushu, Pedro Gómez (1535–1600), the delicate negotiations with the angry Portuguese were concluded successfully.[41] The presence of Nagayoshi and Katsutaka with their following of soldiers in the city served, moreover, as a constant reminder that the Portuguese could no longer behave as if they owned the place. Fróis writes: "as the customs of the Portuguese are very different from the Japanese way of doing things, many riots and disagreements occurred between them, which we always used to remedy and calm down, but those which occurred this year were more intense than usual and almost led them to cut each other's throats, so we had great trouble calming down such dangerous quarrels. Father Pero Gómez was close to death from pure fatigue and distress."[42]

Jeronimo Pereira and the carrack of 1588 left Japan in February of 1589.[43] The Captain Major committed suicide by throwing himself into the sea on 1 April of that year, soon after his return to Macao. It took three days before his corpse was found.[44] Evidently, the profits of the Japan trade had not lived up to expectations. The Macao merchants decided, therefore, to hold off for another year so as to make the Japanese appreciate the arrival of the Portuguese carrack more. Therefore, no ship was sent from Macao to Japan in 1589.[45]

By 26 January 1589, moreover, there were again ten Jesuits stationed in Nagasaki, six padres and four brothers, clearly a formidable team. Among the padres were two Spaniards: Pedro Gómez and Gregorio de Cespedes (1552?–1611), who had spent almost a decade in the Kinai. Next, there were two Italians: Organtino Gnecchi-Soldo (1533–1609), who with eighteen years of experience in the Kinai was the Jesuit with the most intimate knowledge of Japan's new ruler Hideyoshi. Pedro Paulo Navarro (1563–1622) had only just arrived in Japan in 1586. Finally, there were two Portuguese: Antonio Lopes (1545–1598), the Superior of the Nagasaki residence since 1582, and João de Crasto (?–1594), the Society's treasurer. Three of the brothers were highly educated Japanese, including a pharmacist, a scribe and interpreter, and a doctor.[46]

Their number no longer included Gaspar Coelho, who had over the past twelve or thirteen years been particularly involved in the fortification and expansion of Nagasaki. The Vice-provincial was now living in Kazusa, in Arima.[47] Hideyoshi certainly knew about this large missionary presence in the city, but he realized that they were still playing an important role as mediators and interpreters between the Portuguese and the Japanese merchants. For the moment, therefore, he was willing to allow their presence if it was as indispensable as the past trading season had suggested.

While there was still hope for the arrival of the carrack of 1589, Hideyoshi issued a new order appointing Terazawa Shima no kami Hirotaka (1563–1633) and Tōdō Takatora as *bugyō* of Nagasaki on 5 August of that year.[48] Born in Owari, Hirotaka was a direct retainer, who after the Kyushu campaign had received a fief of 60,000 *koku* in Karatsu, on the north coast of Kyushu. Hirotaka received the title *Shima no kami* in 1589.[49] As we have observed, Hideyoshi was in the habit of appointing two men to the same post: in 1587, he had sent Tōdō Takatora and his unknown colleague to Nagasaki; in 1588, because of their availability nearby, he had appointed Asano Nagayoshi and Toda Katsutaka. Thus, in 1589, the two men seem to have been chosen to represent Hideyoshi in Nagasaki, as soon as the news of the carrack's arrival would reach them. But they never needed to go, for no carrack arrived.

We have no documents issued by Hideyoshi between August of 1589 and July of 1591, so he may have been too busy with the siege of Odawara Castle. Nagasaki simply may not have been foremost on his mind. That changed as soon as the carrack of 1590 arrived. On 22 July, Enrique da Costa brought an embassy from the Portuguese Viceroy at Goa, led by the Society's Visitor Alessandro Valignano, to Japan.[50] When Hideyoshi was informed of the arrival of an embassy from the Spanish King, he again sent two men to Nagasaki, Nabeshima Naoshige, who had been appointed *daikan* in 1588, and Mori Iki no kami Yoshinari (?–1611).[51]

The latter was from an old retainer family of the Oda. His older brother Ranmaru (1565–1582) had perished, seventeen years old, together with Nobunaga in the Honnōji conflagration. His father having died in 1570, Yoshinari must have been born between 1566 and 1570. After the Kyushu campaign of 1587, not more than twenty-one years old (but possibly as young as seventeen), he was given the Kokura fief, i.e., two counties in Buzen, with 60,000 *koku*, and at the same time the title of *Iki no kami*.[52] The two men arrived in Nagasaki in October and transmitted Hideyoshi's invitation for Valignano to visit him in the capital.

Hideyoshi must have faced a dilemma. Was he to get angry at a cleric coming as an ambassador? Or was he to respectfully receive an emissary of the Portuguese Viceroy at Goa, himself a representative of the king of Spain and Portugal, Philip II? His decision to receive Valignano indicates that Hideyoshi was eager for trade, and willing to tolerate a limited missionary presence for the moment. We don't hear about any skimming off of the profits from the trade this year, so Hideyoshi probably did not interfere with the trade this season.

On the contrary, Hideyoshi seems to have issued, before the departure of Da Costa's carrack in the spring of 1591, a red-seal permit to the Portuguese promising completely free trade in Japan.[53] The Portuguese may have misunderstood this to mean that their former monopoly and privileges were back in force again. Also, because four years after the publication of the anti–Christian edicts, the churches of Nagasaki still had not been demolished, many were already starting to assume that Hideyoshi silently meant to allow the practice of Christianity.[54]

As for the Jesuits, with Valignano in town as ambassador, they could move back into their old quarters at Morisaki.[55] The envoy had brought back four Japanese youths, who had traveled all the way to Europe and had come back laden with rich gifts.[56] Hideyoshi was eager to meet them. Because of illness, Valignano only left for the Kinai in December, and was finally received by Hideyoshi in the Jurakutei at Miyako on 3 March 1591.[57] Hideyoshi had his doubts about this mission, but he was happy with the gifts it had brought. He well understood, of course, Valignano's secret purpose of trying to normalize the position of Christianity in Japan, but he refused to rescind his prohibition of 1587.[58]

All he would allow was that ten padres could remain in Nagasaki to serve the needs of the Portuguese traders.[59] We are reminded that there already were ten Jesuits stationed in Nagasaki, so here is another indication that Hideyoshi was kept informed of all details concerning the Jesuits. All he did, therefore, was to officially recognize the status quo for the sake of the trade. Clearly, his aim was to accommodate the Portuguese merchants whenever he could do so at no extra cost to himself. Thus the grand result of this embassy, that had cost more than six thousand *ducados*, was that the São Paulo church at Morisaki could now be reopened and used again,[60] even though Japanese Christians were not supposed to worship there. But even this meager result did not last for much longer than a year.

Before the arrival of the next carrack, Hideyoshi issued, on 21 July, another *sadame* or list of stipulations for Nagasaki. It lists some draconian measures to prevent the type of disagreements that had made the trade so difficult in previous years. If two Japanese were to come to blows in the port, both were to be executed "without establishing the rights of wrongs of the matter." If a disagreement occurred between a Japanese and a Portuguese merchant, the matter was to be investigated carefully. In case both parties were found to be equally at fault, the Japanese was to be executed. All merchants were admonished, on pain of death, not to add or mix anything after the prices of the commodities had been established, and to use the same scale for both buying and selling.[61]

The document provides proof (if we needed any) that trouble often occurred in Nagasaki. This had probably worsened after the city had been incorporated into the *tenryō*, or Hideyoshi's domain, and the Jesuits had gone underground. As these rules generally favor the foreign merchants, it is clear that this document was not addressed to them. Rather, it sounds as if Hideyoshi was saying to the merchants of Japan: "Watch your step, keep your cool, and be honest in your dealings. If you don't, your head will come off." It was Hideyoshi's way to create a favorable business climate.

In August of 1591, Nagasaki was again full of soldiers. These were the days of the mobilization for Hideyoshi's upcoming Korean campaign. As usual, Hideyoshi sent two of his representatives to Nagasaki: Nabeshima Naoshige and Mori Yoshinari. One evening Arima Harunobu passed through with his own army, two thousand strong, mustered for transfer to Korea. The atmosphere in the city was thick with animosity between the soldiers of this Christian warlord and those of Naoshige, the successor to Ryūzōji Takanobu, the great adversary of Arima who had died on the battlefield trying to conquer it. The encounter seems to have turned into a real test for Hideyoshi's peace, which only barely held.[62]

*   *   *

A Hapless Captain Major: Roque de Melo

This was the atmosphere to which, on 19 August 1591, Captain Major Roque de Melo Pereira arrived in Nagasaki.[1] The captain came from a minor branch of the illustrious Melo (or Mello) family of Alentejo, the Portuguese flatlands immediately south of the Tejo river, which the family originally may have helped conquer from the Arabs.[2] His parents were Pedro de Melo and Luiza Pereira, both from the small Alentejo town of

Serpa. Pedro was, like his father, grandfather, and great-grandfather before him, the *alcaide mor* or highest judiciary official of the township of Serpa and its surroundings, an office that had, pending approval of the kings of Portugal, become hereditary in this branch of the Melo family. Among Roque's many brothers and sisters, no less than six dedicated their lives to the church.[3]

We know from the royal patent granting him the captaincy of Malacca in 1581 that, at that time, Roque de Melo had already spent twelve years in India.[4] Therefore, he must have left Portugal in 1569. Roque would have been at least in his late teens when he first arrived in Goa, and this puts the date of his birth roughly between 1540 and 1550. We next find him earning his spurs at the siege of Chaul. In 1570–71 that Portuguese settlement on the west coast of the Indian continent was under attack by Nizam Shah, the sultan of Ahmadnahar. The chronicler of the siege mentions Roque de Melo and his brother Henrique on several occasions,[5] the latter perishing on 22 May 1571.[6]

Already on 10 February 1573, this personal loss had resulted in the issue of a patent for a China voyage by the Chancellery of King Dom Sebastião, the text of which states explicitly that it was granted "for the services rendered to Us in the Indies by Roque de Melo, *fidalgo* of the Royal Household, who is still in active service there and who fought in the siege of Chaul, where he was wounded and where his brother Henrique was killed."[7] It is unimaginable that such a quick and timely recognition of Roque's merits and his brother's death could have been made without special connections at court, but, at the same time, it is difficult to see who may have been responsible for this.[8] In any case, just receiving this patent meant very little: it would take Roque de Melo more than a decade and a half before he was able to make use of it.

Thus we clearly see that receiving a royal patent or *alvará* represented only one of the many hurdles that a potential Capitão Mor of the China voyage had to overcome. The next information we have about Roque's career in India concerns his three-year service as Captain of Malacca, between 1582 and 1585.[9] This post in the eastern outreaches of Portugal's thalassocracy in Asia was, with Hurmuz and Goa, one of the three most powerful and lucrative *cargos* of the whole empire. The royal patent was granted on 28 January 1581.[10] Again, this is evidence of Roque de Melo's continued good connections at the new court of Philip I of Portugal (= Philip II of Spain).

It should be noted, again, that at the time of this grant, ten years after the siege of Chaul, Roque de Melo still had not been able to make use of his patent for the China voyage, and so he remained unrewarded for his service during the siege. Neither was his family indemnified for the loss of Henrique, whose memory seems to have faded already to the point that he had become, to the scribe of the Court, simply "a brother of his."[11] It is possible that his family was getting impatient that Roque had still not been able to use the patent for the China voyage and so had started pushing for another reward that might enable him to do so.

An appointment to the Captaincy of Malacca was, of course, the right move, for, as foreseen in the patent itself,[12] in this function Roque de Melo was in a position to get in line for the China voyage. As Captain of Malacca, moreover, he would receive a salary of "six hundred thousand *reis* for each of the aforesaid three years" as well as being the beneficiary of the emoluments and advantages (bribes, extortions) connected with that function, the extent of which was limited mainly to what the conscience of each individual captain would allow.[13]

The grant is also a good indicator of the general confidence that Roque de Melo's record in India had inspired up to that time, for Malacca was one of the few posts in Portuguese India where the incompetent or too flagrantly unjust did not last long.[14] In fact, only one year after this royal grant was made to him, Roque de Melo was sent by Viceroy Dom Francisco de Mascarenhas to replace Dom João da Gama before the latter's time was up. He left Goa on 20 April 1582,[15] and he took over from Dom João on 22 August.[16] Next, there is a four-year gap in the record of his career during which he did not hold any post in the organization of Portugal's thalassocracy in Asia. It is possible that he returned home to Portugal. By 1590, finally, we find him in Macao as the next Captain Major of the Japan voyage.

Commercially speaking, a successful stay in Macao was key to a profitable voyage to Japan. The merchandise to be sold in Japan was acquired mainly during the Canton fairs, which were held twice a year, in October and April.[17] Therefore, a well-organized China-Japan run involved a lengthy stay in Macao. During this time, furthermore, the expertise and the connections of the *moradores* or Portuguese citizens of Macao were absolutely indispensable to negotiate with the Chinese authorities and purveyors of Canton. A successful Captain Major would have to be careful to forge good relationships with these people, among whom many New Christians (or crypto–Jews) could be found.[18]

After their expulsion from Portugal earlier in the century, this group of commercially savvy men had spread throughout the Portuguese thalassocracy. Legally, the captain of the China voyage was the highest authority in Macao during the time of his presence there, but it was imperative for him not to let religious prejudice stand in the way of commercial success. This may have been easier for some than for others. For somebody with Roque de Melo's strict religious background and close relations with the Spanish court, it may have been particularly difficult.[19]

Thus, in August 1591, more than eighteen years after having been granted the voyage, Captain Major Roque de Melo Pereira finally arrived in Nagasaki. To everyone's consternation, his carrack was immediately surrounded by guard boats full of armed men. While it had been the custom since the foundation of Nagasaki for the Portuguese merchants to go ashore as soon as the carrack had anchored, this time no one was allowed to leave the ship. We do not have any account in Portuguese of what actually happened, but in a Japanese document we are told that the carrack was boarded by force and searched on a pretext.

The Portuguese were told that Hideyoshi's representatives in the city, the two ferociously anti-foreign watchdogs Nabeshima Naoshige and Mori Yoshinari, wished to buy all the gold on board, and for that purpose "we were stripped naked and our bodies were searched as if we were servants…. We were prevented from victualing or taking water, and those who tried to get water on their own were whipped and their barrels smashed."[20]

Of course, Roque de Melo fired off a furious complaint to Hideyoshi.[21] It is interesting that he was able to do so, even with a full blockade of his ship by Naoshige and Yoshinari's men. Possibly, some Japanese Christian of Nagasaki had managed to establish contact with the ship, and the Jesuits took care of the rest. Their hand in establishing this prompt link with the center of power in the Kinai can be seen, apart from the excellent Japanese translation of the Portuguese complaints, in its addressee, the Kyoto magistrate (*shoshidai*) Maeda Munehisa (1539–1602). Munehisa seems at this time to have been somewhat favorably inclined to the missionaries.[22] With two sons who had converted to Christianity, he was the most appropriate person with direct access to Hideyoshi to approach the Kampaku on behalf of the embarrassed Portuguese.[23]

Now Hideyoshi could react as a truly magnanimous ruler, protecting the weak, punishing evil, and favoring free trade. He addressed the Captain Major as follows:

> The news that, when the Black Ship arrived in Nagasaki, lower officials of that port behaved illegally and obstructed [the trade], was reported to me in writing and so I have ordered that each of these transgressing lower officials should be punished. You are free to trade not only the gold bars but all other merchandise with anyone. Moreover, if there are still others who obstruct the trade, you should report this to me so they can be swiftly ordered [to desist]. For more details consult with Kuroda Kageyu and Natsuka Ōkura daiyu.[24]

This reply was issued on 26 September, and must have reached Nagasaki in the first or second week of October. Although in this document Hideyoshi reprimands and dismisses the "lower officials" at Nagasaki, who had represented him so badly, the fact that he refrains from mentioning their names indicates that he did not intend to make them pay. Playing out the comedy for their Portuguese spectators to the bitter end, Naoshige and Yoshinari left the city "under the cover of darkness."[25] Hideyoshi also reaffirmed the rights of the Portuguese to free trade and, in line with his by now established practice, he appointed two new men, Kuroda Yoshitaka (1546–1604) and Natsuka Masaie (?–1600), to whom the Portuguese could turn if they needed more help.[26]

Although Hideyoshi pretended that the incident was entirely due to the "illegal" behavior of two ignorant "lower officials," it is difficult to imagine that such a deviation from established custom could have happened without the Kampaku's permission and active connivance. We have seen that, from Hideyoshi's point of view, the Portuguese were in dire need of a lesson as to who was boss in Japan. The dissimulating behavior of Domingos Monteiro in 1587–8, the non-departure of the Jesuits, the in-your-face gall of the most senior Jesuit in Asia, Valignano, to appear as envoy from the Portuguese Viceroy in 1590, all of these affronts to Hideyoshi's self-image as the ruler of the *tenka* had accumulated over the past four years.

It was now Hideyoshi's turn: a strip search of the preening and overbearing Portuguese is just the kind of idea that Hideyoshi himself may have come up with. The foreign merchants were humiliated, it is true, but as it happened on the Portuguese ship, they were so only in front of each other and Hideyoshi's men. No lasting harm was done, no merchandise was stolen or impounded, and no Jesuit letter later mentioned the incident to a European audience. But the message was clear enough. Just as Hideyoshi had warned the Japanese merchants at the beginning of this same trading season, he was now warning the Portuguese to behave while in Japan.[27]

By the beginning of October of 1591, most of the great Japanese merchants, who had come from Kyoto and Sakai to buy the carrack's gold with silver provided by several daimyo,[28] despaired of getting permission to do business. They had waited three months (July through September) and seem to have left Nagasaki before Hideyoshi's new orders finally arrived. So the Portuguese had to wait until the following year to sell their merchandise. These unusual circumstances forced Roque de Melo to stay in Japan for almost fourteen months, until 9 October 1592.[29] His failure to return to Macao in the fall of 1591 or the following spring was again a sign to the merchants of that city that it was better to postpone sending a new cargo to Japan.

During this time, Roque de Melo is likely to have acted as godfather at the baptism of a Japanese samurai.[30] He is also said to have been the "principal founder" of the hospitals and the hermitage of St. Lazarus, which were established to take care of the lepers in the area.[31] There were two hospitals, one for men and one for women, for the lepers were known for their disregard of the sexual mores of healthy people.[32] When Roque de Melo finally returned to Portugal in 1598 or 1599, he brought with him seven baptized Japanese slaves: five women by names of Illena, Ursulla, Sezilia, Izabel, and Lucrecia, and two men, Mathias and Luiz, as well as one freeman by name of Antonio.[33] The wealth he had accumulated during thirty years in Asia, however, was not extraordinary.[34] He died soon after his return.[35]

*   *   *

A Spaniard from Peru: Juan de Solís

In the retinue of Visitor Alessandro Valignano, arriving in Japan in the summer of 1590, there had been a Spaniard from Peru by name of Juan de Solís (1555–1594). Although, for the amount of trouble he managed to stir up, we have exceedingly little information on him, it is clear that he must have been a remarkable character, even for an empire-building Spaniard of his age. The first time Juan de Solís (who was born of a commoner father and a noble mother) appears in the sources, it is as a fourteen-year old retainer of Francisco de Toledo, who had come to Peru as the new Viceroy in 1569.[1]

We hear nothing more about him until he suddenly reappears in Macao, in 1588, as the captain of a Spanish ship from Callao, Peru, that he had managed to sail across the Pacific. Copper not yet having been discovered in the ancient empire of the Incas, Solís had heard it could be exchanged cheaply against Spanish silver in China. He therefore wanted to establish a transpacific link between the New World and Asia. He must have been a dreamer. Or maybe someone set him up. It is unclear what made him think that he could get away with what the Portuguese in Macao considered a clear-cut smuggling operation, contravening their rights guaranteed by Philip II when he took charge of the crown of Portugal.

As soon as he had anchored in Macao, his ship was declared forfeited and sold for a trifle, his crew was arrested and sent on to Goa, while Juan de Solís himself was jailed and his small fortune of six thousand *cruzados* in silver seized. The extraordinary lengths to which de Solís subsequently went to get his money back and use it to invest in Chinese or Japanese merchandise to bring back to Peru indicate that he had probably borrowed most of it, possibly even from the Viceroy Francisco de Toledo himself. In other words, Solís had gambled and he was a dead man unless he was successful. But if he was a dreamer and a gambler, he was also a man of considerable charm and resourcefulness. He had survived a transpacific adventure after all.

His first priority was to get his money out of the hands of the Macao merchants. Allowed to visit a church (it must have been a Sunday), Solís got up on his chair and announced in a loud voice to everybody present all the trials he had experienced upon coming to Macao.[2] It so happened that Visitor Valignano was attending the same mass. The latter had only just arrived in Macao from Goa and was in urgent need of extra funds, for he had been informed of Hideyoshi's proscription of Christianity. Then and there, he suddenly understood that, through Solís' voice, Providence was offering him a solution to his pecuniary problem. He immediately took action to have Juan de Solís released from jail, and then took care that his money, with the Spaniard's grateful permission, was invested to buy a share in that year's cargo for Japan.

So far Jesuit accounts have told a very different story about the relationship between Valignano and Solís.[3] It was only in Macao that the Visitor had heard of Hideyoshi's recent anti–Christian edict and had understood that if his embassy to Hideyoshi was to be effective in getting Japan's ruler to rescind his anti–Christian edict, it needed to be far more splendid than had been prepared in India. In his eagerness to bolster his chances in Japan, the Visitor was prepared to ride roughshod over the interests of others weaker than him. Larger interests were at stake here, after all.

In Goa, he had already forced the four boy "ambassadors" to give up the splendid presents they had received from the various rulers of the Western Mediterranean.[4] Now, he promised Juan de Solís his freedom and profits in the Japan trade. Only a dreamer like Juan de Solís would believe that the Portuguese Captain Major of Macao would allow setting such a pernicious precedent. Thus, Antonio da Costa was informed by the Visitor of the necessity to humor Juan de Solís for the moment.[5] His brother and replacement as Captain Major in Japan, Enrique, was to take him on his ship to Japan.

Juan de Solís never left a detailed account of what happened, or, if he did, it has not survived. Of course, he must have realized that his position as a smuggler was juridically weak. All the same, we do have two short testimonies he gave on 24 and 26 May 1593 in front of the public notary at Manila.[6] They are better than nothing, for without them we would have to rely solely on the Jesuit account of the affair. One thing, for example, that is never mentioned in any of the Jesuit accounts is that Juan de Solís took part in Valignano's embassy to Hideyoshi, and so must have made the whole journey from Nagasaki to Kyoto in the train of the Visitor.[7]

This allows us to date the time of the falling out between Valignano and Solís to after the embassy, probably during the summer of 1591, when "his" silk may finally have been sold, and Valignano no longer saw any need to hide the fact that poor Juan was not going to get a penny of the money he thought he had invested in the carrack's cargo.[8] True to his indomitable nature, Juan de Solís decided to build his own ship to go back to China, make a few trips to Japan, and then return rich to America.

He found an ally in another Spanish merchant, whose name was Antonio Duarte. This elderly trader had arrived in Nagasaki with a large amount of gold, in 1589 or 1590, from New Spain via the Philippines. Fróis writes that "a padre was sent to help him hide this gold," so that it would not fall into the hands of some non–Christian.[9] Antonio Duarte had also lost a large "deposit" of 2500 ducats he had been forced to make by the Portuguese authorities in Nagasaki. When the Jesuits refused to press the case of the Spaniards with the Captain Major,[10] in September of 1591, the two men decided to try and seek justice from the Japanese authorities, first from Nabeshima Naoshige and Mori Yoshinari, Hideyoshi's appointees, later from Katō Kiyomasa (1562–1611),[11] and eventually even from the kampaku himself.

In the course of this litigation, Antonio Duarte died, doubtless of vexation, leaving 6500 cruzados to the Jesuits to be distributed as alms in various ways.[12] Juan de Solís was not ready to be so generous and forgiving, and sometime late in 1591 or early 1592 he left Nagasaki for Satsuma to build his own ship. We need not wonder how he managed to get such a project started, for that domain in southern Kyushu was still eager, just as several others, to compete for foreign trade with Nagasaki, and Antonio Duarte may have helped with the initial financing.

What is surprising, rather, is the desperation with which Juan de Solís tried, on top of everything else, to become a shipwright also.[13] It was while Solís was engaged in building his ship that he was given a chance to take his revenge on the Jesuits. On 26 July 1592,[14] Juan Cobo (1546?–1592), a Dominican friar from the Philippines, arrived in Satsuma with letters establishing his credentials as an ambassador sent by the Governor of Manila, Gómez Pérez de Dasmariñas (1539–1593),[15] to Hideyoshi.[16]

The years between 1587 and 1591 had been good for Hideyoshi. He had accomplished what no other man had done before him, i.e., he had brought all of Honshu, Shikoku, and Kyushu under his rule. He had reason to feel on top of the world. These same years, therefore, with the unification of the *tenka* in sight, were also the time that he and his advisers were looking around for new mountains to scale. Among the projects proposed to him were the conquests of Taiwan,[17] of the Philippines,[18] of India,[19] of Korea, and, most prestigious of all, the conquest of China. It was as if Hideyoshi was picking from a dessert tray after the main dish of the unification, and if in the end he chose to pick (and choke on) the largest piece for the taking, that did not mean he would disdain to swallow any of the smaller pieces if they did not require much more effort than some threats.

This was the direction taken towards the Philippines, where Governor Dasmariñas received, on 31 May 1592,[20] a haughty letter from Hideyoshi, containing the following threats:

> I refrained [so far] from sending my fighting men [against Manila] as I had first intended. After two months I shall betake myself to Nagoya, one of my harbor-towns, where I shall muster my fighting forces. If ambassadors come from the Philippines as a token of the Governor's friendliness, I shall not, as a token of my friendliness, raise my standard, I shall not send my fighting men against the Philippines to conquer them with overwhelming force. My conquest would make the people of the Philippines rue the day when they did not send me ambassadors.[21]

The letter was delivered in Manila by one Gaspar Harada, an emissary and relative of the adventurer Paulo Harada Kiemon.[22] The latter, described as "malicious and shrewd,"[23] was a former Christian, who had once been a rich merchant, but had spent too much and gone bankrupt. He had participated in a Japanese mission to the Philippines in 1589 of between thirty and forty people, who disguised as Christian pilgrims had scouted Manila's defenses[24] and afterwards had reported on their weakness to Hideyoshi.[25] In April of 1592, Governor Dasmariñas had been warned about the same Paulo Harada, this time by Antonio Sedeño, Superior of the Jesuit mission in Manila, who had on 18 April received a top-secret communication from Alessandro Valignano in Nagasaki announcing the ominous coming of Hideyoshi's envoy.[26]

Valignano himself had been the reason why Paulo Harada had decided not to go to Manila as Hideyoshi's envoy. After he had received the document with the Kampaku's ultimatum for the Philippines, Harada had gone to Nagasaki in November of 1591 to equip a ship and try to get letters of recommendation from the Visitor.[27] In this he was not successful. On the contrary, he was told by Valignano that the Spanish might very well hang him. Pretending illness, therefore, he had not traveled to Manila but had sent his nephew Gaspar [Harada Magoshichirō] instead, who had left from Satsuma.[28] The mastermind of the expedition, Paulo Harada himself, awaited its success in the same domain.[29]

Just to be sure that the Governor got his message, which downplayed the imminence of a Japanese attack on the Philippines as well as the need to wait in sending an embassy to Hideyoshi until permission from the King of Spain had been received, Valignano wrote a second letter. This second letter was written in the Jesuits' secret language, Latin, and was smuggled to Manila by a trusted Christian on the very ship that was bringing Gaspar Harada with Hideyoshi's threatening missive.[30] For someone who was publicly advising everyone not to meddle in Japanese politics, Valignano was taking rather imprudent risks with this foray into the secret service business.[31] Of course, it was not in the interest of the Jesuits in Japan to encourage commercial and evangelical competition from the Philippines.[32]

Although early dreams to use their foothold in the Philippines as a jumping board for the conquest of China had turned the head of many a Spaniard,[33] by the time of Gaspar Harada's arrival in Manila wiser counsel had prevailed.[34] Governor Dasmariñas was well aware of the weakness of the colony in both manpower and defense works. After receiving the news of an impending Japanese attack in the early spring of 1592, he first had the Japanese residents of the inner city in Manila moved out into the suburbs into a neighborhood called Dilao.[35]

Then, upon receiving Valignano's messages and Hideyoshi's communication, he asked Juan Cobo for advice. This friar had come to the Philippines in 1588, where he had been active among the Chinese residents of Manila.[36] He was one of the few, it seems, to have made an effort to learn their language and writing system,[37] for when Dasmariñas saw himself faced with Hideyoshi's letter (which looked like Chinese) Cobo was the only one to whom he could turn to tell him its true contents.[38]

In fact, the Governor asked for translations from both Juan Cobo and Gaspar Harada, and the results turned out to be very different from one another. According to Cobo's interpretation, Hideyoshi wanted the Spanish in the Philippines to become his vassals, whereas Gaspar pretended that all the Taikō (Hideyoshi abandoned the title *kampaku* on Tenshō 19.12.22 [5 February 1592]), when his nephew was promoted to it as his official heir. Hideyoshi then assumed the title *taikō* [retired regent]). wanted was friendship and a good relationship with the Governor. Armed with this knowledge, the Governor called together a meeting of Manila's notables in the beginning of June to discuss whether to send an embassy, as Hideyoshi had demanded, or not. On this occasion the Jesuit position represented by Sedeño, to try and temporize, was rejected, and Juan Cobo was chosen to head an embassy to Japan in an attempt to avert a calamity that might reach Manila from the side of Japan.

Upon its arrival in Satsuma, the Spanish mission[39] was soon informed of a nearby Spaniard who was building a ship, and when Cobo and Solís met, they seem to have taken a liking to each other right away. Juan de Solís had much to tell the friar about the troubles he had experienced from the Portuguese, the litigations he was still engaged in, and how he had been defrauded by the Portuguese merchants and the Jesuits. He also had much experience to offer, for he had participated in Valignano's embassy to Hideyoshi of the year before and so was familiar with some of the ceremonial at the Taikō's court. Even more important, he had acquired a trustworthy Japanese interpreter (we know only as Luis[40]), whom he now put at Cobo's disposal.

It was thus natural for Cobo to invite Juan de Solís along on his embassy to Hideyoshi. On their way to Nagoya in Hizen, from where since 25 May of that year Hideyoshi had been overseeing his Korean campaign, they passed through Nagasaki in late July or early August. The Jesuits took notice:

> They first came to Nagasaki to buy here some things they needed, and in this port they were very well received by the Portuguese and the fathers of the Society [Alessandro Valignano and Pedro Gómez],[41] who went out to meet them at sea[42] and brought them charitably home

with them, even though they [Cobo and Lope de Llanos] did not show them any proofs of friendship, for they did not tell the Portuguese nor the fathers of the Society what was the reason of their visit, nor did they bring any letter from the Governor or did they wish to take any of their [the Jesuits'] advice. Rather they showed that they mistrusted them, and the next day they left again even though the fathers bade them to stay longer so that they might inform them better about the local customs and about what they had to do.[43]

In this short description of Juan Cobo's one-night stay in the Jesuit residence of Nagasaki, the foundation is already laid for the Jesuits' later scathing assessment of this mission led by the Spanish friar. It seems that Juan de Solís had foreseen the awkwardness of the situation and had chosen not to go back to Nagasaki with Cobo, but had spent the night one mile outside of Nagasaki.[44] When the Spanish embassy arrived at Seto, they were met by Paulo Harada himself, who took them to Nagoya in litters "on the shoulders of men."[45] The poor appearance of this delegation consisting of three Spaniards, three Chinese, and one Japanese combined with their meager presents did not make a good first impression, especially as compared with Valignano's splendid embassy of the year before.

It may have been on this point that the Jesuits of Nagasaki, Valignano and Gómez, had hoped to convince Juan Cobo to discontinue his embassy, advice the friar had evidently declined to take. So they were made to wait at Nagoya.[46] The time was used by Juan de Solís to get acquainted with the fortress and with his fellow adventurer Paulo Harada, who showed him the city: "this city of Nangoya this witness saw with his own eyes is a city of one hundred thousand or more inhabitants. It was built and populated in five months and is three leagues long, and nine leagues in circumference, and this was done by order of Quambaco [*sic*], from which his great power can be seen."[47]

It was Paulo Harada and his crony Hasegawa Sōnin (1539–1606),[48] instead of the Christian sympathizers among Hideyoshi's men, to whom the Spanish trusted the management of their mission before the ruler of Japan, certain in the knowledge that otherwise the Japanese Christians would inform the Jesuits of every detail concerning their embassy. While waiting for the audience, and with the help of Juan Cobo and his teacher of Chinese, known to us as Juan Sami, Juan de Solís also prepared for Hideyoshi a written petition of his grievances against the Portuguese "who had stolen from him a quantity of gold, silver, and other property. He presented this petition to the king of Japan [i.e., Hideyoshi] on the day when he met him."[49]

This latter occasion took place on 27 or 28 August,[50] and it was Paulo Harada himself who brought the three Spaniards before the Taikō.[51] Hideyoshi, as was his wont, took his time with each member of the embassy and seemed especially interested in what Juan de Solís had to say about the Portuguese and the Jesuits in Nagasaki. Alas, we have only a contemporary Jesuit summary of what happened during the audience, for Juan Cobo never made it back to Manila and, after seeing the consequences of what he had said, Juan de Solís did not give much detail at the inquest held in Manila in May of 1593 either.[52]

This is the Jesuit version of the incident:

Juan de Solís started to falsely accuse the Portuguese in front of the Kampaku, saying that they prevented ships of other nations from coming to Japan and that from him they had stolen money. This was confirmed by the ambassadors [Juan Cobo and Lope de Llano] in such a way that the Kampaku became extremely angry with the Portuguese and called them all kinds of names.... And he said that it seemed as if the Portuguese had made themselves masters of Nagasaki, for they were issuing orders there as if they had conquered it by force, and that he would put a stop to that in a way that the population of the town, which was already very rich, would not increase so much, and that he did not wish the *nao* to go there anymore.[53]

There is one point, however, that remains unmentioned in this representation of what happened during Juan Cobo's audience with Hideyoshi, but was conceivably the most important reason for Hideyoshi's anger against the Jesuits. It was that he heard from Juan Cobo that Valignano had falsely presented a gift to him in the name of the King of Spain: "saying that the King Our Lord sent it to him because he knew that the Taikō did not own any such."[54] Strictly speaking, Valignano had not been lying, for among the gifts he had taken away from the four boy "ambassadors" were several given to them by the King of Spain.[55] Because of his intimate acquaintance with the details of Valignano's embassy, Solís knew that the Visitor had not been straightforward, but rather lawyer-like, about the provenance of the gifts for Hideyoshi, and must have informed Cobo of this.

Hideyoshi's first reaction was to punish the Jesuits for their deviousness and insolence in trying to deceive him, just as he had done in 1588. Terazawa Hirotaka, who had already been named Nagasaki *bugyō* in 1589, was ordered to leave immediately for the city and dismantle the Jesuit church and headquarters at Morisaki. The building materials were to be sent to Nagoya for use in the Taikō's fortress.[56] Terazawa himself had been appointed the year before as one of Hideyoshi's supervisors for the enormous building project Hideyoshi had started there.[57] This time there was to be no bribery to leave the church standing, as Hideyoshi must have made abundantly clear to Terazawa.

When the latter arrived in Nagasaki, on the last day of August, and started to execute his lord's orders, he was met by a delegation of four Portuguese traders, who beseeched him to delay taking down the church until an answer had been received to a message that had been sent to Hideyoshi.[58] Terazawa ignored the request. He also carried a message from Hideyoshi for the Captain Major, the hapless Roque de Melo, "that [the Taikō] was very upset that the Portuguese oppressed foreigners who had come to his land, and prohibited ships and merchants to come to Japan from other parts of the world, and that the next time such things happened he would to order him to cut his belly."[59]

Fróis writes that Hideyoshi's representatives, Terazawa among them, and the party from the Philippines with Juan de Solís arrived in Nagasaki on the same day. The Spanish were lodged in the house of "another Spaniard." Terazawa then "ordered a caller to announce in all the streets of Nagasaki that no one should dare do any harm to the ambassadors from the Philippines. And if they suffered any molestation whatsoever, the whole population of the town would pay for it bitterly."[60]

Terazawa and his companions had come to execute Hideyoshi's revenge on the Jesuits:

> And next they ordered our residences and church to be taken apart, for which they had brought along one hundred and fifty men, who took quite a few days to dismantle the buildings.... And although the Portuguese did what they could to make Terazawa postpone the execution of his orders until the Kampaku had been contacted, they were unsuccessful, so in the end the church and all the houses were destroyed, which had cost around ten thousand cruzados.[61]

Valignano is said to have taken the destruction of the church really hard.[62] It is no wonder he did, especially after he heard about what had happened at Nagoya, and how it had been the grudge held by his former "protégé" Juan de Solís against himself that was responsible for this disaster. Dejected about the dismal result of his second stay, the

Visitor finally left Japan for Macao on 9 October 1592, accompanied by Luís Fróis and Gil de la Mata (1547?–1599), on the carrack of Captain Major Roque de Melo. Fróis would later need two whole pages of his *Historia* to convince his readers (and himself) that the Visitor's embassy, although unsuccessful in its main objective (i.e., the rescinding of Hideyoshi's edict), had nevertheless been "ordered with particular providence of God Our Lord and had been very effective."[63]

Terazawa had also been commissioned by Hideyoshi to investigate Juan de Solís' complaints about having been robbed of his silver by the Portuguese. He was soon told, however, that the forfeiture had taken place in Macao and not in Japan. Naturally, the *bugyō* concluded, that the affair fell outside his jurisdiction. It was unlikely that Hideyoshi would object that he had favored the Portuguese position over the objections of a single Spanish plaintiff.

In any case, the Spaniards seem to have left Nagasaki for Satsuma after only a short four or five-day stay in the city.[64] Juan de Solís, at least, now had the personal permission of the Taikō to continue building his ship. When he arrived in Satsuma (where his ship but for the mast had been ready), however, he found his boatswain dead and the vessel scuttled.[65] It is unclear what happened next. There is some evidence that de Solís traveled back to Kyoto in order to see and complain to Hideyoshi once more.[66]

The rest of the story of Juan de Solís and Juan Cobo is quickly told. In the end, they traveled to Manila on different ships, Cobo leaving first with his teacher of Chinese Juan Sami. This ship was shipwrecked off Taiwan and the men either drowned or were finished off by the natives there.[67] Juan de Solís made it to Manila, arriving on 23 May 1593. He participated in an inquiry by the Governor about Cobo's embassy on the day after his arrival.[68]

In Fróis' words:

> God Our Lord prolonged the life of Juan de Solís [a little longer than that of Juan Cobo] so that he might do penance for the great disorder and scandal that he had caused. When the vessel he had built in Satsuma was ready, he sailed her to the Philippines on her maiden voyage, where he met with great success in his trade. And wanting to start executing his plans from there, the merchants of Manila invested a lot of capital in his ship, and since his departure, we have heard and read from there, that [God] sent him such a heavy and furious storm that no one could humanly escape, and so everyone there is convinced he has perished, especially because they did not receive any news or message from him either from China or from any of its neighboring kingdoms.[69]

"Queira Deos lembrarse de sua alma" [May God remember his soul] is Fróis' final pious sigh about Juan de Solís, intimating that he doubted very much that God would forgive him for all the trouble he had caused the Jesuits, including the loss of the largest church of Nagasaki and the Jesuit headquarters. In other words, Fróis hoped de Solís would burn in hell for the rest of eternity.[70]

* * *

A New Head of the Mission: Pedro Gómez

During the first years after the city's incorporation into Hideyoshi's domain, the appointments of officials to administer it during the trading season notwithstanding, the daily management of Nagasaki remained in the hands of its Christian *tōnin* or headmen.[1] As before, too, the Portuguese in town were under the jurisdiction of the Captain Major. Regrettably, for the years after 1591, there are no more official Japanese documents connected with Nagasaki until after Hideyoshi's death. Thus, pursuing our investigation of Hideyoshi's relationship with the city, we will have to make do with the sources left behind by the Europeans and try to read them from Hideyoshi's point of view.

The new head of the mission to succeed Gaspar Coelho was Pedro Gómez, a New Christian from Antequera near Malaga in Southern Spain. Gómez had been a prodigy among the Jesuits, joining the Society at the age of eighteen. He had come to Portugal two years later, in 1555, and soon was teaching arithmetic, music, geometry, and astronomy at the University of Coimbra. Already in 1565, he was mentioned to Portugal's King Dom Sebastião as a possible choice for a future bishop of Japan.[2] Two years later, in 1567, he professed his four vows,[3] and so was ready for leadership among the Jesuits anywhere in the world. He finally left Portugal for Japan in 1579, forty-four years old, and arrived in Japan four years later, after suffering much hardship along the way.[4]

Gómez had traveled the Cape route via Goa, Malacca, and China. He had been shipwrecked on the Ryukyu islands, and had later been forced to flee from his post in eastern Kyushu when the army of Satsuma invaded.[5] The next year, he had seen all of Kyushu conquered by Hideyoshi and Christianity proscribed. Since then, for the past seven years, he had lived under the cloud of prosecution, managing the mission from Nagasaki as best he could. He had been head of the Jesuit mission in Japan since 1590.[6]

In the *Anua* or Annual Letter of 1593, Gómez dedicated a long section to events in Nagasaki after the destruction of the Jesuit headquarters and church at Morisaki.[7] Terazawa does not seem to have stayed in Nagasaki very long, but he left some of his retainers behind to administer the city in his name.[8] The first establishment of a *bugyōsho* or government office in Hon Hakata-machi is usually dated to this time as well, and therefore it is possible that Terazawa left orders to build this government office. With a permanent representation of the ruler of the *tenka* in the city, Nagasaki came to be placed on the same footing as Kyoto, Osaka, and Sakai, cities that were all governed by direct retainers of Hideyoshi.

Gómez complains that Terazawa and his men were making life difficult for the Jesuits, not just by the destruction of the main church and the confiscation of Morisaki, the land the church and the Jesuit residence had occupied, but also by all kinds of petty harassment. While Terazawa threatened to inform Hideyoshi if the citizens of Nagasaki attended church services, wore veils and rosaries, or held Christian ceremonies on the occasion of weddings and funerals, the new governor never demanded that the population of Nagasaki apostatize.[9]

Terazawa, continued Gómez, is a confirmed heathen and a protégé of Yaku'in Zensō (1526–1599), Hideyoshi's private physician and confidante, who seems to have played an important role at the time Hideyoshi issued his anti–Christian edicts.[10] Gómez calls him a "cruel enemy of Christianity." Terazawa, too, had risen to his present position of power solely because of the Taikō's favor and would do anything to assure himself of his continued patronage. Knowing how much Hideyoshi disliked the padres, Terazawa did not give the Jesuits the slightest chance to befriend him. Worse, he told them that they had no right to stay in Japan, and that not even the letter they had shown him from Maeda Gen'i, governor of Kyoto, gave them that right, because it did not mention any padres by name.

The Jesuits were ordered to pull down a great cross that was still standing in the cemetery of the town, and another that marked the site of the St. Lazarus hospital, where his men also started to dismantle the chapel. Terazawa "threatened to get rid of the Misericordia church, but after he was informed by the city's rulers of the help the poor received in that establishment he allowed it to remain."[11] As usual, there was room for negotiation on the remaining Jesuit establishments in the city, if the Jesuits would come up with "five bars of silver, which are worth more than twenty *cruzados*" for the men Terazawa had left behind.[12]

Gómez complains of other vexations from these retainers and schemes people devised to make some money out of the weak position of the padres. Not all of this is relevant here, and it should be noted that when things were going well for the Jesuits in Nagasaki in the previous years when they were ruling the city, we never get so much information about the city as now in their complaints. Next, Gómez describes another false accusation "by a bad man" before the Kampaku and Terazawa, who had said that the Christians of Nagasaki were "well provided with arms and hoped that there would be an uprising somewhere, when, with the approval of the fathers, they would rise against the Kampaku."[13]

Hideyoshi had ordered the disarming not only of Nagasaki, but the whole of the Kyushu countryside. This is known as the sword hunt or *katanagari* of 1588. It was not really aimed specifically at the Christians. It was just that, in Kyushu, there were so many armed Christians. "He used a great number of his men to carry out his purpose, threatening to crucify those who did not comply so that everyone presented their arms without hiding any away."[14] Hideyoshi's orders were executed with great vigor, so that a huge number of weapons were collected. In Nagasaki alone, four thousand *katana*, five hundred lances, and another five hundred bows and countless arrows, three hundred guns and more than one hundred suits of armor were given up.[15]

Gómez writes that the closer the time for the arrival of the carrack of 1593 approached, the more the padres came to live with a new fear. Since the church and the Jesuit residence in Nagasaki had been destroyed, the non–Christian Japanese seemed to have been generally of the opinion that the Portuguese, aghast and indignant, would not come back to Japan, and so the lucrative trade they had brought would be lost. The more time passed, the more the destruction of the church was condemned by "all the great lords of Japan," who blamed Hideyoshi, saying that if the carrack did not come to Japan any more, this realm would be "lost and ruined."[16]

Most of all, however, these voices blamed Terazawa, because he had pushed Hideyoshi in this matter, and was the principal reason why the Portuguese might be offended. This, however, is followed by a revealing remark of the Vice-provincial to the effect that the Jesuits knew very well that this type of thinking had more to do with samurai disdain for profit making. The Portuguese were in Asia to make profits and nothing else. What the Jesuits feared was that this would now become clear to Hideyoshi as well, and "even if he killed the fathers and destroyed all of Japanese Christendom, the Portuguese would still continue to come to Japan…. And so we dreaded that he might lose all the fear and reluctance to offend the Portuguese that he had had so far."[17]

This was, indeed, the crux of Hideyoshi's problem. He did not know how the Portuguese would react. Would they defend their religion to the end? Or was it possible that they cared more about the profits to be made in Japan? Gómez, on the other hand, knew that Macao could not exist without the Japan trade. In the end, he grew to see the problem as an opportunity to mend fences with Terazawa, using the Brothers João Ruiz (i.e., Rodrigues, 1561–1634) and Cosme Takai (1552–?).[18] A prominent Christian of Nagasaki by name of Antonio Murayama agreed to cooperate with the brothers in this, for he "could provide the necessary access to Terazawa, because every time the Governor came to Nagasaki he would stay at Murayama's house."[19]

This is the first time Antonio Murayama (1566–1619) appears in a contemporary source. Later, during the second half of the Keichō period (1604–1614), he was to become one of the most powerful men in Nagasaki.[20] The three men seem to have gone to Nagoya, where "Antonio Murayama did his job with great care and diligence."[21] In the end, Terazawa agreed to meet with the two brothers sent by Gómez. Possibly, the Governor had grown nervous about the consequences that his acts of the previous year might have, for if the carrack did not come and the trade was lost, he would not only lose Hideyoshi's favor, but he might even be ordered to make amends for his failure by committing suicide in the Japanese manner.[22]

Seen against this background, the arrival of the carrack of 1593 under Captain Major Gaspar Pinto da Roca must have come as a great relief to all the Japanese, while the missionaries just had to make the best of it.[23] The Captain Major visited Hideyoshi in person.[24] Suddenly, being Portuguese was all the rage around Hideyoshi: "every Japanese at court made efforts to obtain at least one article of European dress; some nobles even possessed complete wardrobes of cloaks, capes, ruff shirts, breeches, and hats. The tailors at Nagasaki were obliged to work around the clock to satisfy the demand and some were persuaded to move to the capital, where they could continue to supply the court."[25]

This, partly, was a performance à la Hideyoshi to express his relief about the fact that the trade with the Portuguese was continuing, and partly it was an example of his artful flattery of the traders: by dressing like them he told them how much they were wanted and appreciated. In this atmosphere, there was no denying any Portuguese request. So when Captain Major Gaspar Pinto da Roca asked Hideyoshi for permission to rebuild the church in Nagasaki that had been demolished the year before, the Taikō gladly reversed his position and allowed the Morisaki church to be rebuilt once more.[26]

* * *

The Spanish Spy: Bernardo Avila Girón (1)

Bernardo Avila Girón has always been an enigmatic figure. Because he lived in Nagasaki, on and off for twenty-five years, between 1594 and 1619, his *Report on the Kingdom of Nippon Mistakenly Called Japan* is our most important secular eye-witness account of Christian Nagasaki.[1] In spite of it being the very first book-length *journalistic* account of Japan by a European author, the manuscript has never been published in its entirety. At the time of writing, the author had, except for the letter books published by the Jesuits, nothing to compare his work with. He clearly worked with great diligence on his manuscript, rewriting it several times and sending it off to different people in Spain, possibly in order to get it published or at least to avoid it getting lost. Almost everything we know of his life derives from chance remarks he offers in his own text.

Did he leave a book of lasting value? In a sense he did, but only by default. It is because as yet so few Europeans wrote about Japan (and Nagasaki in particular), that his account remains valuable. His writing style and sense of composition, however, are (to put it mildly) unsophisticated. His reasoning is sometimes hard to follow. In spite of what we know about the many times that this author copied his own manuscript, he seems to have improved it very little, limiting his own editing to adding a few passages here and there. The end result remains a stylistically poor effort. To sum up: Bernardo Avila Girón shares with Francesco Carletti the honor of being the only Europeans to have left secular eyewitness accounts of Japan, as seen from the city of Nagasaki. This value is heightened, again, if we remember that two hundred and fifty years of Bakufu anti–Christian policy has assured that there are very few contemporary Japanese sources left that deal with daily life in Christian Nagasaki.

Avila Girón's book is roughly divided into three parts. The first part deals with every-day Japan that the writer saw around him in the city of Nagasaki as well as during his travels through Kyushu and Honshu. To most scholars today, this is the most interesting and valuable part of the book. To give just one example of information that cannot be found anywhere else: "When I first came to this kingdom in ninety-four, a cow cost between four and five *reales*, and one could get thirty-five *catties*, or more than forty pounds, of beef without bones for one *mas* of silver, but today [1613] I get no more than four pounds because now everyone in this town eats beef, and while the population of this city used to be three thousand inhabitants, now it has more than twenty-five thousand."[2]

In the second part, Avila Girón explains the recent history of the unification of Japan under Oda Nobunaga and Toyotomi Hideyoshi, while in the last part of the book he describes what he has heard and seen with his own eyes of the persecution of Christianity between 1612 and 1619. After an entry referring to 15 March of the latter year, his text breaks off abruptly. The only other news we have of him is a statement dated 28 June 1619 by Padre Antonio de los Martires, Franciscan Provincial of San Jose in the Philippines to the effect that Avila Girón is the official notary of "many other missionaries in that kingdom [i.e., Japan]."[3]

Avila Girón first appears in 1586 as a resident and influential merchant in Manila.[4] We find him next returning to the Philippines on 31 May 1590, in the company of Das-mariñas, the newly appointed governor of this most westerly outpost of the Spanish empire.[5] It is unclear what happened in between those dates, but immediately afterwards, i.e., between 1590 and 1593, it is clear that Bernardo was close to the Governor of the Philippines. Dasmariñas set to work energetically to reinforce the Spanish colonial town of Manila. The year after his arrival, he imposed a two percent export tax on the galleon trade with Acapulco to pay for a wall around the Spanish settlement, later called, after this wall, Intramuros.[6] The wall would be completed (and the tax discontinued) six years later. On 14 October 1593, two days before his scheduled departure for a military expe-dition to the Moluccas, the governor became roaring drunk at a going-away party given by his assistant Pedro de Rojas, who was to be unofficially in charge while the governor was on the warpath.

Barely on his way, on 25 October 1593, Governor Dasmariñas got himself murdered by the Chinese rowers of his own galley. Avila Girón was not part of the expedition and had remained behind in Manila. He writes: "There was great consternation in Manila when the news of the murders reached the city. Feeling ran high against the Chinese population, mingled with fears of a general uprising, for most of the city's forces were absent in the Visayas, awaiting the governor's arrival to proceed against the Moluccas."[7]

In the confusion that followed the governor's death and because no testament of the dead governor could be found, Pedro de Rojas proclaimed himself Governor and Captain General of the Philippines. He immediately ordered Dasmariñas' son Don Luis Gomes Perez Dasmariñas to return to Manila with all the forces under his command at Cebu, about one hundred fifty leagues away.

Pedro de Rojas would remain in this position of power for forty days until, upon the return of Dasmariñas' son Luis, an Augustinian Friar by the name of Diego Muñoz made it known that, before his departure, the late governor had secretly entrusted him with a box of papers.[8] When the box was opened, it became clear that Dasmariñas had meant for his son to continue the government of the Philippines and Rojas had to make way. Still, the forty days he had been in power was the window of time during which Rojas arrested and imprisoned Bernardo Avila Girón.[9]

His reasons are not quite clear. It is possible that Rojas wanted to extort money from Avila Girón, who seems to have committed the crime of *pundunor* ("point of honor"), that is, he probably killed a man who had tried to seduce the native woman he was living with.[10] Avila Girón suggests such a course of events when he writes in the very beginning of his manuscript about conjugal fidelity in Japan: "If a woman is married, she can be trusted completely, for there are no women in the world more honorable and of greater loyalty, for [in Japan] she who makes a wrong choice pays for it with her head. In this, there is better order in Japan than with us, not because the laws of Spain are not just and good, but because some judges ignore them with impunity, and this I know from personal experience in Manila."[11]

Avila Girón goes on to describe what happened to him in Manila after his arrest in 1593. In spite of having provided sufficient testimony given by seven trustworthy witnesses who had testified that he had been wronged by the man he had killed, he was sentenced to death by Pedro de Rojas. He ends this account of his close brush with death with a rhetorical question: "When a Japanese finds his wife alone with any man, even if they are just talking together, he may kill her and does not need any witnesses, and with reason, for what more witnesses does a man need when he finds his wife with another man in his own house?"[12]

The death penalty was pronounced in the beginning of November 1593, but the sentence was not immediately carried out. The subsequent arrival in Manila of the son of his friend, Governor Dasmariñas, saved the writer's neck. We have no information how he spent the next few months, but we know that he left the Philippines in July of 1594. A few months earlier, in May of 1594, a Franciscan friar, by the name of Marcelo de Ribadeneira (1560?–1610), had arrived in Manila straight from Spain.[13] Ribadeneira and his companions, the friars Andres de San Antonio, Agustín Rodriguez, and Jeronimo de Jesus, were eager to go and help their fellow Franciscan Pedro Blásquez (1542–1597), who had gone to Japan the year before.

This was the group Bernardo Avila Girón joined on a Japanese vessel about to return to Japan.[14] We can only guess at his reasons. Even if he was a hot-blooded sinner, he seems to have been a sincere Roman Catholic and a fervent believer in the civilizing mission of the Spanish Crown. He must have had strong backing from the new governor for the Franciscans not to object to his company, for neither party could have known the other. What is more, soon after their arrival in Hirado on 27 August 1594,[15] their ways parted. Avila Girón left for Satsuma,[16] while Ribadeneira and his two companions headed for the Kinai.[17]

The fact that Bernardo went to Satsuma, instead of Nagasaki, indicates that he was careful not to make the same mistake as Juan de Solís had done. He also may have been working towards Solís' goal to establish a direct link between Manila and Japan. As he would write later, in Satsuma Bernardo was shocked to see first-hand Japanese justice at work. A peasant, his wife, and two sons were executed for the non-payment of a tax constituting no more than two bundles of un-hulled rice worth 3 *mas*. By the end of the year, we find him for the first time in Nagasaki.[18] He may have lived outside of Uchimachi, possibly already in the area near the San Miguel church of Rokasu-machi where he later did most of his writing.

He probably had brought considerable financial resources with him, likely in the form of gold, which was cheap in the Philippines.[19] But he was also lucky, for there was no Portuguese ship lying at anchor in Nagasaki Bay that year. For the moment, therefore, he did not need to make a large security deposit with the Captain Major, promising he would not interfere or compete with the Portuguese trade, as we have seen Juan de Solís and others had been forced to do. It is also clear that he was on good terms with the Jesuits in town, led at this time by his fellow countryman the Spanish padre Pedro Gómez.

During the trading season of the next year, 1595, starting with the arrival of Captain Major Manoel de Miranda, Avila Girón absented himself from Nagasaki to stave off inopportune Portuguese demands. He used the occasion to make a trip to neighboring Arima in the company of a Jesuit brother, possibly a Japanese convert interested in improving his Spanish. That would again seem to point at Padre Pedro Gómez, who may have been instrumental in setting this up. The two visited the castle of Arima Harunobu, but the warlord himself was away in Korea, proving his loyalty to Hideyoshi.[20] Afterwards, Avila Girón traveled to Kyoto where he linked up with Marcelo de Ribadeneira again, most likely in the Franciscan convent recently established in the capital.[21]

Avila Girón's presence in the Kinai indicates that his early stay in Japan may have had little to do with trade. Clearly, if he had been an ordinary trader, there would have been no reason to travel all the way there. But if he was not in Japan to trade, then why was he there in the first place? I think that it is likely that he was sent by the younger Dasmariñas to find out if the invasion of the Philippines threatened by Hideyoshi was going materialize in the near future, and, if not, what the chances were of establishing a trade link between Japan and Manila, which was in dire need of raw materials for its defense like iron, copper, saltpeter and sulfur. These were the two questions of the most immediate concern to the Spanish in the Philippines.

It is clear, moreover, that Luis Dasmariñas had been crucial in preventing Bernardo's execution. The new governor of the Philippines, therefore, could demand a risky assignment from the man he had saved from the gallows. Luis Dasmariñas, however, was replaced in July of 1596 with Francisco Tello de Guzman (?–1603) by order of Philip II himself, who thought the son of the murdered governor too young to be in charge of such a fragile and sensitive outpost as Manila.[22] Although, Avila Girón subsequently may have lost his official support for this reason, the money he had brought lasted him until 1597, and he clearly enjoyed living in Nagasaki, where his household included five young female Korean slaves.[23]

A Cockaigne of Sex:
Francesco Carletti (1)

In Japan the missionaries found a society unburdened by the idea of original sin. This challenged some of the most basic foundations of their power over the faithful. Without teaching original sin, the missionaries could not have the same importance in Japan as they had in Europe. So insist on the necessity of teaching this idea they did. It pops up everywhere, but most often in the vicinity of the Portuguese traders. If the Portuguese brought large cargoes of silk every time they arrived in Japan, the missionaries did not fail to bring equally sizeable cargoes of awareness of sin.

It sometimes seems as if the missionaries (not just the Jesuits, but the Dominicans as well) were obsessed with this problem, for they do not stop writing about the great numbers of non-procreative and extramarital sins committed in Japan. Fróis, of course, is as delicate as he can manage, but we may be sure that his brethren in the Society knew exactly what he meant when he was on the topic. We have already noted the roundabout way in which he indicated that the port of Fukuda was providing amenities for the Portuguese sailors in the same way Hirado had done during the 1550s.

In 1583, a new church was started just outside the old town by a Japanese Christian from Sakai, on a spot between two streets that were becoming known as Hakata-machi and Kōzen-machi, the latter named after the rich Hakata merchant Suetsugu Kōzen (1520–1614). Both street names, then, indicate that the people living in the area came from northern Kyushu's traditional and richest merchant community. The fact, however, that a church was deemed necessary in their neighborhood (a mere three minute walk from the site of the older church at Morisaki) indicates that it may have been a disreputable place.

The Hakata merchants, in other words, are likely to have provided "non-Christian" entertainments for those Portuguese who wanted to slip away from the moral conventions imposed by the Jesuits in their citadel. Fróis writes with prudish understatement how Padre Organtino saved the souls of the girls in the neighborhood: "There were a number of girls in town who were in immediate danger of losing their souls, because of the vehement occasions [occaziões vehementes] they had for that. The father worked hard to marry off thirty of them, which he succeeded in doing to the great consolation of their parents and relatives, who because of their poverty had not been able to support them."[1]

Poverty certainly was also a factor in the custom of providing lonely merchants with companions for the duration of their stay in Japan. Bernardo Avila Girón, Francesco Carletti (1572–1639), Francis Caron (1600–1673), and many others essentially tell the same story. Carletti's is the most steeped in the Mediterranean tradition of protecting the virginity of one's daughters and sisters:

> they do not hold the honor of their daughters or sisters in as much esteem, even not valuing it at all. It often happens that a girl's father or mother or brother will discuss her price before she is married, this with no shame on anyone's part, selling her very easily for money, but driven by great poverty, which indeed is very great throughout all that area, and which explains why they enter into every sort of venereal dishonor in such a manner and in such diverse and unheard-of ways that it seems impossible.[2]

He goes on to detail the custom of how the agents of the available girls would come to see the Portuguese merchants in their lodging as soon as they had arrived: "they ask them if they want to buy a virgin or have her in some other way that would please them more, and this for the time that they will be there, or just to have her for some nights or days or months or hours. And they make the arrangements with them."[3] Often it would be the parents, themselves, who made the agreement and received the money: "if the men want them, they bring the girls to their houses to be seen for the first time; or, sometimes, the men go to their houses to see the girls."[4]

"Many of the Portuguese," he concludes, "find this land of Cockaigne much to their liking—and, what is better, it costs them but little. And very often they are given a girl of fourteen or fifteen years, a virgin and beautiful, for three or four *scudos*, more or less, according to the time they want to have her at their disposition, at the end of which they have only to return her to her home."[5] Generous Portuguese merchants who had made a lot of money during their stay in Nagasaki might give their girls "thirty or forty scudos" upon their separation after seven or eight months, and without such a "dowry" "many of them never would be able to marry" one of their countrymen.[6]

In fact, the boundaries between love, house service, and prostitution, again as a result of the non-existence of the idea of original sin, were vague in Japan:

> there are also women who go out by the day, and it is enough to give them any little amount whatsoever, and it never is necessary to discuss the consideration of the money, which is never refused by their parents, they being the ones to whom it is usually given…. There also are women who make arrangements through pimps, and it is enough to give them food and clothing, neither of which costs much, and the rest of whatever they earn stays with the pimps.[7]

Caron reports that, in Hirado in the seventeenth century, such women would expect no more than between three and six *stuyvers* daily for their food, one or two silk dresses of between twenty and thirty guilders and one or two cotton dresses for clothing, and a pair of leather shoes as well as some sandals; while her parents or her master require between ten and thirty guilders. "Then the Dutchman invites everyone for a meal and he is married for the time of his stay in Japan. After his departure some Japanese hurries to marry the woman for her savings."[8]

By the end of the sixteenth century, Nagasaki's sex trade already counted many successful courtesans. This is something we learn from Avila Girón's casual remark that "there is no hooker in Nagasaki without her palanquin."[9] And although we have very few descriptions of these women here is the anonymous voice of a Japanese sex worker inside the confessional:

> When I was a child, I lost both my parents and became an orphan. As I was going alone through the world, I was picked up by a foreigner as his plaything, and stayed for four months in his house as if I were his wife. Then I understood that being a servant is hard, and as I did not have any status nor knew of any pride or shame, I became a prostitute in the red-light district. For three years I sold my body to everyone who fancied me. During this time, I took care to keep my beauty and prevent any calamity by wiping myself with urine or anything else as soon as my client had spent himself and left, so that nothing of him would remain inside my body.[10]

The lack of inhibitions and boundaries of what were considered appropriate sexual relationships was not, of course, limited to those between Japanese and their foreign guests. Here is another (rather outrageous) voice from the confessional. Although it was noted down with much disapprobation by the missionary who received it, he never indicated any doubt as to its essential veracity. For that reason, we may consider it just an admittedly extreme case of lechery, the more so because it is but one among many other such confessions that kept on puzzling the missionaries:

> As you can see, I am still young, and moreover I am not yet familiar with the precise morals of the Christians. Most of my friends are like this as well, so you can imagine my situation. Anyway, I go through life just having fun, participating in linked-verse parties, and all the sex these usually involve, without a thought for the laws of God, His commandments, or any fear of hell, leading an existence like that of the animals clinging to the ugly matters of the body. Everything I think, say, or do finds its origin in carnal desires. So, whenever I feel like having sex with a boy, I act upon my desires looking for a chance to satisfy them. When my eyes are drawn towards some beautiful woman, I won't stop until I have been able to insert my tool into her body. To sum up, I have not accomplished anything, nor followed anybody. All I have done is to dig up sins to be committed.
>
> Even since my last confession, I have often let my seed flow by manipulating myself. Daily I have had sex with other men, I wetting him and he wetting me. It goes without saying that I have also sinned with women. I have slept about four hundred times with single women, and I don't remember how many times with married ones. With some once, with others two, four, five or six times each. Among them there were also women who were my girlfriends for half a year, one year, two months, or even two years. I don't remember how many times I sinned with each individual, it all depended on the opportunity.
>
> Five or six times, I have been able to take away the shame women experience when it is their first time with a man. I seduced one of them by telling her that I would marry her and then after I had had her, I changed my opinion of her and dumped her. Another one disliked me at first but I employed a go-between and insisted so that, in the end, after many false promises, I had my pleasure and did not keep any of them. I threatened the third one that if she didn't do what I said I would strangle her right there and then. In this way I succeeded in my conquest, after which I kept her as my mistress for three months. I only sinned about three times with each of the other three. Whenever I think of all my conquests, I get totally lost and absorbed in my pleasure.
>
> I also boast of my wickedness and tell my stories angling for praise. I even teach the Way of Lechery to those who are not very familiar with it. This too is an everyday occurrence. There really may not be any way to pardon me for what I am going to say next, but as this is a confession I will say it anyway even if it makes me feel ashamed. Three times I have deeply sinned with animals. [The funny thing is that] afterwards I felt pangs of jealousy whenever I saw these animals have sex together. This was about ten times. I have also two or three times acted as a go-between myself. Twice the people I brought together had been alone, once one of them had lived alone without a wife.[11]

*　*　*

The Martyred Mendicant: Pedro Blásquez

Pedro Blásquez arrived in Japan in 1593 on the ship of the Portuguese merchant Pedro Gonzalez de Carvajal,[1] ostensibly as ambassador from the Governor of the Philippines, but in reality to challenge the Jesuit monopoly on mission work in Japan.[2] Blásquez was accompanied by two other friars: Fray Francisco de San Miguel (1545?–1597), and Fray Gonzalo Garcia (1557–1597), who sailed on the junk of Paulo Harada Kiemon.[3] The arrival of these Franciscans in Japan constituted another Spanish attack on Portuguese privilege, similar to the one Juan de Solís had tried. This time, however, it was carried out, not with the surreptitious and unofficial support from the Viceroy of Peru, but with the official sanction of the Spanish church and through the governor of the Philippines, and by implication, the king of Spain (and Portugal!) himself.

The two ships with the friars reached Nagasaki around the same time in the summer of 1593, and the Franciscans were provided lodging by the Jesuits until they were ready to go and visit Hideyoshi at nearby Nagoya.[4] As we have seen from the episode in the life of Juan de Solís, Hideyoshi was eager to establish commercial relations with Manila. Thinking that the Blásquez' embassy provided an opening, he welcomed the Franciscans and, as was his wont, dissimulated, leading Blásquez to believe that it was not Christianity of which he disapproved, but the behavior of the Jesuits. Magnanimously, the Taikō gave permission to establish a residence wherever the Franciscans wanted to settle in Japan, and so the newly arrived emissary chose to start in the capital under Hideyoshi's very eyes.

Significantly, Hideyoshi had not rescinded any of his previous prohibitions, which remained in force. Thus, he had only given permission for the Franciscans to be in Japan. Mistakenly, Blásquez took this for permission to proselytize.[5] Blásquez came back to Nagasaki in the company of Jeronimo de Jesus on 18 December 1594.[6] He may have wanted to see if he could establish a Franciscan presence in the country's only Christian town. Traveling to Kyushu, however, he "fell sick along the way and had such a high fever that he arrived exhausted in Nagasaki. The Jesuits took him in, cured him, and cared for him with much charity until he was healthy again."[7] Recovering in their residence, Blásquez met with his fellow countryman Pedro Gómez, his counter-part among the Jesuits and seven years his senior. Regrettably, neither missionary has left us a report of their first contact and what they discussed.[8]

The two Spaniards had followed very different routes to finally end up in the same place. Pedro Blásquez had always been near the center of Spanish power. He came from near Avila in central Castile. He joined the Franciscans at age twenty-four.[9] Fifteen years later, in 1581, he left Seville for Mexico, where he was active among the Indians of Chichimeca.[10] In 1584, he traveled to the Philippines where he quickly rose to a position of leadership. Before he left for Japan, in 1593, as Governor Dasmariñas' ambassador, he had been in charge of the Franciscan Convent of Manila.[11] Now, at the age of fifty-four, he was for the very first time in his life in a place where he did not know the language of the ruling class and where he could not count on the backing of the authorities for his missionary zeal.

Thus, in spite of the similarities in their common background and calling, the out-look of these two men had been shaped in a very different manner by the road they had followed before meeting each other in Nagasaki. If the differences in their approach of how to proceed in converting the Japanese were not clear to either Gómez or Blásquez after their first meeting, they certainly must have become aware of them after Lent of 1595 had started.

First, the Franciscans moved out of the residence of the Jesuits: "they climbed into the litter of a devout Portuguese by name of Francisco Rodriguez Pinto, who together with other devout Portuguese brought the friars to a hermitage that was next to a lepers' hospital a quarter of a league away from the town."[12] This was the hermitage of St. Lazarus, established by Captain Major Roque de Melo a few years earlier. There they preached and heard confessions to the great surprise of the Christians of Nagasaki, who had not had a chance to practice their religion openly for almost eight years. The Franciscans kept regular church hours and, while taking care of the lepers, they led the faithful in prayer by day and "mortified their flesh" at night. Anyone who wanted, Japanese or Portuguese, could join in.[13]

This open flouting of Hideyoshi's decree upset both the members of the Brotherhood of the Misericordia, who were officially in charge of the leprosarium, as well as the representative of Governor Terazawa resident in the city. At the behest of the Jesuits, who had probably been warned by Terazawa's representative, the members of the Misericordia Brotherhood evicted the Franciscans from the chapel. Blásquez was brought back to Kyoto under guard,[14] but managed to come back to Nagasaki later in the year. Over the summer of 1595, he established a small Franciscan chapel made of wood in the old town cemetery, where until recently a large cross had always stood giving the area its name of Cruz-machi (today the site of Nagasaki City Hall). He named the chapel Our Lady of the Angels, a reference to the annunciation of the immaculate impregnation of Mary by the Holy Spirit, much revered by the Franciscans.

Thus, Blásquez had decided to provide the Christians of Nagasaki with an example of another type of Christianity, based on the life of St. Francis.[15] The Franciscans went barefoot, begged for their food, and dressed only in their grey frocks of roughly woven material, tied at the waist by a rope. This rope ended in the three knots of the Franciscan vows: one knot for perfect poverty, one knot for virginity, and one knot for obedience.[16] With the entry of these Spanish Franciscans, the ideology of the Holy Spirit first found a foothold in Nagasaki.[17] This combined with a natural inclination of the lay Portuguese in town to mistrust the religious monopoly of the Jesuits, was sufficient reason for the *casados* of Nagasaki to be particularly supportive of the efforts of the Franciscans.

For the rest, the years 1595 and 1596 were relatively uneventful in the eyes of the people of Nagasaki. Now we know it was just a case of silence before the storm. With the blatant example of the Franciscans in town, even the prudent Jesuits loosened up a little. There was, for example, again a procession of flagellants on 11 April, Maundy Thursday, which may have been started by the Franciscans, but the Jesuits joined in.[18] That the latter were starting to come out of the woodwork also appears from a notice that they publicly wore their black cassocks at the funeral of the Japanese wife of a Portuguese resident of Nagasaki, by name of Jeronimo Rodriguez, something which they also had not done since 1587.[19] Again, I have to stress here that it is not reasonable to suppose that such flagrantly public transgressions against his edict of 1587 could have been kept hidden from Hideyoshi. Rather, it is likely that reports about Franciscan proselytizing, both in the Kinai as well as in Nagasaki, had been infuriating the Taikō all year long.

When Padre Pedro Martins (1535–1598), sent to Japan as the country's first resident bishop, arrived on 14 August on the carrack of Rui Mendes de Figueiredo, he was received into the city with a solemn parade, accompanying him to the Jesuit headquarters at Morisaki.[20] There he was greeted by the heads of the Jesuit establishments, as well as by representatives of the Christian organizations of the surrounding area.[21] The new bishop did not waste much time in getting down to deal with the Franciscans, whose behavior was imperiling all of Japanese Christendom. He immediately forbade the Franciscans to proselytize and Japanese believers from attending mass said by the Franciscans.[22] One month later, on 13 September, he gave a fiery sermon in which he excommunicated all the Spanish friars active in Nagasaki,[23] announced he would fine anyone bringing friars to Japan 100 *taels* in silver,[24] and threatened to excommunicate any Portuguese or Japanese who would still go to hear mass or take communion at the friars' church in Nagasaki. All aid to the friars was forbidden.[25]

In the next month, October 1596, the Manila galleon *San Felipe*, richly laden and bound for Acapulco, was thrown off course by a violent storm, and ended up being blown all the way to Shikoku. Severely damaged but still afloat, she was pulled ashore by local beachcombers in order to be plundered. Its captain, Matias de Landecho, protested to Hideyoshi, who promptly confiscated the cargo for himself. Next, Pedro Blásquez made the mistake of getting involved, meeting on 29 October with a Spanish delegation from the ship,[26] and claiming that much of the cargo belonged to his order.

That was too much effrontery for Hideyoshi to swallow. Notified of the claims by the Franciscan, he was said to have exclaimed:

> How can it be that these monks, who say that they are so poor, now say that the stuff from this ship is theirs? Certainly I say that they must be men of evil affairs, false and deceitful. Further, having commanded and prohibited their impertinent religion, I know perfectly well that, in spite of my prohibition, they have taught and converted many to Christianity. And they have stayed at this court and in everything acted contrarily. For that reason, they having transgressed against my will, I now command that they be taken prisoners and crucified, together with all who have accepted their religion, in the city of Nagasaki.[27]

In this way, the Taikō killed several birds with one stone. First, he obtained the cargo of the *San Felipe*, valued at more than a million and a half silver pesos. This allowed him to replete his treasury, which his Korean campaigns had left empty.[28] Second, he was putting fear into the hearts of the Christians throughout Japan, but especially those of Nagasaki, and made clear that he was really serious about his prohibition of their religion. Third, he was finally able to strike a heavy blow at the Spanish in Manila, Mexico, and Spain, all three of which had been temporizing and ignoring his diplomatic overtures for several years now.[29]

As a result of Hideyoshi's order, Pedro Blásquez, the other Franciscans of the Kinai, as well as twenty Japanese converts (including three men connected with the Jesuit mission in the capital, arrested by mistake) were jailed on 9 December 1596.[30] On 6 January 1597, Blásquez and the others were taken out of their prisons and led on carts through Miyako with their arms tied and with ropes around their necks. They were preceded by a sign which bore the sentence they had been condemned to. At a temple along the way, a part of the left ear of each of the prisoners was cut off.[31] On 8 January, the whole group was brought to Osaka on horseback, where great throngs of people crowded the streets, because Hideyoshi had just arrived as well.[32] On 9 January, they started their long journey from Osaka to Nagasaki.[33] By 1 February 1597, they had reached Karatsu in northern Kyushu, the castle town of the Governor of Nagasaki. Terazawa Hirotaka being in Korea, they were met by the Governor's younger brother Hanzaburō, who was to be in charge of their executions.[34]

On 4 February they reached Sonogi (present-day Higashi Sonogi-chō on Ōmura Bay). Here, the whole train of dead men walking embarked with their guards in three boats to cross Ōmura Bay to Tokitsu, and travel from there overland to Nagasaki.[35] In Sonogi, too, Murayama Tōan and the Jesuits João Rodrigues and Francisco Pasio (1553–1612) came to meet them.[36] Tōan, as we have seen, was a Nagasaki Christian known for his ability to get along with many different people. His function may have been to smooth out the relations with Hanzaburō and the guards, who had come with the group of convicts from Osaka, and to obtain permission for the Jesuit padres to administer the last sacraments.

Pasio, groomed to be Gómez' successor as head of the mission in Japan, heard the confessions of the three men among the prisoners, who had been connected with the Jesuit mission in the capital. Two of these, Juan de Goto (1578-1597) and Diego Kisai (1533-1597), he then welcomed as brothers into the Society,[37] so that their martyrdom might add the same luster to the Society as that of the Franciscans did for the order of the *fratres minores*. That night, Rodrigues heard the confessions of the Franciscan group.[38]

The next morning, 5 February, all twenty-six were crucified on the spot where the "Western Slope" or Nishizaka of Mt. Tateyama reaches the water of Nagasaki Bay. This was Nagasaki's habitual execution ground, located near the St. Lazarus chapel. The crosses were erected in a semi-circle, with those of the Franciscans in the middle. By Hideyoshi's express orders, the condemned were fastened to their crosses with metal bands, not only around their wrists and ankles, but also around their necks.[39] The use of these iron straps was unusual, for normally in Japan the bodies were fastened to the cross with ropes. In the center stood a sign with the inscription: "Condemned to death on the cross because they preached the forbidden Christian law."[40]

Avila Girón writes:

> Although they did not allow the Japanese to approach, there were a large number of people, men as well as women, on top of the mountain at the foot of which this slope is situated. Many others watched from the tops of the roofs of their houses and these were the upper class of the town, whose moans rose up to heaven and echoed back at them. Everywhere, in the streets, the mountains, and the valleys these echoes went back and forth until they became one single lament.[41]

His countrymen, Marcelo Ribadeneira and his fellow Franciscans of Nagasaki, were watching from the carrack of Ruy Mendes de Figueiredo, whereto, on 13 January 1597, they had been moved as a precaution against a possible outburst of popular sympathy. They would remain under guard on the ship until her departure on 21 March 1598. The carrack had probably anchored, as usual, not far from the mouth of the Urakami river, She would have provided a good view of the execution grounds from the waterside. Therefore, Ribadeneira's account is the best informed we have of the public reaction to the martyrdom.[42]

Everyone was dead by ten in the morning.[43] Next, the Portuguese and the Japanese Christians

> went to catch the blood of the martyrs on pieces of cotton and taffeta that they had brought with them for just that purpose. And the onrush of the Christians who wanted to take home relics was such that the gentiles were powerless to stop them from taking what they coveted, although they wounded many and one person was seriously hurt in the head. But it was no use: they could not prevent them from taking the blood or the soil on which it had dripped. The Christians also cut whatever they could from the crosses and the clothing of the holy martyrs, showing how much they valued these holy relics. When the guards, who had been keeping the ropes and some mantles of the holy friars, saw this they later sold these articles of clothing to devout Christians for a very good price.[44]

The town and its surroundings became obsessed with the corpses. Greed for pieces of clothing went so far that it became necessary to cover the naked bodies of the executed with rags and mats. More soldiers were called up to guard the corpses, as Hideyoshi had ordered that they should hang on their crosses until they had completely decomposed. When the news of the martyrdom spread in the villages around Nagasaki Bay, many more Christians came and the number of guards still proved insufficient. There was the danger, moreover, that these Christians would come at night to steal away the corpses of the martyrs. Therefore, a palisade was built around the crosses so that no one would be able to approach them. Even this did not prevent many Christians from trying to enter the enclosure to worship the corpses.[45]

It was a cold winter. After the initial rush for relics, the bodies of the twenty-six martyrs froze solid and so remained more resistant to the crows and other predators. This, of course, immediately led to stories about their miraculous resistance to decay. On 21 March 1597, the *São Antonio* left Nagasaki Bay, carrying, apart from the four Franciscans who had escaped execution, also the troublesome new Bishop Martins.[46]

Avila Girón describes what happened on Good Friday, the following 18 April, after spring had come and the bodies had thawed out:

At two o'clock in the afternoon, seventy-two days after the holy martyrdom, there were many people on their knees before the holy martyrs praying, as they did out of devotion, especially on a day like that. Suddenly, blood started to flow from the body of the Holy Commissary, Fray Pedro Bautista, out of the wounds made by the lance thrusts, in such quantity that it crossed the body to drip down to the foot of the cross where it soaked into the ground. The Japanese present were struck with wonder and many of them carried the news back to the town.[47]

The town immediately went into an uproar over this "miracle." Men and women started to run to the execution grounds in such crowds that at a distance of more than four hundred paces from the corpses there was no way of getting through, although the road was as wide as the widest street in town. The magistrate of that time ordered a number of police officers to be positioned near the major access roads to the leprosarium. But the people of Nagasaki found a way around these men by climbing Mt. Tateyama and going down to the execution grounds behind their backs. The policemen were recalled as there seemed to be no way to stem the flood of people eager to see the miracle with their own eyes.

Bernardo Avila Girón was turned back by the police in the morning

[I] went back there the same afternoon and saw the Holy Commissary [Pedro Bautista Blásquez], his face very handsome, as if he were asleep, and the right side of his rib cage all bare, for people had cut away his clothing to take as relics. His sacred body was still intact and he was so white and looked so beautiful that it made one happy just to see him. The whole foot of the cross was bathed in his blood, which was of such a beautiful color that it resembled nothing as much as the rising sun. It was a wondrous thing that after so many days the blood would still be so fresh, and that without having flowed before, except on the day of the execution, it would flow on that particular day, Good Friday, the day of Christ's passion, which the Holy Commissary had wished to imitate, and that there were so many people there to witness it.[48]

＊　＊　＊

A Town Under Pressure:
Francesco Carletti (2)

By June, according to one eyewitness, some parts of the corpses were still hanging on their crosses.[1] It seems that the last remains were taken down and buried in October.[2] Each of them was given a proper burial, even though from many of them—and especially from the religious—many of their limbs, chiefly their heads, had been taken as relics.[3]

This had happened despite the fact that there had been guards, and in spite of the prohibitions issued by Hideyoshi and by the Jesuit bishop, who had both forbidden the corpses from being touched under penalty of death.[4] This latter testimony is Francesco Carletti's, from whose fascinating travel account we have already had occasion to quote several times. That the attitude of several scholars towards the value of his testimony is ambivalent,[5] however, is mainly due to the following terrifying short story he tells elsewhere in his account of his stay in Nagasaki.

> These people [i.e., the Japanese] … deal very seriously with adultery, which they punish severely, with death to both parties if they are caught in the act or brought to judgment. Taking the adulterers, man and woman, they put them into a wagon and take them, bound and with their hands behind their backs, to the house of the husband. And in his presence they cut off the man's penis and take enough skin from his body to make a sort of cap, this to put on the head of the adulterous woman. And from near her shameful part they cut a strip of flesh from around the vagina, making a garland of it to place on the head of the adulterous man. And thus ornamented and adorned with those members, they go naked through the city, making a miserable and shameful show of their bodies to all the people during the time when the flowing out of their blood from the wounded parts ends their lives.[6]

It is important to state that, as far as I have been able to check, Carletti is eminently accurate in everything he has written about his stay in Japan and throughout the rest of his travel account. Not a few times he assures his readers of his book that he is making nothing up and only reports what he has seen with his own eyes, eschewing hearsay and speculation. In this passage, too, it is clear that Carletti is speaking of something he has seen with his own eyes. His experience of Japan did not reach beyond Nagasaki, and therefore, if true, his account is based on something he must have seen there, even if he thinks that this type of punishment is a general custom of Japan. In my opinion, it is in this respect only that he exaggerates, for I have not been able to find any other example of this type of gruesome punishment in Japan.[7]

What we need to keep in mind here is that Nagasaki in the 1590s was a place with a different set of moral values from the rest of Japan. In fact, rather than looking for precedents in Japan, the "custom" described by Carletti here has more immediate connections with some ancient European traditions: it resembles nothing so much as a *charivari* [shi-və-'rē], albeit in a rare and particularly gruesome variety.[8] Charivari used to be widespread all over Europe and the northern Mediterranean. They were ways in which small communities enforced their dominant morality. The objects of charivari usually were a man and a woman who had somehow offended against this morality: widows or widowers who remarried, marriages contracted between an old man and a young wife, and most frequently adulterers. Such sinners against morality might suddenly find themselves the object, often at night, of a deafening noise made by a group of youths beating with sticks upon pots and pans, and sometimes engaging in more violent acts, such as the breaking of windows or the kicking in of doors.

"The victims are then taken out of their house and paraded through the streets of the community—on a cart, behind a cart, on a donkey, or on a pole etc.—and may be subjected to other physical trials such as dunking into a stream, a pond, or a river, as well as being led to the periphery of the community and to be abandoned there, sometimes after having been tarred and feathered."[9] Sometimes, such groups of rowdy young people could be paid off, but more often "just like public executions, charivari formed a welcome relief from the dreary routine and monotony of living in an isolated village or provincial town."[10] Consequently, the result often was that the couple realized it was impossible for them to continue to live in the same community any longer.[11]

While most examples of charivari that have been transmitted to us from the sixteenth through the nineteenth centuries seem pretty tame (although not, to be sure, from the point of view of the couple involved), there are a few examples that resemble the scene described by Carletti. Here is an example of a charivari from northern France, dating from 1262: "Whoever is caught in the act of adultery with a married woman, or someone else's woman, will walk the village stark naked, with the woman going ahead holding a rope attached to the testicles of the man behind her. The town crier will precede them calling out: 'Who ever behaves like this will be treated like this. Each of the guilty will pay a fine of 65 *sous*, two-thirds for the seigneur and the rest for the town consuls.'"[12]

Research by classicists has even found examples of charivari among the Greeks of classical Athens.[13] The common denominator of all these examples is the public humiliation combined with some sort of mutilation, precisely the two elements we find in Carletti's account. It is certainly possible that some learned padre in Nagasaki, when asked how people traditionally punish adultery in Christian countries, might have come up with these two characteristics. His Japanese listeners then put these ideas into practice, adding some peculiarly Japanese ideas about adultery.

In his wonderful article on the background, reasons, and psychology of charivari, the Dutch anthropologist Anton Blok has provided some illuminating insights that may help us understand why Carletti's account should be taken seriously. Blok says that, first and foremost, charivari seem to be limited to "small, mostly endogamous, face-to-face communities, where public opinion, to use one of Norbert Elias' ideas, is 'the foundation of everyone's existence.'"[14] This is certainly applicable to Christian Nagasaki, where people tended (and were encouraged by their priests) to marry within the pool of those who were baptized. Although such marriage partners often came from the outside, they would share (or adopt) the Christian norms of the Nagasaki community. It is well known that Japanese society, in general, was (and to a large extent still is) particularly "face-to-face" oriented. All streets of Nagasaki, for example, were organized into tightly run Christian block organizations, where public opinion mattered a great deal.

As if he had Nagasaki in mind, Blok further adds: "these communities often have their own cultural signature and identity, they are not rarely under pressure or are confronted with some sort of demographic, economic, or political crisis."[15] Because he does not add the word "religious" among the different types of crises such communities may face, we have to conclude that he did not know about Carletti's account, which makes his comments all the more relevant here. As for the deeper psychology of charivari, the communal need they seem to fulfill, Blok theorizes that they represent an effort to repair by magical means the boundaries of the community that have been violated. The charivari is a purification ritual that repairs and brings into focus the cultural categories of the habitual order. In this connection, he compares it to the scapegoat, which not only embodies and absorbs impurity, but is also capable of liberating the community from pollution by its violent elimination, in which the whole community participated.[16]

The scene Carletti describes certainly fits this pattern. The executions of twenty-six Christians, almost haphazardly picked up off the streets of Kyoto and then deliberately transported to Nagasaki, had put the city under severe pressure. As far as I have been able to ascertain, nobody has ever asked why these men, who had all been arrested in the Kansai, could not be executed there on the spot. The fact that these men had to travel all the way to Nagasaki means that, for Hideyoshi, the location where the example was set was the important thing, not the victims themselves. The Taikō may even have been waiting for an incident that would provide him with an excuse to set this example. Of course, it is no coincidence that the European victims were all insolent Spanish friars, and not Jesuits who, although manifestly untrustworthy, at least had given proof they feared Hideyoshi. To the pressure of the executions were added the strict orders that the bodies of the crucified should stay where they were until they had rotted and fallen off their crosses by themselves. The Taikō had provided detailed instructions to fasten the bodies more securely than was usual, so that his example should last as long as possible.

There can be no doubt that, with all this, the population of Nagasaki got Hideyoshi's message, loud and clear. But as Christianity is a religion about life after death, which holds that not life but death is the real thing that counts, the population became, if anything, more Christian because of the example set by their martyrs. The latter had all died without a complaint: preaching, praying, or singing, full of joy even, because the death of a martyr for the faith, according to Catholic doctrine, leads straight to heaven. The executions, then, sharpened everyone's awareness of what it meant to be a Christian in Japan. For those who did not yet get the message, Padre Pedro Gómez wrote a short pamphlet "about what martyrdom is, its dignity, its rewards, and what is required for it to be valid, and above all what frame of mind and what gear one needs at such a moment."[17] This was translated into Japanese, printed and distributed in great numbers among the Christians of Nagasaki. Alas, not a single copy seems to have survived.[18]

In other words, the martyrdom may have radicalized the population of Nagasaki as a whole to the point where it could treat adulterers in the fashion described by Carletti. Hideyoshi died the next year. He probably never realized that his example had backfired, at least in the short term, that the Christians of Nagasaki had become more, and not less, Christian. It took his successor sixteen years before he came to the conclusion that Hideyoshi had been right and that he, too, needed to proscribe Christianity throughout Japan. Clearly, Tokugawa Ieyasu (1542–1616) agreed with Hideyoshi on all points: the faith was unnecessary, ridiculous, pernicious even and undermining all normal samurai relationships, but the trade needed to be preserved. This was, as Gómez notes, the reason why there were still padres in Japan:

> Taikō Sama remained convinced that the friars and all other missionaries were either spies for their King, or used their preaching of the Gospel as a cover to conquer the land, just as the pilot [of the *San Felipe*] had said. This would entail throwing all of us out of Japan completely. But happily, the Good Lord has seen fit to implant in his heart the conviction that without our presence there can be no trade between the Japanese and the Portuguese, thus tying his hands where throwing all of us out is concerned.[19]

Thus, the problem remained how to uncouple the trade brought by the Portuguese from the religion brought by the missionaries, who served as go-betweens between merchants from opposite sides of the globe. Hideyoshi's legacy of brute force showed how the Tokugawa would eventually go about accomplishing this same goal.

The Italian Painter: Giovanni Cola

The question presents itself, again and again, what *did* the Japanese converts understand and what did *attract* them to the new religion? It is undeniably true that however mercenary the motives of many converts may have been, such mercenary motives alone do not explain the continued existence of Nagasaki and other, smaller Christian communities in Japan. As we have seen in the last section, after the example Hideyoshi had set, the town is likely to have been left more fervently Christian than ever before, now that it had its own set of martyrs, who had preceded them to Heaven, and now that it owned a rich collection of their relics: pieces of clothing soaked in their blood, body parts, even skulls.[1]

To explore the attraction of Christianity in Japan a bit further, we will have to consider two different, but intertwined, aspects: the universal appeal of the Church in its post–Tridentine garb and its appeal to the Japanese in particular.[2] As mentioned in the section on how Ōmura Sumitada was converted, the Roman Catholic Church has mastered to a high degree the use of images that bypass rational thought and appeal directly to the emotions. The Jesuits were the trendsetters of this device in Japan. As a contemporary Jesuit put it:

> The speech [of an image] is an abbreviated book and brief worship. It is something that speaks without talking and is heard without the ear; something written that everyone understands; a letter that everyone can read; a book for the learned; an attribute that makes manifest things which are past and ancient. It is a mirror that reflects things held in trust [i.e., things that are not actually part of it].... Furthermore, those forms and media [i.e., images] pass deeper into all the interior senses, and the more subtle they are, the more easily they enter and take hold, until the intellect becomes aware of these things, like pictures and phantoms.[3]

Thus, it was of prime importance that a sufficient supply of quality pictures was available to help the missionary effort. This, of course, was not easy to assure. Importing them was uncertain, haphazard, and expensive, and therefore not a long term option, for there were never enough pictures for every missionary and all the churches, which periodically burned or were torn down. Torrès is already likely to have pushed for a solution, but it was while Cabral was superior of the Japan mission that finally someone was found in Europe who was young, talented, and trained enough to be sent to Japan.

His name was Giovanni Cola (1558–1626), known in Japan as Nicolao. He was born in Nola, in the Kingdom of Naples,[4] and he had entered the Society in December of 1577 at the age of nineteen.[5] It is likely that he had learned to paint from his own father or another close family member, for he was sent to Japan after only two years in Rome during which he is said to have mainly studied engraving and metal relief.[6] His mission was so urgent that he was sent off to Portugal even before his novitiate was completely finished.[7] In Portugal, however, Brother Nicolao found himself forced to spend a year in Evora on account of an outbreak of the plague in Lisbon,[8] but in March of 1581, he was finally able to leave for Japan.[9]

His journey was reasonably fast. He arrived in Cochin on 15 October 1581, reached Goa later that year, and left again for Malacca on 26 April 1582 in the company of his fellow Italian, the Jesuit Francesco Pasio (1553–1612).[10] The latter came from Bologna in northern Italy, was five years Nicolao's senior, and had already been ordained a priest before he had left Portugal in 1578.[11] Pasio was destined to become head of the Japan mission, and Nicolao may be considered his protégé. This is important to note, for from the time of his arrival in Japan we find Nicolao behaving with the willfulness and capriciousness often associated with young artists, but generally not with Jesuit brothers.

The two reached Malacca on 14 June,[12] and then Macao on 7 August 1582.[13] There, they arrived too late to sail for Japan and had to wait until the next monsoon. Nicolao used this time to make a large painting of a Salvator Mundi.[14] The two Jesuits finally arrived in Nagasaki on 27 July 1583 on the carrack of Aires de Miranda.[15] After a few months in Nagasaki, during which he seems to have painted another Salvator Mundi,[16] in December of 1584 we find Nicolao listed as a member of the Azuchi residence, east of the capital.[17]

According to the *Anua* or yearly letter of 1584, Fróis was already dissatisfied with him, but was resigned to the fact that Nicolao could not be forced:

> Brother Giovanni Nicolao, the painter, who has already been here and in India for two years, still has not produced anything else but two altar paintings, one in Nagasaki and one in Arima. As we need more than 50,000 pictures for all the Christian households in Japan, we all beg of your paternity that you may send some brother to Japan with some ready-made plates, materials, and instruments so that we can start printing pictures here to be distributed among our flock. The images that would be most useful at this moment are: one of the Savior with the world in his hand, the Transfiguration, the Resurrection, Christ praying in the Dark, images of Our Lady, and the Adoration of the Infant Christ by the Magi, as well as some images of the saints the size of one sheet of paper, and also a lot of paper, for the Christians here would be greatly consoled with such images.[18]

Clearly, the artist in Nicolao had been resisting calls for the mass-production of Christian images. According to John McCall, he was again in Arima painting and teaching in 1585,[19] but at least the teaching part of this statement is belied in another annoyed remark by Luís Fróis, dated 1 January 1587, to the effect that Nicolao had not done any teaching since he had arrived in Japan three-and-half years earlier.[20] That he was much in demand is certain. During the first ten years of his stay in Japan, we find him almost constantly on the road. By 1586, he is said to have made six more smallish paintings,[21] probably of a size that could be easily carried by traveling missionaries, the ones most in demand. In 1586, he was sent to the Kinai again,[22] where he is listed as a member of the Osaka residence in October.[23]

When Hideyoshi closed down all the Jesuit establishments the next year, Nicolao traveled, like all his fellow Jesuits, back to Kyushu. On 26 January 1589, he is listed as a member of the Arie residence, on the Shimabara peninsula, where the Jesuit College had been moved from Azuchi.[24] In the fall of 1590, we find him in Kazusa, Arima. At this time Nicolao finally agreed to start to make prints from copper engravings on the new press that had just arrived that year from Portugal.[25]

This press had been acquired by Diogo de Mesquita (1553–1614) in the early months of 1586,[26] when he had arrived in Lisbon with the delegation of "junior ambassadors" sent by Alessandro Valignano from Japan in 1582.[27] The Visitor brought the press with him from Goa, on his second visit to Japan in 1590. In November of 1592, just after the destruction of the great church of Nagasaki, Nicolao moved his studio from Kazusa to Shiki, on Amakusa island off Kyushu's west coast. Here, the Jesuits had decided to hide from Hideyoshi what was left of their operations. The establishment included, apart from the painting studio, also the Jesuit seminary. At this time, Nicolao finally seems to have accepted a few Japanese disciples to work under him. The Catalogue of members of the Japan mission of November 1592, mentions the names of two Japanese Brothers, "Votavo Mancio and Mancio João."[28] The printing press had already been moved from Kazusa to Shiki in May of 1591.[29]

The next year, 1593, Nicolao was again moving, this time to Hachirao on the Shimabara peninsula, where the Jesuit seminary was hidden in a forest.[30] By 1595, Fróis is reporting a little more positively about Nicolao's efforts:

> Those who are learning how to paint images in oil or water colors and those who are learn-ing the art of engraving are getting better every day, as you probably have already seen from several images we have sent back to Europe over the past several years. Because of their efforts, Japan is acquiring its share of painted and printed images, which is of no small help and consolation for this Christian community.[31]

The seminary was burned in 1595, and Nicolao was forced to move once more, this time back to Arie in Shimabara. There he remained until the seminary was closed in September of 1597, when, in the wake of the executions in Nagasaki, the persecution was intensifying again.[32] It was in Arie that, in December of 1596, Bishop Martins visited Nicolao's studio, an event reported in the annual letter of that year. The studio seems to have been a regular factory of propaganda material:

> From the printing office the Bishop and his entourage went into the studio of the engravers. The young artists were at work with their gravers. The workroom of the painters stirred up especial admiration. These were of various age levels, and were very numerous. With palette in hand, they stood before the canvases and painted pictures in oils. Over the entrance to their house hung a picture of Mary, which a young nineteen-year old Japanese had made in perfect form.[33]

In 1598, the school was moved to Nagasaki, where that summer, in the back of the Jesuit compound at Morisaki, a splendid new building was prepared. Care was taken, however, to keep it hidden from the eyes of occasional passersby.[34] In October of the same year, it is said that there were already seventy students working there.[35] In 1600, however, the school was again removed to Shiki, then back to Nagasaki, and next to Arima again. By October of 1601, the school was again in Nagasaki.[36] It is hard to under-stand, at this distance, the precise rationale for all these moves, especially the later ones, which occurred after Hideyoshi's death in September of 1598, but they are all likely to be connected with the unsettled circumstances in the years before the great Battle of Sekigahara in the fall of 1600.

In the annual letter of 1602, it is again reported that the chronic dearth of paintings was finally getting solved. A reduction of the number of churches, due to Hideyoshi's persecutions, may have been part of the solution:

> In this city the pupils, sixteen or seventeen in number, who are learning how to paint live in a separate building of the seminary. Two of us supervise them. One [Nicolao] came from Rome some years ago and is now a priest. He has educated such diligent students that the churches in Japan have the richest altar paintings, which are undoubtedly comparable to those of Europe. With these and other images printed in great quantities and distributed among the Christians, the devotion and Christian piety are greatly enhanced in these parts.[37]

The school would remain in Nagasaki until 1614. We can get an idea of how truly versatile Nicolao's hands were, when we read that he was also responsible for building clocks, organs, and other musical instruments. When the great church of Nagasaki received its bell tower in 1603, it was Nicolao who had built the mechanism that showed the time in Roman numerals as well as the twelve characters of the Chinese zodiac. The clock also showed the date in both the Western and the Chinese calendars.[38]

Two post–Tridentine images especially carry the emotional appeal important for the Church: that of a mother with her newborn child and that of a dead man hanging on a cross. At first sight, these two images represent birth and death, a beginning and an end. However, it is revealing to observe that, until Hideyoshi's executions, the second of these two images had remained largely unused, suppressed even, by the Jesuits in Japan. Typically, as we have seen above, when Fróis asked in 1584 for plates to print images in Japan, he did not mention a depiction of the crucifixion. Even in its expurgated form (i.e., the presence of a loincloth), Jesus-on-the-cross is such a crude, sledgehammer-like image it can only be shown with the approval and active support of the worldly authorities. It is an image depicting the very essence of worldly authority: the application of the death penalty.

Among the new converts to Christianity in Mexico, for example, used as they were to gruesome and extremely bloody displays of power, this image was an effective, even civilizing, substitute for what had happened on the steps of the Aztec pyramids. But in Japan, where the stateliness of Buddhist imagery had set the tone for the past thousand years, this image could not be shown without offense to the uninitiated. Doctrinally, even mention of the Eucharist was avoided in the presence of non-believers for fear of being accused of cannibalism. We know, moreover, that often a curtain would be hung over paintings, such as the fifteen stages of the rosary, and that the scene of the crucifixion would be painted, purposely, at the very top where it could remain hidden under a rolled-up curtain even when most of the other stages were being shown.[39]

Here is how such a situation is described in an anti–Christian tract, the *Nanbanji kōhaiki*: "Rolling up a curtain of gold brocade, the priests then showed [the believers] the image of a young woman of exquisite beauty holding a small child which, they instructed orally, was the supreme saint who had suckled on her breast. She had a crown of precious stones on her head and was dressed in a coat studded with the seven gems."[40] It was important that the first impression of the uninitiated should be positive, as expressed here in the phrase "exquisite beauty," and not be the one of horror that a crucifixion might invoke. As in so many European churches, at most the image of the scene on Golgotha may have been abbreviated to the depiction of a *Maria Dolorosa*, with one out-sized tear rolling down a lovely cheek to symbolize all the sorrow of a mother who sees her son executed on the cross.

Thus, the secrecy with which the crucifixion was surrounded had made it into a larger mystery in Japan than elsewhere in the Roman Catholic world at the time. Hideyoshi's insistence that the Franciscans arrested in the Kansai should be executed in Nagasaki thus acquires a new dimension. He was, in fact, providing Christian Nagasaki with a *tableau mourant*: the town's first sustained look at one of the two most essential images of its own religion, multiplied by a factor of twenty-six.

What was Hideyoshi trying to do? It is no use arguing that he was just being a crude and cruel ruler, no different from the Romans who had crucified Christ. On the contrary, for a Japanese unbeliever, he was showing a surprisingly sophisticated knowledge of the religion brought by the European missionaries, a knowledge that was denied in its pictorial form to most Japanese Christians, even in Nagasaki itself. This knowledge Hideyoshi is likely to have acquired through his conversations with the Jesuit interpreter João Rodrigues during the decade following his initial prohibitions of 1587.[41]

These conversations, in themselves, prove that Hideyoshi remained concerned and was keeping a close eye on Nagasaki and the Jesuits. His continuing eagerness to learn about Christian doctrine may even signal a degree of uncertainty on his part about whether he had done the right thing. Therefore, the crucifixions of February 1597, while mainly functioning as threats to the population of Nagasaki, should also be interpreted as containing elements of a brutal demystification and bold challenge to the Jesuits and their converts, to the Spanish of the Philippines, and indirectly to the Crown of Spain and Portugal, as well as to the Pope himself.

If the crucifix and the painted image of the crucifixion thus remained mostly un-shown by the church in Japan, the burden of presenting Christianity's public image fell largely to the Virgin Mary, with or without her holy child. At the very core of this image is a reminder of the universal bliss found at a mother's breast. It is the depiction of her tenderness that counts and explains everything.[42] It is in her image that we find the universal appeal of a remembered emotion merging seamlessly with the specific appeal of Christianity in Japan. At least since 1603, the largest church of Nagasaki was dedicated to Nossa Senhora da Assunção or Our Lady of Ascension, so named after the 15th day of August when Mary was believed to have risen up to Heaven. It was the town's most important festival. It is, of course, not likely to have been just a happy coincidence that She, in this way, also effortlessly displaced O-Bon, the most important Buddhist festival of the year, at a time that the Portuguese ships were sure to be in town.

Over the past millennium, ever since the adoption of Chinese civilization, public morality in Japan had become increasingly drenched in a Confucian doctrine that was anything but women-friendly. In the traditional Chinese view, women have no independent social status. All women are supposed to obey their fathers in their youth, their husbands in their prime, and their oldest sons in their old age. Buddhism had added to this trio of Confucian obligations, another five reasons or "obstructions" that kept women from being able to reach enlightenment. Together these two male sticks to beat females were known in Japan as the Five Obstructions and Three Obligations (*goshō-sanjū*), usually used as an expression of disdain for females, "proving" their inferiority to men.[43]

After the breakdown of the ancient *ritsuryō* state and whatever laws still had protected women's rights to inheritance and property, the rise of warrior culture assured that the position of women in sixteenth century Japan had deteriorated to the point where, to large segments of the population, they were considered little better than cattle at the service of their fathers, brothers, or husbands to further the men's interests. Unwanted babies were similarly disposed of without much sentimentality.

As a result, one can imagine the general consternation caused among the warrior class by the sudden appearance of a religion in Japan advertising a woman as its most central image, stressing her sacred role as a mother and the resulting bond with her child. On the other hand, one can also easily understand the great emotional appeal this image must have had for at least the suppressed, female part of the population in so far as it managed to become exposed to the Christian message.[44] This, in fact, was an attraction so powerful that even Hideyoshi could not prevent several women in his own household from becoming fervent followers.[45]

I conclude that a large percentage of those who were genuinely attracted to the message of the missionaries must have been Japanese women. For them, Christian doctrines such as those of the Immaculate Conception of the Mother of God by means of the Holy Spirit and of Original Sin Expiated by the Lamb of God are unlikely to have provided the dominant motivation. Rather more important must have been the suppressed emotions of the time period itself: those concerning the sanctity of life as well as those involved in the bond between mother and child.

Christian communities were, furthermore, taught to help each other and relieve the plight of the sick and the poor as a condition for being a good Christian. One reason why Nagasaki kept on growing steadily ever since its foundation was, as almost every annual letter reports, its Kyushu-wide reputation for the generosity of its charity. With the Jesuits channeling the profits of the trade with the Portuguese as much as possible into the hands of the Christian merchants of Nagasaki, the latter organized themselves into brotherhoods, such as that of the Misericordia, specifically designed to help the poor and destitute. Here is how a fervent Japanese believer, Lucia de Freitas, about to be executed in Nagasaki in 1622, put it to her brothers: "She told them they should never forget to take care of the poor because [such good deeds] are the seed that enriches the sower, and the more you throw the seed at those in need, the more you gain in a bargain with God Our Lord, to whom we lend our riches, and having Him as our creditor He will pay up without fail."[46]

In other words, if one was poor and destitute in turn-of-the-century Japan, one could try and get to Nagasaki, become a Christian, and somebody would provide the bare necessities until one was able to stand on one's own feet again. This may sound like a mercenary motive for becoming a Christian, but we should not underestimate the power of charity to create real Christians out of people who were desperate and grateful to have been given another chance. This in itself may have been, to many, a miracle providing sufficient proof of the existence of the Christian God. In other words, there existed a whole range of motivations for becoming a Christian. In 1609, the anti–Christian ideologist of the new Tokugawa regime, Hayashi Razan, put it in a nutshell: "They often press their faith upon our people, fooling them, and those who like unusual things and those who depend upon the profits of the marketplace often serve that law."[47]

* * *

A Chinese Madonna: Matsupo/Maso

The Funazu-machi area was known for its cheap accommodations. Japanese merchants, itinerant craftsmen, and sailors would all find temporary accommodation here. Its beach provided a convenient place to go ashore from the type of bark used for travel around Kyushu. Foreigners other than the Portuguese, too, would stay here, particularly the Chinese, but the Spanish, Dutch, and English as well. In a curious notice, the English merchant Richard Cocks, for example, noted on 27 December 1616 in his diary that a Chinese merchant—he calls him the China Captain's Brother, and a little later, Captain Whaw—did not charge the English factory for the one-month stay of one of its employees named Wilmott and his Japanese servants in the "China House" of Nagasaki.[1]

It is certain that we have to look for this China House in the Funazu machi neighborhood. It was probably located in Mukai Funazu-machi, for we have a notice for March of 1620, when a Chinese physician and trader called Ishiya Nikan could be reached there, although he owned a house in nearby Naka-machi.[2] Another indication in this direction is that the English themselves also lodged generally in Mukai Funazu-machi, where they called their usual landlord by his Christian name of Andrea.[3] It is possible that, in 1616, Andrea was not able to provide lodging for Wilmott and his servants, for the landlord of the English seems to have gone on overseas trading voyages himself from time to time.[4] Instead, they must have found lodging in the nearby China House through the good offices of Cocks' trading partner Captain Whaw, or, more correctly transcribed: Captain Hua, whose full name was Ou Hua-yu (?–1621).

As we have seen, Hideyoshi was anxious to encourage overseas trade after his victory in Kyushu and his prohibition of Christianity in 1587. At the same time, he organized the extermination of the pirates along Japan's coastal areas. This was the time when he ordered the attainder of Fukabori Sumimasa,[5] who had a long record of preying on Chinese merchant shipping.[6] Between 1588 and 1592, many Chinese ships again reached Nagasaki. But the Japanese invasion of Korea ruined this early Chinese trade in the Nagasaki area, for when the Koreans requested help from China to repel the Japanese, the Ming emperor responded with a large emergency force. And so the trading activities of the Chinese merchants were restricted again.[7] But it seems that they never ceased completely to come.

By the beginning of the seventeenth century, there is evidence of a small community of Fujianese, who were to remain the main group of Chinese in Nagasaki until the 1630s.[8] Ou Hua-yu was such a Chinese merchant from Fujian. He may have first arrived in Japan in 1595 or 96,[9] and, as Richard Cocks mentions, he was generally known as the "younger brother" of the boss of all the Chinese in Japan, Li Tan, who himself was based in Hirado.[10] This does not necessarily mean that the two were blood relatives, rather that the one had pledged his allegiance to the other, creating a bond "as tight as that between brothers," most likely because they were both from the same city (Quanzhou?) in Fujian province. In 1599, Ou Hua-yu and his "elder brother" are known to have been among the founders of a Chinese cemetery at Inasa, a hamlet outside Nagasaki on the western shore of the bay, right across from Funazu-machi.[11]

According to tradition, a Chinese temple, later known as the Pure Land Sect temple Goshinji, was also built there in 1597.[12] It was the first non–Christian religious structure to be erected since the founding of the Jesuit town. Later, the temple's nickname became *kaburaya* or "whistling arrow," as if to commemorate the coming of an anti–Christian offensive from the Buddhists, starting from here.[13] At first, the "temple" is likely to have been a simple structure dedicated to the goddess Ma-tsu or Ma-tsu-po (known in Japanese as Maso), who protects Chinese sailors at sea. After 1614, or possibly even before, her shrine may have been moved to the "China House" in Mukai-Funazu machi, whence it later ascended the foothills of Mt. Tateyama. In 1628 it found a place inside the Fukusaiji temple, newly built by the Fujianese of Zhangzhou in Shimo Chikugo-machi.[14]

To understand the ambiguous nature and the essential liminality of the Funazu-machi neighborhood, it is necessary to go a little deeper into the religion of the Chinese at this point. The Nagasaki historian Nishikawa Jōken wrote in 1695:

> The first of the Chinese deities is Maso. The Chinese ships coming to Nagasaki will shoot their cannon when they reach the entrance of the bay. When they drop their anchors, they sound their cymbals and drums to celebrate. After unloading their cargo, they take the image of Maso and bring it ashore. When the time has come to sail back home, they bring her back on board sounding their cymbals, drums, and trumpets all along the way. Upon the deity's

arrival at her ship, all the other boats in the harbor also sound their cymbals and drums. This is a Chinese custom.[15]

At first, these statues of Ma-tsu may have been placed in the inns where the Chinese stayed in Nagasaki or in the houses of their Japanese business relations. Later they were likely to have been placed in the meeting hall (or "China House") for the Chinese speaking the same dialect. The Western literature on Ma-tsu and the spread of her cult, summarizing and interpreting a veritable mountain of Chinese sources, is unusually varied and complex.[16] Here space will not allow anything but the most cursory introduction to this subfield of Chinese religion. I will limit myself to those points that seem important to understand the Chinese of Christian Nagasaki at the beginning of the seventeenth century.

Studies of the Ma-tsu cult usually start with an account of a semi-historical personage from the Lin family in Fujian, who would during the Ming dynasty also become known as Tien-fei, the Heavenly Concubine, which was later upgraded during the Qing to Tien-hou or Heavenly Consort.[17] Her birth and death dates are usually given as 960–987.[18] James Watson has reminded us of Wolfram Eberhard's conclusion, in his study of the aboriginal cultures of South China, that such traditional accounts might be the result of a Han cooptation of a water spirit cult of the seafaring Yueh people.[19] However this may be, the official Chinese tradition started during the Tang dynasty.

Professor Yang sums up the Ma-tsu tradition as follows:

> While still a young girl, she was able to perform miracles, and she refused to be married. Soon after her death, sailors struggling in storm and other dangers on the high seas frequently claimed to have seen the apparition of her image, which led the ship to safety. In subsequent centuries down to the modern period, stories of the miracles of T'ien-hou continued to be told by sailors returning from dangerous voyages up and down the China coast. As a consequence, there were temples dedicated to this goddess in all coastal provinces as well as in localities along major navigable rivers.[20]

There are two elements in Ma-tsu's story that have puzzled Western researchers for generations. On the one hand, in most versions, there is an overt reference to and connection of Ma-tsu with the Buddhist female deity of mercy, Kuan-yin (Jpn. Kannon). On the other hand, there is the unspoken suggestion that she died a virgin. This is fleshed out in some detail in more elaborate accounts, where she is said to have died wearing a red dress on the ninth day of the ninth month.[21] These details suggest that one crucial element was left out of the official accounts, i.e., that Ma-tsu committed suicide and chose to die on a specific day, one of the five magical days of the year, the ninth day of the ninth month, which was known for its particular promise that "If you ascend to a high place ... you can avert disaster."[22]

For this reason, when Chinese sailors after a close brush with death at sea would manage to get back to shore, they would report that they had seen Ma-tsu in her red dress in the clouds, on top of the mast,[23] or just hovering over the sea.[24] "All of a sudden," says one account, "a bright light appeared in the sky, the clouds opened and a human form appeared on top of the mast. She remained there for a while busy with something, then took the helm and only disappeared after the danger had passed."[25] James Watson reports, further, that in many of the oral versions of this myth, it is clear that Ma-tsu not only saved sailors at sea, but also had "a special relationship with spinsters and other unmarried women."[26] In some accounts, she refused to marry and "became notable as a seer or medium. One oral account from Taiwan reports that she voluntarily ended her life with a total fast. A number of women in the New Territories of Hong Kong maintained quite firmly to me that T'ien Hou killed herself rather than marry an older man chosen by her parents."[27]

What seems to point further in this direction is the red gown in which she is said to have died and in which she appears to sailors at sea. Watson writes: "the appearance of a female spirit in a red gown is an unambiguous symbol of suicide in Chinese peasant society. Women who have reached the end of their patience sometimes commit suicide in a red wedding gown. This extra measure gives the deceased's spirit awesome powers." The red wedding dress, says Watson, "symbolizes the liminality of a woman as she is transferred between two families. Suicide in this liminal state creates an uncontrollable ghost, one without ties to any kin group."[28]

In other words, the historical Ma-tsu may have wanted to take revenge on those who wanted to marry her off against her will by committing suicide on the night before her wedding, and she took care to do so on a day which would reverberate to maximum effect throughout Chinese history. Seen in this light, her elevation over the centuries to a goddess of ever-higher rank may be explained as having been fueled by a continuously felt need to placate her angry ghost. In this way, the historical Ma-tsu acquired a status in Chinese society quite different from, but, where the veneration in which she was held is concerned, quite comparable to the Virgin Mary in Europe.

By mid–Ming times, Ma-tsu's cult had spread throughout Fujian, into Vietnam, the Malaysian peninsula and beyond.[29] The spread of the cult, both within and outside of Fujian was further aided by the deity's adoption as the patron deity of the Fujian merchant guilds,[30] the members of which founded many temples in her honor in overseas Chinese communities.[31] In these overseas shrines, typically, Ma-tsu is accompanied on each side by two other divinities: Thousand-Mile-Eye and Good-Wind-Ear.

These are said to be brothers, and are both hideously ugly. Thousand-Mile-Eye is a giant with an indigo blue face, eyes like shining lights, and an enormous mouth with protruding fangs. Thousand-Mile-Eye has a hand shielding his eyes as if he were scanning the horizon.[32] Good-Wind-Ear has a body like the shell of a pumpkin, a mouth like a pot of blood with teeth like daggers. He has scarlet hair and two horns on his head. They are armed with halberds.[33] Good-Wind-Ear has turned his head a little and cups his ear with his hand to better listen. De Groot writes: "One should not look too far for the origins of these two figures. It is probable that they are the rather bizarre personifications of the two principal qualities that distinguish a good sailor, that of paying attention to the least breeze, and that of being able to see far ahead and know how to choose the shortest route through the waters."[34]

Europeans have always been surprised to learn about the Virgin Ma-tsu, because of her similarities to the Virgin Mary. Just like Mary was the Mother of Jesus, Ma-tsu was called "Holy Mother of the Heavens" and "Queen of Heaven." Almost all Chinese ships

> have her image on board in a small open shrine on the port side. Mornings and evenings incense and candles are lit for her, and when the ship sails out on a journey it is usual to make her a large offering. On the days dedicated to the festival of this deity, seaports are decorated with colorful banners and greenery. Plays are enacted in her honor on the large ships and small vessels cooperate to stage their own. On all ships large or small offerings are made according to the means and degree of devotion of the crews."[35]

The confusion about this Chinese goddess has always been greatest in Macao, which was originally established on a promontory with a shrine dedicated to her. In truth, when

Maso and Her Two Guardians (Nagasaki Ten-kōdō).

the Portuguese spoke of their city as the "City of the Mother of God in China," they were identifying, consciously or unconsciously, Ma-tsu with their own Virgin Mary.[36]

That these were two very different deities, only those who lived in China could know. Thus, just like the Jesuits did in Macao, where everyone pretended that Ma-tsu was nothing but an imperfect Chinese version of the Virgin Mary (who, by the way, is also said to help sailors at sea), the Jesuits in Nagasaki may have taken the position that a shrine dedicated to her could serve as a first step to the conversion of the Chinese. This is one solution to the dilemma that the early existence of a shrine or temple in Inasa poses, and it includes the (speculative) possibility that such a shrine or shrines may have existed in Funazu-machi as well, even before 1614. The presence of Maso, possibly already on the spot where later the Fukusaiji would be built in 1628,[37] furthermore, may explain the real reason behind the expansion, as a religious counterweight, of the Lazarus chapel right next door around this time. As we have seen, this chapel had existed in this neighborhood since 1592. It was upgraded to a full-fledged parish church, the São João Bautista, with its own native priest, Paulo dos Santos (1570?–1637), in 1606.[38]

In view of this history of confusion around and deliberate fudging of the status of this Chinese goddess, it is not surprising that when the Tokugawa Bakufu finally decided to crack down on Christianity in Nagasaki, Maso was suspected of being a Christian deity in disguise. This was the reason why she needed to be hidden away in Buddhist temples that the Chinese started to build in the 1620s.[39] When that did not seem convincing enough, Chinese Obaku Zen Buddhist monks with impeccable pedigrees were invited by the Chinese community in Nagasaki to take charge of these temples.[40] Ironically, the Tokugawa Bakufu was so taken by these men that the Zen sect they brought to Japan received its official sponsorship and was able to establish other temples outside Nagasaki in the Kinai.[41] Possibly it is for this reason that Maso's worship has survived in Nagasaki to this day.

*   *   *

The Eyes and Ears of Ieyasu: Ogasawara Ichi'an

Where the foreign trade was concerned, Hideyoshi and his successor, Tokugawa Ieyasu, were convinced that the trade brought by the Portuguese should serve their purposes, not those of the Jesuits. The Taikō had tried, with mixed success, to impose a privileged position for himself as the first buyer of each cargo brought to Japan. After him, Ieyasu did the same, sending agents from his household to buy foreign goods in the city. While Ieyasu was setting up his new administration, he had a great need for foreign goods, especially silks, both in quantity and quality. It was the task of the official he sent to Nagasaki to purchase these goods at the lowest possible price before Japanese merchants could buy their share.[1]

With suspicion of the missionaries on the increase, these agents also became charged with intelligence gathering, and later with the enforcing of measures to counter the power of the padres. As Bishop Cerqueira wrote in 1606:

> There came to this city of Nagasaki a person closely connected with the Kubo Sama [Ieyasu] … with the competence and power, given him by the same Kubo, to lay down the law in the dealings and trade of the Portuguese *nao*, which at that moment had come to this port, and to supervise the government of this city for the time he was here; and apart from this he was also given the task to gather information and inquire into everything going on in these lower parts of Japan in order to be able to inform the Kubo later, as the watchful spy that he was."[2]

The term *olheiro* ("overseer"), derived as it is from *olho* (Port. "eye") and translated here as "watchful spy," suggests that Bishop Cerqueira was trying to render the Japanese term *me-tsuke* (i.e., someone who "attaches" his eyes to things) or *yoko-me* (lit. someone "looking from the corner of one's eye," or "sidelong glance" > "spy") with the closest Portuguese term he knew. Such terms employed to designate these shogunal agents reflected their function inside a system of government for the city that had started out, as we have seen, largely autonomous, but which during the first half of the seventeenth century grad-ually became more and more subjected to these shogunal agents.[3]

The usual term for these officials during the reign of Hideyoshi was *daikan*,[4] a term which seems to have been in use during the administrations of Ieyasu and Hidetada as well.[5] During the rule of the first Tokugawa shoguns, however, the term *bugyō* was employed interchangeably with *daikan*, as we can see in Cocks' diary when he uses the phrase "the emperours dico [*daikan*] or Bongew [*bugyō*]."[6] Other terms were *komabutsu goyō* or "[official] in charge of foreign goods," and *karabune no ito bugyō* or "official of the silk of the ship[s] from China."[7] Again, in the contemporary sources of the early Kan'ei period, i.e., the 1620s, there still was no official title for the shogun's representative in Nagasaki, but slowly, especially in Nagasaki itself, a preference appeared for the use of the term *Nagasaki bugyō*.[8] It was only from 1638 onwards that the title *Nagasaki bugyō* was used systematically to indicate the officials sent out from Edo to supervise the admin-istration of the city of Nagasaki.

But if there was no agreement on the official title of the highest authority in Nagasaki (we shall call him here the Nagasaki Governor), there certainly was, from early on, a competitive awareness among the Japanese officials involved in the government of Nagasaki that such a post existed. We notice them jockeying with each other behind the scenes for the shogun's trust in order to get appointed. In the first ten years of the Toku-gawa Bakufu, eight men and one woman were directly involved, to varying degrees, in this competition. Some of them honored family ties above all else, while others committed themselves to temporary alliances if it suited their purpose of the moment. Implacable enemies were created by this competition, and although no deaths are officially recorded in connection with it, at least two of these protagonists suddenly disappear without a trace or explanation from our sources.

Although Terazawa was, in name and title, still Nagasaki's chief official, by 1601 Ieyasu had second thoughts about letting him continue to govern the city in his name. He needed someone more closely allied to himself, whom he could trust to always provide him with accurate information. In 1600, when Horatio Neretti had trouble selling his 2500 piculs of raw silk (instead of the usual 1500 or 1600 piculs, or between ninety and ninety six thousand kilograms),[9] the Jesuits had been scrambling for capital in Nagasaki. Without the capital of the great merchants from the Kinai, who had stayed away this year because of the great battle looming between eastern and western Japan, the Christian merchants of Nagasaki were unable to come up with the necessary funds to buy such an outsized cargo.[10]

Therefore, the Portuguese asked Ieyasu's help in disposing of their accumulated wares. After his victory at Sekigahara, Japan's new ruler responded by sending his retainer Ogasawara Ichi'an to Nagasaki. We have no birth or death dates for Ichi'an. He does not appear in that great compilation of Bakufu retainers, the *Kansei Chōshū Shokafu*. All we know is that he was somehow related to the old daimyo of Mikawa, and was living in seclusion as a *rōnin* in the Higashiyama area of Kyoto. As he cannot be found in any genealogy, he may have committed some kind of crime or been involved in a fight, for which he was cut off from his family and exiled to Kyoto.[11]

It is likely that he took the tonsure at this time, and became a Buddhist of the Ikkō sect of the Pure Land denomination.[12] Thus, he was known as the lay monk Ogasawara Tamemune Nyūdō Ichi'an. The choice of the Ikkō sect may seem strange at first sight for a close associate of Ieyasu, who had done battle with the sect in his younger years,[13] but it may indicate that one of his functions was to keep an eye on this trouble-prone form of Buddhist religious practice. As a lay monk, Ichi'an was a fervent practitioner of the tea ceremony. This allowed him to get to know all the great merchants of the Kinai.[14]

Apart from his well-known connection with Nagasaki, Japanese scholars have been able to come up with only two other incidents in Ichi'an's life. Between 14 and 17 June 1582, Ichi'an seems to have visited the Tokugawa retainer Matsudaira Ietada (1555–1600),[15] who wined and dined him for four days. Clearly, Ietada's purpose was to obtain inside information on the situation in Kyoto for Ieyasu. Therefore, at least one scholar has concluded that, in reality, Ichi'an was Ieyasu's spy stationed in Kyoto, who had disguised himself as the dissipated lay monk Ichi'an, interested in the tea ceremony.[16]

Thus, when almost twenty years later Ieyasu had achieved what he had originally set out to do, he may have rewarded Ichi'an for his long-time service with a mission to Nagasaki that could be profitable in more ways than one. Ichi'an must have left Kyoto in the company of a number of great merchants shortly after the Japanese New Year of Keichō 6 (1601). Among the men accompanying him was Hasegawa Nami'emon Shige-yoshi (1562–1606), the oldest of three brothers who later also played important roles as "eyes and ears" of Ieyasu in Nagasaki.[17]

Obtaining the support in Nagasaki of the *machi-doshiyori* (or mayors) Takagi Luis and Takashima Jeronimo, Ichi'an was able, between the months of February and April, to broker a deal for his consortium of merchants to buy the whole Portuguese silk cargo outright at a very high price.[18] The success of this mission contrasted sharply with the failure of Terazawa's agent in Nagasaki to buy silk of the very best quality for the new hegemon of Japan at this same time. At first, the Jesuit interpreter João Rodrigues was blamed for this.[19] It is likely that, later that year, Ichi'an was among the "various persons," who helped exonerate Rodrigues before Ieyasu.[20] Emphatic support for Rodrigues' innocence by a long-time retainer like Ichi'an would serve to make Terazawa's sudden loss of influence with Japan's new ruler a little more understandable.[21]

No new carrack came to Nagasaki in 1601. Three ships had left India, but one perished on the coast of Canton. The two others were caught in the same typhoon and arrived in Macao with so much damage that they could not continue their voyage.[22] The year after, in 1602, Dom Paulo de Portugal finally came to Japan in person. His carrack reached the Gotō islands on 11 July,[23] and Nagasaki a few days later. If he expected to sell his silk at the same high prices of the year before, he was in for a rude surprise. The 2500 piculs brought by Neretti had flooded the market. Those who had bought in 1601 at high prices did not want buy any more, for fear they might be ruined.[24]

Pretending to have been misled by the Portuguese as to the value of the raw silk, these merchants now lodged a complaint with Ieyasu against the Portuguese, which involved the Jesuit missionaries. Ieyasu ordered an investigation, at which Rodrigues represented the Jesuits. In the end, an amicable settlement was arranged with low prices paid for the silk this year. It is hard to see what actually occurred, but Professor Nakada has proposed a solution that has the virtue of explaining the appearance of a new trade organization monopolizing the silk trade with Macao, the *itowappu nakama*.[25]

Even though, he writes, Dom Paulo had not brought an especially large cargo, the merchants allied to Ichi'an would not have been able to make a profit if others were allowed to buy this year's cargo at low prices. Therefore, they may have petitioned Ieyasu to decree that only those who bought last year would be allowed to purchase the silk this year, at the lowest possible price.[26] From the fact that this was indeed the result, we know that from then on it would be these men, mostly the friends of Ogasawara Ichi'an from Kyoto, Osaka and, Sakai allied with the principal silk traders of Nagasaki, who would dominate the silk trade, set the price of the silk products, and provide the Tokugawa shoguns with the tool they needed to manipulate the trade brought by the Portuguese. It was a seminal moment in the history of the Portuguese-Japanese relationship.

At the Japanese New Year of 1603, João Rodrigues and Murayama Tōan (1566–1619) made a New Year's visit to Ieyasu as the representatives of Nagasaki. For his efforts to bring about the settlement of the year before (and thus having cooperated with the Bakufu against the interests of the Portuguese), Rodrigues was honored by being received before all other monks who had come to see Ieyasu. He was allowed to sit closer to Japan's ruler than even the daimyo.[27] Murayama is mentioned by Avila Girón as the man who had originated the idea of the bulk purchase of the silk by privileged merchants. Now they were asked to report on Terazawa's tenure as Governor of Nagasaki. Rodrigues, at least, is likely to have eloquently represented the exasperation of the Jesuits with the man who had destroyed their churches and caused them so many headaches over the past thirteen years.

As a result of this report, Terazawa was relieved from his post,[28] while Murayama became one of the "mayors" governing the internal administration of Nagasaki.[29] The departure of Terazawa as Nagasaki *daikan* was also symbolically important as a change of guard from Hideyoshi's to Ieyasu's rule in Nagasaki. It also marks the point of divergence between Murayama and the Jesuits, for with an appointment by Ieyasu, Murayama was no longer dependent on the padres for his position and influence in Nagasaki. This is the first information we have of Tōan occupying any official post in Nagasaki. It is unlikely that he was already made *daikan* by Hideyoshi, as Japanese sources dating from the eighteenth century have it.[30]

Rodrigues, on the other hand, with his appointment as buyer for Ieyasu's household and his position as Procurador of the Society, had become the chief intermediary between the Japanese and the Portuguese traders, and the most powerful Jesuit in Nagasaki to boot. Possibly in recognition of this, he had been allowed by Alessandro Valignano to take his fourth vow on 10 July 1601,[31] i.e., a mere five years after his ordination in Macao in 1596.[32] From now on, among the Jesuits in Nagasaki, Rodrigues ranked only just below Valignano, the Visitor, Luis Cerqueira, the Bishop, and Francisco Pasio, the Vice-provincial (who had replaced Pedro Gómez in the fall of 1600).

In this way, the stage had been set for a clash between Murayama Tōan and João Rodrigues, both eager to increase their influence with Ieyasu at the expense of the other. That same New Year of 1603 further saw the official appointment of Ogasawara Ichi'an as the new "governor" of Nagasaki. On the surface, this may seem an extraordinary advance for somebody of his background: a dissipated monk was appointed to a position that had heretofore only been given to samurai of daimyo rank. The appointment, then, reinforces the impression that Ichi'an may have been serving Ieyasu in some secret capacity for a long time.[33] On the other hand, in view of the fact that Nagasaki represented the hub of Japan's foreign relations, and the fact that monks had been involved in the conduct of diplomacy since long before the Tokugawa came to power, the choice of Ichi'an was not all that unusual.[34]

On the contrary, the choice of a Buddhist monk as the administrator of Christian Nagasaki served notice to the town that the Christian monopoly over the souls of the city's inhabitants was about to end.[35] Here too, we see discord looming, and it will not surprise anyone to learn that Ichi'an's tenure ended in a fight with the city's local administrators, the Christian *otona*. For the moment, however, Ichi'an left for Nagasaki with his newly acquired following of ten *yoriki* or samurai followers, one of the perks of the position of Nagasaki Governor under the Tokugawa.[36] His task was three-fold: his first duty was to cooperate with Rodrigues to buy silk for Ieyasu, to represent the Bakufu's policies towards the foreigners and regulate the trade they conducted at Nagasaki. Ichi'an, therefore, was known as the "director of the business with the Portuguese."[37] It was in order to be able to function smoothly as the privileged buyer for the shogun that the new Governor was given the power he wielded. Ichi'an's second, and more covert, duty was to deal with the problem of Christianity in Japan. As we have seen in the last section, the Chinese may have been able to establish a foothold for Ma-tsu in Funazu-machi in the beginning of the seventeenth century. It is not impossible that they received permission to do so from the lay monk Ichi'an.

No Portuguese ship reached Nagasaki in 1603. On 30 July of that year, the carrack *Santa Catarina* belonging to Captain Major Gonçalo Rodrigues de Souza, had been ready to leave for Japan, but she was captured by Dutch corsairs just outside of Macao's harbor. Her cargo, sold at Amsterdam, yielded 3.5 million guilders.[38] In 1604, the Captain Major was João Cayado de Gamboa, who left Macao on 19 July and arrived in Nagasaki on 14 August.[39] The Bakufu had prepared for his arrival. On 31 May of that year, Ieyasu's secretaries Honda Kōzuke no kami Masazumi (1565–1637) and Itakura Iga no kami Katsushige (1545–1624) signed an order that no merchants other than the privileged ones who had been buying the silk in 1601 and 1602 were allowed to enter Nagasaki until the silk price had been set.[40]

Upon Cayado's arrival, the cargo seems to have been sealed and heavily guarded until the authorities at Suruga had been informed.[41] The precedents of the previous years were now, clearly with Ieyasu's approval, used to establish a new way to conduct the trade. The Portuguese were forced to agree on a bulk price for the silk before they were allowed to sell any of their other wares. The new system became known as the *pancada* and in Japanese as the *itowappu* system. It immediately resulted in lower profits for the Portuguese and gave the new Governor ample opportunity to line his own pockets.[42] The Portuguese did, of course, everything in their power to try and subvert it by selling clandestinely to free-lance traders through the intermediary of the Jesuits.

For this reason, Ichi'an's power was strengthened in 1604 and 1605 with such measures as the registration of everyone aboard the incoming ships, the making of a complete inventory of the cargo, the sealing of the bales until permission was given to unload, the stationing of officials on the ships to enforce these measures, etc.[43] Ichi'an, moreover, was confronted with the same problems presented by the different jurisdictions of Nagasaki's Inner and Outer Towns, with which Terazawa Hirotaka (and before him the Jesuits) had already wrestled. In Bishop Cerqueira's words: "it happened sometimes that criminals who had broken the laws of Nagasaki only needed to take one step to find themselves safely in the district belonging to the Lord of Ōmura."[44]

Just as was the case in the Funazu-machi area where the Chinese had their meeting hall, the power of the Jesuits reached only imperfectly into the lower reaches of the Nakajima River. The Jesuits had long considered the right bank a place for the town to expand. They may have hoped they would somehow be able to induce Sumitada (and later his son Yoshiaki) to cede this area to the Society as well. Although after Hideyoshi's takeover of the town, this became a moot point in so far as the Jesuits were concerned: it did not stop the area from being rapidly developed, just as the planners in the Society had foreseen.

Because Uchimachi had to be provided with daily necessities (even water!) from Ōmura, we find that the streets built between the city walls and the Nakajima River were mostly concentrations of suppliers of certain bulk goods. Apart from the ancient fishing village that became known as the fish market of Uo-no-machi, there was, for example, Zaimoku-machi, the street of the lumber dealers. Next door, in Kōya-machi, lived the cloth dyers, in Fukuro-machi the rice dealers, in Sakaya-machi the wine and liquor dealers, in Daiku-machi the carpenters, and in Okeyamachi those who manufactured tubs of all sizes.

All the people of these streets considered themselves to be respectable professionals, and so here the streets were named after their professions. As Ōmura was officially a Christian domain, there was no problem in enforcing baptism for everyone living in Sotomachi or the Outer Town, as the area slowly had become known during the 1590s. Ichi'an and the Nagasaki members of the silk monopoly guild (*itowappu nakama*), including Murayama Tōan as well as João Rodrigues, who represented the Jesuits, could all agree that it was essential for the government of Nagasaki that Sotomachi be subject to the same regulations as Uchimachi.

This became all the more acute with the establishment of the new trading system, which seemed to encourage smuggling goods from the Portuguese ships to the territory of Ōmura Yoshiaki to be sold there at higher prices to Japanese merchants not belonging to the *itowappu nakama* group. Therefore, when Ichi'an returned to Suruga in the fall of 1604, he presented Ieyasu with persuasive arguments to confiscate Sotomachi and add it to the *tenryō*. One year later, with a *hōsho* (official document) issued by five officials of Ieyasu's cabinet, the confiscation became a fact on 23 October 1605.[45]

It goes without saying that the expropriation was a major economic blow to Ōmura Yoshiaki, who although "indemnified" for his loss of Sotomachi with land producing a tax income of a little under 1900 *koku* from five villages around Urakami,[46] lost the much higher income he received from taxes, supplying Uchimachi with water and other essential commodities, trade, and smuggling. It is no wonder that he set out to blame and take revenge on those that he could harm. Ichi'an with his close connection to Ieyasu was out of his reach, and so were the *machi-doshiyori* as officials of the *tenryō*. The Jesuits were another matter, however, and to Yoshiaki their involvement in the whole affair seemed clear. Already during the summer of 1605, while the matter was still under discussion between Bakufu retainers in Kyoto, Yoshiaki, who was in the city as well, started to suspect the Jesuits of being behind the whole idea.[47]

It is likely (although for obvious reasons undocumented) that the Society had been pestering him about Sotomachi since he had succeeded his father as the lord of Ōmura in 1587.[48] Next, at Ieyasu's insistence and because of his disgust over having Sotomachi taken away from him, Yoshiaki ordered the padres out of his domain on 24 February 1606,[49] and renounced Christianity himself a little later.[50] It is certain that, by this early act of apostasy, he safeguarded the Ōmura domain for himself and his descendants. Yoshiaki ordered the common people of his domain to become members of the Jōdo sect.[51] Taking his cue from Katō Kiyomasa,[52] he and his retainers became members of the Nichiren sect in November of 1606.[53]

In the Jesuit archive in Rome, there exists a document in Spanish with the verbose title *Translation of a letter written by Ogasawara Ichi'an, who came on behalf of Daifu*

Sama [i.e., Tokugawa Ieyasu] *as Governor of Nagasaki to deal with the ship of the Portuguese and the other foreign ships sailing to this port of Nagasaki.*[54] This is the only document supposedly written by Ichi'an that has been preserved, and its general drift is clear. Its stated purpose was to declare on paper that the Society of Jesus had had no involvement in the Sotomachi/Urakami exchange that had angered Yoshiaki so much.

Although purporting to be "a translation," the Japanese original has not been preserved. The "translation," moreover, does not show the terseness characteristic of Japanese documents. On the contrary it is extremely repetitive and contains several expressions that may be doubted to have been in the vocabulary of Ieyasu's spy.[55] However, if there was a need for all this smoke, we may be sure there was a fire somewhere. The matter is obliquely referred to in the third paragraph of the document. The most important step in the process that culminated in the confiscation of Sotomachi had been when Ichi'an, sometime in late 1604, had convinced Ieyasu of the necessity for such a move.

As Ichi'an himself wrote (according to this Spanish document): "I myself made a sketch of the city and the township of Ōmura Dono [= Sotomachi] and showed it to His Majesty, informing him in detail of everything that I had seen and experienced." Thus, it seems that the key to convincing Ieyasu had been "a sketch of the city and the township of Ōmura Dono." Where had this "sketch" so suddenly come from? It is unlikely that, in the short time he spent in Nagasaki, Ichi'an would have had the time to spare for such a complicated project as making an accurate map of the area around Nagasaki Bay, quite apart from having the desire, manpower, and ability to execute it.

On the other hand, an up-to-date map of Nagasaki and its environment must have been kept in the Jesuit compound at Morisaki. Therefore, if a map was shown to Ieyasu, it almost certainly originated with the Jesuits. Most likely it was Rodrigues himself who had provided Ichian with the map in question,[56] but it was important for the Society to deny his involvement to the outside world.[57]

* * *

Anti-Christian Cabal: The Hasegawa Siblings

Although Ichi'an had been successful in the matter of adding Sotomachi to Nagasaki's administration (something that the Jesuits and Terazawa had failed to accomplish over the past two decades or so), he was unable to hold on to his job as Governor. Maybe his fall was caused by the envy of others at Ieyasu's court. With the transfer of Sotomachi to the *tenryō*, the stakes in the power game around Nagasaki had been raised immeasurably.[1] The enlargement greatly strengthened the power of the Governor (at least while he was in Nagasaki), but Ichi'an, who had made many enemies and had few allies, was probably an easy target in Fushimi and Suruga. At this point, after the transfer of Sotomachi, he was up against, among others, the powerful alliance of the Hasegawa siblings, one sister and three brothers.

It is probable that the key figure of the alliance was the girl, O-Natsu no kata (1581–1660), who became Ieyasu's concubine in 1597 when she was sixteen years old and the future hegemon of Japan was fifty-four. She was a daughter of Hasegawa Saburōzaemon Fujinao, himself a son of Shindō Yoshitoshi, a member of the Kitabatake family of court nobles.[2] Fujinao had served the Hōjō until 1590, and after their fall he had retired to his home in Ise.[3] O-Natsu soon made herself indispensable to Ieyasu. Only two years after entering his household, she was already successful in getting a plum appointment for her oldest brother, Nami'emon Shigetoshi (1562–1606), who was sent in 1599 by Ieyasu as chief administrator to Sado Island, famous for its goldmines.[4] We have already noted above his subsequent appointment in 1601 to accompany Ichi'an to Nagasaki as a buyer for Ieyasu.[5]

In this same function he again went to Nagasaki in 1605 with the title of *sōyaku*,[6] or "counterpart" to Ichi'an.[7] That year, the two men bought fifty thousand *kin* (30,000 kilograms) of raw silk on Ieyasu's behalf to be sent to Fushimi Castle.[8] It is likely that such bulk purchases of the Bakufu were conveyed to the Kinai with boats and labor of the western daimyo. Now such services were no longer requested by a letter from the hegemon, but the ability to requisition them had become part of the power of the Nagasaki Governor.[9]

In 1606 this power of the Nagasaki Governor vis-à-vis the western daimyo was further expanded with a decree ordering that Chinese ships arriving in the domains of the western daimyo should be inspected and a list of their cargo should be made, which was to be sent forthwith to Nagasaki in order to be reported to the ex-shogun at Sunpu Castle in Shizuoka. Until the Nagasaki Governor had been informed of what goods to purchase from the ship, trade should be halted. The Governor could send someone to the domain in question to inspect the ship, or he could order the ship to come to Nagasaki.[10] This decree not only strengthened the Bakufu's hold over foreign policy,[11] it also provided opportunities to interfere in the internal affairs of all coastal domains, which so far had only marginally been incorporated into the new state.[12]

In the company of Ichi'an and Hasegawa Nami'emon traveling to Nagasaki in the spring of 1605, there had also been Nami'emon's younger brother Chūbei Fujitsugu (?–1665).[13] His is the most shadowy presence in the family alliance. He may not have been as ambitious as his two brothers (he survived them both by about half a century) and he must have been the youngest of the three, although the year of his birth is not known.[14] He had already accompanied his older brother on his mission to Sado Island in 1599,[15] and he is said to have visited Nagasaki every year as Ieyasu's silk buyer,[16] but it is not quite clear when these yearly visits started and when they came to an end.

In any case, we read in one of the Jesuits' letters that "two principal persons" had come to Nagasaki to buy "various merchandise" for Ieyasu.[17] Hindered ("impediti") by the Procurador (i.e., Rodrigues), they had been unable to accomplish their "designs," and for this reason submitted to Ieyasu "a treatise of forty-eight chapters against Rodrigues in particular and the Society in general."[18] We are probably justified in recognizing the Hasegawa brothers in these "two principal persons."

The Jesuits were always vulnerable targets at Ieyasu's court. What complicates the matter here is that Hasegawa Nami'emon may have started his move for the position of Nagasaki Governor by a side attack upon the Jesuits, whom he knew to be allied, temporarily at least, to his real target, Ichi'an. By now, Nami'emon knew all the key players in Nagasaki: the *otona* of Uchimachi, Murayama Tōan, *otona* (or *daikan*) of Sotomachi, and the Jesuits. Through his sister, he was intimately familiar with the alliances around the ex-shogun himself in Fushimi and Sunpu, and Shogun Hidetada in Edo.

Then, in the spring of 1606, Ichi'an recommended that Ieyasu receive Bishop Cerqueira, who had already been in Japan for eight years but had never dared come to

Honshu yet.[19] This was probably a mistake on Ichi'an's part, for it made his temporary alliance with the Jesuits public. That summer of 1606 Ichi'an seems to have traveled to Nagasaki in the company of another brother of O-Natsu and Nami'emon, Sahyōe Fujihiro (1568–1617).[20] Sahyōe's task is described as *komabutsu goyō*, i.e., he was "in charge of foreign goods."[21] At the same time, Chūbei and a member of another old merchant family associated with Ieyasu, Chaya Kiyotsugu, were also sent as *mekiki* or "connoisseurs" of silk.[22] The Hasegawa family and the Chaya family had long been closely linked.[23]

Conspicuously missing from this line-up of Bakufu officials coming to Nagasaki in 1606 is Nami'emon, who is said to have died on 29 August in Kyoto that very year.[24] It is unclear how or why he disappeared so suddenly from the scene, a fact that arouses our suspicion that there may have been more to this death than we are told. That summer the Portuguese ship arrived in Nagasaki on 14 August after having weathered a typhoon on 31 July.[25] Its Captain Major was Dom Diogo de Vasconcelos,[26] whose ship was extraordinarily well-armed with forty pieces of artillery.[27] Again, the negotiations of the Portuguese with the elders of the silk guild seemed to go nowhere, and the Japanese side was ready to call it quits and go home.

Without the services of João Rodrigues as an intermediary between the elders and the Portuguese merchants, the trade would have been impossible, writes Francisco Pasio in a letter dated 18 October 1606, soon after the trading season was over.[28] Professor Gonoi Takashi concludes that Hasegawa Sahyōe must have become extremely frustrated that he had been unable to effect a breakthrough in the stalled negotiations by himself, even though he was the one representing Ieyasu.[29] With their elder brother dead but with their sister still very much in place behind Ieyasu, the two Hasegawa brothers, Sahyōe and Chūbei seem to have indicted Ichi'an after the trading season.

The case was heard by the shogun in the first month of the new year of 1607. Rodrigues is said to have tried to intervene on Ichi'an's behalf, but if he did he was not successful.[30] The *machi-doshiyori* Takagi Luis and Takashima Jeronimo are known to have traveled to Sunpu that spring to explain Ichi'an's failure in the accounting of the Nagasaki trade of the year before.[31] It is unclear what exact charges had been brought against him. They may have had to do with the collection of the taxes in Nagasaki, which had become more complicated after Sotomachi had been added to the *tenryō*.[32] Another distinct possibility is that lax supervision on Ichi'an's part had been the cause that a large part of the raw silk imported in 1604 and 1605 had not been sold under the conditions imposed by the new *itowappu* guild and was spoiling the market for the *machi-doshiyori* of Nagasaki, who doubled as members of the *itowappu* guild.[33]

Such charges might have been enough to relieve Ichi'an from his post as Governor of Nagasaki, but the fact that he was exiled to "a distant island," as he was later that year or early in 1608,[34] seems to point in the direction of a graver offense than mere financial impropriety. If he was the long-time associate of Ieyasu that his appointment indicated in the first place, then the punishment of exile must have been the result of a crime that would have resulted in an ignominious death for anyone less well-connected than Ichi'an. Neither the Japanese sources nor those of the Jesuits, however, help us piece together what happened. In any case, the result of Ichi'an's demise as Nagasaki Governor was the appointment of Nami'emon's brother Sahyōe to the position.[35]

The new governor's task was not simple. In Uchimachi and the trade, he would have to deal with his natural opponent, João Rodrigues (representing the Jesuits) and the Town Elders (representing the Nagasaki merchant class and allied to the Jesuits). In

Sotomachi, he had to get along with the *daikan*, Murayama Tōan, who had risen to one of Nagasaki's top positions at the same time as Rodrigues. Both men had almost simultaneously arrived in the area. Rodrigues may have been slightly earlier, having arrived in Japan, i.e., Nagasaki, in 1577.[36] Tōan, on the other hand, was not far behind. We do not know exactly when he first arrived in Nagasaki, but from the fact that he was able to marry into a powerful local family, the Nishi from Ōura,[37] in 1586, he must have arrived in the late 1570s or early 1580s. Five years Tōan's senior, Rodrigues had risen in the Society through his exceptional verbal and social skills. Simultaneously, Tōan had risen in Nagasaki's merchant world to one of the most respected and powerful positions through his wit, shrewd business sense, and charisma.

Tōan's great advantage over Rodrigues was, however, that once in Nagasaki he did not go anywhere else, but was able, during the roughly twenty-five years before 1605, to slowly build up a network of supporters in the city. Rodrigues, having joined the Society in 1578, only arrived to live in the city around 1590, well after Hideyoshi had taken the town away from the Society. As we have seen, Rodrigues, in fact, became the Society's liaison man with Hideyoshi and later also with Ieyasu, but in Nagasaki his influence remained limited to the backrooms of the Jesuit policymakers at Morisaki. In other words, in Nagasaki, Rodrigues was quintessentially a man behind the scenes.

Avila Girón writes that when he came back to Nagasaki in 1607 he found that Murayama Tōan

> had already been appointed [to Nagasaki *daikan*] and knew how to comport himself so well that he became immensely rich and powerful. Because such displays of power often entail disorderly conduct, this man also hurt himself through his lifestyle, particularly by his unbridled pursuit of women, which caused much unpleasantness between him and his wife and sons. He spent money prodigally on these women and kept many of them in different places, although they did not do him much good at all, because he brought back from court many lumps in his loins, of such small sizes that it took him many months before he could get rid of them and even risked his life, and even now he is not quite cured of them.[38]

From 1606 onwards, moreover, the new and implacably anti–Christian *bugyō* Hasagawa Sahyōe came to Nagasaki, where power was divided between him, Rodrigues and Tōan. Naturally, Sahyōe leaned towards Tōan, who, although a Christian, was a layman increasingly at odds with the Jesuits. Just after he had arrived in Nagasaki, Sahyōe needed Tōan more than Tōan needed Sahyōe. Both had received their appointments in their respective jurisdictions from Tokugawa Ieyasu himself. At court in Sunpu, Sahyōe may have been the one with the better connections, but in Nagasaki Tōan outshone him on all fronts. Tōan governed up to forty-six streets as Nagasaki *daikan,* while Sahyōe, as Nagasaki *bugyō*, only ruled nineteen. What is more, the day-to-day government of Sahyōe's territory, *uchimachi*, was in the hands of the town elders, and basically all Sahyōe could do was represent Ieyasu's interests to them. As a non–Christian, Sahyōe was doomed to remain an outsider, eyed with suspicion by the whole city. He needed an ally.

Tōan, on the other hand, had no rivals for power in the outer town. Even though he was not one of the city's founders, he was Nagasaki to his core. The town had been very good to him. Its international atmosphere was the medium in which he had flourished and where he had risen from a humble servant boy in the service of a Hakata merchant, possibly Suetsugu Kōzen himself, to his present position as Ieyasu's representative (*daikan*) in the Outer Town. Tōan may not have been as fluent in Portuguese as Rodriguez had become in Japanese, but a working knowledge of the foreign language was all Tōan needed. After all, he was in Japan.

Charismatic, he was careful to entertain good relations with the forty-six street elders of the outer city.[39] A pragmatist, he was also willing to cooperate with Sahyōe, because he correctly perceived that Sahyōe's presence would help keep the Jesuits off his turf. Sahyōe would turn out to be an implacable opponent of the presence of the Jesuits in Japan. This is perfectly in line with the forty-eight article complaint against the Society that may have been submitted to Ieyasu by his brothers in 1605.

In the years after 1606, moreover, Murayama Tōan is likely to have informed Hasegawa of the mechanics of the trade. In this way, Rodrigues, who was the principal Jesuit official able to circumvent Bakufu control, became a marked man. Behind the scenes, in close proximity to Ieyasu, O-Natsu fostered this common anti–Christian stance of the Hasegawa family as one way to take over power in Nagasaki. Through such moves by the people of his surroundings, we see that Ieyasu was already leaning more and more towards an outspoken, anti–Christian stance, but he certainly received anti–Jesuit input from other directions as well.

Since 1600, when the first Dutch ship had made it all the way across the Pacific to Usuki on the east coast of Kyushu, the Portuguese and the Jesuits were no longer the only Europeans in Japan.[40] One of the crew of the ship, its first mate, the Protestant Englishman William Adams, managed to capture Ieyasu's fancy and was adopted into Ieyasu's retainer band as a full-fledged *hatamoto*, or banner man, with a small fief in Miura.[41] While the Jesuits' advice to Ieyasu had been to quickly crucify any Dutch pirates who reached Japanese shores, Adams retaliated by bad-mouthing the Jesuits. The idea, for example, that since Hideyoshi had been commonly held among the Japanese upper-class, i.e., that the Jesuits were indispensable intermediaries for a smooth conduct of the trade, may have been one of the first to come under fire in the private conversations between the shogun and the sailor.

Ieyasu encouraged Adams and the other members of the Dutch crew to contact their compatriots in Asia and telling them that they would be welcome as trading partners in Japan.[42] Still, it would take until 1609 before the next Dutch ships actually arrived. The establishment of a Dutch trading factory in Hirado that year must be considered a crucial event in the history of Christianity in Japan,[43] for if the Dutch could trade in Hirado without any help from the Jesuits, then the Portuguese could be expected to do the same in Nagasaki. It is, of course, no coincidence that the next year, in 1610, the Bakufu started to experiment with this very idea by ordering the exile of the one Jesuit who had been considered the most crucial for the trade for the past twenty years: João Rodrigues.

* * *

The Last Conquistador: André Pessoa

Fear of Dutch competition in Asia kept the Portuguese carracks away from Nagasaki in 1607 and 1608. No ships even arrived from Goa in Macao during these years.[1] It is not to be wondered, then, that the Captain Major who made it to Nagasaki in 1609 was a particularly pugnacious Portuguese from Malacca called André Pessoa (1560–1610).[2] Pessoa's early career, just as was his later one, was marked by violence. This much is clear from a feisty protest he sent Philip II, when he was back in Lisbon in 1591.

In this letter to the King's Cabinet, he summed up his merits to the crown up to that time. He had started his career as a servant to the King (*moço da Camara*). Shot through the throat in 1584 at Terceira, one of the Azores, he nevertheless made it to Goa that same year. After that he had served for five years in the Spice Islands, where he fought the English intruding upon the monopoly that the Portuguese had carved out for themselves. He went back to Lisbon in 1590 to try and get recognition for his services to the Crown, but was only rewarded with posts he knew he would be unable to take up for many years.[3]

Although he could barely talk because of the wound in his throat he had received seven years earlier,[4] Pessoa went back to India, and from there to Malacca. He is said to have taken part in André Furtado's expedition to the Spice Islands in 1601–1603. He was again wounded while directing the defense of the fortress Malacca during the Dutch siege from May to August 1606. In October of the same year, he engaged the Dutch fleet as commander of the galleon *São Simão*, was captured by his enemies, and released after a ransom was paid. As a reward for his service, Viceroy Martin Afonso de Castro granted him the next China voyage.[5] In February 1607, he left Malacca on the *Nossa Señora da Graça* protected by five galleons, and arrived in Macao in August of the same year.

Before he could make the Japan-run included in his license for China, however, Pessoa had to deal, at the end of November 1608, with a series of incidents caused by rowdy sailors from the domain of Arima, who were making the streets of Macao unsafe for the Chinese population.[6] Pessoa cornered the band in two houses, one of which he destroyed with heavy caliber artillery, while those who had taken refuge in the other surrendered.[7] These men were only allowed to go back to Japan after having signed a document stating that the troubles had been entirely their own fault. Next, Pessoa was brazen enough to sail for Japan in person.

Leaving Macao on 16 May 1609, he arrived in Nagasaki on 26 June after a long and difficult crossing.[8] He had on board 300,000 *kin* of raw silk, a two years' supply,[9] as well as twelve new missionaries.[10] Pessoa's troubles started immediately upon dropping anchor in the bay. Told that he would have to allow a permanent presence of Japanese officials on board, who would prepare an inventory of the cargo, keep a register of all individuals on the ship, as well as give or deny permission to anyone wanting to go ashore, Pessoa was unwilling to allow such infringement of his authority on his own ship.[11]

Hasegawa Sahyōe, for his part, could not possibly fail to enforce these regulations with the first Portuguese ship that had entered Nagasaki Bay since his appointment, especially because his predecessor had lost his position over this same problem. Not interested in coming to an agreement with Sahyōe, Pessoa decided to send an embassy to Ieyasu to hand over several letters from the Macao authorities requesting that the ancient privileges of the Portuguese in Japan be restored.[12]

Hasegawa kept on negotiating until he reached an agreement with some of the traders to bring their wares ashore, of which he then bought the most valuable part at a price he set himself.[13] Meanwhile, Sahyōe's brother Chūbei and the Kyoto merchant Chaya Matashirō had arrived in Nagasaki from Sunpu as Ieyasu's *mekiki* or expert buyers. Thus, Ieyasu was well represented in the city and there was no necessity to make concessions to the recalcitrant Pessoa. To report on the situation, Hasegawa Chūbei accompanied the Portuguese delegation under Mateo Leitao back to Sunpu.[14]

The embassy included João Rodrigues as well,[15] who must have known that Chūbei was a formidable opponent. The Portuguese were made to wait until after the Dutch had been received, even though the latter had arrived in Sunpu later than the Portuguese delegation.[16] Next, Rodrigues managed to obtain an order from Honda Masazumi on 24 August, forbidding Japanese vessels to sail for Macao in order to avoid the troubles caused by the sailors from Arima the year before.[17] This order convinced Hasegawa Sahyōe and Murayama Tōan in Nagasaki that Rodrigues' influence in Japan should be curbed.[18]

With the negotiations about the raw silk cargo stuck once more, in the end the Bakufu decided to use force and teach Pessoa a lesson. He and many of his fellow Portuguese over the past years had been behaving in a manner altogether too oblivious of the new central authority established in Japan. We are reminded of Hideyoshi's decision to do the same in 1591 when Roque de Melo, more cautious or timid than Pessoa, had come to Japan.

Ieyasu must have had three reasons for forcing the issue over control of the trade. First, he was well aware that it would be difficult for Macao to exist without the Japan trade. Second, he probably believed that, even in case the Portuguese would stop coming to Japan, the Spanish, the Dutch, and the Japanese Red-Seal ships would be able to bring the necessary goods from overseas. Third, the Portuguese were still secretly selling raw silk outside the *pancada*. The excuse for an attack on the Portuguese ship, however, was found in the role Pessoa had played in dealing with the crew of the red-seal ship from Arima in Macao the year before.[19] For this reason, it was Arima Harunobu who was given the task to destroy the Portuguese ship.

The secret order to attack may have been brought to Nagasaki by Hayashi Razan's younger brother Nobukiyo. The sequence of movements of the two brothers as told in Razan's *Nagasaki itsuji*, a "hidden account" of Nobukiyo's journey to Nagasaki in 1609–1610, seems to point in this direction. At this time, Razan still was an obscure scholar, who had been employed by the Bakufu for his knowledge of Chinese since 1605.[20] His younger brother was completely unknown and therefore well-suited to be a secret messenger. In August of 1609, Razan got married in the capital to Kame, an eleven-year old daughter of the Arakawa family.[21] After their marriage, he suddenly left for Sunpu "in the fall." This may have been any time from the beginning of September onwards. Next, in November, Nobukiyo went "for some reason" to Nagasaki.[22]

In December, Razan returned to his home in the capital, where he received a letter from Nagasaki by Nobukiyo informing him that "there was no snake."[23] This expression leads us to suspect that Nobukiyo's mission had potentially been a dangerous one. If we may believe Razan, this news caused a veritable paroxysm of brotherly love in him, which we find described in *Nagasaki itsuji*. In others words, Razan was relieved that Nobukiyo's dangerous trip had been accomplished without incident and would benefit his career as a Bakufu official. Razan wrote this short piece in February 1610 after Pessoa's carrack had been destroyed and he had been reunited with his brother on 8 February 1610.[24] The text gives a factual account of the attack on Pessoa, but the word *itsuji* of its very title suggests some other, hidden meaning.

Next, during the month of December, soldiers from Arima were gradually brought into the city. On the afternoon of 3 January 1610, before the attack was to take place, seven or eight Portuguese merchants based in Nagasaki left their property and servants in town and went aboard the Portuguese ship.[25] It is probable that these were men fearing for their lives, as they were known to have subverted the *itowappu* system during the past years by secretly selling raw silk to merchants outside the *itowappu* guild.[26] They were betting on the wrong horse, however.

Avila Girón was in Nagasaki at the time:

> More than three thousand soldiers had come from Arima and these and many others from this town boarded many craft to go for the *nao* that night. The Portuguese ship could not sail out of the bay for reason of the wind blowing in from the sea, but at around nine o'clock that night with the enemy closing in on her she blasted away with a few of her artillery pieces doing much damage among her attackers. She blew her trumpet [in triumph] and hoisted her sails but could not get any further than Tomachi, a dependence of Nagasaki about half a league from here, where she came to a stop in full view of the city.[27]

Remarkable is that Avila Girón relates that men from Nagasaki itself were participating in the attack on the Portuguese ship. Thus, Arima Harunobu may have been able to call up men from two *machi* traditionally allied or beholden to Arima: Shimabara-machi and Kabashima-machi. He would have received support from both Hasegawa Sahyōe and Murayama Tōan, both powerful enough to call up men from other segments of the town, such as Katsuyama-machi and the other wards of Sotomachi. The Jesuits seem to have been divided on whom to support along national lines: the Japanese brothers prayed in their church for the victory of Arima Harunobu, while the Portuguese padres rooted for Pessoa.[28]

During the three days that the battle was a stand-off, Arima Harunobu and Hasegawa Sahyōe held talks about the situation at the residence of Murayama Tōan,[29] while Hasegawa Chūbei worked around the clock to construct, on top of two boats, a floating attack tower with which to approach the Portuguese ship.[30] By 6 January, the northwesterly wind calmed down and the carrack was able to make a little headway towards the entrance of the bay, where she became immobilized again near Fukuda. Again, it is Bernardo Avila Girón who has left us the most trustworthy account of the battle:

> At nightfall the *nao* had again a little wind, which made her hoist her sails, but it soon died down and allowed the approach of the tower, which went for the stern of the *nao* propelled by oars, so that the guns of the *nao* could not do it any harm whatsoever. The *nao* was surrounded by a great number of vessels and so many bullets rained down on her that no one could escape them. In this way, they killed about half of the few men they had on board.
>
> The men on the *nao* shot many pots and bags of powder at the vessels surrounding them, and from these bags, when they cut them open to hurl them, much powder spilled into the waist and onto the scene of battle. It so happened that a soldier was holding a powder pot with its fuses already lit in order to hurl it at a vessel, when they shot him through his right hand, which was holding it, and made him drop it into the waist, where it broke open and set fire to all the powder which lay scattered around there, burning the soldier and everyone around him. The fire reached the sail, and the whole ship started to burn so that the crew was forced to withdraw to the prow castle. No more than two Japanese managed to enter the ship and Andre Pessoa dispatched them both with his own hands in the gangway below the poop deck.
>
> Pessoa seeing that his ship was on fire and he and his men could no longer use her to hide away, he understood that the Japanese were going to enter, extinguish the fire, and take possession of everything inside. So he determined that there was no longer any way out and that he in the first place was certain to die. He called the constable and ordered him to set fire to the powder magazine, which was well furnished. Hearing this, the factor Pedro Estorci said: "I don't know if Your Mercy should order such a thing in good conscience." But the Captain did not answer him. He put his sword on top of a berth and his shield next to it. Then he took a crucifix in his hand and left. The next moment, the *nao* blew up with a crash and a boom so loud that for one moment this whole city shook.

> The first movement of the powder was upwards, throwing a great quantity of silk baskets, silver chests, and other things, which had been standing in the upper berths of the rear castle, up into the air. With this movement the prow of the *nao* dipped down and left those who had been standing there floating in the water…. The second movement of the powder was downwards, and it did so with such force that it took the *nao* with it into the ocean and buried her deeply in thirty-five fathoms of water, where she has remained until today, even though Sahyōe has tried and spent what he could to raise her, but he has not been successful.[31]

The affair left "more than two hundred Portuguese dead, 200,000 *ryō* of silver and 200,000 *kin* of raw silk, precious fabrics, gold, and countless other articles to rot" at the bottom of Nagasaki Bay.[32] The Jesuit Rodrigues Giram estimated the total loss at one million *cruzados*.[33] In the wake of this show of force, Hasegawa took a hard line toward the Portuguese remaining in Nagasaki: Portuguese assets were confiscated, and "for a time it seemed possible that they themselves, and even the Jesuits, might lose their lives"[34] After journeying to Sunpu to discuss the situation with Ieyasu, Sahyōe released the assets of the Portuguese, assured them that they could continue to reside in Japan, and eased the stringent restrictions on their commercial activities. However, when the next trading carrack arrived in 1612, Hasegawa's three regulations were put into effect.[35]

Hasegawa accomplished one more thing in Sunpu. He obtained Ieyasu's permission to send João Rodrigues into exile. The Jesuit probably sailed in March on a junk that carried the Portuguese traders who had cooperated with Hasegawa and therefore not been on Pessoa's carrack when she exploded.[36] This order to exile Rodrigues was the clearest sign so far that the days of the Jesuits in Japan were numbered. Ieyasu was convinced that there were enough Japanese experts in the Portuguese language now in Nagasaki to dispense with the services of the padres. As predicted in Philip Curtin's theory, the Jesuits had outlived their usefulness as cultural brokers.[37] The Hasegawa cabal had won: Sahyōe would be Governor of Nagasaki until his death in 1617 and O-Natsu became the recipient of possibly as many as four trading licenses or *shuinjō* in the years that followed.[38]

The trade had to continue, of course, although after what had happened to Pessoa in January 1610 no one in Macao was sure how to go about reestablishing the link with Nagasaki. In April 1611, a small ship carried the Jesuit Rui Barreto (1549–1611) to Macao.[39] He may have been sent to encourage the Macaonese to come and make up. So, in June of the same year, a small junk brought Dom Nuno de Soutomaior as an envoy from the city.[40] Trading was allowed again on condition that the Portuguese agreed to subject themselves to the new regulations. A ship carrying this good news arrived in Macao from Nagasaki in October.[41]

The next year, to make sure the merchants from Macao would not hesitate to come to Japan, a ship carrying a personage no less than the Vice-provincial, Francisco Pasio left Nagasaki for Macao on 22 March 1612 with a personal message from Ieyasu expressing his desire to continue the trade.[42] As a result, on 17 August of that year, Captain Major Pedro Martins Gaio came to Nagasaki on the galleon *San Felipe e Santiago*,[43] accompanied by another small galleon *de aviso*.[44] The two vessels carried only thirteen hundred *piculs* of raw silk.

At the same time, however, the Japanese and Chinese Red-Seal ships, as well as the Spanish, had increased the available quantity of the best silk available in Nagasaki to five thousand *picols*,[45] so prices could remain low. By now, many Chinese were starting to circumvent the legal restrictions on trade with Japan by shipping large amounts of silk to Cochin, where it was bought by Japanese Red-Seal traders piloted by Portuguese seamen.[46]

The *itowappu* system was now in place. With the Nagasaki Governor controlling the negotiations, clearly the Jesuits were no longer indispensable intermediaries. For the first time, the control over the profits of the trade was completely in Japanese hands. This can also be seen from the fact that 1612 was the first year that the payment for the silk was done completely in government-minted *chōgin* silver, up to twenty percent less pure than the previous *haifuki gin*,[47] thus imposing a whopping twenty percent tax on the total volume of the trade to go into Bakufu coffers. This regulation was extended to the Red-Seal trade as well.[48] Before 22 October 1612, the small galleon *de aviso* left Nagasaki to bring this disappointing news to Macao.[49]

In March 1613, Dom Nuno's galleon left Nagasaki for Macao.[50] No official Japan voyage reached Nagasaki from Macao this year.[51] On 18 September 1613 it was reported in Sunpu that a fleet of fifteen Japanese ships bringing silk thread and foreign goods from Nagasaki to the Kansai had met with a violent storm and suffered much damage. When, the day before, they had put into port in Ise, three ships belonging to Hasegawa Sahyōe (and therefore probably carrying many goods destined for Ieyasu) were still missing. Other ships of this fleet may have belonged to the western daimyo. As a result of the disaster, the price of silk on the markets of Kyoto and Sakai shot up.[52] With the market in Japan depleted of its silk supply, 1614 was promising to become a good year for the trade.

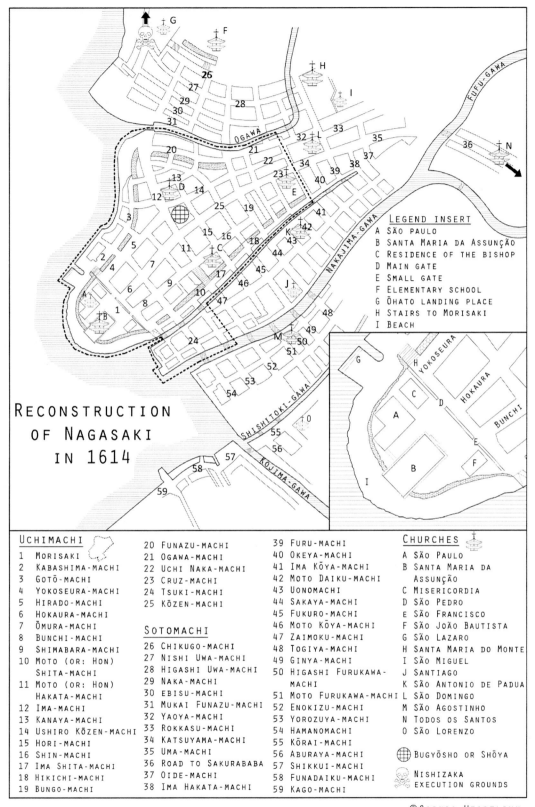

Reconstruction of Nagasaki in 1614

© Saskia Hesselink

The Second Prohibition:
Tokugawa Ieyasu

With the wisdom of hindsight, we now know that things started to change rapidly for Japan's Christians with a letter sent by Hasegawa Sahyōe on 22 December 1613 and received a few days later by the rector of the Miyako College, Gabriel de Matos (1571–1634).[1] The padre had just arrived in the Capital on 17 December to take over the mission from Pedro Morejon (1563–1639), who was getting ready to leave the region, where he had been the head of the church over the previous decade. And now, here was a letter informing the new rector that Ieyasu had decided that Christianity was a pernicious faith and would no longer be allowed in Japan.

Sahyōe's letter was short, in keeping with the style of official communications in Japan:

> To the Senhor Padre of the residence on Fifth Avenue in Miyako. I send the bringer of this letter with the purpose to inform you that the King [Ieyasu] has heard that innumerable Christians of this city of Miyako have gone to worship the cross on which Jirōbyōe, a Christian from Nagasaki, is crucified at this moment for having broken the law which forbids the exchange and transport to Kyushu of unmarked silver. The King has said that a religion that teaches the adoration of a breaker of the laws of the realm, a thief, and a great crucified sinner, and all those others who have been decapitated or burned, that such a religion is inspired by the devil, and a great crime, which worries me very much. Because I have heard this I am greatly concerned, and for this reason I am sending you this man to inform you. The eleventh day of the eleventh month. Hasegawa Sahyōe.[2]

Immediately, the padre sent a Japanese brother with a present for the Governor to ask him to be an advocate for the Christians before Ieyasu, because as Governor of Nagasaki, who had many times condemned criminals to death, he could testify that he had never seen or heard of the city's Christians worshipping such criminals.[3] Sahyōe at first refused to receive the messenger, and when in the end he did, it was only to berate him for having come at all. Ieyasu's decision had been taken and there was nothing he could do anymore.[4]

What Matos did not know yet at that time was that it was Sahyōe's own denunciation of Christianity to Ieyasu and his advisers, who were hunting near Kyoto at the time, that had finally triggered decisive action on the part of the retired shogun.[5] Two months earlier, in October, Sahyōe and his brother Chūbei had been in Hirado checking out the facilities of the newly established Dutch and English factories there. Evidently, they had concluded that the ships of these two nations could replace those of the Portuguese, in case the latter decided to abandon the Japan trade.[6]

The document prohibiting Christianity that the priest Sūden finished composing for Ieyasu on 31 January 1614 was distributed throughout Japan in February.[7] With it,

Ieyasu banished all missionaries, ordered the closing of all churches, prohibited the outward or secret practice of Christianity by any Japanese, and gave notice that anyone ignoring these orders would be executed.[8] On 28 January, Ieyasu had already ordered his retainer Ōkubo Sagami no kami Tadachika (1553–1628) to come and see him in Sunpu.[9] The latter came back from Edo to his castle in Odawara on 4 February, and after the Japanese New Year went on to Sunpu, where on 13 February he had his meeting with Ieyasu and was appointed General Commissioner in Charge of the Expulsion.[10]

At that time, the ex-shogun must have given him precise orders on how to deal with the Christians of Kyoto and Osaka.[11] These instructions do not yet seem to have included the right to impose the death penalty, but torture of the disobedient resulting in death was allowed.[12] On 25 February, Tadachika arrived in the Capital, where he was lodged in the residence of the former magistrate of Nagasaki, Tōdo Takatora.[13]

Although none of these moves by the authorities were as yet known in Nagasaki, the Christian feast of 9 February 1614 is not likely to have been celebrated in Nagasaki with the same innocence as the holiday of Epiphany (6 January) had been.[14] The former was a moveable holiday, celebrated only in Japan. It fell on the same day as the first day of the first month of the Japanese New Year. Over the past sixteen years (since 1598), the Japanese holiday had been transformed into a new Christian holiday named the feast of *On-mamori no Santa Maria* or Saint Mary Who Protects Us. On this day, the Bishop of Japan had been in the habit of performing a solemn ritual to call upon the Virgin to protect the Christians.[15] This allowed Japanese Christians to celebrate a Christian feast on the same day as their gentile brethren did.[16]

Ash Wednesday fell in the following week. This was the start of Lent, a forty-day period of mourning and penitence, without public entertainments or festivities. The faithful, donning clothes of a dark and somber color, went to church barefoot to receive a mark on their forehead made with the ashes of the burned palm leaves used on the Palm Sunday of the previous year, so they could show in public that they were doing penance.[17] Lent was not only a time of fasting on Saturdays and other forms of self-chastisement,[18] but it was also the annual season to prepare for baptism.

It is likely that the official news and the text of Ieyasu's prohibition reached Nagasaki in that same first week of Lent. As if God had decided to strike Nagasaki with calamity upon calamity, Bishop Cerqueira died on Sunday 16 February,[19] leaving behind much confusion and strife about who was to succeed him as the head of the church in Japan. He was buried in the cemetery of the Misericordia church.[20] Ten days later, upon his arrival in the capital, Ōkubo Tadachika issued orders that all the missionaries of the Kinai should make themselves ready to leave for Nagasaki.[21] This news, again, is likely to have been sent on to Nagasaki immediately, arriving there in the second week of March.

It is clear, however, that by the third week of February, the Christian leadership in Nagasaki had already understood that things were really heating up this time, for on 25 February they sent their most venerable and well-known member, Diogo de Mesquita,[22] to try and visit Ieyasu in person.[23] Among all the Jesuits in Nagasaki, Mesquita had managed to have the best relationship with Hasegawa Sahyōe.[24] Inspite of being ill, he accepted the commission to travel to the Kinai. In Osaka, he waited one month for permission to travel on to Suruga until he was told that he would not be allowed to do so.[25]

In Kyoto, the destruction was starting on the day after Tadachika's arrival in the city.[26] The *Tokugawa jikki* reports laconically:

Ōkubo Sagami no kami Tadachika had been ordered to go to Kyoto to take care of the inves-tigation of the Religion of the Heavenly Lord. Today he burned one church and demolished another one. He sent the *bateren* [padres] to Kyushu. It is said that all the people who did not want to apostatize were put naked into rice bags, which were piled along the river between Shijō and Gojō. At first they were reciting prayers, but when nobody seemed to care about them and they realized they were going to die of hunger and would earn no merit or fame, they all wanted to apostatize. They asked for help from their guards, who laughed a lot at this and freed them from their bags.[27]

It was still cold in Kyoto, and to be piled on top of one another had the effect of crushing those underneath while those on top were freezing.[28] This torture may have taken several days, so the rumors reaching Nagasaki must have become a steady stream since the beginning of March. At ten o'clock on the night of 11 March, the missionaries from Kyoto and Osaka arrived in Nagasaki in eight large *funes*, transport craft that had sailed from Osaka in record time.[29] They were joined by the missionaries of the Augus-tinian mission in Bungo on 15 March.[30]

Palm Sunday was 23 March. A procession composed of the clergy and laity used to carry palm leaves from a chapel or shrine outside the town, where the palms were blessed, to the main church. At this time, however, it is likely that the procession was kept simple in order not to further excite the authorities. The three days after Palm Sunday were tra-ditionally dedicated to the most thorough cleaning of the year with no time spent on cooking, for on Wednesday evening everything had to be ready for the celebration of Maundy Thursday.[31]

Maundy Thursday fell on 27 March. This was the end of Lent, when the penitents could finally break their fast. In Nagasaki, it was also traditionally the day of a procession by all the one hundred members of the Misericordia Brotherhood, whose participation was mandatory.[32] In 1614, it would have been Valentim Carvalho, replacing Bishop Cerqueira, who absolved the penitent from their sins, received new members into the church, and presided over the rest of the Holy Week's festivities.

For the following week, we have a notice from Kuroda Nagamasa (1568–1623), daimyo of Fukuoka, who on Thursday 4 April sent his retainer Okōchi Kuranosuke a letter in which he enjoined him to be sure to receive Governor Hasegawa Sahyōe in an appropriate manner when he passed through the domain on his way to Nagasaki.[33] Sahyōe's status as Ieyasu's representative in Kyushu was growing every year, and the respectful attitude of the daimyo was the most accurate gauge of the growing importance of the Nagasaki *bugyō*. The persecution of Christianity in Japan would soon elevate the position of the Nagasaki Governor to where he could issue commands to the daimyo of Kyushu.[34] Governor Sahyōe arrived from Sunpu in the Capital on 23 April.[35]

On Wednesday 30 April, Takayama Ukon and Naitō Jōan, two prominent Christian samurai and former retainers of Hideyoshi, arrived in Nagasaki.[36] These two men were the highest-ranking Christians left in Japan, for by this time all Christian daimyo and other direct Bakufu retainers had already apostatized. Takayama and Naitō's refusal to do so had condemned them to exile, not just to some lonely island off the coast, like emperors and other ranking officials were, but out of Japan altogether. For the moment, they were lodged in the Jesuit residence at Todos os Santos, where Ukon Dono behaved as if he had chosen to join a religious order. While waiting to depart for the Philippines, he seems to have been completely absorbed in prayer and "spiritual exercises."[37]

With each rumor and prisoner reaching Nagasaki from the Kinai, the impending, yearly arrival of the Governor came to be increasingly feared. The Governor had been writing letters announcing the impending departure of all the padres and the coming destruction of all the churches. Rumors ran that he had volunteered to make the whole population of Nagasaki into apostates, and that he would do so with the help of torture and killing. In response, possibly influenced by their lingering Easter mood, Nagasaki's Christians indignantly declared they would die for their faith rather than abandon it. Some organizations encouraged the signing of oaths to that effect.[38] It seemed no longer possible to avert a bloodbath that would make Hideyoshi's *tableau mourant* appear like child's play.

*   *   *

The Last Processions:
Bernardo Avila Girón (2)

With the return to Nagasaki of Diogo de Mesquita from his failed mission to Ieyasu, it was generally understood that the worldly means of the faithful to avert their impending doom had been exhausted. This only fueled the religious frenzy buzzing through the city. It was still widely believed that if only its inhabitants could prove themselves worthy of being saved, God could not fail to come to their rescue. It was now up to Nagasaki's Christians to convince the Omnipotent of the need for His intervention to effect an immediate change of mind in the ruler of Japan.

Gabriel de Matos has summed up for us the different methods employed in Nagasaki to get the Good Lord's attention. First, Carvalho ordered all the padres to say mass four times a week and the brothers to pray four times the entire crown of the rosary. All members of the Society should flagellate themselves twice a week, once in private and the second time all together in Church during the Holy Sacrament. They should all fast as well as recite special prayers for this time of need.[1]

But the missionaries were not the only ones trying to establish a direct line to communicate with the Almighty. The whole population of Nagasaki did its best as well. First, they decided that the largest house in each street should serve as the reception area for all the members of the street organization, who, dividing themselves up into different shifts, prayed continuously for forty hours at a time without interruption. This was not done just once, but many times over.[2] Next, they came together to study the articles of their faith and to prepare themselves through "spiritual exercises" for martyrdom. Every day, "six, seven or more" preachers would leave the Jesuit College to instruct the citizens of Nagasaki about the precise requirements of martyrs for the faith and how one could prepare oneself for that moment.[3]

Then there were the public atonements for past sins with horrific self-inflicted torments, which also served to show the determination of the believers, signifying that even though they might be killed by similar punishments inflicted on them by the authorities, they would not abandon their faith. While we have no particular information about the Easter processions of 1614 (thus leading us to suspect they may have been rather subdued affairs, characterized by fearful caution), now that all hope had come to be vested in the Good Lord alone, all over town processions were held with ever increasing intensity.

During the three weeks between Friday 9 May (the day after Ascension) and 29 May (Corpus Christi), countless processions were held throughout the city. It began, writes

Gabriel de Matos, with the Christians from the parish of the Todos os Santos Church. As we have seen, this church was located at Sakurababa and represented the oldest Christian community around Nagasaki Bay. These parishioners "organized a procession of some seven hundred people, which went all the way through town stopping at all the churches," until it reached the great Jesuit church at Morisaki.[4]

A witness has left a description of a veritable Grand Guignol of self-inflicted punishments:

> Some walked dressed in the same hempen rice bags tied up with many ropes as they had heard had been the punishment of the Christians elsewhere in Japan. Others went about as if crucified, carrying large crosses to which not only their arms had been fastened but their whole torso down to their belts. Again others carried muskets that had been lashed to their legs so tightly that it looked like the barrels had penetrated their flesh.... Others went about in groups tied together with thick ropes, which held their necks in a tight loop, as if they were shackled. They too suffered greatly from the least disruption of their walking pace by any of their group.[5]

Outside of these group torments, many penitents

> went naked from the waist upwards, with their torsos wrapped in thorny vines, on top of which they wore a mat woven of thin reeds serving to make the thorns enter their flesh. Others used oyster shells strung tightly together, instead of thorns, to cover themselves, and suffered great pains in this way. Then, there were those who carried two boulders hanging down from both ends of a pole that rested on their shoulder. This required much effort not only because of the weight of the stones but also to control their swinging. There was one man who carried two entangled snakes over his naked flesh that would bite him from time to time as proven by the wounds he had already. Some walked while beating their chests with rocks. Then there were those who were tied to crosses carried on the shoulders of others, and these crosses would be erected in the courtyard of each church where the procession halted.[6]

The Dominican missionary Jacinto Orfanel (1578–1622), who has also left us a description of this first procession, mentions that Murayama Tōan and his sons participated in it,[7] while Avila Girón explains the reaction of the Nagasaki *daikan* in more detail: "Tōan was in his country house in Mogi a league from here, where he was never short of women, or rather he lived there like a Turk in his seraglio, when the news of the start of the present persecutions and the impending exile of the padres reached him. Everybody expected the Governor would have little trouble in making him leave his faith, for he barely seemed to live a Christian life at all."[8]

In spite of his well-known life of debauchery, however, Murayama

> has surprised us all and showed us that even though he had all these weaknesses he still valued the salvation of his soul and did not want to lose it, and I hope that we may all give such proofs as he did.... For when he learned that the padres would be expelled from Japan and that the Christians of Miyako were already being persecuted, the first thing he did was to throw all the ladies who had been weighing on his conscience out of his house, giving them all a dowry so they could get married and live like honest women. He fired some of his servants who had helped him recruit and drag these women to his house, giving them more than he owed them, and so he put his house in order.[9]

Next, Tōan went to confess himself

> with great proofs of grief and repentance. He came back home and reconciled himself with his wife and sons. He made his accounts with his managers in order to know how much silver, gold, jewelry and other valuables he owned. He readied himself for whatever Our Lord would be pleased to order be done with whatever he owned and even with his life for the

faith he professed. He started to perform many acts of penitence and during the first procession here that left from Todos os Santos he carried a heavy cross that cut so deeply into his shoulders that he was covered in blood. He, his wife, and his sons also walked in the other processions either publicly or covertly with much devotion and satisfaction.[10]

After this first procession, other parishes organized similar processions. For the next eight days, one procession after the other would leave their neighborhood church from noon until nightfall. Sometimes three or four processions would be making a stop at the same church.[11] Morejon wrote about this time that "there was not scarce any one person in all the city, man, woman, nor child that did not, some once, some twice, some thrice go in these processions, doing some penance or other therein."[12] While some of these processions may have been small affairs, they were numerous, and for more than two weeks "every night large groups of penitents chastising themselves made the rounds of the city's churches."[13]

The next great procession was held on Monday 12 May.[14] It again left from the Todos os Santos church, and more than three thousand people participated. Avila Girón describes them as tied up with ropes, cords, and chains. Some had their arms stretched out on heavy beams, which they carried on their backs. Others had boulders slung around their necks. There were those, men as well as women, caning themselves or their companions with bamboo sticks split at the end into thin strips, their blood flowing freely. "It was as if people were saying: If what you want is for us Christians to suffer, here are the tools of our suffering! Of course, from now on, we will kiss them and embrace them in reverence. Because we believe that Our Lord will give us the fortitude to throw away our lives for our faith."[15]

On Wednesday 14 May no less than seven different processions were held. In one of these Tōan and his family appeared again barefooted and with crowns of thorns on their heads, both of their arms bent backwards and tied together at the biceps, holding a cross in their bound hands. The procession carried a wooden placard on a long pole listing the names of those who had prepared it and those who were participating. "We are weak, sinful people" it proclaimed, "we ask for the blessings of the Almighty so that we can die in unison for our faith in Our Lord who atoned and was humiliated for our Sins. We swear that with His blessing we will throw away our lives for Our Lord."[16] The population of Nagasaki seemed as in a daze; many "still did not understand in what way they had sinned and for what they should search their conscience."[17] On Thursday three more processions were held, and on Friday three more during the day and one at night. More than five hundred penitents took to the streets on Saturday.

The largest of these processions were those organized by the mendicant orders, the Dominicans and the Augustinians, less experienced with Japan and therefore less cautious than the Jesuits and the Franciscans. On Pentecost, Sunday 18 May, Nagasaki seems to have been quiet, with everyone going to mass, but on the following Monday, demonstrations started again with a procession leaving the Santo Domingo Church with three thousand men, women, and children, whipping each other "in an atrocious manner" and passing by seven other churches before returning to the church of the Dominicans in Katsuyama-machi.[18]

By 1614 Nagasaki counted fifteen churches and chapels,[19] most of them built by the Jesuits. Three churches were run by other orders: the Santo Domingo, run by the Dominicans, the Santa Cruz (also known as the San Francisco) run by the Franciscans, and the San Augustino, run by the Augustinians. The San Francisco church had been rebuilt in

Cruz machi in 1611, the site of the old cemetery. This was in Uchimachi, located in the area now called Sakura-machi.[20] The Augustinians were the most recent to join the effort to convert the Japanese, so they could only establish themselves in the least desirable part of town, across the Nakajima river in the area of the Kawata, or untouchables.

To live on the opposite side, i.e., the left bank of the river, was to come down in the world. Just as on the right bank, however, here too the streets were named after the occupations of their inhabitants. The Kawata, or leather workers, lived in Kegawa-machi. Because conditions in Nagasaki were relatively benevolent for the Kawata, and Hideyoshi's Korean invasions had provided ample work (gloves, boots, chaps, jackets) in the years between 1592 and 1598, this community seems to have grown very quickly.[21]

A community of leatherworkers was an indispensable asset for a port town like Nagasaki, which imported deerskins from Siam, Cambodia, Cochin China, the Philippines, and Taiwan. The Kawata had chosen a site between the Nakajima river and a stream, which drained the mountainside. The stream still exists, although it is channeled largely underground today. It is called the Shishitoki-gawa or Deer-Dismembering river, a distant echo of the artisans and their bloody trade who used to live here.[22] The new neighborhood came to include specialist manufacturers of bows, arrows, drums, and armor, all of which use animal products.

This was the area where Friar Hernando de Ayala (1575–1617) had built the São Agostinho church in 1612. Its principal entrance gave onto [Moto] Furukawa machi,[23] while the land around it stretched all the way from the Nakajima riverbank halfway up to present day Teramachi.[24] Attached to the church was a building known as the Zeniya, which distributed alms to the poor of Nagasaki. Its parish counted four thousand families and around ten thousand Christians.[25] On 20 May, at two thirty in the afternoon, a procession left from this church. It was as if it had become a contest between the different orders about who could mobilize the longest procession, with the most horrifying scenes.

Thursday 29 May was Corpus Christi. This holy day had, since 1605, become an important feast in Nagasaki. Corpus Christi is a complicated holiday. It celebrates the doctrine of transubstantiation, the sacramental change of the host into the body of Christ. It is a typical Tridentine holiday, in that the Church Council issued, on 11 October 1551, a decree characterizing it as a "triumph over heresy" and condemning anyone refusing to celebrate the Blessed Sacrament in procession.[26] For this reason, it also came to be considered an obligatory holiday to be celebrated in Spain's overseas empire, where the initial temporal conquest was consolidated and confirmed by its ongoing "spiritual conquest."

In that respect, celebrating Corpus Christi started late in Nagasaki: fully twenty-five years after the usurpation of the Portuguese throne by the Habsburgs. The procession organized on the day of Corpus Christi, therefore, had become a victory procession by this time. Ostensibly "the victor was Christ himself, embodied in the consecrated host."[27] Christ had conquered sin and death, and, since Trent, heresy was the principal sin that deserved death. The obligation for everyone to participate, moreover, reveals a subtext of the essentially coercive nature of this festival. We are not surprised to see the Society of Jesus, still the dominant religious power in Nagasaki, as its organizers.

Since it is a Eucharistic feast, the sacrament forms the center of the procession.[28] Over time, the procession became essentially a recreation of the social hierarchy of the environment in which it took place, with the degree of proximity to the Eucharist symbolizing the degree to which one had risen in society. It goes without saying, therefore, that Corpus Christi processions always (even today) cause much jockeying for position by different social groups. This is one of the instruments the church has devised to enforce and strengthen its influence, because it usually dominates the decision-making process as to who may walk where in the procession.

The Eucharist itself is, it goes without saying, carried in a costly and ornate vessel by the highest participating prelate, who in his turn is surrounded by other priests. The closest a layman can approach the Eucharist is as one of the six or eight canopy-bearers, protecting the Eucharist, The canopy covers the bearer of the Eucharist and the other clerics who are his closest associates. All other societal groups: the medium and lower-ranking officials, the army, the guilds, the educational establishment, the leisure associations etc. either precede or follow the Eucharist, in the ascending and descending order of their respective social prominence and power, each bearing the banner of their organization.

Churches ring their bells when the procession is approaching. Its route is strewn with sweet-smelling herbs, such as thyme and rosemary. Rose leaves are also popular, because the liturgical color of the festival is red. In some places the procession is "announced by the purest of the pure, by children,"[29] often disguised as angels, by virtue of their pre-sexual nature. Because the procession is essentially one fueling and channeling social competition, often great sums are expended for its displays, which may include elaborate tabernacles for the Eucharist, sumptuous canopies, banners, and *tableaux vivants*, paid for by the different groups making up the congregation. In Nagasaki, these groups were most often the streets, which functioned, as we have seen, as groupings of certain specific professions.

As Spanish dominance in its overseas possessions was often reinforced by the Corpus Christi festival, it is not surprising to find our Spanish eyewitness, Bernardo Avila Girón, to have been particularly attuned to this event taking place in Nagasaki this year for the last time:

> In front went fifty Japanese children exquisitely dressed with candles in their hands. After them came 216 *irmãos* [brothers] and *dōjuku* [associates], who study to become priests, also with candles in their hands and dressed in short white outfits. Then followed four richly dressed little angels. Next followed a gilded platform from which hung many chains of large amber beads, relic boxes, and many other jewels, an incense box with many chains, amber, and relics. On this platform stood a pretty Infant Jesus. This was preceded by eight large burning wax candles, and followed by a choir of singers. Next, walked more than fifty padres of the Society dressed in surplices and stoles. Twenty of them wore capes.[30]

The procession showed its very contemporary concerns:

> Next came an enormous banner, which showed on one side a chalice and host, and on the other side a scene with Abraham brandishing a knife over his humble son Isaac on an altar piled with firewood. A sincere Portuguese carried this banner, dressed in deep red damask. He was followed by four angels with candles in their hands, preceded by another choir of singers. Next came twelve large, wax candles set in candelabras of colored varnish, each of which held a rose of gilded brass. About one hand palm below this rose, each happened to have a golden Jesus. The people who carried these were also dressed in dark purple.[31]

The banner picturing *Abraham brandishing a knife over his humble son Isaac* is clearly a reference to the predicament in which Nagasaki (Isaac), at this very moment, found itself vis-à-vis Ieyasu (Abraham), including the hope that, just like in the Old Testament, God would intervene in the coming sacrifice and stay Ieyasu's hand. God must intervene, otherwise Christian Nagasaki would die. The description continues:

After this came the Holiest Sacrament on a richly decorated golden *custodia* of beautiful craftsmanship. The Provincial, Padre Valentim Carvalho, carried it on a small, wooden tray lined with damask assisted on each side by the deacon and sub-deacon, all three walking at ease and with much decorum. The Sacrament was covered by a beautiful, expensive canopy of embroidered velvet carried with eight poles by the highest ranking people of the town, all wearing dark red clothing.[32]

These "highest ranking" people, of course, included the *machidoshiyori,* the *daikan,* and possibly the *provedor* of the Misericordia brotherhood of this year. The Jesuits, mindful of the impression the processions would make in faraway Suruga, forbade this one to leave the Jesuit compound at Morisaki. There the crowd was so thick, it was impossible to move, whether inside the church or outside, in the gardens or on the square. The three streets, Bunchi-machi, Hokaura-machi, and Yokoseura-machi, which came out onto the Jesuit compound were all completely filled with people.[33]

In Japan, the persecution of Christianity inevitably halted these processions, so they never attained the status, as well as the social significance, of the Corpus Christi processions in the Americas, where the festival of the conquering body of Christ came to reaffirm, reenact, and was identified with the actual conquest drama of the Spanish over the Indians.[34] In Nagasaki, by contrast, the soul of the city was retaken by the Japanese authorities, and the conquest-signifying element of Corpus Christi was transferred to a new pagan festival, first organized in 1634 by order of the Nagasaki Governor when most of the town's population had already apostatized.

It should be noted that this first festival, organized by the military authorities, had as its theme Empress Jingu's legendary invasion of Korea,[35] as if organizing the festival in Nagasaki was just as much a "spiritual" conquest as an invasion of foreign territory.[36] In other words, if there is one clear predecessor for the famous Nagasaki Okunchi festival still celebrated today, it is the Corpus Christi procession of the decade between 1605 and 1614. The sword of conquest cut both ways.

* * *

The City Occupied:
Yamaguchi Naotomo

In spite of the precautions taken, all these processions throughout the city caused quite a bit of commotion. This frightened the men who had been left behind by Hasegawa Sahyōe while he was spending his usual time at court. Pedro Morejon and Gabriel de Matos report that these officials wrote letters that "the city was all in an uproar, united and resolved not to obey the shogun's orders and not to let the padres leave the country,"[1] painting the situation in the most ominous manner possible, and warning him he should be careful while traveling to and entering the city. As fate would have it, the messenger carrying these letters missed Sahyōe and his brother Chūbei, who had already left for Nagasaki, so that the letters were delivered to their sister.

That was, of course, exactly the wrong person to receive this information:

She being a wicked woman, a Gentile and an enemy to the Christian faith, went weeping with the letters to the Shogun, and related the matter in such manner, as though doubtless her brethren were both of them slain already at Nagasaki. Wherewithal the Shogun was so moved to anger and indignation, that laying his hand upon his sword, he swore, that if Nagasaki were near at hand he would go there himself in person, and put it all to the sword and fire. And fearing lest Sahyōe alone would not be able to rule the Christians and bring them to order and obedience, he commanded that Surugadono, one of the principal Captains he had in Fushimi, should go there with all his soldiers.[2]

"Surugadono" refers to Yamaguchi Suruga no kami Naotomo (1546–1622),[3] the Fushimi *bugyō* at the time, although his departure for Nagasaki would not take place until more than a month later.[4] The Hasegawa brothers, Sahyōe and Chūbei, arrived in Terai, the harbor of the Saga domain, on 11 June.[5] From there, they traveled on to the mostly Christian domain of Arima, where on 15 June Sahyōe ordered Arima Naozumi (1586–1641) to call together all the leaders of the Christian organizations and brotherhoods so he could tell them what they had to do in order to avoid Ieyasu's wrath, threatening them in the direst possible terms to abandon their religion.[6] Leaving by boat from Kuchinotsu, the brothers arrived in Nagasaki on 23 June.[7]

Contrary to what he had been told, Sahyōe found the city quiet and peaceful.[8] All its devout Christians were fasting on the night before the birthday of John the Baptist, the fourth day of the Cycle of St. John, which continues through the days of Saint Peter and Saint Paul on 29 and 30 June. On the day after his arrival, 24 June, Sahyōe sent the city official in charge of daily affairs of the year (*nengyōji otona*) and one of his retainers to the Jesuit Provincial Valentim Carvalho to announce that all padres had to leave Japan in October for Manila or Macao. The friars of the mendicant establishments were also punctiliously informed.[9]

Three days later, on 27 June, Captain Major João Serrão da Cunha reached Japan on the *Nossa Senhora da Vida*, appearing mistakenly on the other side of the Nagasaki peninsula before Himi in Tachibana Bay.[10] It would take him ten more days before he entered Nagasaki Bay.[11] 2 July was the day of Mary's Visit to Elisabeth. This was the day when the Misericordia brotherhood traditionally chose its board of guardians. We can be sure this custom was still observed in 1614, for the Misericordia kept on choosing its officers at least until 1619.[12] The results of the election were announced on the following day, when the new Mesa or Board of the brotherhood took its oath.

On 7 July the carrack finally entered Nagasaki Bay. When the news reached Ieyasu, about two weeks later, he was said to have been very happy and to have asked if the trade would continue even if he expelled the padres from Japan.[13] Because the Captain Major of this year also held the rights to the voyage of the following year (1615) and shared in the rights of the one in the year thereafter (1616) with others,[14] he of course wanted to continue to come to Japan, "but as he much regretted us being expelled from Japan, not only because the Christians of this country would remain behind without the support of their shepherds and masters, but also because he would sorely miss us in the conduct of his trade, he decided to intervene for us with Sahyōe."[15]

He told the Governor that he proposed to travel to Suruga in person in order to ask Ieyasu himself to allow the missionaries to remain in Nagasaki, and if this was not possible, to at least allow that they could keep a toehold there. Sahyōe, however, advised against this, saying that for the moment there was nothing to be done about the missionaries and that Ieyasu's orders had to be obeyed. He promised to write to his sister and the ruler himself and counseled the Captain Major to just send a Portuguese with an expensive present. Thinking of the great cost his embassy would entail, the Captain Major decided that it was better not to flout this advice and make an enemy out of Sahyōe.

Therefore, he sent the scribe-of-the-people, or the second-ranking official chosen by the merchants of Macao, with six other Portuguese. Although he was able to present a petition to Ieyasu through the intermediary of his closest advisors, this remained without effect. Rather, as Sahyōe had predicted, Ieyasu got irritated, saying that "if the believers in our holy faith multiplied too much, it would lead the Christians to obey him no longer, and that we had already asked for only a toehold in Taico's time, but even so we had spread all over Japan since that time, and that because we would now do the same, he would not allow any Padre to remain in Japan."[16]

On 27 July Yamaguchi Naotomo left Fushimi with five hundred riflemen in order to eradicate the religion of the Heavenly Lord in Nagasaki.[17] At the same time, the formerly Christian warlord Arima Naozumi was commanded to move his fief to Hyūga in Eastern Kyushu, where Takahashi Mototane (dates unknown) had just been attaindered. In their place Nabeshima Katsushige of Saga, Terazawa Hirotaka of Karatsu, and Ōmura Sumiyori (1592–1619), Yoshiaki's son, were appointed caretakers of the Arima domain. For the taxes, however, they were obliged to follow Sahyōe's orders, so for all practical purposes it was the Governor of Nagasaki who was the de facto lord of the domain neighboring Nagasaki.[18]

When Arima's retainers proved unwilling to obey their lord and apostatize, Naotomo was allowed to call up the forces of Satsuma to chase them away.[19] While Naotomo was traveling to Kyushu, hundreds of other soldiers from Ōmura, Arima, Hirado, Hizen, and Satsuma gathered in Nagasaki to help execute Ieyasu's orders and prevent the outbreak of an expected rebellion among the citizenry.[20]

Next, on 9 August, Arima Naozumi came to Nagasaki to take his leave from Governor Sahyōe, who had been instrumental in having him attaindered of his patrimonial fief.[21] It is hard to imagine that Naozumi was unaware of that fact. That evening, there was another fast among the Christians of Nagasaki to prepare for the celebration of St. Lawrence on the next day. This saint was claimed by Spain as her native son, and the recently built palace of the Spanish king, the Escorial, was dedicated to his memory.[22] The largest church of Nagasaki, the Santa Maria da Assunção at Morisaki, possessed a copy of the tabernacle of the San Lorenzo church in the Escorial.[23] Thus, clearly, St. Lawrence's feast day was observed in Nagasaki in honor of the king of Spain.

Two days after St. Lawrence, on 12 August, Yamaguchi Naotomo arrived in the city at the head of his five hundred riflemen.[24] The Dominican Orfanel wrote admiringly about him that "he would not allow any of his men to fall in love, or to be attentive to and think about women; and when he found out that they had disobeyed him in this respect, he would send away those who were not his own men, and cut off the heads of those who were. For he said that anyone so carried away could not properly serve his lord: which words, for sure, were not lacking in reason."[25]

Thus reinforced, Sahyōe could announce the next day, 13 August, that if any missionary had not yet found a ship on which he would leave Japan, he should do so forthwith. The Dominicans, Franciscans, and Augustinians answered that they all had found a ship. Questioned which ship, they said it was the one of Esteban d'Acosta, which was scheduled to leave for Manila.[26] On the evening of 14 August, Nagasaki fasted in preparation for the holiday of the next day, Mary's Assumption into Heaven.

Traditionally, this was Nagasaki's most important holiday, ostensibly as the day of the "completion" of the town's founding in 1571. In the same way as the Christian holiday celebrated on the day of the Japanese New Year, this holiday fell on the day of the most important Buddhist holiday of the year, Obon, and because by this time of the year the Portuguese were sure to be in port to lend their support to the occasion.[27] We do not hear of any public celebrations on this day, but Sahyōe chose it to send warnings, once more, to all the missionaries in Nagasaki that they all without fail had to leave Japan in the fall.

Three days later, he set the final departure date for the missionaries. In a message to the *nengyōji* and police officers (*yokome*) of Nagasaki, he told them to inform all the missionaries of the different orders, as well as the Japanese clerics, that they were to embark by the 15th day of the 9th month, which fell this year on 18 October.[28] Ieyasu had set the date by which the padres should be gone as the "ninth moon which signifies the end of autumn in Japan."[29] This year, the ninth moon started on Tuesday 4 October and would have been full on Tuesday 18 October. It might still be visible for a week to ten days longer, so this left the Governor some leeway, if needed.

Avila Girón reports that on this day, 18 August, a contingent of soldiers from Satsuma arrived in Nagasaki in nine ships. Most left again shortly after,[30] but the *karō* or senior retainer Mihara Shō'emon Shigetane and another retainer identified only as Iga no kami stayed with around two hundred men.[31] If the nine ships mentioned by Avila Girón each carried roughly one hundred men, the Satsuma contingent sent by the daimyo Shimazu Iehisa (1576–1638) may have counted close to one thousand samurai.

It would, of course, have been too great an imposition on the city and its surroundings to feed so many soldiers if there was no clear military need for them. Thus, seven of the ships returned to Sendai, the nearest port of the Satsuma domain, where they could be kept at their domain's expense ready to join their comrades in Nagasaki, if the need arose.[32]

There are no further data available for August and the beginning of September. We may be sure that the mood in Nagasaki continued to be depressed and fearful of what the coming weeks were to bring: the expulsion of the padres, the destruction of the churches, and possibly a bloodbath in the city for its refusal to apostatize. The birth of Mary used to be celebrated in Nagasaki on 8 September, but it is doubtful whether the holiday got much attention this year.

On 11 September, Hasegawa Chūbei and Chaya Kiyotsugu left Nagasaki to report to Ieyasu's advisor Honda Masazumi.[33] They had been summoned back to Sunpu to report on the situation in Nagasaki, and probably went to reassure Ieyasu that an overt rebellion by the Christians of Nagasaki seemed unlikely, and that, therefore, the preparations for the coming attack on Hideyori's remaining forces in Osaka castle did not need to be interrupted.[34]

Avila Girón reports that in the "middle of September," Sahyōe

> called together all the *machi-doshiyori* (mayors) and *otona* (street headmen) of Nagasaki and asked each of them individually and then all of them as a group to swear an oath that no one living in their ward would aid any padre or *hermano*, or extend any help to them whatsoever so that they might continue to stay in Japan. If this oath was broken, they and their families would lose their heads and their property. All the *otona* then were forced to sign this oath, and they were ordered to require he same of all the street elders (*kumi no oya*) in their wards.[35] In the end, Sahyōe sent one of his men who went around the whole town to collect signatures from all the people of Nagasaki. I myself was forced to do the same.[36]

On 25 September the theft of the painting of Mary Mother of God from the altar of the Santa Maria da Assunção (or the Hishōten Santa Mariya as it was called in Japanese) church at Morisaki was discovered, proof of the chaos that was starting to reign in the Jesuit compound just before the departure of the missionaries.[37] On 27 September Hasegawa Chūbei and Chaya Kiyotsugu arrived in Sunpu, where they reported the arrival of the Portuguese on 7 July and conferred about the expulsion of the Evil Lot. This time in the record Chūbei bears the title of *bugyō* and Kiyotsugu is called a *kanshō* or trade official.[38]

From the beginning of October the Christians of Nagasaki and the area surrounding the city hurried to come to confession. They came from all over Kyushu, some even from as far away as the Kinai, fearful that they would not get a chance to receive the sacrament of absolution for a long time. In less than four weeks, about six thousand believers were heard and absolved in the confessional.[39] On Saturday 11 October Sahyōe sent a message to all religious orders and the parish priests that they were to embark by Thursday 16 October of the following week and wait on their ships until it was time to sail. The padres answered that they were ready to embark and that the only thing that held them ashore was the fact that their ships were not yet ready for them.[40]

On Tuesday 14 October, the Dominicans destroyed the crosses of their monastery and its graveyard in Katsuyama-machi, and burned them together with other implements used in their ceremonies. Those whose family members lay buried there hastily came to collect their bones for reburial in a safer location.[41] The following day, with much crying and sobbing the last mass was read in the *Santo Domingo* Church. Afterwards, the holy sacrament was destroyed in the presence of many Japanese as well as Spanish residents of Nagasaki.[42] However, that Thursday, neither the missionaries nor the ships on which they were to leave Japan were ready, and Sahyōe must have agreed to a two-week delay of the embarkation.

Until the very last moment before their departure, the Jesuits and the mendicants engaged in unseemly fights about filling the vacancy left by the demise of Bishop Cerqueira.[43] In large measure this controversy centered on the problem of who was to determine which of the missionaries would be allowed to stay behind in Japan. Where the Jesuits were concerned, it was Carvalho who made that decision. The other orders, however, knew that to submit in this respect would also oblige them to follow the leadership of the Jesuits during the coming persecutions.

Carvalho only wanted the physically fit and relatively unknown to stay behind and go underground. The elderly and those with known physical weaknesses would have to leave, even those who were too fat and would not be able to keep up with their minders when on the run. But Carvalho's choices could also affect the delicate balance between the fathers of different nationalities in Japan. Being Portuguese himself, in the end Carvalho approved the illegal stay of seven Portuguese padres and one Portuguese brother, five Italian padres, (but only) two Spanish padres, four Japanese padres and eight Japanese brothers, thus establishing a Portuguese voting block that would not be easily outnumbered.[44] The average age of the padres remaining behind was 44.6 years.[45] In the end, of course, it all mattered very little.

On Saturday 25 October, Sahyōe sent another messenger to all the missionaries, ordering them to leave the city by the next Monday. He again received the answer from the Jesuits that everyone was ready to go, but that the ships were not. In reply, Sahyōe ordered the padres to board the ships in so far as possible, while the rest should leave their compound at Morisaki to go to Fukuda and wait there until their ships were ready.[46] The next day, the last mass was celebrated at Morisaki.[47]

The following day, Monday 27 October, the altar was taken down and destroyed, so as to avoid its desecration at the hands of the soldiers. All the padres left the compound for Fukuda, where they were lodged in little fishermen's huts, carefully watched by soldiers sent by Yamaguchi Naotomo.[48] Only the Provincial Valentim Carvalho and two of his assistants were allowed to stay in Morisaki until their ship was ready.[49] That same afternoon, Sahyōe took possession of all the churches to billet the soldiers of the different domains.[50] Until then, they may have camped outside the city.

Orfanel reports: "It was sad to see the poor Christians of Nagasaki, walking through their streets from church to church, wailing and crying, and looking at those walls not knowing what to say."[51] The men from Ōmura were housed in the São João Baptista church in Chikugo-machi.[52] That same afternoon, Mamiya Gonzaemon Isasada, who had come to Nagasaki with Yamaguchi Naotomo in August, left the city for Osaka to report to Ieyasu on the progress in expelling the missionaries.[53]

In the next few days, as soon as the missionaries had left town, Sahyōe started a drive to make the whole city sign an oath, invoking *kami* and *hotoke*, that no one would give lodging to any missionary.[54] This must have caused quite a bit of bitter hilarity among the city's population, which gladly went along with this order to swear such an easy oath. As an anonymous confession has it:

> Now restrictions have been placed on Christianity and a *bugyō* has come to where I live [who requires] that all Christians place their signature on a document promising that they will not provide lodgings to padres and includes an oath to make it more binding. I have made this promise just like all my neighbors…. Once I had to swear by all the *kami* and *hotoke* of Japan. This was no problem for me, I thought, for *kami* and *hotoke* serve no purpose, so I was not signing any real oath at all, but just something serving to fool the pagan *bugyō*.[55]

In the early morning of Wednesday 29 October, our Spanish eyewitness Bernardo Avila Girón visited Morisaki. Soldiers armed with sticks were posted at the main entrance. They told him that the gentiles from Hirado had entered the compound and even had brought their horses to be stabled there.[56] Valentim Carvalho and his assistants were scheduled to leave at sunrise that morning. With the departure of the Provincial from Nagasaki, Yamaguchi Naotomo considered his task in Nagasaki as completed, for on this day he wrote a letter to Shimazu Iehisa announcing the departure of the missionaries from Japan and ordering the daimyo of Satsuma to consult with Governor Sahyōe where the further treatment of the Nagasaki Christians was concerned.[57]

*　*　*

The Destruction of the Churches: Hasegawa Sahyōe

Two days later, Saturday 1 November was All Saints. This was the day on which the members of the Misericordia brotherhood used to go in procession to Nishizaka, Nagasaki's execution grounds, in order to collect the bones of those executed over the past year in order to give them a Christian burial in their cemetery. With so many soldiers from the surrounding domains in the city, it is highly doubtful that this public ceremony could have been observed this year. Instead, Governor Sahyōe called all the *machidoshiyori*, the *otona* and other officials of Nagasaki together to announce that he had been ordered to destroy all the churches. Happily, he said, the padres had already left the city, so the work could begin right away. When they heard this announcement, the *otona* were perplexed. They said they would like to discuss this matter with others who were not present at this moment and requested permission to defer their answer.[1]

On the same day, the Hosokawa retainer Maki Same no suke and three company commanders were sent to Nagasaki from the Kokura domain in northern Kyushu. Accompanying them were Shimozu Hanzaemon and Nakagawa Gohei, men of the senior Hosokawa retainer Nagaoka Okinaga, who were dispatched at the head of one hundred musketeers. The whole Hosokawa force may have numbered between three and five hundred men. The six commanders were ordered to coordinate their movements so as not to expose the domain to shame. They traveled by boat along the coast, but no soldiers were allowed to go ashore anywhere along the way. If any purchases of firewood or other necessities needed to be made, each boat was allowed to send one trustworthy member of its rowing crew ashore. Hanzaemon and Gohei were given the right to punish whosoever disobeyed their orders.[2]

The next day, Sunday, 2 November, the *otona* reported back to the *bugyō* with the answer that the citizens of Nagasaki were all very tired and poor, and requested the *bugyō* to order someone else to perform the job of destroying the churches. Sahyōe answered that he understood their position and that he would turn elsewhere. But, he added, they should not get upset if the whole town, or even their own houses, would be filled with the people doing the job. So he contacted the daimyo of Hizen, Isahaya, and the others who were already in the city to undertake the task.[3] This was the first Sunday in almost half a century (i.e., since 1568 or 1569) without mass said in public in the area around the Bay of Nagasaki.

On Monday, 3 November, two thousand soldiers belonging to the contingents of various Kyushu daimyo were sent in three groups to Fukuda, Kibachi, and Fukabori anchorages and points of departure at the entrance of Nagasaki Bay to make sure that no padres would leave their ships to hide themselves in the neighborhood. On this day, the retainers of the daimyo of Hirado started to dismantle the Santa Maria da Assunção and São Paulo churches of the Jesuit compound at Morisaki.[4] The work would take five days.[5] Afterwards, the men of the *itowappu* guild (the *itowappu shukurō*) took over a part of the site and, from 1615, conducted the negotiations with the Portuguese to set the silk price in the same rooms in which they had always been held.[6]

On Wednesday, 5 November, the men from Ōmura, led by Yoshiaki's son Sumiyori,[7] started to take down the Santa Maria do Monte (or: Yama no Santa Mariya) church at the foot of Mt. Tateyama. This was the most easily visible church of Nagasaki from the sea.[8] As the work took three full days, we may be sure that this church had grown into a sizeable structure since its last rebuilding in 1612. Already in 1609 there had been three chapels next to the main building, in one of which mass was said from time to time.[9] It would take a lifetime before, in 1671–2, the Tateyama *bugyōsho* or Governor's Office was built on the same spot.[10] Avila Girón lived only 200 paces away from the site.[11]

On Thursday, 6 November, two ships left the harbor of Nagasaki and sailed (or were towed) to the entrance of the bay where the rest of their passengers were to embark. They were joined the next day by a third vessel. The three ships finally left Japan consecutively on 7, 8, and 9 November. The first ship under Manuel Gonzales was bound for Macao, mostly carrying Jesuits, the second under Esteban d'Acosta was heading for Manila, carrying Takayama Ukon, Naitō Jōan, their companions, most of the mendicants leaving Japan, as well as twenty-three Jesuits (eight priests and fifteen brothers).[12]

The third junk under Francisco Domingo was bound for Siam, but would stop at Macao to allow its passengers to disembark.[13] These ships were most likely Chinese style junks, rented with funds from the missions. They would have had a Portuguese captain and a mixed Chinese and Japanese crew. They were not part of the trading mission brought from Macao by João Serrão da Cunha, who would only leave Japan in March of 1615.[14]

Numerous escorts, manned by men called up by Governor Sahyōe and Yamaguchi Naotomo, accompanied the junks two miles out to sea. The samurai aboard these vessels did not dare go too far in this unfamiliar territory: "When these guard boats had accompanied our ship two miles out into sea, they turned back. Immediately, three other boats appeared from between some islands. Two of the Dominicans, two of the Franciscans, and the five parish priests went on board, each of the boats taking three religious and going back to shore its own way. This happened at nightfall, and on the way everyone changed into civilian clothing."[15]

This may sound as if the return to land would be an easy feat, but Pedro Morejon shows that it was nothing of the kind:

> Everyone [in Nagasaki] wanted to hide a padre in their house, and asked for this honor with great insistence from the superiors of the Society. Some schemed to get a father by going out to sea in their boats to follow the ships carrying the missionaries into exile, in order to try and get hold of a padre, putting themselves in great danger, not only from the numerous spies and guards, but also exposing themselves to drowning in the high waves of winter. In this way, some only made it back after many days, half-dead from hunger and with the skin chafed off their hands from the effort they had made rowing against the wind and rain.[16]

Avila Girón supposes that Sahyōe silently allowed many priests to remain behind. The Governor did not make any list of who was in Japan at the time, and he did not keep a strict count of who went aboard the ships. If Sahyōe had really wanted to be sure none of the embarked missionaries came back to shore, he writes, the Governor should have had their ships accompanied until they had passed the Gotō islands or left Satsuma past Ryūkyū.[17] He may have taken a bribe.

After having finished with the Yama no Santa Mariya church, the men from Ōmura started "with great fury" (says Avila Girón) to dismantle the São João Baptista church in Chikugo-machi on Sunday 9 November. Others from the same domain started that same day on the São Agostinho church in Furukawa-machi.[18] Orfanel caught the sounds and the mood of the city in these days:

> Nothing could be heard but the noise of striking blows, of pulling nails out of boards, falling and breaking tiles, and crumbling walls. These were the same walls that had once enclosed the hearts of the Christians, who went around sadly and with hanging heads. On top of that, they had to put up with the insults of the gentiles who filled the city and ran about everywhere their faces smiling with satisfaction and mocking them with blasphemies. This hurt all the more when they realized that without their padres they were orphans now, which they had never thought possible.[19]

On the same day Yamaguchi Naotomo seems to have worried that he might not have enough manpower to keep the work of the demolition going if the people of Nagasaki erupted in rebellion over the destruction of their churches. So he wrote to Shimazu Iehisa that "recently the daimyo of Kyushu had been coming to see him, each bringing fifty or a hundred men to put at his disposal," so it would be better for Iehisa to do the same.[20]

On Monday 10 November, an enigmatic messenger from the Toyotomi faction in the Kinai by name of Takaya Shichirōbei arrived in Nagasaki.[21] Shichirōbei is said to have been a Nagasaki merchant, and upon his arrival in Nagasaki he asked to see Takayama Ukon. The man seems to have carried a proposal to the Christian samurai that Ukon take up command of the Toyotomi forces in the defense of Osaka Castle, which was about to be invested by the Tokugawa.[22] Finding that Ukon had left the area for the Philippines only two or three days earlier, the messenger continued on his way to Satsuma with the same request, presenting Shimazu Iehisa with a *wakizashi* by Nagakata Masamune and a letter from Hideyori on 1 December.[23]

As we have seen, the daimyo had already thrown in his lot with the Tokugawa, so he must have refused the request. What happened to the messenger of this dangerous communication is not recorded. Meanwhile, our Spanish eyewitness Avila Girón could no longer keep track of the crews of the different domains doing the demolition work. He reports that

> On [Tuesday] 11 November they started on the San Antonio de Padua and on 12 November on the church of the Apostle São Pedro and the Santo Domingo church, which to our great sadness they had destroyed by [Thursday] 14 November, so that on [Friday] 15 November they could start on the church [dedicated to] the angelic Padre San Francisco and the one [dedicated to] the Apostle Santiago [Saint James].... This church, being small, was demolished on that same day.[24]

The church dedicated to San Antonio de Padua had been built in 1606 with funds donated by Murayama Tōan. The *daikan* had wanted to provide a church for his own son Francisco, who had been ordained by Bishop Cerqueira that year. It is not quite clear where the church stood, but it was probably somewhere along the right bank of the Naka-jima River, either in Uo-no-machi or in Moto Daiku-machi.[25] In 1612 the church was finally said to have been finished.[26] The São Pedro Church stood in Ima-machi, and the São Domingo Church in Katsuyama-machi, while the Santiago Church was located in Sakaya-machi.[27]

Avila Girón then tells the story of how, on Monday, 17 November, a whole company of the demolition crew of the São Francisco Church was caught underneath when its roof and that of the large chapel came crashing down. This church had just undergone a major reconstruction and had not been put back into use yet.[28] Finally, God seemed to be exacting some revenge: "In this way, they paid for the laughs and the mockeries that had accompanied their work so far. It was noteworthy that, in spite of their usual caution, many died doing the demolition work. They tried to hide the dead from us, for they thought they were disgraced if we knew that Suruga dono did not have much reason to blaspheme."[29]

An apostate, by name of Dufan Lian, who used to be a brother in the Society and now was a married man in Nagasaki,[30] reported that the commander had said: "Let's see if, within fourteen days, the God of the Christians will mete out some punishment to those [who destroy his holy places], as they say He usually does to those who persecute the faith, or if, as is more likely, He does not come to the aid [of the Christians] at all."[31] To the Christians of Nagasaki it was self-evident that God would punish those who were involved in the demolition.

The demolition caused other deaths as well. Avila Girón reports that even before the demolition started in Morisaki "some men from Hirado were killed for the theft of something quite unimportant, and on the grounds of the São João Baptista church a boy who was caught stealing a persimmon was also killed."[32] Richard Cocks, the English merchant who had arrived in Japan the year before, in 1613, wrote in a letter from Hirado to his patron Lord Salisbury on 10 December that "not so much as a piece of timber saved but cost him his life who carried it away; and amongst the rest, one saving but a picture or painted piece of paper, & being found with it, had his head cut off and his body quartered."[33]

Avila Girón continues:

> They demolished, destroyed, burned and carried away the materials of these nine churches, their bell towers, and time pieces so that no church remained standing except the Misericordia, which was surrounded and by order of the *bugyō* used to store away the *tatami*, doors, partitions, and other materials they had taken from the other churches, for they had no time to dispose of them properly.[34]

Next, to the great surprise of the Christians of Nagasaki, the soldiers who had destroyed the churches were withdrawn and embarked for Arima on 17 November.[35] The expected razzias, tortures, and accompanying bloodbath did not materialize, but instead were reserved for the Christians of Arima, where for ten days Governor Sahyōe and Yamaguchi Naotomo terrorized the Christian population, helped by a force of ten thousand soldiers from Satsuma and Hizen.[36] When they returned to Nagasaki on 25 November, they intended to subject the city to the same treatment and make apostates of all the city's inhabitants.

Fate, however, intervened. The winter siege of Osaka Castle was just about to start, and the decision to leave the Christians of Nagasaki alone for the moment must have been made by Ieyasu himself,[37] who called up his retainers in the city to come and participate in the decisive battle with the Toyotomi.[38] Governor Sahyōe, his brother Chūbei, Yamaguchi Naotomo, Mamiya Gonzaemon, and a representative of Shimazu Iehisa all arrived in Ieyasu's camp before Osaka Castle on 27 December.[39] Thus, they are likely to have left Nagasaki together around the middle of December.

Of Sahyōe, who brought Ieyasu cannon he had bought from the Dutch,[40] it is reported that just before leaving he had "burned publicly in a courtyard before his house a great number of rosaries, images, crosses, and other symbols of the Christians that he had brought from Arima. At this time his men hit the Dominican Padre Fray Alonso de Navarrete, who, disguised as a Spanish layman, happened to pass by there and had rushed to extract from the fire what he could."[41]

*   *   *

An Early Apostate: Chijiwa Miguel

If a list were made of the ten most famous Japanese Christians of the sixteenth and seventeenth centuries, the four samurai boys who, in 1582, were sent by Valignano on a propaganda mission to Europe would certainly have to feature on it.[1] All of them intelligent, their subsequent fates provide a microcosm for the Jesuit mission in Japan. They all joined the Jesuits on 27 May 1591, less than a year after their return to Japan.[2] Three of them were ordained priests on 21 September 1608.[3] One died fairly young at age forty-two.[4] Of the two other priests, one died in Macao in 1629,[5] and the other was tortured to death in Nagasaki in 1633.[6]

The splendid success achieved by the Jesuits with these three men, however, was darkened by the fourth to the point of relegating the whole group to virtual oblivion in subsequent Jesuit historiography. Chijiwa Miguel (1570?–1633), possibly the most sensitive and intelligent of the four, has not had, until very recently,[7] a good press: he became the first of Japan's famous Christians to apostatize. He lived in Nagasaki for a good part of his life after rejecting the faith.

Miguel was born around 1570, the second son of Chijiwa Awajima no kami Naokazu (also known as Choku'in), a younger brother of Arima Yoshisada and Ōmura Sumitada who had been adopted into the Chijiwa family of long-standing retainers to the Arima House.[8] They ruled from Chijiwa on the northwest coast of the Shimabara peninsula. Both of Miguel's parents were Christians, although it is not known when they were baptized, his father as João and his mother as Jeronima.[9] In 1569, Naokazu built Kamakasa Castle in Chijiwa, but he died fighting off the forces of the Ryūzōji early the next year. Miguel's older brother, thirteen-year old Sumikazu, avenged their father's death by taking the head of his killer. Three or four years later, Jeronima and Sumikazu's little brother fled Arima to take refuge in Ōmura. When in 1577, the Chijiwa stronghold was finally taken by the Ryūzōji army, Sumikazu committed a rather un–Christian *seppuku* or suicide. He is said to have been twenty-five years old.[10]

Although Miguel was now in name the head of his family, his domain had been annexed by the Ryūzōji. The boy and his mother were living with his uncle Ōmura Sumitada, who in 1580 entered him as a student in the Jesuit seminary in Arima. There, he was known as a warm-hearted and gentle boy.[11] In the spring of 1581, he was baptized by Alessandro Valignano himself. His godfather, whose name he received, was the Captain Major of that year, Miguel da Gama, a descendant of the famous Vasco da Gama.[12] One year later, on 20 February 1582, Miguel left for Europe as "envoy from Ōmura and Arima."[13] With his companions, he sailed on the carrack of Captain Major Ignacio de Lima, who gave Valignano, the boys' Jesuit minder, Diogo de Mesquita, and the boys themselves his own cabin and treated them as well as he could.[14]

After reaching Lisbon in August of 1584, the boys and Mesquita, traveled on to Spain.[15] While visiting Toledo, Miguel came down with some infectious disease (smallpox?) that he may have contracted upon reaching Europe.[16] Still, he seems to have been well enough to dress up as a samurai in *hakama, tabi, zōri* and carrying two swords to meet the King of Spain, Philip II, on Wednesday 24 November 1584.[17] After visiting the Escorial Palace, three days later, the group traveled on to Italy, and arrived in Rome on 22 March 1585.[18] The next day, the boys were granted a private audience with the eighty-four year old Pope Gregory XIII, who died soon after the audience, while the boys were still in Rome. For this reason, one month later, on 26 April 1585, they were able to meet the new Pope Sixtus V as well, and attend his accession ceremony on 1 May.

Having been made citizens of the eternal city, the group left Rome on 13 June. The return trip took them through northern Italy, where they were received like royalty in Pisa, Florence, Venice, and Milan, before embarking in Genoa for Barcelona. From there they traveled by coach to Madrid and back to Lisbon. They left for India on 18 April 1586.[19] The group spent the winter of 1586-7 in Mozambique,[20] and arrived in Goa on 29 May 1587.[21] Accompanied by Visitor Alessandro Valignano and two Arabian horses, provided by the Portuguese Viceroy as a present for Hideyoshi, they arrived in Macao on 28 July 1588.[22] The Jesuits and their charges finally returned to Japan on 21 July 1590,[23] where Miguel was welcomed in Nagasaki by his cousins Ōmura Yoshiaki and Arima Harunobu.[24]

Fróis has described this moment for us in his *Historia*:

> And because Dom Miguel was sick in bed when they arrived, as he had been all the way from China, Dom Protasio [Arima Harunobu] first greeted the Padre Visitor, Dom Mancio and the other *fidalgos* who had come out to receive him on the *nao*, and then went straight to see Dom Miguel, and stayed with him at his bedside for three hours or more, talking about a great many things, and showing him so much love and treating him with such exquisite care that one might almost have thought it excessive.[25]

Harunobu expressed his envy

> for all the things that he [Miguel] had seen and all the honors he had received from His Holiness and the other kings and lords of the Christian world, of which he wanted to be informed in all detail. He marveled, as did all the others, at the clothing they were wearing. And hearing about the great familiarity with which they had been treated by His Holiness the Pope and His Majesty the King of Spain, he said that he finally understood what he had never understood before, and that if he had known six years ago what he knew now, he would have sent his brother Dom Leão, who was the same age as Dom Miguel.[26]

Miguel's mother was next. As most of the principals involved in this reunion after eight years of absence, she had trouble recognizing her son:

> [Because they had grown up so much,] Dom Miguel did not recognize his cousins, although he had immediately recognized Arima Dono, who was already a grown-up man when he had left Japan. Dom Martinho did not recognize his own brother, nor did his brother recognize him. And what is more, Dom Miguel's mother did not recognize her son, nor did the mother and father of Dom Martinho recognize theirs, while Dom Julião's sisters did not recognize their brother either. The same thing happened when Dom Mancio's mother from Hyūga came to visit him in Nagasaki.[27]

Thus, there can be no doubt that the trip had changed all four boys to the point that even their parents did not recognize them any longer. The trip to Europe seems to have been a particular eye-opener for Miguel. On the plus side, we may agree with the assessment of the boys' hagiographer Guido Gualtieri that "in matters of letters as well as of music these young Japanese have profited so much in a comparatively short space of time that they have become able to play several musical instruments well, and the clavichord exceedingly well. And, indeed, practicing assiduously during their home trip, they gave a successful public concert in Macao on European instruments."[28] They would do so again upon meeting Hideyoshi on 3 March 1591. On the other hand, visiting the Portuguese settlements in China, Malaysia, India, and Africa, the boys had been distressed because: "Everywhere we went, we saw Japanese, who had been sold as slaves."[29]

As for their progress in "letters," we have an example of a letter in Latin said to have been written by Miguel.[30] In Goa, Hara Martinho even gave a speech in Latin that was later printed.[31] However, these texts seem too accomplished to have been written without extensive assistance from the European padres, the more so because we find Miguel in 1593 still only studying Latin at the second level.[32] All in all, it would take him more than a decade to digest all the impressions he had absorbed during the eight years of his journey to Europe and back. For the moment, he was content to keep following the lead of the Jesuits, and participate in Valignano's embassy to Hideyoshi. After the travelers' performance, in the Jurakutei, on the harp, clavichord, violin, and lute,[33] the Taikō asked Miguel his name and whether he was related to Arima Harunobu.[34]

As we have seen, the four travelers entered the Society of Jesus at the Colegio in Amakusa in July of the same year. Miguel's mother, mindful that he was the only legitimate heir that the Chijiwa family had left, seems to have done all she could to prevent his becoming a cleric, going as far as having his cousin Arima Harunobu intervene on her behalf with Alessandro Valignano.[35] Persevering in face of such opposition, Miguel's motivation to join the Jesuits must have been strong, at least when he started out.

On 1 January 1593, Miguel is labeled in a Society Catalogue as "thin and weak," possibly as a result of the long trip to and from Europe and the strenuous regimen imposed during his novitiate.[36] After taking his vows that same year on 25 July, Miguel continued his studies in Amakusa,[37] where he studied Japanese with another brother, Ungyo Fabião, later to become well-known as the author of *Ha-Deusu* (1621), the most notorious anti–Christian treatise of his time (written in Nagasaki).[38]

The next decade was the time when Miguel must have slowly lost his faith. Regrettably, these are also the years that we have no information at all about his development or movements. It is generally agreed that Miguel left the Society sometime between 1598 and 1603.[39] If we try to narrow this down to a specific year, it seems that 1601 is the most likely to have been a watershed for Miguel.[40] We know that early in that year Itō Mancio and Nakaura Julião were given permission to go to Macao to study at the Jesuit College, while this permission was withheld from Miguel and Hara Martinho. Such a trip to Macao, as we have seen in the cases of Luis d'Almeida and João Rodrigues, was often a preamble to being ordained.

Although no one was ordained in Macao at this point, it was clear that, inside the Society, Mancio and Julião had become the frontrunners of the four. While Hara Martinho seems to have been resigned to staying behind in Japan, Miguel may have been upset and indignant enough to leave the Society.[41] Stationed in Ōmura, he also may have received a negative evaluation from his superior Afonso de Lucena.[42] Valignano's withdrawal from active involvement in managing the Japan mission and the resulting resurgence of those in the Society who discriminated against the Japanese brothers must have been among his reasons as well.[43] Some writers think that the fact that Miguel was behind the others in his study of Latin played a role.[44] While any of these factors may have triggered his decision, I think that Miguel's subsequent history shows that the real reason lay deeper and may even have been perceived earlier by his Jesuit mentors than by Miguel himself.

Lucena has the following to say on the subject:

> When, some time ago, the lord of Ōmura and some of his vassals and relatives abandoned their faith, he [Miguel] also apostatized and became a heathen; or rather he became a heretic or atheist (for, as he did not worship Shaka or Amida, he was no heathen). I recognized that he had lost the holy faith from his heart, when I had a long conversation with him after his apostasy. He thought so little of Christ Our Lord that he compared him to Mohammed. And just as this maledict Mohammed thought of Christ, i.e., that he is not God himself, so this maledict Miguel thinks as well.[45]

As we read here, the step to apostasy occurred at the time Ōmura Yoshiaki abandoned the faith, i.e., in 1606, and so this passage refers to a time possibly five years after Miguel left the Society. Obviously, however, the two steps are related to each other. If we step over the evident disapproval of the padre about Miguel's rejection of Catholic dogma, we have to admit that Miguel was making a very valid and intelligent comparison between Christ and Mohammed, something that may seem obvious today, but must have been a revolutionary observation in his own time, certainly in Japan.

But there was more. After leaving the Society, Miguel soon married and entered the service of Ōmura Yoshiaki. The two events likely were connected, with his cousin and new liege lord acting as a go-between in setting up Miguel in a new life outside of the Society.[46] In any event, Miguel received an income of six hundred *koku* from land at Kamiura Ikiriki (present-day Tarami, Ōmura City).[47] As an Ōmura retainer, Miguel had opportunities to travel again, this time to Manila, where he had not been on his first trip outside Japan.[48] According to documents left in the Ōmura domain, he was overseas in the company of another retainer by the name of Ureshino Han'emon.[49] In Manila, he finally had the freedom to observe with his own eyes the results of a successful Christian invasion.

The *Ōmurake hiden*, or "Secret History of the Ōmura Houser" reports that it was Miguel who advised Yoshiaki in 1605 that Christianity was nothing but a device for the conquest of foreign lands: "From his youth he had been a student of that sect, and he went all the way to Rome, where through his diligence he reached the innermost recesses [of the doctrine]. After he returned home, he told Lord Yoshiaki in secret: 'That faith is extremely pernicious. Outwardly, it purports to deal with the afterlife and salvation, but in reality it represents a plot to grab foreign lands.'"[50] The document concludes: "When we explore the inner doctrine, with Seizaemon as our indispensable guide, [we see that] the Christians reject the customs we practice at home and the laws issued by the authorities. They make light of their official duties and work only for the church."[51]

Ironically, during the controversy over the exchange of Sotomachi for Urakami and the subsequent expulsion of the Jesuits from the domain in 1606, Hara Martinho traveled several times to Ōmura to represent the Jesuit point of view.[52] His arguments were heard in the domain by his old traveling companion Miguel.[53] In just five years, the two men had come to take up diametrically opposite positions. Later, after Yoshiaki had ordered to put the Jesuits in his domain under arrest, the Dominicans tried to get permission to replace them.

Because Yoshiaki himself was still at court, it was the warlord's younger half-brother, Suminao (who had originally been baptized Linus), and Miguel who received the mendicants and refused their inopportune request with the words: "Those fathers [i.e., the Jesuits] were still in Ōmura, and it would not be honorable for their lord to banish one father [Afonso de Lucena], who had loved him and knew him since he was a boy, and replace him with others whom he did not know."[54]

Not long after this meeting, the Dominican friar Tomas de Santo Espiritu Zumarraga (1577–1622) wrote bitterly:

Although we did not get to talk to the Lord of the domain…, we were received by some of the leaders, among whom was the lord's brother and his cousin [i.e., Miguel] who is the great nobleman who was sent to Spain by the Jesuits. This fellow's possessions, his house, furniture, and all his land, after a careful accounting, amount to less than nothing, although he prospers at the moment and has an income of fifteen hundred ducats every year, but he also has the obligation to serve his cousin, who has given him this, with as many soldiers. When he takes it away, he will have exactly nothing. Less than two hundred pesos remains to him of this income every year to spend on his table. These are the so-called lords who went to Spain, and to whom the Pope, the King, and all the nobility [of Portugal, Spain, and Italy] showed off their power. The other three are brothers in the Society, and would, if they were laymen, have even less than this one.[55]

The mendicant continues in the same disparaging vein:

We are told that this so-called lord who visited Rome speaks very badly [of our Christian religion], going as far as saying that the Ten Commandments are very different in Spain and in Japan, and that the clergy is not respected in Spain at all. Some people have come to tell us that it is a scandal he is believed, just because he is an eyewitness. God knows the truth of this, all we can say is that if he wants to dishonor the Jesuits, he only has to take himself as an example and tell what happened to him: how they pretended in Spain he was a member of a great family, and only said so to get money for their mission. May God guide him by the hand and may He give that what they say about him is false, although we ourselves saw very bad signs in his face and actions.[56]

From this rather ominous entry in the letter of the Dominican friar, we see that Miguel needed to watch his step and be careful of what he said in the still Christian domain of Ōmura, where many resented his puncturing of Jesuit balloons. This became even more imperative after Miguel got into trouble with Ōmura Yoshiaki (1610?) and had to flee to Arima. According to Lucena, Yoshiaki intended to have him killed and put the blame for the prohibition of Christianity on his shoulders.[57] According to the *Ōmurake hiden*, however, it was the Christians of Ōmura who had intended to kill him with poison.[58]

The domain of Arima, however, turned out to be unsafe for Miguel as well. Poison having failed, he was wounded there with a knife, possibly by his own servant or someone in the pay of his cousin Arima Harunobu.[59] Miguel survived the injury, according to Lucena, "because weeds never perish."[60] Exactly *when* this attack occurred is unclear.[61] It may have been during the confusion of 1612, when Harunobu lost his domain and was commanded to commit suicide by Ieyasu.[62]

In any case, it was probably in this same year of 1612 that Miguel and his family fled to Nagasaki.[63] It is unthinkable that, by this time, a notorious apostate like Miguel could find refuge in Uchimachi, the Funazu-machi area, or the right bank of the Nakajima River, which were still firmly administered by the respective brotherhoods of the Jesuits, the Franciscans, and the Dominicans. However, the left bank of the river, imperfectly overseen by the Augustinians, would have been a good environment for a fugitive to hide out. This was where the untouchable skinners or Kawata lived. Nearby, a street had been built for the cutlers, who provided the Kawata with the knives they needed for their trade. Another unsavory profession concentrated here were the silver dealers of Ginya-machi, a disreputable lot in Christian eyes because of their involvement with money lending and counterfeiting.[64]

What is more, at the point where the Shishitoki stream joined the Kojima River (today: Dōza River), a rivulet coming down from Mt. Atago, there lived the most discriminated group of all: the Koreans. In status-conscious Japan, most of this former human loot, originally brought to Japan to be sold as slaves, was forced to live on the left bank of the Nakajima River, unless they were owned outright or employed by more respectable people elsewhere in town. I think that, having been abroad and seen many countries, of all these groups of people Miguel and his wife would have preferred to live among the Koreans, where they may have found more sympathy for their plight as fugitives in their own land than anywhere else.

The next person on record to have met Miguel is the English merchant Richard Cocks (1566–1624), who came to Nagasaki on, or shortly after, 9 December 1613.[65] As an Anglican, he was not warmly received in the city, where (as he recalled in 1620) there "were soe many prists & Jesuists, w'th their p'takers, that one could not passe the streetes w'thout being by them called Lutranos & herejos."[66] Cocks was in Nagasaki "to the entent to [have bought a] junk to have made a voyage for Siam [and have saved the monsoon], as Captain John Saris left order," as he put it in his barely literate style in a report about his first year in Japan written on 25 November 1614.[67]

The Englishman's search for a seaworthy vessel was not successful, but it must have taken him all over town, even into neighborhoods not usually frequented by merchants from overseas. Two weeks later, on 10 December 1614, Cocks wrote in a letter to his patron, Lord Salisbury: "Only it was my chance to be shewed one of these supposed princes, a pore bare fellow whoe now hath forsaken his Christian faith and is turned pagon."[68] There can be no doubt as to who of "princes" is meant here. It seems that Miguel was poorly dressed and may have looked down and out. Cocks is as condescending and dismissive of his social status as Zumarraga was eight years earlier.

Afonso de Lucena still places Miguel in Nagasaki in 1622 and 1623,[69] although we know that he moved back to Ōmura during the last years of his life. After the deaths by poison of Ōmura Yoshiaki in 1616 and his successor Sumiyori in 1619,[70] the situation in the domain greatly changed and the fact that Miguel was one of Japan's first apostates, who had virtually saved the domain for the Ōmura family had turned into a badge of honor. This was, of course, sufficient reason to invite Miguel back to take up his former lands in Kamiura Ikiriki.

That at least is one conclusion possible to draw from the inscription on a gravestone recently discovered at the site.[71] According to this inscription (paid for by his youngest son Genba Seizaemon, who had married into the Ōmura family) Miguel died on 23 January 1633, two days after his wife had passed away,[72] thus showing his devotion to his companion of three decades.[73] As for his reasons to leave Nagasaki, it is possible that Miguel left the city because he felt the pressure of the Nagasaki Governor to assist him in the suppression of Christianity and he did not want to be forced into becoming an informer of the kind that Nagasaki was beginning to sprout after 1616.[74]

* * *

The Taiwan Expedition: Murayama Tōan

Murayama Tōan would not have been the man he was, i.e., "the richest man in Japon & com vp of base parentage by his subtill & craftie wyt,"[1] if he had not thought of a few plans to save the citizens of Nagasaki and their Christian faith. We are reminded of the vow he made during his return to the church in 1614, readying himself "for whatever Our Lord would be pleased to order be done with whatever he owned and even with his life for the faith he professed," as Avila Girón reports so verbosely.[2]

At first, like many of his fellow citizens of Nagasaki, Tōan supported the Toyotomi, under siege in Osaka castle by the Tokugawa forces during the winter of 1614–15, and after a stalemate and truce, again in the early summer of 1615. Before the second siege, Murayama secretly sent his own son, the parish priest Francisco Murayama, with four hundred men to reinforce Hideyori's defenses.[3] If the Toyotomi held out, at least Western Japan might be spared further persecutions of its Christians.

From an autograph letter dated 2 June 1615, we know that Tōan was at that moment in or near the capital,[4] no doubt anxiously following the developments around Osaka castle,[5] which only two days later would fall to the Tokugawa. On 7 June, possibly after having learned of his son Francisco's death, Tōan left for the Kantō to mend his relations with Ieyasu, his support for the defeated Toyotomi side still a secret.[6]

Waiting for an audience with Ieyasu cannot have been easy for a known Christian from Nagasaki. But Tōan was rich, well-known, and he had been appointed to his position as the *daikan* of Sotomachi by Ieyasu himself. Eventually, he would be able buy himself into Ieyasu's vicinity again. In any case, he now had plenty of time to think how he could please Japan's ruler. The first indication of this is contained in the diary kept by Richard Cocks in an entry for 21 October that he wrote to his associate William Eaton in Osaka to find out if it is true that Tōan had been "apoynted to make warse against the Chinas."[7]

The term "apoynted" is curious, for it suggests that the task, at least initially, was not undertaken voluntarily. Next, we learn that, on Sahyōe's recommendation, a Red Seal license was issued to Tōan for trade with Taiwan on 31 October 1615.[8] These two snippets of information seem to contradict each other, but only for as long as it takes us to remember the concept of what we would call today "plausible deniability." In reality, then, the Red Seal license must have represented Ieyasu's permission, order, or approval to conquer the island.

A few days later, Cocks wrote that the China Captain in Hirado, Li Tan, had received the news that Nagasaki's Governor had held back a small junk to carry soldiers to Taiwan.[9] This is another sign that, by this time, Tōan's new project had support at all levels of the Tokugawa Bakufu. Thus, we are beginning to see the outline of a new plan, which may have been proposed to Ieyasu sometime during the fall of 1615.

It was a dream of conquest of the large island south of the Ryukyu chain. In this new domain, eminently situated to serve as a base for Japanese trading throughout Asia, Christianity would be allowed. At first, Tōan's friends the Dominicans would supply spiritual support.[10] Japan's Christians would form the bulk of its population, and the colony would be led and fed by the business acumen of the citizens of Nagasaki. Had Christians not provided the spearhead of one of Hideyoshi's armies in Korea in the 1590s as well?

There was, moreover, an ominous precedent for this invasion, dating back only a few years earlier. In March of 1609, Ieyasu had issued a secret order to Arima Harunobu: "Faraway countries such as Siam and Cambodia all send tribute and traders to Japan, but nearby Taiwan has never sent an embassy so far."[11] The expedition to reconnoiter and conquer Taiwan was sent on its way in the spring of 1611. The men from Arima ended up fighting the Taiwanese aboriginals, abandoning their dead, attacking a few Chinese ships at anchor, and bringing back a number of captives to be shown to Ieyasu. These were later sent back to Taiwan loaded with presents.[12] The net effect of the expedition, however, had been to leave Harunobu broke and unable to defend himself when the Okamoto Daihachi affair exploded in his face in 1612.[13]

Governor Sahyōe had been involved up to his neck in these affairs of the Arima domain, and, therefore, had seen firsthand the effectiveness of ordering such an enormous undertaking if one wanted to bring down a lord from an old and well-established samurai family of the area. As governor of Nagasaki, moreover, Sahyōe cannot have approved of Tōan's openly pro–Christian attitude during the processions of 1614, especially as seen in contrast to the prudent attitude of the *machi-doshiyori* who had forbidden their streets to participate in the demonstrations.

Therefore, if there was anyone in Nagasaki who needed to be brought down in Sahyōe's eyes, it was Tōan. For these reasons, it is not at all impossible that the proposal to order another Taiwan expedition may have come from his direction.[14] Thus, with the stone of an invasion around his neck, Tōan returned to Nagasaki in February of 1616 to supervise the preparations for the expedition in person.[15] By 7 March Richard Cocks had caught on as well: "Also, it is said that the Emperour hath appointed one Tuan Dono, a rich man of Langasaq,' that at his owne charge [he shall go to the] wars and take in an island called Fermosa [off the coast of] China, for w'ch occation he is now making [ready juncks and] other provision."[16]

A Dominican testimony, dating from 1620, assesses the expedition as follows:

> The emperor [Ieyasu] had ordered.... Tōan to undertake this project. He had accepted the mission and offered to undertake it at his own expense. For this purpose he had brought together a number of large vessels with numerous and very good crews. He handed all this to his son Shuan because he recognized that, although he was only a youth, he was full of energy and good judgment, and so he made him commander of all the men who had joined the expedition.[17]

Thus, a fleet of thirteen ships left the harbor of Nagasaki in the first half of May.[18] We do not have much information about the equipment the fleet carried or how they planned to take Taiwan. Some of the ships were large enough to carry twenty-five to thirty rowers on each side.[19] A storm on the way, however, scattered the ships. Some ended up on the Ryukyu islands, others on Taiwan, a third part on the Chinese coast, while the commander Murayama Shuan himself eventually reached Cochinchina.[20]

Likely, the expedition had left Nagasaki too late to sail with the north-south monsoon, which may have turned around south-north at the very moment they were at sea, scattering the ships and spoiling their impact when some of them finally reached Taiwan. Another testimony of more than thirteen years after the event mentions that there were between three and four thousand soldiers on the ships, who were able to take Taiwan, but, for lack of supplies, did not manage to hold on to it very long.[21]

The size of the ships and the number of soldiers suggest a considerable investment in this venture on Tōan's part. It is noteworthy, too, that this whole fleet could be assembled in Nagasaki in a little over half a year. If we go back and try to trace the fate of the expedition step by step, we find that, on 15 May 1616, Cocks noted that the fleet was making a stop at the Gotō islands to wait for reinforcements from Miyako.[22] Among Cocks' papers there are two more references, dated five days apart between 17 and 22 July, to what happened with Tōan's fleet. This information, says Cocks, was provided by Ou Hua-yu, the Chinese merchant living in Nagasaki mentioned above, who reported the return of three of Tōan's ships.[23]

The ships which Tōan had sent to conquer Taiwan, Cocks writes, did not succeed, for their belligerent intent had been discovered before they arrived. The fleet lost one ship and all its crew, who sliced open their own bellies when they were surrounded by the Taiwanese natives and saw no way of escaping. The rest of the fleet did not dare go ashore, but sailed for the coast of China, where they killed more than twelve hundred Chinese and confiscated all the vessels they found, throwing their crews overboard. Therefore, it seemed likely that no junks from China would visit Japan that year. Informed of this, the Chinese of Nagasaki decided to report it to Ieyasu, which they hoped would cause Tōan to lose his life and property.[24]

It should be remembered that this "news" comes from an untrustworthy source, for naturally all Chinese in Japan would have been opposed to an expedition to conquer Taiwan and establish a colony or trading post on the island. Such a conquest might have made their Japan trade superfluous. It is possible, therefore, that parts of this "report" are somewhat exaggerated. The Chinese of Nagasaki, it is clear, would have liked to see Tōan ruined and his property confiscated.[25] There were others just as eager to see to this as well.

For lack of any Japanese sources dealing with these events, the Chinese materials about this expedition (some of which seem to corroborate Cocks' story) are all the more precious.[26] According to one of these, two ships under the command of a man called Akashi Dōyū (Michitomo?) anchored at Dongyong in the county of Minxuan in Fujian in late June 1616.[27] The Japanese ships were very large, about 24 meters long, and carried, apart from four horses, a large supply of weapons and countless leather boxes [ammunition?].[28]

The Japanese were reported to have said they had come to Taiwan and Fujian to look for Tōan's son who "had been sent as an envoy" and had not returned yet. They had also had occasion to teach the violence-loving natives of Taiwan a lesson.[29] This news was quickly sent to the provincial capital and from there forwarded to the Chinese court. Meanwhile, the Japanese made a prisoner of a Chinese official.

His name was Dong Ba-qi, and he had volunteered to approach the foreign vessels in order to reconnoiter.[30] When the ships left, they took Dong along with them to Japan. The following year, on 23 May 1617, the same man called Dōyū returned, now saying he had come as an envoy from the ruler of Kyushu, Murayama Tōan, who had been invested by the ruler of Musashi with the supervision over the Chinese who came to trade in Japan.[31]

When this news reached the court, the vice-minister for naval affairs, Han Zhong-yong, hurried to the coast and went on board the Japanese ship to interrogate the Japanese envoy about the invasion of Taiwan.[32] The envoy told him that

> a trading fleet of eleven ships had left Japan the year before. They had encountered rough weather and lost sight of each other. Two of the ships under the command of Murayama Tōan's son still had not returned to Nagasaki. Seven of the others had fought with Chinese soldiers in Zhejiang. The two ships under the command of Dōyū had been cast upon the coast of Fujian at Dongyong.[33]

Evidently, hasty preparations had not been good for the discipline of the crews. Many probably were unemployed riff-raff from Nagasaki's harbor side.[34] Dōyū's two ships returned to Nagasaki with their Chinese prisoner after several other ships of the fleet had already limped back into Nagasaki Bay. At this point, Tōan must have decided that his only way out of the failure was to pretend the expedition had been sent as an embassy to China. Treating Dong Ba-qi with all possible honors, he ordered Dōyū to return to China in his name to try and establish commercial relations with the Chinese instead of attempting the conquest of Taiwan again.

When Dōyū was finally asked by Naval Affairs Minister Han Zhong-yong about his purpose in coming to China once more, he said that "he now wished for nothing else but to return to Japan with an official letter from the Ming Court stating that it had appreciated and was aware of Murayama Tōan's great honor and fame. For the rest, they wished that from now on Japanese and Chinese might be able to start trading harmoniously without any belligerent intentions towards each other."[35]

This request for a letter from the Ming court praising Tōan rings very true. After the failure to conquer Taiwan, there was nothing that could save Tōan any longer, except perhaps a letter from the Emperor of China. The answer of the Ming official was that, based on the experiences of the Chinese since before Hideyoshi's invasions of Korea (1592–

8), the Satsuma conquest of Ryukyu (1609), and the recent Taiwan expeditions (1611, 1616), there was no other way for them but to distrust and hate the Japanese.[36] Thus, Tōan's envoy was forced to return to Japan empty-handed.

Finally on 22 July 1617, Cocks quotes a letter from Jorge Durões, a Portuguese resident of Nagasaki, who reported to the English factory that the last three of Tōan's ships had returned from Cochin China at the end of June.[37] Later, the Dominican Francisco Morales would write:

> About [Murayama] Shuan Juan, his wife wrote to me to say that when he had gone to Cochin China two years ago, he was stricken with a terrible torment [i.e., storm], so that he begged Our Lord to extend his life if there was still any way in which he could serve Him, and that might take his life now if he had somehow offended Him. But the torment ceased and Shuan arrived in Cochinchina, where he built a small church for the Japanese Christians who lived there.[38]

This is the last news we have of the ill-fated expedition that must have cost Tōan a sizeable part of his fortune.[39] He was left much weakened and out of favor with the court of Tokugawa Hidetada, who now ruled Japan after his father Ieyasu had died in 1616. In fact, Tōan was nothing more than a sitting duck.

✳   ✳   ✳

Dangerous Litigation: Murayama Tōan vs. Suetsugu Heizō

The first to realize this may have been the underground Jesuits of Nagasaki. There is an interesting letter written by Mateo de Couros (1567–1632), that seems to confirm this:

> I asked the two *otonas* or headmen of this city [Luis Takagi's son Pedro and Machida João], that in their complaint against the said Tōan they would make common cause with Heizō, and that they would give me sworn testimony that the Society had had nothing to do with this business, which they gave me in two copies, which I am now sending to Your Reverence via the Philippines. The signature of Heizō is lacking because he was at court at the time [the certificate was composed].[1]

Here we see the mayors of Nagasaki plotting with the Provincial of the underground Jesuit mission in Japan to bring Tōan down. It is not clear from this letter (which is dated well after Tōan was jailed) when this collaboration between the mayors and Heizō started. Their resentment towards Tōan, accumulated over the years, must have been considerable, largely mirroring that of the Jesuits, who had raised Tōan to power only to see him turn against them and support the Dominicans.

In the fall of 1617 sixty-four year old Takagi Luis officially announced to the Bakufu authorities in Edo that he was retiring from his position as official of Uchimachi, and that his son Sakuemon (1588–1641) would succeed him.[2] The person introduced by Mateo de Couros to the mayors in the fragment quoted above, Suetsugu Heizō, came from an old Hakata family that had been involved with Nagasaki since the 1580s. Heizō's father, the Christian merchant Suetsugu Kōzen Cosme put up the capital for an expansion of Uchimachi along the land tongue toward Mt. Tateyama in order to house a number of new immigrants from Hakata.[3]

The Suetsugu family had always considered Hakata the main base of their commercial operations, and their involvement in Nagasaki had remained on a subsidiary basis. Kōzen himself, for example, never moved to Nagasaki. His son Heizō was born in Hakata in 1573 and baptized João. He was Kōzen's second son and therefore free to move to Nagasaki, which he seems to have done sometime during the 1590s.[4]

The Tokugawa period sources we have left dealing with him may be slightly more trustworthy than usual because it is certain that the Suetsugu family kept their own records in Hakata.[5] Thus it is reported of Heizō that before moving permanently to Nagasaki, he used to come to the city from Hakata every year during the trading season.[6] When he started to live in Nagasaki, it was, curiously, not in Kōzen-machi, but in nearby Kanaya-machi, the street of the iron dealers, where he is said to have risen to *otona* or street elder.

Heizō was involved in the Red Seal trade from the very beginning, and his is one of the first names to be mentioned in a Red-Seal letter giving permission for a voyage to Annam and dated 1604.[7] Until 1617, then, when Heizō became forty-four, he was part of that large group of rich Nagasaki merchants who represented as *otona* the streets where they lived in the city government.[8] It seems that by that time Heizō had already discontinued his involvement in the Red-Seal trade, concentrating instead on the buying and selling of silk. Richard Cocks, for example, who knew Heizō personally, never mentions that he was trading with foreign countries.[9]

More importantly, Heizō seems to have been one of Nagasaki's first apostates from this *otona* class. Although the exact date of his apostasy in front of Bakufu authorities is not known, it is likely it occurred sometime during his litigation with Tōan.[10] Mateo de Couros may even have been aware of this when he invited him into the conspiracy with the mayors of Nagasaki. Heizō was useful, of course, as front man for the attack on Tōan. Later, after Heizō was appointed Nagasaki's *daikan*, Couros may have hoped that he would protect the Jesuits in return.

According to a letter written by the Jesuit Francisco Vieira (1555?–1619), Heizō's resentment towards Tōan also considerably predated his attack upon the *daikan*. Vieira writes that Heizō had prepared himself with documents and proof for ten or twelve years before making his move against the official of Sotomachi.[11] He started his attack by pressing Tōan for repayment of a debt which dated to the time of his father Kōzen and Tōan refused to acknowledge. A violent discussion followed and the affair was brought before Shogun Hidetada's council.[12]

Although, again, just as with the Taiwan expedition we have no contemporary Japanese sources referring to this cause célèbre (not even a reference in the *Tokugawa Jikki*), we can surmise from the scattered information in the sources compiled by the foreigners in Japan that the litigation between the two men lasted for about one year, between the summer of 1617 and the summer of 1618.[13] Apart from the debt, Heizō seems to have brought a whole array of other charges against Tōan.

Cocks' diary has an entry for 14 June 1618, where the diarist quotes a letter from Jorge Durões. This Nagasaki merchant had informed the English factor that Tōan stood accused of murdering seventeen or eighteen people, among whom a family that had not wanted him to have their daughter.[14] Such charges were not sufficient, however, to topple an administrator appointed by Ieyasu himself: "the councell tould Feze Dono they would haue hym to take in hand matters of leeveing & not dead people."[15]

Heizō also offered money to the Bakufu. Appointed to Tōan's position, he promised he would pay the Bakufu five thousand *ryō*, instead of the three thousand that Tōan paid.[16] Although it was true that the taxes paid by the inhabitants of Sotomachi did not even come close to five thousand *ryō*, the more mobility there was in the plum positions of the tax collectors the better it was for the state. So here was an argument that needed to be taken seriously.

We may surmise that, on the whole, Tōan had become a sort of an obstacle, not only in the Bakufu's conduct of foreign policy, but also in its efforts to get a firm grip on Nagasaki, the country's most important import and export center. Since the days of Hideyoshi, Tōan had gathered immense riches, prestige and power, and had become like the mayor of an independent town. Eventually, the Bakufu decided that he needed to be removed.[17]

On 8 February 1618, Cocks noted in his diary that Heizō had passed by Hirado on his way to court, where he had indicted and "utterly undon Tuan."[18] Although this may have been cause for joy among some people of Uchimachi, to the people of Sotomachi, Heizō's victory was a disaster. His public statement that he would extract five thousand *ryō* in taxes seemed to guarantee their impoverishment.[19] They tried to appeal to the Bakufu, but it was too late.[20]

Heizō, however, was not satisfied, he still feared Tōan's wealth and influence in the city. Therefore, he stepped up the pressure and "apeached Twan & his children as Christians & maintayners of Jesuistes and fryres whoe were enemies to the state."[21] According to this testimony, then, it was Heizō who brought Christianity into the litigation. On this point, of course, Tōan could retaliate.

The Jesuit Francisco Vieira reports that one of Tōan's assistants in his litigation with Heizō was a man who had been living in Nagasaki since 1615: "an apostate and former *dōjuku* of the Society, called Fabião, who accused us at court, on Tōan's behalf, that there were still many of us in Japan, because he knew us and in particular those of us who were living in Nagasaki, even giving the names of the houses where we were usually hiding."[22]

In front of two members of the *rōjū*,[23] the highest council of the Bakufu, Tōan added to this that Heizō himself also was a Christian and that he "wanted his office to be better able to hold on and hide the fathers of the Society in Nagasaki of whom there were still many in Japan, for it seemed to him that as the King had exiled those fathers and did not want them in Japan, he would not give Heizō his position [if he would use it to give shelter to the padres]."[24]

With the introduction of Christianity into the conflict, the litigation was taking a more ominous turn for the whole city of Nagasaki. It is likely that this was the first time Edo officials became aware that there still was a sizeable number of padres living in and around Nagasaki. When the litigants were asked the question if they themselves were Christians, Heizō denied this, but Tōan bravely answered in the affirmative. Heizō's gumption was too much for Simão, a long-time *dōjuku* of the Jesuits, who had also been brought to the proceedings by Tōan.[25] Simão is said to have called out that Heizō was a liar, that he was a Christian as well, and that he had participated in the 1614 processions just like Tōan.[26]

As it turned out, Heizō had the more powerful ammunition to sway the shogun's council, having been informed by someone in Tōan's household about the involvement of the family in the return of Tōan's son Francisco after the expulsion of the priests in 1614 and his support for Hideyori:

He accused him of having had a son who was a priest and therefore exiled from Japan, but who had come back to support the army of Osaka. This Tōan could not deny, but he said that he had not known of his son's return to Japan nor of his presence in the army of Osaka. But such excuses are not admitted in Japan, where parents often pay for the misdeeds of their sons and vice versa. They removed him from his functions and exiled him together with his son Shuan, who was assisting him in these proceedings, but they left him his silver, and his wife and the rest of his sons remained free.[27]

In view of the later persecutions in Nagasaki, it is remarkable that at this date, more than four years after Ieyasu's prohibition, it was still not considered a crime to be a Christian in private in Edo. Tōan, therefore, was not convicted because he was a Christian, but because his son had flouted the shogunal order of exile by coming back to Nagasaki and supporting Hideyori's forces in Osaka.

Again, the date of the new verdict is uncertain. Cocks noted in his diary, on 19 August 1618, that he had heard from William Adams that Tōan had lost his trial, that all his possessions had been confiscated, and that his life was "at the Emperor's pleasure."[28] It is possible that the mayors of Nagasaki were present in Edo when the verdict was announced.[29] If he had been an ordinary merchant, Tōan would have been executed, but as a former member of the ruling class, he was sent into exile in the beginning of December 1618, either in Kai, or to "an island in the vicinity of Edo."[30]

The most important outcome of the litigation for Nagasaki was that it had proved that there were still a number of padres in the city and its surroundings. Thus, both the new *bugyō* and the new *daikan* were warned, on pain of being put to death themselves, that they had better round up all of these illegal aliens.[31] With this clear mandate, they returned to Nagasaki in August of 1618.

* * *

The New Governor: Hasegawa Gonroku (1)

Since 1606, at the very outset of his tenure, Nagasaki Governor Hasegawa Sahyōe had become influential in the domains surrounding the city, when Ieyasu ordered that all foreign merchandise arriving anywhere in Kyushu had to be submitted to his scrutiny before it could be sold. Next, in 1612, Sahyōe became paramount in the neighboring domain of Arima, when he was appointed, again by Ieyasu, to the position of supervisor over Arima Naozumi, Harunobu's son.[1] Starting in 1614, his power was again increased in order to deal with the suppression of Christianity. This time, he received the right to call up soldiers from all the powerful *tozama* lords of the domains of Satsuma, Kumamoto, Saga, and Fukuoka. This was something quite different from being able to command forces from the smaller neighboring domains, such as Ōmura, Arima, Isahaya, and Hirado.[2]

Gradually, therefore, Sahyōe became preoccupied with the problem of how to transfer the powerbase, carved out by himself with the support of O-Natsu, his sister, to someone else upon his death. This, possibly, was one of the reasons why Sahyōe tried hard to be invested with the domain of Arima, an ambition that ultimately remained unfulfilled. Sahyōe's successor in Nagasaki turned out to be a man simply called Gonroku. Later he became Hasegawa Gonroku Fujimasa (?–1630), variously described as Sahyōe's nephew, his son, and his younger brother.[3] In spite of this, Gonroku is not even mentioned as a Hasegawa family member in the great compilation of Bakufu retainers, although he never lost his rank, nor was he ever exiled or condemned to commit *seppuku*.[4]

Gonroku, therefore, likely was of *chōnin* or commoner extraction, who won Sahyōe's confidence with his commercial ability, and in the end was adopted by him.[5] Gonroku's first trace in the record dates from 1609, when he was awarded a Red-Seal license for Luzon on the recommendation of Honda Masazumi.[6] Four months later, he received another Red Seal license for the Philippines.[7] In both cases, Gonroku is likely to have functioned as a front man for his "uncle" Sahyōe's overseas trading ventures. Next, Gonroku appears in the diary of a tea master from Fukuoka, Kamiya Sōtan, who from 1612 mentions Sahyōe attending his gatherings.[8] On such an occasion, on 18 May 1613, Sahyōe introduced Gonroku officially as "his nephew" to this company of well-connected tea drinkers.[9]

After his successful four-month stay in Nagasaki and Arima between August and December 1614, Sahyōe was rewarded with an appointment to the position of *mandokoro* or shogunal representative in another trading city, i.e., Sakai, on 23 January 1615.[10] From this time on, Sahyōe mainly resided in or near this port city to supervise its rebuilding from the ashes left by the flames of war and to suppress Christianity in this community that had had such frequent contact with Nagasaki over the past several decades.[11]

Sahyōe's star, however, which seemed to shine so brightly at the Bakufu's firmament in the first half of 1615, quickly faded. It may be that, as Pagés has written, he was denounced for his rapacity and tyranny by the citizens of Sakai.[12] It is also true that he became too ill in his last years to perform adequately in the different functions he had been charged with. In the summer of 1616, Sahyōe may have visited Nagasaki for the last time. He continued to be represented there by his protégé Gonroku.[13]

One of Sahyōe's last acts, as the commissioner in charge of suppressing Christianity in and around Nagasaki, was a letter he wrote to Gonroku, most likely at the behest of his superiors in the Bakufu, in the summer (July?) of 1617.[14] In this letter he ordered the arrest and execution of those who had hidden the Dominican friar Alonso de Navarrete (1571–1617) and the Augustinian friar Hernando de Ayala (1575–1617), who had just been arrested in Nagayo, Ōmura, on 29 May.[15]

For fear of popular unrest, the friars had been quickly beheaded three days after their arrest on Takashima island in Ōmura Bay.[16] One year earlier, on 18 September 1616, Hidetada had issued his own prohibition of Christianity, which referred to the edict of 1614 as an anti–Christian law, "the meaning of which had [or: should have?] by now penetrated to the lowest classes in society."[17] What was new in the *interpretation* of the old law, from now on, was that helping padres to hide automatically became a capital offense.

Two of the friars' Japanese helpers, Gaspar Ueda Hikojirō and Andre Yoshida, had presented themselves at the Nagasaki *bugyōsho* with a request to be arrested as well, but Gonroku had refused to comply. On Sahyōe's orders, the two men were arrested on 21 August and beheaded on 1 October 1617.[18] They were the first laymen to be executed for their faith in Nagasaki since 1597. Sahyōe himself died in Kyoto on 24 November that year.[19]

Around the same time, Gonroku received a temporary appointment to replace his "uncle."[20] Pagés, quoting some letter filled with the Jesuit belief in a just universe, writes that Sahyōe "ended up like the apostates, a desperate death. His decomposing blood caused him intolerable pains, and the infection of his wounds caused everyone, including his family, to keep away from him. He expired in convulsions of pain and rage."[21] How much truth this contains and how much wishful thinking, it is no longer possible to say.

Until the litigation between Tōan and Heizō, most Bakufu officials had believed that the banishment of 1614 had accomplished practically the whole task of the suppression of Christianity they thought necessary for the stability of the new society they were fashioning. For that reason, in the years immediately following the expulsion, there had been few arrests and executions throughout the country (thirteen executions in 1615, and only twelve in 1616). The persecution seemed to be on a backburner. It is true, of course, that in 1615, soldiers had been stationed around the Misericordia Church to prevent the people of Nagasaki from holding religious meetings there,[22] and that the next year, at Hidetada's orders, a religious register was compiled of all Nagasaki's inhabitants.[23]

As for the missionaries, this relative respite was used as a chance to smuggle new forces into the country: about twenty missionaries, foreign and Japanese, entered clandestinely during 1615–1616.

> At first, the administrators of Nagasaki had been unaware of it, and their surprise was great when they sensed it and succeeded in arresting two out of seven smugglers. A temporary satisfaction was broken by disappointing shock, which was replaced by irritation, anger, and hatred; all this was intensified by the rebuke from the higher authorities and was followed by the determination to execute the suppressive measures more vigorously.[24]

These same years, just before and after Sahyōe's death, were full of tensions for Hasegawa Gonroku. If the interdiction of Christianity had not been pressed with much urgency, it was at least partly due to a rekindling of the power struggle around the post of Governor of Nagasaki, in which Gonroku was only one of the competitors. On 20 July 1615, for example, Cocks mentions a rumor that Hasegawa Chūbei would be appointed Nagasaki *bugyō*.[25] Chūbei, indeed, would have been the logical choice, and might have been appointed if Ieyasu had not died and his sister O-Natsu had not been chased from court in 1616, the year before Sahyōe's death.[26]

What is more, in 1616, Murayama Tōan still may have been jockeying for the position as well, and he too would have had a chance of being appointed if his Taiwan expedition had been successful.[27] In the end, Tōan's fall, engineered by Mateo de Couros, Takagi Pedro, and Suetsugu Heizō, assured Gonroku of his continued tenure, so he too must be counted among the league of Nagasaki men opposing Tōan.

On 5 February 1618, not quite two and a half months after Sahyōe's death, Cocks mentions another rumor to the effect that Sahyōe's son was likely to be appointed Governor of Nagasaki,[28] and that Gonroku would just be his representative in Nagasaki.[29] So, even in 1618, Gonroku still was not sure whether he would be able to hold on to the post for which Sahyōe had groomed him. From August 1618 on, at any rate, the provisional governor saw himself faced with strict orders to clamp down on Christianity in Nagasaki on the one hand, and the necessity of cooperating with the new *daikan* Suetsugu Heizō on the other. Although Heizō's jurisdiction counted twice as many streets or *machi* as Gonroku's, the latter was more powerful in the all-important matter of trade.

The difference between the two officials lay mostly in the fact that Heizō was considered a local official or *jiyakunin*, while Gonroku shared his jurisdiction over Uchimachi with other *jiyakunin*, the mayors or *machidoshiyori*, two of whom, the so-called *nengyōji*, took care of most day-to-day business for him. Gonroku, also, did not reside permanently in Nagasaki, but only came to the city during the trading season, usually arriving in July and leaving again for Edo in December.[30] Thus, he was the one who received the direct orders from the Council of Elders, who had invested him with the authority to enforce these orders.

Ultimately, the suppression of Christianity was his responsibility.

On 15 December 1617, Jeronimo Rodrigues (1567–1628) had still been able to write from Macao in the annual letter of the Jesuits that

> everyone in Nagasaki has religious images in their houses, and many of those are in places where the whole world can see them. The citizens of Nagasaki also own spiritual books, and they wear their rosary beads and *Agnus Dei* amulets visibly on their chests; they recite the Christian doctrine and psalms in many houses; and they hold their funerals freely in public cemeteries, where chapels still stand as before.[31]

In 1618, Gonroku and Heizō arrived in Nagasaki later than usual, probably because they had had to wait in Edo for the final verdict on Tōan. When they reached the city in the second half of August, the town was rife with rumors about the arrival of new missionaries (no less than fourteen had arrived that summer).[32] It was politic, however, to move slowly for the moment. Pagés writes that Gonroku and Heizō dissimulated about their true intentions for two months, between late August and late October,[33] and this seems to be in keeping with a realistic appraisal of the situation in which they found themselves.

Upon their return to the city, they had found a fleet of four Portuguese galliots, commanded by Captain Major Antonio de Oliveira de Moraes.[34] The Captain Major had lost two similar vessels on the way due to bad weather. But with the remaining four he had succeeded in destroying one lone Dutch pinnace in an accidental encounter.[35] As Gonroku and Heizō had returned from Edo with a full program of anti–Christian ordinances to implement (which naturally would be easier to do without four well-armed Portuguese ships in the harbor), the Portuguese were given a good price for their silk and then sent on their way unusually early, so that they arrived in Macao on 1 November.[36]

Upon their departure, they were warned that, from now on, the Portuguese were forbidden on pain of death to secretly engage in activities supporting the missionaries.[37] At the same time new orders for the suppression of Christianity were announced throughout the city, prohibiting upon "the gravest penalties [i.e., being burned alive], to give shelter to the missionaries, for the brotherhoods to come together, to hold prayer sessions in the graveyards or on the sites of the razed churches, and to possess any image or symbol of the Christian religion."[38]

A system of rewards for informants was also introduced: thirty bars of silver were to be rewarded to anyone whose information led to the arrest of a priest.[39] This amount, at forty-three *momme* per bar of silver, represents a sum of 1290 *momme*.[40] This considerable sum of money made becoming an informer for the Bakufu particularly attractive for the less scrupulous among the Christians of Nagasaki. So it is not surprising that the number of arrests suddenly started to rise. The Dominican Orfanel writes about this time:

> They also arrested those who read Christian literature in some Christian study groups and put up thirty bars of silver as a reward for denouncing a missionary. These were exhibited on the square, in a high spot, with a placard beneath it saying: "This silver will be given to whoever discovers a thief or a missionary...." It so happened that they were looking throughout the city for certain thieves and had originally (a few days earlier) exhibited the silver and the sign beneath it to find them, and because a little later they were also looking for the missionaries they just added the phrase "or a missionary."[41]

During November and December of 1618, Gonroku and Heizō organized a house-to-house search for hidden padres throughout the whole city and collected signatures from all its householders. As we have seen, in the fall of 1614 Sahyōe had already made the citizens of Nagasaki swear an oath, street by street, that on pain of death and confis-cation of all their property no one was to shelter padres, friars, brothers, or their helpers. When Hidetada had passed his own anti–Christian legislation in September 1616, placards were erected throughout Nagasaki spelling these orders out once more and specifying that all members of the ten-family groups into which each street of Nagasaki was organ-ized would be co-responsible if one of the households were found to have been hiding a padre.[42]

This happened at a time when there were forty-nine padres and brothers left in Japan,[43] the majority of whom was hiding in and around Nagasaki. Now the house-to-house search was accompanied with a new drive to collect signatures from all of the city's householders. Signing meant that all ten householders and their families would be pun-ished for an infraction against the new ordinance committed by anyone belonging to their group. At this time, i.e., in November and December 1618, the householders were made to sign these documents once more with the addition that the person in whose house a padre would be found would be burned alive with his whole family, while all the others of his group of ten households would be decapitated.

At the very same time, on 25 November 1618, the city also saw its first autodafé. Twelve people, the members of three families (including the wives and children) of the boat owners who had helped to bring Tōan's son Francisco back to Nagasaki in 1614, were burned alive.[44] This example was, of course, timed to go with the signing of the oaths and was designed to instill fear into everyone who was hiding padres in Nagasaki. All trustworthy Christian sheep of the city were involved, on a rotating schedule, in the effort to provide their shepherds with shelter and protection, while "many spies and other ver-min walked around the city in disguise day and night in order to discover where the priests were hidden."[45]

All this time, the Murayama family, too, had been sheltering Dominican and Fran-ciscan friars in their different residences around town.[46] But so strong still was their prestige that even after Tōan's exile the Murayama households could not be raided without solid evidence. Instead, on the night of 13 December 1618, men of the *bugyōsho* knocked at the gate of the house of Domingos Jorge (1576–1619), a Portuguese merchant, who lived in Bunchi-machi, near the former Jesuit compound at Morisaki.[47] There they found two Jesuits: Padre Carlo Spinola (1565–1622), the treasurer of the Society, Brother Ambró-sio Fernandes, formerly of the Jesuit Navy,[48] and João Chūgoku (1573–1622), a Japanese brother.[49]

> And because this was a house of a Portuguese, it did not concern anyone else, for the for-eigners such as the Portuguese and Chinese, although they have regular homes with wives and children and live in this city, do not belong to any groups or registers of their street, and for this reason their neighbors' affairs are of no concern to them and neither are theirs to those who live in the same street, for they are exempt from this law, and if any missionary is found in the houses of the Portuguese, only the householder, his wife, and children are exe-cuted.[50]

On the same night men of the new *daikan* Suetsugu Heizō raided the house of Cosme Takeya Sozaburō, a Korean, who likely was living somewhere on the left bank of the Nakajima river. They arrested the head of the household and two Dominican friars:

Angel Ferrer Orsucci (1575–1622) from Lucca in Italy and the Spaniard Juan de Santo Domingo (1587–1619). Both friars had arrived in Japan, disguised as Spaniards from the Philippines, exactly four months earlier.[51]

The next day, 14 December 1618, all the arrested were led before Governor Gonroku, who "wanted to hear from their own mouth that they were missionaries and the name of the order to which they belonged, and, after a short interview, he informed them of the will of the sovereign. The accused answered that they were acting at the orders of another sovereign, superior to those on earth, who was God Almighty."[52] All the missionaries and their servants were sent to the Suzuta jail in Ōmura, while their hosts, the Korean Cosme Takeya, his seven neighbors and Domingos Jorge were locked up in the Nagasaki jail.

To make sure the mayors knew of the annoyance felt by the Bakufu authorities over the attitude of the people of Nagasaki towards the prohibition of Christianity, on 16 December 1618, Gonroku informed Takagi Sakuemon (Pedro) in writing, sending him a letter with praise for his own apostasy, but, above all, threats for the Christians of Nagasaki and himself if he failed to report the whereabouts of the missionaries in hiding.[53]

On 20 January 1619, Gonroku jailed Kuroji Pablo, a Nagasaki *otona* or street elder, whom he had appointed to guard the thirty bars of silver that were exhibited in public during the day to excite the greed of potential informers. The man's only crime seems to have been that he had refused to serve in this capacity any longer and be exposed to all the abuse and criticism of his fellow-citizens for aiding and abetting the persecution by the authorities.[54]

Five days later, on 25 January, Gonroku left Nagasaki for Edo.[55] In his absence, his retainer Sukedayu represented his master and made sure no missionaries remained in the city, forbidding the reading of religious texts or listening to religious sermons, as well as holding prayer meetings.[56] The first reward of 1619 was likely given to an informer by name of Kusari João, who pointed out to the *yokome* (or spy) Yasuemon that the house of Yoshida Shō'un, a cloth dyer of Kōyamachi, was likely to hold a hidden padre.[57]

A raid in the night of 14 and 15 March resulted in the arrest of the Spanish friar Alonso de Mena (1578–1622).[58] Working quickly, Heizō's men tortured Mena's servant, who betrayed the information that there was another friar hiding in the residence of Tōan's eldest son, Toku'an. The same day, Francisco Morales, a Spanish Dominican, was seized there:

> They gave me time to put on my habit which I did with great satisfaction, for it seemed to me as if I was entering the order of Our Father Santo Domingo once more. They took the cords off [from around my waist] and tied them tightly around my neck and bound my hands behind my back with the same rope. Tied up in this way, I went around noon through town, which was quiet in spite of my arrest. It seemed to me that I had never in my life been honored as much. There were five [of us Dominicans] in Nagasaki and, as Your Reverence knows, when we used to appear in the streets people would come out of their houses to kiss our habits with great reverence, but I was never honored as much as now that I walked around tied up like a robber.[59]

Toku'an himself was not at home, but informed of the friar's arrest by his wife, he rushed back to be arrested as well. He had prepared the white habit of his brotherhood for the time that he would be arrested: "Toku'an also walked with his hands tied up and everyone came out to kiss his habit as well. Many women, from grief or reverence, broke through the cordon of the many policemen around us, who did not mind this too much."[60]

All Toku'an's property was confiscated. Only his wife, who was brought up in the Suetsugu household, went free. She cut her hair to signal her dedication to a religious life.[61]

This arrest set in motion the total destruction of the Murayama family. The crime here was compounded, as Morales explained in an account written from jail in 1620, by the fact that "Tōan was at that moment in exile [with his third son] because of his [second] son the priest, so that this crime of [his first son] Toku'an looked like recidivism."[62] Still, it took until the fall of 1619 before Tōan and his third son Shuan were recalled to Edo from their place of exile.

This long delay indicates that the Council of Elders was extremely reluctant to order the execution of someone who had been appointed to an important official position by Ieyasu himself. It is also possible that they had had enough of listening to new charges brought by Heizō, and only took action on Tōan's case after hearing new testimony from Governor Gonroku. The latter visited Edo in September of 1619. The governor had just obtained a new and valuable source of information on the padres in and around Nagasaki in the person of a Japanese priest ordained in Rome, who had recently apostatized. His name was Araki Thomé.

* * *

In Pursuit of Ordination:
Araki Thomé

Araki Thomé or Thomas Araki (1583–1646) was one of the first priests to be caught in the new net set out by the Nagasaki authorities. He has deserved his bad reputation, for he clearly succumbed to the temptation of power: for more than two decades, between 1619 and 1639, he wielded the authority of his former priesthood, his familiarity with the Christian networks, and his knowledge of Latin and the Christian doctrine in the service of successive Governors of Nagasaki.

It is this renegade we have to try and understand next. Araki was born somewhere in Hizen, possibly Arima, with several handicaps: he was of low birth and had only a Christian mother to bring him up.[1] It may have been for this reason that he was not allowed by the Jesuits to pursue his calling to become a priest, for the Jesuits preferred boys from samurai or at least rich merchant families to enter the Society.[2]

There were other possible reasons, however, why Thomas did not pursue his calling in Japan. The historian Gonoi Takashi thinks that he must have studied Latin for several years in the Nagasaki seminary, but he points out that around the time that Araki might have joined, the Society was in serious financial trouble. In 1600, a junk carrying Jesuit capital was shipwrecked and the yearly carrack from Macao did not appear. With its limited budget and numerous expenses, the mission obviously had to get rid of all unnecessary outlays.

It was decided, therefore, to let go of all the *dōjuku* or associates and to admit no Japanese into the order for the moment.[3] For these reasons, Araki may not have seen any other way to become a priest than by going to Rome himself. The idea alone shows the dimensions of Araki's ambition. It is likely that he was not supported by his Jesuit mentors in this plan, and that therefore the most obvious route to Europe, via Macao and Goa, was closed to him.

The world, however, had become round in Japan as well, so there was another way. In these years around the turn of the century the route between Nagasaki and Manila had been well traveled by Japanese merchants for over a decade, and so there were any number of junks leaving the port for the Philippines every year. From there, Araki could reach Acapulco, travel overland to Vera Cruz, the Spanish port on Mexico's Caribbean coast, and sail for Sevilla from there.

Araki seems to have left Japan in 1602, and to have passed through Mexico in 1603.[4] Between 1604 and 1610, he was in Rome, studying theology at the Gregorian University, "the seminary established by order of the council of Trent, where the teachers were Jesuits."[5] Pagés mentions, without any particular innuendo, that the Jesuit Cardinal Roberto Bellarmino (1542–1621) had taken a special liking to Araki and often recited the Book of Hours with him.[6]

We know that on 8 February 1607 Araki wrote a letter from Rome to the Jesuit fathers in Japan. It must have been extremely satisfying for him to do so. On 10 October 1608 Vice-provincial Francisco Pasio sent him a reply in Japanese, which echoes the surprise, admiration, and misgivings about Araki's accomplishment that the padres of the Japanese mission felt.[7]

At age twenty-seven, after six years of study in Rome, Araki was ordained in 1610.[8] He left Rome for Spain in June of 1611.[9] On 4 July of that year, he presented a "memorial" to the *Consejo de Indias* of the Spanish King, in which he called himself Pedro Antonio.[10] The letter glows with self-confidence, and we learn a few more details about the dangers of the voyage that Araki had undertaken to get to Rome.

In addition to Latin, Portuguese and Italian, it is clear that Araki had also become fluent in Spanish along the way:

[My name is] Don Pedro Antonio Araki, priest and native of Japan. I came from the Kingdom of Japan in order to receive instruction in the faith. I came to the Philippines with this
intent and to take care of certain business that I had there. Governor Don Pedro de Acuña
gave me letters of introduction to Your Majesty, as did the Count of Monterrey in New Spain,
who was Viceroy [of Mexico] at that time. During my journey to Spain, [we were waylaid] by
pirates near Havana, who robbed me of these letters and everything else I carried, as can be
seen from the certificate that was given to me by Don Juan Andrade Colmero, who commanded the fleet that brought me from the Philippines to New Spain, and by Don Lorenzo
de Olivares, alderman of the city of Madrid, who served as a lieutenant on the same fleet.
These gentlemen are presently living in Madrid.[11]

After this name-dropping introduction, Araki continues grandiloquently:

I went on to Rome to conduct my business with the Pope and I spent more than six years
studying theology in the papal seminary until I was ordained a priest. After I had finished
my studies, I returned to Spain in June in order to humbly request permission from Your
Majesty to go back to the Kingdom of Japan, either by the eastern or by the western route,
whichever will present the most convenient opportunity to bring with me twelve or thirteen
preachers of the Holy Gospel. At the same time, [I request] to be given a pious subvention
that will enable me to bring these preachers, with which Your Majesty will do great service
for Our Lord and the Christians of Japan, and will induce them, when they know of this
mercy, not only to yield to the faith, but also to the rule of Your Catholic Majesty.[12]

He could not have put it in starker terms. Araki had learned his theology lessons well: preachers were in the front-line of the Spanish conquest these days, just as the Japanese authorities feared. As we can read here, Araki intended to bring his own small army of missionaries to Japan so that back home he would no longer be dependent on the

Jesuits. He drops the numbers "twelve or thirteen" here, or precisely the number of disciples mentioned in the New Testament. Again, the size of his ambition as well as his obvious dreams of power can be gauged from this memorial.

From two letters written in Japan after Araki had already left Rome, we learn more about the misgivings the Jesuit padres had about the newly ordained Japanese priest. The first one is by Bishop Cerqueira, written on 10 October 1612. The bishop felt relieved that Araki had been behaving well in Rome:

> I remain consoled with the good news Your Reverence has sent me about the Japanese Father Antonio, that he is virtuous, for this is the most important. In scholarship, on the other hand, mediocrity will suffice. If he comes back to serve here in this church there will be no end of things for him to do. But as for his sustenance, it would be best if he brought it along himself.[13]

One year later, on 4 October 1613, the Italian missionary Celso Confalonieri (1557–1627), no doubt informed of Araki's ordination, still showed misgivings: "although exceptionally intelligent, his will was not strong, and therefore he should never have been sent to Rome."[14] Both Jesuits, then, seem to have been aware of some character flaw in Araki that he might learn how to hide, but that would not be easily overcome. It is clear that both these Jesuits feared his return to Japan.

The future would prove them right. Araki arrived in Macao on 7 August 1614, after three years of arduous travel.[15] Four months later, the following December, the junks carrying the missionaries exiled from Japan by Ieyasu arrived in the Portuguese port on the Chinese coast. Obviously, Araki's grand project of returning to Japan with his own followers had become impossible, and with that realization he needed to recast his dreams of power and glory upon his eventual return to Japan.

For the moment, he was content to regale the Japanese students at the Macao seminary with stories about his experiences in Europe.[16] Araki seems to have known that the directives had changed and that no more brothers of the Society would be ordained without express permission from Rome. When told of this, several of them decided to leave Macao for Manila and India to see if conditions for getting ordained were better there.[17]

In August 1615, Araki came back to Japan and straightway went into hiding.[18] At first, he seems to have been well received wherever he went in Nagasaki. In a letter, dated 20 March 1616, the new Vice-provincial Jeronimo Rodrigues (1567–1628) wrote about him:

> In this [i.e., last year's] carrack, Araki Thomé returned [to Japan], who is also known as Padre Antonio, the Japanese priest who was ordained in Rome. Here [in Nagasaki], they tell a thousand stories about his dignities and the honors [he received in Europe]. He of course does not mind telling about his adventures. If someone like him arrives there [in Rome] again, it would be most advisable not to ordain him, but to send him here and there, and then, if he obeys well, to ordain him only when they know him better. Araki exerts himself much in this association of the parish priests.[19]

In other words, Araki had aligned himself with the parish priests and mendicants in opposition to the Jesuits immediately upon his return to Japan. A few months later, Jeronimo Rodrigues mentions Araki again in a letter dated 18 July 1616, complaining that he walked around while praying with his rosary, a right reserved to priests of higher rank than him. Araki, however, had retorted to this objection that he had received the right to this privilege from the pope himself. Rodrigues then remarks that someone [arrogant and ambitious] like him would never have been ordained in Japan.[20]

Proud to show off his priestly status to the Japanese, Araki must have been easy to spot and track by informers. On 10 August 1619, he was taken into custody by the officers of the Nagasaki *bugyōsho*.[21] Mateo de Couros writes: "This sorry fellow had already long been corrupted by the flesh, such as is the custom here, and not only the servants of the Governor attest that they arrested him inside a pavilion where he was spending time with his niece with whom he was rumored to be living in sin."[22]

The first thing he did was to surprise his captors with some unusual acrobatics: "Being held under guard in the Governor's residence, he fled from there jumping over walls and gates. It seems, however, that someone convinced him two days later that to flee when one is arrested for the faith is dishonorable, and so he returned. He and other clerics were brought to the Ōmura jail."[23] According to another report, on this occasion he was wearing the robes he had used when he was studying in Rome.[24]

Thus, after his second arrest, Araki was held in the infamous Suzuta prison in Ōmura, where at that time the Jesuits Carlo Spinola (1565–1622) and Ambrósio Fernandes (1551?/3?–1620), the Dominicans Francisco de Morales (1567–1622) and Tomas de Zumarraga (1577–1622), the Franciscans Alonso de Mena (1578–1622) and Apolinar Franco (1575–1622) and their respective Japanese helpers were being held as well.[25]

Pacheco reports:

His rationality was already rather poor, but after about twenty days in jail he showed that he had completely lost his mind. Not being able to bear the harsh conditions in the cramped jail any longer, he gave up his faith and rank as a cleric, and promised to stop preaching the law of Christ Our Lord. He wrote to the heathen governor that, having studied in Rome himself, he had realized that there was nothing certain in the law of the Christians, and begged to be released from jail.[26]

His request not having been answered as soon as he had hoped, he made a second, more formal declaration of his apostasy, which was made public by the office of the Nagasaki Governor. With this, Araki had become the first priest to apostatize in Japan, and all Japanese Christians were in shock.[27]

He was released from prison to become a walking advertisement for the Bakufu's anti–Christian policy. Not long afterwards Araki was told to accompany Governor Gonroku to Edo to bear witness that the latter was doing his job.[28] According to testimony from Orfanel, he was dressed in his priestly robes on his departure from Nagasaki. The Dominican adds that Araki's head was freshly shaved in a crown as well, in the manner of priests.[29]

The Governor of Nagasaki, Orfanel writes,

boarded the ship for Edo in the company of Araki. He had his meals together with him, and acted in a friendly manner in many other things. This was because he wanted to present Araki to the shogun. I have received information that when they reached Kami [i.e., Kansai area], Araki gave Gonroku a list of all the fathers in Japan, with details of who was in which province. Because he had given this list, as I am told, of how many fathers there were in Japan, and in which provinces and houses they were staying, we feared that this was the end of everything. But Providence ordered that no one listened to him, because he did not appear before the shogun nor before the governors of the realm.[30]

Another report of the same trip written by the Jesuit Matteo de Couros was:

Gonroku asked him [Araki] whether the Dutch would join the Portuguese and Spanish if they planned to conquer Japan. To which he answered that they were all like dogs inside one house, fighting and biting each other while there is no one around, but making common cause as soon as an outsider appears to threaten them. Gonroku answered that is what the present and previous shoguns think as well. That is: our desire to spread the Christian faith is nothing but a way to make Japanese Christians help in the conquest of Japan on behalf of the King of Spain and the other European nations.[31]

In spite of the friendly intimacy he had enjoyed with Gonroku, upon their return to Kyushu, Araki was put back into jail on Ikinoshima, in the domain of Hirado,[32] where Gonroku thought he could still serve as an informer for a while. The following year, on 6 February 1620, Francisco Pacheco, who was in charge of the Japanese Christians around Kyoto at the time, wrote down his assessment of the impact Araki had had in Edo:

> I think that he [Thomas Araki], because he was treated well by Gonroku Dono, told him all he knew about Europe, and what is more, about the great enemy of the Society, Tōan, who was the key person among the four who govern the town—I have already sufficiently informed your Eminence about this person—that five years ago, at the time of the war in Osaka, he had supplied men and food to Hideyori, the son of Taikō, the previous ruler of Japan. Gonroku subsequently told this to the shogun and his councilors.[33]

Pacheco concludes:

> As a result, three or four days after his arrival in Edo, then, two things happened. One was the autodafé of the glorious martyrs from Miyako, and the other was the death of Tōan and his son and the confiscation of all their property. Tōan's death has other reasons as well, but people who are familiar with the situation say that it is because of his connection to Hideyori. That also is what is shown by the manner in which he was executed, for the shogun ordered his whole progeny to be exterminated.[34]

What could Araki have added to the charges against Tōan that Heizō had already brought over the past two years? Clearly, Pacheco did not know precisely either. But how could he have known, while in hiding out in the Kansai, what had been said in the Suzuta prison where Araki had been locked up before his apostasy? While the Jesuits imprisoned there are not likely to have opened up to him, the Dominicans clearly had not been so careful.

Therefore, while Araki was still trusted in jail as a fellow priest at odds with the Jesuits (ordained in Rome even!), he must have been able to learn where everyone had been before their arrest as well as the names of those who were still in hiding. Consequently, he was able to tell Gonroku that all the Dominicans of Japan, and some Franciscans as well, had mainly relied upon the Murayama family to survive thus far. This must have been the proverbial straw that broke the camel's back.

At last, the taboo on executing a man who had been appointed by Ieyasu himself was breached.[35] Orders were given to exterminate Tōan and all his offspring. The first to be executed were Tōan himself and his third son Shuan who had accompanied him into exile. Their decapitation took place in Edo on 1 December 1619.[36] Tōan's oldest son Toku'an had already been burned alive two weeks earlier, on 18 November, in a second autodafé staged in Nagasaki to burn him in public together with four other men, three of whom had also been convicted of housing padres.[37] Two more sons, Pedro (1599–1619) and Paulo (1601–1619), were executed in Kyoto later that same December.

Mateo de Couros writes:

> Paulo, the younger of the two, had fled to a branch temple of the Hokke sect. They say that he served the superior there as the instrument of his abominations. And also that this same bonze had wanted to save him, saying he had already abandoned his faith in Christ, but that this had not helped him. The Christians from here, who were in the capital at the time, say

that this bad apple did not give any proof of dying in the faith of Christ Our Lord, and that the bonzes of the Hokke sect took away his corpse and took care of his funeral ceremony.[38]

Tōan's three remaining sons, Manoel (1596–1620), Diego (1606–1620), and Miguel (1608–1620) were decapitated in Nagasaki on 24 July 1620. Of Manoel it is said that he had been an avid collector of relics of the saints, having saved five corpses of martyrs and eighty fingers that had been cut off different confessors. In his testament, he legated these treasures to the Franciscans and Dominicans.[39] At the time of the execution of her last three sons, Tōan's wife Nishi Justa, who had at first remained under house arrest with some of her daughters, was thrown into the Nagasaki jail for refusing to apostatize. So were her daughter-in-law Takagi Catharina, Shuan's wife, and their three children: seven-year old Antonio, three-year old Maria, and two-year old Justa.[40] Their executions (and those of Toku'an's wife Maria and their infant son Ignacio), however, still lay more than two years in the future.

*   *   *

Changes in the City: Hasegawa Gonroku (2)

When Hasegawa Gonroku returned to Nagasaki on 14 November 1619, he clearly had orders to increase the pressure on the city's Christian community once more, just as those he had brought the year before. Four days after his arrival in the city, a new autodafé was organized in which Toku'an and others who had hidden padres in their houses were burned alive. Next, on 27 November, twelve men whose crime was to have lived in the same streets as those burned nine days earlier were beheaded in public.[1]

At the last moment, one of the men, thinking of what would become of his wife and children if he died in this manner, decided to apostatize: "they pulled him from prison, and the servants of the Judge brought him home and returned all his former possessions to him. His wife and children, however, left by the back door while he was entering through the front door, saying that they did not want to live with someone who had abandoned God and that they should kill her and the children in place of her traitorous husband."[2]

After the executions, Gonroku is said to have built a temple for the militant Ikkō sect.[3] Slowly, the governor was getting more confident in exercising his authority in Nagasaki. He forbade the citizens of Nagasaki to visit the cemeteries or the ruins of the churches to perform religious acts, or even to possess religious images. By implication, however, people in Nagasaki were still allowed to practice their beliefs as long as it was done inside each individual household without the aid of religious images.[4] It would take until 1622 until the faith itself was officially prohibited in the city. At the same time, circulation by missionaries in the city became more difficult as the street gates were closed at night, and by day it was no longer allowed to go about in a closed palanquin.[5] The Governor's men also started to enter the houses of the citizens of Nagasaki at will.

Here is the plaintive voice of a padre:

It seems that only in Nagasaki devils may walk around without chains, for since the year [1618] … it went from bad to worse, with Judases everywhere on the look-out for fathers. They suddenly enter houses to search them, such trouble! The punishments are so severe that not only the property of the householder is confiscated and he himself is burned alive, but they are also killing the people of his ten-household group and confiscating all their property as well. There are apostates walking around in Nagasaki who make a living this way, for whoever denounces a father gets half of the property confiscated in connection with his arrest. In short, it is no longer possible to live in Nagasaki, and so the city is doomed in this way.[6]

Next, in the months following his arrival in the city, Gonroku gave orders to destroy, one by one, all the remaining buildings that had any connection with Christianity and had been spared so far because of their social usefulness. Although unused, the Misericordia or St. Elisabeth church in Moto Hakata-machi was still standing, its time piece still chiming time,[7] and so were smaller churches and chapels that had somehow escaped the fury of 1614: the São Lorenzo chapel of the Korean community in Kōrai-machi,[8] the São Miguel at the foot Mt. Tateyama,[9] the Santa Clara near the Ōhashi Bridge in Urakami,[10] and a chapel in Inasa of which not even the name remains.

Mateo de Couros reports:

After Gonroku had started to persecute the living here, he went after the dead as well, giving orders to dig up all those who had been buried in the three cemeteries of the Misericordia, the Santa Cruz, and the Santa Maria [churches], and to bury them in the São Miguel cemetery, which lay outside the city proper. For some days one heard nothing throughout town but wailing and sobbing inside the houses and workmen hauling through the streets the caskets that they use to bury the bodies of the dead here. Among these, we also transported the body of Bishop Cerqueira, which had been interred in the Misericordia cemetery with all the others of our Society.[11]

Couros writes sarcastically:

Next came the persecution of the poor, who lived in some ten establishments like hospitals in different areas of the city. These were all destroyed and their inmates evicted by order of the governor, while the three houses for the lepers located outside the city were burned. Thus, through this inhuman cruelty, more than four hundred people became homeless. However, all found shelter through the great devotion and charity of the Christians; and the members of the Society took care that no one remained unattended.[12]

The property of the different religious orders was now distributed among those who were considered to be helpful in the suppression of the Evil Faith. The Takagi family had already been rewarded for the public apostasy of Luis and his son Pedro Sakuemon with a plot of land that had been part of the Jesuit compound at Morisaki. His example evidently was, in the eyes of Bakufu officials, of great propaganda value.

Suetsugu Heizō received the site of the Santo Domingo church and monastery,[13] building his official residence with lumber that was left from the church and "placing himself on the spot where we used to keep the Most Holy Sacrament."[14] Materials from the destroyed Misericordia and Santiago churches and hospitals were used to expand the jail that had been built in 1615 in Cruz-machi on the site where formerly the São Francisco church had stood.[15] The site of the Misericordia church and cemetery was given to a man called Denyo Kantetsu (1587?–1650), who had answered the Bakufu's call for Buddhist priests to come and settle in Nagasaki. Hailing from Yasutake village in Chikugo, Denyo had not, according to tradition, been able to find a place to stay in Christian Nagasaki when he first arrived there, sometime in 1615.

Finally, he found lodging with Iseya Dennojō, a brothel owner in Furu-machi.[16] With the help of the *bugyōsho*, he built a small retreat there, which he called the Chūdōin. In October of 1617, he visited Edo, where he was received in Chiyoda Castle by Shogun

Tokugawa Hidetada and received two sets of seasonal clothing, and likely a promise of support for his efforts in Nagasaki.[17] Now, with a sizeable plot, Denyo could plan to build Uchimachi's first Buddhist temple. It would become known as the Daikakuzan Daionji of the Pure Land Sect.[18]

Orfanel, who was still at large in the surroundings of Nagasaki, writes:

> At the end of August or the beginning of September of 1621,[19] some bonzes or heathen priests of the Devil tried to build a temple dedicated to their master on the spot where in more peaceful times the Church and Casa of the Misericordia used to stand. The Christians came to ask us whether, if they were forced to provide labor by the heathen governor, they would be allowed to supply it. We answered them that they absolutely could not do so, although there were certain things which they would be allowed to do, such as leveling the site, but to help build a pagan temple would be a scandal in Nagasaki, where no one had ever done anything like it before, but everyone had always indignantly and resolutely refused such requests.[20]

If that was the Dominican position on the issue, others were more accommodating: "So the Christians decided not to help build the temple, but they changed opinion afterwards, at least some of them, who were the richest and most easily scared, saying they had been told by other fathers (whom they had consulted) that they could help, as long as it was not to pay for the main altar and the cloth that hangs over it, which is called Butsudan in Japan."[21]

At the same time, the site of the former São João Bautista church and hospital was given to a Buddhist priest of the Nichiren sect called Honsui'in Nichi'e (ca. 1580–1642).[22] This priest originally came from Kumamoto and had acquired experience converting Christians since arriving in Ōmura in 1606, where he had risen to be head priest of the Honkyōji temple. He came to Nagasaki in 1616, and in 1620 started to build a temple with the support of the Nagasaki *bugyō*, the lord of Ōmura, and the *machi-doshiyori* Takagi Sakuemon, who had converted to the Nichiren sect.[23]

This temple became known as the Honrenji or Seirinzan, which still exists today.[24] The cherry trees that had been planted nearby, twenty-three years earlier, to mark the spot where Nagasaki's first twenty-six martyrs had died were uprooted and thrown into the sea.[25] In this way, another sacred spot with "altars near each tree, unto which place many hundreds went every day to pray" was destroyed.[26] As can be seen from the last two of these allocations of property left open by the destruction of the churches, the Bakufu had started to realize that if Christianity was to be suppressed in Nagasaki, some other religion, more obedient to the government's commands and wishes, had to be substituted. It would take some time before there was any organized religious establishment in Japan enshrining the Tokugawa government itself.[27]

Nagasaki, it is clear, could not wait for this, and (supposedly) already in 1614 a call had gone out to enlist Buddhist priests in the cause of the government.[28] The Bakufu was not fastidious about who could apply for its support, for the post–Christian religious history of Nagasaki shows a surprising variety of sects that at one time or another tried to gain a foothold in the city. More than thirty temples and shrines were built in Nagasaki during the thirty years between 1620 and 1650, or an average of more than one temple a year.[29]

In this manner, Nagasaki became a laboratory-like environment for experiments with mind-control of its population, and some of the measures that were first tried out in Nagasaki were later adopted throughout the whole country.[30] Although the system to divide the population of villages and towns into groups of ten households with common responsibilities is an old Chinese technique to assure compliance with government decrees through the creation of a mixture of threat, shame, and mutual suspicion, this system had been unknown in Nagasaki before the prohibition of 1614. In Nagasaki, on the contrary, it had always been the brotherhoods of the different parish churches that had fulfilled this organizational function.

A witness, writing in 1622, reports on the recent institution of this system in Nagasaki:

> They use this custom in populous cities with many transients, like Miyako, in order to govern them better and to prevent capital crimes, concerning which they announce in public (or rather they lay down the law to the headmen of the streets) that if anyone commits an evil act, not only the actual criminal but also all those who belong to his group of householders will be executed. He who is the headman of the street then orders the man who in each street has the duty to announce such matters to everyone, and this man goes from house to house to advise the inhabitants of the official orders. For performing this task, the people of the street give him some silver every year, and as all the streets are clearly divided by gates, it is easy to know where to go. In this way, no one in any neighborhood agrees to any malfeasance for everyone fears to incur the above mentioned penalties.[31]

In 1621, these ten-household groups were reduced to five households living in close proximity of each other.[32] This was a rational measure in that otherwise the number of innocent victims would become far too large every time someone was arrested for having sheltered a padre, at the a time when there still more than sixty padres in Japan.[33] Thus, this reduction, on the one hand, may be seen as a compassionate measure, most likely to have been championed in Edo by Hasegawa Gonroku, who seems to have had a decided and open dislike of unnecessary bloodshed.[34] On the other hand, the reduction also encouraged the denunciation of priests by those who had kept quiet about their whereabouts as long as they had been part of a ten-household group in which such a priest was hidden, for they were sharing in the responsibility. By becoming part of a different group of householders, it became easier denounce the householders or *yadonushi* involved in hiding the priests in what had become another group.[35]

* * *

The Summer of 1622:
Bento Fernandes

If only there were sources left to fill the deafening void concerning the eradication of Christianity in Nagasaki. Important deliberations and discussions must have taken place in Chiyoda Castle between the shogun and his advisers, but these did not produce any surviving paper trail. The crucial meeting of the shogun's councilors with Hasegawa Gonroku is likely to have taken place in late May or early June of 1622. Upon that occasion, the *bugyō* was given a number of death sentences that had been decided upon, and he received clear orders on how to proceed when he returned to Nagasaki, especially concerning the manner in which the convicted were to die that summer.[1]

Two matters relating to the suppression of Christianity in Kyushu had been before the shogun's council. The first had come from Hirado, where the Dutch had proven that two Europeans sailing on a Japanese vessel from Manila, who had fallen into their hands in 1620 pretending to be merchants, were in reality two friars, one an Augustinian and the other a Dominican, who had been trying to enter Japan by stealth.[2] Both missionaries as well as the captain of the vessel were to be burned alive for flouting Japan's anti–Christian legislation, while the rest of the crew and passengers were to be beheaded as accomplices. The executions were to take place in Nagasaki, as soon as could be organized after Gonroku's return to the city that year.

The second matter was of earlier date. It was the final outcome of the case of Murayama Tōan, which had taken such an ominous twist with the arrest of Araki Tomé and the information he had supplied to the Bakufu of the large number of priests still in hiding in and around Nagasaki. As we have seen above, Araki's betrayal had first led to stricter supervision of Nagasaki's Christians, the institution of a reward system for the arrest of undergound missionaries, and soon, also, to the actual arrest of five friars.

These European missionaries and their Japanese assistants had been in the Ōmura jail since 1619, where they had joined other religious who had been caught previously. They were all being held in unspeakable conditions until an example could be made of them. In those unrecorded meetings in the spring of 1622, Hidetada and his advisers must have decided that the time had come for another gruesome example that would show the people of Nagasaki that Hideyoshi had been both modest and clement, in the number of people he had executed as well as in the manner of execution he had decreed. Orders were given for a second autodafé that year to be held soon after the first, in which twenty-five missionaries and their helpers would be burned, the wood for which was to be supplied by all the people of Nagasaki. A yet indeterminate number of others, largely women and children, were to be beheaded at the same time.

Thus, in the summer of 1622, the gloves were coming off in the handling of foreign missionaries in Nagasaki. The first execution of fifteen people took place on 19 August, and the second of fifty-five people on 10 September, with three more decapitated in the same spot on the next day. Thus, within one month, an unprecedented seventy-three Christians (among them eleven European padres) were executed. All of these dates fell in the midst of the trading season. In other words, the timing of the executions indicates that they were not just intended to frighten the population of Nagasaki, but were also meant to be witnessed by a foreign audience. By this time, foreigners in Nagasaki were no longer exclusively Portuguese, Spanish, African, Indian, or Italian, but now there were also often Chinese, Dutch, and English traders in the city. What is more, quite a few Chinese and even some Dutchmen had made the city their permanent home.

Two types of punishments were decreed: a simple, merciful beheading for those involved without bearing direct responsibility, and a long drawn-out roasting on a slow fire for those deemed responsible for the crimes committed. All missionaries who were still free in or around Nagasaki felt a strong obligation to attend and report on these executions, regardless of the danger involved if they were also caught.[3] Their eyewitness testimony would become a vitally important part of the martyrdoms themselves, and assure their place in the annals of the Church.

As there were still at least five priests hiding around Nagasaki, we have ended up with a rich trove of eyewitness accounts of these executions. They provide detailed information on what was then (and still is) considered a seminal martyrdom for the Japanese Church. We can, on the one hand, compare these accounts with the findings of modern studies on the nature and character of public executions, and on the other hand with other Christian martyrdoms reported from the late Roman Empire.

However difficult it had been to fit Christian teachings into the web of customs of Japanese society, the concept of martyrdom fitted very easily, because of the Japanese tradition of glorifying a chosen death. An authority on early Christain martyrdoms, Professor Bowersock, writes:

> Without the glorification of suicide in the Roman tradition, the development of martyrdom in the second and third centuries would have been unthinkable. The hordes of voluntary martyrs would never have existed. Both Greek and Jewish traditions stood against them. Without Rome, a *martus* would have remained what he had always been, a "witness" and no more. But the spread of the Roman *imperium* brought with it the glorification of Lucetia and Scaevola in legend and the heroic suicides of Stoic philosophers [e.g. Seneca] in recent memory.[4]

In contrast to Araki Tomé, most missionaries who remained in Japan or were smuggled into the country after 1614 were eagerly awaiting their own martyrdom. There were two rewards for being martyred, both of course predicated upon complete faith in the teachings of the Church. First, there was the personal reward of going straight to "heaven" or "paradise." How this life after death was actually envisioned by the believers is difficult to reconstruct. It may have been deeply personal and different for each believer.

Second, there was a this-worldly reward: the belief that the blood of the martyrs is the seed of the church. As the history of the Church has shown over and over, the steadfastness of the martyrs in the face of death has always impressed those who witnessed their deaths and made them conclude that such superhuman defiance of pain and death was sufficient proof of the truth of the teachings of Christ. The horrendous story of Christ himself, who was said to have chosen to die on the cross, had served throughout the ages as the beacon for all martyrs.

Because of the enthusiasm for martyrdom exhibited by the early Roman Christians, the Church soon decided to clamp down on so-called voluntary martyrdom.[5] This was a lesson, then, that the Japanese Church did not have to relearn. The missionaries did not encourage believers to just go up to the persecuting authority and present themselves as martyrs-to-be. To be betrayed, however, was another matter. Once one's cover was blown, and one was asked the all-important question about one's beliefs, the Christian and aspiring martyr was expected to tell the truth, even if telling the truth meant an awful death.

Up to that moment, however, the missionaries and their helpers had an obligation to elude the authorities by all means at their disposal. Although such efforts to remain underground can be evaluated in different ways (what are heroics for fellow-believers is nothing but senseless vanity to non-believers), it cannot be denied that the lives of these men contained many elements of the adventures experienced by other underground operatives, such as thieves, murderers, and spies.

The underground missionaries may have had most in common with spies. Like spies, they were not motivated by the immediate gratification of their desires that characterizes thieves and murderers. Both underground missionaries and spies are convinced that their efforts are dedicated to some higher goal to improve the lot of mankind, such as the spread of freedom or a similar ideal. Both have in common that they must operate in enemy territory and so feel the necessity to remain unobserved, to travel incognito, to familiarize themselves quickly with new surroundings, to depend on their skills to disguise themselves, and to deal with a wide variety of people.[6]

Here we will take a look at one of the greatest experts of this game, the life of a man who was so skillful in eluding the Tokugawa authorities that his own name is still virtually unknown, even among experts of the Christian experiment in Japan today, in spite of his having left us extensive written eyewitness testimony of the reality of the persecution.[7] His name is Bento Fernandes (1579–1633).

Bento (i.e., Benedict) was born in Borba, Alentejo, as the son of Miguel Fernandes and Isabel Affonso around 1579.[8] At the unusually young age of eleven he entered the Jesuit novitiate in Evora, and later graduated from the university in the same city.[9] He was officially admitted into the Society on 22 March 1597, and left for the Indies, twenty-three years old, in April 1602.[10] He arrived in Macao the next year,[11] and stayed in the city for three years. This long period indicates that he may originally have been designated for the China mission. After a few years of study, however, his superiors probably decided that he did not have the patience needed for the acquisition of the scholastic accomplishments in the Chinese Classics that were rapidly becoming *de rigueur* for that mission field. On 14 August 1606, therefore, he arrived in Japan on the carrack of Diogo de Vasconcelos.[12] From Nagasaki, he was sent to Arima to study Japanese.[13] By October of 1607, he is already listed as the padre in charge of the Kami-gyō residence in the capital with a Japanese brother named Shimizu Rafael under him.[14]

His study of Chinese during his years in Macao must have given him an edge over his fellow students in Arima, at least where the acquisition of Japanese vocabulary derived from Chinese was concerned. He remained part of the Kyoto residence for the next five years, during the quietest period the mission had experienced since 1587. Thus, he must have had ample time to perfect his command of the language, acquiring the Kyoto-accent and vocabulary, a skill much sought after by the Jesuit missionaries in Japan.

In 1612, Fernandes transferred to the residence of Shimo-gyō in the capital, and in February of 1613 he is listed as one of two advisers to the rector of the Kyoto residence.[15] As the rector was the superior of all the Jesuits in and around the capital, we may conclude that in six short years Fernandes had risen in the Jesuit hierarchy to a position that signified considerable trust in his judgment. He was thirty-three years old. At this time, one year before the second prohibition of Christianity, he was sent to Nagasaki.[16] It is no longer clear what his mission was, but we are not surprised to see him take there, on 1 January 1614 (the holy day of Jesus' Circumcision), the four vows only the most highly ranked of the Jesuits were allowed to make.[17]

In November of 1614, Fernandes is described as in good physical condition with a good command of Japanese.[18] By that time, he must have left for the Kansai again, where he remained in hiding around the capital while the other missionaries were exiled.[19] On 10 December 1614, when the Tokugawa forces were gathering to invest Osaka castle, Fernandes was present inside.[20] He managed to escape from the burning castle, however, and returned to Kyoto on 21 January 1615.[21]

Fernandes remained around the capital for more than two years,[22] but on 3 September 1617 he was back in Nagasaki again.[23] On 25 February of 1618, however, Fernandes was again in Kyoto,[24] where he attended a grand execution of martyrs for their faith on 6 October 1619.[25] In February 1620, Fernandes was planning to leave for Edo via Suruga to see what could be salvaged from what was left of the Christian communities in the Kantō.[26] He finally arrived in the shogun's capital on 19 March, where he stayed for fifty days, leaving again on 8 May to visit the Japan Sea coast.[27] On 14 January 1621, he was ordered back to Nagasaki, a journey he is most likely to have made by boat, traveling along the coast at night.

Quite apart from how one evaluates the motives and purpose of such extensive travel throughout Japan, the historian remains speechless with amazement at the sheer effort and gall involved. It is no small matter for a foreigner to escape detection in Japan in this manner for so long. It goes without saying that, wherever and whenever possible, Fernandes had to avoid the public roads, which he could only use with his face covered. He had to skirt all checkpoints of the different domains he passed through, a crime carrying the death penalty in itself. He had to cross mountains and swim across rivers. He had to find shelter and food along the way, etc. etc.

It is clear that however accomplished he was in the Japanese language, his skill would not have sufficed for him to make all these travels by himself without attracting undue attention. The extent of Fernandes' travel, then, indicates to us also the extent of the Christian network as it still existed throughout Japan in the second decade of the seventeenth century. Fernandes, it goes without saying, was completely dependent upon Japanese Christians to provide him with information about the route ahead, with guides and provisions along the way, and with the means of transportation where available.

It is likely that he was always accompanied by one or two acolytes he completely trusted, men he had known since the time he was stationed in the capital, who admired him and were of high accomplishments in their own right, who knew, for example, how to bluff their way around country bumpkins along the road. The number of roles the man with the covered face could have played in their company is almost endless: from the poor disfigured servant, via the holy man who had made a vow of silence, to the nobleman of high rank traveling incognito to or from the capital on some unknown but essential purpose.

Having returned to Nagasaki, he was known under different false, Japanese names, such as Jorita Seiemon and Sukenojō. He is reported to have been admired by many for "his good character and his mastery of Japanese."[28] We may add that he must also have been a master of disguise. And it was in disguise that Fernandes must have attended the executions of 1622, of which he became the most important reporter. Eleven years later, on 30 July 1633, Fernandes was caught himself and died in October at age fifty-four from torture in one of Nagasaki's torture pits, his eyeballs having fallen from their sockets.[29]

We have two separate accounts from his hand of the events of the summer of 1622. One, concentrating on the executions of nine European missionaries on 10 September, can be found in the Jesuit archive in Rome.[30] The other is a little-known account preserved in the Biblioteca Publica of Evora, which also deals with that event but focuses on the lay people involved.[31] This latter account is especially valuable because it is one of the very few Jesuit sources dealing exclusively with individual members of the missionaries' flocks. On this occasion, then, these little sheep of ordinary Japanese Christians were, in the eyes of the author himself, made extraordinary by their willingness to suffer death for the belief system taught them by the Europeans.

*   *   *

A Japanese Padre:
Kimura Sebastião

At the end of June, the sun rises in Nagasaki shortly after five am, so it is likely that it was still quite dark, when, in the wee hours of 30 June 1621, Gonroku's men from the *shōya* or Governor's office converged on Antonio Korea's house in Hama-no-machi. For a long time, Hama-no-machi had been among the poorest sections of town. Situated as it was at the point where the Nakajima River flows into Nagasaki Bay, the street took its name from the word *hama*, meaning "beach" or "seashore." Work on expanding the ward into the shallow waters of the bay had already started in 1609.

By 1621, Hama-no-machi was well on its way to become what it still is today: one of Nagasaki's most popular shopping districts, with easy access to the bay and the sea beyond. This was the area where Antonio Korea (1582?–1622) had managed a shop for many years.[1] As his sobriquet indicates, Antonio had originally come to Japan as a captive from Hideyoshi's Korean campaigns. He seems to have been taken prisoner by a warrior from Isahaya. This was the domain bordering Ōmura, where the Jesuit Rui Barreto (1549–1611) had settled as a missionary.

It was Barreto who baptized the Korean prisoner-slave and gave him his Christian name of Antonio.[2] The desperate Koreans brought as slaves to Japan during the 1590s were especially targeted for conversion by the Jesuits.[3] From Isahaya, Antonio was sold to a new Christian owner in Nagasaki, who eventually set him free, provided him with one of his other slaves for a wife, and a little money to set up a household of his own.[4] By dint of honesty and hard work, Antonio did well for himself. He eventually managed to become a member of the Misericordia brotherhood, quite a mark of distinction in Christian Nagasaki, certainly for an ex-slave.[5]

Fernandes writes: "In business he was strictly honest and without guile, something rare for small-scale merchants, and because he had been poor he never forgot the needy, whom he helped according to his means. He held his wife and family to high Christian standards and practice."[6] Antonio's wife Maria was born in 1579 in Odamura, in Hizen. She had been sold into slavery in Nagasaki in 1583 or 1584, a victim of the wars still raging in Kyushu at that time.[7] She was baptized by her new owner and was lucky never to have been sold overseas. She may have been around thirty when she consented to marry Antonio, while her Korean husband was somewhat younger than she.

After trying for a few years to have children, the couple adopted an orphan boy, baptized João, born around 1610. Their own marriage had probably taken place well before that, possibly as early as 1607. In 1618, when Maria was almost forty years old, she suddenly conceived and bore a little son of her own. The couple was so impressed with what they understood to be an unexpected gift from God that they called the boy Pedro, after the apostle Peter, and promised to bring him up to serve the church.[8]

When the raid on their shop took place, Gonroku's men knew exactly where to go. A Korean woman, who served in Antonio's household, had betrayed them the day before to obtain the considerable reward for catching a priest. The servant must have been familiar with Antonio's household, where padres and their helpers were regular guests and lodged for a few nights before they had to move on. Since the start of the persecutions in 1614, Antonio had vowed to save at least thirty-three cruzados a year to help the padres.[9]

Padre Kimura Sebastião (1565–1622) had come to Antonio's house on the night of 28 June, for he had been invited to celebrate mass on the occasion of the holiday dedicated to the Catholic Saints Peter and Paul. St. Peter, apart from being young Pedro's patron saint, is known as the heavenly doorkeeper. He is the patron of the Church and the Papacy, and is considered both powerful as well as accessible to ordinary believers.[10] Paul, the apostle of the gentiles, was martyred under Nero in Rome, and became the patron saint of the Jesuit missionaries in the sixteenth century.[11]

In Nagasaki the two saints were worshipped on the same day, 29 June.[12] When Padre Kimura and his two assistants arrived, therefore, it was clear that they were going to stay at least two nights. Antonio had prepared bedding for them "in a small second story that the worthy Korean had constructed inside his house for such lodgers."[13] Padre Kimura is said to have joked "from time to time that as long as he did not sleep under a roof covered with tiles [he was referring to Nagasaki's jail], he would not be able to get any rest."[14]

From these two pieces of information, we may conclude that Antonio's house was originally a very simple single-story structure, probably just covered with shingles. On the night of 29 June, a neighbor came to warn Antonio that he was about to be arrested, but Antonio laughed the matter off, refusing to be worried. He must have strongly believed that God would not allow such an important servant of the church as Padre Kimura to be taken to jail.[15]

Kimura Sebastião was born into a Christian family in Hirado in 1565, the year of the attack by the domain on the Portuguese at Fukuda. His great-grandfather is said to have been baptized by Francis Xavier, i.e., the founder of the Japanese mission himself.[16] At age twelve, Sebastião became a live-in servant to Padre Sebastião Gonçalves (1533–1597), who had replaced Baltasar da Costa as Hirado's superior in 1576.[17] After three years of service, Sebastião was able, at the special recommendation of Gonçalves, to enter the Arima seminary at the foot of Hinoe Castle in Arima in 1580.[18]

Again two years later, in 1582, Sebastião entered the Society as a novice in Usuki, Bungo, where for two years he was under the supervision of the strict Spanish padre, Pedro Ramon (1550–1611).[19] After his novitiate, he was sent as a brother to the capital to serve under the veteran Padre Organtino.[20] By the time he came back to Kyushu in 1587,[21] at age twenty-two, he had acquired a good command of the refined speech of the capital.

In Kyushu followed more years of study: in 1589 he is recorded to have been engaged in the study of Western philosophy and Japanese literature in the Colegio at Kōchiura on Amakusa.[22] In October 1594, Sebastião left Japan for Macao in the company seven other promising Jesuit brothers of the Japan mission, four Japanese and three Europeans.[23] In Macao, he studied for three years the "casos" [examples] of moral dilemmas, a discipline that was the specialty of the Jesuits.

Afterwards, he was ordained sub-deacon,[24] indicating approval for his eventual ordination as a priest in Japan. In other words, wherever he went among the Jesuits, Sebastião had received the enthusiastic support of his superiors. Unwavering faith, absolute obedience, combined with an ability to absorb and retain knowledge must have been foremost among the ingredients that went into the making of this Japanese Jesuit, who would be the first native Japanese to be ordained, one year after his return to Japan in 1600.[25]

After his ordination, he was sent to Amakusa, which had become part of the domain of the anti–Christian daimyo Katō Kiyomasa.[26] More than a year later, in 1603, the mission at Kōchiura, where Padre Kimura was stationed,[27] was closed when Terazawa, daimyo of Karatsu, took over the island.[28] Padre Kimura then joined the Shiki residence.[29] Thus, he became familiar with the reality of the persecution at its earliest stage. Being Japanese, however, he had no trouble blending into his surroundings and could proselytize and administer the sacraments without fear of discovery wherever he was unknown to the authorities. He became one of the earliest wandering priests of the Society. In 1606 we find him in Bungo, and in 1607 in Kazusa (Shimabara), in 1612 in Nagasaki, in 1613 in Saga, in 1614 in Chikuzen and Chikugo.[30]

After the prohibition of 1614 we lose track of him until 23 February 1619, when he was back in Nagasaki.[31] One year later, on 9 February 1620, Padre Kimura received the singular honor of being the first native Japanese priest to be allowed to swear the four oaths of the highest-ranking Jesuits.[32] There is no better gauge to measure how highly he was valued among the European Jesuits in Asia. Here was a native priest who had proven all his life to be one of them in all respects, but superior to all of them in his ability to preach to the Japanese while staying ahead of the law.

By the time of his arrest in June 1621, Padre Kimura had been on the run for the better part of eighteen years. This realization gives an extra poignancy to his words, quoted above, about not being able to get any rest until he would be sleeping under the tiled roof of a jail. His ability to escape detection so far may, on the one hand, have made him careless about his safety, even if he was not actually convinced that God was protecting him. At the same time, he must have been very tired as well, and thus, paradoxically, he may have welcomed his arrest. Now, all that was left for him to do was to suffer his earthly punishment. Compared to more years as a fugitive in an increasingly hostile environment, it may have seemed the lighter burden.

Two servants had accompanied Padre Kimura to Antonio's house. We only know the name of the older one, i.e., Akahoshi Tomé (1565–1622). Of the younger one, we know nothing but that he was "a servant boy who was being trained to be the Padre's *dōjuku*" [helper or associate].[33] When the padre was caught, it was this boy who was with him and so he was tied up as well. The older servant was hiding somewhere else:

> the police officers took and tied up the Padre, and were ready to go without bothering about the other servant [Tomé], because they did not see him. So he left his hiding place, and, introducing himself to the officers, forcefully told them that he was the Padre's real *dōjuku*, and not the boy that they had caught. Therefore, they should tie him up and take him away with his Padre. So they let the boy go, and arrested and tied up Tomé.[34]

The latter had originally been a samurai from Higo, where he had converted to Christianity when Hideyoshi's retainer, the Christian daimyo Konishi Yukinaga was lord of half that province. After Yukinaga's death and the take-over of the domain by Katō Kiyomasa in 1600, Tomé had abandoned his position to follow the Jesuits, whom he served in the most menial jobs in spite of his proud background. He had left with the padres for the Philippines in 1614, but had since returned to Japan, fifty years old, feeling he could better serve the Christian cause in his native land.

Padre Kimura, Akahoshi Tomé, and Antonio Korea were taken to the *shōya*, where they were interviewed by a man named Sukedayu. This was the given name (his family name has not come down to us) of Hasegawa Gonroku's representative in Nagasaki during the time the Governor spent in Edo. After the interview, Antonio was brought to Nagasaki's jail in Cruz-machi, while Padre Kimura and Akahoshi Tomé were sent the next day to Ōmura. It is said many women followed Padre Kimura's *kago* or palanquin until Nagayo.[35]

In Ōmura, they were held in the notorious Suzuta prison, a jail built on a promontory, like a fortress, to hold the arrested padres and their helpers until the Bakufu decided their fates. Evidently the authorities feared that if so many priests were kept under detention in Nagasaki, this might provoke an armed revolt by Nagasaki's Christians to set them free. Fernandes reports that during the first ten days Antonio spent in jail, he felt very guilty for having been the cause for the arrest of Padre Kimura, but that he later he understood that "this was not the work of humans but that the Lord himself in his unfathomable providence had ordered this and wanted these padres to be arrested."[36]

At the time of Antonio's arrest, his wife Maria "wished very much to be arrested for her faith as well and to accompany him to jail. Because she was a woman, however, she was handed over to the people of her street until her case had been decided."[37] Clearly, Gonroku did not want women in his jail in order to avoid all the abuse this would have entailed. He must have left strict orders, to both Sukedayu, Suetsugu Heizō, the mayors and the street elders of all the wards that women after their arrest would become the responsibility of the streets where they lived until they were convicted.

Even though she was supposed to be under house arrest, for a while Maria managed to visit her husband every day in jail, until she was advised "that such frequent visits might become the pretext for curtailing [the rights to visits for] all the others."[38] For this reason, she limited her visits to one every three days. Obviously, her "house arrest" was of the very mildest kind, only requiring her word that she would not try to escape and so put everybody's life in jeopardy. On 9 September, Gonroku called her to his office, and ordered her to apostatize. When she refused, she was finally allowed to accompany her husband and children to jail, where she received a last visit from her mother and friends. "She cut her hair and gave it to her beloved mother as a keepsake and token of love."[39]

* * *

The Ten-Family System: Hama-no-machi Antonio

Of the fifty-five people executed on 10 September 1622, the raid on Antonio Korea's house is the only case of which we know where, when, and (more or less) how the arrest took place. It is therefore especially informative to see how the denunciation and co-responsibility systems set up in Nagasaki during the preceding years worked in practice. Three male signatories of Antonio's Hama-no-machi *kumi* register accompanied the Korean to jail.

The first was sixty-two year-old Kawano Shichi'emon Bertolomeu, originally from Shimabara, where he had been baptized at the age of seven in 1566 or 1567. He had come to Nagasaki in 1614, when under the leadership of Hasegawa Sahyō'e the persecutions in Arima had become very violent. Fernandes tells how Bertolomeu was acquainted with someone known to be an informer for the Governor. For this reason, rumors had started to run about Bertolomeu as well, and he was eager to prove he was no informer himself: "he hastily went to the Governor's mansion, where the officials already knew he was part of the same *kumi* as Antonio, and so tied him up and put him in jail."[1]

Every time he was called from jail before his judges, who encouraged him to apostatize and save his life, Bertolomeu refused to do so. Because of his signature on the register of the *kumi*, he was only guilty by association. His death by beheading would be quick and merciful, and, as a martyr, it would earn him entrance into Paradise. For a fervent believer of his age, it was too good a deal to let slip through his fingers. When his wife and children came to visit him in jail he told them of his good fortune. His oldest son, he said, "should keep his severed head in his house to remind him of his father who gave his life for the love of God, so that this memory would help him to live virtuously, and that, once in paradise, he would not forget them."[2] The son obviously had already established his own household and was no longer part of Bertolomeu's family register in Hama-no-machi.[3]

The second man to accompany Antonio to jail in the arrest of Padre Kimura was Tanda Ya'ichirō Damião (1580?–1622). According to Fernandes, he was born in Nagasaki, where he was baptized when he was eight days old, as was the custom in the Christian families of the city. From the age of thirteen, he lived with the Jesuits as a servant. Later, he married and became a merchant. He owned a house in the street of Antonio Korea, to whose *kumi* he belonged. The house was actually rented to another Christian, and Damião himself lived in another street nearby.

Hearing that the men of Antonio's *kumi* would be called by Sukedayu, he went to the *shōya* where the Governor's representative asked him who had signed the register, because he was not living in the block where the padre had been arrested. Damião answered that he had signed the document himself. Hearing this Sukedayu ordered him sent to jail, so they tied him up and brought him there. In spite of having signed the register, Damião too could easily have escaped a death sentence if he had been willing to apostatize.

This, however, he was not willing to do. When his wife Gracia came to visit him in jail, he told her to remain steady in the faith.[4] Damião may not have been very confident about her constancy. He was called to the *shōya* twice, where the *bugyō*'s men tried to persuade him to abandon his faith, but like Bartolomeo he refused to do so. "And before being called to receive his final sentence, one of our Japanese fathers slipped into the jail with great courage and danger to his life to hear the confessions of Damião and his fellow prisoners."[5]

This latter detail is also reported for several others. The act of hearing confession is to provide the believer with a direct conduit to God, who hears and absolves through the priest. The priest administers the sacrament as a confirmation of God's absolution. To provide such a channel on the day before the prisoners would be given their last chance to apostatize is to make such an act almost unthinkable. It shows that the Jesuits were actively encouraging and (almost) forcing martyrdom on people. Fernandes admits this quite clearly: "we made it a point to go and hear the confessions of those who needed to be consoled, especially in such a time of need. But the men and women who were to be called before the officials had precedence, in the eyes of the Father Rector, over any others, and he took care that the sacrament of the Eucharist might be administered to those who deserved it."[6]

On 9 September, the day before the executions, Damião was called once more by Gonroku. He was told that the only way to save his own life and that of his four-year old son Miguel was by "turning his back on his faith." However, "neither his will to live nor the sight of his innocent son sufficed to break the spirit of this soldier of Christ."[7] At this final refusal, Gonroku angrily confirmed his sentence and that of his four-year old son.

On his way back to the jail, Damião encountered his wife and told her that she should not be sad to see her son go to the gallows "because God was bestowing upon the two of them the singular honor of having the name of their beloved son added to the list of such distinguished martyrs." Again he repeated that she should remain constant and "exert herself all the more in the service of God, and to do nothing that would offend the Lord."[8] It seems obvious from all this that Damião's wife (who may not have been as fervent a Christian) was not convinced of the necessity to lose her son in this manner.

The third to accompany Antonio to jail was thirty-four year old Yamada Domingos. He was an older brother of the merchant Yamada Antonio, who had been beheaded three weeks earlier, on 19 August 1622, for sailing as a merchant on the vessel of Joachim Hirayama, who had given passage to the priests Zuñiga and Flores.[9] The Yamada family was originally from Nagato, the westernmost part of Honshu, where they had served the Mori. Domingos' grandfather had been baptized by Cosme de Torrès, when he was proselytizing in Yamaguchi during the first half of the 1550s. Later, after the wars that destroyed the Mori, he had ended up in Bungo where his son Pedro, the father of Domingos and Antonio, was born and baptized. Pedro served the Jesuits as a *dōjuku* for a long time, mainly following Baltazar Lopes (1533–1605), whom he accompanied to India in 1576 and with whom came back to Japan the next year.[10]

Upon his return, Pedro married and his son Domingos was born and baptized in Kuchinotsu. Later, after his father's death, Domingos left for Nagasaki where he lived with his mother Magdalena in the vicinity of Antonio Korea. After Antonio was arrested, the men of the *shōya* sent for Domingos and asked him if he knew that Padre Kimura had been staying in his street. He answered that although he had not known about it, it did not matter because he was of the same *kumi* as Antonio Korea and had signed the same oath as he did, which was the same as knowing it. For giving this defiant answer, he was sent to jail. Being led before Gonroku on 9 September, the day before the scheduled executions, Domingos was given a last chance to apostatize. But he refused to do so in view of "his position as the elder brother of the blessed Antonio, and as a descendant of someone who from infancy had drunk the milk of the law of the Gospel in this land."[11] This answer earned him his death sentence.

One other man accompanied Antonio to jail. This was Fuchinoue Shichirōemon Tomé (1543–1622). About seventy-eight years old by the time of Padre Kimura's arrest, he was a native from Amakusa, where he had served as a tax collector. Ieyasu's prohibition order had been executed on the island with particular ferocity. Tomé and a friend were tortured for being Christians by being tied to a post naked and left out in the cold for two days and one night in order to make them apostatize. The friend was killed and Tomé was told to leave the domain. So he went to Nagasaki with his family.[12] His wife having died some years previously, he gave all his possessions to his oldest son and dedicated his life to his religion. He prayed so much, says Fernandes, that he was rarely seen without his rosary in his hands. As he was a member of Antonio's *kumi,* he was called to the *shōya* and went eagerly, determined to give his life for the faith.

This determination, however, pitted him against his son André, who took the position that the house where Tomé was living had belonged to his elder brother. The latter had signed the *kumi* register, but had recently died. So, according to André, he was now the main householder living there, and it was his duty to go and take the family's responsibility before the governor. Shortly after his father had left for the *shōya*, André went there himself also, but the father had left instructions for the neighbors not to let the young man enter the Governor's office on any account. The neighbors, therefore, went after him and caught up with him in front of the *shōya's* gate, where they forcibly restrained him from entering and took him back to Hama-no-machi. Inside the Governor's office, the officials found out that Tomé had not signed the register himself, but that it bore the signature of his eldest son. For that reason, they told him to stay at home under the supervision of the other inhabitants of his street. The old man was very disappointed to hear this, for it sounded to him as if he was not worthy to be put into jail.

He told the officials to put him in jail together with the others anyway, because he belonged to the same *kumi* as Antonio Korea. But no one listened to his entreaties, and he returned home dejectedly.[13] When one of Gonroku's men came to his house to make an inventory of its contents, which had all been forfeited because of Padre Kimura's arrest, Tomé tried again to convince him of his desire to be put into jail. The official explained to him that although he would lose all his property, he was not in any danger of being executed, for he had not signed the register himself, but his dead son had done so. The old man, however, kept on insisting that he wanted to be arrested and be condemned to death so much, that the official got angry and "remarked sourly that it was 'because there were people holding opinions like these that there was no lack of accommodations for the missionaries,' even though that was against the laws of the Lord of the land. He told him he was a dangerous fellow and likely to commit such crimes."[14]

When Gonroku arrived in Nagasaki in 1622, he brought with him a mandate "not to leave anybody alive who had been found to have lodged preachers of the Gospel or those of their *kumi*."[15] On 9 September, he called Tomé to his office once more and told him to apostatize. Tomé refused. The Governor told him that he was sentencing him to death, but Tomé was hard of hearing and did not understand what he was being told. In a loud voice he demanded to know if he would be executed with the others of his street. Upon being informed that the old man was deaf and worried he was not going to be among those condemned to death, Gonroku raised his voice in order to be understood by the old man and told him that he had already been sentenced to die with them and did not have to worry. On his way to jail, he saw his son, who asked him what the outcome of his meeting with the Governor had been. The old man answered him that he now was part of that lucky group of martyrs scheduled to die the next day.[16]

Apart from Antonio's wife Maria, two other women were put under house arrest in connection with Padre Kimura's arrest. The first was a thirty-five year old widow who was born in Nagasaki in 1586 and baptized eight days after her birth in the Morisaki church. For some reason, Fernandes does not give her Christian name, but only mentions that her deceased husband's name was Ogata Domingos. As usual, Fernandes mentions nothing but virtues about the future martyr. Although she had found herself a poor widow at a young age, she had refused to remarry. She lived in the street of Antonio Korea and was a member of his *kumi*. Her property was confiscated. Being called to the *shōya* by Gonroku's men, she was asked who had signed the register for her family. She answered that her husband had signed before he "had embarked." When she was asked where her husband was now, she said that he had gone "to make his living on the other side."[17] She likely was not quite right in the head. She was sent home again.

When Gonroku returned to Nagasaki in the summer of 1621, he had her come to his office and asked her if she was a Christian, which she affirmed with enthusiasm. Gonroku informed her that if she did not apostatize she would be burned alive. But the widow said that she would on no account do such a thing, even if they burned her. For this answer she was sent back in the care of her neighbors in Hama-no-machi.

The next year, Gonroku again called all the women who were under detention in their own streets. He now had clear orders from the shogun's advisers how to proceed with them. The widow of Ogata Domingos appeared before him on 5 September, and when Gonroku asked her who she was, she answered that she was a widow and in charge of her own household, which belonged to the same *kumi* as that of Antonio Korea. Gonroku told her to apostatize so that they could put this whole affair behind them. She returned to Hama-no-machi with the other women. Rumor had it that this would be the first time that women would no longer be pardoned. The widow started to prepare for her death and sew the clothing in which she and the others of her street wished to die.[18] She gave away everything she still possessed to the poor. Her slaves and servants she set free and sent away. On 8 September, she invited her father, mother, and all her other relatives to a last meal together.[19]

That same night, her street elder called her to his house and asked her if she knew what she had to answer the next day when she was called to the governor's office. She answered him that there was nothing much to say. The next day, she was one of the first to present herself at the office of the Nagasaki Governor. When Gonroku saw the determination with which she answered him, he sentenced her to death. She was brought to jail, where she cut off her hair, which she sent to her parents as a keepsake together with "the whip with which she had been in the habit to discipline herself and the sackcloth in which she had done penance."[20]

One other woman was put under house arrest. Catarina, also a widow, had been born in Chikugo. She had been taken prisoner during the wars of the 1580s and sold to Nagasaki. There she had converted, receiving baptism in the Morisaki church. She was set free and married. A few years later, her husband died while they were living on Antonio Korea's street. They belonged to the latter's *kumi*, the register of which her husband had signed. Her property was confiscated and she was put under detention on her own street until her case came up.[21]

Three times she was called to the mansion of the Governor. Each time, it caused friction between her and her son João, who contended that now that his father was dead the requirement to appear before the *bugyō* applied to him. His mother retorted that the house belonged to her as long as her son had not officially registered it in his own name. As she was the owner of the house, she should go. The two became so adamant in their disagreement that the mother asked her neighbors and acquaintances to restrain her son and make him obey. At last he gave up and let his mother go.[22] In the *shōya*, Catarina was told to go home and put herself under the surveillance of her neighbors. Like the others, she received her final death sentence on 9 September after she had refused to apostatize.

As we can see from the above account of the people belonging to Antonio's *kumi*, there were seven households that became involved in the arrest of Padre Kimura. Of these the representatives of four households had signed the register in person. Of these four householders, two had sons registered as a member of the *kumi* who were executed because of their fathers' refusal to apostatize.

Moreover, if Fernandes is correct in telling us that the change from a ten-household based *kumi*-system to one comprising only five households took place in 1621,[23] this must have happened after Gonroku arrived in the city on 29 July.[24] Thus, in this case, Gonroku's men were still operating under the old, ten-household system.[25] Seven of these ten households provided members ready to die for their faith, a total of twelve people. This means that the representatives of the remaining three households must have apostatized, and probably some male members belonging to the first seven households did so as well.

As we saw above, in Fuchinoue Tomé's household also lived his son André, while the widow Catarina lived together with her son João. If these two men were spared (their names are not among those executed), they must have apostatized. This throws a different light on the generosity contests they waged with their respective parents, as reported by Fernandes. It becomes clear that both these sons would have apostatized before the *bugyō* and so saved the lives of their parents *as well as* their own. Foreseeing this, both parents appealed to the neighbors in support of their parental authority.

Such details are left unmentioned by Fernandes. But from the fact that we can distill this information from his account at all, we may surmise that in the final count he must have considered the Hama-no-machi case an exceptional success.[26] A high percentage of the households involved (70 percent) had provided martyrs to the Church. This becomes all the more apparent when we consider that the three other *kumi* involved in the executions of 1622 had provided far fewer people willing to die for their faith, and thus, by implication, a much higher number of apostasies.[27] In the trials preceding the executions of the Christians, the secular power of the authorities was pitted against the sacral power of the church. "If a magistrate could force a Christian to recant, he won; if not, he lost."[28] In the case of Antonio's *kumi* of Hama-no-machi, then, Hasegawa Gonroku had clearly lost.[29]

*   *   *

The Corral of the Martyrs: Sukedayu

Fernandes describes how this group of twelve Christians from Hama-no-machi (as part of the larger group of thirty to be executed) was brought to the execution grounds on the morning of Saturday 10 September 1622. They all left their jail singing and walked "eagerly and happily" to their deaths.[1] There is no reason to dismiss such descriptions of eager martyrdom as fabrications or ascribe them to any rose-colored glasses before Fernandes' observing eyes. Such attitudes on the part of martyrs are also amply attested from earlier Christian literature. Professor Bowersock writes in his study of Christian martyrdoms in the Roman Empire about "frequent reports of radiant joy, smiles, and even laughter among the Christians on their way to a martyr's death."[2]

In the Gesù Church, not far from the Piazza Venetia in Rome, hangs a painting of the events that took place in Nagasaki on 10 September 1622.[3] It was done in distemper on paper that was later varnished and glued onto wood, and was most probably produced in Macao shortly after the executions, possibly even as early as 1623, by a Japanese painter-acolyte of the Jesuits.[4] This conclusion is especially suggested by the details of the costumes of the spectators depicted on this painting, and among these details it is above all the patterns discernible on the veils worn by the women of Nagasaki in the painting that remind the viewer of similar designs that can be found on certain painted screens of the period (*nanban byōbu*).[5]

The focus of the painting is a corral, an elliptical space marked off by a bamboo fence, into which the viewer is looking from some imaginary high vantage point, hovering somewhere above the city of Nagasaki, as if one were an angel in Heaven. The fence divides the painting immediately into two very different spaces. Outside the fence, we find soldier-guards and masses of spectators, and inside the fence we see the victims and their executioners.

The Executions of 10 September 1622 (Gesù Church, Rome).

The corral was built for the occasion on the last of the foothills of the western slope of Mt. Tateyama, the mountain towering behind the old town, before it reaches the point where the Urakami River flows into Nagasaki Bay.[6] The fence looks a little flimsier than it is likely to have been in reality, a device that allowed the painter to depict all the detail happening within the corral, even what is happening next to the fence close to the ground, something that would otherwise be obscured by the fence itself.

In the upper left corner of the corral, we see a red carpet spread out over a big rock. On it stands one man, who holds a staff in his right hand and stretches out his left hand. He is looking out over twenty-eight warriors, fourteen on his left and fourteen on his right. Eight of these men hold the decorative lances that symbolize the power of the Nagasaki *bugyō*. The man has two swords stuck in his sash, and he seems to be barefoot. He dominates the execution grounds and it seems reasonable to identify him as Sukedayū,[7] the vice-governor below Hasegawa Gonroku, whose exalted status and possibly his personal preference would have prevented his attending the executions in person.[8] Altogether, we see forty-three officials inside the fence. Not all of these can have been men from the *shōya*, for only from 1638 onwards was the Nagasaki *bugyō* assigned an official following of five *yoriki* and twenty *dōshin*.[9] Therefore, most of these soldiers and guards are likely to have been called up from neighboring domains, such as Hirado and Ōmura.[10]

In the second chapter "The Spectacle of the Scaffold" of his well-known study *Discipline and Punish*, Michel Foucault has analyzed the nature of public executions, drawing largely upon materials derived from the French monarchy. He describes, in turn, the significance of the most important elements common to the dramas on the scaffold: the suffering victim and his struggle, the king and his representatives, the public watching the execution, and the printed accounts published later. It is testimony to the astuteness of Foucault's analysis that his conclusions can be applied to other historical contexts.[11] The depiction of the execution grounds on the Gesù painting reminds us that:

A whole military machine surrounded the scaffold: cavalry of the watch, archers, guardsmen, soldiers. This was intended, of course, to prevent any escape or anger on the part of the people, any attempt to save the condemned or to have them immediately put to death; but it was also a reminder that every crime constituted as it were a rebellion against the law and that the criminal was an enemy of the prince.[12]

The central focus of the area inside the fence is on a row of twenty-five stakes with firewood piled up around them:

The evening before someone is to be burned, it is announced by the town crier hitting his cymbal that every household has to bring two, three, four or five bundles of firewood (more or less depending on the number of people to be burned) to the spot where the execution is to take place. According to custom, every street has a headman who is charged with the task of supervising that every household provides this wood irrespective of the fact whether they are Christians or gentiles.[13]

The firewood was then arranged around as many posts as there are people to be burned

and at a distance of about one and a half fathoms [about nine feet] from these posts an opening is left to bring in the delinquents, who are then tied with a thin rope to one hand and pulled as high as it may reach, while the other hand remains loose, and the feet are tied to the lower end of the post. Then they close off the entrance and pile more wood evenly around them and when it is high enough they set fire to it on all sides, so that the poor victims are suffocated or roasted rather than burned.[14]

On the Gesù painting, flames are starting to rise from the firewood at various places. A victim is tied to twenty-two of the stakes, while three of the stakes are left empty. The victims dressed in black are those affiliated with the Society of Jesus (10), those in white with the Dominicans (7), and those in brown or grey with the Franciscans (5). Before, and to the viewer below, the pyre are thirty other Christians, condemned to be beheaded.[15] Nine executioners have just started this task. Six of the victims already have their heads cut off, their bodies are lying on the left. Four of the heads (two women, a child and a man's) are exposed on the exhibition shelf that has been erected behind them, in between their bodies and the pyre. The fifth head of a child is just being raised by one of the executioners to be impaled upon the huge iron spikes lining the center of the shelf. A sixth head, freshly cut, is being picked up by another executioner. Among the twenty-four remaining Christians about to die by their executioners' swords, there are twelve women and seven children ranging in age from infant to adolescent.

In contrast to those condemned to die by the sword on this painting, we do not have to guess at the identities of the victims tied to the stakes. The painter has helpfully provided their names, even if some of this writing has become unreadable with the passage of time.[16] Among the twenty-five victims executed in this manner are nine European clerics, one Jesuit priest, five Dominican and three Franciscan friars. Even so, the black gowns of the Jesuits seem to dominate the painting. The reasons for this are ideological. The painting is hanging, after all, in the church of the Jesuits and was clearly made by a Jesuit acolyte. Therefore, it is important that a simple count of the people at the stakes would lead the viewer to believe that the majority executed upon this occasion had been people who died as martyrs affiliated with (i.e., provided to the Church by) the Jesuits. In reality, the mendicant priests outnumbered the Jesuits by eight to one.

This, of course, was due to the success of Araki Thomé's betrayal on the one hand, and the superior ability of the Jesuits to elude the authorities on the other. The ideological goal of the painting, however, was reached by only depicting those who could be called "martyrs for the faith." As in the eyes of Church authorities the martyrdom of three of the Dominicans were in doubt, the stakes of these men were left empty.[17] This had the convenient effect of putting the black robes of the one Jesuit and his Japanese affiliates in the majority.

By rights, however, the martyrdom of 10 September 1622 belonged to the Dominicans. The order would never recover from the combined blows of Araki's betrayal and the executions in Nagasaki. Afterwards, only three Dominicans remained in hiding in Japan, one of whom (Diego Collado) would leave the country for Manila in November of the same year.[18] Reinforcements were sent the next year[19] and the year after,[20] but there were no longer any Dominicans in Nagasaki.

To the right of the corral, among the soldiers from Ōmura, stand two palanquins, a high-ranking official and an upper-class *bushi* with their eleven followers. Among this group there are also six foreigners. They may be Dutch or English, who have come from Hirado to watch the executions. Thus, one of the palanquins may belong to the daimyo of Hirado. From the laughing faces of these foreigners, we may read, simultaneously, Jesuit disapproval of the Protestants as well as the eagerness of these men to show that they are not very upset by what they are seeing. The stability of their trade depended on proving that their own religion was different from that of the Portuguese and Spanish. Eight non-warriors, standing behind them, may be Nagasaki officials or merchants.

To the left of the corral, we see seven boats floating in the bay. These carry a total of thirty-two people, mostly (twenty-two) women. These women are looking up towards the execution grounds and seem to be praying. All the women and children, together one hundred and fifty-three people on this painting are likely to be Christians. There are ninety-eight warriors involved in the execution, either as guards or executioners. There are another one hundred and forty other spectators, warriors or *bushi*, town's people or *chōnin*, and peasants, as well as a total of fourteen foreigners. On the boats, we find seven warriors and three captains. All together there are four hundred and forty-one people in the painting.[21]

There are several shortcomings in this painting. I have already pointed out the obvious, pro–Jesuit bias in its arrangement. The skill of the painter, also, is evidently not of the highest order, viz. the awkwardness of the perspective. Rather than for its artistic qualities, it should be valued as a historical source. Although the painting is large, measuring 135 cm by 155 cm, the crowds of Japanese Christians that attended these executions must have been far larger than could conveniently be depicted on this surface. Some estimates mention as many as thirty thousand,[22] an unlikely sixty thousand,[23] or even an impossible one hundred thousand spectators.[24]

We know that other paintings were made of this same event as well. The Jesuit Superior of Manila, Garcia Garces, wrote in 1623 for example that several paintings of the executions had reached Manila.[25] Thus, it is more than likely that the Dominicans and/or the Franciscans produced their own versions of this scene as well. None of these have survived, however, so the Gesù painting is valuable just for being the only painting of the executions to have come down to us.

Five strange figures hide among the crowd of spectators. The first of these figures sits with the women at the bottom of the painting and is clad in a brown *nagasode* (long-sleeved kimono). The figure has long hair, the head covered with a *mugiwarabōshi* or broad-rimmed, conical straw hat. The second figure is also dressed in brown, but has a white, tasseled veil under a similar straw hat. We see other figures with such straw hats combined with drab robes as well: one near the fence, one a little further up the mountain, and one in one of the back rows. Itinerant Buddhist monks often wore such broad-rimmed, conical straw hats. Apart from that, they are also a good way to hide one's face. It is not impossible, therefore, that with these figures the painter has meant to suggest the presence of several other European missionaries in disguise, who would later compose the eyewitness accounts of the event we possess.

When the procession that had left Nagasaki's jail with its accompanying mass of spectators reached the execution grounds, Padre Kimura spoke to the crowds from Nagasaki in a loud voice, telling them

> how happy he was, how eager to suffer martyrdom, and how relieved his soul felt now that it saw the stakes and the firewood that would serve to burn him. The only thing he wanted people to understand and show to everyone present was the pleasure and joy he felt communicated to him by the goodness of the Lord. He said much more about this but it was hard to hear him in the din of the crowds.[26]

When Antonio's wife Maria saw him, she showed the padre her son whom she carried on her shoulders. She "told him that today she was offering this little boy whom she loved so much to God, who had given him to her."[27] The moment was short and fleeting, but the padre showed his approval and admiration for the strong faith of his former host. Maria was, in fact, sacrificing everything she had on earth. According to Fernandes, she was the only one here who gave up everything she had: her property, her house, her husband, her children, as well as her own life.[28]

Because time was pressing, however, the police officers pushed the prisoners from Nagasaki inside the bamboo fortress. Entering the corral, the group from Nagasaki was told to stand in line along the fence. Four of the prisoners, however, were pulled apart, for they were to share the ordeal in fire with the prisoners from Ōmura. Antonio Korea was among these four. Two of the other three were, like him, householders responsible for having lodged padres and their helpers. In contrast to those condemned to a simple beheading, the guilt of these four had been weighed and found to be heavier than that of their wives and children, and therefore deserving of a much harsher punishment. They had originally been lodged in the Nagasaki jail, apart from the padres, because it was hoped that a sojourn in that terrible place might induce their apostasy and that of their families.

Having refused to apostatize, they had compounded their original guilt to the point where they now had to suffer the same punishment as the padres and their helpers. Because these four victims were the first to be assigned a stake on the pyre, we see them occupying the first four stakes on the left in the Gesù painting, with Antonio from Hama-no-machi in the third position dressed in the black costume of the Misericordia Brotherhood. Fernandes writes: "During the time that these soldiers were preparing the execution, the innocent children … were running around inside the corral, so happily and cheerfully that it was a pleasure to see them. Although the corral was a battlefield surrounded by soldiers from Ōmura and Hirado, equipped for war with lances, matchlocks, and Japanese bows, these little innocents did not know what fear was."[29]

About the on-going battle of the scaffold, Foucault writes: "From the point of view of the law that imposes it, public torture and execution must be spectacular, it must be seen by all as its triumph. The very excess of the violence employed is one of the elements of its glory: the fact that the guilty man should moan and cry out under the blows is not a shameful side-effect, it is the very ceremonial of justice being expressed in all its force."[30] It follows, therefore, that those who do not show signs of suffering win their battle with the authorities. This is an important point to remember when analyzing the accounts of the martyrdoms, which often speak of the "victories" gained by the martyrs. Such victories refer to suffering in patience, without crying out, not, of course, to surviving the ordeal.[31]

The rationale of the Roman Catholic Church we find on a continuum of reversed earthly values: to part with one's property and give to the poor is to buy credit with God, to confess one's sins and to chastise oneself is to purify one's heart. Because to suffer is to acquire merit, and to be executed for the faith is to be chosen by God to enter Paradise, it follows from this that to live when one has a chance to die a martyr is sadness, and to die a gruesome death instead is cause for joy.

Upon a signal from Sukedayu, five executioners started with the beheadings. They unsheathed their swords and from both sides of the line "in an instant, heads started to jump away from their bodies."[32] It is said that, when heads are cut with the speed allowed by the extreme sharpness of a Japanese katana, the pressure in the arteries of the victim pushes the head away from the body. The higher the pressure, the further the head "jumps." In samurai folklore, this has given rise to stories about heads of fiends flying around trying to do one last dastardly deed (like biting the executioner's nose or ear).[33] Of the pious widow Catarina, from Hama-no-machi, Fernandes reports that her head "jumped with a strange nimbleness pronouncing those sweet words Iesus y Maria three times while it was leaping more than an arm's length away from her body."[34] "In spite of this," our chronicler asserts, "the innocent children among the victims did not become afraid nor even started to cry, something very unusual for their age.[35] At this time, the Christians watching this battle … raised their voices invoking the sweet names of Jesus Maria … and because this multitude of Christians was countless, the noise of these invocations was so loud that it reverberated through the valley into the mountains."[36]

Thirty heads fell in a very short time. They were put on the stakes that had been prepared, as we can see on the Gesù painting, with their faces turned towards those to be roasted. Of Antonio from Hama-no-machi, it is reported that he was particularly interested to see how his friends and relatives had died: "the spectators noticed that Antonio stared at the heads of the lucky ones who had already gained Victory with their beheading. He showed himself very happy to see them and seemed to give thanks to God to be able to see that his friends and, most importantly, his sons and wife had ended and completed their lives in such a heroic manner."[37]

It was his turn next. Fernandes reports: "And as the fire lit up, the screaming of the spectators became so loud that it was not possible any longer to hear anything else."[38] Thus, the noise of the maddened crowds must have drowned out the singing that the condemned at their posts had started.[39] As it had rained that morning, the firewood was wet, so the smoke must have been thick for a while and when it cleared, many of the victims likely had already passed out or died. Fernandes writes:

> Everyone saw that our foreigner, who had come as a prisoner from Korea, showed so much courage and remained so steadfast that he did not yield to any of the Japanese or Europeans. He stayed so still and without moving on his spot that it seemed as if he had no need for the ropes to keep him in place. And when the force of the fire increased he expired saintly and valorously giving his blessed soul to God Our Lord, purified as it was in the fire of martyrdom.[40]

But, even inside the fire, there were degrees of severity in punishment. Those who were weak from their time in prison, such as most of the Europeans, passed away quickly after the smoke and heat overwhelmed them. Others lasted longer because they had been given the spots further away from the heat of the firewood. Padre Kimura had been singled out by his executioners for the cruelest spot. It is likely that this was because he was the only native Japanese priest among those executed on this day. In the eyes of the authorities, his disobedience was of the most outrageous kind. Being an upper-class male who should have known better than being fooled by the foreigners, his uncompromising attitude towards his faith must have been considered particularly offensive and distasteful, and of a completely different order than the effrontery of the Europeans.

Padre Kimura "was so far from the flames that not even his clothes caught on fire. His torment lasted for close to two hours, during which he continued to stand up without moving with his customary calm and composure, with such control that it seemed as if the fire did not affect him at all."[41] Not everyone, however, was as lucky as those who died quickly, or as heroic as those who suffered for a long time like Padre Kimura. After the fire had been lit, three men decided that they were not prepared to die for their faith in this manner. Two had recently been admitted in jail as "terceiros" into the Dominican order, the third was one of those who had provided shelter to the padres. They undid the ropes that tied them to their stakes, and fled running through the corral trying to find a place where they could jump through the fire. When they came running out, they were crying *Namu Amida Butsu* or "Hail to the Amida Buddha," thus indicating their willingness to apostatize. Sukedayu, however, decided it was too late and ordered his men to use their lances to drive the men back into the ring of fire.

*   *   *

Repressive Measures: Tokugawa Iemitsu

In 1623, Tokugawa Iemitsu (1604–1651), even more eager than his grandfather and father to eradicate Christianity throughout Japan, succeeded to the position of shogun.

One of the first important tasks he faced was how to deal with Christian Nagasaki. The new shogun, still guided by his father and his advisers, decided to systematically undermine each support upon which Christian Nagasaki had been able to exist. Ships entering Nagasaki Bay were so closely visited that between 1622 and 1630, no Jesuit managed to enter Japan, and between 1624 and 1629 no member of any order at all.[1] At the same time, the hunt for hidden priests went on inexorably, so that by the end of the decade their number was reduced to a handful, who had been scattered throughout Japan and were completely unable to cope with the task of caring for what was left of Japan's Christendom.

Without the constant encouragement, reinforcement, and absolution of the padres, Christian piety, blind religious fervor, and stubborn determination slowly had to make way for a more realistic appraisal of the situation. Life was literally made impossible for anyone who wished to hold on to his Christian beliefs in public.[2] Nagasaki was turned into a city of apostates. The measures aimed at accomplishing this were implemented by a succession of Nagasaki *bugyō* between 1622 and 1629. It is not always clear which decisions were taken in Edo and which by the officials on the spot. In general, most cases involving the European missionaries were at first decided in Edo Castle, while those of the many Japanese supporting them were often summarily executed in the city itself.

On the whole, the policy was designed to suppress Christianity while preserving Nagasaki's by now traditional function as the country's most important link with the world outside Japan. For a few years, however, the eradication was thought more important and received precedence over the trade. On 12 January 1623, for example, the chief factor of the Dutch traders in Hirado wrote that no ships would be sent from Nagasaki to Siam that year, because the captains and crews of these ships "mainly consist of Christians, who are suspected of smuggling papists into the country."[3]

One month and a half later, on 25 February, Padre Baltasar de Torres (1563–1626) wrote to the General of the Society that of the twenty-eight Jesuits still in Japan twenty-three were padres, of whom one third was old and tired of the past ten years of persecution. He added that it had become impossible to replace them with younger ones because of the thorough visitation and supervision of foreign shipping arriving in Nagasaki.[4]

In November 1623, the Augustinian friar Vicente de Santo Antonio Simoens (1590–1632) reported that Hasegawa Gonroku had gone

> to the Emperor's court with his subaltern called [Suetsugu] Heizō, an apostate, who is our fiercest persecutor here. After many discussions before the Emperor on the question whether there still were Christians in Nagasaki or not, with the apostate always taking the position that there were [still many], the Emperor ordered the expulsion of all the Spanish from this city, including those who had married Japanese women. This new order was sent by express mail to be announced immediately.[5]

A whole array of new measures resulted from these discussions in Edo Castle reported by the Augustinian friar. That winter, a register was compiled of all the Europeans in the city:

> The police went around all the streets and entered all the houses of the Europeans, writing down the names of the whole family and asking especially the women and the servants if they were Japanese or of European descent, even noting down their ages. On this list they not only put Europeans but also those Koreans, Chinese, and Japanese who went around dressed like Portuguese, because it seems they even abhor European dress these days.[6]

Next, not only the Spanish, but "all Europeans,"[7] who had married Japanese wives in Nagasaki were ordered to leave Japan with their sons by the end of 1624. Traffic between Nagasaki and the Philippines was less regulated than that between Nagasaki and Macao, and many ships owned by Japanese and Portuguese merchants were constantly arriving from Manila during the time the winds were blowing north. Christian penetration of Japan from that direction, therefore, had proven easier and more successful over the past ten years, so that the Bakufu came to the conclusion that "as long as there were Spanish living in the city or coming as merchants, there could not fail to be missionaries as well, because they would disguise themselves [as Spanish laymen]."[8]

Therefore, Japanese merchants were forbidden to travel to Manila, and all shipping originating in the islands was barred from doing business in Japan. In this atmosphere, it is no wonder that a Spanish embassy that had been sent from Manila to improve relations was refused by the Bakufu early in 1624.[9] It is illuminating (and illustrative of the thinking in Edo Castle) to read the reasons why. First, the Japanese objected that the embassy had not been sent by the Spanish king, but originated in the Philippines, where the ecclesiastical authorities were more powerful than the Governor himself. Second, similar embassies had been sent before and had proved to be nothing but an excuse to start spreading "a false and diabolical law ... with which they misled [the shogun's] vassals and sowed disorder in his domains."[10]

Any Japanese, in fact, who was still professing to be a Christian was now barred from leaving the country altogether, but non–Christians, including apostates, were still allowed to travel overseas.[11] From this time, also, Portuguese pilots were no longer allowed to steer Japanese ships.[12] Dutch and Italian pilots quickly took their place on the large vessels sailing for the great merchants,[13] while the captains of smaller ships sailing for their own account often did without.[14]

On 3 March 1624 Padre João Baptista de Baeça wrote that officials had come to Nagasaki to enforce the departure of the Spanish and Portuguese merchants from the city, to take down all the crosses, and to destroy the gravestones of the Christians. How ideologically driven the persecution had become, and how deep the misunderstanding was between the Japanese Christians and their remaining shepherds on the one hand and the Bakufu authorities on the other, can be read from the surprise, expressed in Jesuit letters, at how petty and virulent the enforcers were becoming. Padre Rodrigues Giram reported in the *Anua* of 1624, that even those who sold rosary beads or recited prayers with their rosaries were being punished.[15] It was, however, just such individual refusals to abandon the faith in public that infuriated the officials. The misunderstanding was between those who believed in the absolute truth of what they were taught and those who saw it for nothing else but the ideology of a competing empire.

The Bakufu had a point, of course, in this assessment. At the same time, however, its very violent, petty, and prolonged response to the Christian challenge showed how very threatened the men in power must have felt in the face of this tenacious, foreign doctrine. For the next few years, everyone who furthered the cause of Christianity was hunted down, registers were compiled of everyone living in the city, and people were being questioned if they had ever performed official duties for the Church.[16]

On 30 November 1624, the Dutch Chief Factor Cornelis van Neijenroode wrote from nearby Hirado to his superior in Batavia: "When the Portuguese galliots were about to depart on the seventeenth of this month, the Governor of Nagasaki ordered an autodafé for two Japanese who had lodged papists in their homes so that the ships would be able to bring this news to Macao. The five Portuguese imprisoned [in Nagasaki] daily expect the same fate."[17] The Dutchman continued to report that no one was allowed to leave the city. Everyone had to stay inside. No boats were permitted to sail from Hirado to Nagasaki.[18] The Portuguese residents of Nagasaki married to Japanese women, he wrote in another letter, had been forced to depart and only been allowed to take their sons with them. They had had to leave their wives and daughters behind. Some Portuguese, who had left the year before, had come back to Nagasaki to trade this year, but were not allowed to stay in their own houses. If they wanted to see their wives, they had to send for them in the house of an apostate innkeeper.[19]

Orders had come down from Edo, he explains, not to allow Portuguese merchants to lodge in any household that was still headed by a Christian or to conduct their business with Christians. "Recently ... more than one thousand have apostatized in spite of all the efforts made by the many papists who are still in and around Nagasaki to prevent this. It is almost unbelievable how much trouble and danger that these papists are exposed to for trying to help the Christians and stay alive in Nagasaki."[20]

On 20 February 1625, the Jesuit padre Mateo de Couros wrote that Japanese outside Japan could only return if they were ready to apostatize.[21] Later that year, the same padre gave an example of what had happened to a junk from Cambodia, which carried a number of Japanese Christians as members of its crew: "when the pagans disembarked, the Christians had to stay on board the ship. She was surrounded by armed guards, who did not allow them any supplies, even water. The crew remained constant for as long as they had provisions, but in the end they all, except one, apostatized out of hunger and thirst."[22]

Paperwork also increased. To obtain permission to leave from Nagasaki for Southeast Asia, Japanese captains had to go to the Governor's office where they had to swear an oath that no one of their crews was a Christian who had not apostatized.[23] As for ships arriving in the harbor of Nagasaki, no one was allowed to come or bring anything ashore before the arrival of the harbor officials on the ship, irrespective of her nationality, be it Japanese, European, or Chinese. Portuguese ships were now required to bring a list of everybody on board, signed by the town councilors of Macao and the Captain Major.[24] No one who was not on the list was allowed to come ashore. This list was checked upon arrival and again at the time of departure.

In 1625, Governor Hasegawa Gonroku boarded the Portuguese galliots in the company of his associate, the apostate priest Araki Thomé, who helped him check the list of all those embarked against those actually on the ship.[25] After the trading season of that year, Gonroku forced Captain Major Agostinho Lobo to stay behind in Japan because he had not brought a list of all those embarked on the five ships, which had come that year with far too many unknown young men on board.[26] All merchandise and luggage was also closely inspected, and no one was allowed to bring anything, not even letters or books, for the padres any longer. Before Gonroku left for Edo that year, he called all the street elders of Uchimachi to his office and forced them to sign an oath that, on pain of death, no one in their wards would be baptized, no one would read "spiritual books," and no one would propagate "the things of our Holy Law."[27]

A Hard-Liner:
Mizuno Morinobu

These new regulations caused much hardship, and not only to the population of Nagasaki. It seems that the persecution also was taking its toll on the city's governor of the past ten years. A Dutch report has: "Governor Gonroku did not seem to have much taste for shedding blood, so that he was always sick or pretending illness, as I was able to see for myself. When I visited him he seemed to be tortured by something, so that he could not sleep by night or by day, as he told me, and for this reason he had been applying continually to be discharged from his position. This he finally obtained in 1626."[1]

The last time Gonroku travelled back to Edo from Nagasaki, he visited Hirado on 2 February 1626. Chief Factor Cornelis van Neijenroode reports that the Governor had offered him on that occasion "the choice of thirty-five houses and properties, formerly owned by the Portuguese in Nagasaki, in order to reside there and conduct our trade."[2] A month later, on 3 March 1626, the chief factor wrote down rumors he had heard in Hirado that the governor had been relieved of his charge, and that someone else had been appointed in his place. The man was described as

> a great lord in his own right, brought up in Edo, and a great enemy of Christianity. It is thought that this is the reason for his appointment. He has not yet arrived, but it is certain that [when he does] things will change greatly in Nagasaki. The previous [two] governors have been ordinary townsmen, who did not keep a grand retinue, but from now on the government of the city will, in contrast, have a samurai character.[3]

The new governor was Mizuno Kawachi no kami Morinobu (1577–1636), a member of an old Tokugawa retainer family from Mikawa, who had served Ieyasu since before his campaign against Uesugi Kagekatsu in 1600.[4] He arrived in Nagasaki on 17 June 1626,[5] and immediately ordered an autodafé of nine missionaries, three of whom were Europeans, two of them recently caught in Arima. The burning took place on 20 June.[6]

The occasion is illustrative because, apart from the missionaries, there were five Portuguese (two of them pilots) who were also scheduled to be executed for supporting the padres. They escaped this punishment, however, by their public "apostasy, idol worship, and being shaved in the Japanese manner."[7] What is more, there was still a chronic shortage of pilots in Nagasaki.

"One or two days later," Mateo de Couros wrote after this autodafé,

> the Governor ordered the public burning of all the property that had been confiscated from the missionaries since December of 1618…. A great quantity of books, almost all we had owned, our records, and the letters of all the previous Vice-Provincials and Generals of the Society went up into flames at that time, as did many ornaments, some of them very beautiful, even the chalices, which the apostate cleric [Araki Thomé] threw into the fire with his own hands, many reliquaries, some of them made of gold and other large ones of gilded silver with beautiful crystal of Milan, and others of finely worked gold filigree …. Many beautiful oil paintings and engravings … all were burned to ashes, which were thrown into the sea.[8]

This public performance of apostasies and autodafé was followed by a second autodafé, less than one month later, on 12 July, of eight Japanese Christians who had been convicted of sheltering the padres.[9] They all remained constant. It is probable that these sentences had been confirmed in Edo beforehand. They made the change in government more terrifying and ominous of things yet to come, the more so because during the last year of his tenure as governor, Gonroku had not ordered any executions at all.

Where the trade was concerned, the new governor required everyone to list the amounts of money sent overseas as capital to be employed in the trade between Nagasaki and Macao. Because the order was accompanied by the regulation that if anyone was found later not to have divulged his assets, he was to be executed, almost everyone complied. The total came to the enormous sum of 230,000 *cruzados*. The governor decreed "that those who apostatized would receive their rightful share, and those who refused to do so would lose their investment. This caused many to abandon their faith, especially among the richest citizens of Nagasaki."[10]

Mizuno seems to have been determined but calm, pressing his case "with friendly words, as if he was just giving advice. Those who are poor and in want, he threatens very sharply if they do not want to apostatize, but if on the contrary they are willing to listen to him, he makes many promises to help them obtain money and property, and to be helpful in all kinds of ways."[11] The new governor acquired the reputation of someone who kept his word to those who apostatized

> giving houses to one and land to another, which used to be the property of those who have been killed. Others, again, he makes the hosts of the Chinese, who have come this year with more than sixty, large and small junks. When those Chinese sell their merchandise, the governor makes them pay ten percent to their hosts to pay for their candlelight. In this manner many of the poor, who did not know how to make a living, obtain a small income.[12]

For a while the apostates who were allowed to lodge the Portuguese were in a minority and so prices for lodging the Portuguese merchants doubled. The merchants from Macao were no longer allowed to hire Christian servants,[13] or even to talk to Japanese Christians.[14] At this time, citizens of Nagasaki were only allowed to travel freely within a radius of one mile from the city, whether by land or by sea. If they wanted to travel further, they had to be registered in a Buddhist temple.[15]

To make things worse, no one was allowed to emigrate any longer. Those who had left the city to live somewhere in its surroundings were called back, and had to present themselves in the company of their street elder and their families at the Governor's office. The new governor also sent out callers throughout the streets of Nagasaki announcing that it was now forbidden to employ Christian craftsmen, such as carpenters or coopers, and for any craftsman not registered in a Buddhist temple to engage in his trade.[16]

Officials were sent to all the *machi* to register the apostates, and require them to perform *fumie* or "stepping upon a religious image" with their feet.[17] At first these images were paper ones that had been confiscated from the Jesuit printing press. Later, when the numbers of apostates grew, more durable images were required, and they were made in wood or copper especially for the purpose. After this proof of loyalty to the Tokugawa regime, the apostates were required to sign or press their seal in a register. This is the first instance of what would later, during the 1630s, become a custom enforced throughout the whole country, becoming one of the hallmarks of the Tokugawa regime only abandoned in the nineteenth century. Those who did not want to comply with the registration process simply fled into the mountains where many of them died of exposure, hunger, and thirst.[18] After the trading season, by the beginning of October, the Portuguese were sent back to Macao. No one was allowed to stay behind.

Before departing for Edo to report on the progress he had made in the eradication of Christianity,[19] the governor "called all the apostate Christians, or new heathen, in their best clothing to his office on 8 October [1626]. They numbered more than fifteen hundred. He spoke to them in polite language and made further promises of his help and favor in order to get others to apostatize by this example."[20]

The next year, Mizuno Kawachi was back in Nagasaki on 24 July 1627. On 26 July he ordered the two former mayors Machida João and Gotō Sōin Thomé, who still had not apostatized, to leave for Edo. As soon as these men had been sent off to Edo, Governor Mizuno dealt with the rest of Nagasaki's upper class. He closed and posted guards before the gates of the residences of nine of the town's remaining principal Christians, who were told to make public apostasies. Only one complied with the orders of the governor. The other eight were sent off to Edo as well, while Mizuno confiscated the property of these men.[21]

In 1627 no ships arrived from Macao, where the Dutch were blockading the harbor.[22] Only a small junk carrying correspondence made it to Nagasaki. The letters were closely scrutinized by several men in the employ of Mizuno Morinobu, such as Araki Tomé and Antonio Neretti.[23] It may have been unfortunate in more ways than one that there was no trading this year, for it gave the governor and his men more time to deal with the suppression of Christianity. Another large autodafé took place on 16 August 1626, similar to the one of 1622, but on a somewhat smaller scale: ten Japanese were beheaded and eight religious were roasted to death on the slow fire: three European Franciscans, three naturalized Koreans, and two Japanese.[24]

With each year that passed, the Bakufu became more impatient with the population of Nagasaki. When Mizuno Morinobu traveled to Nagasaki for the third time in 1628, he had in his pocket a letter addressed to him by the Shōgun's Council which contained the outcome of its deliberations on the cases of several Christians from Nagasaki that the governor had brought back to Edo for the council to decide. The document left no doubt about the manner in which he was to act to those who had transgressed against the new laws ("In each case, the men and their sons shall die, while their wives, daughters, servants, slaves, and other property shall all be confiscated [and sold]"), and how the Governor was to increase the pressure on those who were still clinging to their Christian identity in Nagasaki ("they shall be made to do the dirty work available in town. It goes without saying that they will be given a hard time").[25]

This year, the governor started to systematically enforce apostasies throughout town. Those who refused to apostatize were no longer allowed to go out, but were forced to stay in their homes. Their doors and windows were hammered shut with nails, so that they would die of hunger. Those who did not own a house but were renting were expelled from their homes and forced to flee into the mountains around the city, where they too died within months, mostly of hunger and exposure.[26] Meanwhile, the governor raised the reward for informers for information leading to the arrest of a padre from thirty to one hundred bars of silver,[27] but as there were fewer and fewer padres left in the area this did not lead immediately to more arrests.

Trade with the Dutch was interrupted, ostensibly because of a violent dispute that had arisen between traders from Nagasaki and the Dutch Governor of Taiwan. The Japanese merchants (who were sailing on a ship owned by Suetsugu Heizō) resented the way they had been treated by the Dutch. Therefore on 29 June 1628, pretending to have come to take their leave, they took the Dutch Governor of Taiwan, Pieter Nuyts, hostage. As heedless of their own lives as was fashionable among Japanese sailors of their day, they managed to force the frightened Dutch Governor into buying his own release by sending a number of his subordinates to Japan.

When this group of Dutchmen arrived in Nagasaki, they were detained for almost two and a half years. On 31 July 1628, Pieter Muyser, the senior officer of the group, wrote:

> Our case is held up by the terrible persecution of the Christians pursued once more because of the return of Kawachi Dono, the Governor of this town. The citizens and those living in the direct surroundings of the town are caught by the hundreds, treated in a very severe manner, and finally thrown into the hot sulphureous springs of Arima and Bungo. These days that we were being held here, callers went out throughout the city announcing that those who were still professing to be Christians should present themselves at the Governor's office before 5th of this moon, which corresponds to 4 August, in order to apostatize.[28]

After that date, all would be burned. This decree caused many to flee "leaving everything behind, their house, their garden, and other possessions, so that whole shopping streets remain empty, all their inhabitants having fled. This destruction is just too miserable to observe."[29]

The trade with the Portuguese came to a standstill as well, again ostensibly because of an incident that had occurred in Siam, where in May a Spaniard, by name of Don Juan de Alcaraso, had burned a Japanese Red-Seal junk belonging to Mayor Takagi Sakuemon.[30] When Captain Major Antonio Monteiro Pinto arrived with five galliots, he was held responsible for this act of aggression, because Spain and Portugal were still under the same crown.[31] The whole Portuguese fleet found itself suddenly embargoed[32] and forced to remain idly at anchor in the bay.

Neither of these interruptions of the trade were what they seemed, i.e., problems caused by foreigners that needed to be sorted out by the Bakufu before the trade could be allowed to continue. That, of course, was the *form* in which these matters were presented to the people of the two nations involved.[33] In reality, all trade *needed* to be suspended in order to give the Governor of Nagasaki a chance, once and for all, to deal with Christianity in Nagasaki. There simply may not have been enough trained manpower at his disposal to do the two jobs of eradicating Christianity and supervising the trade at the same time. It is also possible that the Bakufu wanted to avoid advertising the clean-up, the necessity for which may have been considered a loss of face. After all, a whole city had been ignoring its anti–Christian legislation for the past fourteen years. It would not do, therefore, to have merchants from all over Japan in the city, or in nearby Hirado, at this time. What is more, suspending the trade with the Europeans mostly hurt the Christian merchants of Nagasaki and Hirado.[34] Both the Portuguese and the Dutch, then, became unwitting victims of this internal policy matter, which must have been the real reason for the suspension of the trade. In order to make this less obvious, in the end the Portuguese trade was suspended for three years, and the (less important) Dutch trade for four.

Contrary to the Bakufu's wishes, however, a record of the violence was created by the Dutch.[35] Three hundred and forty-eight Christians were brought to Arima to be tortured "with hot water that was poured over, burned with red-hot irons, beaten with reeds, left stark naked out in the heat of the sun for days, at night in the cold, and many other torments, such as tubs filled with snakes set in front of them with the threat to put them inside, making roasters with wood underneath and threatening to roast their children on top of them in front their own eyes."[36] The victims were not allowed to die, but on the verge of death were nursed back to health to be tortured again when they had regained their forces. "With women and virgins they behaved in such an abominable manner that I would be ashamed to say it out loud, let alone write it down, from which I will therefore refrain."[37]

Some suffered their torments for three or four weeks, others longer, but eventually most apostatized. "By the end of September, there were only five or six of the whole group left who had not yet abandoned their faith. The flesh on their bodies had rotted, so that they stank like leek onions from all the pus and boils."[38] These last remaining holdouts continued to be tortured until they died a martyr's death. "The Lord of Arima had taken charge of these tortures, because he was of the opinion that Kawachi Dono was too soft on these people."[39]

What the Japanese authorities pursued was the example they wanted to set. When such staunch Christians finally apostatized, others might come to realize that resistance was futile and apostatize more quickly. By the end of December 1628, the last three people of the group finally died: "They were so exhausted and emaciated that they slumped down dead where they were seated, one about a day and a half after the others."[40]

* * *

The Climax of the Persecution: Takenaka Shigeyoshi

Just when one thought that the persecutions could not get any worse, they got more terrible than ever. Mizuno Morinobu was appointed Governor of Osaka on 7 March 1628.[1] As indicated above, he may not have had sufficient taste for the type of work the Bakufu required in Nagasaki. It took until the next year before the next governor was able to get to Nagasaki. On 27 July 1629, Takenaka Uneme no Shō Shigeyoshi (1588–1633), made his entry into the city.[2] He was the son of a Toyotomi retainer, Takenaka Shigetoshi (1562–1615), who in 1601 had been given the domain of Funai in Bungo, the old castle town of Ōtomo Sōrin.[3] Shigeyoshi had succeeded his father in 1615, and had been employed as a judge and spy by the Bakufu. When he arrived in Nagasaki, he already had a reputation of being "very severe."[4]

His task was the total eradication of Christianity from the city and its surroundings. For this he had brought with him around four hundred soldiers, among whom there were thirty mounted samurai with their servants. These samurai with their followers were lodged outside the city. They came to the governor's office at daybreak and left again after sunset at night.[5]

The second day after his arrival in Nagasaki, Takenaka had several posts erected with fire wood arranged around them, a threat to all those still hiding missionaries in their houses. His predecessor Governor Mizuno had compiled a register with all the names of the streets of the city and the names of all householders which had so far refused to apostatize. Governor Takenaka now closed off all the roads giving access to the city, over the water and overland, so that no one could flee. He gave orders that he was not to be disturbed for anything unrelated to the Christian problem. Therefore, all business was suspended. The gates of the streets were closed earlier, well before dark, and only reopened after sunrise the next day in order that there might no longer be any traffic taking place in the dark. For the time being, these gates were no longer manned by the locals, who were all suspected of being Christian sympathizers, but by the governor's own men.

Next, the men of the new governor visited all the households still registered as

Christian, in the company of the elder of the street in question. These street elders had already been forced to apostatize by Governor Mizuno, so by this time only those willing to serve the Bakufu were left in such positions.[6] Every householder was asked if he was still a Christian. Those who answered negatively would be left alone, while those who dared confirm that they were still Christians would be asked to apostatize on the spot.

If they refused to apostatize, they were sent to the Governor's office, where they were locked up in a fireproof warehouse. Then

> they would ask his wife, his children, and the other members of his household the same question. If they also refused, they would make a complete inventory of all the property, nailed all doors and windows closed, and put their seals on them, taking the people out of the house. If these people apostatized, they would also make the inventory, but leave the people inside the house as care-takers of the property.[7]

The householders were sent to the sulfurous hot springs of Arima. At night, they were put inside grass huts in which it was impossible to sit upright. These were mounted on wooden platforms which were sticking out over the water. Each hut contained a large number of people and was closed off so that the inmates would have only the fumes and the stench of the water to breathe. From time to time, those who seemed to be asleep or on the verge of death were pulled out so that they might be forced back in again as soon as they had recovered. Only those willing to apostatize were allowed to come outside and stay there.

As soon as it was day, those who were still holding out were put next to the water, "where very small ladles of this water were thrown all over their bodies, with the exception of their heads, while they were steadily asked if they were not ready to abandon their faith."[8] The water was so hot and acidic that it penetrated through their skins as far as the bones. It would have been too dangerous to throw it on their heads, for the goal was apostasy, not death. There were very few who were able to bear this torture for more than three days. The men from the Governor's office kept on torturing different groups of householders from Nagasaki during the whole month of August.

The women were treated differently. "Those who were living without husbands or sons and those who were widows were also sent, if they were very old, to the hot springs. Some of the young women they sent naked on hands and feet through the streets of the town."[9] They were exposed to all the horrors that the disdain of the torturers could inflict upon them, and that sometimes recall the crimes committed by Emperor Buretsu, more than eleven hundred years earlier.[10]

After everyone had apostatized, the governor made every householder, from the smallest to the largest household, sign a register that they were no longer Christians nor were lodging any more Christians in their homes.[11] Thus, in a span of forty-five days, Governor Takenaka had achieved what his two predecessors had not been able to accomplish in fifteen years. After these gruesome months, the roads were opened again, and Nagasaki was in business once more. By the end of September, Takenaka sent all of his own retainers back to his domain, not keeping more than the thirty men he was assigned as his ordinary following in Nagasaki.[12] As far as Takenaka was concerned, he had solved the problem of Christianity in Nagasaki, where everyone now was officially registered as an apostate.

All that was left was some mopping up of individual Christians who had for some reason been overlooked, who had been out of town, or who had revoked their previous apostasy. The Governor spent three more terrible years in Nagasaki doing just that, continuing the custom of *fumi-e*, or "stepping on the picture," to catch those who still considered themselves secret Christians, and devising new forms of torture to produce apostates. Meanwhile, he enriched himself as much as he could. In this respect, he clearly went too far, even in the eyes of his superiors. On 21 March 1634, he and his son Gensaburō were forced to commit *seppuku* or ritual suicide.[13]

*   *   *

The Brave Ex-Mayor: Machida João

After Governor Mizuno arrived in Nagasaki on 24 July 1627, he had called the two mayors who still had not apostatized to his office.[1] They were Machida João and Gotō Thomé. The governor dissimulated and told the two old men he had been unable to meet with them the year before, but that he now wanted to make their acquaintance. After an exchange of compliments, Mizuno simply gave them permission to go home again. Later on the same day, their sons Machida Sŏemon Pedro and Gotō Shinzaemon Paulo,[2] who had succeeded to the position of their fathers, were also called to the governor: "He told them that he had conferred about their cases at court, reporting [to the shogun and his advisers] that they and their fathers were still Christians, who did not want to obey the shogun. He was now notifying them in the shogun's name that if they did not abandon the Law of God, they should go to court and present themselves there."[3]

As we have seen in the case of Murayama Tōan, the Tokugawa authorities greatly hesitated to take punitive measures against anyone of the governing class or those who had been received inside the shogun's Castle. This would have greatly diminished the awe required from the population for the ruling class as a whole. What is more, it is clear that the Bakufu had by now come to understand that simple executions would only increase the "stubbornness" of the Christians. Creating hardship, then, was the route chosen for converting Nagasaki to Buddhism. For this reason, it issued the order for these men to come to Edo.

Meanwhile, Governor Mizuno warned the lords of Arima and Ōmura to hold their troops in readiness in case unrest broke out in Nagasaki over the departure of the two former mayors and their families. Therefore, the area around the city filled with the sounds of arms, horses, and men, frightening and sowing confusion among its inhabitants.[4] In the end, it was decided that the two men and their sons men should leave quietly by boat on the night of 30 July, lest their departure become a noisy demonstration of loyalty by thousands of Nagasaki citizens.[5]

The mayors of Nagasaki had been in the habit of alternating, in pairs among each other, their duty of making New Year's visits to the lord of the *tenryō*, all the way in the Kantō. For that reason, the trip was not new to these men, nor was it particularly arduous, traveling all the way by boat to Osaka, as they were. Upon their arrival in the city at the end of the Inland Sea, they were well received by Christians and gentiles alike.[6] As everyone must have realized, their journey could only end in death. Upon their arrival in Edo, the two men and their sons presented themselves before "the governors, who did not respond to them other than by asking why they did not want to stop being Christians, as the shogun had ordered?"[7]

Because these were Christians in exile, no one dared provide them with lodging, so they ended up living in make-shift shacks along the Sumida River. The other group of dignitaries from Nagasaki, also sent to Edo by Governor Mizuno, found the mayors and their families living in these huts along the river. This story is also told by the Dutchman Pieter Nuyts in his report of his failed embassy, for which he was in Edo at this time.[8] In the end, Gotō Thomé is said to have died of exposure on the last day of 1627.[9]

It is not clear at which level the decisions concerning these people were made, but the first officials they are likely to have encountered must have been their counterparts, the Edo Governors or *machi bugyō*.[10] It was by order of one of the "governors" that the whole Christian group from Nagasaki finally found lodging in a Buddhist temple.

The group was called to "judgment" a second time, when

they were only asked if they were going to obey the shogun, their lord. They answered humbly that they would obey him completely in everything, as they had always done. Only in matters that went against their religion, which did not forbid, but rather obliged them to better serve their lords and the government of the country, they could not do so, because they had been Christians since infancy, with the permission of all the ancient lords of Japan: Nobunaga, Taikō-Sama [Hideyoshi], Daifu [Ieyasu], and the Shogun himself,[11] who all had always favored Nagasaki in this matter.[12]

What is interesting in this quote is not so much the content itself. Rather, it is the fact that here (for the first time?) Japanese Christians dared enunciate in the very center of Tokugawa power the cardinal principle that had made Christianity taboo in Japan, i.e., that this religion taught that there was a limit to the obedience that one human being could owe to another. Unspoken, but behind this idea, was the denial of divine status to any human, a problem we have also seen Hideyoshi wrestling with. In this respect, the disobedience shown by these Christians foreshadowed the long debate on loyalty among the intellectuals of the different Confucian schools that Tokugawa Japan was to give rise to in subsequent centuries.[13]

In the late 1620s, the Tokugawa authorities were still convinced that they could stop the diffusion of such dangerous ideas and enforce their notion of limitless loyalty upon the nation. When the group from Nagasaki was called a third time, it was to the office of the "Governor Yemondonne." This was Matsudaira Masatsuna (1576–1648), a retainer of Ieyasu who had become Hidetada's adviser, and whose court title "Emon no suke" or "Emon no daifu" was used to identify him inside the Tokugawa bureaucracy.[14] This time, Machida João was the only one of the old guard left to represent Nagasaki before the officials of the Bakufu. The former mayor of Nagasaki did not do what clearly was expected of him, that is to simply announce his own and the group's apostasy. Instead, he presented a petition asking for religious freedom for his city, stating that "Whatever prohibitions of Christianity had been issued before, the lords of Japan have always permitted the citizens of Nagasaki to be Christians because they are merchants and their city the principal port for the Christian ships."[15]

Masatsuna promised to show the petition to the closest associate of the former shogun Hidetada himself, the president of his advisory council. It is likely that Doi Toshikatsu (1573–1644) was meant here, called "the greatest instigator of this prosecution."[16] Again, we may marvel at the stubborn gumption with which Machida João insisted on bringing up the question of freedom of religion for Nagasaki, with its underlying problem of the impossible divinity of rulers.[17] It goes without saying that his petition had no chance among men who were in the midst of deifying the founder of the Tokugawa Bakufu.[18]

Epilogue:
Nagasaki in the 1630s

Catholic historians have always been concerned with the exact number of those who died for the faith. Already in the seventeenth century, there were those who made the attempt to compile complete lists.[1] This was not out of historical interest, rather it was a vital part of the intellectual life of a practicing Roman Catholic, to whom the highest ideal has always been the entrance into Heaven. And there is no surer way to enter Heaven than through dying as a martyr for the faith.

This is one of the reasons why although executions went up during Mizuno Morinobu's tenure as Governor of Nagasaki, they went down again under his successor Takenaka Shigeyoshi, who is known for his particular ferociousness as a prosecutor of Christians. But Takenaka was clear about one thing: he wanted to avoid making martyrs through executions of Christians for their faith. He clearly was aware that if someone succumbed to hardship, this would not formally qualify him or her for martyrdom. So he preferred organizing hardship of all kinds of extreme forms over organizing executions.[2]

The ultimate concern with Heaven has remained the same since the seventeenth century, but the historical methods of Catholic historians since the days of Bartoli, Crasset, and Charlevoix have greatly improved. In the twentieth century, the quest was enriched with the participation of Japanese historians who added information from Japanese sources to the search for the martyrs, which used to be conducted exclusively on the basis of materials in European languages. It goes without saying that this long tradition of searching for the martyrs of Japan, remains an on-going quest which is not likely to be exhausted any time soon.

As is clear from the information brought together above, it is also a quest that is not likely to tell the story of all that was suffered by Nagasaki's Christians because of the persecution. In spite of four centuries of sleuthing, we do not have complete records of the executions. Many of the names of the victims are irretrievably lost. All we can say is that there likely were more executions than those we know of. What is more, the categories I have established are, to a certain degree, arbitrary. Until 1639, Nagasaki was a town of immigrants, both Japanese and foreign. For the purposes of my analysis, I have taken everyone who lived in Nagasaki before his or her arrest to be a "citizen" of Nagasaki.

Executions of Nagasaki Christians (1617–1639)[3]

	Burned Alive			Decapitated			Anatsurushi		
	Men	Women	Children	Men	Women	Children	Japanese	Europeans	
							Men	Women	Total
1617	2								2
1618	3	3	7						13

	Burned Alive			Decapitated			Anatsurushi			
	Men	Women	Children	Men	Women	Children	Japanese Men	Japanese Women	Europeans	Total
1619	5			11						16
1620				2		2				4
1621				2						2
1622	27	1		29	14	13				84
1623										0
1624	2									2
1625										0
Subtotal under Hasegawa Gonroku (9 years)										**123**
1626	23				3	1				27
1627	9	2		5	1	7				24
1628	13	1		8	1	11				34
Subtotal under Mizuno Kawachi Mitsunobu (3 years)										**85**
1629	1			1	1					3
1630	3			1	1	3				8
1631										0
1632	10			4						14
Subtotal under Takenaka Uneme Shigeyoshi (4 years)										**25**
1633	16	8	1	3			22		8	58
1634[4]		1					3	2	3	9
1635[5]	3	3					1?	?	?	7?
1636	1					1	?	?		2?
1637[6]		1					17?	17?	3	36?
1638									1	1?
1639	1[7]									1?
Total	**118**	**20**	**8**	**66**	**21**	**38**	**43?**	**19?**	**14**	**347?**

Out of a total of 373 executions of Christians in Nagasaki between 1597 and 1639,[8] forty-eight were those of European missionaries. The number of executed was much higher among the mendicants than among the Jesuits (fifteen Franciscans, twelve Dominicans, seven Augustinians, and one Holy Trinity friar, vs. only ten European Jesuits), even though in Japan European Jesuits always overwhelmingly outnumbered the mendicants, in Nagasaki as elsewhere.

What is more surprising is that, up to as late as June 1626, only one European Jesuit priest had been executed in Nagasaki.[9] This means, of course, that Jesuits were harder to arrest than the mendicants. This is likely to be due to three factors: the Jesuits were more careful, they had better connections, and they spoke better Japanese.

When we look at the figures for the executions of the Japanese members of the different religious orders active in and around Nagasaki, a very different picture emerges. The number of executions of Japanese Jesuits (32) almost equals that of the Japanese members of the three main mendicant orders taken together: twelve Franciscans, nineteen Dominicans, and three Augustinians (34). These latter three figures, as indicated above, are debatable, because of the rather loose criteria I have employed in including someone as a member of a mendicant order.[10]

If we now contrast these figures with those of the lay people executed in Nagasaki (principally between 1617 and 1637), we find the following result: a total of 101 missionaries, both foreign and Japanese, vs. 234 lay people, 169 of whom were said to be living in Nagasaki at the time of their arrest, while 65 people were brought to Nagasaki in order to be tortured and executed in public there. Of the 169 people living in Nagasaki, ninety-one were males over fifteen years old, including three native Portuguese, forty-two were women, and thirty-six were children fifteen years and younger, some as little as two years old.[11]

The corresponding figures for those who came from elsewhere are: forty-two men (including thirteen Japanese based in the Philippines), fifteen women, and eight children. What can be said about these executions of lay people is that the overwhelming majority was executed for aiding and sheltering the missionaries, while a few were executed for being somewhere at the wrong time. If one thing is clear from a study of the executions in Nagasaki, it is that the Bakufu aimed at the elimination of foreign and Japanese missionaries from Japan as well as at the complete destruction of the support networks established by the different missionary orders.

It did not, however, bother to execute anybody for their inner beliefs, unless the victims themselves insisted, by refusing to apostatize, that they were to be included among those executed.[12] Quite a few of the lay women from Nagasaki executed there between 1617 and 1639 fall into the latter category, and so we end up with the conclusion that in a city which had lost 15 to 20,000 inhabitants in the first three years of the persecution after 1614, there were fewer than forty-two women left who were prepared to die voluntarily for their beliefs.

Even if we suppose that this figure (because of the insufficiency of our sources) is ridiculously low, and assume that we have lost records of half or even eighty percent of such women, then the truer figure might approach as many as three hundred women executed for their faith, which still would represent only two percent of the female population of Nagasaki by 1639.

This is not to belittle the sacrifice of those who died for their faith. It is just to point out the ruthless effectiveness of Bakufu policy in dealing with a city that it knew to be completely Christian and to stress that the object of this policy was to spare the city of complete destruction. In this connection, it is illuminating to look at these numbers of people executed in Nagasaki and compare them to the numbers of Christians executed elsewhere in Japan, most obviously in that other great event of the 1630s, the Shimabara rebellion, where the number of summary executions of Christians after the fall of Hara Castle must be counted in the tens of thousands.[13]

In July of 1633, a new and particularly repellent form of torture or execution was adopted, in which the victims were hung upside down in pits filled with excrement.[14] As we have seen, by this time there were no longer large numbers of Christians left in Nagasaki, which made it possible to treat each new case of a refusal to apostatize in an individualized manner. At the same time, the stakes were raised with a torture more gruesome even than the sulfurous hot springs of Arima.

As the figures show, this new *anatsurushi* method was not particularly effective in producing apostasies, except from European Jesuits.[15] Still, during the second half of the 1630s, it became the preferred punishment for those who were still refusing to apostatize. Its awfulness, therefore, is more a measure of the government's resentment towards such obstinate resistance than that it earned its validation through success.

As stated above, our figures of Japanese Christians executed for their faith become more uncertain after 1634. This is because with the virtual extinction, imprisonment, or apostasy of all European missionaries in Japan, there were no longer any eyewitnesses left who could send back such information to Europe where it would be valued and preserved. To Bakufu or domain officials, these were not deaths deserving to be recorded and remembered.

Portuguese merchants, moreover, recorded only the deaths of their fellow country-men. So, although we know that the pace and fury of the executions was increasing, we become more and more at a loss of how to track them. Also, it is not always clear who succumbed to the torture of being hung in the pit and who apostatized, saving his or her life.

For these reasons, the number executed for their faith up to and including 1632 is far more likely to be correct than our figures for the years following 1633. From 1638 onwards, the only trustworthy witnesses of the persecutions left in Japan were the Dutch. The drawback of their testimony is, however, that as Protestants they were not particularly interested in the deaths of Roman Catholics.

The Dutch would not go out of their way, for example, to record the exact numbers, names, ages, and sexes of those executed, unless it was somebody they knew about through their trading activities. So we frequently end up with such vague expressions that "a number of Japanese" were executed for having been found to be Roman Catholics. This would go on with some frequency for the rest of the seventeenth century.

Thus, by the beginning of the fourth decade of the seventeenth century Christian Nagasaki had ceased to exist. All of its inhabitants had been forced to become members of the different Buddhist sects that had established branches in the city.[16] The ideological war against Christianity, however, continued unabated in Nagasaki.

In 1634, the Suwa shrine, established on the slope of Mt. Tateyama in 1626, held its first festival procession through the city. The theme of the procession was the Korean expedition of the legendary Empress Jingū, a clear reference to the fact that the new religious authorities in the area still considered Nagasaki a "foreign land" or maybe rather "occupied territory."[17]

By the time of the Shimabara Rebellion (1637–8), the city was fearful but quiet. The mayors seem to have come together at the residence of Suetsugu Heizō's son to discuss measures to keep their town peaceful and orderly at all costs.[18] Guards were posted at all access routes to Nagasaki: at the Mogi pass, the Himi pass, at Tomachi, and Tokitsu, allowing no rebel to pass and to stir up trouble around Nagasaki Bay.

For this act of cooperation, the mayors were praised by the *rōjū* Matsudaira Izu no kami Nobutsuna, who made a point of passing through Nagasaki after quelling the Shimabara rebellion, arriving in the city on 29 April 1638.[19] One month earlier, Nobutsuna had been in charge of the bloodbath in which thirty-seven thousand insurgents lost their heads.

It is likely that at this time Nobutsuna gave orders to improve the city's defense system, establishing look-outs at the bay's entrance at Nomosaki, on the top of Hinoyama, at Kosedo, and Hōkazan. Two boats, manned by five oarsmen each, with the words "Nomo shogunal reporting boats" on the sails, and with masts painted black in the middle and white at each end, were attached to the post. Two men were on watch, alternating every twenty days, throughout the year. When a foreign ship appeared, she was first sighted at Nomo, the signal being taken up at Kosedo and passed on to Jūzenji mura (the present Jūnin-machi), and from there to the Governor's residence.[20]

How far the former Christian leaders of the city had come is proven by the cases of the sons of Suetsugu Heizō and Luis Takagi, who on 1 June 1640 were received in audience in Edo Castle and received one hundred bars of silver for their efforts to keep Nagasaki out of the confrontation in Shimabara.[21] The belatedness of these rewards should warn us that something else is likely to have been going on.

We should not forget that it was in the previous year, 1639, that the Bakufu had finally taken the step to send the Portuguese back to Macao without allowing them to trade and denying them any further permission to come to Japan.[22] Without the foreign trade there was, of course, no reason for the existence of Nagasaki. The first to have been aware of that fact must have been the leaders of the town which had already abandoned its religion in order to be able to continue the trade.

Although the official sources do not mention it, it is likely that the city's leaders had petitioned the Bakufu for the transfer of the Dutch factory from Hirado to Nagasaki, when they arrived in Edo in January of 1640 for their usual New Year's visit. That they were successful is proven by this reward they received five months later, during which time they are known to have been waiting in the shogun's capital.[23] Thus, Nagasaki's failure to render help to the rebels of Amakusa and Shimabara was rewarded with the Dutch trade. The decision to move the factory was abruptly announced to the Dutch on 11 May 1641. The forced move from Hirado to Nagasaki took place during the following month, after which the Dutch found themselves sequestered on the same artificial island, which had since 1636 separated the Portuguese from the rest of the city.[24]

This was an artificial land-fill of a surface of slightly over 3924 *tsubo* (or about 3.27 acres), built since 1635 on the beach below Morisaki.[25] Material for the land-fill was obtained by destroying the very tip of Morisaki where the Hishōten Santa Mariya (Nossa Senhora da Ascensão) church had stood. In this way, the site of Japan's oldest and biggest church completely disappeared, and so could no longer provide physical support for any Christian-tainted nostalgia.[26] The remaining lower-lying land around Morisaki's perimeter became known as Edo-machi, a new street, which had come into existence by an order originating in Edo. The whole project was financed by twenty-five merchants from Nagasaki, whose descendants owned the buildings on the island until well into the nineteenth century.

In this way, Nagasaki's livelihood was buttressed with the Dutch trade, which complemented the trade that was already brought to Nagasaki in Chinese vessels. Together, the Chinese and the Dutch would continue Nagasaki's by now traditional function as Japan's main port of entry for products from overseas, overshadowing Kagoshima, Tsushima, and Hakata for the next two centuries. Even without Christianity, Nagasaki remained a cross-roads and meeting place with other cultures, albeit one strictly controlled and regulated.

With the departure of the missionaries and the destruction of the churches, the city came to be much more firmly administered as part of the personal domain of the Tokugawa shoguns. It is useful to ask in how far it had ever been an independent city. From the point of view of the Portuguese, Nagasaki must have seemed far beyond the pale of their formal empire. Until 1641, the formal Portuguese thalassocracy only reached as far as Malacca.

Between Ceylon and Malacca, however, along the coasts of Bengal, Burma, Siam, and Cambodia, the Portuguese presence was more tenuous and less formalized, consisting of Portuguese communities that were dependent on local authorities.[27] Beyond Malacca, in the Indonesian archipelago and along the coast of China, Portugal was represented mainly by individuals, especially after the loss of Ambon (one of the spice islands) to the Dutch in 1605.

The latter two areas are known today as Portugal's informal empire, where the power of the king of Portugal reached only sporadically in the form of his approval of the *camara* or city councils and his appointment of the bishops.[28] These were the lands where private Portuguese hired themselves out to local rulers as mercenaries, sometimes doubling as pirates or robbers roaming the seas and the continent of Asia for their own account. By some estimates, the number of Portuguese soldiers involved in enterprises outside Portugal's formal thalassocracy may have been larger than those employed in the service of the King and his Captains.[29]

In this context, we can see elements of the Portuguese informal empire in both Macao and Nagasaki. Whereas the Captain Major with his patent from the Portuguese king had some real authority in Macao, in Japan this authority was until 1587 shared with the Jesuits, and after that with Hideyoshi's representatives. In the case of Nagasaki, we could say that after 1600 the authority of the king of Portugal mainly reached the city in the form of his right to appoint the bishop residing there. It follows that, when Bishop Cerqueira died early in 1614, the last trace of Portugal's influence in the city disappeared with him.

The prohibition of Christianity was the result of two different discussions in the highest echelons of the Tokugawa Bakufu. The first discussion had been going on ever since Hideyoshi's first prohibition of Christianity and concerned the degree to which the missionaries were thought to be necessary for the trade, brought by the empire-building Portuguese to Nagasaki. The second discussion concerned Christianity as the aggressive ideology of the Europeans in Asia. This latter discussion necessarily involved the development of a Japanese ideology to support first Hideyoshi's unification of Japan and later that of the Tokugawa.

Without a doubt, the two discussions were linked, at first under Hideyoshi in Fushimi and Ōsaka, and later under the Tokugawa in Edo and Sunpu. However, the second discussion took quite a bit of time in picking up steam, and in fact only got going well after the first discussion had already come to a definite conclusion with the expulsion of the padres in 1614.[30] It was only the unexpectedly stubborn resistance of the Japanese Christians that led to more and more thorough measures, first in Nagasaki and gradually to include the whole country, which were aimed at trying to close off any ways the "evil religion" could enter or continue to exist in Japan.

These measures continued during the 1630s. On 6 April 1633, the bakufu issued a list of seventeen articles, which prohibited foreign travel by Japanese nationals on ships that did not have formal permission from the authorities for that purpose. Japanese who had lived abroad for some time were forbidden to return. The same list of articles reiterated the prohibitions against Christianity issued by Ieyasu in 1614 and Hidetada in 1616. These seventeen articles were promulgated once more on 23 June 1634. At that time, three new articles were added, forbidding foreign missionaries from coming ashore in Japan, and all Japanese from leaving Japan for any reason.

The next year, on 12 July 1635, these orders were tightened once more. This time, all Japanese ships were prohibited from leaving the country. Finally, on 22 July 1636, the bakufu sent a list of nineteen new articles to the governors of Nagasaki. These raised the rewards for denouncing Japanese Christians, expelled from Japan the children of mixed marriages, and tightened prohibitions, already in place, against contact with overseas family members. Even correspondence with such family members was no longer allowed.[31]

The importance of the Christian episode in Japanese history, and especially Christian Nagasaki, is not necessarily linked to whether or not Christians survived in Japan. Far more pervasive was its effect on subsequent Japanese intellectual discourse in a peculiarly negative form, sometimes called "anti-Christianity,"[32] which remained for the rest of Japan's early modern period an important part of the ideology of the country's ruling class.[33] In this form, it continued to inform Tokugawa diplomacy,[34] religion,[35] literature,[36] legislation, and history writing.[37]

If Christianity had been unimportant, anti–Christianity would not have been so pervasive in Tokugawa Japan. Opposing the teachings of the padres, then, provided a sort of negative paradigm within which the Tokugawa authorities felt most comfortable. Paradoxically, therefore, in order to understand the roots of the Tokugawa mindset, its religious policy-making, its legislation, and much of its relations with the outside world, it is necessary, as we have done here, to study the history of the labors of the padres during Japan's "Christian century."

Where the key question of the divinity of human rulers is concerned, it would take until the Shōwa emperor's New Year's Day "declaration of humanness" of 1946 that a Japanese head of state formally abdicated his own divine status.[38] Forced to do so by the new authority in Japan, the emperor issued an imperial rescript stating: "The ties between us and our people have always stood upon mutual trust and affection. They do not depend upon mere legends and myths. They are not predicated on the false conception that the Emperor is divine and that the Japanese people are superior to other races and fated to rule the world."[39]

It is to be hoped that these words have finally settled the problem.[40] It is also sobering to realize that, after more than three centuries, the debate was essentially decided in favor of the position the Nagasaki Christians, represented by Machida João, had dared take in the shogun's capital early in 1628. Centuries of persecution, a number of catastrophic wars, as well as a conclusive and humiliating defeat of the Japanese nation had been necessary to get to that point.

Glossary

alvará	[Portuguese]	patent, permit
anua	[P]	yearly letter
bakufu	[幕府]	military government headed by a shogun
bugyō	[奉行]	governor
bugyōsho	[奉行所]	governor's office [aka *shōya*]
bushi	[武士]	warrior, samurai
capitão mor	[P]	captain major
casa	[P]	Jesuit residence
casado	[P]	married settler
chōnin	[町人]	commoner, townsman
consejo de Indias	[Spanish]	council of the Indies during the dual monarchy
daikan	[代官]	representative official
daimyō	[大名]	domainal lord
dōjuku	[同宿]	helper, servant
dōshin	[同心]	constable, low-ranking official
fidalgo	[P]	nobleman
fudai	[譜代]	hereditary retainer
fusta	[P]	small galley
hōsho	[奉書]	letter written in the name of the shogun
hotoke	[仏]	Buddha and Bodhisattvas
irmão	[P]	brother
itowappu	[糸割符]	system of the bulk purchase of silk
itowappu shukurō	[糸割符宿老]	merchant elite controlling the bulk purchase
jitō	[地頭]	shogunal agent
jinaichō	[寺内町]	temple town
ji'yakunin	[地役人]	local official
jizamurai	[地侍]	land owning samurai
kami	[神]	deities, deified ancestors
kamon	[家紋]	family crest
kampaku	[関白]	Hideyoshi's title up to 1592.02.05
kanshō	[官商]	trade official

karō	[家老]	senior retainer
katana	[刀]	Japanese sabre, sword
katana-gari	[刀狩り]	sword hunt
koku	[石]	47.654 U.S. gallons; 5.119 U.S. bushels
kokujin ryōshu	[国人領主]	landed samurai
kumi	[組]	group of households in a street block
kumioya	[組親]	leader of a group of households
machi	[町]	ward, street block
machidoshiyori	[町年寄]	town elder, mayor
mekiki	[目利]	specialist, connoisseur
metsuke	[目付]	spy
monjo	[文書]	[original] document
morador	[P]	resident
mordomo	[P]	leader of the Misericordia Brotherhood
namban	[南蛮]	Southern Barbarian [i.e., Portuguese in Japan]
namban byōbu	[南蛮屏風]	painted screen depicting the Portuguese
nao	[P]	Portuguese ship of the *caravela redonda* type
nengyōji	[年行事]	street official
otona	[乙名]	street elder
padre	[P]	priest, father
padroado	[P]	royal authority over ecclesiastical offices overseas
pancada	[P]	[blow>] agreement to sell the silk cargo in bulk
pilota	[P]	pilot
procurador	[P]	chief financial officer of a Jesuit mission
provedor	[P]	chief financial officer, purveyor
rōjū	[老中]	council of the shogun's advisors
seppuku	[切腹]	ritual suicide
shōya	[庄屋]	government office
shugenja	[修験者]	mountain ascetic
sotana	[P]	black cassock
sotomachi	[外町]	outer town
tabi	[足袋]	Japanese [cotton] socks
taikō	[太閤]	Hideyoshi's title after 1592.02.05
tenka	[天下]	domains included in Hideyoshi's polity
tenryō	[天領]	Hideyoshi's and Ieyasu's own domains
tōnin	[頭人]	head man
uchimachi	[内町]	inner town
yadonushi	[宿主]	householder [especially those accused of sheltering priests]
yashiki	[屋敷]	mansion, official residence
yamabushi	[山伏]	mountain priest, warrior monk
yokome	[横目]	spy
yoriki	[与力]	police official

Notes

Abbreviations Used

ADC	Academia das Ciencias (Lisbon, Portugal)
AFH	*Archivum Franciscanum Historicum*
AGI	Archivo General de Indias (Sevilla, Spain)
AGS	Archivo General de Simancas (Valladolid, Spain)
AIA	*Archivo Ibero-Americano*
ANTT	Arquivo Nacional da Torre de Tombo (Lisbon, Portugal)
APT	Archivo Provincial de Toledo (at Alcala de Henares, Spain)
ARSI	Archivum Romanum Societatis Iesu (Rome, Italy)
BA	Biblioteca Ajuda (Belem, Portugal)
BNL	Biblioteca Nacional Lisboa
BNM	Biblioteca Nacional Madrid
DNS	*Dai Nihon Shiryō*
BPE	Biblioteca Publica Evora (Evora, Portugal)
BPJS	*Bulletin of Portuguese-Japanese Studies*
HD	*Hanshi daijiten* (Tokyo: Yūzankaku)
JapSin	*Japonica-Sinica* section at ARSI and KB
JJRS	*Journal of Japanese Religious Studies*
KB	Kirishitan Bunko (Sophia University, Tokyo, Japan)
KBKK	*Kirishitan bunka kenkyūkai kaihō*
KCSF	*Kansei chōshū shoka fu* (Tokyo: Zoku Gunsho Ruijū Kanseikai)
KD	*Kokushi daijiten* (Tokyo: Yoshikawa Kōbunkan)
KK	*Kirishitan kenkyū*
MFA	Mello Family Archive (Serpa, Portugal)
MN	*Monumenta Nipponica*
NA	Nationaal Archief (The Hague, Netherlands)
ND	*Nagasaki dansō*
NFJ	Nederlandse Factorij Japan at NA
NKBT	*Nihon koten bungaku taikei* (Tokyo: Iwanami shoten)
NR	*Nihon Rekishi*
NSHK	*Nagasaki Shiritsu Hakubutsukan Kanpō*
NSS	*Nagasaki shishi*
NZM	*Neue Zeitschrift für Missionswissenschaft*
OSS	Ōmura Shiritsu Shiryōkan (at Ōmura Municipal Library, Japan)
RAH	Real Academia de la Historia (Madrid, Spain)
RK	*Rekishi kyōiku*
SHJ	Shiryō hensanjo (Tokyo University, Japan)
SHJKK	*Tōkyō Daigaku Shiryō Hensanjo Kenkyū Kiyō*
SZ	*Shigaku zasshi*
TASJ	*Transactions of the Asiatic Society of Japan*
TJ	*Tokugawa Jikki* (Tokyo: Yoshikawa Kōbunkan)
Vocabulario	*Vocabulario da Lingoa de Japam* (Nagasaki: Jesuit Press 1604)

Part One: Founding Fathers
Introduction

1. Disney 2009, vol. 2, ch. 16.
2. Robinson 1992.
3. Especially in China (*folangji*) where the rumors of their guns preceded the Portuguese themselves. See the fascinating etymologies collected by Chase 2003, pp. 242–3 (n. 10).
4. For role of raiding in the establishment of the Portuguese thalassocracy, see Newitt 1986, p. 20 ff.
5. Thomaz 1964.
6. Chang 1934.
7. Flynn and Giráldez 1995.
8. For Chinese opinions of the Portuguese see Fok 1987 and Porter 1999.
9. Berry 1994.
10. Shapinsky 2009.
11. So 1975; Wang 2002.
12. Von Glahn 1996, p. 128.
13. Yamamura and Kamiki 1983.
14. Lidin 2002.
15. Flynn and Giráldez 1994.
16. On the founding of Macao, see: Montalto de Jesus 1926; Rego 1946; Boxer 1960, 1969a; Braga 1949; Egerod 1959; Ptak 1980; Porter 1993, 1999.
17. Schurz 1939.
18. Boxer 1963.
19. Caraman 1976; Cushner 1980; Konrad 1980.
20. Spence 1984; Mungello 1985; Hsia 2010.
21. Elison 1972, p. 224.
22. Fróis' *Historia* 3, 1982, pp. 138–9.
23. *Constitutiones* Ch 2. 5, Ganss 1970, p. 255. Aveling 1982, p. 117.
24. Léon Bourdon (1993) has shown how the mission had largely exhausted itself and was on the verge of collapse at the time Cosme de Torrès decided to pursue the establishment of a Christian port-settlement, see chapter 11, pp. 317–8; pp. 320–22; ch. 12, pp. 374–6; ch. 13, pp. 379–406.
25. Kishino 2001.
26. Curtin 1984, p. 3. Cooper 1972, p. 433 quotes Ma-

noel Dias' words: "many Portuguese declare that it is impossible in Japan to conduct the business of the carrack, sell the silk peacefully and return on time, if the Fathers do not help."

27. Bourdon 1993, passim.

28. Costa 1998, pp. 94–5.

29. Berry 1982.

30. Hesselink 2012.

31. Curtin 1984, p. 3.

32. Only eight Japanese brothers (out of an approximate total of more than two hundred who were accepted into and had committed their lives to the Society, i.e., less than four percent) were ordained between 1600 and 1614.

33. Lucena/Schütte 1972, p. 82.

From Hirado to Yokoseura:
Luis d'Almeida (1)

1. Melchior Nunez Barreto (1520?–1571) to the Gen. Goa 24 I, 30 quoted in Schütte 1975, p. 42.

2. Bourdon 1949, p. 71.

3. Nieremberg 1984, pp. 3–4.

4. Elison 1973, p. 208. Gonoi 2006, pp. 110–1 points out that Almeida continued to be involved in the practise of medicine.

5. Nieremberg 1984, pp. 5–6.

6. Fróis' *Historia* 1, pp. 130–1.

7. *Cartas* Evora I, p. 87v.

8. Bourdon 1993, p. 429.

9. Nieremberg 1984, p. 6. Gonoi 2013, p. 4.

10. Fróis' *Historia* 1, p. 274; Okamoto 1974, pp. 371–2; Toyama 1981, p. 88.

11. Bourdon 1993, pp. 419–29.

12. Fróis' *Historia* 1, p. 270; Fróis' *Geschichte*, pp. 152–3.

13. On Bartolomeu Konoe, see Gonoi 2013, pp. 7–8.

14. Matsuda 1978, p. 33 has the distance as 6 *leguas* or 36 kilometers.

15. Fróis' *Historia* 1, pp. 270–1; Fróis' *Geschichte*, p. 153.

16. On the problem whether, strictly speaking, Sumitada deserves to be called a *daimyo*, see Elisonas 2007, p. 34. Elisonas cites Sumitada's oath of loyalty sworn to Ryūzōji Takanobu on 12 July 1576 as one argument against considering him an independent warlord. This argument, however, would only be valid for the period of eight years between 1576 and 1584, when Takanobu died. More important is the argument that the domain of Ōmura was too small and Sumitada too weak to deserve the title.

17. Okamoto 1974, p. 534; Toyama 1981, p. 88; *idem* 1986, pp. 223, 228.

18. *Cartas* Coimbra, ff. 290–1; Schütte 1971, p. 5; Toyama 1981, p. 89; Bourdon 1993, p. 435.

19. Okamoto 1974, p. 378; Boxer 1963, p. 28. Cf. also Fróis' *Historia* 2, p. 79: where he mentions that every year, at the time of the likely arrival of the *nao*, a light craft was sent out into the ocean by the padres to make contact with the Portuguese before anyone else "so that the captains majors know where to go and which places to avoid."

20. Okamoto 1974, p. 380; Nieremberg 1984, p. 7.

21. *Cartas* Evora I, f. 109r. Bourdon points out that Sumitada seems to have backtracked on his first promises to Domingos Riveira and Bertolomeu Konoe, for now Yokoseura bay was to be divided into two halves: one to be given to the Jesuits to administer while Sumitada kept the other half for himself (Bourdon 1993, p. 435).

22. Nieremberg 1984, p. 7.

23. Bourdon 1993, pp. 435–6.

24. *Cartas* Evora I, f. 119r; Fróis' *Historia* 1, p. 290.

Becoming a Christian:
Ōmura Sumitada (1)

1. Fróis' *Historia* 1, pp. 292–3.

2. *Cartas* Evora I, p. 119r.

3. Fróis' *Historia* 1, p. 288.

4. The text has "eight days after Brother Luis d'Almeida's departure [for Satsuma]." With Almeida having left in the third week of Lent, i.e., the week between March 8th to March 15th, Sumitada's arrival in Yokoseura must have taken place between March 16th and March 23rd. Gonoi 2013, p. 11 places it on 22 March 1563.

5. *Cartas* Coimbra, p. 393r.

6. Bourdon 1993, p. 441.

7. Fróis *Historia* 1, p. 277. Torrès' own letter describing these events has not been preserved (cf. Schütte 1975, p. 68). Still, a copy of this lost letter is likely to have been the source for Fróis' description.

8. Fróis *Historia* 1, pp. 277–8.

9. Francisco Xavier, for example, used paintings of the *Madonna and Child* and the *Annunciation* when he first arrived in Kagoshima. See: Schurhammer 1933, p. 116; Bailey 1999a, p. 188. Almeida, too, always carried an image of the Virgin Mary while traveling throughout Japan (Sakamoto 1999, p. 122).

10. McCall 1947, pp. 124–5; Bailey 1999b, p. 60; Newitt 2005, p. 100.

11. Etchū 1988, p. 239.

12. Fróis *Historia* 1, p. 278.

13. Knauth 1972, p. 97.

14. Bourdon 1949, p. 73.

15. Fróis' *Geschichte* 1926, p. 342.

16. Originally Ōmura Sumitada's boy lover (Toyama 1981, p. 40). The source uses his Christian name Luis, and so Matsuda 1978, p. 32 concludes that Shinsuke had already been baptized by Luis d'Almeida when he had visited Ōmura in July of 1562. Gonoi 2013, p. 14, however, places his baptism at the same time as Sumitada's.

17. Fróis' *Historia* 1, p. 279.

18. *Ibid.*

19. *Ibid.*

20. As told in the *Vita Constantini*, attributed to Eusebius. The original phrase in Latin *In hoc signo vinces*, moreover, was alive and well in contemporary Portugal, for the Portuguese kings often had gold coins struck which displayed this phrase. For such coins under D. Sebastian (1557–1578) and D. Henrique (1578–1580), see: João Medina, n.d., vol. 6, pp. 216, 224, 226 (the one struck for D. Sebastian carries the date 1562!).

21. Elison (1973, pp. 89–90) argues persuasively for an economic/strategic basis for Sumitada's conversion; Toyama (1981, pp. 172–3), basing himself on local sources of the Ōmura domain, gives greater weight to Sumitada's superstitious side and argues for a typical Japanese religious eclecticism on his part, converting to Christianity while remaining also, at least at first, a believer in Buddhist and Shinto deities. Thus, at the time of his baptism he was merely adding another source of divine support to a very shaky temporal position (*ibid.*, p. 172). To Catholic writers, both in the West and in Japan, it goes without saying that Sumitada was a paragon of Christian *virtud*.

22. Fróis' *Historia* 1, pp. 279–80.

23. *Ibid.*

24. Arima Yoshisada (1521–1577).

25. Fróis' *Historia* 1, p. 280.

26. Bourdon 1993, p. 441ff shows how Torrès astutely led Sumitada towards his baptism by playing him off against his relatives in Arima, while all three principal actors (Sumitada, Yoshisada, and Sengan) were becoming more and more inclined to give in to Torrès' demands as,

during the course of 1563, their sense of urgency about the coming war with Ryūzōji Takanobu increased. According to Bourdon, their negotiations with the Jesuits were wrapped in "une lourde atmosphère de marchandages, sinon même de chantages" (p. 450).

27. *Cartas* Coimbra 1570, p. 348r.

28. *Cartas* Evora I, p. 119r.

29. *Ibid.*, p. 118r–v.

30. Fróis' *Historia* 1, p. 280.

31. The text has "Dom Bartholomeo," but this is an anachronism for Sumitada had not been baptized yet.

32. Fróis' *Historia* 1, p. 295.

33. *Cartas* Evora I, p. 134v, i.e., between 30 and 35 kilometers.

34. *Ibid.* Gonoi 2013, p. 13, identifies Almeida's host as Tomonaga Sumiyasu.

35. Probably April 28th or 29th 1563.

36. "tres Portugueses honrados," *Cartas* Evora I, p. 134r.

37. "tres Portugueses, pessoas de qualidades," Fróis' *Historia* 1, p. 281.

38. *Cartas* Evora I, f. 134v and Fróis' *Historia* 1, p. 281.

39. Alvarez-Taladriz 1973, p. 199 thinks one of them may have been Bartolomeu Vaz Landeiro. On him see: Okamoto 1974, p. 426; Boxer 1963, pp. 41–2; Souza 1986, pp. 36–7; Sousa 2010.

40. Evidently by now it was the end of May: Torrès left Yokoseura on May 21st, stayed a night in Ōmura and went back on the 22nd, two days later on the 24th Sumitada sent him a message, and five days later he came to Yokoseura (29th?).

41. *Cartas* Evora I, p. 135r; Fróis' *Historia* 1, p. 281.

42. *Cartas* Evora I, p. 135r.

43. It would take until 1574 before Sumitada fulfilled these expectations of the Jesuits. Cf. Letter by Michael Vaz in Real Academia de la Historia (hereafter RAH), Cortes 562, 9/2663, ff. 130r.

44. *Cartas* Evora I, p. 134v.

45. *Ibid.*

46. In contrast, Fróis records the date of the baptism of Ōtomo Sōrin with great precision: "Aos 28 de Agosto, dia do gloriozo doutor Santo Agostinho, pela menhã...." (*Historia* 3, p. 27).

47. Schütte 1975, p. 68.

48. Fróis' *Historia* 1, p. 281.

49. Pacheco 1969, p. 137; Etchū 1988, p. 239. Gonoi 2013, p. 14 mentions the possibility that Tomonaga Sumiyasu (Shinsuke) was baptized Luis at this time.

50. Some Jesuit historians seem to be inclined to think that Pentecost (30 May 1563) would have been the most appropriate time for the baptism: Schütte 1968, pp. 471, 711, 980; and Wicki in Fróis' *Historia* 1, p. 282, note 21. I see no reason to doubt this, but note that, in view of the hurried nature of the event, it may not necessarily have happened on an important holy day at all, and 31 May or any day in the beginning of June are just as likely as the day of Pentecost, in fact more likely in the light of my argument. Bourdon 1993, p. 444, n. 135 places the baptism in the middle of June.

51. He was in Shimabara at this time (Nieremberg 1984, p. 8).

52. His letter of 17 November 1563, when he was back in Yokoseura, includes the following line: "On June 25th, a letter from Father Cosme de Torrès reached me ... and he also gave me the news of the baptism of Lord Ōmura with twenty-five of his principal retainers...." Academia das Ciencias (Lisbon, hereafter ADC), *Cartas*, vol. 3, 1563–68, f. 52r; *Cartas* Evora I, p. 126r. There is a similar factual notice in a letter Almeida wrote the next year (on 14 October 1564), *cf.* ADC, *Cartas* vol. 3, 1563–68, f. 110v.

53. When Valignano tried his hand at writing a history of the mission, he did the same: "Vomuradono, que en las continuas platicas con los nuestros estava y muy movido y determinado de ser Christiano, se resolvio *en el mes de Junio deste año 63* de cumplir su deseo y habitarse [miswriting for *baptizarse*] iuntamente con muchos de sus hidalgos" (italics added, *Principio e progresso da Religião Christãa no Japão*, BA 49-IV-53, f. 365r). On this manuscript, see Schütte 1954b.

54. *Cartas* Evora I, p. 135r.

55. Sanskrit name: Maric(h)i—in India and Tibet a goddess of light, associated with the sun and dawn, and with weapons in six hands.

56. The text has *galo* (rooster), but this is possibly due to a contemporary confusion with the weather vanes on top of European church towers. Toyama thinks this is likely to have been the Marishiten shrine on Torikabutoyama in Nakadake, Ōmura (Toyama 1981, p. 62; *idem* 1986, p. 272).

57. *Cartas* Evora I, p. 135v; Okada 1977, p. 67; Toyama 1981, p. 170.

The Mission's Superior: Cosme de Torrès

1. I have not been able to identify Torrès' original affiliation.

2. Knauth 1972, p. 38.

3. Schütte 1975, p. 1312.

4. Matsuda 1978, p. 23.

5. For the different categories of the Jesuits, see Ganss 1970, p. 81.

6. Cooper 1974, p. 197.

7. Fróis' *Historia* 1, p. 336.

8. Schütte 1975, p. 1321.

9. Nieremberg 1984, pp. 8–9.

10. Padres: Torrès, Monte, and Fróis; brothers: Fernandez and Almeida; novices: Jacome Gonçalves and Michael Vaz. Among the *dōjuku* must have been Uchida Tomé, Torrès' *dōjuku*, as well as the Japanese man called Melchior we have encountered in the company of Luis d'Almeida.

11. Again, the crucial detail of Sumitada's location is omitted, but it seems to have been somewhere less than one day's travel from Yokoseura.

12. *Cartas* Evora I, p. 127v.

13. *Ibid.*, p. 128r.

14. *Ibid.*, p. 128v.

15. *Cartas* Evora I, pp. 132r–v.

16. JapSin. 5a, f. 27v; *Cartas* Evora I, p. 132v.

17. Matsuda 1978, p. 16.

18. Toyama 1981, p. 26.

19. This alliance was cemented through the exchange of three women: Ōmura Sumikore received Haruzumi's aunt (in reality an adopted daughter of Takazumi, his grandfather and Sumitada's great-grandfather) into his household. Arima Haruzumi received one of Sumikore's daughters, a younger sister of his son Sumisaki, who in his turn was married to one of Haruzumi's own daughters (Toyama 1981, p. 12).

20. Sumisaki's own son, Matahachirō (later Taka'akira), was born in 1534 of a liaison with a daughter of Suzuta Sumitane. The latter was an Ōmura retainer, of whom the *Ōmurake oboegaki* says that he had plotted with the House of Arima, the result of which was a grave defeat for the Ōmura. After peace had been made with the house of Arima, this man had been forgiven and his daughter was taken into the Ōmura household. The precise details of this affair are lost, but what seems clear is that many in the Ōmura household, not least of course those with close ties to Arima, considered the succession by the grandson of a traitor an impossibility.

21. Matsuda 1978, p. 16.
22. Toyama 1981, p. 27.
23. BNL COD 4534, f. 436v; *Cartas* Evora I, p. 137r.
24. Fróis' *Historia* 1, p. 335.
25. *Ibid.*, p. 336.
26. One obvious reason why Torrès was not asked to profess the fourth vow was, of course, because Fróis himself had not yet reached this exalted position.
27. Fróis' *Historia* 1, p. 337.
28. *Ibid.*, pp. 337–8; Toyama 1981, p. 165.
29. Fróis' *Historia* 1, p. 338. On the basis of a letter by Fróis dated 14 November 1563, Gonoi 2013, pp. 18–19, argues that the attack on Dom Luis in reality may have taken place on 17 August and the uproar in Yokoseura on 18 August 1563.
30. Bungo is an ancient *kuni* in north-eastern Kyushu, i.e., a province of the ancient Chinese-style or *ritsuryō* system of government dating from the 8th century. Although by the sixteenth century such administrative units had no longer much political significance, as geographical terms they were still very much part of everyday speech.
31. Fróis' *Historia* 1, pp. 338–9.
32. *Ibid.*, p. 339.
33. *Ibid.*
34. *Ibid.*, pp. 339–40. The date of the destruction of Yokoseura as well as the identity of those who burned the town differ when we compare the account in Fróis' *Historia* with letters written by him and Almeida closer to the events in question (Gonoi 2013, pp. 20–1).
35. We have letters written in Yokoseura by Torrès (20 October 1563; JapSin. 5, 22–23v); Fróis (14 November 1563: JapSin 5, 25v–27; *Cartas* Evora I, pp. 131v–137); Almeida (17 November 1563: *Cartas* Evora I, pp. 118–131v). These are all likely to have been written before the departure of the *nao*.
36. Okamoto 1974, p. 387.
37. Fróis' *Historia* 1, p. 353; Nieremberg 1984, p. 9.
38. Schütte 1968, p. 496.
39. *Cartas* Evora I, p. 203v: Baltasar da Costa recounts the death of six relatives of "Catandono," who was responsible for cutting down crosses both in Hirado as well as in Yokoseura.
40. Okada 1977, p. 80.

A New Anchorage:
Luis d'Almeida (2)

1. Toyama 1981, p. 165. In that case he would have re-converted to esoteric Shingon, for both temples were connected with the worship of Tarazan Daigongen (*ibid.* p. 166; see also: Fróis' *Historia* 1, p. 338 who also mentions that Sumitada found refuge in Taradake). However, Toyama 1986 argues for a *shukke* (or adoption of the status as a Buddhist monk) on the part of Sumitada in 1574 (p. 220).
2. Nieremberg 1984, p. 9.
3. *Cartas* Evora I, pp. 130r–v.; Okada 1977, p. 78; Bourdon 1993, pp. 445–9.
4. Nieremberg 1984, p. 10.
5. As with so many of such texts, the original document has been lost and we only know it in a later copy. The document was first published in Toyama 1986, p. 414 (doc. 147).
6. Toyama 1981, p. 33; Toyama 1986, p. 188. These formal arrangements were made as late as 1586, when war threatened.
7. Although Sumitada had converted to Christianity, there was one corner of the castle where a statue of the Thousand-Armed Kannon stood (Toyama 1981, p. 166).
8. "le chenal de Hariwo, qui, de plus en plus étroit à mesure qu'on s'y engage, et balayé par de très violents

courants de marée, était encombré en son beau milieu par deux gros pâtés de roches presque à fleur d'eau, si bien qu'aucun navire à voile de quelque tonnage ne pouvait s'y risquer" (Bourdon 1993, p. 433).
9. Toyama 1986, p. 40. The name Tomachi is usually derived from Tohachi, i.e., a hamlet of eight households.
10. Toyama 1981, p. 32.
11. Matsuda 1970, p. 55.
12. Takeno 1976, p. 57.
13. Translated from Toyama 1986, p. 414 (doc. 147).
14. Juan Fernandez writes in his letter of 1565.09.23 that the *nao* had first visited Yokoseura, but seeing that the port was still in ruins it had set sail for Hirado, when on its way it was met by Baltasar da Costa's messenger (*Cartas* Evora I, p. 203r). See also: Fróis' *Historia* 2, p. 79.
15. *Ibid.*, p. 65; also Nieremberg 1984, p. 12.
16. Toyama 1981, p. 120.
17. We note that these Asian converts were given biblical names that corresponded to their non-white heritage.
18. ADC *Cartas*, vol. 3, ff. 207v–208r. Printed versions in *Cartas* Alcala, ff. 238v–239v; *Cartas* Evora I, ff. 204–205.
19. Toyama 1986, p. 418 (doc. 153).
20. Schütte 1968, p. 714; Pacheco 1969, p. 225.
21. Fróis' *Historia* 2, pp. 71–2.

A Knight in Superior Armor:
Dom João Pereira

1. For a more detailed survey of these men, see Hesselink 2012.
2. Boxer 1963 calls such an appointment a "patent."
3. Felgueiras Gaio 1938, vol. 22, p. 173.
4. For the details, see Hesselink 2012, pp. 15–16.
5. ANTT *Chancelaria D. João III*, liv. 33, f. 44, transcribed in Thomaz 1964, doc. 156.
6. Jacinto de Lima's list, p. 53.
7. Entered the order on 1 November 1533 (Jacinto de Lima, p. 41).
8. Couto, Dec. VII, Liv. III, Cap. I, p. 191.
9. Couto, Dec. VII, Liv. VIII, Cap. XIII, p. 284.
10. *Ibid.*
11. *Ibid.*, Dec. VII, Liv. X, Cap. IX, p. 513.
12. Hesselink 2012, pp. 16–17.
13. Fróis' *Historia* 2, p. 73.
14. *Ibid.*
15. Toyama 1986, p. 420 (doc. 156). The letter collection of which these letters from Sumitada to Kanetsugu form a part, the *Fukuda monjo*, has a copying history (cf. Toyama 1986, pp. 430–4), that makes them rather vulnerable to criticism and doubt as to their historical value. See also the following note.
16. This date accords wonderfully well with a letter written by Balthasar da Costa from Hirado on 22 October 1565, the day after the defeated men from Hirado had returned home (JapSin 6, 12–13v; *Cartas* Evora I, fols. 202v–203r). Da Costa mentions that the fleet had been away for five days, meaning that it left on 17 October and executed its surprise attack the next morning. It may have taken the severely damaged Hirado fleet longer than a day to return to its home base. It is details such as this date that may help in establishing the credibility and value of the *Fukuda monjo*.
17. *Cartas* Coimbra, p. 584v; *Cartas* Evora I, p. 203r.

The Chinese in Nagasaki Bay:
Nagasaki Sumikata

1. *Cartas* Evora I, ff 159v–172.
2. Nieremberg 1984, p. 12; Pacheco 1969, p. 225.
3. See especially Pacheco 1969; *idem* 1970; Schütte 1971.

4. Wang 1990, p. 408.
5. Itabashi 1971, pp. 17–8.
6. Wang 1990, p. 411.
7. The classic study of maritime China is Wiethoff 1963, p. 133.
8. *Ibid.*, p. 139.
9. *Ibid.*, p. 142.
10. *Ibid.*, p. 144.
11. *Ibid.*, p. 145.
12. *Ibid.*, p. 146.
13. *Ibid.*, p. 175.
14. *Ibid.*, p. 177.
15. *Ibid.*, p. 182.
16. *Ibid.*, p. 183.
17. Wang 1990, p. 408. Insulinde is the term I have adopted to avoid the anachronism of "Indonesia."
18. Ptak 1994, pp. 287–90, esp. n. 8 for bibliographical references.
19. Itabashi 1971, pp. 20–1.
20. Lin 1990, p. 183.
21. Fróis' *Historia* 2, p. 392.
22. Lin 1990, p. 185.
23. *Ibid.*, p. 186.
24. *Ibid.*, p. 187.
25. Toyama 1984, p. 84, quoting *Nagasaki kyū narabi ni shoki kyoyō*.
26. The grave of the latter still exists, but the key character on the gravestone, indicating where he came from (Fuzhou?), has become illegible (Li 1963, p. 9).
27. Li 1991, pp. 46–7. Chinese also settled on the opposite side of the bay, at Inasa, especially after 1580, when it became difficult for non–Christians to remain in or near the new town of Nagasaki (Orita 2001, pp. 6–9).
28. Hotei 2005, p. 55.
29. Matsuda 1970, p. 55.
30. Toyama 1986, p. 188.
31. *Ibid.*

A Man for the Jesuits:
Ōmura Sumitada (2)

1. *Cartas* Evora I, p. 228v. Torrès, however, in his letter of 24 October 1566 (JapSin. 6, ff. 134r–v; *Cartas* Evora I, ff. 205v–206r) seems to suggest that the nao had already arrived in May.
2. See Toyama 1981, p. 112.
3. *Ōmurake oboegaki*, cited in Toyama 1981, p. 112.
4. Toyama 1981, p. 124.
5. JapSin. 6 134–134v; *Cartas* Evora I, ff. 205v–206v; Schütte 1975, pp. 74–77.
6. Cf. Pacheco 1970, p. 309: "Letters written by Cosme de Torrès and Belchior de Figueiredo are also missing, and these were the two missionaries most directly concerned with the founding of the port. Complying with his obligation as superior, Torrès had written every year to Rome or Goa, but his last known letter was written in 1566. Did he stop writing from that date onwards? It would be somewhat strange if he had."
7. Schütte 1968, pp. 883, 993.
8. July 1566; September 1566: Nieremberg 1984, p. 13.
9. JapSin 6, 134r–134v; *Cartas* Alcala, f. 240r (italics added).
10. *Ibid.*
11. Cabral was another missionary born in Goa. He arrived in Japan in 1564 and was sent back to India again, because of his tuberculosis, in December of 1566 (Fróis' *Historia* 2, p. 71). A letter from his hand is preserved in *Cartas* Alcala, ff. 263r–265r; *Cartas* Evora I, ff. 228–230.
12. Pacheco 1969, p. 226.
13. *Cartas* Alcala, f. 263v.
14. *Cartas* Evora, f. 137v.
15. Actually, Sebastian would only ascend his throne on his fourteenth birthday, 20 January 1568. At the time of his coronation, the king's tutors and advisers were all Jesuits (Alden 1996, p. 81).
16. Takeno 1976, p. 57.
17. If the succession took place after the arrival of the nao, it may have occurred precisely because this year the nao did not come to Fukuda. The involvement of Arima in this case is also suggested by an entry in the *Ōmura-ke hiroku* that has the Jesuits petitioning Yoshisada for intercession in the matter of allowing the Portuguese ships into Nagasaki Bay (*Nagasaki kenshi, taigai kōshōhen*, p. 51, translated in Gonoi 2013, p. 22).
18. Wang 1990, p. 411; Ikuta 1992a, p. 431.
19. Etchū 1988, p. 239.
20. Letter of 20 October 1565: JapSin 6, 4–5v; quoted in Schütte 1975, p. 69.
21. Fróis' *Historia* 1, p. 335: "grande gentio."
22. Toyama 1981, p. 167; another similar donation is recorded for 1568 (Toyama 1981, pp. 75–6).
23. *Cartas* Evora I, f. 252v.
24. Toyama 1981, p. 125; Pacheco 1965, p. 32: this is the time Jesuit historians prefer as the "discovery of the bay of Nagasaki" by Luis d'Almeida. See also, following Pacheco, Etchū 1988, pp. 239–40.
25. Schütte 1971, p. 4.

Nagasaki Bay in 1568:
Gaspar Vilela

1. This is likely to be the voice of Dirk China, or Dirk Gerritsz Pomp from Enkhuizen, the first Dutchman to visit Japan and China (twice in the early 1580's) serving as the gunner of the nao. He later befriended Jan Huygen van Linschoten in Goa, serving as his informant, see *Itinerario*, vol. 5 (1939), pp. 250–1.
2. *Cartas* Evora I, p. 255r.
3. *Ibid.*
4. *Cartas* Evora I, f. 252v.
5. Nieremberg 1984, p. 13.
6. Pacheco 1969, p. 225.
7. Luís Fróis, however, was not. He was in Sakai at this time, cf. *Cartas* Evora I, ff. 240v–242r; ff. 250v–252r.
8. BNL COD 4532, f. 61r. This *Copia de huma* [carta] *de hum homem Portugues que escreveu de Japão aos 15 de Agosto de 1569 aos Padres e Irmãos da Companhia de Jesus em Portugal* (ff. 59r–65r) is a little known letter written by one of the Portuguese laymen who travelled with Torrès to Ōmura in October of 1568, possibly Gamboa or Gouvea. It provides a few details not found in any Jesuit letter.
9. Schütte 1975, p. 394. The names are unidentifiable.
10. BNL COC 4532, f. 61r.
11. Schütte 1975, p. 394.
12. Etchū 1988, p. 240.
13. Schütte 1975, p. 394.
14. Pacheco 1969, p. 226.
15. Nowadays, the spot of the Shuntoku temple.
16. *Cartas* Evora I, f. 283.
17. Pacheco 1969, p. 32.
18. Miguel Vaz in *Cartas* Evora I, f. 253r. In reality, these baptisms did not take place until 1570, when they were forced by an ultimatum of the new superior Francisco Cabral (*Cartas* Evora I, fol. 297).
19. Pacheco 1969, p. 230.
20. After his *gempuku* (coming-of-age) ceremony known as Yoshizumi, and later famous as Ōmura Yoshiaki (Toyama 1981, p. 30).
21. Toyama 1981, p. 126.
22. BNL COD 4532, f. 61v.

23. In September, he was still in bed in Kuchinotsu with a swollen arm, but on 1569.02.23 he is recorded to have left Ōmura for Amakusa (*Arumeida nenpu* 1984, pp. 13–14).

24. BNL COD 4532, f. 61v.

25. BNL COD 4532, ff.108v–111v; JapSin 7 II 3–8v; *Cartas* Evora I, ff. 301v–305. Fróis' rendering of it in his *Historia* 2, pp. 324–6, leaves out much relevant detail.

26. Vilela does not recognize the baptisms performed by Almeida the year before. About the baptisms he performed in Nagasaki and the number of Christians there, we have different testimonies: "six hundred" (letter of an anonymous Portuguese, possibly Manoel Travassos, close to Vilela, dated 15 August 1569 in *Cartas* Evora I, f. 288r); "three hundred" (letter by Miguel Vaz dated 3 October 1569 in *Cartas* Evora I, f. 269r); "four hundred" (letter by Almeida dated 22 October 1569 in *Cartas* Evora I, f. 280v); "eight hundred" (letter by Almeida dated 15 October 1570 in *Cartas* Evora I, f. 294v); "fifteen hundred" (letter by Vilela himself dated 4 February 1571 in *Cartas* Evora I, f. 303r).

27. *Cartas* Alcala 1575, ff. 312v. See also: BNL COD 4532, ff. 109v.

28. *Todos os Santos*: probably, then, the little church was finished around 1 November 1569. Today, the spot is again occupied by a Buddhist temple, the Shuntokuji.

29. *Cartas* Alcala 1575, ff. 312v. See also: BNL COD 4532, ff. 109v.

30. See Hesselink 2004, pp. 186–7.

31. *Cartas* Alcala 1575, ff. 313r. See also: BNL COD 4532, ff. 109v.

32. *Cartas* Alcala 1575, ff. 312v–314r. See also: BNL COD 4532, ff. 109v–110v.

33. Fróis' *Historia* 1, p. 294.

The Busy Scribbler: Luís Fróis

1. On him see Hesselink 2012, pp. 9–10 and 13, also notes 37 and 50. Schütte 1975, p. 395 says that Manoel Travassos, Bertolameu de Gouvea, Francisco Ferreira, and Baltasar Gamboa visited Sumitada in Ōmura.

2. *Cartas* Evora I, f. 318v.

3. Pacheco 1969, p. 228.

4. Toyama 1981, p. 113.

5. Elison 1973, p. 93.

6. Toyama 1981, p. 128.

7. The title is, of course, a misnomer, for it should properly have been called "The History of the Christian Mission in Japan, 1549–1593."

8. Fróis' *Historia* 2, p. 376.

9. Figueiredo was in Bungo, see: Schütte 1975, p. 75; and JapSin 6, ff 193–196v; *Cartas* Evora I, ff. 243–246v for a letter written by him from Bungo on 1567.09.27.

10. Pacheco 1969, p. 225.

11. Schütte 1968, p. 577.

12. Schurhammer and Voretzsch (1926) translate the same word as "unpassend," performing the same type of tour-de-force as I do with my "unbecoming" (cf. Fróis' *Geschichte*, p. 433).

13. Fróis' *Historia* 2, pp. 376–7.

14. Nieremberg 1984, p. 10. Schütte 1968, p. 560, has Fróis leaving Takushima on 10 November, but this may be one of the rare instances where Schütte is mistaken.

15. Letter written by Fróis on 15 November 1564 (JapSin. 5 136–139v; *Cartas* Evora I, ff. 157v–159v).

16. Schütte 1968, p. 577.

17. Schütte 1968, p. 632.

18. We do not have a precise date for Figueiredo's return from Teguma. Pacheco 1969, p. 225.

19. "fazendo primeiro os consertos necessarios com Dom Bartholomeo, começou o Padre…."

20. Fróis' *Historia* 2, p. 324; Schütte 1968, p. 472.

21. Toyama 1981, p. 128.

22. Fróis' *Historia* 2, p. 377; Fróis' *Geschichte*, pp. 432–3. Figueiredo was stationed in Nagasaki between August 1570 and May 1574 (Schütte 1968, p. 472).

23. Pacheco 1970, p. 309.

24. The confusion was so great that, as recently as 1970, the city celebrated the 400th anniversary of its founding. See: Matsuda 1970, Matsuura 1970, Pacheco 1970.

The Founding of Nagasaki: Francisco Cabral

1. Torrès' recall can only be inferred by analogy, because he died before the *nao* left that year. The recall of Vilela is a fact (Franco 1717, p. 199).

2. Vilela was an orphan brought up by friars of the military order of Saint Benedict, in Avis, archbishopric of Evora (Franco 1717, p. 175). Like Torrès, he was already an ordained priest when he joined the Jesuits. It should be noted that both priests showed a propensity to emotionalism and a propensity to manipulate the emotions of their congregation, cf. Torrès' behavior on 15 August 1563, the day of his profession of the three vows in Yokoseura, and Vilela's elaborate orchestration of the passion weeks of 1569 and 1570 in Nagasaki. Such behavior was later condemned as very "un-Jesuit." These "unseemly" elements were, for example, discreetly pruned from Vilela's letters in the Evora edition of the *Cartas* (1598).

3. He sailed on the carrack of Manoel Travassos (Boxer 1963), accompanied by Alessandro Valla-Reggio and Jacome Gonçalvez on 30 October 1570 (Schütte 1968, p. 315).

4. Elison 1973, p. 13, calls him in a peculiar mixture of Spanish and Portuguese: "*hombre criado del Rei, fidalgo y muy fidalgo.*"

5. He was sent off to the fishing village of Kōchiura off the coast of Amakusa, see Schütte 1975, pp. 90–93.

6. Nieremberg 1984, pp. 15–6. The new superior must have been told to avoid southern Kyushu.

7. Cf. Höpfl 2000.

8. Matsuda 1967, p. 610.

9. *Ibid.*

10. *Ibid.*

11. Wicki 1956, p. 419.

12. Schütte 1975, p. 43.

13. Alvarez-Taladriz 1954, p. 112.

14. Matsuda 1967, p. 610.

15. Schütte 1968, p. 42.

16. Matsuda 1967, p. 610.

17. Schütte 1975, p. 151.

18. Schütte 1968, p. 530.

19. Francisco Cabral arrived in Shiki with his companions on the junk of Esteban Leyte (Schütte 1968, p. 315).

20. JapSin 6, f. 294, cited in Matsuda 1967, p. 611; Schütte 1975, p. 86.

21. Matsuda 1967, p. 612.

22. *Ibid.*

23. Matsuura 1970, p. 27.

24. Matsuda 1970, p. 55.

25. Boxer 1963, p. 35; Pacheco 1969, p. 230.

26. Cabral is referring to his own conversion of Tomachi Shigekata!

27. RAH, Cortes 562, f. 62r.

28. "nangraisaqui," JapSin 7 I, 71r.

29. *Ibid.*; also in: RAH Cortes 562, f. 51v.

30. *Cartas* Evora I, ff. 316v–7r.

31. JapSin 7 III 68r–69v; *Cartas* Evora I, pp. 317–318. Anno 1974, pp. 32–3, points out that, according to con-

temporary standards these gentile samurai from Shiki were perfectly within their rights to execute those who had fled their domain illegally.

32. Amino 1978, pp. 336–53.

33. JapSin 14 II, f. 236, quoted in Rodrigues 2006, p. 42.

34. Koga 1957; Watanabe 1964; Matsuura 1970; Matsuda 1970; Etchū 1978a; Takeno 1976; Anno 1974, 1992.

35. Matsuura 1970, p. 25. Not being based on contemporary documents, none of the information in this paragraph and the next can be considered "hard fact."

36. *Ibid.*

37. Anno 1992, pp. 183–8 points out that other *machi* may have been established at the same time.

38. Etchū 1978c, p. 214.

39. Avila Girón mentions it as one of only four machi which did not pay attention to the image of the Virgin Mary when it was carried around on festival days.

40. Etchū 1978a, p. 37.

41. Matsuura 1970, p. 26. Another etymology has that it was populated by people of different geographical units (*bun*) from Ōmura (Koga 1957).

42. Schütte 1975, p. 394. Pirez calls him "Sanquam" [=Sankan 三官], which seems to indicate he was a merchant of considerable stature (no. 3!) among the Chinese in Kyushu.

43. Letter of 15 December 1566: *Cartas* Alcala, f. 264r.

44. Also called Yoshisada (Takeno 1976, p. 55). He died on Genki 2.06.14 [6 July 1571], just after he had helped to found Nagasaki.

45. Nakamura 1964, p. 16, has Hirado no Yoyemon.

46. Watanabe 1964, p. 326.

47. Matsuura 1970, p. 25.

48. Toyama 1986, pp. 228–9.

49. On Hirado-machi, see Hesselink 2009. Hirado-machi took over the leadership of Yokoseura-machi before the start of the Kan'ei period (1624), see Nakamura 1964, p. 16.

50. Takeno 1979, p. 43.

51. Takeno 1976, p. 58.

52. Etchū 1978c, p. 214.

53. This, at least, is the message we get when we look at the earlier specimens of the *nanban byōbu*.

No Place for the Fainthearted: Belchior de Figueiredo

1. Alvarez-Taladriz 1954, p. 114, n. 28.

2. *Ibid*, p. 115, n. 28.

3. Schütte 1975, p. 43.

4. Letters by Figueiredo, from Ōmura: *Cartas* Evora I, ff. 204–205; from Arima: *Cartas* Evora I, ff. 205–205v; from Bungo: JapSin 6, ff. 193–196v; *Cartas* Evora I, ff. 243–246v; JapSin 6, ff. 254–256v; *Cartas* Evora I, ff. 277–279v.

5. RAH, Cortes 562, p. 620.

6. Letters from Nagasaki: Matsuda 1967, p. 617; letter of 23 September 1572: RAH, Cortes 562, ff. 85r–107v; letter from Kuchinotsu 29 September 1572: JapSin 7 I, 97–98; *Cartas* Evora I, fol. 338v.

7. Schütte 1975, p. 81.

8. Fróis' *Historia* 2, p. 367; Schütte 1968, p. 525.

9. Fróis' *Historia* 2, pp. 371–2; Boxer 1963, pp. 37–8. Others have off the coast of Amakusa.

10. Gonsalo Alvares, Manoel Lopes, João Velho, Diogo Fernandes, Antonio Nunes (Fróis' *Historia* 2, p. 371).

11. Cooper 1974, p. 240.

12. Toyama 1981, p. 76.

13. Toyama 1986, p. 41.

14. Toyama 1986, pp. 40–41.

15. Toyama 1981, p. 18.

16. Fróis' *Historia* 2, p. 375.

17. *Ibid.*

18. Next, we find Cabral leaving Kuchinotsu for Takase in Higo on 7 September (Matsuda 1967, p. 629; Alvarez-Taladriz 1954, p. 112), suggesting that, after his failure to sneak by Fukabori, Cabral had indeed taken the arduous Mogi road to get to Shimabara. He finally arrived in Bungo by the end of the month (Schütte 1968, p. 578).

19. Fróis *Historia* 2, Chapter 100 (pp. 389–96).

20. *Ibid.*, p. 390.

21. *Ibid.*

22. *Ibid.*, pp. 390–1.

23. Although Elison 1973, p. 94, identifies the father in charge of Nagasaki at this time as Gaspar Coelho, it surely was Belchior de Figueiredo.

24. Uo-no-machi along the Nakajima river, in Tokugawa times still the site of Nagasaki's fish market.

25. Fróis' *Historia* 2, pp. 391–2.

26. *Ibid.*, p. 392.

27. *Ibid.*, pp. 392–3.

28. *Ibid.*, p. 393.

29. *Ibid.*

30. *Ibid.*, p. 394.

31. Again, the names of these four brave Christians from Shiki are missing. This time it is easy to see why. Such names of men who disobeyed clear orders from a padre did not need to be preserved for posterity.

32. *Ibid.*, p. 396.

33. *Ibid.*

34. Schütte 1968, p. 472; p. 525. On 6 October 1574, Padre Francisco Stephanonio, just arrived in Japan, still places Figueiredo in Ōmura in his letter to Emanuel Texeira of that date (JapSin 7 I, f. 241v). Miguel Vaz writes, on 1 October 1575, that Figueiredo had gone to Goto. (JapSin 7 III, ff. 277v–278r).

35. Schütte 1968, p. 588.

Christian Champion: Caspar Coelho (1)

1. Today, Porto is Nagasaki's "sister-city."

2. ARSI, Goa 24 I, ff. 126–27v; quoted in Schütte 1975, p. 109. In fact, in 1579, Coelho had only been in Japan eight years.

3. Fróis mentions Coelho as the superior of Kyushu in 1576 (*Historia* 2, p. 451). By 1579, the following missionaries were stationed in Kyushu: João Battista di Monte (eighteen years of experience in Japan), Luís Fróis (sixteen years), Belchior de Figueiredo (fifteen years), Baltasar Lopez (ten years), and Sebastian Gonçalvez (seven years).

4. Schütte 1975, p. 43.

5. Toyama 1981, p. 171.

6. RAH, Cortes 562, f. 129v–130r.

7. Bourdon 1993, p. 21.

8. Letter of 3 August 1575 (RAH, Cortes 562, f. 130r–v).

9. Toyama 1986, p. 414 (doc. 147).

10. Some Buddhist temples were left standing to serve as Christian churches. Sumitada himself, for example, was buried in 1587 on the grounds of the Hōshōji, dating from the 14th century and a branch temple of the Saidaiji, a Nara temple of the Shingon sect (Toyama 1981, p. 173).

11. Fróis' *Historia* 2, p. 430.

12. Quoted in Toyama 1981, p. 176.

13. Toyama 1981, p. 177.

14. Fróis' *Historia* 2, p. 431.

15. Toyama 1981, p. 164.

16. Schütte may have had these numbers in mind when he wrote that Coelho was operating "with much success" in Ōmura (Schütte 1968, p. 472).

17. Cf. Coelho's letter of 5 October 1575 in *Cartas* Evora I, fol. 353.

18. Ikuta 1992b, p. 455.
19. Vaz' letter of 3 August 1575, RAH, Cortes 562, f. 133r.
20. Anno 1974, p. 32; Anno 1992, p. 238.
21. RAH, Cortes 562, f. 133r.
22. Toyama 1981, pp. 189–192.
23. *Ryūzōji monjo* printed in *Saga-ken shiryō shūsei komonjo hen* vol. 3, pp. 75–6 has the phrase *Tendō kore wo hanare karasa*. According to Higashibaba 2001, p. 39, "karasa" = *garasa* = *graça*, while *tendō*, albeit of Confucian origin, is "one of at least four alternatives to Deus" (*tenson* 天尊, *tentei* 天帝, *tenshu* 天主, ibid. p. 87), therefore: "the grace of God."
24. Toyama 1981, p. 192.
25. Toyama 1981, pp. 198–9.
26. An attempt at reconstructing the tumultuous history of Nagasaki of these years, mainly based on Edo period sources, is made in Anno 1992, pp. 236–56.
27. Letter of Cristobal de Leon dated 15 September 1576 in RAH, Cortes 562, ff. 156r–v. See also the letter by Gregorio de Cespedes dated 7 October 1577 in RAH, Cortes 562, 181v–82r.
28. RAH, Cortes 562, ff. 156v.

The "Donation" of Nagasaki: Alessandro Valignano

1. Fróis' *Historia* 2, p. 452.
2. *Ibid.*, p. 453.
3. Arima Shigezumi (Harinobu)'s year of birth is uncertain. He is said to have been the second son of Arima Yoshisada (KD, vol. 1, p. 349).
4. Fróis' *Historia* 2, p. 499.
5. Fróis' *Historia* 3, p. 131. Okada 1977, p. 146.
6. Cieslik 1962a, p. 4. How Valignano knew to go to Kuchinotsu and not to Nagasaki is a mystery, unless he had been informed by Domingos Monteiro, the Captain Major of the year before, who is on record as having brought the Visitor a letter from Cabral (cf. letter from Cabral to the General 15 October 1578 in JapSin 8 I, f. 203v). Needless to say this letter has not survived.
7. Moriyama 1966, p. 222.
8. Schütte 1968, pp. 45–50.
9. On Valignano, see Elison 1973 and Moran 1993.
10. Cooper 1974, p. 34.
11. Kleiser 1938, p. 71.
12. Toyama 1981, p. 178.
13. E.g., Elison 1973, pp. 94–101.
14. Kataoka 1970, p. 40.
15. E.g., Cieslik 1962a and Kataoka 1970.
16. I.e., 30 *kin* in silver or 3000 *koku* of rice (Takeno 1976, p. 61). Altogether, Sumitada may have received between 2300 and 2400 cruzados (23–24 *kin* in silver) a year in income from Nagasaki in anchorage tax, custom duties, land tax, and occasional presents from the Jesuits before the donation (Takeno 1976, p. 62).
17. Schütte 1971, p. 15.
18. Cieslik 1962a, p. 5.
19. According to a letter Valignano wrote to Theotino de Bragança on 15 August 1580 (*Cartas* Evora I, fols. 478–479v), the visitor reported that Sumitada feared the increasing ability of Ryūzōji Takanobu to simply take Nagasaki away from him, and therefore proposed to outfox the lord of Saga by giving the town away before Takanobu could take it (*cf* also: Toyama 1981, pp. 192–3). It is hard to see the significance of this, for if the town were incorporated into the Saga domain, the Jesuits would immediately find another port for the *nao* in a domain that was more receptive to their missionary work. It is doubtful, therefore, that this was an argument any Jesuit would have mentioned to Valignano. To find it in a letter written by

the Visitor means that it may have been Sumitada himself who mentioned it, or that Valignano misinterpreted what Sumitada told him.
20. Cieslik 1962a, p. 8.
21. Schütte 1971, p. 14.
22. Toyama 1981, pp. 193–4.
23. According to Cieslik 1962a, p. 5, Valignano's reason for delaying his decision was that, if Nagasaki was to be a Jesuit foothold in Japan, this needed to be the common decision of all the fathers in Japan. This does not seem likely because the Jesuit document accepting Nagasaki on behalf the Jesuits is dated 9 June 1580 (Pacheco 1969, p. 232), while the *consulta* debating it was held the month after.
24. Toyama 1981, p. 77.
25. Attending were: Alessandro Valignano, Francisco Cabral, Gaspar Coelho, Lourenço Mexia, Luis d'Almeida, and Antonio Lopez.
26. Portuguese version: JapSin 2a, f. 25r–26r; Spanish version: JapSin 2a, 62r–63r.
27. JapSin 2a, 25v–26r and 62v. The latter version is a translation of the former and, being an interpretation of the original rather than an official document, its language is occasionally slightly more concrete and precise. My English translation takes into account both versions.
28. There is much lawyer-like debate on this point. Kataoka (1970, p. 43) reasons that the acceptance must have taken place between the donation [which he dates as 9 June 1580] and Valignano's first report to the General of the Society on the acceptance of Nagasaki [dated 15 August 1580, *Cartas* Evora I, fols. 478–479v].
29. Alvarez-Taladriz 1954, p. 76*; Schütte 1971, pp. 18–9.
30. Schütte 1951, p. 430; see also Elison 1972, p. 224.
31. Schütte 1951, p. 430. Alvarez-Taladriz 1954, p. 76*.
32. Alvarez-Taladriz 1954, pp. 79–80.
33. JapSin 46, f. 50, cited in Schütte 1964, p. 26.
34. RAH: Cortes 562, f. 290v.
35. *Ibid.* "la cerca … al derredor de una tapia muy fuerte."
36. Parker 1996, pp. 12–13; and 2002, pp. 196–202.
37. Moran 1993, p. 161.
38. Schütte 1951, pp. 321–31.
39. Schütte 1975, p. 122.
40. ARSI Goa 13 I, f. 216v.
41. Cabral left Kuchinotsu on 19 February 1583 (Alvarez-Taladriz 1954, p. 113).
42. See for example Boxer 1951, p. 141.

The King-Sized Admiral: Ambrósio Fernandes

1. See Schütte 1971, p. 15; Anno 1992, p. 240.
2. Matthew 1988, p. 283.
3. Valignano, *Apologia*, ed. Alvarez-Taladriz 1998, p.167.
4. Alvarez-Taladriz 1973, p. 87, n. 197; also p. 127.
5. Alvarez-Taladriz 1988, p. 141.
6. Alvarez-Taladriz 1954, p. 80; Ruiz-de Medina 1999, p. 422 has 1555, but without source notation; *Varones Ilustres* 1887, vol. 1, p. 364 has 1551.
7. Schütte 1972, p. 78.
8. "Et ego agnosco fratrem Ambrosium, iesuitam, qui erat dux cuiusdam navigii parvuli ad modum trirremis custodiens civitatem et portum…" (Ribadeneira, *Responsiones* 1605–08, quoted in Castro 1979, p. 246).
9. JapSin 36, 201v, cited in Ruiz-de Medina 1999, p. 422.
10. Ruiz-de Medina 1999, p. 422.
11. Schütte 1975, p. 587.
12. In this year, Fernandes was stationed in Kazusa (Schütte 1975, p. 272).

13. Etchū 1978a, p. 67.
14. Alvarez-Taladriz 1954, p. 80; Schütte 1975, p. 311.
15. Schütte 1975, p. 443; Pacheco 1985, p. 13.

Militant Missionaries: Gaspar Coelho (2)

1. ARSI Goa 13 I, f. 216v.
2. Letter of Valignano to the General of 28 October 1583 (JapSin 9 II, 170r): "porque ni sabe la lengua ni ay esperança de la poder aprender."
3. Toyama 1981, 204.
4. Fróis' *Historia* 4, 1983, p. 50.
5. Murdoch 1925, p. 220; Toyama 1981, p. 205.
6. The Jesuit sources give the date of the battle, according to the Julian calendar, as 24 April 1584 (See Elisonas 1991, p. 344, n.52). The Japanese sources connected with the battle are collected in DNS 11-6, pp. 161–366.
7. *A vos vinhamos todos buscar!* (Fróis' letter of 31 August 1584 in *Cartas* Evora, vol. 2, fol. 118).
8. The editor of the *Cartas* left out the unedifying moral to the tale that Fróis had originally added: "A boy of 14 or 15 years old hugged Takanobu, with whom, they said, the latter had entertained a relationship that was neither very blessed nor very chaste, for wherever he [Takanobu] went he would always take two or three of those boys with him on horseback; they [the men from Satsuma] killed him [the boy] there on the spot, for he [Takanobu] did not need any other guardian angel to accompany him on his pilgrimage to Hell" (BNL COD 11098, f. 197r).
9. Fróis' *Historia* 4, p. 63.
10. Moriyama 1966, p. 226; Okada 1977, pp. 153–4.
11. See map, page 12.
12. Schütte 1972, p. 122.
13. Aduarte 1962, p. 407; Elison 1973, p. 114.
14. Bernard 1938, p. 113; Gense and Conti 1957, p. 264.
15. Bernard 1938, p. 113; Aduarte 1962, p. 408.
16. JapSin 10 I 23–24v. See also: Takase 1977, Ebisawa 1981, p. 108, and Miki 1983, p. 131.
17. *Uwai Kakken nikki* in *Dai Nihon Kokiroku*, vol. 2 (1955), pp. 49–50. I am grateful to Professor Yamaguchi Takamasa for his kind help in reading parts of this Satsuma dialect text with me on 5 July 2006.
18. *Ibid.*
19. Pobre's *Historia* (ed., Martinez Perez 1997, p. 132). Pobre's account was written between 1598 and 1603. Thus he is not an eyewitness, but reports information he heard while he was in Nagasaki in 1598. On Juan Pobre and his *Ystoria*, see Boxer 1969a.
20. *Uwai Kakken nikki* in *Dai Nihon Kokiroku*, vol. 3 (1957), p. 50.
21. Pobre's *Historia* (ed., Martínez Perez 1997, p. 132).
22. *Uwai Kakken nikki*, p. 47.
23. Fróis' *Historia* 4, p. 69.
24. *Ibid.*
25. Fróis' *Historia* 4, p. 289.
26. *Anua* of 1586, JapSin 45 IIb, f. 115r.
27. It was probably for the New Year's ceremony of 1586, that Antonio Lopes went to Satsuma "levando comsigo hum Irmão japão e alguns christãos velhos, dos principaes de Nangazaqui" (Fróis' *Historia* 4, p. 290).
28. Knauth 1972, p. 112.
29. Fróis' *Historia* 4, p. 216; Alvarez-Taladriz 1972c, p. 59, n. 40.

Part Two: Brave New World

The Conqueror of Kyushu: Toyotomi Hideyoshi (1)

1. Cooper 1972, p. 429.

2. Boxer 1951, p. 106. According to Lobato 1999, p. 289, these profits rose from around 100,000 cruzados per voyage in the 1560's to 200,000 cruzados in the 1580's.
3. Numbers of troops in Berry 1982, pp. 83, 89.
4. There exist twelve texts, dating from 1587 to 1592 and issued in Hideyoshi's name, which deal with the trade in Nagasaki. These texts can be divided into three groups. The first group, dating from July 1587, comprises the two documents proscribing Christianity and the slave trade (translations of these can be found in Boscaro 1973, Elison 1973, and Kouamé 2011). The second group consists of six documents, issued in 1588, 1589, and 1591, which concern the general management of the city and the trade. The third group consists of four documents, dating from 1591 and 1592, and deal with specific complaints of European traders. The relevant volumes of series 11 of DNS dealing with these years have not yet been published.
5. Fróis' *Historia* 4, p. 217; Schütte 1972, p. 113.
6. Schütte 1968, p. 671.
7. Fróis' *Historia* 4, p. 288.
8. *Ibid.*, pp. 221, 288.
9. *Ibid.*, pp. 288–9.
10. *Ibid.*, p. 227. Padres present were: Francisco Calderon, Gregorio de Cespedes, João de Crasto, Luís Fróis, Organtino Gnecchi-Soldo (Boxer 1951, p. 140).
11. Fróis' *Historia* 4, p. 228.
.12. *Ibid.*, p. 229.
13. *Ibid.*, p. 229.
14. *Ibid.*, p. 233.
15. *Cartas* Evora II, f. 176v.
16. Schütte 1968, p. 601.
17. Schütte 1972, pp. 122–3, n. 34.
18. *Ibid.*, pp. 135–7.
19. Schütte 1968, pp. 499, 698–9.
20. Although it seems a little early in the year, this is the date given in BA 49-V-3, f. 8v–9r.
21. Fróis' *Historia* 4, p. 366.
22. Shimizu 1969, p. 11.
23. Fróis' *Historia* 4, p. 366; Schütte 1975, pp. 395–6.
24. JapSin 51, f. 40, cited in Schütte 1975, p. 400; also: Fróis' *Historia* 4, pp. 372–3.
25. Fróis' *Historia* 4, p. 390.
26. Alvarez-Taladriz 1973, p. 87, n. 197; also p. 127.
27. "El cuambaco, enfadado desto, volbió el rostro a otra parte sin hablar más en la materia." Declaration of Juan de Solís, AGI Filipinas 6, no. 4148, printed in Iwasaki Cauti 1992, p. 145.
28. *Cartas* Evora II f. 199v.
29. Fróis' *Historia* 4, p. 397.
30. *Ibid.*, p. 398.
31. Alvarez-Taladriz 1972c, p. 41.

The Slave Trader: Domingos Monteiro

1. Okamoto 1936, p. 466.
2. Sousa 2010, pp. 148–9.
3. Valignano's *Adiciones* pp. 287–8, quoted in Okamoto 1936, p. 605.
4. For other New Christians living in Nagasaki and involved in the slave trade, see JapSin 12, II, f. 213v, quoted in Moran 1993, p. 26. The whole question of the slave trade is treated in Okamoto 1936, pp. 755–67; see also Maki 1961, and Nelson 2004.
5. Okamoto 1936, p. 461.
6. Okamoto 1936, p. 489.
7. SHJ ms *Kyūshū godōzaki* by Ōmura Yūki, quoted in Maki 1961, p. 190.
8. Cocks' *Diary* 1, pp. 184, 366 for prices in 1616.
9. JapSin 10 II, 271–274; transcribed in Alvarez-Taladriz 1972a, p. 50, n. 17.
10. *Ibid.*
11. Prisoners taken in a "just" war were recognized by

the Jesuits as legitimate slaves (Nelson 2004, p. 467). In 1598, Bishop Cerqueira, a recent arrival in Japan, came to the conclusion that the majority of the people sold as slaves in Japan had been obtained illegally (Pagés 1869, vol. 2, p. 72).

12. Guzmán 1601, vol. 2, p. 680; italics added.

13. *Inventarios do Padre Francisco Rodrigues* at ANTT, Ms. da livraria 805, f. 98v.

14. BNL COD 6904, ff. 165r–66v.

15. According to Japanese estimates, between 20,000 and 30,000 Koreans were brought to Japan as slaves, but according to Korean estimates the number was higher than 100,000 (Gonoi 2003, p. 50).

16. *Goshuin shishoku kokaku* monjo, quoted in Watanabe 1939, pp. 462–3; Boscaro 1973, pp. 225–35; Shimizu 1977: pp. 268–9; Kouamé 2011, pp. 166–8.

17. Fróis' *Historia*, vol. 4, pp. 395.

18. The story has been retold many times: Anesaki 1930, pp. 215–9; Okada 1977, pp. 191–3; Ebisawa 1995, pp. 286–7. Catholic authors tend to stress Hideyoshi's drunkenness that night and the "sudden reversal" of his stance towards Christianity. In English the best account has been Elison 1973, p. 115 ff.

19. *Matsurake monjo*, quoted in Nagayama 1927, no. 9; Watanabe 1939, pp. 464–5; Kobata 1951, pp. 115–6; Boscaro 1973, pp. 235–41; Elison 1973, pp. 115–6; Ikuta 1992b, p. 466; Kouamé 2011, pp. 158–9.

20. Japanese historians have traditionally tried to see the two edicts as directed to different audiences, the first one for internal consumption and the second one directed towards the foreigners, or the first one for the Kinai region and the second one for Kyushu. For a summary of this discussion among Japanese historians, see Anno 1995, especially pp. 322–32. In an essay of considerable subtlety, Shimizu Hirokazu has shown that such distinctions are artificial, and that the second edict was used both to notify the Hakozaki and Ise shrines, the leadership of the Jesuits and the Captain Major, as well as forming the basis of the text for public announcements in the cities of Hideyoshi's *tenka* (Shimizu 1995, pp. 376–7).

21. On Hideyoshi resenting the Portuguese for not bringing the carrack to Hakata, see also Ebisawa 1995, p. 288.

Rewriting History: Luís Fróis

1. Berry 1982, p. 92.

2. Quoted in Boscaro 1973, p. 220.

3. The first to question this assessment was Elison 1973, p. 119 ff.

4. Quoted in Delplace 1909, vol. 1, p. 24. 3

5. See Bourdon 1993 for the failure of the Yamaguchi mission (1557), ch. 11, pp. 317–8; for the failure of the Hirado mission (1559), pp. 320–22; for the chronic lack of funds, ch. 12, pp. 374–6; for the failure of the Miyako mission (1559–1560), ch. 13, pp. 379–406.

6. A fact later also acknowledged by Hideyoshi when, in 1595, he appointed Padre João Rodrigues as his agent to buy silk in China to the amount of 2000 *koku* of rice (Cooper 1974, p. 107).

7. While in the twelve years before 1562, the Jesuits possibly baptized some six thousand Japanese, in the twenty-four years that followed the number of baptized reached an impressive 170,000 (Costa 1998, pp. 94–5).

8. At this very moment, Valignano also filled the function of Provincial of the order in Goa.

9. Laures 1957, p. 10.

10. Boxer 1951, p. 149.

11. On 14 October 1590, Valignano wrote a letter to the General of the order, Claudio Aquaviva, in which he accused Coelho of having hidden a letter with this order from the other Jesuits in Japan (JapSin 11 II 235–235v, partly transcribed in Alvarez-Taladriz 1972c, p. 47, n. 13, p. 69, n.70). Thus, a letter that no one had seen except, according to Valignano, the dead Coelho himself was the only proof that the Visitor could adduce to the other Jesuits that Coelho had not followed his orders! Needless to say, there is no trace of such a letter in any archive that has preserved Jesuit letters.

12. Even this point is debatable, however, for Fróis was always writing, and so it is difficult to pinpoint the exact moment when he started his *Historia*.

13. Although by a willing and active participant in the clean-up effort, Fróis' work continued to contain too many traces of the aggressive mission policy the Jesuits had pursued during the more than twenty-five years before 1587, as we have amply demonstrated above. For centuries, therefore, it was not considered fit for publication by the managers of the order. It was only in the late twentieth century that a Jesuit edited this *magnum opus* for publication. Another major work by an author (not nearly as stylistically accomplished as Fróis) did not survive at all: Michael Cooper has concluded that João Rodrigues' history of the first forty years of the mission, dealing with the years 1552–90, was "already lost by the middle of the eighteenth century" (Cooper 2001, p. XXIX).

14. Crucial letters by Torrès and Figueiredo connected with the founding of Nagasaki are all missing (Pacheco 1970, p. 309). One of the most important documents, the *Regimentos*, detailing how power should be exercised in Nagasaki in the years after 1580, was composed by Alessandro Valignano himself. We are not surprised to read that it "regrettably has not come down to us" (Cieslik 1962a, p. 9; also: Alvarez-Taladriz 1954, p. 77). The drawing of Nagasaki's defense works that once accompanied the manuscript of Valignano's *Sumario* is also missing (Alvarez-Taladriz 1954, p. 80). We have found traces, furthermore, how even the published letter collections were re-edited to conform with the new party line: the *Cartas* editions of Coimbra (1570) and Alcala de Henares (1575) were made superfluous by a monumental new edition published in Evora in 1598, from which, for example, Michael Vaz's involvement in the founding of Nagasaki had been excised. It takes a really trusting soul to believe that all this is due to coincidence.

15. Okamoto 1936, p. 476.

16. Domingos Monteiro died the following year (Schütte 1975, p. 407). According to Fróis (JapSin 45 Ib, f. 126r), to send these emissaries was another idea agreed on by the Jesuit conclave held at Hirado in the summer and fall of 1587.

17. Fróis' *Historia* 5, p. 23.

18. Schütte 1968, pp. 612, 627.

Master of the *Tenka*: Toyotomi Hideyoshi (2)

1. On Tenshō 15.05.08-09 (13–14 June 1587): Hinotani Teruhiko and Emoto Hiroshi [eds.] *Taikōki*, p. 245; KCSF vol. 2, p. 334; Okada 1977, p. 188.

2. Nakada 1983b, p. 5.

3. Wicki *Documenta Indica*, vol 18, p. 615, cited in Costa 1998, p. 511. We have no contemporary Japanese sources about this trip, but the *Nagasaki jikki nendai roku*, a compilation of the Dutch interpreters' guild of Nagasaki of later date, has: "these men had associated with the Portuguese ships over the past decades and were believers in the evil law of the Christians. His Excellency heard that they opposed the Way of the Gods and the Law of the Buddha and had destroyed shrines and temples. Saying this was illegal to the highest degree, they were quickly chased away" (*Nagasaki jikki nendai roku* 1999, p. 11).

4. JapSin 45 II b, f. 112r (Fróis' *Anua* 1587).

5. In 1587, there were already three churches in the Nagasaki area: the church at Morisaki (later called the Assunção church), the Misericordia church at Hakata-machi (since 1583), and just outside the city proper the Todos os Santos church at Sakurababa (since 1568).

6. JapSin 45 II b, f. 115r (Fróis' *Anua* of 1587).

7. Shimizu 2001a, p. 337. As Tōdō Takatora was paired up with Terazawa Hirotaka (1562-1633) to deal with Nagasaki in 1589, they may have come together to transmit Hideyoshi's orders in 1587 as well. That, at least, seems to be the conclusion drawn by Takeno 1976, p. 67.

8. *KD* vol. 10, p. 181.

9. Testimony of Jeronimo Pereira in Alvarez-Taladriz 1973, p. 129, note 62.

10. *Nabeshima Naoshige kōfu* (quoted in Shimizu 1969, p. 12) has "a fine of six *momme* in silver is imposed on each man and woman throughout the city." There are copies in the Tokyo National Museum and the Nagasaki Prefectural Library, both entitled *Naoshige kō santoku fu* (*Kokusho sōmokuroku*). There are similar entries in the *Zoku Nagasaki kan* and the *Nagasaki shūkai*.

11. Fróis' *Historia*, vol. 4, p. 418. One bar of silver (*ichimai*) was worth 4 *taels*, 3 *mas* in Japanese currency or 4 *cruzados*, 6 *vintis* in Portuguese currency (Shimizu 2001a, p. 345, citing Fróis' *Anua* of 1588). A sum of 600 *ichimais* would therefore amount to 2418 *taels* or 241,800 silver *momme*. Theoretically, then, this sum divided by 6, or 40,300, would give us the number of Nagasaki citizens in the summer of 1587. However, this number is about ten times too large (see: Takeno 1976, p. 65, who estimates the population of Nagasaki at 4,000 at this time).

12. Shimizu 2001a, p. 338.

13. Schütte 1971, p. 23.

14. *Ibid.*

15. Shimizu 2001a, p. 336, citing Fróis.

16. Shimizu 1969, p. 13. The *Nagasaki Kokinshūran* has Jinzaemon leaving the domain in 1588 (Woolley 1881, p. 129).

17. Schütte 1968, pp. 700-1.

18. Shimizu 1969, p. 13.

19. JapSin 10 II 282r-285v, transcribed in Alvarez-Taladriz 1974a, pp. 7-16; quoted in Takase 1977, p. 126; Sakamoto 1981, p. 134.

20. 25 July 1587-27 April 1588: Shimizu 1969, p. 13; Shimizu 2001a, pp. 338-9.

21. Sumitada had died on 25 May 1587.

22. *Anua* of 1587, quoted in Kataoka 1970, p. 46.

23. Moriyama 1966, p. 227; Shimizu 2001a, p. 340.

24. The original documents of two have been lost. Their text, however, is preserved in the *Nagasaki jitsuroku taisei* (1760-4) compiled by Tanabe Shigehiro (*KD*, vol. 10, p. 573).

25. *Nabeshima monjo*, quoted in Nagayama 1927, no. 10; Watanabe 1939, p. 455; *Saga-ken shiryōshūsei komonjo hen*, vol. 3, 1958, p. 278 (no. 17); Shimizu 1969, p. 14; Shimizu 1977, p. 269; the orginal is reproduced in Kōbe shiritsu hakubutsukan/ Kobe City Museum 1998, no. 91. See also: Nakada 1983b, p. 6.

26. KCSF vol. 13, p. 285. In 1591, he would change his personal name to Naoshige.

27. Shimizu 1969, p. 14.

28. Shimizu 1969, p. 15.

29. Matsuda 1970, p. 133.

30. *Nagasaki jitsuroku taisei*, p. 5; Cieslik 1962a, p. 11 and Shimizu 1977, p. 270.

31. *KD* vol. 12, p. 80. Since 1587, he was also lord of Ōzu Castle in Iyo (Ehime) with 160,000 *koku* (*KD* vol. 2, p. 617).

32. Shimizu 2001a, p. 342.

33. Tsang 2007, p. 24.

34. Boxer 1963, p. 51; Schütte 1975, p. 228. Usually, the news of the arrival of the Portuguese carrack preceded its actual anchoring in Nagasaki bay, so we often end up with two different (but consecutive) arrival dates.

35. Alvarez-Taladriz 1973, p. 129, note 62. I have not been able to find the original source quoted here.

36. Iwao 1959, p. 64.

37. Coelho in *Cartas* Evora II, fl. 244; Okamoto 1936, p. 681.

38. Gonoi 1972, pp. 38-9.

39. Thus, it may have been around this time that the great merchants of Japan established permanent offices in Hon Hakata-machi, next to what used to be the first moat or Ichinohori, which had been filled in for expansion of the city's defense works in 1580-2. With Hideyoshi himself encouraging the trade, the voices of these great merchants were to become increasingly important in city affairs, and so naturally their offices eventually became the locus of the city government. When Hideyoshi decided to establish a *bugyōsho* or permanent representation of his authority in the city in 1592, it was not located in one of the original six *machi*, where the Jesuits had their headquarters, but in this same area of Hon Hakata-machi (Etchū 1980, p. 165).

40. *KD* vol. 5, p. 935. The other one was Ishida Mitsunari (1560-1600).

41. Pereira sent his own emissary, Manuel Lopez, to Hideyoshi, who was received in audience on 10 October 1588 (Boscaro 1973, p. 220). A document preserved in the collection of the Matsura family contains an order by Hideyoshi for the daimyo of Hirado to supply boats to ship cargo, i.e., the raw silk Hideyoshi had bought, from Nagasaki to Osaka (Kobata 1951, p. 117). The order states shortly that the Matsura are to follow the directions of Konishi Izumi (=Ryūsa). Although the document was issued on 22 October, it only seems to have arrived in Hirado on 20 December 1588. It is difficult to account for this delay, especially because the silk may have been sent before the latter date.

42. *Anua* written at Kazusa on 20 September 1589, RAH Cortes 562, ff. 460v-461r.

43. Boxer 1963, p. 51.

44. Schütte 1975, p. 404.

45. A Spanish vessel from Manila and a Portuguese vessel, however, were blown off course and entered Amakusa's Sashinotsu and Satsuma's Kataura harbors. To the latter port, Hideyoshi sent Ishida Mitsunari with 20,000 pieces of silver to buy up the silk and assert his precedence over the Shimazu (Shimizu 1969, p. 16).

46. Pharmacist (boticairo): Sugi Gomes (1543?-1623), see Schütte 1975, p. 1303. Scribe and interpreter: Takai Cosme (1552-?), see JapSin 25, f. 37, cited in Alvarez-Taladriz 1972b, p. 68, n. 67; doctor Yōhōken Vicente (1539?-1609).

47. Gonoi 2002, p. 368.

48. Shimizu 2001a, p. 343. Also: *Zōho Nagasaki ryakushi,* cited in Ushiki 1966, p. 61; Etchū 1980, p. 168.

49. KCSF vol. 11, p. 42. If this is correct, his appointment to Nagasaki *bugyō* must date from 1589, rather than from 1588 as most authors (Ushiki 1966, p. 61; Etchū 1980, p. 168; Shimizu 2001a, p. 343) have it. This year also fits much better with Hideyoshi's appointment habits.

50. There is some uncertainty about who was Captain Major this year. JapSin 31a, f. 3r and AGI Filipinas 6, no. 4148 (quoted in Iwasaki Cauti 1992, p. 146) both have Henrique da Costa. Wicki mentions João da Gama (Fróis' *Historia* 5, p. 361, n. 4), but without a source location I consider this a mistake. The embassy has been described many times: Murdoch 1925, vol. 2, pp. 261-4; Kleiser 1938, pp. 70-98; Boxer 1951, p. 153; Boxer 1963, pp. 54-5; Cooper 1974, pp. 75-82; Cooper 2005, pp. 155-8.

51. Kleiser 1938, p. 79 quotes an unidentified Jesuit source as having "Kango no kami" (*Kaga no kami* 加賀守) and "Ikonokami" (*Iki no kami* 壱岐守). *Kaga no kami* refers to Nabeshima Naoshige. *KCSF* vol. 13, pp. 285–6, does not mention when Naoshige received this title. In 1588, Naoshige was still known as Hida no kami. It is likely that he received the new title when he took over the Saga domain in the spring of 1590 (KCSF, *ibid*.).

52. *KD* vol. 4, p. 232. Later, he changed his name to Mōri Katsunobu and participated in the Korean campaign. He was attainted by Tokugawa Ieyasu after Sekigahara and from then on forced to live under the tutelage of the Yamanouchi in Tosa.

53. The red-seal document in question has not survived, but we will have occasion to come back to this document below.

54. "...porque viendo [los cristianos del Japón] que Cambaco no tocaba en aquella Yglesia y cassas estando en lugar tan público, cobrauan mucho ánimo porque les pareçía que tácitamente consentía que los padres perseuerassen en el Japón" (anonymous, RAH, Cortes 9/2665, f. 171).

55. Fróis' *Historia* 5, p. 187.

56. Cooper 2005, pp. 157–8.

57. Schütte 1968, p. 56.

58. Hideyoshi's negative answer to the Viceroy's letter brought by Valignano was crafted on 23 July 1591 by the priests Yūsetsu Suihō 有節瑞保, Seigo'in Dōchō 聖護院道澄, Seishō Shōdai 西笑承兌, Yuian Eitetsu 惟杏永哲, the court noble Kikutei (Imadegawa) Haruki 菊亭晴季, and the *renga* poets Satomura Shōha 里村紹巴 and Satomura Shōshitsu 里村昌叱, who all came together at Maeda Gen'i's mansion to discuss the problem with Hideyoshi (*Rokuen Nichiroku* 鹿苑日録 entry for Tenshō 19.06.03, quoted in Erkin 2002, p. 49). I am grateful to Professor Matsui Yōko for alerting me to this reference.

59. Schütte 1970, p. 24.

60. Pacheco 1977, p. 53.

61. *Saga-ken shiryō shūsei komonjo hen* vol. 3, p. 280 (Nabeshima monjo no. 20); Shimizu 1977a, p. 271. An approximate translation was published in Boxer 1963, p. 319. The Portuguese King had already issued an order against such abuses on the side of the Portuguese in 1570 (Nakada 1983b, p. 7). See for example: "E porque sou outros sim informado que os Portugueses que vão tratar ao Japão mudão os pesos e balanças, vendendo por humas e comprando por outras, tudo em grande prejuizo dos Japões, ... ordeno e mando que daqui em diante os Portugueses comprem e vendem por hum mesmo peso e balança" Alvará de Dom Sebastião, Sintra, 20 September 1570 (BNL Fundo Geral 4534 ff. 144–6).

62. Fróis' *Historia* 5, p. 357.

A Hapless Captain Major: Roque de Melo

1. BA 49-IV-57, f. 176r. Also: Fróis' *Historia* 5, p. 355.

2. Felgueiras Gaio 1938, vol. 6, tomo 18, pp. 139, 176.

3. Andrade Leitao *Nobiliario de Portugal* at BA 49-XII-37, pp. 237–8. Also: *Livro das gerações e nobreza de Portugal* BNL COD 1327, f. 91v.

4. ANTT *Chancelaria D. Henrique*, liv. 46, f. 234r.

5. Antonio Pinto Pereira, vol. 2, pp. 60; 70; 121r.

6. *Ibid.*, vol. 2, p. 145r.

7. ANTT, *Chancelaria D. Sebastião*, liv. 32, f. 300v.

8. According to Diego do Couto. Dec. VIII, Cap. XXXIII, p. 307, another future Capitão Mor of the Japan voyage, João Cayado de Gamboa (1604), also fought in the same siege of Chaul. Although his father occupied an important position in the Indian bureaucracy, he was not rewarded at this time.

9. Lobato 1999, p. 357.

10. ANTT, *Chancelaria D. Henrique*, liv. 46, f. 234r.

11. Henrique does not appear in most genealogies of the Melo family, an exception is *Livro das gerações e nobreza de Portugal* (BNL COD 1327, f. 91v).

12. ANTT, *Chancelaria D. Henrique*, liv. 46, f. 234r.

13. Hesselink 2012, pp. 11–12.

14. See above: A Knight in Superior Armor: João Pereira.

15. Couto, Dec. X, Liv. II, Cap. IX, p. 212.

16. Couto, Dec. X, Liv. III, Cap. II, p. 275. Cardon 1947, p. 199 mentions that the transfer of the command over the Famosa fortress took place on 19 August 1582.

17. Carletti 1966, pp.175–6.

18. Sousa 2010, p. 145.

19. There seems to be some evidence that Roque de Melo was involved in the Inquisition of Goa to enforce Portuguese laws against Judaism. Evidence from the documents connected with his inheritance, moreover, show that Roque was not particularly successful in amassing great riches during his thirty-year stay in Asia (see MFA, maço 15, no. 1).

20. *Saga-ken shiryō shūsei, komonjo hen* vol. 3, pp. 283–4 (*Nabeshima monjo*, no. 23). The document seems to be a Japanese translation of a Portuguese complaint addressed to Hideyoshi.

21. *Ibid.*, pp. 282–3 (*Nabeshima monjo*, no. 22) and the document mentioned in the preceding note, which seems to have been appended to it. Cooper 1974, p. 86 mentions that the message was sent on 23 August, or four days after the arrival of the nao. Although I have not been able to confirm this date, it fits the situation as reported in the surviving Japanese documents. The date on these documents, however, is 2 September (Tenshō 19.07.15), which may be explained as the date of their translation into Japanese after their arrival in the Kinai.

22. Cooper 1974, pp. 87–90. Munehisa was also known as Gen'i Hōin. For his letters, see: Alvarez-Taladriz 1966c and Berry 1983.

23. Erkin 2002, p. 51.

24. *Saga-ken shiryō shūsei komonjo hen* vol. 3, pp. 284–5 (*Nabeshima monjo*, no. 24). It is likely that this is Hideyoshi's response to Roque de Melo's complaint of 23 August of that year (Cooper 1974, p. 87).

25. Cooper 1974, p. 87.

26. For Kuroda Yoshitaka see: KCSF vol. 7, pp. 202, 205. For Natsuka Masaie see: KD vol. 10, p. 708.

27. *Saga-ken shiryō shūsei komonjo hen* vol. 3, p. 280 (*Nabeshima monjo*, no. 20).

28. Iwao 1959, p. 64.

29. Alvarez-Taladriz 1973, p. 203, n. 138.

30. See my article "A Metal Dealer and Spy from Nagasaki in Manila in the First Quarter of the Seventeenth Century" in Jane Kate Leonard and Ulrich Theobald [eds.]. *Money in Asia (1200–1900): Small Currencies in Social and Political Contexts*. Leiden: Brill Publishers, 2015, pp. 487–508.

31. Alvarez-Taladriz 1973, p. 203, n. 138; see also: Pacheco 1977, p. 62.

32. Ribadeneira 1947, p. 353.

33. MFA, maço 15, no. 1. I am grateful to Matilde and Francisco Gago who generously granted me access to the papers of the Mello family archive at Serpa.

34. For a calculation of his accumulated wealth, see my forthcoming article "A Portuguese Nobleman Makes No Fortune in Asia: Roque de Melo Pereira."

35. The headship of his branch of the Melo family was taken over by his younger brother Francisco, who was professed as a member of the order of Christ on 26 December 1603 (MFA, maço 15, no. 48).

A Spaniard from Peru: Juan de Solís

1. Iwasaki Cauti 1992, p. 129.
2. Blair and Robertson vol. 9, p. 42, have de Solís going up into the pulpit.
3. Beginning with Valignano himself in 1591 (see Alvarez-Taladriz 1972b), and in print with Guzmán 1601 (f. 482), who translated Fróis' account (*Historia* 5, pp. 360–1) literally into Spanish. The Jesuit version stresses how ungrateful de Solís was for the "compassion" Valignano had shown him ("because he was a foreigner"), and the "favors" he had received from the Visitor. See also: RAH 9/2665, ff. 265r–287v; JapSin 31, 1–51v.
4. Elison 1973, p. 133.
5. There is some uncertainty about who was Captain Major this year. JapSin 31a, f. 3r and AGI Filipinas 6, no. 4148 (quoted in Iwasaki Cauti 1992, p. 146) both have Henrique da Costa. Wicki mentions João da Gama (Fróis' *Historia* 5, p. 361, n. 4), but without a source location I consider this a mistake.
6. Transcribed in Iwasaki Cauti 1992, pp. 143–5: Appendix I: Declaración de Juan de Solís sobre la embajada del Padre Fray Juan Cobo al Japón (AGI, Patronato 25, r. 50); and pp. 145–7: Appendix II: Declaración de Juan de Solís acerca de la destrucción de la iglesia de la Compañía de Nagasaki (AGI, Filipinas 6, no. 4148).
7. *Ibid.* p. 146.
8. Likely because the money had been spent by Valignano himself: it is significant to note that the figure of Valignano's expenses for the embassy, i.e., 6000 *ducados*, mentioned by the Jesuits, is exactly the amount that Juan de Solís was claiming he was owed (Kleiser 1938, p. 84; Cooper 1974, p. 82; Iwasaki Cauti 1992, p. 147).
9. Fróis' *Historia* 5, p. 361.
10. Iwasaki Cauti 1992, p. 148.
11. Guzmán 1601, f. 483.
12. Alvarez 1940, p. 300.
13. Iwasaki Cauti 1992, p. 148.
14. Schilling and Lejarza 1934, p. 498.
15. He had arrived in Manila as the new Governor on 31 May 1590 (Schilling and Lejarza 1934, p. 498).
16. For accounts of the early relations between the Philippines and Japan see: Paske-Smith 1914, Bernard 1938, Iwao 1943, Irikura 1958.
17. Testimony of Antonio Lopez 1 June 1593 (Blair and Robertson vol. 9, p. 39).
18. According to the same witness, who participated in Juan Cobo's embassy, the conquest of the Philippines had already been assigned by Hideyoshi to Hasegawa Hōgen Sōnin (cf. Blair and Robertson vol. 9, p. 39).
19. See Hideyoshi's letter to the Viceroy Duarte de Menezes of Tenshō 19.07.25 (12 September 1591) in Murakami 1929, pp. 26–9.
20. Schurz 1939, pp. 105–6.
21. Translated from a contemporary Spanish translation in Gense and Conti 1957, p. 291. See also: Perez 1915, pp. 407–8; Murakami 1929, pp. 29–30; Irikura 1958, p. 54.
22. Iwao 1985, p. 52.
23. Schilling and Lejarza 1934, p. 496.
24. Gómez Pérez Dasmariñas to the King of Spain 1592.05.31, quoted in Colin/Pastells vol. 2, p. 49; also with some orthographic differences in Iwasaki Cauti 1992, p. 121, transcribed from AGI Filipinas 18-B.
25. Colin/Pastells vol. 3, p. 445.
26. *Ibid.* The letter was brought to Manila on the ship of Pedro Liao Chen [Ryōchin], a Chinese convert to Christianity, and carried by Marco Antonio, an Italian. They had sailed from Hirado on 1592.03.04 and arrived in Manila on 18 April 1592 (Colin/Pastells vol. 2, p. 50).
27. Colin/Pastells vol. 3, p. 445.
28. Schilling and Lejarza 1934, p. 498.

29. Colin/Pastells, vol. 2, p. 48.
30. The letter is printed in Colin/Pastells vol. 3, pp. 445–6.
31. Irikura 1958, p. 57.
32. Iwasaki Cauti 1992, p. 125.
33. Bourdon 1960; Wicki 1961; Boxer 1969b.
34. Knauth 1972, p. 48.
35. Iwao 1943, pp. 12, 19.
36. Schilling and Lejarza 1934, p. 498.
37. Arnaiz 1939, p. 634.
38. *Ibid.*, pp. 302–3.
39. It included Juan de Cobo, Captain Lope de Llanos, and three Chinese: Juan Sami, Cobo's teacher of Chinese (Arnais 1939, p. 304), his son Francisco de Lordui (Alvarez 1940, p. 299), and Antonio Lopez (Bernard 1938, p. 124).
40. Bernard 1938, p. 124.
41. Fróis' *Historia* 5, p. 418.
42. Meant here is the landing near Morisaki called Ōhato, not even five minutes' walk from the Jesuit establishment. In the Bunroku period (1592–5) this beach was transformed into an actual pier with a landing of hewn rock, and an official *bansho* was built to house a guard (Watanabe 1964, p. 347).
43. RAH, Cortes 565, f. 171, quoted in Iwasaki Cauti 1992, p. 133. Also, a similar account in Fróis' *Historia* 5, p. 418.
44. Fróis' *Historia* 5, p. 417. Going ashore somewhere along the bay, Juan de Solís is likely to have stayed the night with the relatives of his interpreter, Luis, who must have come from a Christian family in the Nagasaki bay area of independent means, but not from the city itself, for in that case he would have been prevented by the *tōnin*, acting on behalf of the Jesuits, from serving Juan de Solís after his falling out with Valignano.
45. Iwasaki Cauti 1992, p. 133.
46. According to Solís' testimony they waited only a week (Blair and Robertson, vol. 9, p. 35), but he is likely to have wanted to stress the success of Cobo's mission by shortening the time they had to wait for an audience.
47. Blair and Robertson vol. 9, p. 35.
48. Vassal of Oda Nobunaga, who was the first to report the latter's assassination to Hideyoshi, also known as Hōgan (KCSF 13, pp. 324–5), which is the *Fungen* of the Spanish sources (e.g., Perez 1915, p. 404).
49. Testimony of Juan Sami 24 May 1593 transcribed in Iwasaki Cauti, p. 134; see also Blair and Robertson vol. 9, p. 42.
50. Hideyoshi left Nagoya for Kyoto on 29 August 1592 (Alvarez 1940, p. 661), so the embassy must have taken place before that date. Also, the Spanish translation of Hideyoshi's answer to Dasmariñas, given by Alvarez, is dated "*Tenshō … mizunoe tatsu* [i.e., 20th year], 7th month, 21st day" (i.e., 28 August 1592). This letter Juan Cobo is likely to have received on the occasion of the audience.
51. Blair and Robertson vol. 9, p. 38.
52. Blair and Robertson vol. 9, pp. 33–38.
53. Fróis' *Historia* 5, pp. 418–9; a similar entry can be found in RAH Cortes 565, f. 170. See also Murdoch 1925, p. 267.
54. Iwasaki Cauti 1992, p. 141. The reference *en rreconoçimiento que* [Hideyoshi] *no hauía tal* is possibly to a recent European invention, such as for example the wheel lock pistol. Boxer (1931, p. 71), mentions that "in 1588 Dom Duarte de Menezes, the Viceroy at Goa, included a pair of pistols in the presents which he made to the Kwambaku Hideyoshi."
55. The horses brought had been given to the Japanese boy ambassadors by the Indian Viceroy at the express command of the King of Spain (Yūki 1994). This letter of the king was also helpful in convincing the Viceroy of the

necessity to cooperate with Valignano in sending him back to Japan as his ambassador (30 October 1588:Valignano to the General JapSin 10 IIb, ff. 338v–339r).

56. Schütte 1975, p. 498.
57. On 25 November 1591 [Tenshō 19.10.10] Terazawa had been appointed *fushin bugyō* 普請奉行 for Nagoya Castle (Ide 1975, p. 24).
58. JapSin 31, f. 23.
59. RAH Cortes 565, f. 170, transcribed in Iwasaki Cauti 1992, p. 150.
60. Fróis' *Historia* 5, p. 420.
61. *Ibid.*
62. Schütte 1971, p. 25.
63. It is, of course, no coincidence that Luís Fróis, the spin doctor of the Jesuit mission in Japan, spun a detailed web about all the excellent results the embassy had produced (cf. JapSin 51e, ff. 363r–367r), but no one was fooled in Goa (cf. letter by Francisco Vieira to Claudio Aquaviva of 23 November 1593, *Documenta Indica*, vol. 16, p. 432, quoted in Wicki 1985, p. 269, n. 8) or Rome (cf. letter by Claudio Aquaviva to Valignano of 16 January 1595, ARSI Gall. 44, f. 27v–28r, quoted in Wicki 1985, p. 269, n. 9). Fróis is less exuberant in his *Historia* 5, pp. 318–20. Valignano's own assessment of his embassy can be found in Alvarez-Taladriz 1972b.
64. Fróis' *Historia* 5, p. 423: "elles se partirão hum dia de muita chuva, secretamente."
65. Testimony of Francisco Lorduy de Oñate in Blair and Robertson, vol. 9, p. 43.
66. *Ibid.*
67. Drowned: Gonoi 2002, pp. 348–9; finished off by the natives: Fróis' *Historia* 5, p. 455. See also: Juan Pobre's *Historia*, quoted in Schilling & Lejarza 1934, p. 499.
68. Colin/Pastells vol. 2, p. 65.
69. Fróis' *Historia* 5, p. 427.
70. Guzmán, another Jesuit writer of the late 16th century, was of the same opinion: "Manifesto castigo de Nuestro Señor" (Guzmán 1601, p. 513).

A New Head of the Mission: Pedro Gómez

1. Shimizu 1969, p. 17.
2. Schütte 1939, p. 240.
3. Schütte 1939, p. 239.
4. Fróis' letter of 2 January 1584 in *Cartas* Evora II, fol. 124; Schütte 1975, p. 176.
5. Schütte 1968, p. 663.
6. Lopez Gay 1964, p. 59.
7. The letter is dated 15 March 1594 (RAH Cortes 565, ff. 1–18).
8. The names of Okada Gonbei and Taniyama Genzō are mentioned in Hayashi Akira and Miyazaki Shigemi *Tsūkō Ichiran* vol. 139, p. 47. Etchū 1980, pp. 169–70, mentions Sano Sōzaemon.
9. RAH Cortes 565, f. 2v–3r.
10. Fróis' *Historia* 4, p. 400.
11. RAH Cortes 565, f. 3r.
12. *Ibid.*
13. *Ibid.*, f. 4r–v.
14. *Ibid.*
15. *Ibid.*
16. *Ibid.*, f. 4v.
17. *Ibid.*
18. See Cooper 1974, p. 97; on Cosme Takai, see Schütte 1975, p. 1304.
19. RAH Cortes 565, f. 5r; JapSin 52a, f. 8v.
20. On Murayama, see Alvarez Taladriz 1966a, 1966b, 1967.
21. RAH Cortes 565, f. 5r; JapSin 52a, f. 8v–9r.
22. Murdoch 1925, p. 269.
23. JapSin 52a, f. 9r; Cooper 1974, p. 99.

24. Fróis' *Historia* 5, p. 506; Miyake 1956, p. 83.
25. Cooper 1974, p. 104.
26. For the church as rebuilt at this time see: Ōsaka Castle screen, right wing, upper part of panels 1–3, see Sakamoto 2008, p. 2.

The Spanish Spy: Bernardo Avila Girón (1)

1. The best copy is preserved in the Escorial Library (ms O. III. 19). There are other copies in BNM (Mss. 19628) and in ARSI (JapSin 58b). I have also used the microfilm copies of these manuscripts at SHJ and KB. There are still other copies as well, see: Schilling and Lejarza 1933, pp. 517–27.
2. Schilling and Lejarza 1934, pp. 16–17.
3. Schilling and Lejarza 1933, p. 493.
4. Alvarez-Taladriz 1966b, p. 400.
5. Schilling and Lejarza 1934, p. 498.
6. Schurz 1939, p. 180.
7. *Ibid.*, p. 84.
8. Rios Coronel 1621, ff. 9v–10r.
9. Schilling and Lejarza 1934, p. 498.
10. Schilling and Lejarza 1933, p. 486; 1934, p. 18.
11. Schilling and Lejarza 1934, p. 18.
12. *Ibid.*
13. Schilling and Lejarza 1933, p. 488.
14. Castro 1979, p. 192.
15. *Ibid.*
16. Schilling and Lejarza 1934, p. 34.
17. Fray Andres de San Antonio had died at sea before Taiwan, *cf.* Castro 1979, p. 192.
18. Himeno 1986, p. 43.
19. AGI, patronato 46, ramo 31; SHJ 7519-29-2, f. 94.
20. Schilling and Lejarza 1934, pp. 27–9.
21. Castro 1979, p. 193.
22. Rios Coronel 1621, p.15r; Schilling and Lejarza 1935, p. 103, n. 1.
23. Schilling and Lejarza 1935, pp. 226–7.

A Cockaigne of Sex: Francesco Carletti (1)

1. Carletti 1966, p. 127.
2. *Ibid.*
3. *Ibid.*
4. *Ibid.*, p. 128.
5. *Ibid.*
6. *Ibid.*
7. *Ibid.*
8. Caron 1648, p. 20.
9. Schilling and Lejarza 1934, p. 265.
10. Collado 1632, p. 42; Ōtsuka 1961, pp. 32–3.
11. Collado 1632, pp. 42–4; Ōtsuka 1961, pp. 33–5.

The Martyred Mendicant: Pedro Blásquez

1. Gense and Conti 1955, p. 166.
2. See Cooper 1974, p. 126.
3. Gense and Conti 1955, p. 166.
4. Cooper 1974, p. 126.
5. Boxer 1963, p. 58.
6. Avila Girón, ch. XV quoted in Himeno 1986, p. 43.
7. Juan Pobre *Istoria*, c. 13, fol. 50, quoted in Alvarez-Taladriz 1973, p. 203, n. 136.
8. See Pedro Chirino, *Historia* Ms. lib. II, cap. XIV, quoted in Perez *San Pedro Bautista* 1916, pp. 220–1, n. 2; and Ribadeneira 1947, pp. 352–3.
9. Willeke 1990, p. 165.
10. Schilling and Lejarza 1934, p. 501.
11. Willeke 1990, p. 165.
12. Juan Pobre *Istoria*, c. 13, fol. 50, quoted in Alvarez-Taladriz 1973, p. 203, n. 137.
13. Ribadeneira 1947, p. 353.

14. Elisseeff 1986, p. 227.
15. Castro 1979, p. 195.
16. Cf. *Kobe shiritsu hakubutsukan nanban byōbu* by Kanō Naizen, right wing, first panel.
17. For the ideology of the Holy Spirit among the Portuguese in Asia, see Hesselink 2012, pp. 20–29.
18. Ribadeneira quoted in Perez' Jerónimo de Jesús 1923, p. 514; also quoted in: Alvarez-Taladriz 1973, p. 180. Gonoi 2003, p. 50, mentions 'a procession of penitents' on the next day, Good Friday, as well.
19. Alvarez-Taladriz 1973, p. 238, n. 28.
20. Schütte 1968, p. 52; Alvarez-Taladriz 1973, p. 86, note 194.
21. Cieslik 1963, p. 16; Schütte 1968, p. 52; Alvarez-Taladriz 1973, p. 86, note 194.
22. Cieslik 1962b, p. 95.
23. Cooper 1974, p. 132. At this moment, there were three Franciscans active in Nagasaki: Fray Augustin Rodriguez, Fray Bartolomeo Ruiz, Fray Marcel de Ribadeneira (Uyttenbroek 1958, p. 20).
24. Perez' San Pedro Bautista 1916, p. 251.
25. *Ibid.* p. 252.
26. Cooper 1974, p. 133.
27. Carletti 1964, p. 119. The last remark marks this fragment as a summary in Carletti's own words, rather than Hideyoshi's, for the decision to have the executions take place in Nagasaki was only made in January 1597.
28. Gense and Conti 1957, pp. 283–4.
29. Hideyoshi seems to have gone out of his way to provide Padre Gil de la Mata with two complete sets of high quality Japanese armor packed in their usual lacquered boxes, when, on 9 October 1592, the missionary left Japan to travel back to Europe. Gil de la Mata met with Philip II for two hours on 18 December 1594 to present the gifts (ARSI, Hispania 138, f. 67 quoted in Lopez Gay 1964, p. 111; cf. also Schütte 1961, p. 20).
30. Schilling and Lejarza 1934, p. 524.
31. Schilling and Lejarza 1934, pp. 536–9.
32. Schilling and Lejarza 1934, p. 540.
33. Cooper 1974, p. 136.
34. *Ibid.*, p. 137.
35. What is little known is that Captain Matias de Landecho of the *San Felipe* and his suite seem to have followed the Franciscan group. Arriving in Nagasaki on the night of 4 February, they stayed in the house of Antonio Garces de Miranda, a rich Portuguese *casado*. When they visited the Jesuits to see if the Franciscans could not be rescued, Padre Gómez advised them that there was nothing that could be done anymore (Tellechea 1998, pp. 54, 140).
36. Cooper 1974, p. 137.
37. The third, Pablo Miki (1564–1597), was already a member of the Society (cf. Uyttenbroek 1958, p. 21).
38. Franciscans: 1. Fray Pedro Bautista Blásquez; 2. Fray Gonzalo García (1557–1597); 3. Fray Francisco de la Parilla (1544–1597); 4. Fray Martin de la Ascension de Aguirre (1567–1597); 5. Fray Francisco Blanco (1569–1597; 6. Fray Felipe de las Casas (1567?–1597). Japanese converts: 1. Cosme Takiya (1559–1597); 2. Miguel Kozaki (1551–1597); 3. Ventura de Miyako (1570–1597); 4. Gabriel from Ise (1578–1597); 5. Thomas Dangi (1555–1597); 6. Paulo Suzuki (1548–1597); 7. Francisco Yokichi (1551–1597); 8. Thomas Kozaki (1582–1597); 9. Pablo Ibaraki (1543–1597); 10. Leon Ibaraki Karasumaru (1548–1597); 11. Juan Kinuya (1569–1597); 12. Matthias; 13. Joaquin Sakakibara (1557–1597); 14. Luis Ibaraki (1585–1597); 15. Antonio de Nagasaki (1584–1597); 16. Pedro Jukijiro; 17. Francisco Gayo of Kyoto (1570–1597). For more information on these individuals, see Alvarez-Taladriz 1973.
39. JapSin 58b, f. 172v–3r. See also Carletti 1964, p. 106.
40. Uyttenbroek 1958, p. 28.

41. Schilling and Lejarza 1934, p. 546.
42. Ribadeneira 1947, lib. V, ch. XVIII, p. 476. For a more detailed description of the execution, see also chapters XIX, XX, XXI of Ribadeneira's account.
43. Ribadeneira 1947, p. 496.
44. *Ibid.*, p. 483.
45. *Ibid.*, p. 497.
46. Juan Pobre, Agostin Rodriguez, Bartolomeo Ruiz, and Marcel de Ribadeneira (Uyttenbroek 1958, p. 32).
47. Schilling and Lejarza 1934, p. 549.
48. *Ibid.*, p. 550.

A Town Under Pressure: Francesco Carletti (2)

1. Carletti 1964, p. 105.
2. Ribadeneira 1947, p. 504, mentions that the corpses hung on their crosses for nine months. Avila Girón's account essentially agrees with this (Schilling and Lejarza 1935, pp. 105–6). Carletti remains vague about when exactly they were taken down: "during my stay" (Carletti 1964, pp. 120–1).
3. Ribadeneira 1947, p. 504.
4. Carletti 1964, pp. 120–1.
5. Jorissen 2002, pp. 44–9, thinks that Carletti is making all of this up. But he also writes that it is possible that Carletti met Fróis on his deathbed and was given a copy of the *Tratado* to read, while shortly after stating that is possible that Carletti did not visit Japan at all. In short, according to Jorissen, anything is possible. What he thinks is impossible, however (i.e., that Carletti witnessed the remains of the 26 martyrs on their crosses upon his arrival in Japan in June 1597, four months after they had been executed), is, on the contrary, eminently possible, especially when one reads the accounts of how securely they had been fastened (*ibid.*, pp. 105–6). Elisonas 2009, p. 78 is a little vaguer, but also clearly has this passage in mind when he disparages Carletti's testimony.
6. Carletti 1964, pp. 126–7.
7. The closest is a law issued in Kanpō 1 (1741): "persons who, while attempting to commit adultery had wounded the woman's husband, should be led through the streets, and after that decapitated and their heads exposed" (Kuechler 1885, pp. 132–3).
8. Remarkable is that Carletti came from Florence, a city where *charivari* were unknown (Trexler 1981, p. 165).
9. Blok 1989, p. 272.
10. *Ibid.*
11. The literature on *charivari* is extensive. For France, see Davis 1975, pp. 97–123 and Jacques Le Goff and Jean-Claude Schmitt (eds.) 1981.
12. Rébouis 1881, p. 35. There is an illustration of this custom in *Les Coustumes de Toulouse*, a manuscript dated 1297 held in the Bibliothèque Nationale de France, fol. 60. For another gruesome charivari from the Crimea, see: Saintyves 1935, p. 29.
13. LeGoff and Schmitt, p. 118.
14. Blok 1989, p. 267, quoting Elias' untranslatable German term: *Existenzbegründend.*
15. *Ibid.*, p. 268.
16. *Ibid.*, p. 273.
17. JapSin 54a, f. 4r.
18. Schütte 1939, p. 242.
19. JapSin 52d, f. 306r.

The Italian Painter: Giovanni Cola

1. According to Ribadeneira 1947, many of these had been exported to Manila, Malacca, and Goa. Some had even been sent to Spain for preservation in the Franciscan convent of Salamanca (Ribadeneira 1947, pp. 503–4).

2. Cf. DeBergh 1980/2000, pp. 408–9.
3. British Library Harley 5478, fol. 280a, quoted in Bailey 1999c, pp. 88–9.
4. Vlam 1976, p. 252.
5. McCall 1947, p. 126.
6. *Ibid.*, p. 127.
7. Vlam 1976, p. 253.
8. *Ibid.*
9. Schurhammer 1933, p. 118.
10. Vlam 1976, p. 254.
11. Gonoi 2002, pp. 346–7; Lopez Gay 2001, p. 27 has 1554 as his birth year.
12. Vlam 1976, p. 254.
13. McCall 1947, p. 127.
14. Vlam 1976, p. 261.
15. Alvarez-Taladriz 1972c, p. 45, n. 5; McCall 1947, p. 127 gives 20 July 1583 as the arrival date, Schütte 1975, p. 1254 has 25 July 1583.
16. McCall 1947, p. 127.
17. Schütte 1975, pp. 164–5.
18. JapSin 9 II, 329: Fróis' *Anua* of 13 December 1584.
19. McCall 1947, p. 130.
20. JapSin 10 II, 223r–v, quoted in Schütte 1975, p. 517, n. 5.
21. McCall 1947, p. 127.
22. JapSin 51a, f. 20.
23. Schütte 1975, pp. 209, 225.
24. Schütte 1975, p. 272.
25. Schilling 1931.
26. Pacheco 1971, p. 440.
27. Fróis 1942; Cooper 2005.
28. Schütte 1975, p. 291.
29. The 600-page work on the lives of the saints of the church *Sanctos no Gosagvuio no vchinvqigaqi* still bears a 1591 imprint at Kazusa, while the Roman catechism *Dochirina kirishitan* was published in the same year in Amakusa. Both works use the Roman alphabet to print translations of Western texts into Japanese. See also Schütte 1975, p. 518, n. 6.
30. Schütte 1975, p. 517, n. 5.
31. JapSin 52a, f. 97, 141.
32. Schütte 1975, p. 517, n. 5. It seems that a number of the painting students had moved to Nagasaki in 1597, where they, at Terazawa's insistence, had to leave Morisaki to go into hiding at Todos os Santos (JapSin 52d, f. 308r).
33. *Anua* of 1596, quoted in McCall 1947, p. 133. I have not been able to find the Portuguese original of this quote.
34. Schütte 1975, p. 517, n. 5.
35. *Ibid.*
36. Valignano writes in a letter dated 15 February 1601 that the move back to Nagasaki occurred four months earlier (JapSin 14 I, f. 101, cited in Schütte 1975, p. 517, n. 5).
37. *Anua* of 1602, BA 49-IV-59, f. 81; also Guerreiro 1603, vol. 1, p. 179.
38. Kataoka 1979, p. 132.
39. I know of only two paintings done in Japan depicting the crucifixion. Both are contained in lacquered cabinets elaborately decorated with mother-of-pearl in lays on hinged doors that could be locked and behind which the paintings could be safely hidden away (see *Dai Zabieru Ten*, nos. 195 and 197).
40. Ebisawa 1964, pp. 30–1; Millioud 1895, pp. 282–3. The policy of the Jesuits to omit mention of Christ's suffering and the crucifixion can also be found in the 1596 and 1610 translations of Thomas a Kempis' *Imitatio Christi* (*Contemptvs mvndi jenbu* and *Kontemutsusu munji*) and in the 1599 translation of Luis de Granada's *Guia de Peccadores* (*Kia to Hekataru*), see Farge 2002, pp. 27–8; 58–60.
41. Alvarez-Taladriz 1973, p. 179, n. 45; Cooper 1974, pp. 83, 88, 107, 116.

42. Gutiérrez 1971, pp. 151–2.
43. Ôsumi 2002, p. xxviii.
44. In this connection, it is probably not without significance that one of the most famous Christian propaganda treatises written by the Japanese Jesuit brother Fabian Fukansai, the *Myôtei mondô* (after 1603), is presented in the form of a dialogue between two women. In other words, this text was especially aimed at literate women, a public that was very difficult for male Jesuit proselytizers to approach through direct contact.
45. Gonoi 2005, pp. 75–105; Kitagawa 2007.
46. BPE Codex CXVI 1–31, f. 87v.
47. *Razan sensei bunshū*, vol. 1, 1918, p. 246.

A Chinese Madonna: Matsupo/Maso

1. SHJ Cocks' *Diary* 1, p. 374.
2. *Suetsugu monjo*, quoted in Kawashima 1921, pp. 152–3. The Fujian Chinese of Nagasaki still have their China House, known as the Fukken Kaikan, now located in Kannai-machi, the area formerly (1688–1868) known as the Tôjin yashiki.
3. For the Japanese called Andrea, see: SHJ Cocks' Diary, vol. 1, pp. 62, 65–6, 72, 96 (1615); vol. 2, pp. 217–8 (1618), p. 328; vol. 3, pp. 14, 80, 82, 109, 141, 145, 151 (1620–1) etc.
4. SHJ Cocks' *Diary* 2, pp. 217–8, 229.
5. *Saga-ken shiryō shūsei*, vol. 4, no. 381.
6. Fróis' *Historia* 2, p. 392.
7. Chang 1970, p. 60.
8. Wang 1990, p. 417. According to an entry in the *Tokugawa jikki*, 80 ships "from different countries in the Western Ocean" reached Nagasaki in 1611 (TJ 1, p. 559).
9. Li 1991, p. 98.
10. Iwao 1958; Wills 1979, pp. 216–8.
11. Li 1979, p. 534; Li 1991, pp. 91–6.
12. Etchū 1998, p. 34.
13. Fujiwara 1990, p. 72.
14. Wang 1990, p. 418; *NSS Butsujibu* 2, pp. 249–52; Li 1979, p. 533.
15. *Ka'i tsūshōkō*, vol. 2, quoted in Li 1979, p. 530.
16. Valentijn 1726, vol. V, p. 252; De Groot 1886, pp. 262–7; Werner 1932, p. 503; Duyvendak 1938, p. 344; Chen 1940, p. 239; Braga 1949, pp. 107–8; Saso 1965, pp. 41–46; Wiethoff 1966; Yang 1967, pp. 72–3; Eberhard 1968, pp. 402–4; Chen 1974, p. 103; Salmon/Lombard 1980, p. 124; Watson 1985; Ter Haar 1990. In Japanese, there is the exhaustive work of Li Hsien-chang 1979.
17. For the story of her official ranking, see Wiethoff 1966.
18. Other dates: 713–56; 907–60; 1101–26 (Werner 1932, p. 503).
19. Watson 1985, pp. 298–9.
20. Yang 1967, pp. 72–3. For a more extensive treatment see: De Groot 1886, pp. 262–7.
21. Duyvendak 1938, p. 344.
22. On the festival of the ninth day of the ninth month, see Eberhard 1968, pp. 357–60.
23. Wiethoff 1966, p. 320.
24. Duyvendak 1938, p. 344.
25. De Groot 1886, p. 263.
26. Watson 1985, p. 297.
27. *Ibid.*
28. *Ibid.*, n. 15.
29. Watson 1985, p. 303.
30. Ter Haar 1990, p. 375.
31. For Vietnam, see Chen 1974, p. 103; for Java see Salmon/Lombard 1980, p. 124; for Taiwan see Saso 1965.
32. De Groot 1886, p. 267.
33. *Ibid.*
34. *Ibid.*

35. De Groot 1886, p. 265.

36. Braga 1949, p. 105.

37. According to Li 1979, pp. 532–4, it is likely that the temple was built to replace or enlarge the pavilion for Matsu-po on the same spot. Until at least the Shōhō period (1644–47), the main deity venerated at this temple was Mat-tsu-po.

38. Pacheco 1977, p. 62.

39. The histories of the Chinese temples are marred by a lack of original sources. In seems clear, however, that of the four Chinese temples in Nagasaki, only the Shōfukuji 聖福寺 (which was only established in 1672 by traders from Canton) did not originate in a shrine dedicated to Maso. In 1623, traders from Jiangsu and Zhejiang established the Xingfusi (Kōfukuji) 興福寺 (or Nanking) Temple in Irabayashi (*NSS Butsujibu* 2, p. 151; Chang 1970, pp. 113–4; Li 1979, p. 540; Wang 1990, p. 418). In 1628, merchants from Fujian built the Fujisi (Fukusaiji) 福済寺 in Chikugomachi. In 1629, merchants from Fuzhou built the Chongfusi (Sōfukuji) 崇福寺 (or Fuzhou) Temple on the mountainside behind Ima Sukkui machi and Ima Kago machi (*NSS Butsujibu* 2, pp. 364–5; Wang 1990, p. 418; Baroni 2000, p. 32 has 1635).

40. The Fukusaiji acquired its full Buddhist form only at the beginning of the Kei'an period (1648–52) with the arrival of Obaku Zen priest Yun-qian (died 1673) in 1650 (Li 1979, pp. 532–40). This was late in comparison with the Kōfukuji and Sōfukuji, which respectively had already changed to the Zen sect in 1632 and 1635. In 1654, Yinyuan, another Obaku Zen priest, came to Nagasaki in the company of some 30 Chinese disciples to be abbot of the Kōfukuji and Sōfukuji (Baroni 2000, pp. 35–6, 45).

41. Baroni 2000, pp. 180–8.

Eyes and Ears of Ieyasu: Ogasawara Ichi'an

1. Shimizu 1984, p. 413.

2. Bishop Cerqueira in a letter dated 10 March 1606 (JapSin 21 I, f. 95r). I am grateful to Ms. Madalena Ribeiro for letting me copy me her flawless transcription of this hard-to-read letter on 28 July 2008.

3. See: Earns 1987.

4. Shimizu 1977, 1984, p. 409.

5. Shimizu 1984, p. 410.

6. *Ibid*. Although I have not been able to locate this particular phrase in SHJ Cocks' diary, it is clear that he uses the two terms interchangeably.

7. Cf. Shimizu 1984, p. 425.

8. The best example is the document addressed to *Nagasaki Gobugyōsho Sama* by the interpreter Kichibei in Kan'ei 4.06.29 (Ōmura Shiryōkan, ms. no. H-122-1).

9. Gonoi 1972, p. 39; Nakada in *NKS taigai kōshōhen*, p. 88, has 250,000 *kin*.

10. Gonoi 1972, p. 39.

11. Nakada 1983a, p. 10.

12. Etchū 1978b, p. 59.

13. Tsang 2007, pp. 201–222.

14. There even seem to have been marriage relations between the house of the Shinshū Ogasawara and that of the Kyoto merchant Chaya Shirōjirō Kiyosuke (?–1596), who himself was descended from a vassal of that branch of the Ogasawara family (Nakada 1983b, p. 10).

15. KCSF vol. 1, pp. 156–9.

16. Shimizu 1975a, pp. 67–8.

17. Shimizu 2001b, p. 35.

18. Nakada 1983b, p. 10. Nakada in *NKS taigai kōshōhen*, p. 87; Costa 2001a, p. 86.

19. Guerreiro 1930, p. 175.

20. Guerreiro 1930, pp. 175–6; Cooper 1974, p. 199.

21. Terazawa, after all, had transferred his loyalty to Ieyasu immediately upon Hideyoshi's death and he had performed important military services for him in the Kantō as well as on the battlefield of Sekigahara. See: KCSF 11, p. 42 and HD 7, p. 169.

22. Branquinho 1993, p. 96.

23. BA 49-IV-59, f. 79v; JapSin 14 I, f. 109; 34, f. 16.

24. *NKS taigai kōshōhen*, p. 85.

25. Professor Nakada's interpretation of the *itowappu yuishogaki* (cf. *NKS taigai kōshōhen*, p. 85).

26. *NKS taigai kōshōhen*, p. 85.

27. Doi 1971, p. 204.

28. Etchū 1980, p. 173. He immediately retaliated. In 1604, the Jesuits reported that Terazawa had decided that he would stop at nothing to come back into Ieyasu's graces. He ordered all the Christians of his domain in Karatsu to leave, destroyed the two churches that were left and confiscated their properties (Cieslik 1963a, p. 26).

29. Schütte 1971a, p. 30.

30. Francisco de Morales wrote in 1620: "[Tōan] corrió en paz con sus riquezas y oficio por espacio de 14 años favorecido del emperador y de los tonos principales de Japón" (Muñoz 1967, p. 46), which, in view of the loss of his position as *daikan* in 1617, would indicate again that Tōan only from 1603 onwards had had any official function.

31. Cooper 1974, p. 197.

32. Gonoi 2002, pp. 362–3.

33. Shimizu 1975a, p. 68.

34. *Ibid.*, p. 74.

35. Nakada 1979, p. 47.

36. TJ, vol. 1: p. 81. At the same time, Okuyama Shichi'emon from Ōmura and Yatsuyama Tō'emon from Satsuma were appointed *chōshiyaku*.

37. Shimizu 1984, p. 413.

38. Boxer 1968, p. 50.

39. BA 49-V-5, f. 54v.

40. *Itowappu yuisho*, DNS 12-2, p. 229, quoted in Shimizu 1977a, p. 275. Also in *Tsūkō ichiran* 153, p. 247, where it is said that this document was addressed to Takagi Sakuemon.

41. Shimizu 1977b, p. 32.

42. Etchū 1980, p. 174.

43. Shimizu 1984, p. 414.

44. Cerqueira 10 March 1606 in JapSin 21 I, f. 95r.

45. Cf. *Nagasaki o-kura-iri kae-chi no mokuroku koto* printed in *Ōmura shishi*, vol. 1, pp. 71–2.

46. *Ibid.*: Nishimura, Kitamura, Azebettō, Hokamemura, Part of Ienomura. Matsuda 1970, pp. 134–5 has: Nishi Urakami, Koba, Kitamura, Ienomura, and Nishimura.

47. In the summer of 1605, Yoshiaki wrote letters back to his domain ordering his retainers not to go to church and to stay away from the priests (JapSin 21 I, f. 95v; Yūki 1984a, p. 11).

48. Bishop Cerqueira wrote, in 1606, that he had tried a last-minute effort to have Yoshiaki renounce his rights to Sotomachi to the *machidoshiyori* of Nagasaki in exchange for a certain fixed income, but that Yoshiaki had reneged on his agreement and had demanded the return of the document he had already signed (JapSin 21 I, f. 96v).

49. In a letter to Pasio of that date, Yoshiaki ordered him to recall all the padres and brothers from Ōmura (Schütte 1968, p. 184). The reason he gave was that he had been ordered to eradicate Christianity from his fief by Tokugawa Ieyasu (Yūki 1984a, p. 16; Fujiwara 1990, p. 69). Pasio says that when Tokugawa Ieyasu heard what had happened at Ōmura, he was annoyed, for when he himself had earlier requested Yoshiaki to abandon Christianity he had been refused, but now he had done so because of a simple grudge against the Jesuits (Pacheco 1966, p. 14).

50. Pacheco 1965, p. 34.

51. The first to introduce Jōdo Buddhism into the Ōmura domain was an ex-follower of Katō Kiyomasa, the monk Shaku Dōkan (Kojima 1991, p. 153).

52. When Kato Kiyomasa heard about Yoshiaki's apostasy, he sent a Nichiren priest with the request that "because they were already political allies, they might also become religious allies." (Pacheco 1966, p. 14). Yoshiaki accepted his offer and ordered work started on the first Nichiren temple, the Honkyōji, to be built in his domain (Kojima 1991, p. 152).

53. Pasio 12 February 1607, quoted in Yūki 1984c, p. 44; also Yūki 1984a, pp. 2, 17.

54. JapSin 14, I, 152r–153r.

55. It is doubtful, for example, that expressions such as "the Society did not intervene" or "the church did not intervene or bear any responsibility at all in this matter" were used in the original Japanese document. That the original is likely to have mentioned João Rodrigues by name (instead of "the Society" or "the Church") may be concluded from two other letters, one by Honda Masazumi and the other by Okamoto Daihachi, which are preserved with the letter written by Ichi'an and both absolve Rodrigues by name. Only the letter by Okamoto, himself a Christian, uses the expression "the Church."

56. Rodrigues' involvement in the affair is also clear from Brother Gaspar Sadamatsu's accusation, mentioned by Mateo de Couros in 1612: "Brother Gaspar was the first to tell Ōmura-dono how in Nagasaki, on the orders of Father Francisco Pasio, Father João Rodrigues, the Interpreter, drew a map of the same city in order to give to the Lord of the Tenka, with the intention that he should take over for himself part of the same city which belonged to Ōmura-dono because it would be better administered if he possessed it all" (Cooper 1974, p. 209). Noting that Brother Gaspar was a native from Ōmura, Cooper draws the exact opposite conclusion from the one presented here).

57. More smoke was produced on 20 February 1607, when the Jesuits held an inquiry rigged to "prove" that they had not been involved in the transfer (cf. Yūki 1984c). Nine "trustworthy" witnesses were asked to confirm or deny 8 propositions that were formulated in such a way that any witness could exculpate the Society without lying. Seven (six of them Jesuits: two padres and four brothers) of the witnesses confirmed all eight statements exculpating the Jesuits. Jeronimo Takashima refused to confirm two of the propositions and João Machida refused to confirm four of them.

The two machidoshiyori agreed in their refusal to confirm proposition no. 6: "If it was not a falsehood that the Society of Jesus had sent a map depicting Nagasaki and the town of Ōmura Yoshiaki. Not in this case nor in any other case have we ever given any map of this town or of the territory of Ōmura Yoshiaki either to the shogun or anyone else." Note that the proposition does not say: 1. if such a map existed; 2. if anyone could have copied it. That the inquiry was rigged is also evident from the fact that the main person involved, João Rodrigues, was not called as a witness even though he was in the area, for two-and-a-half months later he accompanied Vice-provincial Pasio to Ieyasu, leaving Nagasaki on 5 May 1606.

Anti-Christian Cabal:
The Hasegawa Siblings

1. Etchū 1980, p. 174.
2. TJ 2, p. 140; KCSF vol. 13, p. 124. Shimizu 2001b, p. 32.
3. Earns 1979, p. 16.
4. KCSF vol. 13, p. 124.
5. Shimizu 2001b, p. 35.

6. Shimizu 1984, p. 425. Shimizu 2001b, p. 35
7. Written with the characters 相役 (the same word written with the characters 雑役 means "odd-job man").
8. Itowappu go-yuisho cited in Shimizu 1977b, p. 31. It was transported overland from Nagasaki to Kokura. From there, Ieyasu ordered the daimyo of Higo, Hosokawa Etchū no kami, to transport the silk by boat to Fushimi (Nagasaki shohatsusho, quoted in Shimizu 1975b, p. 63).
9. Shimizu 1975b, p. 64.
10. Shimizu 1977b, p. 32. The daimyo themselves knew that they had to tread carefully where foreign ships were concerned, and thus they allowed the Nagasaki Governor to interfere in their domains' internal affairs where these matters were concerned.
11. The 1606 order does not seem to have been limited to Chinese ships, for the Dutch ships which arrived in Hirado in 1609 were also forced to hand over a list of the cargo to the Nagasaki Governor (Shimizu 1977b, p. 33). In 1613, however, the Dutch were free to unload their cargo in Hirado without notifying the Bakufu officials in Nagasaki.
12. Shimizu 1984, p. 414.
13. Shimizu 2001b, p. 39.
14. Cf. Ōsaka Tōjinki, Keichō 19.11.27, quoted in DNS 12–16, p. 412.
15. KCSF 13, pp. 124–5.
16. Shimizu 2001b, p. 39.
17. Letter by Organtino Gnecchi Soldo 28 March 1607, JapSin 14, 278v.
18. Cooper 1974, p. 253.
19. BA 49-IV-59, f. 385r: apart from Ichi'an, the visit is said to have been arranged with the help of "o principal Gouvernador desta cidade." It is clear who is meant here for the only person in Nagasaki who was more of a "principal gouvernador" than Ichi'an himself was Murayama Tōan, who governed a greater number of streets in Sotomachi than Ichi'an did in Uchimachi.
20. Shimizu 1984, p. 425.
21. Ibid.
22. Earns 1979, p. 16. It is not clear if the four men traveled together as a group.
23. In 1603, Hasegawa Sahyōe lost his heir, Matashirō, whom he had adopted from the Chaya family. Matashirō originally was the second son of Chaya Kiyonobu (who died 1596). Because his older brother died, Ieyasu ordered him to return to the Chaya family and continue its line (Nakada 1983b, p. 11).
24. I.e., Keichō 11.07.26 (KCSF 13, p. 124). TJ (vol. 1, p. 414) calls him the Nagasaki bugyō at the time of his death.
25. BA 49-IV-59, f. 319, cited in Costa 2001b, p. 88.
26. Boxer 1963, p. 70; Pacheco 1993, p. 341.
27. Sugidani 1993, p. 229.
28. Doi 1971, p. 207.
29. Gonoi 1972, p. 58.
30. Earns 1979, pp. 14, 27, n.2.
31. Shimizu 1975a, p. 70.
32. However, as Shimizu 1975a, pp. 70–1 has already pointed out there is no evidence that "Murayama Tōan, who shared tax collecting responsibilities in Nagasaki with Ichi'an, was called to Sunpu as well, so this remains rather difficult to understand."
33. Shimizu 1975a, pp. 71–2. From this time on, the finances of the city were entrusted to the machidoshiyori (NPL Machidoshiyori yuishogaki, quoted in Shimizu 1975a, pp. 70–1).
34. Chayake kyūki, the diary of Chaya Shirōjirō, quoted in Shimizu 1975a, p. 73.
35. TJ vol. 1, p. 99, lists Sahyōe's appointment under 1603, which is clearly a mistake, because it also lists Ichi'an's appointment for "that year's [1603] spring" (p. 81).

36. Cooper 1974, p. 23.
37. On the Nishi family, see Hesselink 2015.
38. Avila Girón, Escorial ms, f. 191v.
39. In the summer of 1618, in Tōan's most desperate hour while the Bakufu was deliberating his fate, the 46 *otona* of *sotomachi* sent a petition to Edo on Tōan's behalf. The document arrived too late to have any effect, but its existence alone testifies to Tōan's exceptional political ability of having made friends with all the *otona* in his jurisdiction.
40. The standard work on the journey is still Wieder 1923–5.
41. On Adams, see: Rundall 1850.
42. Cf. Van Opstall 1972, p. 137.
43. Hesselink 1984, p. 14.

The Last Conquistador: André Pessoa

1. Bishop Cerqueira, letter 9 October 1609, RAH 9/2666, f. 309r.
2. André Pessoa (1560–1610) was born the son of Lorenzo Pessoa and Francisca Calado at Azambuja, on the Tejo, district of Lisbon. From 1577 on, he served as a soldier in the Indies and on the Azores (Boxer 1951, pp. 269–71, cited in Gonoi 1976, p. 344).
3. Scribe of the Portuguese fortresses at Hurmuz and Malacca (AGS, *Secretarias Prouinciales*, libro 1458, no. 36, 1 February 1591).
4. "estar oje com a falla quasi perdida com se nelle enxerga por causa das feridas que teue na terçeira" (*ibid.*).
5. Boxer 1968, pp. 52–3, without giving a source, writes that he bought the patent for 41,000 *serafines*.
6. Rodrigues Giram March 1610, quoted in Gonoi 1972, p. 53.
7. Boxer 1929, 1951, pp. 270–1; Alden 1996, p. 133.
8. Cieslik 1974, p. 3. Gonoi 1976, p. 303 has 29 June; Boxer 1963, p. 72 has July. All of these may be correct depending on what one calls "arrival" (being first sighted, appearing at the entrance of Nagasaki Bay, dropping anchor inside the bay etc.).
9. Nakada in *NKS taigai kōshōhen*, p. 91.
10. Kojima 1991, p. 197.
11. Gonoi 1972, p. 53; Innes 1980, p. 259.
12. Gonoi 1972, p. 53.
13. 50,000 taels (*ryō*), cf. Rodrigues Giram February 1610, quoted in Gonoi 1972, p. 54.
14. Gonoi 1972, p. 57.
15. Cooper 1974, p. 262.
16. Van Opstall 1972, p. 142.
17. Boxer 1951, p. 272, gives a translation of the order.
18. Doi 1971, p. 210. Nine years later, Mateo de Couros would write that it had been Murayama Tōan who had persuaded Sahyōe to convince Ieyasu to order Arima to attack and take Pessoa's ship (Alvarez-Taladriz 1966a, p. 95).
19. Gonoi 1972, p. 58.
20. Ooms 1985, p. 73.
21. Hori 1964, p. 138.
22. *Ibid.*
23. *Nagasaki itsuji* in *Razan sensei bunshū*, 1918, p. 246.
24. *Ibid.*
25. Rodriguez Giram, March 1610, cited in Gonoi 1972, p. 58. Hayashi Razan mentions the same date for Hasegawa's order to attack the ship (*Razan sensei bunshū* 1918, p. 247).
26. Gonoi 1972, p. 58.
27. Schilling and Lejarza 1935, p. 125.
28. Yūki 2001, pp. 26–7.
29. Schilling and Lejarza 1935, pp. 124–5.
30. KCSF 13, pp. 124–5.
31. Schilling and Lejarza 1935, pp. 125–7.

32. *Nagasaki itsuji* in *Razan sensei bunshū*, 1918, p. 247. Similar figures are mentioned in TJ 1, p. 501.
33. According to Afonso de Lucena this figure included the loss at 3,000 piculs of raw silk, worth about 700,000 cruzados, and 300,000 cruzados in silver (quoted in Gonoi 1972, p. 55). According to TJ (vol. 1, p. 501), all that was saved was "3000 kin of silk and 5000 miscellaneous small boxes which had been stored in the churches of Nagasaki."
34. Innes 1980, p. 261. According to Mateo de Couros, Murayama Tōan was in a position to enrich himself with the merchandise, already brought ashore, of those Portuguese who perished with Pessoa (Alvarez-Taladriz 1966a, p. 95).
35. *Ibid.*
36. Boxer 1963, pp. 78–9.
37. Curtin 1984, p. 3; see also: Hesselink 2012, pp. 2, 30–1, n. 140.
38. One for Cambodia and one for Vietnam, in 1613 (TJ 1, p. 608; Shimizu 2001b, pp. 33–4), and possibly two others in 1615 and 1616 (Iwao 1958, chart p. 220). After Ieyasu's death she had to leave Court and retired to Nakano, where she lived as the nun Sei'un'in with an income of 500 *koku* (TJ 2, p. 98). Later she was given a residence near the third moat of Edo Castle, which she left again for a house in Koishikawa (Peri 1923, p. 53). She died at the advanced age of 80 in 1660 (Earns 1979, p. 27, n. 13).
39. JapSin 36, f. 14, cited in Costa 2001b, p. 91. 10 July 1611: A junk leaving Macao for Nagasaki is wrecked off the coast of Fujian and the survivors are killed by the Chinese (JapSin 15 I, f. 193; also 100v, cited in Costa 2001b, pp. 90–1). Among them was Padre Rui Barreto (Schütte 1968, p. 343).
40. Boxer 1963, p. 79.
41. Costa 2001b, p. 91.
42. RAH, Cortes 9/2666, ff. 267–70, cited in Costa 2001b, p. 91.
43. Boxer 1963, p. 80.
44. Costa 2001b, p. 91.
45. Takeno 1969, p. 23, gives these figures as respectively 14,000 *kin* and 20,000 *kin*.
46. Letter of Valentim Carvalho dated January 1615, quoted in Gonoi 1972, p. 52.
47. The export of *haifuki-gin* had already been forbidden on Keichō 14.09.30 (27 October 1609), cf. Taya 1984, pp. 445–6, quoting *Tōdaiki*. *Haifuki* silver was obtained by the use of bone ashes to separate lead from silver when smelting the ore.
48. Gonoi 1972, p. 47.
49. JapSin 35, f. 8, cited in Costa 2001b, p. 91.
50. JapSin 15 II, f. 240, cited in Costa 2001b, p. 92.
51. Boxer 1963, p. 82.
52. Shimizu 1972b, p. 64, quoting the *Tōdaiki* (Keichō 18.08.04). TJ 1, p. 629, mentions the same under the entry for 20 September 1613, which is possibly the day that the news reached Sunpu.

Part Three: Forging a Yamato Soul

The Second Prohibition: Tokugawa Ieyasu

1. Matos 1616, f. 35r–v.
2. JapSin 16 I, f. 49; also quoted, slightly differently, in a letter by Gabriel de Matos on 21 March 1614 (JapSin 16 II, f. 56r). Also in: Matos 1616, ff. 35r–v.
3. JapSin 16 II, f. 56v.
4. Matos 1616, ff. 38v–39r.
5. *Ibid.*, f. 38v. Later, after his death, Francisco Pacheco would give Sahyōe his due, calling him "the author and origin of this persecution" (letter of 5 March 1618, JapSin 36, f. 114r).

6. Farrington 1991, p. 1520; SHJ Cocks' Diary, p. 152.
7. DNS 12–13, pp. 190–1, quoting *Ikoku nikki.* See also: Takagi 2004, p. 65.
8. *Ibid.*
9. DNS 12–13, p. 189, quoting *Sunpuki.*
10. *Tsuihō sōbugyō,* see DNS 12–13, p. 191, quoting *Ikoku nikki.*
11. DNS 12–13, p. 189, quoting *Tōdaiki.*
12. Matos 1616, f. 42r–v.
13. KCSF vol. 11, p. 381.
14. For holidays celebrated in Christian Nagasaki, see RAH 9/7236, ff.56v–57v.
15. Higashibaba 2000, p. 47.
16. Avila Girón mentions this holiday (Schilling and Lejarza 1934, p. 264), which was promulgated by the newly arrived Bishop Cerqueira in one of his first episcopal decrees, issued after a *consulta* held in November 1598 (Schütte 1954a, pp. 7–8). The holiday is not mentioned on the Old Church Calendar, published in Murakami 1942. It is not likely that Bishop Cerqueira performed the ritual this year, for he was in the final stage of his struggle with cancer (Cieslik 1963c, p. 58).
17. For the customs associated with Lent, see Weiser 1952, pp. 182–3.
18. On fasting in Nagasaki, see: Costa 1998, pp. 359–60.
19. Avila Girón, Escorial ms., f. 172v.
20. JapSin 35, f. 137.
21. Matos 1616, f. 39r.
22. Valignano had died in 1606 in Macao, Organtino in 1609 in Nagasaki, and Pasio in 1612 also in Nagasaki.
23. Avila Girón, Escorial ms, f. 172v.
24. Matos 1616, f. 39r; Cieslik 1963a, p. 36.
25. Pacheco 1972, p. 238. The sixty-one year old padre may have made it back to Nagasaki by the beginning of May in the certainty that he was to be expelled from Japan. In his last act of resistance, he managed to die somewhere on the beach near Fukuda or Kibachi on 4 November, a few days before he would have had to embark (Cardim 1646, pp. 41–4, pl. 9; Moran 1993, p. 19; Gonoi 2002, pp. 344–5). According to *Varones Ilustres* 1887, vol. 1, p. 363, Mesquita died on 14 November 1614.
26. DNS 12–13, pp. 432–3, quoting *Tōdaiki.*
27. TJ 1, p. 646.
28. Crasset 1689, vol. 2, book 14, p. 254.
29. They were rounded up on 25 February, and brought to Osaka the next day. They sailed on 28 February (Avila Girón, Escorial ms, f. 172v), which leaves only twelve days for the boat trip to Nagasaki and their arrival on 11 March (*ibid.,* f. 173r).
30. *Ibid.,* f. 174r.
31. Weiser 1952, p. 188.
32. Russell-Wood 1968, p. 20
33. Keichō 19.02.25, cited in Shimizu 1975b, p. 65.
34. Shimizu 1975b, p. 61.
35. DNS 12–14, p. 914, for Keichō 19.03.15, quoting *Jikei keiki.* TJ 1, p. 336.
36. Avila Girón, Escorial ms, f. 174r
37. DNS 12–14, p. 1030, quoting Colin/Pastells' *Labor Evangelica,* Lib. IV, Cap. 28.
38. Avila Girón, Escorial ms, f. 184r.

The Last Processions: Bernardo Avila Girón (2)

1. Matos 1616, p. 71v.
2. Avila Girón, Escorial ms., ff. 189r–v.
3. Matos 1616, p. 72r.
4. Matos 1616, p. 72v.
5. *Ibid.,* pp. 72v–3r.
6. *Ibid.,* pp. 73r–v.

7. Orfanel 1633, p. 29v.
8. Avila Girón, Escorial ms, ff. 192r–v.
9. *Ibid.,* f. 192v.
10. *Ibid.,* f. 192v–193r.
11. Matos 1616, p. 74r.
12. Morejón 1619, p. 292.
13. Matos 1616, p. 74v.
14. Morejón 1619, pp. 291–2.
15. Cf. Avila de Girón, Escorial ms., f. 185r.
16. *Ibid.,* ff. 185r–v.
17. *Ibid.,* f. 185v.
18. Avila Girón, Escorial ms, ff. 186r–v.
19. The precise number depends on the definition of Nagasaki. By 1610, Nagasaki's Korean inhabitants, for example, had their own chapel dedicated to San Lorenzo the Spanish Martyr, with its own brotherhood (Schütte 1968, p. 743). This was located in what is now Kajiyamachi, but at the time seems to have been called Kōraimachi or Korea Town (Gonoi 2003, p. 52). There were churches (chapels?) in Urakami and other hamlets around the bay as well.
20. Etchū 1984, p. 22.
21. Kawata came to Nagasaki from Ōmura, Hirado, Saga, Karatsu, Hakata, and even as far as Sakai (Isomoto 1985, p. 53; Fujiwara 1990, p. 66).
22. Carletti, transl. Weinstock 1964, pp. 130–1.
23. Roughly up to the spot where now the Mizuho Ginkō (formerly Daiichi Kangyō) is located.
24. Pagés 1869, p. 231.
25. I.e., the Italian Pedro Paulo Navarro (1563–1622), in Japan since 1586, and since 1592 one of the three best European speakers of Japanese (cf. Schütte 1975, pp. 287, 313).
26. Dean 1999, p. 8.
27. Dean 1999, p. 7.
28. Rubin 1991, p. 246. I am grateful to Professor Frances Ramos for pointing this reference out to me on 21 November 2004.
29. Rubin 1991, pp. 250–1.
30. Avila Girón, Escorial ms., ff. 188r–189r.
31. *Ibid.*
32. *Ibid.*
33. *Ibid.,* fol. 189r. Matos 1616, p. 76r.
34. See Dean 1999, passim.
35. Hesselink 2004, pp. 186–7.
36. For the idea of "spiritual conquest," see for example Ricard 1933.

The City Occupied: Yamaguchi Naotomo

1. Morejón 1619, p. 294.
2. Morejón 1619, pp. 295–6, with a few modernizing modifications.
3. KCSF 4, pp. 325–7.
4. Crasset vol. 2, Book 14, p. 275. Also in: DNS 12–14, p. 928.
5. Sugidani 1993, p. 261, n. 30.
6. Avila Girón, Escorial ms. f. 193r.
7. Morejón 1619, p. 296.
8. Pagés 1869, pp. 276–7.
9. Morejón 1619, p. 296.
10. Avila Girón, JapSin. 58, f. 245r.
11. Morejón 1619, p. 297; Pagés 1869, p. 277; Boxer 1963, p. 83.
12. Its *provedor* in this year was Kusuriya Miguel.
13. Matos 1616, p. 76v.
14. João Serrão da Cunha had bought two Japan voyages in Goa in 1610 for 27,000 *pardaos serafines.* He lost out on the second voyage (1615), and fought it in court until the late 1620s, when he was instead rewarded with the governorship of the Cape Verde Islands (Boxer 1963, p. 82, idem 1968, p. 65).

15. Matos 1616, p. 77r.
16. *Ibid.*, p. 78r.
17. TJ 1, p. 667; *Tsūkō Ichiran*, vol. 5, p. 158.
18. Shimizu 1975b, p. 59.
19. TJ 1, p. 667.
20. Kojima 1991, p. 226.
21. Avila Girón, Escorial ms., f. 202r.
22. Farmer 1978, p. 238.
23. Schütte 1970, p. 3. For a description of the tabernacle see Lozoyo 1967, p. 30.
24. Avila Girón JapSin 58, 245r; Matos 1616, p. 76v. For some reason, *Tsūkō Ichiran* has 27 August 1614 (Kan'ei 19.07.22), but it is quoting doubtful Tokugawa sources of later date.
25. Orfanel 1633, p. 30r.
26. Orfanel 1633, p. 37r.
27. Orfanel 1633, p. 37r; Pagés 1869, p. 277.
28. Avila Girón, Escorial ms, f. 203r.
29. Matos 1616, p. 78r.
30. Avila Girón, Escorial ms, f. 203r–v.
31. DNS 12–14, p. 905. Avila Girón says they soon left for Arima (Escorial ms., f. 203v).
32. It seems that lots were drawn, cf. DNS 12–14, p. 903, quoting *Satsuma kyūki*. I have not been able to identify Iga no kami. On Keichō 19.08.12 (15 September 1614), Sahyōe wrote Shimazu Iehisa that Iga no kami could return to the domain. He would consult with the remaining Satsuma retainer in Nagasaki, Mihara Shō'emon Shigetane, in case he needed more manpower (DNS 12–14, p. 905).
33. As reported by Hasegawa Sahyōe in a letter to Shimazu Iehisa dated Keichō 19.08.08 (DNS 12–14, pp. 409–10).
34. The mail ordering them back had arrived on the night of 8 September, cf. Avila Girón, Escorial ms., f. 203v.
35. For the officials of Nagasaki's street organizations see Hesselink 2009, pp. 10, 17, notes 37 and 38.
36. Avila Girón, Jpn transl. pp. 445–6; Aduarte 1963, p. 14.
37. Avila Girón, Jpn transl. p. 447.
38. TJ 1, p. 677, entry for Keichō 19.08.24.
39. Matos 1616, pp. 78r–v.
40. Avila Girón, Jpn transl. p. 448.
41. Orfanel 1633, p. 38r.
42. *Ibid.*
43. Cieslik 1963b, p. 40; Alvarez-Taladriz 1967a, p. 88; Kataoka 1989, p. 54; Costa 1998, p. 790.
44. Gonoi 1978, p. 20. For the mendicants, see Orfanel 1633, p. 39v; Pagés 1868, vol. 1, pp. 355–6.
45. Six men in their thirties, eight in their forties, and four in their fifties, with ten men over forty-five years old. The average age of the *iruman* was forty-five (with four in their thirties, two in their forties, and one each in their sixties and seventies), cf. Gonoi 1978, p. 20.
46. Orfanel 1633, p. 38v.
47. Morejón 1619, pp. 304–5.
48. *Ibid.*, p. 305.
49. *Ibid.*, p. 305. Avila Girón, Jpn. transl. p. 450.
50. Pagés 1869, p. 283.
51. Orfanel 1633, p. 38v.
52. Avila Girón, Escorial ms. f. 208r.
53. Avila Girón, Escorial ms., f. 173r. For some reason, Avila Girón calls him the "son" of Yamaguchi Naotomo, but I have not been able to track this elusive character down in KCSF or any other Tokugawa source. He would later return again to Nagasaki in the tenth month, and presumably leave again with Yamaguchi Naotomo in the eleventh month (DNS 12–16, p. 412).
54. Orfanel 1633, p. 115v.
55. Collado 1632, p. 57.
56. Avila Girón, Escorial ms, f. 207v.
57. Shimizu 1975b, p. 60.

The Destruction of the Churches: Hasegawa Sahyōe

1. Avila Girón, Escorial ms., f. 208r; Orfanel 1633, p. 40r.
2. DNS 12–14, pp. 908–09.
3. Avila Girón, Escorial ms., f. 208r.
4. Jesuit documents use the terms São Paulo and Nossa Senhora da Assunção without ever specifying whether these are the same church or not. I conclude there was a large Assunção Church as well as a smaller chapel dedicated to St. Paul.
5. The *Kiyō zakki* (dating from 1697) has Nabeshima Shinano no kami Katsushige "burning" this church (DNS 12–14, p. 916). But Katsushige was preparing to participate in the siege of Osaka at this time (KCSF, vol. 13, p. 287). Similarly, several other sources have Terazawa Hirotaka "burning" churches in Nagasaki, but he was not in Kyushu either at this time (KCSF, vol. 11, p. 42). All of this gives an idea of the unreliability of these later Tokugawa sources.
6. Anno 1992, p. 174.
7. KCSF, vol. 12, p. 200.
8. Pagés says that the men from Ōmura were led by "le rénégat Jendgiro" (DNS 12–14, p. 971).
9. Schütte 1971a, p. 31.
10. Today the spot is occupied by the Nagasaki Museum for History and Culture.
11. Avila Girón, Escorial ms., f. 208v.
12. Pagés, 1869, p. 278.
13. Avila Girón, Escorial ms., f. 209r.
14. JapSin 58, f. 410, cited in Costa 2001b, p. 93.
15. Orfanel 1633, p. 39r.
16. Quoted in Colin/Pastells, vol. III, p. 418.
17. Avila Girón, Escorial ms., f. 209r.
18. Avila Girón, Escorial ms., f. 209v.
19. Orfanel 1633, p. 40v.
20. DNS 12–14, p. 908.
21. DNS 12–14, p. 1031, quoting Colin's *Labor Evangelica*.
22. On the same day, Ieyasu ordered Terazawa Hirotaka to consult with Hasegawa Sahyōe about the padres of Nagasaki, as Sūden notes down in his diary (Shimizu 1975b, p. 60). Terazawa Hirotaka had arrived in Sunpu from Edo to see Ieyasu. He was to travel on to his Karatsu fief immediately and confer with the Nagasaki *daikan* Hasegawa Sahyōe Fujihiro about the expulsion of the Bateren (TJ 1, p. 690).
23. KCSF 2, p. 342.
24. Avila Girón, Escorial ms., f. 209v.
25. Cieslik 1963b, p. 37 has Uonomachi, but in another article of the same year (Cieslik 1963c, p. 77) he opts for Furukawa-machi on the left bank, as does Miyazaki 1985, p. 40; Pacheco 1975 mentions Moto Daiku-machi as its location.
26. Ribeiro 1936, p. 49; Cieslik 1963c, p. 71.
27. The *Kiyō zakki* says that it was Matsura Iki no kami who "burned" the São Pedro church (DNS 12–14, p. 916). The bell of the Santiago church is still preserved in the Hachimangu of Takeda City in Ōita prefecture (Etchū 1978a, p. 81). Etchū conjectures that it may have been brought back to that city by Nakagawa Hisamori (1594–1653), daimyo of Oka-han. As we know that Hisamori participated in the preparations for the winter offensive against Osaka Castle and was in Osaka from the "tenth month" (November) guarding the Tenman Gate (KCSF vol. 5, p. 28; HDJ vol. 7, p. 466), his window of opportunity for having been in Nagasaki on 11 November to participate in the destruction of the Santiago church is rather small. The trip to Osaka, by boat, would have taken at the very least ten days for Hisamori and his men.
28. Orfanel 1633, p. 40v.

29. Avila Girón, Escorial ms., ff. 209v–10r.
30. There is no record in the Jesuit sources about this man. He may have been an early apostate of Chinese descent, erased from memory by his resentful Jesuit superiors.
31. Avila Girón, Escorial ms., f. 210r.
32. Avila Girón, Escorial ms., f. 208r. Persimmons were just coming in season.
33. Farrington 1991, p. 257.
34. Avila Girón, Escorial ms., f. 210r.
35. *Ibid.*
36. Pagés 1869, pp. 284–5; see also Ruiz-de Medina 1999, pp. 339–40 for the gruesome details.
37. On 14 November 1614, a message had reached Sunpu from the Nagasaki Daikan Hasegawa Sahyōe that on 27 October [09.24] Takayama Ukon Nyūdō Nanbō, Naitō Hida no kami bō, as well as more than one hundred believers in the religion of the Heavenly Lord had been exiled to Macao (TJ 1, 695: Keichō 19.10.13).
38. This may have been the content of the orders carried by the *tsukaiban* Mamiya Gonzaemon [on Keichō 19.10] to Nagasaki (DNS 12–16, p. 412).
39. TJ 1, pp. 734–6; DNS 12–16, p. 412.
40. Shimizu 1975b, p. 61.
41. Orfanel 1633, p. 50r; Earns 1979, p. 18.

An Early Apostate: Chijiwa Miguel

1. For the mission see: Abranches, Okamoto, Bernard 1942 and Cooper 2005; for an analysis of the propaganda side, see Elisonas 2007.
2. Schütte 1972, p. 129.
3. Schütte 1968, p. 743.
4. Mancio Itō (1570–1612) died on 13 November 1612 (Gonoi 2002, pp. 352–3).
5. Martinho Hara (1568–1629) died on 23 October 1629 in Macao (Alvarez-Taladriz 1974b, p. 122).
6. Julian Nakaura (1567–1633) died on 21 October 1633 in the pits in Nagasaki (Cardim 1646, pp. 201–4, pl. 74; Schütte 1968, p. 362).
7. See Elisonas 2001, 2007.
8. See genealogical chart.
9. Alvarez-Taladriz 1954, p. 90.
10. Miyazaki 2000, pp. 110–4.
11. *Ibid.*, p. 113.
12. *Ibid.*, p. 114. Dom Miguel's *alvara* can be found in ANTT, section *Chancelaria D. Sebastião e D. Henrique*, vol. 29, ff 6v–7r. For his descendance, see *Nobiliario de Portugal*, BA 50-IV-1, p. 691v.
13. Schütte 1972, p. 129.
14. Yūki 1993, pp. 339–40.
15. Cooper 1974, p. 71.
16. Miyazaki 2000, p. 117.
17. BNL 11098, f. 29v.
18. Cooper 1974, p. 71. For more information on the European leg of the trip, see also Elisonas 2007.
19. Toyama 1981, p. 187.
20. Yūki 1994.
21. Toyama 1981, p. 187.
22. Yūki 1994.
23. Schütte 1972, p. 129.
24. Miyazaki 1984, p. 25.
25. Fróis' *Historia* 5, pp. 187–8.
26. *Ibid.*, p. 188.
27. *Ibid.*
28. Gualtieri 1586. Passage translated in Harich Schneider 1973, p. 21.
29. De Sande 1590, in dialog XIV, pp. 138–9.
30. JapSin 33, f. 47r.
31. Laures 1957, pp. 29–30.
32. Miyazaki 1984, p. 25.

33. Cooper 1974, p. 80.
34. Kleiser 1938, pp. 35–6.
35. Sakamoto 1981, p. 163.
36. Schütte 1975, p. 318.
37. JapSin 12, 178r–v, quoted in Schütte 1939; also Schütte 1975, p. 290.
38. On Fabian and *Ha-Deusu*, see Elison 1973, pp. 142–84; 259–91.
39. Alvarez-Taladriz 1954, p. 87; Schütte 1972, p. 130.
40. Sakamoto 1981, pp. 159–60.
41. Miyazaki 1984, p. 28.
42. Sakamoto 1981, pp. 266–7.
43. Sakamoto 1981, p. 164.
44. Miyazaki 1984, p. 29.
45. Schütte 1972, pp. 132–3.
46. Miguel may have married a daughter of one of the branches of the Ōmura family (Miyazaki 2000, p. 111), or possibly a daughter of the Asada 浅田 retainer family. She bore him four sons: Tomanosuke, Saburōbei, Kiyo-[or Sei-?]suke, and Genba (Miyazaki 2000, p. 113).
47. Miyazaki 2000, p. 113. On the spot where Miguel and his wife may once have lived now stands the [Tarami] Kumano jinja, known locally as the Chijimiya.
48. *Ōmurake-ki*, aka *Kaden shiryō*: DNS 12–13, p. 441.
49. Miyazaki 2000, pp. 113, 117.
50. Quoted in Kojima 1991, p. 159; Miyazaki 2000, p. 119.
51. DNS 12–13, p. 441.
52. Pacheco 1965, p. 35.
53. Yūki 1990, p. 20.
54. Schütte 1972, pp. 222–3.
55. Muñoz 1967, pp. 3–4.
56. *Ibid.*
57. Schütte 1972, pp. 132–3. Ōishi 2005, pp. 63–5, connects this with a complicated plot by Yoshiaki and his chief retainer Ōmura Hiko'emon, which aimed at getting rid of Christian family members so their holdings might be confiscated.
58. Miyazaki 2000, p. 119.
59. *Ibid.*, p. 118.
60. Schütte 1972, pp. 132–3.
61. Morejón says "a few years before 1619" (quoted in Alvarez-Taladriz 1954, p. 87).
62. DNS 12–9, pp. 330–358. This is the so-called Okamoto Daihachi affair, when Ieyasu found out that Harunobu had tried to bribe Honda Masazumi's retainer Okamoto Daihachi, a Christian, to try and regain territory around Nagasaki. The ex-shogun ordered Harunobu to commit *seppuku*, and had Daihachi burned alive. The affair caused the prohibition of Christianity in the Tokugawa domain (TJ 1, p. 580).
63. Miyazaki 2000, p. 118.
64. JapSin 21 I, f. 95r
65. Cf. Danvers 1896, vol. 1, pp. 196–7
66. Farrington 1991, p. 794.
67. Danvers 1896, vol. 1, pp. 196–7; Farrington 1991, pp. 224–8.
68. Farrington 1991, p. 257.
69. Schütte 1972, pp. 134–5.
70. *Ōmurake hiroku*, *Ōmurake maki* 4, quoted in Miyazaki 2000, p. 119.
71. *Nagasaki Shinbun* of 2004.02.29. Ōishi 2005.
72. Ōishi 2005, p. 83.
73. His posthumous name was Honjūin Jōan, 本住院 常安. Honjūin is also the name of the Asada family temple, the Honjūin Jishōji 本住院自證寺, cf. Ōishi 2005, p. 133.
74. There exists a manuscript *Kirishitan Kanagaki*, possibly written by Miguel (cf. Elisonas 2001, 2007, pp. 48–9).

The Taiwan Expedition: Murayama Tōan

1. SHJ Cocks' *Diary*, vol. 2, p. 66 (20 April 1617).
2. Avila Girón, Escorial ms., f. 193r.
3. Elison 1973, p. 436, translates a section of a letter by Hayashi Razan to Ishikawa Jōzan in which the ideologist mentions "a secret dispatch of soldiers and supplies." Hori 1964, p. 395 considers this information false. Kojima 1991, p. 201, however, quotes a Jesuit source saying that Tōan paid for and "sent weapons and four hundred soldiers to Osaka Castle."
4. The letter written by Hasegawa Gonroku is addressed to the *machidoshiyori* of Nagasaki and preserved at NPL. See Shimizu 2001b, pp. 44–5.
5. According to the Dominican friar Francisco Morales, Tōan "estubo en el ejercito del Emperador," i.e., was part of Ieyasu's army (Muñoz 1967, p. 46).
6. Kojima 1991, p. 243.
7. SHJ Cocks' *Diary* vol. 1, p. 105 (11 October 1615 on the Julian calendar).
8. Genna 2.09.09, printed in Murakami 1929, p. 334; Iwao 1926, p. 13.
9. *Ibid.*, p. 119.
10. Alvarez-Taladriz 1967, p. 90.
11. DNS 12–6, p. 132.
12. Kojima 1991, pp. 256–9.
13. See above An Early Apostate: Chijiwa Miguel, note 62.
14. Kojima 1991, p. 244.
15. Avila Girón quoted in Alvarez-Taladriz 1967a, p. 90.
16. I.e., 25 February 1616 on the Julian calendar (Danvers 1900, vol. 4, p. 49; Farrington 1991, p. 378).
17. Francisco Morales (shortly after 24 July 1620), printed in Muñoz 1967, pp. 45–6.
18. Kojima 1991, p. 246, quotes Cocks as giving the date of 29 March, but Cocks gives no such date anywhere. The 29th day of the 3rd month, however, corresponds to 14 May 1616. Aduarte 1963, vol. 2, p. 258, mentions 4 May 1616.
19. Aduarte 1963, vol. 2, p. 258.
20. *Ibid.*, p. 259.
21. DNS 12–26, pp. 909/53: Letter of Jacob Specx, the Dutch chief factor in Hirado at the time of Tōan's expedition, dated 15 December 1629 and addressed to the Directors of the Dutch East India Company.
22. SHJ Cocks' *Diary* vol. 1, p. 223, under 5 May 1616.
23. SHJ Cocks' *Diary* 1, pp. 260–1. The two references do not give exactly the same information, but the later entry is clearly the more coherent. It is possible that the communication Cocks received from Nagasaki was written in some kind of pidgin Portuguese that he only came to fully understand after a few days of reflection.
24. Richard Cocks to Richard Wickam (Danvers 1900, vol. 4, p. 130; Farrington 1991, p. 444).
25. Kojima 1991, pp. 248–9.
26. DNS 12–26, pp. 899–909. I am grateful to Professor Hui-Wen Koo of National Taiwan University for discussing these materials with me on 26 January 2010.
27. *Ibid.*, pp. 901–4: *Chong xiang ji* by Dong Ying-ju (cited in Kojima 1991, pp. 251–2).
28. *Ibid.*, p. 906: *Dongyong zheng wo* chapter in the *Yongchong xiaopin* by Zhu Guo-zheng.
29. *Ibid.*, pp. 901–2.
30. *Ibid.*, p. 902.
31. *Huang ming shilu* quoted in Kojima 1991, pp. 264–5.
32. DNS 12–26, p. 901: *Dongxi yangkao*.
33. *Ibid.*, p. 901; cited in Kojima 1991, p. 267.
34. Kojima 1991, pp. 274–6, believes that the fleet employed the last of the *wakō* pirates converted to Christianity.

35. DNS 12–26, p. 901; Kojima 1991, pp. 268–9.
36. *Ibid.*, p. 901; Kojima 1991, p. 269.
37. SHJ Cocks' *Diary* 2, p. 119.
38. Muñoz 1967, p. 73.
39. Even after the Taiwan expedition, Francisco de Morales estimated his fortune to be around 100,000 ducats (Iwao 1926, p. 111).

Dangerous Litigation: Murayama Tōan vs. Suetsugu Heizō

1. Alvarez-Taladriz 1966a, p. 98, quoting Mateo de Couros' letter of 23 February 1619 addressed to Luis Pinheiro, Procurador in Madrid (APT legajo 996). The certificates preserved at RAH, Cortes 567, Legajo 13, no. 27 (new no. 2679) and APT Legajo 955 are printed *ibid.* on pp. 98–100, and both dated 1 March 1618. The position of "mayor" (in Couros' letter still *otona*) was later known as *machidoshiyori*.
2. Etchū 1968, p. 9; idem 1978b, pp. 61, 63. It is not quite clear whether this occurred in 1617 or 1618. Both Takagi seem to have received clothing with the shogun's crest and bars of silver as a reward for what obviously were official apostasies (*Nagasaki machidoshiyori hattan yuisho*, which however does not specify the date, see Shimizu 1992, p. 3).
3. One of the streets built at that time, Kōzen-machi (or: Hon/Moto Kōzen-machi), was even called after him and would later form the nucleus of a whole neighborhood with streets variously known as Ura Kōzen-machi, Ushiro (or Nochi) Kōzen-machi, and Shin Kōzen-machi (not named as such until 1672, cf. Watanabe 1964, p. 338), which kept their association with the Suetsugu family. The same general area is still called Kōzen-machi today.
4. Heizō's older brother was called Sōtoku, Christian name: Jacobo (Toyama 1984, p. 77). He lived permanently in Hakata (Alvarez-Taladriz 1966a, p. 110).
5. Known as the *Suetsugu monjo*, preserved at SHJ.
6. DNS 12–32, pp. 291–2: *Kiyō kokin monogatari*.
7. DNS 12–1, p. 907, the Red-Seal letter was awarded on Keichō 9.08.26 [19 September 1604].
8. By this time, Nagasaki counted about 65 *machi*, 19 in Uchimachi and 46 in Sotomachi (and so the city had already grown to more than three quarters of the size (80 *machi*) at which it would remain for the rest of the Tokugawa period.
9. His son, Heizō II Shigesada, however became a well-known investor in the Macao-Nagasaki trade from the 1620's onwards (Oka 2001).
10. According to the *Nagasaki meika ryakufu*, cited in Alvarez-Taladriz 1966a, p. 112, n. 23, Heizō's apostasy occurred on 7 December 1616. Etchū 1980, p. 184, places it in the summer of 1616. Both of these guesses are rather too early in my opinion. A more likely date is sometime between the summer of 1617 and the summer of 1618. On the importance of such apostasies, see Hesselink 2009, p. 17.
11. Alvarez-Taladriz 1966a, p. 106.
12. DNS 12–32, p. 291.
13. I.e., the Jesuit and Dominican letters, and the diary of Richard Cocks. On 19 August 1618, Cocks noted: "Touan Dono hath lost his processe, and all his goodes confiscat, & his lyfe at Emperours pleasure." (SHJ Cocks' *Diary* vol. 2, p. 344).
14. This is a charge that also appears in Avila Girón, Escorial ms. ff. 191v–192r.
15. SHJ Cocks' *Diary* vol. 2, pp. 296–7.
16. Alvarez-Taladriz 1966a, quoting Mateo de Couros' letter of 23 February 1619.
17. Kojima 1991, pp. 283–4.
18. SHJ *Diary* vol. 2, pp. 242–3. See also a letter dated

5 March 1618 by Francisco Pacheco (1565–1626) to the General of the Society, the writer already knew the news (JapSin 36, f. 114r).

19. Alvarez-Taladriz 1966b, p. 406. When it became clear that Heizō could not come up with five thousand *ryō*, Tōan's "competitors" (says Avila Girón) put up close to 2000 *ryō* to make up the difference (*ibid.* p. 407).

20. *Ibid.*, p. 407.

21. SHJ Cocks' *Diary* vol. 2, p. 297.

22. JapSin 17 Ib, f 179v: letter from Francisco Vieira to Mutio Vetelleschi, dated 16 October 1618. On Fabian, see Ide 1966, 1973, 1974, 1977, 1997; Cieslik 1972; Elison 1973, pp. 142–84, 259–91; Sakamoto 1981; Mayer 2000.

23. JapSin 17 Ib, f 194v: letter from Francisco Vieira to Nuno Mascarenhas, dated 20 February 1619.

24. JapSin 17 Ic, f. 240r: Letter of Francisco Vieira to the General dated 23 February 1619.

25. Alvarez-Taladriz 1966a, p. 97.

26. Alvarez-Taladriz 1966b, p. 409.

27. Muñoz 1967, p. 46. A similar version is told by Avila Girón (Alvarez-Taladriz 1966b, pp. 409–9).

28. SHJ Cock's *Diary* vol. 2, p. 344.

29. That, at least, is one interpretation of the tradition in the Takagi family that, as a reward for being one of the first of Uchimachi's ruling elite to reject Christianity, Luis' son Saku'emon had received from the shogun, in September of 1618, seasonal clothing, silver, and the right to build a house on a site in Hokaura-machi that had formerly housed part of the Jesuit compound (cf. *Jōkyō Takagi Sakuemon kakiage*, in *Tsūkō ichiran* 193, vol. 5, pp. 161–2, which dates this to Genna 4.10.29 [15 December 1618], see also Etchū 1978b, p. 63.

30. Kai: Kojima 1991, p. 293, no source reference. Island: Elison 1973, p. 163, no source reference.

31. JapSin 17 Ic, f 238r: "porque hum so que bella se achasse, a Gonrocu se avia de cortar a cabeça, e a Feizō crucificar." Cf. also *Tsūkō ichiran* 193, vol. 5, p. 162.

The New Governor: Hasegawa Gonroku

1. Matos 1616, f. 2v; Pagés 1869, p. 214. At the same time, Nabeshima Katsushige was ordered to provide military assistance in case Arima retainers resisted Sahyōe's orders (Shimizu 1975b, p. 57).

2. To make things abundantly clear, Honda Masanobu wrote a *hōsho* on Keichō 19.11.27 [27 December 1614] to Ōmura Sumiyori that he was to follow Sahyōe's orders in all matters concerning the suppression of Christianity (Shimizu 1975b, pp. 60–1).

3. DNS 12–28, p. 218. See also Shimizu 2001b, pp. 41–2.

4. Sahyōe had four sons, about whom very little is known (KCSF vol. 13, pp. 124–5). They may have been born too late in his life to succeed him at the time of his death. During a visit to Hirado by Sahyōe and his brother Chūbei in October 1613, the latter wanted a monkey from the English ship "for his Brothers children." (Farrington 1991, p. 1520). After Sahyōe's death, his sister O-Natsu adopted several of his offspring. Later, Ieyasu's grandson, Iemitsu, awarded the youngest, Hachizaemon, an income of 400 *koku* in 1625 (TJ 2, p. 140).

5. Shimizu 2001b, pp. 41–2.

6. Dated 13 October 1609 [Keichō 14.09.16], cf. Shimizu 2001b, p. 43.

7. Dated 4 February 1610 [Keichō 15.01.11]: cf. Kawashima 1921, p. 87; also Shimizu 1984, p. 427.

8. *Kamiya Sōtan nikki*, entry for Keichō 17.05.08, quoted in Shimizu 2001b, p. 42.

9. Entry for Keichō 18.06.26, quoted in Shimizu 2001b, p. 42.

10. TJ 1, p. 758: Keichō 19.12.24. This is the date of an

informal notice, i.e., the date that Hidetada was informed on this day of Ieyasu's decision (Shimizu 1975b, p. 61). The official appointment occurred on the 15th day of the first month of the Japanese New Year (12 February 1615).

11. Shimizu 1975b, p. 62. In Sakai, Sahyōe was assisted by the merchant Hiranoya Tōzaemon (Massarella 1990, p. 200). Several months later, on 28 June 1615, he received another appointment, this time as *daikan* of Ozushima, an important port on the Inland Sea between Sakai and Nagasaki (TJ 2, p. 48). According to Shimizu Hirokazu, Ieyasu must have meant to accomplish more with these appointments than just the suppression of Christianity: Sahyōe was effectively given control over all the shipping between Nagasaki and Sakai along the Inland Sea in order to assure that the foreign goods brought to Nagasaki would find their way smoothly to the markets of the Kinai (Shimizu 1975b, p. 62). Sahyōe's appointment to the post of 'commissioner of shipping in Osaka' (*Osaka funabugyō*) also fits into this pattern, although the date of this appointment does not seem to be recorded anywhere (*ibid.*, p. 64). His official appointment to *bugyō* of Sakai followed on 22 June (*Sunpu nikki*, quoted in DNS 12–21, p. 167).

12. Pagés 1869, p. 319.

13. Shimizu 2001b, p. 47. For Sahyōe's final years, we are almost completely dependent on the scattered information that the English merchant Richard Cocks noted down: see SHJ Cocks' *Diary* 1, pp. 157, 251, 278, 310, 319, 345, 347, 349, 375; vol. 2, pp. 37, 54, 78, 80, 85, 138, 162, 172, 187. See also: Etchū 1980, pp. 182–3; and DNS 12–27, p. b65.

14. Pagés 1869, p. 369.

15. Hartmann 1965, p. 65.

16. Sicardo 1698, p. 154; Cieslik 1963a, p. 39.

17. DNS vol. 12–25, pp. 349–50; Shimizu 1977a, pp. 289–90.

18. Ruiz-de Medina 1999, pp. 373–4.

19. KCSF, vol. 13, p. 124, also SHJ Cocks' Diary 2, p. 203 (date according to the Julian calendar).

20. DNS 12–28, p. 214.

21. Pagés 1869, p. 386.

22. Kataoka 1989, pp. 119–20, citing *Anua* of 1615 by Mateo de Couros, dated 15 March 1616 (JapSin 58, f. 292, I have not been able to locate this reference).

23. Cieslik 1951, p. 121, no source reference.

24. Anesaki 1936, p. 19.

25. SHJ Cocks' *Diary* vol. 1, p. 33, also cited in Earns 1979, p. 18.

26. To make things even more unclear, Gonroku seems to have had a younger brother, by name of Sakichi or Sankichi, who received on 7 March 1618 in Gonroku's name a New Year's gift from Richard Cocks (SHJ Cocks' *Diary* vol. 2, p. 255. A return present arrived at the Englishman's lodgings in Nagasaki on 21 March 1618 (*ibid.*, p. 264, Julian calendar 11 March 1618).

27. Etchū 1980, p. 184.

28. This is likely to have been his eldest son Hirosada, aka Sahyōe (KCSF vol. 13, p. 125).

29. SHJ Cocks' *Diary* vol. 2, p. 246, also cited in Shimizu 2001b, p. 49.

30. Shimizu 2001b, p. 47.

31. Schütte 1975, p. 722.

32. In July 1618, the Jesuits Giovanni Matteo Adami (1576–1633), and Francisco Vieira (1555?–1619), the brothers Antonio da Ponte (?–?) and Thomas Tsuji (1571–1627) arrived in Japan from Macao (Pedro Morejón, quoted in Perez 1914, p. 41; Schütte 1968, pp. 203, 350; Gonoi 2002, pp. 358–9). The Japanese brothers Aleixo Shiga Shinji (1565–?) and Tadeu (1568–1627) arrived from the Philippines, but the first was immediately expelled from the Society (Alvarez-Taladriz 1974b, p. 127), while the second traveled on to Macao (Schütte 1968, p. 350; 1975, p. 795).

On 12 August: the Franciscans Antonio de San Buenaventura Casal (1588–1628), Diego Pardo de San Francisco (1575?–1632?) and Martin de Pineda (?–1622?) arrived in Nagasaki accompanied by the Dominicans Angel Ferrer Orsucci (1575–1622) and Juan de Santo Domingo (1587–1619) as well as the Augustinians Bartolome Gutierrez (1580–1632) and Pedro de Zuñiga (1579–1622) (cf. Perez 1914, p. 2; Uyttenbroek 1958, p. 117; Hartmann 1965, p. 77; Willeke 1990, p. 203; Ruiz-de Medina 1999, p. 447). In September, the Franciscan Francisco Galvez (1575–1623) arrived from the Philippines (Perez, Ricardo de Santa Ana 1921, p. 65).

33. Pagés 1869, p. 392.
34. Branquinho 1993, p. 97.
35. Carta de João Rodrigues Girão, BNL ms 26, no. 18, quoted in Coutinho 1999, p. 129.
36. Boxer 1963, p. 97.
37. Shimizu 1984, p. 416.
38. Pagés 1869, p. 392; Hartmann 1965, p. 77.
39. Called the *kenshōsonin* system. Kataoka 1970, p. 37; Cieslik 1963a, p. 40.
40. JapSin 17, f. 238, cited in Gonoi 1978, p. 37 (letter by Francisco Vieira, dated 15 February 1619): 30 bars of silver is "more than 120 *cruzados.*"
41. Orfanel 1633, pp. 91r–v.
42. Orfanel 1633, p. 115v.
43. Anesaki 1930, pp. 653–4, quoted in Kataoka 1963, p. 8.
44. Ruiz-de Medina 1999, p. 396. On this occasion, the Kawata of Kawaya-machi refused to have anything to do with the executions on the grounds that being a Christian is no crime (letter of the Dominican friar José Salvanez de San Jacinto, dated 25 March 1619, in Delgado 1985, pp. 44–5).
45. JapSin 17 Ic, f. 238r: letter of Francisco Vieira to Mutio Vitelleschi of 15 February 1619.
46. Alonso de Mena (1578–1622), for example, hid for two years between 1614 and 1616 in Tōan's main residence in Katsuyama-machi (Alvarez-Taladriz 1966b, p. 404) and so did Juan de Santa Maria for a while after returning to Nagasaki from the high seas in 1614 (*ibid.*, p. 409). Francisco Morales (1567–1622) hid in the house of Tōan's eldest son Toku'an (Alvarez-Taladriz 1967a, p. 98). Pedro Bautista Porres y Tamayo, the elected regional superior of the Franciscans in Japan, also hid in the same house for two years (Willeke 1990, p. 179). Shorter stays at one of the houses of the extended Murayama family are recorded for Alonso de Navarrete (1571–1617), Jacinto Orfanel (1578–1622), and Juan de los Angeles Rueda (1578?–1624).
47. JapSin 59 I, f 75v, cited in Ruiz-de Medina 1999, p. 418; Pagés 1869, p. 393.
48. See above: A King-Sized Admiral.
49. Ruiz-de Medina 1999, pp. 457–8.
50. BPE Codex CXVI 1–31, f. 85v.
51. Ruiz-de Medina 1999, p. 447.
52. Pagés 1869, p. 394.
53. *Tsūkō ichiran*, vol. 5, p. 162, quoted in Shimizu 1977, p. 292.
54. Orfanel 1633, pp. 91v–92r.
55. *Ibid.*, p. 92r.
56. Shimizu 2001b, p. 58.
57. JapSin 59 179v; Orfanel 1633, p. 100r; Kojima 1991, p. 303.
58. Alvarez-Taladriz 1967a, p. 86.
59. Letter of 16 February 1620, printed in Muñoz 1967, p. 42.
60. *Ibid.*
61. Alvarez-Taladriz 1967a, p. 98. Maria (1588–1621) was a niece and adopted daughter of Suetsugu Heizō.
62. Muñoz 1967, p. 47.

In Pursuit of Ordination: Araki Thomé

1. In 1608, his mother was living in Amakusa (JapSin. 33, f. 80).
2. Letter by Celso Confalonieri of 4 October 1613, cited in Takase 1994, p. 602.
3. Gonoi 2007, pp. 36–7.
4. Takase 1994. p. 599.
5. *Ibid.*, p. 600.
6. Pagés 1869, p. 373.
7. JapSin. 33, f. 80, printed in facsimile in Obara 1981, [p. VI]. I am grateful to Professor Gonoi for discussing this letter with me on 24 July 2007. Although Kōta Shigetomo in "Schurhammer-shi wo hou" (*Zenshū* vol. 4, pp. 477–8) pretends that this letter could be an autograph of Pasio himself, Gonoi 2007 identifies the writer as Pasio's secretary Gonzalo Fusai.
8. Schütte 1968, p. 235; Matsuda 1978, p. 225.
9. Takase 1994, pp. 599, 603.
10. For Araki's use of these names, see also Schütte 1968, p. 234; Takase 1994, p. 595.
11. AGI Indif. 1434, quoted in Gil 1991, p. 125.
12. *Ibid.*
13. JapSin 15 IIa, f. 166.
14. Cieslik 1995, pp. 279–80. I have not been able to locate this letter.
15. JapSin 16 IIa, f. 1r (Latin letter from Araki to the Pope of 3 January 1615).
16. Charlevoix, admitting the truth of Araki's allegations, reports that he informed the Japanese members of the Society in Macao that "a certain order" of Spanish friars [i.e., the Dominicans] was preparing an invasion of Japan (Charlevoix 1736, vol. 2, ch. XIV, sect. 8, p. 233).
17. Among them were Pedro Kibe, who seems to be the only one to have been supported by the Jesuits. He was ordained in Rome in 1620 (Kataoka 1979, p. 149). All others went over to the mendicants: Juan Miyazaki (?–1633) was ordained in Manila in 1619 by the Franciscans (Uyttenbroek 1958, p. 94); Luis de Santo Tomas Matsuo (?–1626) and Tomas de San Jacinto Nishi Rokuzaemon (1590–1634), both were ordained in Manila in or after respectively 1623 and in 1627 by the Dominicans (Gonoi 2002, pp. 360, 367); Vicente de la Cruz Shiozuka (1576–1637) first became a Franciscan tertiary in Manila in 1619, and a Dominican in 1636 (Gonoi 2002, pp. 362–3); Jacobo de Santa Maria Tomonaga Gorōbyōe (1582–1633) was ordained in Manila by the Dominicans in 1626 (Kataoka 1979, p. 148); Tomas de San Augustin (1602–1637) was ordained by the Augustinians in 1627 at Cebu (Kataoka 1979, p. 149).
18. Cieslik 1995, p. 280.
19. JapSin 16 I, f. 305v.
20. JapSin 17, f. l v, quoted in Takase 1994, p. 610.
21. Pagés 1869, p. 409.
22. JapSin 35, f. 137r.
23. JapSin 37, f. 70: letter by João Baptista de Baeça written on 20 October 1619.
24. JapSin 38, f. 58r.
25. Muñoz 1967, p. 171.
26. JapSin 38, f. 58r, quoted in Takase 1994, p. 611.
27. Charlevoix 1736, loc. cit.
28. Alvarez-Taladriz–1966b, p. 415.
29. Orfanel 1633, p. 97r.
30. JapSin 38, f. 58r–v, letter by Francisco Pacheco of 6 February 1620, quoted in Coutinho 1999, p. 86.
31. JapSin 35, f. 137r, letter by Mateo de Couros of 20 March 1620, quoted in Takase 1994, p. 613.
32. Orfanel 1633, p. 99v; Pagés 1869, p. 419.
33. JapSin 38, f. 58v.
34. *Ibid.* See also Charlevoix 1736, vol. 2, ch. XIV, sect. 8, p. 233; Kojima 1991, pp. 311–2 and Takase 1994, p. 613.

35. From this, it can be easily understood why later Edo period writers thought it so important to impute Tōan's appointment to Hideyoshi.

36. Elison 1973, p. 163; Kojima 1991, p. 323.

37. I.e., Domingos Jorge, Juan Yoshida, and Cosme Takeya. The fourth was the Jesuit Brother Leonardo Kimura, who had been languishing in the Nagasaki jail since 1615, and may have been so close death that it was judged better to make a public example of him now, instead of having him die an unadvertised death in jail (Pagés 1869, pp. 420–4; Ruiz-de Medina 1999, p. 418).

38. Alvarez-Taladriz 1966a, p. 101.

39. Pagés 1869, p. 436.

40. Pagés 1869, p. 416, note 1.

Changes in the City:
Hasegawa Gonroku (2)

1. Ruiz-de Medina 1999, p. 421.

2. José de San Jacinto, *Relacion Breve*, in Muñoz 1967, p. 173.

3. Shimizu 2001b, p. 58, the temple did not survive.

4. Gonoi 1978, p. 37; Etchū 1980, p. 185.

5. JapSin 59, f. 250v: *Anua* of 1620, dated Macao 10 April 1621, also cited in Rodrigues 2006, p. 105.

6. Letter by João Baptista Porro to Pedro Morejón, dated 6 October 1621, quoted in Schütte 1975, p. 906.

7. At least it was still chiming on 5 January 1616 (Pacheco 1977, p. 61).

8. It was destroyed on 12 February 1620 (Gonoi 2003, p. 52).

9. Pacheco 1977, p. 68.

10. Pacheco 1977, p. 65.

11. JapSin 35, f. 137–8: letter by Mateo de Couros dated 20 March 1620, quoted in Pacheco 1977, p. 69.

12. *Ibid.*

13. After the destruction of the Dominican church in 1614, this land had reverted to its original owner Murayama Tōan (Pacheco 1977, p. 67; Etchū 1978a, p. 137).

14. José de San Jacinto (1580–1622), quoted in Alvarez-Taladriz 1966a, p. 111, n. 21.

15. JapSin 34, f. 178r (see also: Pacheco 1972, pp. 250–1; Gonoi 1981, p. 4; Miyazaki 1985, p. 34). Where once the leper's hospital stood in Urakami, now stands Sanō jinja 三王神社 in Sakamoto-machi (Pacheco 1977, p. 64).

16. NMM Ms *Yoriai machi yuisho oboegaki*. Also: *NSS Butsujibu* 1, p. 82; Etchū 1980, pp. 173,181; Hesselink 2004, p. 202.

17. *NSS Butsujibu* 1, p. 83.

18. It became a branch temple of Chion'in (Etchū 1998, pp. 39–40). It was moved in 1648, after the Kawata had been removed from the general area of Kawaya machi (Fujiwara 1990, p. 73).

19. Cf. also: Etchū 1984, p. 17.

20. Orfanel 1633, p. 134r.

21. *Ibid.*

22. Both Nichi'e and Denyo (together with three other priests) are known as *Kirishitan taiji gosō* or "Five Priests Exterminators of Christianity," who are supposed to have planned, coordinated, and executed the "conquest" of Christianity in Nagasaki. This, once more, is a legend dating from the second half of the Tokugawa period.

23. Etchū 1998, p. 42.

24. It is said that because Nichi'e was brought up by Katō Kiyomasa's mother, who had retired as Seirin'in, he named his temple after her and enshrined in it a statue he had carved of her.

25. Delgado/Sakuma 1976, p. 70; Orfanel 1633, p. 106r.

26. Letter of Richard Cocks in Nagasaki to Sir Thomas Wilson in London, dated 10 March 1620 (Farrington 1991, p. 780).

27. This establishment, when it took shape in the 1630s and 1640s, became what we now know as Tōshō (or: Light Shining in the East)-worship, which enshrined Tokugawa Ieyasu as its main deity. Later, a *massha* or branch shrine dedicated to this deity was added to the Suwa shrine, but it is no longer known at what time this occurred (*NSS Jinja Kyōkai-bu*, vol. 1, p. 344).

28. Etchū 1998, p. 39.

29. Cf. *NSS Butsujibu*, 2 vols.

30. I.e., the change from a 10-family system (*jūningumi*) to a 5-family (*goningumi*) system, the temple registration system, and the *fumie* system all originated in Nagasaki.

31. BPE, codex CXVI-1-31, ff. 71–71v.

32. *Tratado dos gloriosos martyres*, BPE Codex CXVI 1-31, f. 71v; Kataoka 1963, p. 9 mentions 1622 as the year of the reduction.

33. Anesaki 1930, pp. 653–4, quoted in Kataoka 1963, p. 8.

34. This is the conclusion drawn in Earns 1979. It may also be an indication of Gonroku's original *chōnin* upbringing.

35. Higashibaba 2001, p. 143.

The Summer of 1622: Bento Fernandes

1. Pagés 1869, pp. 495–6.

2. On 22 July 1620, Pedro de Zuñiga and Luis Flores were arrested off Taiwan by the *Elisabeth*, an English ship, later commandeered by the Dutch, who triumphantly turned ship, cargo, crew and passengers over to the Bakufu. Although bound for Nagasaki and with a crew based in the city, the case mainly played out in Hirado where the prisoners were kept. It seems to have especially angered Hidetada, when he was told that another Dominican, Diego Collado, had tried to free the two friars from their captivity (see: Hartmann 1965, pp. 82–95; Ruiz-de Medina 1999, p. 440; Gonoi 2002, p. 361).

3. The Japanese Jesuits, such as Nakaura Julian, are also likely to have attended in disguise. If they wrote any accounts in Japanese, these have not survived. Printed accounts can be found in: *Relacion breve* 1624, a Jesuit pamphlet in Spanish (RAH Cortes 566, f. 378v–379r); Garces 1624, pp. 7r–19v and 43–45r, in Spanish; a Dominican *Relacion Verdadera* 1624 in Spanish; (Dominican) Carrero 1626, reprint 1868, pp. 245–7 in Spanish; (Dominican) Orfanel 1633, pp. 166r–177v in Spanish; Gysbertsz 1637, pp. 4–6 in Dutch, may also be based on an eyewitness account; (Jesuit) Crasset 1689, vol. 2, pp. 369–90 in French is also likely to be derived from an eyewitness account. There may have been eyewitness accounts in English as well, although I have not been able to locate any.

4. Bowersock 1995, pp. 72–3.

5. *Ibid.*, pp. 4, 18, 20.

6. A recent book analyzes the task of the spy as follows: "For the task of the spy is not so very different from that of the novelist: to create an imaginary, credible world and lure others into it by words and artifice" (Macintyre 2010, p. 63).

7. See JapSin 60, ff. 221–256v; BPE Codice CXVI-1-31.

8. Franco 1714, p. 256.

9. DNS 12-35, p. b74; Ruiz-de Medina 1999, 713.

10. Schütte 1975, p. 1169.

11. *Ibid.*, p. 453.

12. *Ibid.*, p. 491.

13. *Ibid.*, p. 502.

14. *Ibid.*, p. 507. The brother would later be dismissed from the Society (Schütte 1968, p. 344).

15. Schütte 1975, p. 557. The other adviser was Christovão Ferreira.

16. Yūki 1997, p. 60.
17. Schütte 1975, p. 595.
18. *Ibid.*, p. 580.
19. *Ibid.*, p. 423.
20. Yūki 1997, p. 60.
21. *Ibid.*, p. 61.
22. JapSin 35, ff. 155–6 (letter by Fernandes from Miyako to Antonio Mascarenhas, dated 6 February 1606).
23. APT, E-2: 103–7–8.
24. Schütte 1975, p. 772.
25. Yūki 2003, p. 3.
26. Schütte 1975, pp. 815, 831.
27. Yūki 1997, p. 61.
28. Ruiz-de Medina 1999, p. 713.
29. Yūki 1997, p. 54
30. JapSin. 60, ff. 242v–249r in Portuguese (dated 16 December 1622).
31. *Tratado dos gloriosos martyres*, BPE Codex CXVI 1–31, ff. 45r–92r in Portuguese (dated 3 August 1623).

Japanese Padre: Kimura Sebastião

1. His Korean name has not been transmitted. Fernandes mentions that his Japanese name was Genzaemon (cf. *Tratado dos gloriosos martyres*, BPE Codex CXVI 1–31, f. 67r). According to Francisco Carrero 1868, p. 246, Antonio was 40 years old at the time of his execution.
2. BPE Codex CXVI 1–31, f. 67r.
3. For Korean Christians in Japan, see: Ruiz de Medina 1987, 1988, and Gonoi 2003. For a similar strategy of the Jesuits in the New World, see Reff 1991.
4. *Tratado dos gloriosos martyres*, BPE Codex CXVI 1–31, f. 67v.
5. JapSin 34, f. 179r: Leonardo Kimura mentions Hama-no-machi Antonio in his letter from the Cruzmachi jail dated 25 October 1619 (Miyazaki 1985, p. 35).
6. *Tratado dos gloriosos martyres*, BPE Codex CXVI 1–31, f. 67v.
7. *Ibid.*, f. 70r.
8. *Ibid.*
9. *Ibid.*, f. 67r.
10. Farmer 1978, p. 321.
11. Farmer 1978, pp. 314–5.
12. Cf. the Christian calendar in RAH 9/7236, ff. 56v–57v.
13. *Tratado dos gloriosos martyres*, BPE Codex CXVI 1–31, f. 67v.
14. *Ibid.*
15. *Ibid.*
16. Cieslik 1963a, p. 5.
17. *Ibid.*, p. 9.
18. *Ibid.*, p. 11.
19. *Ibid.*, p. 12; Yūki 2001, p. 32.
20. Cieslik 1963a, p. 12
21. Yūki 2001, p. 4.
22. Yūki 2001, p. 32.
23. Yūki 2001, p. 14; Cooper 1974, p. 108 gives March 1596 as the departure date of the group.
24. Yūki 2001, p. 32.
25. Sebastião Kimura was ordained on 21 September 1601 (Ruiz-de Medina 1999, p. 449).
26. Cieslik 1963a, p. 24.
27. Gonoi 2002, p. 364.
28. Cieslik 1963a, p. 24.
29. *Ibid.*, p. 26.
30. *Ibid.*, pp. 28–37.
31. Alvarez-Taladriz 1966a, p. 94.
32. Cieslik 1963a, p. 42.
33. JapSin 60a, f. 30r.
34. *Ibid.*
35. Yūki 2001, p. 8.

36. *Tratado dos gloriosos martyres*, BPE Codex CXVI 1–31, f. 68r.
37. *Ibid.*, f. 70r.
38. *Ibid.*, f. 70r.
39. *Ibid.*, f. 70v.

The Ten-Family System: Hama-no-machi Antonio

1. *Tratado dos gloriosos martyres*, BPE Codex CXVI 1–31, f. 72v.
2. *Ibid.*, f. 73v.
3. Bertolomeu had another son, called Pedro six years old, who was executed on 11 September, the day after his father had been beheaded, likely because he had been forgotten on the day before (Ruiz de Medina 1999, p. 465).
4. *Tratado dos gloriosos martyres*, BPE Codex CXVI 1–31, f. 74r.
5. *Ibid.*
6. *Ibid.*, f. 70r.
7. *Ibid.*, f. 74v.
8. *Ibid.*
9. He was among those arrested off Taiwan on 22 July 1620 by the *Elisabeth*.
10. Schütte 1968, p. 316.
11. *Tratado dos gloriosos martyres*, BPE Codex CXVI 1–31, f. 75r.
12. *Ibid.*, ff. 75v–76r.
13. *Tratado dos gloriosos martyres*, BPE Codex CXVI 1–31, f. 76r–v.
14. *Ibid.*, f. 76v.
15. *Ibid.*
16. *Ibid.*, f. 77r.
17. *Ibid.*, f. 77v.
18. *Ibid.*, f. 77v–78r.
19. *Ibid.*, f. 78r.
20. *Ibid.*, f. 79r.
21. *Ibid.*
22. *Ibid.*
23. *Ibid.*, f. 71v.
24. Orfanel/Collado 1633, p. 163v.
25. See also Garces 1624, p. 44v.
26. An earlier arrest in this same street had produced only two martyrs who could have saved their lives by apostatizing, Chū João and Itō Takasō João (cf. JapSin 34, f. 82r; Ruiz de Medina 1999, p. 431).
27. This is the reason why we do not have the names of these other streets. The *kumi* of Murayama Tokuan André, Takeya Cosme, and Yoshida Shōun João (all executed on 18 November 1619, cf. Ruiz de Medina 1999, pp. 418–9) produced only martyrs from twelve different households (out of a total of thirty), or an average of four households per *kumi*, i.e., only 40 percent. Some of these martyrs were also executed on 10 September 1622 (others had already been executed on 27 November 1619, cf. Ruiz de Medina 1999, pp. 419–21).
28. Potter 1993, p. 64.
29. This is the kind of "triumph" referred to in the title of Carrero 1868.

The Corral of the Martyrs: Sukedayu

1. *Tratado dos gloriosos martyres*, BPE Codex CXVI 1–31, ff. 88r–v.
2. Bowersock 1995, p. 59.
3. Size: 135 by 155 cm. See *Dai Zabieru Ten*, no. 133, p. 109.
4. Possible candidates are Niwa Jacobo (1579–1638), cf. McCall 1948, p. 56; Tadeu of Usuki (1568–1627); and Pedro João from Kuchinotsu (1566–?), all active in Macao in the early 1620's.

5. See Sakamoto 2008, pp. 20 (panel 1), 30 (right wing, panel 2), 138 (panel 1), 135 (right wing, panels 2 and 6), 252 (panel 1). Even today Christian women in Nagasaki still wear elaborate lace veils over their hair when they go to mass, as I was able to observe in the company of Geoffrey and Naoko Tudor during Easter mass in the Urakami Cathedral in 2000.

6. Out of the devastation of the area caused by the atomic bomb, dropped over Urakami on 9 August 1945, the Catholic Church was able to purchase the site of the execution grounds during the days after World War II. Today the site houses a church, a monument to the first martyrs executed there in 1597, and a small museum dedicated to Christianity in Japan.

7. *Tratado dos gloriosos martyres,* BPE Codex CXVI 1–31, ff. 90r.

8. JapSin 60, f. 247r.

9. According to the *KD* vol. 10, p. 580.

10. We see, for example, the *mitsuboshi kamon* (three-dot family crest) of the daimyo of Hirado on the *maku* (curtains) of two of the boats on the lower left. Fernandes writes: "the soldiers from Hirado … came by boat and thirty lancers jumped ashore to guard [the corral] on this side, while those from Ōmura did the same on the mountainside. In this way, [the corral] was like fortress completely surrounded by armed soldiers." (JapSin 60, f. 246v–7r).

11. E.g., Potter 1993.

12. Foucault 1977, p. 50.

13. Gysbertsz 1637, p. 4.

14. *Ibid.*

15. For their names see Ruiz de Medina 1999.

16. From left to right, [the numbering is mine:] 1. *fr. Ant.o Catodo* [Sanga Antonio, 1569–1622], dressed in black; 2. *Paulo casero do P.e frei Joseph* [Tanaka Paulo Ri'emon, 1576–1622] dressed in white; 3. *Ant.o casero do P.e Sebastião* [Antonio Korea, 1582–1622], dressed in black; 4. *Lucia casera do P.e fr. Ricardo* [Lucia de Fleites, 1584–1622, a Franciscan tertiary], dressed in dark grey; 5. *P. Carlos de Espinola da Comp.a de Jesus* (1565–1622), dressed in black; 6. *P.e frei Angel Ferrer do ordo pre*[dicatore]*s* [Angel Ferrer Orsucci,1575–1622], dressed in white; 7. *P.e frei Ioseph de San Jassinto* [José Salvanez de San Jacinto, 1580–1622], dressed in white; 8. *P.e fr. Jacintho Orfanel pre*[dicatore]*s* (1578–1622), dressed in white; 9. *P.e Sebastião* [Sebastião Kimura], dressed in black; 10. [caption unreadable, possibly representing Pedro de Avila, 1591–1622] dressed in Franciscan brown and barefoot; 11. *P.e frei Alonso de Mena dominico* (1578–1622), dressed in white; 12. [caption unreadable, possibly representing Vicente Ramirez de San José, 1597–1622], dressed in brown and barefoot; 13. [caption unreadable, possibly representing Ricardo de Santa Ana Trouvé, 1585–1622], dressed in Franciscan brown and barefoot; 14. *P.e fr. Francisco de Morales dominico* (1567–1622) dressed in white; 15. [caption unreadable, but likely to represent Satsuma Leon], a Japanese cleric, dressed in brown and barefoot; 16. *Ant.o* [Kyūni Antonio, 1572–1622, a novice], dressed in black; 17. [caption unreadable, possily representing Sanpō Pedro, 1580–1622, a novice], dressed in black; 18. [caption unreadable, possibly representing Akahoshi Tomé, 1565–1622, a novice], dressed in black; 19. [caption unreadable, possibly representing Fusai Gonzalo, 1580–1622, a novice], dressed in black; 20. *Sumpo Miguel da Comp.a Japão* [Satō Shunpō Miguel, 1590–1622, a novice], dressed in black; three empty posts; 24. *Luis irmão da Comp.a* [Kawara Rokuemon Luis, 1583–1622, a novice], dressed in black; 25. *Aleixo* [unreadable, *catequista?*] *do P.e frei Ioseph* [Sanbashi Saburō Alejo, 1601–1622], dressed in white. For short biographies see, Ruiz de Medina 1999. p. 4.

17. A similar device had been employed by the Franciscans when they had the 1597 martyrdom depicted with only 23 martyrs, leaving out the three Jesuits who had been executed at the same time (see the print entitled "Drieëntwintig christelijke martelaren in Japan" in the Rijksmuseum of Amsterdam by the Flemish engraver Rafaël Sadeler, 1560–1628).

18. Domingo de Castelleto (1592–1628); Pedro Vasquez de Santa Catalina (1591–1624). Tomas de Santo Spiritu Zumarraga (1577–1622) was still in the Suzuta jail in Ōmura, where he had been since his arrest on 23 July 1617 (Ruiz-de Medina 1999, p. 466). It is unclear why he was not among those executed on 10 September 1622. Possibly, he was too ill to even stand up to perform on the pyre. He died in jail on 29 September 1622 (Ocio/Neira 2000, p. 84; Gonoi 2002, pp. 352–3 has October).

19. On 19 June 1623, Luis Beltran Exarch (1596–1627), Lucas del Espiritu Santo (1594–1633), and Domingo Ibañez de Erquicia (1589–1633) arrived in Satsuma.

20. Juan de los Angeles Rueda (1578?–1624) died on the Ryukyu island of Ishigakishima (Gonoi 2002, pp. 352–3).

21. I am grateful to Padre Daniele Libanori, of the Gesù Church, who provided his detailed photographs of the painting for my analysis.

22. Cieslik 1963a, p. 50.

23. Pardo de San Francisco 1625, p. 42b.

24. Sicardo 1698, p. 221. Cf. Bowersock 1995, p. 48: "The fame of the martyrs is manifest from the crowds that attended them. The Martyr Acts abound in references to the uproar of crowds."

25. Garces 1624, p. 12r.

26. João Rodriguez Giram, *Annua 1622* in JapSin. 60, f. 15r.

27. *Tratado dos gloriosos martyres,* BPE Codex CXVI 1–31, f. 70v.

28. *Ibid.,* f. 71r.

29. *Ibid.,* f. 90r.

30. Foucault 1977, p. 34.

31. As Tertullian has it: "Crudelitas vestra gloria est nostra," quoted in Bowersock 1995, p. 20.

32. *Tratado dos gloriosos martyres,* BPE Codex CXVI 1–31, f. 90r.

33. E.g., the heads of the rebel Taira no Masakado and that of the robber Shutendōji.

34. JapSin 29 I 57; Garces 1624, p. 40r; Ruiz-de Medina 1999, p. 462.

35. In contrast, we have an eyewitness account of the execution of four-year old Onizuka Luis on 12 July 1626, which sounds more credible: "The little kid ran terrified among the dead bodies not knowing whom to turn to until his little head was cut off at one stroke…" (JapSin 61, f. 159r, cited in Ruiz-de Medina 1999, p. 557).

36. *Tratado dos gloriosos martyres,* BPE Codex CXVI 1–31, f. 90r–v.

37. *Ibid.,* f. 69v.

38. *Ibid.*

39. *Ibid.,* f. 91r.

40. *Ibid.,* f. 69v.

41. João Rodriguez Giram, *Annua 1622,* in JapSin. 60, f. 19r.

Repressive Measures: Tokugawa Iemitsu

1. Gonoi 1978, p. 41.

2. On the Bakufu policy towards private religious faith, see Nosco 1996.

3. NA *Overgekomen Brieven* VOC 1078 f. 27v, SHJ 7598-60-5, p. 34.

4. JapSin 38, f. 262, letter dated 25 February 1623. A similar complaint was raised by João Baptista Baeça in his letter dated 12 March 1623 (JapSin 34a, f. 115v).

5. Cabrita 1967, p. 75.
6. JapSin 60, f. 465v: Anua of 1624 by João Rodrigues Giram dated 28 March 1625.
7. I.e., mainly the Portuguese, cf. JapSin 34, 121v, letter of João Baptista Baeça, dated 30 January 1624.
8. Bibliotheca Vaticana, Barberini Lat. 3505, p. 778.
9. Nakada 1979, p. 58.
10. JapSin 60, f. 464v.
11. JapSin 60, f. 463v.
12. Shimizu 2001b, p. 60, citing *Honkōkokushi nikki* 5, in Zoku Gunsho Ruijū kanseikai, 1970, p. 231.
13. E.g., the Dutchmen Pieter Jansz Quick, Frans Jacobsen Visser, Vincent Romeijn (1569–1642), and the Italian Nicolao Marin (?–1631?), the latter two living in the parish of the São João Baptista Church in Chikugo-machi (cf. Iwao 1966, pp. 46, 58; idem 1985, pp. 250, 260). It seems, however that the demand for European pilots was so great that exceptions were made. In 1627, we have a notice about a Spanish pilot by name of Mateo Alvarez still in Nagasaki (OSS no. H-122-1, item 12, see also: Gonoi 1984, p. 49). He was burned for aiding missionaries on 8 September 1628 (Ruiz de Medina 1999, p. 605).
14. Efforts were also made to produce native Japanese pilots familiar with European navigation techniques, but the mathematics involved seem to have stumped most candidates. Japanese pilots: Ikeda Yo'emon, author of the *Genna Kōkaiki* (cf. Kawashima 1921, ch. 8; Arima 1964, p. 119; Iwao 1985, pp. 180, 259); and Kawafuchi Kyūzaemon (Iwao 1985, p. 186). Tenjiku Tokubei, who fourteen years old enlisted as a *kaki-yaku* or secretary and first sailed from Nagasaki for Siam on 4 December 1626, may also have wanted to become a pilot. On him, see: Péri 1923, pp. 111–2; Fujita 1931, pp. 165–80; and Iwao 1985, p. 199.
15. JapSin 60, f. 466v.
16. JapSin. 34, f. 123r. A past of having served the Jesuits would pursue some citizens as late as 1643, see Hesselink 2009, p. 30 (no. [55.], case of Kamiya Denbei).
17. *Outgoing letters Hirado*, Cornelis van Neijenroode to Pieter Carpentier 30 November 1624, NA NFJ 482 f. 35; SHJ 7598-8-3, p. 38.
18. *Outgoing letters Hirado, ibid.*, f. 41; SHJ 7598-8-3, p. 44.
19. *Outgoing letters Hirado*, same to Jacob Constant 30 November 1624, *ibid.*, SHJ 7598-8-3, pp. 60–1.
20. *Outgoing letters Hirado*, same to Pieter Carpentier 17 January 1625, *ibid.* SHJ 7598-8-3, p. 73.
21. JapSin 37b, f. 225v. See also: JapSin 36, f. 273r: letter of Giovanni Battista Zola dated 3 November 1625.
22. Mateo de Couros 26 October 1625 (BA 49-V-8, f. 52, quoted in Coutinho 1999, p. 94).
23. JapSin 37b, f. 225v.
24. JapSin 37b, f. 229v, letter of Mateo de Couros dated 30 October 1625.
25. *Ibid.*
26. JapSin 35, 179r, letter of Bento Fernandes dated 18 December 1625.
27. JapSin 60, 10v: *Anua* of 1625, dated 15 March 1626.

A Hard-Liner: Mizuno Morinobu

1. Gysbertsz 1637, p. 8.
2. Heeres 1898, p. 225.
3. *Outgoing Letters Hirado*, NFJ 482 f. 142v, SHJ 7598-8-4, p. 28.
4. KCSF 6, p. 108.
5. Gysbertsz 1637, p. 9.
6. Francisco Pacheco (1566–1626) and Giovanni Zola (1575–1626), were caught shortly after one another in Arima, and Baltasar de Torres (1563–1626) near Nagasaki (Ruiz-de Medina 1999, pp. 552–6).
7. Gysbertsz 1637, p. 9.

8. JapSin 37b, f. 237v: letter of Mateo de Couros to the General, dated 5 October 1626. See also: Morejón 1631, p. 39r.
9. Ruiz-de Medina 1999, pp. 557–8.
10. JapSin 37b, 238r.
11. Gysbertsz 1637, p. 11.
12. *Ibid.*
13. JapSin 37b, 238r.
14. Pagés 1869, p. 634.
15. JapSin 61, f. 6v: Anua of 1625 by João Rodrigues Giram, dated 15 March 1626.
16. JapSin 37b, 238r.
17. Cieslik 1951, p. 121.
18. An example can be found in Hesselink 2009, p. 54 [no. 179]: the case of Shō'emon's wife's mother. Also in: *Nagasaki zakki*, Kan'ei 3, quoted in Nakamura 1964, p. 21.
19. Morejón 1631, p. 39v.
20. Gysbertsz 1637, pp. 11–12.
21. Yūki 1984b, p. 2.
22. Branquinho 1993, p. 97.
23. He signed his name to a document, dated Kan'ei 4.06.29 [10 August 1627], composed by four Nagasaki interpreters preserved at OSS, no. H-122-1. Willem Jansz describes him as "a shrewd *rapado* or shaved bonze, by name of Antono Noret, sworn interpreter of Nagasaki, born in Korea, and very fluent in both Portuguese as well as Latin which he can read and write, brought up a Roman Catholic and experienced in matters of the church." (NA, Collectie Sweers, van Vliet, Specx. Eerste afdeling, no. 5, f. 239v; SHJ 7598-18-27, p. 30.
24. Ruiz de Medina 1999, pp. 583–9.
25. Shimizu 1977, p. 296. Originally in *Sokkyohen*, also in *Tōbu jitsuroku* printed in *Naikaku bunko shozō shiseki sōkan* vol. 2, pp. 505–6 (Tokyo: Shiseki kenkyūkai, 1981).
26. Pagés 1869, p. 646.
27. Kataoka 1963, p. 13.
28. NA VOC 1101, f. 161r; SHJ 7598-60-12, p. 35.
29. *Ibid.*
30. NA NFJ 482, f. 340, SHJ 7598-8-5, p. 91: *Outgoing Letters Hirado*, Cornelis van Nijenroode to Pieter Muyser, dated 27 September 1628.
31. Boxer 1963, p. 115.
32. Boyajian 1993, p. 234.
33. A similar situation occurred in 1648–9 when the Dutch were led to believe that the help they had given to a Portuguese ambassador was the reason their right to be received by the shogun was suspended, while in reality the Bakufu was pursuing a different agenda, see Hesselink 2002, pp. 136–8, 159–60.
34. Small-scale trade with the Chinese seems to have continued this year. Muyser reports the arrival of two Chinese junks on 2 August 1628.
35. Gysbertsz 1637 was translated into English in Boxer 1935, pp. 73–88; and into Japanese by Kōda Shigetomo, see Caron 1967, pp. 193–218.
36. Gysbertsz 1637, p. 17.
37. *Ibid.*, p. 18.
38. *Ibid.*, p. 18.
39. *Ibid.*, p. 19.
40. *Ibid.*, p. 20.

The Climax of the Persecution: Takenaka Shigeyoshi

1. KCSF 6, p. 108.
2. Gysbertsz 1637, p. 20.
3. HD 7, p. 406.
4. Gysbertsz 1637, p. 20.
5. *Ibid.*, p. 20.
6. Hesselink 2009, p. 17.
7. Gysbertsz 1637, p. 22.

8. *Ibid.*, p. 23
9. *Ibid.*, p. 24.
10. *Nihon Koten Bungaku Taikei*, vol. 68, pp. 16–17 (Buretsu 8.03, corresponding with the year 506). See also Aston 1956, vol. 1, pp. 406–7.
11. Gysbertsz 1637, p. 25.
12. *Ibid.*, p. 26. Also: Toyama 1988, p. 29.
13. KCSF 6, p. 306. For more details, see *Tsūkō ichiran*, vol. 4, *maki* 139, pp. 517–9.

The Brave Ex-Mayor: Machida João

1. We have seen that the Takagi were the first of Nagasaki's ruling class to apostatize. Luis Takagi died on 21 January 1630. Takashima Ryōetsu Jeronimo died on 18 August 1622 (*Nagasaki meika ryakufu*, p. 600; Iwao 1963, p. 3 has 16 August 1622). He was never forced to apostatize.
2. Shinzaemon is likely to be a mistake for Shōzaemon.
3. Morejón 1631, p. 41r.
4. *Ibid.*
5. *Ibid.*
6. *Ibid.*, p. 41v.
7. *Ibid.*, p. 42r.
8. NA VOC 1101, f. 463v; SHJ 7598-60-8, p. 31. On the embassy, see Katō 1981, pp. 86–7.
9. *Ibid.* According to the *Nagasaki meika ryakufu*, p. 595, Gotō Tomé died on Kan'ei 4.11.24.
10. Decisions as to their final fate were probably made by the *rōjū* in consultation with the shogun himself.
11. Curiously, although Iemitsu had succeeded his father as shogun in 1623, the text seems to refer to Hidetada here.
12. Morejón 1631, p. 42r.
13. For the debate on loyalty, often combined with "filial piety" in the term *chūkō* 忠孝, see: Ooms 1985, Paramore 2009, passim.
14. KCSF 4, pp. 394–5: Masatsuna was back in Edo after a trip to Aizu in 1627, and before he was to accompany Hidetada on a pilgrimage to Nikkō in 1628. I am grateful to Prof. Komiya Kiyora for his help with this identification on 24 May 2010.
15. Morejón 1631, p. 42v. The petition was signed by Machida João and his son Pedro, Gotō Paulo, Kazariya João and his brother Tomé (sons of Justino and Justa, founders of the Misericordia Church), Yokose Domingo and his brother João, Tachibana Pedro, Shiraishi André, Nomura João, Tsuruya Leão, Korogawa João, and Tsushima Lope (*ibid.*).
16. *Ibid.* Here called "president mayor privado." On Doi, see Hesselink 2002, p. 65.
17. According to Ruiz de Medina (1999, p. 688), Machida João was burned alive in Nihonmatsu in Ōshū. One of his relatives (a son? or younger brother?), Matias (1581–1634), entered the Society in 1613 and became Valentim Carvalho's secretary, a sign of very good connections. He left for Macao in 1614, and was ordained in 1624. He was active as a priest in Cochin-China between 1630 and 1634, but he died in Macao on 13 March 1634 (Gonoi 2002, pp. 364–5).
18. Ooms 1985, pp. 50–62; Boot 2000.

Epilogue: Nagasaki in the 1630s

1. Cf. Cardim 1646, Bartoli 1660, Sicardo 1698.
2. Elison 1973, 185–91; Hur 2007, p. 56.
3. Main source: Ruiz de Medina 1999. Ruiz-de Medina's work is innovative in several respects, not least because he makes a great effort to be fair to all those who died for their faith in Japan. His work is useful, also, in

that it is very inclusive, for he has decided to employ a rather loose definition of what constitutes a martyr, i.e., anybody who died because of the persecutions. He includes of course those publicly executed, but also those who died during torture or due to deprivations connected with their arrest, their loss of property, their physical or mental health, or any other cause that can be directly attributed to the prohibition of Christianity in Japan.
4. Some of these from a letter by Willem Versteghen to Nicolaes Couckebacker, dated 7 September 1634, at SHJ (7598-8-1 thru 4).
5. From a letter by Willem Versteghen to Nicolaes Couckebacker, dated 12 October 1635 (*ibid.*).
6. Some of these from a letter by Willem Versteghen to Nicolaes Couckebacker, dated 24 August 1637 (*ibid.*).
7. A Portuguese layman by name of Duarte Correa.
8. This figure includes the 26 executions of 1597.
9. Carlo Spinola on 10 September 1622.
10. It is sometimes difficult, also, to distinguish between members of a religious order and hangers-on of that order. The Dominicans, for example, accepted women as tertiary members, that is: lay people fully committed to the support of the order. By contrast, in the case of the Jesuits, it is usually clear who was admitted into the order and who was not. It is therefore difficult to compare these numbers. The number of Europeans executed for their faith in Nagasaki is likely to be as correct as we can get, but many of these missionaries were not arrested in or around Nagasaki, but were transported, often over a considerable distance, to be publicly tortured and executed in Nagasaki.
11. One pregnant woman was executed.
12. This changed later on in the seventeenth century, see Nosco 1996, pp. 147–55.
13. 20,000 by some estimates (e.g., Ruiz de Medina 1999, pp. 253, 740).
14. For a description, see Hesselink 2002, p. 68.
15. No mendicant succumbed, and even the number of European Jesuits succumbing was less than ten, see Hesselink 2002, pp. 49–69, 88–104.
16. See Hesselink 2012, p. 14, n. 21.
17. See Hesselink 2004, pp. 186–90.
18. Etchū 1978b, pp. 66, 69.
19. TJ vol. 3, p. 103.
20. Woolley 1881, p. 145, quoting *Kokinshūran*.
21. TJ vol. 3, p. 182; SHJ *Daghregister Hirado* 4, p. 206. Both sources give the same date (Kan'ei 17.04.12 = 1 June 1640), something which always considerably hardens the reported facts. The *Nagasaki meika ryakufu*, p. 582 (understandably, but inaccurately) dates the reward to 1638.
22. For accounts of the expulsion of the Portuguese, see Boxer 1951, pp. 383–9; Yamamoto 1995, pp. 68–82; Coutinho 1999.
23. Entry in SHJ *Daghregister Hirado* 4, p. 206. The Dutch, however, were not informed of what they had been up to and swallowed the rationale for their rewards wholesale.
24. TJ vol. 3, p. 222. The island was originally called Tsukijima (the "man-made island"). It later became better known as Deshima, or the "island sticking out" [into Nagasaki Bay].
25. On Deshima, see Baba 1935; Yūki 1985; Yoshimura 1986; Nagasaki-shi Dejima shiseki seibi shingikai 1989.
26. See also Etchū 1999 and Hesselink 2004, p. 188 on this problem.
27. On the Portuguese in Siam, see: Halikowski Smith 2010; in Cambodia, see: Bierman 1935; in China, see: Ferguson 1902.
28. On Portugal's inofficial empire, see Newitt 2001 and 2005, and Disney 2009, vol. 2.
29. Disney 2009, vol. 2 , p. 192.

30. Ooms 1985; Paramore 2009.

31. For a more detailed description of these measures, see Yamamoto 1995, pp. 28–56.

32. Hur 2007.

33. See Paramore 2009.

34. This topic has been traditionally connected with anti–Christianity, e.g., Boxer 1951; Asao 1975; Toby 1977; Yamamoto 1995; Hesselink 2002; Arano 2003.

35. The topic is treated in Hur 2007.

36. Cf. Elison 1973, pp. 319–89.

37. These last two topics have not yet received exhaustive treatment. Some examples of anti–Christianity in the legal system can be found in Hesselink 2004, p. 189.

38. For the history of the *ningen sengen*, see Moore 2011, pp. 92–7, who specifically credits MacArthur's desire to Christianize Japan with both the motivation for the declaration and the climate in which it occurred. In other words, the declaration represented the price Hirohito was willing to pay for his own survival and that of the Imperial Institution. When those were assured, Hirohito and his family abandoned their feigned interest in Christianity (Moore 2011, pp. 103–19, 139–41).

39. Quoted in Lu 1997, p. 467.

40. Although the *ningen sengen* has been criticized for its failure to specifically deny the "reputed descent from the sun goddess, Amaterasu Ōmikami" (Bix 2000, p. 561), theologically speaking it represented a revolution in the thinking of the imperial court.

Bibliography

Sources in Manuscript Form

In Japanese

- *Hasegawa Gonroku yori Nagasaki machidoshiyori e ateraru gojō* [Letter from Hasegawa Gonroku to the Nagasaki City Elders] at NPL.
- *Nabeshima Naoshige kōfu* [Record of Lord Nabeshima Naoshige] at SHJ.
- *Nagasaki konryū narabi ni shoki kyoyō* [On the Founding of Nagasaki with an Extract of Various Records] at NPL.
- *Nagasaki machidoshiyori hattan yuisho* [On the origins of the Nagasaki *machidoshiyori*] at NPL, NMM.
- *Suetsugu monjo* [Documents Preserved in the Suetsugu Family] at SHJ.
- *Yoriai machi yuisho oboegaki* [Memorandum on the History of Yoriai Ward, 1734] by Ashikari Zendayu at NMM.

In Portuguese/Spanish

- Andrade Leitao. *Nobiliario de Portugal* at BA 49-XII-37.
- Avila Girón, i.e., *Relacion del Reyno del Nippon a que llaman coruptamente Japon* [An Essay on the Kingdom of Nippon Mistakenly Called Japan] by Bernardo Avila de Girón, 1615, the best copy of which is preserved in the Escorial Library (ms O. III. 19). There is another copy in BNM (Mss. 19628). I have also used the microfilm copies of these manuscripts at SHJ.
- *Chancelarias D. João III, D. Henrique, D. Sebastião* at ANTT.
- *Japonica-Sinica*, this is the largest archive of letters and reports written by the Jesuit missions in Japan and China (as well as Cambodia and Vietnam) to their fellows and superiors in Europe, at ARSI (microfilm copies are at KB). For a catalogue of the individual documents see Obara 1981. Other places where such letters or their copies are preserved include ADC, APT, BA, and RAH.
- *Inventarios do Padre Francisco Rodrigues*, at ANTT, ms. da livraria 805.
- *Livro das gerações e nobreza de Portugal*, at BNL COD 1327,
- *Tratado dos gloriosos martyres … no Reino de Figen*

o anno de 1622 feito pollo Padre Bento Fernandes da Companhia de Iesu (Codice CXVI-1-31) at BPE.

In Dutch

- *Daghregister Hirado* at SHJ (no. 7598-1-1 thru 4).
- *Memorie ende Aenteeckeninge van het gepasseerde dat Willem Janssen in Nagasacqui is geweest to 13 Maert dat met de Joncq Zeelandia naer Batavia is vertrocken. Anno 1630* at SHJ (7598-18-27).
- *Nicolaes Couckebacker Afgaande en Ingekomen Papieren en Boeken gehouden in't Comptoir Firando. Ontfangen Brieven Sept. 12, 1633–Jan 16, 1639 Kopie Boek*, 4 vols. at SHJ (7598-8-1 thru 4).

Sources in Print

Abranches, J.A., Yoshitomo Okamoto, and Henri Bernard. *La première ambassade du Japon en Europe 1582–1592*. Tokyo: Sophia University, 1942.

Aduarte, Diego. *Historia de la Provincia del Santo Rosario de la Orden de Predicadores en Filipinas, Japon y China*. Edicion Manuel Ferrero, 2 vols. Madrid: Departamento de Misionologia Española, 1962–3.

Alden, Dauril. *The Making of an Enterprise: The Society of Jesus in Portugal, Its Empire, and Beyond*. Stanford: Stanford University Press, 1996.

Alvarez, J.L. "Dos notas sobre la embajada del Padre Juan Cobo" in MN vol. 3, 2 (1940): 657–64.

Alvarez-Taladriz, José Luis, ed. Alessandro Valignano's *Sumario de las cosas de Japon (1583). Adiciones del sumario de Japon (1592)*. Tokyo: Sophia University, 1954.

_____. "Fuentes Europeas sobre Murayama Toan (1562–1619) I. El pleito de Suetsugu Heizo Juan contra Murayama Toan Antonio (1617–1619), según el Padre Mattheus Couros, Provincial de la Compañia de Jesús en Japón" in *Tenri daigaku gakuhō*, no. 51 (1966a): 93–114. Alvarez-Taladriz, José Luis. "Fuentes Europeas sobre Murayama Toan (1562–1619) II. Murayama Toan Antonio, según Bernardino de Avila Girón" in *Kobe gaidai ronsō*, vol. 17, 1–3 (1966b): 395–418.

_____. "Una carta inedita de Maeda Geni (1593) al P. Pedro Gómez, S.J." in *Ōsaka gaikokugo daigaku gakuhō*, no. 16 (1966c): 1–26.

_____. "Fuentes Europeas sobre Murayama Toan

(1562–1619) III. La familia Murayama según escritos de Religiosos de la Orden de Santo Domingo" in *Kobe City University Journal*, vol. 18, 2 (1967a): 85–104.

_____. "Transito de Don Bartolome de Omura del Purgatorio del Padre Tsukasa al Paraiso" in *Tenri daigaku gakuhō*, no. 77 (1972a): 24–39.

_____. " Relación del P. Alejandro Valignano, S.J. sobre su Embajada a Hideyoshi (1591)" in *Ōsaka gaikokugo daigaku gakuhō*, no. 28 (1972b): 43–60.

_____. "El Padre Viceprovincial Gaspar Coelho 'Capitan de Armas or Pastor de Almas'" in *Sapientia*, no. 6 (1972c): 41–79).

_____, ed. *Documentos Franciscanos de la Christiandad de Japon (1593–1597). San Martin de la Ascension y Fray Marcelo de Ribadeneira Relaciones e Informaciones*. Osaka: n.p., 1973.

_____. "A cada cosa su nombre y a Dios el que corresponde" in *Ōsaka gaikokugo daigaku gakuhō*, no. 32 (1974a): 1–20.

_____. "Hermanos o Dogicos?" in *Sapientia*, no. 8 (1974b): 97–132.

_____. "Apuntes sobre la fusta del P. Gaspar Coelho, Viceprovincial de Japon (1583–1587)" in *Sapientia*, no. 22 (1988): 133–49.

_____, ed. *Alejandro Valignano Apologia de la Compañia de Jesus de Japon y China (1598)*. Osaka: n.p., 1998.

Amino Yoshihiko. *Mu'en, kugai, raku: Nihon chūsei no jiyū to heiwa*. Tokyo: Heibonsha sensho 58, 1978.

Anesaki Masaharu. *Kirishitan dendō no kōhai*. Tokyo: Dōbunkan, 1930.

_____. "Psychological Observations on the Persecution of the Catholics in Japan in the XVII Century" in *Harvard Journal of Asiatic Studies*, vol. 1 (1936): 13–27.

Anno Masaki. "Chūsei toshi Nagasaki no kenkyū" in *NR*, no. 310 (1974): 27–51.

_____. *Kōshiron: Hirado, Nagasaki, Yokoseura*. Tokyo: Nihon Editā Sukūru Shuppanbu, 1992.

_____. "'Kirishitan kinrei' no kenkyū" in Fujino Tamotsu, ed. *Kinsei shakai to shūkyō* (*Ronshū bakuhan taiseishi*, vol. 9). Tokyo: Yuzankaku, 1995, pp. 321–57.

Arano Yasunori. "Edo bakufu to Higashi Ajia" in Arano Yasunori, ed. *Edo bakufu to Higashi Ajia*. Tokyo: Yoshikawa Kōbunkan, 2003, pp. 7–181.

Arima, Seiho. "The Western Influence on Japanese Military Science, Shipbuilding, and Navigation" in *MN*, vol. 19, 3–4 (1964): 352–79.

Arnaiz, Gregorio. "Observaciones sobre la embajada del Dominico P. Juan Cobo" in *MN* vol. 2, 2 (1939): 634–47.

Asao Nobuhiro. *Sakoku*. Tokyo: Shōgakkan, 1975.

Aston, William G. *Nihongi. Chronicles of Japan from the Earliest Times to A.D. 697*. London: Allen and Unwin, 1956.

Aveling, J.C.H. *The Jesuits*. New York: Stein and Day, 1982.

Avila Girón, Bernardo. See: Manuscripts in Spanish (above), also: Schilling and Lejarza (1933–1935, and in Japanese: Sakuma, Aida, and Iwao 1965).

Baba Makoto. "Deshima no kenkyū" in ND, no. 16 (1935): 32–43.

Bailey, Gauvin Alexander. "The Art of the Jesuit Missions in Japan in the Age of St. Francis Xavier and Alessandro Valignano" in *St. Francis, an Apostle of the East*. Vol. 1 *The Encounter Between Europe and Asia During the Period of the Great Navigations*. Tokyo: Sophia University Press, 1999a, pp. 185–209.

_____. *Art on the Jesuit Missions in Asia and Latin America 1542–1773*. Toronto: University of Toronto Press, 1999b.

_____. "'Le style jésuite n'existe pas': Jesuit Corporate Culture and the Visial Arts" in John O'Malley e.a., eds. *The Jesuits: Cultures, Sciences, and the Arts 1540–1573*. Toronto: University of Toronto Press, 1999c. pp. 38–89.

Baroni, Helen J. *Obaku Zen. The Emergence of the Third Sect of Zen in Tokugawa Japan*. Honolulu: University of Hawai'i Press, 2000.

Bartoli, Daniello. *Dell'Historia della Compagnia di Giesu, Il Giappone seconda parte dell'Asia*. Roma: Varese, 1660.

Bernard, Henri. "Les débuts des relations diplomatiques entre le Japon et les Espagnols des Iles Philippines (1571–1594)" in: MN, vol. 1, 1 (1938): 99–137.

Berry, Mary E. *Hideyoshi*. Cambridge, MA: Harvard University Press, 1982.

_____. "Restoring the Past: The Documents of Hideyoshi's Magistrate in Kyoto" in *Harvard Journal of Asiatic Studies*, vol. 43, 1 (1983): 57–95.

_____. *The Culture of Civil War in Kyoto*. Los Angeles: University of California Press, 1994.

Bierman, Benno M. "Los Portugueses y españoles en Camboja al fin del siglo XVI" in *AIA*, vol. 22 (1935): 261–70; 455–8.

Bix, Herbert P. *Hirohito and the Making of Modern Japan*. New York: HarperCollins, 2000.

Blair, Emma H., and James A. Robertson, eds. *The Philippine Islands 1493–1898*. 50 vols. Mandaluyong, Rizal: Cachos Hermanos Reprint Edition, 1973.

Blok, Anton. "Charivari's als purificatie-ritueel" in *Volkskundig Bulletin*, vol. 15, 3 (1989): 266–80.

Boot, W.J. "The Death of a Shogun: Deification in Early Modern Japan." In John Breen and Mark Teeuwen, eds., *Shinto in History. Ways of the Kami*. London: Curzon, 2000, pp. 144–166.

Boscaro, Adriana. "Toyotomi Hideyoshi and the 1587 Edicts Against Christianity" in *Oriens Extremus*, vol. 20, 2 (1973): 219–41.

Bourdon, Léon. *Les routes des marchands Portugais entre Chine et Japon au milieu du XVIe siècle*. Lisboa: [n.p.], 1949.

_____. "Un projet d'invasion de la China par Canton à la fin du XVIe siècle." In: *Actas do III Colóquio Internacional de Estudos Luso-Brasileiros*. Lisboa: n.p., 1960, pp. 97–121.

_____. *La Compagnie de Jésus et le Japon*. Lisbon/Paris: Fondation Calouste Gulbenkian Centre Culturel Portugais/ Commission Nationale pour les Commémorations des Découvertes Portugaises, 1993.

Bowersock, G.W. *Martyrdom and Rome*. Cambridge: Cambridge University Press, 1995.

Boxer, Charles Ralph. "The Affair of the Madre de Deus: A Chapter in the History of the Portuguese in Japan." *Transactions of the Japan Society* (London), vol. 26 (1929): 4–94.

_____. *A True Description of Japan by François Caron and Joost Schouten*. London: Argonaut Press, 1935.

_____. *The Christian Century in Japan, 1549–1650*. Berkeley: University of California Press, 1951.

_____. "Missionaries and Merchants of Macao, 1557–1687" in *Actas do III Colóquio Internacional de Estudos Luso-Brasileiros, Lisboa 1957*. Coimbra: Imprensa de Coimbra, 1960, pp. 210–24.

_____. *The Great Ship from Amacon: Annals of Macao and the Old Japan Trade, 1544–1640*. Lisbon: Centro de Estudios Ultramarinos, 1963.

_____. *Fidalgos in the Far East 1550–1770*. The Hague: Nijhoff, 1948. Reprint: New York: Oxford University Press, 1968.

_____. "Friar Juan Pobre of Zamora and His Lost and Found 'Ystoria' of 1598–1603 (Lilly MS. BM 617)" in: *Indiana University Bookman*, vol. 10 (1969a): 25–46.

_____. "Portuguese and Spanish Projects for the Conquest of Southeast Asia, 1580–1600" in *The Journal of Asian History*, vol. 3, no. 2 (1969b): 118–36.

Braga, J.M. *The Western Pioneers and Their Discovery of Macao*. Macau: Imprensa Nacional, 1949.

Branquinho, Isabel. "Os capitães-mores da viagem do Japão" in *Oceanos*, no. 15 (1993): 92–8.

Cabrita, José, ed. *Beato Vicente de Santo António. Cartas do Japão: A alma dum santo revelada em suas cartas*. Faro: n.p., 1967.

Caraman, Philip. *The Lost Paradise: The Jesuit Republic in South America*. New York: Seabury Press, 1976.

Cardim, Antonio Francisco. *Fasciculus e Iapponicis Floribus, suo adhuc medentibus sanguine compositus*. Rome: Corbelletti, 1646.

Cardon, R. "The Old Church on the Malacca Hill" in *Journal of the Malayan Branch of the Royal Asiatic Society*, vol. 20, pt. 1 (1947): 188–234.

Carletti, Francesco. *My Voyage Around the World*. Translated by Herbert Weinstock. New York: Random House, 1964.

_____. *Reise um die Welt*. Translated by Ernst Blum from a newly reconstructed Italian text by Gianfranco Silvestro (Turin: Guilio Einaudi, 1958). Tübingen/Basel: Horst Erdman Verlag, 1966.

Caron, Françoys. *Beschrijvinghe van het Machtigh Coninckrijcke Japan*. Amsterdam: Ioost Hartgers, 1648.

_____. *Nihon Daiōkokushi*. Transl. by Kōda Shigetomo. Tōyō bunko no. 90. Tokyo: Heibonsha, 1967.

Carrero, Francisco. *Triunfo del Santo Rosario y Orden de Santo Domingo en los reinos del Japon desde el año del Señor 1617 hasta el de 1624*. Manila: Colegio de Santo Tomas, 1868.

Cartas que os padres e irmãos da Companhia de Iesus que andão nos Reynos de Iapão escreuerão aos da mesma Companhia da India, & Europa, des do anno de 1549 ate o de 66. Coimbra: Antonio de Marijs, 1570.

Cartas que los padres y hermanos de la Compañia de Iesus, que andan en los Reynos de Iapon escrivieron a los de la misma Compañia, desde el año de mil y quinientos y quarenta y nueue, hasta el de mil y quinientos y setenta y vno. Alcala: Iuan Iñiguez de Lequerica, 1575.

Cartas que os padres e irmãos da Companhia de Iesus escreuerão dos Reynos de Iapão & China aos da mesma Companhia da India, & Europa. 2 vols. Evora: Manoel de Lyra, 1598.

Castro, M. de. "Fr. Marcelo de Ribadeneira" in Victor Sánchez and Cayetano S. Fuertes, eds. *España in Extremo Oriente*. Madrid: Editorial Cisneros, 1979. pp. 181–246.

Chang, Aloysius. "The Chinese Community of Nagasaki in the First Century of the Tokugawa Period (1603–1688)." Unpublished Ph.D. dissertation St. John's University, New York, 1970.

Chang, Tsie-tse. *Sino-Portuguese Trade from 1514 to 1641. A Synthesis of Portuguese and Chinese Sources*. Leiden: Brill, 1934.

Charlevoix, Pierre François Xavier de. *Histoire et description générale du Japon*. 2 vols. Paris: Julien-Michel Gangouin [and others], 1736.

Chase, Kenneth. *Firearms: A Global History to 1700*. Cambridge: Cambridge University Press, 2003.

Chen, Chingho A. *Historical Notes on Hoi-An (Faifo)*. Carbondale, IL: Center for Vietnamese Studies Southern Illinois University, [1974].

Chen, Ta. *Emigrant Communities in South China: A Study of Overseas Migration and Its Influence on Standards of Living and Social Change*. New York: Institute of Pacific Relations, 1940.

Cieslik, Hubert. "Die Goningumi im Dienste der Christenüberwachung" in MN vol. 7, no. 1–2 (1951): 102.

_____. "Kirishitan chigyō Nagasaki" in KBKK vol. 6, 3 (1962a): 1–11.

Cieslik, Hubert. "Zur Geschichte der kirchlichen Hierarchie in der alten Japanmission" in *Neue Zeitschrift für Missionswissenschaft*, vol. 18 (1962b): 42–57; 81–107; 177–195.

_____. *Kirishitan jinbutsu no kenkyū*. Tokyo: Yoshikawa Kōbunkan, 1963a.

_____. "Keichō nenkan ni okeru shikyō keiei no seminario ni tsuite" in NSHK no. 4 (1963b): 28–41.

_____. "The Training of a Japanese Clergy in the Seventeenth Century." In J. Ruggendorf, ed. *Studies in Japanese Culture*. Tokyo: Sophia University, 1963c, pp. 41–78.

Cieslik, Hubert. "Fabian Fukanden nōto" in KBKK vol. 15, 3 (1972): 244–250.

_____. "The Case of Christovão Ferreira" in MN vol. 29 (1974): 1–54.

_____. *Kirishitan-shi no mondai ni kotaeru Kirishitan shikō*. Nagasaki: Seibō no kishisha, 1995.

Cocks, Richard. *Diary Kept by the Head of the English Factory. Diary of Richard Cocks, 1615–1622*. 3 vols. Tokyo: Historiographical Institute, University of Tokyo, 1978–80.

Colin, Francisco/ Pablo Pastells. *Labor evangelica, ministerios apostolicos de los obreros de la Compañia de Iesus, fundacion, y progressos de su provincia en las islas Filipinas.* Barcelona: Henrich, 1900–1902.

Collado, Diego. *Niffon no cotobani yō confesion.* Roma: Sacr. Congreg. De Propag. Fide, 1632 [Reprint Tokyo: Kazama shobō, 1961].

Cooper, Michael, ed. *The Southern Barbarians: The First Europeans in Japan.* Tokyo: Kodansha International, 1971.

_____. "The Mechanics of the Macao-Nagasaki Silk Trade" in MN, vol. 27, 4 (1972): 423–33.

_____. *Rodrigues the Interpreter: An Early Jesuit in Japan and China.* New York: Weatherhill, 1974.

_____, ed. *João Rodrigues's Account of Sixteenth Century Japan.* The Hakluyt Society, 3rd series, vol. 7. London: Hakluyt Society, 2001.

_____. *The Japanese Mission to Europe, 1582–1590: The Journey of Four Samurai Boys Through Portugal, Spain and Italy.* Kent, UK: Global Oriental, 2005.

Costa, João Paulo Oliveira e. *O Cristianismo no Japão e o episcopado de D. Luis de Cerqueira.* Ph.D. thesis, Universidade Nova de Lisboa, 1998.

_____. "O Colégio de Macau e a missão do Japão (1594–1614) in Jorge dos Santos Alves, ed. *Portugal e a China: Conferências nos Encontros de História Luso-Chinesa.* Lisbon: Fundação Oriente, 2001a, pp. 61–87.

_____. "A Route Under Pressure; Communication Between Nagasaki and Macao (1597–1617)" in BPJS, vol. 1 (2001b): 75–95.

Coutinho, Valdemar. *O Fim da Presença Portuguesa no Japão.* Lisbon: Sociedade Histórica da Independência de Portugal, 1999.

Couto, Diogo do. *Da Asia: dos feitos, que os Portuguezes fizeram na conquista, e descubrimento das terras, e mares do Oriente.* 15 vols. Lisbon: Livreria Sam Carlos, 1974 (reprint of 1778–1788).

Crasset, Jean. *Histoire de l'Eglise au Japon.* 2 vols. Paris: Michallet, 1689.

Curtin, Philip D. *Cross-cultural Trade in World History.* Cambridge: Cambridge University Press, 1984.

Cushner, Nicholas P. *Lords of the Land: Sugar, Wine, and Jesuit Estates of Coastal Peru, 1600–1767.* Albany, NY: SUNY Press, 1980.

Dai Zabieru Ten—St. Francis Xavier—His Life and Times, Exhibition Catalogue of the Great Xavier Exhibition, organized for the 450th anniversary of Xavier's arrival in Japan in 1999 by the Tōbu Museum of Art and the Asahi Shinbun.

Danvers, Frederick Charles, and William Foster. *Letters Received by the East India Company,* 6 vols. London, 1896–1902 (reprint Amsterdam, 1968).

Davis, Natalie Z. *Society and Culture in Early Modern France.* Stanford: Stanford University Press, 1975.

Dean, Carolyn. *Inka Bodies and the Body of Christ: Corpus Christi in Colonial Cusco, Peru.* Durham, NC: Duke University Press, 1999.

Debergh, Minako. "Deux nouvelles études sur l'histoire du christianisme au Japon" in Stephen Turn-

bull, ed. *Japan's Hidden Christians 1549–1999,* vol. 1 *Open Christianity in Japan 1549–1639.* Richmond (Surrey)/Tokyo: Curzon Press/Edition Synapse, 2000, pp. 396–416, 167–215.

De Groot, J.J.M. *Fêtes annuellement célébrées à Emoui (Amoy): etude concernant la religion populaire des Chinois.* 2 vols. Translated by C.G. Chavannes. Annales du Musée Guimet, vol. 11 Paris: Ernest Leroux, 1886.

Delgado Garcia, José. *El beato Francisco Morales, O.P., martyr del Japon (1567–1622). Su personalidad historica y misionera.* Madrid: Instituto Pontifico de Teologia/Misionologia, 1985.

_____, ed. and Sakuma Tadashi, transl. *Fukusha Hose de San Hashinto Sarubanesu O.P. shokan—hōkoku.* Tokyo: Kirishitan bunka kenkyūkai, 1976.

Delplace, L. *Le catholicisme au Japon.* 2 vols. Bruxelles: Albert Dewit, 1909–10.

De Sande, Duarte. *Diálogo sobre a Missão dos Embaixadores Japoneses à Cúria Romana.* Translation from the Latin by Américo da Costa Ramalho. Macao: Comissão Territorial de Macau para as Comemorações dos Descobrimentos Portugueses/Fundação Oriente, 1997.

Disney, Anthony R. *A History of Portugal and the Portuguese Empire.* 2 vols. Cambridge: Cambridge University Press, 2009.

Doi Tadao. *Kirishitan gogaku no kenkyū.* Rev. ed. Tokyo: Sanshōdō, 1971.

Duyvendak, J.J.L. "The True Dates of the Chinese Maritime Expeditions in the Early Fifteenth Century" in *T'oung Pao,* vol. 34 (1938): 341–412.

Earns, Lane R. "Nagasaki bugyō Hasegawa Gonroku ni tsuite" translated by Fumiko Earns in NSHK no. 20 (1979): 14–30.

_____. "The Development of Bureaucratic Rule in Early Modern Japan: The Nagasaki Bugyō in the Seventeenth Century." Unpublished Ph.D. dissertation, University of Hawaii, 1987.

Eberhard, Wolfram. *The Local Cultures of South and East China.* Leiden: Brill, 1968.

Ebisawa Arimichi. *Nanbanji kōhaiki. Jakyō tai'i. Myōtei mondo. Hadaiusu.* Tōyō bunko no. 14. Tokyo: Heibonsha, 1964.

_____. *Kirishitan dan'atsu to teikō.* Tokyo: Yūzankaku, 1981.

_____. "Kirishitan kin'in no saiginmi: Tenshō kinrei ni tsuite" in Fujino Tamotsu, ed. *Kinsei shakai to shūkyō (Ronshū bakuhan taiseishi,* vol. 9). Tokyo: Yuzankaku, 1995, pp. 278–319.

Egerod, Søren. "A Note on the Origin of the Name Macao" in TP vol. 47 (1959): 63–66.

Elisseeff, Danielle. *Hideyoshi: Bâtisseur du Japon Moderne.* Paris: Fayard, 1986.

Elison, George. Review of Michael Cooper, ed. *The Southern Barbarians: The First Europeans in Japan* in MN vol. 27, 2 (1972): 222–7.

_____. *Deus Destroyed. The Image of Christianity in Early Modern Japan.* Cambridge: Harvard University Press, 1973.

Elisonas, Jurgis. "Christianity and the Daimyo" in John W. Hall and James L. McClain (eds). The Cambridge History of Japan, vol. 4 Early Modern

Japan. Cambridge: Cambridge University Press, 1991, pp. 301–72.

———. "Acts, Legends, and Southern Barbarous Japanese," in Jorge M. dos Santos Alves, ed. *Portugal e a China: Conferências nos Encontros de História Luso-Chinesa*. Lisbon: Fundação Oriente, 2001, pp. 15–50.

———. "Journey to the West" in JJRS, vol. 34, 1 (2007): 27–66.

———. "Nagasaki: The Early Years of an Early Modern Japanese City" in: Liam M. Brockey, ed. *Portuguese Colonial Cities in the Early Modern World*. Burlington, VT: Ashgate, 2009, pp. 63–102.

Erkin, H. Can. "Toyotomi seiken ni okeru gaikō kinō no keisei" in NR no. 655 (2002): 39–53.

Etchū Tetsuya. "Ruisu Sakuyemon, Petoro Sakuyemon ga deta Takagishi shoke ni tsuite" in KBKK vol. 10, 2 (1968): 7–12.

———. *Etchū Tetsuya no Nagasaki hitori aruki*. Nagasaki: Nagasaki bunkensha, 1978a.

———. "Machidoshiyori daikan Takagike keifukō (jō)" in ND, no. 61 (1978b): 50–77.

———. "Nagasaki ni okeru nanban bunka" in KBKK vol. 19, 1 (1978c): 207–218.

———. "Nagasaki ni okeru shoki kinkyō seisaku no ichi kōsatsu" in KK vol. 20 (1980): 159–189.

———. "Nagasaki ni okeru saisho no minato to hori ni tsuite" in ND 69 (1984): 108.

———. "Nagasaki bunkashi josetsu" in Yanai Kenji, ed. *Sakoku Nihon to kokusai kōryū*. Tokyo: Yoshikawa kōbunkan, 1988, pp. 237–257.

———. *Nagasaki bunka kō*. Nagasaki: Junshin Daigaku Hakubutsukan, 1998.

Farge, William J. *The Japanese Translations of the Jesuit Mission Press, 1590–1614*. Lewiston, NY: Edwin Mellen Press, 2002.

Faria, António Machado de. "Cavaleiros da Ordem de Cristo no Século XVI" in *Arqueologia e Historia*, 8a serie, vol. 6 (1955): 13–73.

Farmer, David Hugh. *The Oxford Dictionary of Saints*. Oxford: Clarendon Press, 1978.

Farrington, Anthony. *The English Factory in Japan 1613–1623*. 2 vols. London: British Library, 1991.

Felgueiras Gaio. *Nobiliário de Famílias de Portugal*, ed. by Agostinho de Azavedo Meirelles and Domingos de Araujo Affonso. Braga: Pax, 1938.

Ferguson, Donald. *Letters from Portuguese Captives in Canton, Written in 1534 and 1536*. Bombay: Education Society's Steam Press, Byculla, 1902.

Flynn, Dennis O., and Arturo Giráldez. "China and the Manila Galleons" in A.J.H. Latham and H. Kawakatsu. *Japanese Industrialization and the Asian Economy*. New York: Routledge, 1994, pp. 71–90.

———. "Born with a 'Silver Spoon': The Origin of World Trade in 1571" in *JWH*, vol. 6, 2 (1995): 201–21.

Fok, K.C. "Early Ming Images of the Portuguese" in Roderich Ptak, ed. *Aspects in History and Economic History, Sixteenth and Seventeenth Centuries*. Stuttgart: Franz Steiner Verlag, 1987, pp. 143–55.

Foucault, Michel. *Discipline and Punish: The Birth of the Prison*. Translated by Alan Sheridan. New York: Pantheon, 1977.

Franco, Antonio. *Imagem da virtude em o noviciado da Companhia de Jesus do Real Collegio do Espiritu Santo de Evora do Reyno de Portugal*. Lisbon: Na Officina Real Deslandesiana, 1714.

———. *Imagem da virtude em o noviciado da Companhia de Jesu na Corte de Lisboa*. Coimbra: no Real Collegio das Artes da Companhia de Jesu, 1717.

Frois, Luis. *Die Geschichte Japans. 1549–1578*. Translated by G. Schurhammer and E.A. Voretzsch. Leipzig: Asia Major, 1926.

———. *Tratado dos Embaixadores Japoes que forão de Japão a Roma no anno de 1582*. See: Abranches, J.A. et al. (1942). *La première ambassade du Japon en Europe*.

———. *Historia de Japam*. 5 vols. Edited and annotated by José Wicki. Lisbon: Biblioteca Nacional, 1976–84.

Fujita Motoharu. "Tenjiku Tokubei toten kōrokō" in *Rekishi to chiri*, vol. 27, 1 (1931): 165–180.

Fujiwara Arikazu. "Nagasaki ni okeru Kirishitan danatsu to hisabetsu buraku" in *Hōseishi kenkyū* no. 40 (1990): 61–65.

Ganss, George E. see: Loyola, Ignatius de.

Garces, Garcia. *Relacion de la Persecucion que huvo en la Iglesia de Japon*. Mexico: Diego Garrido, 1624.

Gense, J.H., and A. Conti. *In the Days of Gonzalo Garcia 1557–1597*. Bombay: St. Xavier College, 1957.

Gil, Juan. *Hidalgos y Samurais. España y Japón en los siglos XVI y XVII*. Madrid: Alianza Editorial, 1991.

Gonoi Takashi. "Keichō 14nen (1609) no kiito bōeki ni tsuite" in SZ vol. 81, 11 (1972): 37–64.

———. "1610-nen Nagasaki oki ni okeru Madore-de-Deusugō yakiuchi ni kansuru hōkokusho" in KK vol. 16 (1976): 301–364.

———. "Kinseika no senkyōshi no dōkō to Nagasaki" in NR, no. 361 (1978): 18–44.

———. "Iezusu kaishi Kimura Reonarudo to Nagasaki rō" in *Nagasaki shishi geppō*, no. 3 (1981): 2–4.

———. "Kan'ei nenkan, Furanshisukokai no zaibutsu to Manira hasen ni tsuite" in NR no. 437 (1984): 47–64.

———. *Nihon kirishitanshi no kenkyū*. Tokyo: Yoshikawa Kōbunkan, 2002.

———. "Hiryo Chōsenjin to kirishitokyō: 16, 17 seiki nikkan kirishitokyō kankeishi" in SHJKK, no. 13 (2003): 41–59.

———. "Bungo ni okeru kirishitan bunka" in *Ōita kenritsu rekishi hakubutsukan kenkyū kiyō*, no. 7 (2006): 94–116.

———. "Kyōku shisai Araki Tomasu ni kansuru mikan shokan ni tsuite" in: *Sapientia* no. 41 (2007): 25–40.

———. Yokoseura no kaikō to shōbō ni tsuite in *Sapientia* no. 47 (2013): 1–28.

[Gualtieri, Guido.] *Newe warhafte auszführliche Beschreibung der Jüngstabgesandten Japonischen Legation ganzen Raisz ausz Japon bisz gen Rom und widerumd von dannen in Portugal, bis zu ihrem abschid ausz Liszbona. Auch vonn grossen Ehren so ihnen allenthalben von Fürsten unnd Herrn erzaigt und was sich sunst mit ihnen verlossen*. Dilingen: Joann Mayst, 1587.

Guerreiro, Fernão. *Relaçam annual das cousas que fizeram os padres da Companhia de Iesus na India, & Iapão nos annos de 600. & 601.* Evora: Manoel de Lyra, 1603.

_____. *Relação anual das coisas que fizeram os padres da companhia de Iesus nas suas missões do Japão, China, Cataio, Tidore, Ternate, Ambóino, Malaca, Pegu, Bengala, Bisnagá, Maduré, Costa da Pescaria, Manar, Ceilão, Travancor, Malabar, Sodomala, Goa, Salcete, Lahor, Diu, Etiopia a alta ou Preste João, Monomotapa, Angola, Guiné, Serra Leoa, Cabo Verde e Brasil nos anos de 1600 a 1609.* [New edition edited by] Artur Viegas. 3 vols. Coimbra: Imprensa da Universidade, 1930 [1600–1603], 1931 [1604–1605], 1942 [1607–1609].

Gutiérrez, Fernando G. "A Survey of Nanban Art" in: Cooper 1971, pp. 147–206.

Guzmán, Luis de. *Historia de las Missiones que han hecho los Religiosos de la Compañia de Iesus, para Predicar el Sancto Euangelio en la India Oriental, y en los Reynos de la China y Iapon.* 2 vols. Alcala: Iuan Gracian, 1601 [Tenri University Library Facsimile Reprint, 1976].

Gysbertsz, Reyer. *De Tyrannije ende Wreedtheden der Iappanen.* Amsterdam: Fredericksz Stam, 1637.

Halikowski Smith, Stefan. "No Obvious Home: The Flight of the Portuguese "Tribe" from Makassar to Ayutthaya and Cambodia during the 1660s" in *International Journal of Asian Studies*, vol. 7, 1 (2010): 1–28.

Harich Schneider, Eta. "Renaissance Europe through Japanese Eyes. Record of a Strange Triumphal Journey" in *Early Music* (1973): 19–25.

Hartmann, Arnulf. *The Augustinians in Seventeenth Century Japan.* New York: Augustinian Historical Institute, 1965.

Hayashi Akira, and Miyazaki Shigemi, compilers. *Tsūkō Ichiran.* Ed. Kokusho kankōkai, 8 vols. Osaka, Seibundō, 1967.

Hayashi Razan. *Razan Sensei Bunshū.* 4 vols. Edited by Kyōto Shisekikai. Kyōto: Heian Kōkogakkai, 1918–20.

Heeres, J.L., ed. *Daghregister gehouden int Casteel Batavia vant passerende daer ter plaetse als over geheel Nederlandts-India.* The Hague: Nijhoff, 1896–1898.

Hesselink, Reinier H. *Twee spiegels op Cambang.* Utrecht: H&S, 1984.

_____. *Prisoners from Nambu. Reality and Make-Believe in Seventeenth-Century Japanese Diplomacy.* Honolulu: University of Hawaii Press, 2002.

_____. "The Two Faces of Nagasaki: The World of the Suwa Festival Screen" in MN, vol. 59, 2 (2004): 179–222.

_____. "An Anti-Christian Register from Nagasaki" in BPJS, no. 18/19 (2009): 9–66.

_____. "I Go Shopping in Christian Nagasaki: Entries from the Diary of a Mito Samurai, Ōwada Shigekiyo (1593)" in BPJS, no. 22 (2015).

_____. "The *Capitães Mores* of the Japan Voyage: A Group Portrait" in *International Journal of Asian Studies*, vol. 9,1 (2012): 1–41.

_____. "A Metal Dealer and Spy from Nagasaki in Manila in the First Quarter of the Seventeenth Century" in Jane Kate Leonard and Ulrich Theobald, eds. *Money in Asia (1200–1900): Small Currencies in Social and Political Contexts.* Leiden: Brill, 2015, pp. 487–508.

Higashibaba, Ikuo. *Christianity in Early Modern Japan: Kirishitan Belief and Practice.* Leiden/Boston: Brill. 2001.

Himeno, Jun'ichi. "Hisenkan to mibun <Kirishitan jidai> gaikoku shiryō ni miru hisabetsu buraku no seisei" in *Nagasaki buraku kaihō kenkyū,* no. 13 (October 1986): 37–74; no. 15 (October 1987): 15–51.

Hinotani, Teruhiko, and Emoto Hiroshi, eds. *Taikōki.* In *Shin Nihon koten bungaku taikei,* vol. 60. Tokyo: Iwanami Shoten, 1996.

Höpfl, Harro. "'*Suaviter in modo, fortiter in re*': Appearance, Reality and the Early Jesuits" in Stephen Linstead and Heather Höpfl, eds.: *The Aesthetics of Organization.* London: Sage, 2000, pp. 197–211.

Hori Isao. *Hayashi Razan.* Tokyo: Yoshikawa Kōbunkan, 1964.

Hotei Atsushi. *Nagasaki ishi monogatari: ishi ga kataru Nagasaki no oitachi.* Nagasaki: Nagasaki bunkensha, 2005.

Hsia, R. Po-chia. *A Jesuit in the Forbidden City: Matteo Ricco 1552–1610.* Oxford: Oxford University Press, 2010.

Hur, Nam-lin. *Death and Social Order in Tokugawa Japan. Buddhism, Anti-Christianity, and the Danka System.* Cambridge: Harvard University Press, 2007.

Ide Katsumi. "Haikyōsha Fukansai Fabian bannen no ichishiryō" in KBKK vol. 9, 3 (1966/10): 26–31.

_____. "Haikyōsha Fukansai Fabian no shōgai" in *Hiroshima kōdai kenkyū kiyō,* vol. 7, 2 (1973): 1–16.

_____. "Fukansai Fabian *Myōtei mondō* jōkan 'Zenshū no koto' ni tsuite" *Shigaku kenkyū* no. 121–122 (1974): 87–104.

_____. "Haikyōsha Fukansai Fabian no shōgai (hosetsu)" in *Shigaku,* vol. 48, 1 (1977): 23–31.

_____. "Kōchū Habiancho 'Hadeusu' (1620 nen)" in *Kirishitokyō shigaku* vol. 51 (1997): 93–127.

Ide Tamotsu. *Karatsujō Terazawa Godaiki.* Karatsu: Karatsu shinbunsha, 1975.

Ikuta Shigeru. "Sekai kōro no shuten Nagasaki" in *Higashi Shinakai to seiyō bunka (Umi to rettō bunka* vol. 4). Tokyo: Shōgakkan, 1992a, pp. 413–42.

_____. "Supein teikokuryō 'Nihon' no yume" in *Higashi Shinakai to seiyō bunka (Umi to rettō bunka* vol. 4). Tokyo: Shōgakkan, 1992b, pp. 443–78.

Innes, Robert LeRoy. *The Door Ajar: Japan's Foreign Trade in the Seventeenth Century.* 2 vols. Ph.D. dissertation, Ann Arbor: University of Michigan, 1980.

Irikura, James K. *Trade and Diplomacy Between the Philippines and Japan, 1585–1623.* Ph.D. dissertation, New Haven: Yale University, 1958.

Isomoto Tsunenobu. *Yoki hi e no kiseki.* Nagasaki: Nagasaki-ken buraku kenkyūjo, 1985.

Itabashi Susumu. *Nanbansen ga kita koro—Hirado, Nagasaki kirishitanki.* Shiseidō shinsho no. 48. Tokyo: Shiseidō, 1971.

Iwao Sei'ichi. "Nagasaki daikan Murayama Tō'an to sono botsuraku" in *Rekishi chiri*, vol. 47, 2 (1926): 7–27 (107–27).

_____. *Early Japanese Settlers in the Philippines*. Tokyo: Foreign Affairs Association of Japan, 1943.

_____. *Shuinsen bōekishi no kenkyū*. Tokyo: Kōbundō, 1958 (reprinted as *Shinpan shuinsen bōekishi no kenkyū*. Tokyo: Yoshikawa kōbunkan, 1985).

_____. "Japanese Gold and Silver in the World History" in: Nihon Yunesuko Kokunai Iinkai, ed. *International Symposium on History of Eastern and Western Cultural Contacts* (28 Oct.–5 Nov. 1957). Tokyo: [n.p.], 1959, pp. 63–7.

_____. "Nagasaki no machidoshiyori Gotō Shōzaemonden ho'i: shoki Nagasaki ginza no kinō ni tsuite no ichi kōsatsu" in *Nihon daigaku shigakkai kenkyū ihō*, no. 5, 6 (1963): 1–9.

_____. *Shuinsen to Nihon machi*. Tokyo: Shibundō, 1966, 1985.

Iwasaki Cauti, Fernando. *Extremo Oriente y Peru en el siglo XVI*. Madrid: Editorial Mapfre, 1992.

Jorissen, Engelbert. "Exotic and "Strange" Images of Japan in European Texts of the Early 17th Century: An Interpretation of the Contexts of History of Thought and Literature" in BPJS, vol. 4 (2002): 37–61.

Kansei chōshū shokafu. 27 vols. Tokyo: Zoku gunsho ruijūkanseikai, 1964.

Kataoka Yakichi. "Hakugaika no kirishitan—Nagasaki ni okeru yadonushi no gyōseki wo chūshin toshite" in KBKK, vol. 6, 4 (1963): 7–14.

_____. "Nagasaki no kyōkai chigyō mondai ni tsuite" in ND no. 50 (1970): 35–52.

_____. *Nihon kirishitan junkyōshi*. Tokyo: Jijitsūshinsha, 1979.

_____. *Nagasaki no kirishitan*. Nagasaki: Seibō no kishisha, 1989.

Katō Eichi. "Sakoku to bakuhansei kokka" in Katō Eichi and Yamada Tadao (eds). *Sakoku*. Tokyo: Yūhikaku, 1981, pp. 54–115.

Kawashima, Motojirō. *Shuinsen bōekishi*. Kyoto: Naigai shuppan kabushiki kaisha, 1921.

Kishino Hisashi. "Furanshisuko Zabieru no Higashi Ajia fukyō kōsō" in SHJKK, no. 11 (2001): 188–94.

Kitagawa, Tomoko. "The Conversion of Hideyoshi's Daughter Gō" in JJRS, vol. 34, 1 (2007): 9–25.

Kleiser, Alfons. "P. Valignanis Gesandtschaftsreise nach Japan zum Quambacudono Toyotomi Hideyoshi 1588–1591" in MN vol. 1, no. 1 (1938): 70–98.

Knauth, Lothar. *Confrontación transpacífica: El Japón y el Nuevo Mundo Hispánico 1542–1639*. Mexico: Universidad Nacional Autónoma de México, Instituto de Investigaciones Históricas, 1972.

Kobata Atsushi, ed. *Hirado Matsurake shiryō*. Kyoto: Kyoto daigaku bungakubu kokushi kenkyūshitsu, 1951.

Kōbe shiritsu hakubutsukan/Kobe City Museum, ed. *Nanban bijutsu serekushon/Nanban Arts Selection*. Kobe: Kōbe-shi tai'iku kyōku, 1998.

Koga, Jūjirō. *Nagasaki kaikōshi*. Nagasaki: Koga Jūjirō-Ōikō kankōkai, 1957.

Kojima Yukie. *Nagasaki daikan Murayama Tōan: sono ai to ainan*. Nagasaki: Seibo no kishisha, 1991.

Kokushi daijiten henshū iinkai, ed. *Kokushi daijiten*. 15 vols. Tokyo: Yoshikawa kōbunkan, 1979–97.

Konrad, Herman W. *A Jesuit Hacienda in Colonial Mexico: Santa Lucia, 1576–1767*. Stanford, CA: Stanford University Press, 1980.

Kouamé, Nathalie. "Une «drôle de répression» Pour une nouvelle interprétation des mesures antichrétiennes du général Toyotomi Hideyoshi (1582–1598)" in: Arnaud Brotons e.a., eds. *État, religion et répression en Asie. Chine, Corée, Japon, Vietnam (XIIIe–XXIe siècles)*. Paris: Éditions Karthala, 2011, pp. 149–82.

Kuechler, L.W. "Marriage in Japan. Including a Few Remarks on the Marriage Ceremony, the Position of Married Women, and Divorce" in TASJ vol. 13 (1885): 114–37.

Laures, Johannes. *Kirishitan Bunko. A Manual of Books and Documents on the Early Christian Mission in Japan*. Tokyo: Sophia University, 1957 (reprint Rinsen shoten, 1985).

LeGoff, Jacques, and Jean-Claude Schmitt (eds.). *Le Charivari. Actes de la table ronde organisée à Paris (25–27 avril 1977) par l'École des Hautes Études en Sciences Sociales et le Centre National de la Recherche Scientifique*. Paris: Mouton, 1981.

Li Hsien-chang. "Nagasaki: Tōjin kihajimeta shoki no koto" in *Kakyō seikatsu*, vol. 2, no. 4 (1963): 1–9.

_____. *Maso shinkō no kenkyū*. Tokyo: Taisan Bunbutsusha, 1979.

_____. *Nagasaki tōjin no kenkyū*. Nagasaki: Shinwa ginkō furusato shinkō kikin, 1991.

Lidin, Olof G. *Tanegashima: The Arrival of Europeans in Japan*. Copenhagen: Nordic Institute of Asian Studies, 2002.

Lima, Jacinto Leitão Manso de. See: Faria, Antonio Machado de.

Lin Renchuan, "Fukien's Private Sea Trade in the 16th and 17th Centuries" translated by Barend ter Haar. In: Eduard B. Vermeer, ed. *Development and Decline of Fukien Province in the 17th and 18th Centuries*. Leiden: Brill, 1990, pp. 163–215.

Linschoten, Jan Huygen van. *Itinerario Voyage ofte schipvaert van Jan Huyghen van Linschoten naer Oost ofte Portugaels Indien 1579–1592*. 3 vols. Edited by H. Kern and H. Terpstra. Linschoten Vereeniging, vols. 57, 58, 60. The Hague: Nijhoff, 1910, repr. 1955.

_____. *Itinerario Voyage ofte schipvaert van Jan Huygen van Linschoten naer Oost ofte Portugaels Indien 1579–1592*. 2 vols. Edited by J.C.M. Warnsinck. Linschoten Vereeniging, vol. 43. The Hague: Nijhoff, 1939.

Lobato, Manuel. *Política e Comércio dos Portugueses na Insulíndia: Malaca e as Molucas de 1575 a 1605*. Lisboa: Instituto Português do Oriente, 1999.

López Gay, Jesús. *El matrimonio de los japoneses. Problema, y soluciones según un ms. Inédito de Gil de la Mata, S.J. (1547–1599)*. Roma: Libreria dell'Università Gregoriana, 1964.

_____. "Father Francesco Pasio (1554–1612) and His

Ideas About the Sacerdotal Training of the Japanese" in BPJS vol. 3 (2001): 27–42.

Loyola, Ignatius de. *The Constitutions of the Society of Jesus.* Translated with an Introduction and Commentary by George E. Ganss. St. Louis: Institute of Jesuit Sources, 1970.

Lozoyo, Juan de. *The Escorial: The Royal Palace at La Granja de San Ildefonso.* Translated by James Brockway. New York: Meredith Press, 1967.

Lu, David J. *Japan: A Documentary History.* New York: M.E. Sharpe, 1997.

Lucena, Afonso de. *De algumas cousas que ainda se alembra o Padre Afonso de Lucena que pertencem à Christandade de Ōmura [1578-1614].* See: Schütte, Josef Franz (1972).

Macintyre, Ben. *Operation Mincemeat: How a Dead Man and a Bizarre Plan Fooled the Nazis and Assured an Allied Victory.* London: Bloomsbury, 2010.

Maki Hidemasa. *Nihonhōshi ni okeru jinshin baibai no kenkyū.* Tokyo: Yūhikaku, 1961.

Martínez Pérez, Jesús. *Fray Juan Pobre de Zamora. Historia de la pérdida y descubrimiento del galeón "San Felipe"* Ávila: Institución "Gran Duque de Alba" de la Excellentissima Diputación Provincial de Ávila, 1997.

Massarella, Derek. *A World Elsewhere: Europe's Encounter with Japan in the Sixteenth and Seventeenth Centuries.* New Haven: Yale University Press, 1990.

Matos, Gabriel de. *Relaçam da perseguiçam que teve a Christandade de Iapam desde Mayo de 1612 até Novembro de 1614.* Lisboa: Pedro Crasbeek, 1616.

Matsuda Ki'ichi. *Kinsei shoki Nihon kankei nanban shiryō no kenkyū.* Tokyo: Kazama shobō, 1967.

_____. *Ōmura Sumitada kō to Nagasaki Jinzaemon. Nagasaki kaikō yonhyakunen kinen.* Sasebo: Shinwa Ginkō Zaibikai, 1970.

_____: *Ōmura Sumitada-den.* Tokyo: Kyōbunkan, 1978.

Matsuura Naoji. *Kaikō yonhyakunen Nagasaki no rekishi.* Nagasaki: Nagasaki Bunkensha, 1970.

Matthew, K.M. *History of the Portuguese Navigation in India (1497-1600).* Delhi: Mittal, 1988.

Mayer, Oskar. "Fukansai Fabian and Kirishitan: A Paradigm of Modern Awareness" in Stephen Turnbull, ed.: *Japan's Hidden Christians 1549-1999,* vol. 1. *Open Christianity in Japan 1549-1639.* Richmond (Surrey)/Tokyo: Curzon Press/Edition Synapse, 2000, pp. 23–43.

McCall, John E. "Early Jesuit Art in the Far East I–V" in *Artibus Asiae,* vol. 10, 2 (1947): 121–137; vol. 10, 3 (1947): 216–233; vol. 10, 4 (1947): 283–301; vol. 11, 1–2 (1948): 45–69; vol. 17, 1 (1954): 39–54.

Medina, João, ed. *História de Portugal: dos tempos préhistóricos aos nossos dias.* Vol. 5: *Os Descubrimentos. II Os Impérios.* Amadora: Ediclube, n.d.

Miki Sei'ichirō. "Kirishitan kinrei no saikentō" in KK vol. 23 (1983): 115–138.

Millioud, Alfred. "Histoire du couvent catholique de Kyoto" [*Nanbanji kōhaiki*] in *Revue de l'histoire des religions,* vol. 31 (1895): 270–91, vol. 32 (1895): 25–50.

Miyake Hidetoshi. "Nagasaki bugyō Hasegawa Sahei ronkō—kinsei gaikō seisaku no ichikōsatsu" in *Shien* 69 (1956): 75–97.

Miyazaki Eiichi. "Chijiwa Migeru no shōgai to shison" in *Ōmura shidan* no. 51 (2000): 107–126.

Miyazaki Kentarō. "Tenshō kenŏshisetsu no jinbutsu kenkyū" in ND no. 68 (1984): 21–49.

_____. "Reonarudo Kimura no Kurusu machi-rō yori no ichi shokan no kenkyū" in ND no. 70 (1985): 26–40.

Montalto de Jesus, C. A. *Historic Macao: International Traits in China Old and New.* Macao: Salesian Printing Press and Tipografia Mercantil, 1926.

Moore, Ray A. *Soldier of God. MacArthur's Attempt to Christianize Japan.* Portland, ME: Merwin Asia, 2011.

Moran, J.F. *The Japanese and the Jesuits. Alessandro Valignano in Sixteenth-Century Japan.* New York: Routledge, 1993.

Morejon, Pedro. *A Briefe Relation of the Persecution Lately Made Against the Catholike Christians, in the Kingdome of Iaponia* [1619] Transl. by W.W. Gent. N.p., 1619. (London: Scolar Press [Reprint], 1974).

_____. *Relacion de los martyres del Iapon del año de 1627.* Mexico [City]: Iuan Ruyz, 1631.

Moriyama Tsuneo. "Shimabara-han" in Kodama Kōta and Kitajima Masamoto (eds.) *Dainiki Monogatari hanshi,* vol. 7 *Kyūshū no shohan.* Tokyo: Jinbutsu ōraisha, 1966, pp. 217–257.

Mungello, D.E. *Curious Land. Jesuit Accomodation and the Origins of Sinology.* Honolulu: University of Hawaii Press, 1985.

Muñoz, Honorio. *Epistolario de los MM. Dominicos de Japón.* [Manila: Convento de Santo Domingo, 1967].

Murakami Naojirō. *Ikoku ōfuku shokanshū / Zōtei ikoku nikki shō.* Tokyo: Shunnansha, 1929.

_____. "An Old Church Calendar in Japanese" in MN, vol. 5, 1 (1942): 219–224.

Murdoch, James. *A History of Japan.* Vol. 2 *During the Century of Early Foreign Intercourse (1542-1651).* London: Kegan Paul, Trench, Trubner, 1925.

Nagasaki jikki nendai roku. Ed. Kyūshū daigaku daigakuin hikaku shakai bunka kenkyūka Kyūshū bunkashi kenkyūjo shiryōshū kankōkai. Fukuoka: Kyūshū bunkashi kenkyūjo, 1999.

Nagasaki jitsuroku taisei, Tanba Kankichi and Morinaga Taneo (eds.) in *Nagasaki sōsho,* series 1, vol. 2. Nagasaki: Nagasaki bunkensha, 1973.

Nagasaki-kenshi: taigai kōshō hen. Nagasaki: Nagasaki-ken, 1985.

Nagasaki meika ryakufu, edited by Kanai Toshiyuki and printed in: Nagasaki shiyakusho, ed. *Zōho Nagasaki Ryakushi. Nagasaki sōsho,* vol. 3. Nagasaki: Fujiki Hakueisha, 1926, pp. 547–627.

Nagasaki shiyakusho, ed. *Nagasaki shishi. Chishihen butsujibu* 2 vols.; *Jinja-kyōkaibu* 1 vol.; *Meishō kyūsekibu* 1 vol.; *Tsūkōbōekihen Seiyōshokokubu, Tōyōshokokubu,* 2 vols.; *Fūzokuhen* 2 vols. Osaka: Seibundō, Reprint 1967 (originally published in Nagasaki 1923-1938).

Nagayama Tokihide. *Zōtei Kirishitan shiryōshū—Collection of Historical Materials Connected with the Roman Catholic Religion in Japan*. Nagasaki: Taigai shiryō hōkan kankōkai, 1927.

Nakada Yasunao, ed. *Kinsei taigai kankeishi ron*. Tokyo: Yūshindō kōbunsha, 1979.

———. "Itowappu nakama no seiritsu ni tsuite: Itowappu yuishogaki no hattan kiji no shinpyōsei wo megutte" in [*Chūō daigaku bungakubu*] *Kiyō shigakka*, no. 28 (1983a): 1–60.

———. "Hideyoshi—Ieyasu seiken to Nagasaki" in *Rekishi techō* vol. 11, 12 (1983b): 4–12.

Nakamura Tadashi. "Jinbetsuchō yori mita kinsei shoki no Nagasaki Hiradomachi" in *Kyūshū shigaku*, no. 26 (1964): 12–28.

Nelson, Thomas. "Slavery in Medieval Japan" in MN vol. 59, 4 (2004): 463–92.

Newitt, Malyn. "Prince Henry and the Origins of European Expansion" in Malyn Newitt (ed.). *The First Portuguese Colonial Empire*. Exeter: Exeter University Press, 1986, pp. 9–35.

———. "Formal and Informal Empire in the History of Portuguese Expansion" in: *Portuguese Studies*, vol. 17 (2001): 1–21.

———. *A History of Portuguese Overseas Expansion, 1400-1668*. New York: Routledge, 2005.

[Nieremberg, Juan Eusebio and Alonso de Andrade]. *Varones Ilustres de la Compañia de Jesus*. Tomo I: Mision del Japon. Bilbao: Administracion del "Mensajero del Corazon de Jesus," 1887.

Nieremberg, Juan Eusebio. "Ruisu de Arumeida den" translated by Sakuma Tadashi in KK vol. 24 (1984): 19–27.

Nosco Peter. "Keeping the Faith: Bakuhan Policy Towards Religions in Seventeenth Century Japan" in P.F. Kornicki and I.J. McMullen (eds.). *Religions in Japan. Arrows to Heaven and Earth*. Cambridge: Cambridge University Press, 1996, pp. 135–155.

Obara, Satoru, ed. *Kirishitan bunko. Iezusukai Nihon kankei monjo*. Tokyo: Nansōsha, 1981.

Ocio, Hilario, and Eladio Neira. *Misioneros Dominicos en el Extremo Oriente, 1587-1835*. Manila: Orientalia Dominica, 2000.

Ōishi Kazuhisa. *Tenshō ken'ō shisetsu Chijiwa Migeru no boseki hakken*. Nagasaki: Nagasaki bunkensha, 2005.

Oka Mihoko. "A Great Merchant in Nagasaki in 17th Century: Suetsugu Heizō II and the System of Respondência" in BPJS, vol. 2 (2001): 37–56.

Okada Akio. *Kirishitan daimyō*. Tokyo: Kyōikusha (Kyō'ikusha rekishi shinsho no. 86), 1977.

Okamoto Yoshitomo. *Jūroku seiki Nichiō kōtsūshi no kenkyū*. Tokyo: Rokkō Shobō [Reprint of 1936, 1952], 1974.

Ōmura shishi hensankai. *Ōmura shishi*. 2 vols. Ōmura: Ōmura shiyakusho, 1972.

Ooms, Herman. *Tokugawa Ideology. Early Constructs*. Princeton, NJ: Princeton University Press, 1985.

Orfanel, Jacinto. *Historia Eclesiastica de los sucessos de la Christiandad de Iapon desde el año de 1602, que entro en el la Orden de Predicadores, hasta el de 1620*. Madrid: Viuda de Alonso Martin, 1633.

Orita Takeshi. "Chūgoku bōeki no utsuri kawari" in Nagasaki Chūgoku kōryū kyōkai, ed. *Nagasaki kakyō monogatari: Chūgoku bōeki, tōjin yashiki, Nagasaki kakyō*. Nagasaki: Nagasakiken Rōdō kinko, 2001, pp. 6–26.

Ōsumi Kazuo. "Historical Notes on Women and the Japanization of Buddhism" translated and adapted by Cecilia Segawa-Seigle and Barbara Ruch in: Barbara Ruch, ed. *Engendering Faith. Women and Buddhism in Japan*. Ann Arbor: Center for Japanese Studies/University of Michigan, 2002, pp. xxvii–xlii.

Ōtsuka Mitsunobu, ed. *Koryādo Zangeroku*. Tokyo: Kazama shobō, 1957, 1961.

Pacheco, Diego. "Nagasaki sotomachi to Urakami kanchi mondai ni tsuite" translated by Sakuma Tadashi in KSK vol. 16 (1965): 31–37.

———. "El primer mapa de Nagasaki" in *Boletin de la Asociacion española de Orientalistas*, Año II (1966): 9–20.

———. *Nagasaki wo hiraita hito: Kosume de Tōresu no shōgai*. Translated by Sakuma Tadashi. Tokyo: Chūō shuppansha, 1969.

———. "The Founding of the Port of Nagasaki and Its Cession to the Society of Jesus" in MN, vol. 25, nos. 3–4 (1970): 303–323.

———. "Diogo de Mesquita, S.J. and the Jesuit Mission Press" in MN, vol. 26, nos. 3–4 (1971): 431–443.

———. "Nagasaki Santiago byō'in no kane" translated by Sakuma Tadashi in KK vol. 14 (1972): 231–255.

———ego. "Nagasaki no kyōkai, 1567-1620" in ND, no. 58 (1975): 1–18.

———. "Iglesias de Nagasaki durante el "Siglo cristiano" 1568-1620" in *Boletin de la Asociación Española de Orientalistas* (1977): 49–70.

[Pacheco, Diego] Yūki Ryōgo. "Nagasaki sotomachi no mondai: 1605nen–1607nen" in ND no. 68 (1984a): 1–20.

———. "Nihon ni okeru saigo no kirishitan otona" in ND no. 69 (1984b): 1–5.

———. "Nagasaki sotomachi tochi kōkan mondai: sono ni" in ND no. 69 (1984c): 7–48.

———. "Deshima no tanjō" in ND, no. 70 (1985): 4–25.

———. *Os quatro legados dos dáimios de Quiuxu após regressarem ao Japão*. Macau: Instituto Cultural de Macau, 1990.

———. "Nagasaki ni okeru Makao no Kapitan Mōru" in *Portuguese Voyages to Asia and Japan in the Renaissance Period. Proceedings of the International Conference Sophia University, Tokyo September 24-26, 1993*, Tokyo: Portuguese Embassy in Japan, [1993], pp. 337–344.

———. "A Present of Arabian Horses" translated by Fumiko F. Earns in *Crossroads* no. 2 (1994).

———. *Bento Fernandesu, Japão, 1579-1633, De Borba no Alto Alentejo a Colina Nishizaka em Nagasaki*. Macau: Edição bilingue Portuges-Japones, 1997.

———. "Nihon ni okeru saisho no hōjin shisai" in ND no. 90 (2001): 1–36.

———. "Genna daijunkyō no gonin no intonsha" in KBKK no. 121 (2003): 1–25.

Pagés, Léon. *Histoire de la religion chrétienne au Japon*. 2 vols. Paris: Douniol, 1869.

Paramore, Kiri. *Ideology and Christianity in Japan*. New York: Routledge, 2009.

Pardo de San Francisco, Diego. *Relacion verdadera y breve de la persecucion y Martirios que padecieron por la confession de nuestra Santa Fee Catholica en Iapon, quinze Religiosos de la Prouincia de S. Gregorio, de los Descalços del Orden de nuestro Seraphico P. San Francisco de las Islas Philipinas*. Manila: Thomas Pimpin, 1625.

Parker, Geoffrey. *The Military Revolution: Military Innovation and the Rise of the West, 1500-1800*. Cambridge: Cambridge University Press, 1988, 1996.

Paske-Smith, M.T. "Japanese Trade and Residence in the Philippines: Before and During the Spanish Occupation" in TASJ vol. 42 (1914): 683-710.

[Pereira, Antonio Pinto]. *História da Índia no tempo em que a governou o Visorei Dom Luís de Ataide*. Coimbra: Nicolao Carualho, 1617 (reprint: Lisboa: Imprente Nacional—Casa da Moeda, 1987).

Perez, Lorenzo, ed. *Relaciones de Fr. Diego de San Francisco sobre las persuciones de christianismo en el Japon (1625-1632)*. Madrid: Gabriel Lopez del Horno, 1914.

_____. "Cartas y Relaciones del Japon. Cartas de San Pedro Bautista" in AIA vol. 4 (1915): 388-418; 6 (1916): 197-309; 9 (1918): 55-142, 168-263; 10 (1918): 26-70; 11 (1919): 232-292; 13 (1920): 29-60, 145-197, 321-375; 14 (1920): 161-206; 15 (1921): 166-208, 332-359; 16 (1921): 54-105, 163-219; 17 (1922): 29-78; 19 (1923): 145-194.

_____. "Fray Jeronimo de Jesus restaurador de las misiones del Japon. Sus cartas y relaciones (1595-1604)" in AFH vol. 16 (1923): 507-44; 17 (1924): 98-117; 18 (1925): 90-113, 559-80; 19 (1926): 385-417.

_____. "El Beato Ricardo de Santa Ana y otros martires del Japon en el siglo XVII" in AIA vol. 15 (1921): 26-66.

Peri, Noël. *Essai sur les relations de Japon et de l'Indochine aux XVI et XVII siècles*. [Hanoi:] Extrait du Bulletin de l'Ecole française d'Extrème-Orient, vol. 23, 1923.

Porter, Jonathan. "The Transformation of Macao" in *Pacific Affairs*, vol. 66, 1 (1993): 7-20.

_____. "The Troublesome Feringhi: Late Ming Chinese Perceptions of the Portuguese and Macau" in *Portuguese Studies Review*, vol. 7, 2 (1999): 11-35.

Potter, David. "Martyrdom as Spectacle" in Ruth Scodel, ed. *Theater and Society in the Classical World*. Ann Arbor: University of Michigan Press, 1993, pp. 53-88.

Ptak, Roderich. *Portugal in China. Kurzer Abriss der portugiesisch-chinesischen Beziehungen und der Geschichte Macaus im 16. und beginnenden 17. Jahrhundert*. Bad Bol: Klemmerberg Verlag, 1980.

_____. "Sino-Japanese Maritime Trade, circa 1550: Merchants, Ports and Networks" in Roberto Carneiro and A. Teodoro de Matos [eds.]. *O Seculo christão do Japão* Lisbon, 1994, pp. 281-311.

Razan sensei bunshū, see Hayashi Razan.

Rébouis, Hippolyte, ed. *Les Coutumes de Clermont-Dessus en Agenais 1262*. Paris: L. Larose, 1881.

Reff, Daniel T. *Disease, Depopulation, and Culture Change in Northwestern New Spain, 1518-1764*. Salt Lake City: University of Utah Press, 1991.

Rego, Antonio da Silva. *A presença de Portugal em Macau*. Lisbon: Agência Geral das Colónias, 1946.

Relacion breve de los grandes y rigurosos martirios que el año passado de 1622 dieron en el Iapon a ciento y diez y ocho iustissimos Martyres, sacada principalmente de las cartas de los Padres de la Compañia de Iesus que alli residen: y de lo que han referido muchas personas de aquel Reyno, que en dos Nauios llegaron a la Ciudad de Manila a 12 de Agosto de 1623. Madrid: Andres de Parra, 1624. (Cortes 566, ff. 378r-379v).

Relacion verdadera del excelente martyrio que onze religiosos de la sagrada Orden de Predicadores padecieron por Christo nuestro en el Imperio del Iapon los años de 1618 y 1622, y de Religiosos de la Orden del Padre Serafico San Francisco descalços, y de otros assi Religiosos, y Clerigos, como seglares, niños, y mugeres valerosas. Valencia: Miguel Sorolla, 1624.

Ribadeneira, Marcelo. *Historia de las Islas del archipiélago filipino y reynos de la Gran China, Tartaria, Cochinchina, Malaca, Siam, Cambodge y Japón*. [Barcelona 1601] edicion J.R. de Legísima. Madrid: La Editorial Católica, 1947.

Ribeiro, Vítor. *Bispos Portugueses e jesuítas no Japão. Cartas de D. Luiz Cerqueira*. Lisbon: Academia das Ciências, 1936.

Ricard, Robert. *La "conquête spirituelle" du Mexique. Essai sur l'apostolat et les méthodes missionaires des ordres mendicants en Nouvelle-Espagne de 1523/24 à 1572*. Paris: Institut d'Ethnologie, 1933.

Rios Coronel, Hernando de. *Memorial y Relacion para Su Magestad del Procurador de las Filippinas de lo que conviene remediar y de la riqueza que ay en ellas y en las Islas del Maluco*. Madrid: Viuda de Fernando Correa, 1621. [translation in: Blair and Robertson, vol. 19, pp. 189-297].

Robinson, Kenneth R. "From Raiders to Traders: Border Security and Border Control in Early Choson, 1392-1450" in *Korean Studies* 16 (1992): 94-115.

Rodrigues, Helena Margarida Barros. *Nangasaqui Nanban: Das Origenes À Expulsão dos Portugueses*. Unpublished MA thesis presented to the Faculdade de Ciências Sociais e Himanas at the Universidade Nova de Lisboa, 2006.

Rubin, Miri. *Corpus Christi: The Eucharist in Late Medieval Culture*. Cambridge: Cambridge University Press, 1991.

Ruiz de Medina, Juan. "Corea en la mente evangelizadora Europea desde 1566" in *Boletin de la Asociación Española de Orientalistas*, vol. 23 (1987): 359-68.

_____. "Sobre los orígenes de la Iglesia coreana" in *Hispanica Sacra*, vol. 40 (1988): 541-66.

_____. *El Martirologio de Japon 1558-1873*. Roma: Institutum Historicum SJ, 1999.

Rundall, Thomas. *Memorials of the Empire of Japon*

in the XVI and XVII Centuries. London: Hakluyt Society, 1850. Reprint: New York: Burt Franklin, n.d.

Russell-Wood, A.J.R. *Fidalgos and Philanthropists: The Santa Casa da Misericórdia of Bahia, 1550–1775.* Berkeley: University of California Press, 1968.

Saga-ken shiryō shūsei kankōkai, ed. *Saga-ken shiryō shūsei. Komonjo-hen,* vol. 3. Saga-shi: Saga kenritsu toshokan, 1958.

Saintyves, P. "Le charivari de l'adultère et les courses à corps nus" in *L'ethnographie,* vol. 31 (1935): 7–36.

Sakamoto Masayoshi. *Nihon kirishitan no sei to zoku: haikyōsha Fabian to sono jidai.* Tokyo: Meicho kankōkai, 1981.

Sakamoto Mitsuru. "The Rise and Fall of Christian Art and Western Painting in Japan" in *St. Francis, an Apostle of the East.* Vol. 1. *The Encounter Between Europe and Asia During the Period of the Great Navigations.* Tokyo: Sophia University Press, 1999, pp. 120–35.

_____, [et al.]. *Nanban byōbu shūsei.* Tokyo: Chūō kōron bijutsu shuppan, 2008.

Sakuma Tadashi, Aida Yū, Iwao Sei'ichi, eds. *Abira Hiron Nihon ōkoku-ki.* In: *Daikōkai jidai sōsho,* vol. 9. Tokyo: Iwanami Shoten, 1965.

Salmon, Claudine, and Lombard, Denys. *Les Chinois de Jakarta. Temples et vie collective.* Ann Arbor: University Microfilms International, 1980.

Saso, Michael R. *Taiwan Feasts and Customs. A Handbook of the Principal Feasts and Customs of the Lunar Calendar on Taiwan.* Hsinchu (Taiwan): Chabanel Language Institute, 1965.

Schilling, Konrad. *Das Schulwesen der Jesuiten in Japan (1551–1614).* Münster (Westfalen): Regensbergschen Buchdruckerei, 1931.

Schilling, Dorotheus O.F.M, and Fidel de Lejarza, eds. "Relacion del Reino de Nippon por Bernardino de Avila Girón" in *AIA* vol. 36 (1933): 481–531; 37 (1934): 5–48, 259–75, 392–434, 493–554; 38 (1935): 103–130, 216–39, 384–417.

Schütte, Joseph Franz. "Drei Unterrichtsbücher für Japanische Jesuitenprediger aus dem XVI Jahrhundert" in *AHSI,* vol. 8 (1939): 223–256.

_____. *Valignanos Missionsgrundsätze für Japan.* 2 vols. Rome: Edizioni di Storia e Letteratura, 1951, 1958.

_____. *On Mamori no Santa Maria: Das Fest Unserer Lieben Frau, der Schutzherrin Japans, am japanischen Neujahrstag.* Rome: Institutum Historicum Societatis Jesu, 1954a.

_____. "Valignano's Japangeschichte: Bemerkungen zu Form und Inhalt" in *Analecta Gregoriana,* vol. 72 (1954b): 109–40.

_____. *Documentos sobre el Japon conservados en la Coleccion "Cortes" de la Real Academia de la Historia.* Madrid: Imprenta y Editorial Maestre, 1961.

_____. *El "Archivo del Japon" Vicisitudes del archivo jesuítico del Extremo Oriente y Descripción del fondo existente en la Real Academia de la Historia de Madrid.* Vol 20 of *Archivo documental Español publicado por la Real Academia de la Historia.* Madrid: 25 Años de Paz, 1964.

_____. *Introductio ad Historiam Societatis Jesu in Japonia 1549–1650.* Romae: Apud Institutum Historicum Societatis Jesu, 1968.

_____. "Nagasaki no sōritsu to hatten ni okeru Iezusu no 'konpania' (1567–1570, 1571–1614)" in *ND,* no. 50 (1971): 1–34.

_____. *Erinnerungen aus der Christenheit von Ōmura.* Tokyo: Sophia University, 1972.

_____. *Monumenta Historica Japoniae I: Textus catalogorum Japoniae aliaeque de personis domibusque S.J. in Japonia informationes et relationes 1549–1654.* Rome: Apud "Monumenta Historica Soc. Iesu," 1975.

Schurhammer, Georg. "Die Jesuitenmissionare des 16. und 17. Jahrhunderts und ihr Einfluss auf die japanische Malerei." In: *Jubiläumsband, Deutsche Gesellschaft für Natur- und Völkerkunde Ostasiens anlässlich ihres 60-jährigen Bestehens 1873–1933.* Teil 1 (Tokyo 1933): 116–26.

Schurz, William L. *The Manila Galleon.* New York: Dutton, 1939.

Shapinsky, Peter D. "Predators, Protectors, and Purveyors. Pirates and Commerce in Late Medieval Japan" in *MN,* vol. 64, 2 (2009): 273–313.

Shimizu Hirokazu [Kōichi]. "Hideyoshi seiken to Nagasaki: Bateren tsuihōreigo no Nagasaki shihai wo chūshin toshite" in *RK,* vol. 17, 2 (1969): 11–21.

_____. "Nagasaki daikan Ogasawara Ichian ni tsuite" in *ND* 57 (1975a): 65–77.

_____. "Kinsei shotō Nagasaki daikan no ichi yakuwari ni tsuite: toku ni Hasegawa Fujihiro wo chūshin toshite" in *ND* 58 (1975b): 50–70.

_____. "Kirishitan kankei hōsei shiryōshū" in *KK* vol. 17 (1977a): 251–438.

_____. "Kinsei shotō Nagasaki bugyō no ichi kōsatsu" in *Chūō shigaku* no.1 (1977b): 26–46. Reprinted in Fujino Tamotsu, ed. *Kyūshū to tenryō. Kyūshū kinseishi kenkyū sōsho,* vol. 4. Tokyo: Kokusho kankōkai, 1984, pp. 405–35.

_____. "Nagasaki machidoshiyori hattan yuishogaki" in *Chūō Daigaku ronshū,* vol. 13 (1992): 1–15.

_____. "Bateren tsuihōrei no happu wo megutte" in Fujino Tamotsu, ed. *Kinsei shakai to shūkyō (Ronshū bakuhan taiseishi,* vol. 9). Tokyo: Yuzankaku, 1995, pp. 360–83.

Shimizu Hirokazu. *Shikihō seiken to Kirishitan: Nichiō kōshō no kigen to tenkai.* Tokyo: Iwata shoin, 2001a.

_____. "Hasegawa Gonroku kō" in *Gaiseishi kenkyū,* no. 1 (2001b): 28–70.

SHJ Cocks' *Diary,* see Cocks, Richard.

Sicardo, José. *Christiandad del Japon y dilatada persecucion que padecio. Memorias sacras de los martyres de las ilustres Religiones de Santo Domingo, San Francisco, Compañia de Jesus y crecido numero de Seglares; y con especialidad de los Religiosos del Orden N.P.S Augustin.* Madrid: Francisco Sanz, 1698.

So Kwan-wai. *Japanese Piracy in Ming China During the 16th Century.* East Lansing: Michigan State University Press, 1975.

Sousa, Lucio de. *The Early European Presence in China, Japan, the Philippines and Southeast Asia*

(1555-1590): *The Life of Bartlomeu Landeiro*. Macao: Fundação Macao, 2010.

Souza, George Bryan. *The Survival of Empire. Portuguese Trade and Society in China and the South China Sea, 1630-1754*. Cambridge: Cambridge University Press, 1986.

Spence, Jonathan. *The Memory Palace of Matteo Ricci*. London: Baker and Taylor, 1984.

Sugidani Akira. "17 seiki shotō, Hizen koku Nabeshima ryō ni okeru Dominikokai" in Fujino Tamotsu sensei no kanreki kinen kai [eds.] *Kinsei Nihon no seiji to gaikō*. Tokyo: Yuzankaku, 1993, pp. 225-63.

Taikōki, see Hinotani Teruhiko and Emoto Hiroshi, eds.

Takagi Shōsaku. "Hideyoshi's and Ieyasu's Views of Japan as a Land of the Gods and Its Antecedents: With Reference to the 'Writ for the Expulsion of the Missionaries' of 1614" in *Acta Asiatica*, no. 87 (2004): 59-84.

Takase Kōichirō, "Kirishitan senkyōshi no gunji keikaku" ch. 3 in *Kirishitan jidai no kenkyū*. Tokyo: Iwanami shoten, 1977.

Takase Kōichirō. "Korobi bateren Tomasu Araki" in *Kirishitan jidai taigai kankei no kenkyū*. Tokyo: Yoshikawa kōbunkan, 1994, pp. 595-630.

Takeno Yōko. "Hosokawa-han to Nagasaki bōeki no sui'i—saikoku hōkensei to taigai bōeki no ichi kōsatsu" in RK vol. 17, 2 (1969): 22-27.

Takeno Yōko. "Bōeki toshi Nagasaki no kensetsu to chōsei soshiki" in *Fukuoka daigaku shōgaku ronsō* 21-1 (1976): 55-72.

_____. *Han bōekishi no kenkyū*. Kyoto: Minerva shobō, 1979.

Taya Hirokichi. "Nagasaki no ginza" in Fujino Tamotsu, ed. *Kyūshū to tenryō. Kyūshū kinseishi kenkyū sōsho*, vol. 4. Tokyo: Kokusho kankōkai, 1984, pp. 439-458.

Tellechea Idígoras, J. Ignacio. *Nagasaki. Gesta martirial en Japón (1597). Documentos*. Bibliotheca Salmanticensis Estudios 202. Salamanca: Universidad Pontifica, 1998.

Ter Haar, Barend J. "The Genesis and Spread of Temple Cults in Fukien" in Eduard B. Vermeer, ed. *Development and Decline of Fukien Province in the 17th and 18th Centuries*. Leiden: Brill, 1990, pp. 163-215.

Thomaz, Luís Filipe Ferreira Reis. *Os Portugueses em Malaca (1511-1580)*. 2 vols. Tese de Licenciatura em Historia, Faculdade de Letras, Universidade de Lisboa, 1964.

Toby, Ronald P. "Reopening the Question of Sakoku" in *Journal of Japanese Studies* vol. 3, no. 2 (1977): 323-63,

Toyama Mikio. *Ōmura Sumitada*. Tokyo: Seisansha, 1981.

_____, Katō Akira, Nakano Takeshi, Shiozaki Hiroaki, and Katayose Toshihide. *Waga machi no rekishi: Nagasaki*. Tokyo: Bun'ichi Sōgō Shuppan, 1984.

_____. *Chūsei Kyūshū shakaishi no kenkyū*. Tokyo: Yoshikawa Kōbunkan, 1986.

_____. *Nagasaki bugyō: Edo bakufu no mimi to me*. Tokyo: Chūō Kōronsha (Chūō shinsho 905), 1988.

Trexler, Richard C. "De la ville à la Cour: La déraison à Florence durant la République et le Grand Duché" in Jacques Le Goff and Jean-Claude Schmitt. *Le Charivari. Actes de la table ronde organisée à Paris (25-27 avril 1977) par l'École des Hautes Études en Sciences Sociales et le Centre National de la Recherche Scientifique*. Paris: Mouton, 1981, pp. 165-76.

Tsang, Carol Richmond. *War and Faith: Ikkō Ikki in Late Muromachi Japan*. Cambridge: Harvard University Asia Center, 2007.

Tsūkō Ichiran, see Hayashi Akira and Miyazaki Shigemi.

Ushiki Yōko. "Bōeki toshi Nagasaki ni tsuite" in *RK* vol. 14, 11 (1966): 60-72.

Uwai Kakken. *Dai Nihon kiroku: Uwai Kakken nikki*. 3 vols. ed. Tōkyō daigaku shiryōhensanjo. Tokyo: Iwanami shoten, 1954-7.

Uyttenbroek, Thomas. *Early Franciscans in Japan*. Himeji: Committee of the Apostolate, 1958.

Valentijn, François. *Oud- en Nieuw Oost-Indien*. 5 vols. Dordrecht: Joannes van Braam / Amsterdam: Gerard Onder de Linden, 1724-6.

Van Opstall, Margaretha E. *De reis van de vloot van Pieter Willemsz Verhoeff naar Azië 1607-1612*. The Hague: Nijhoff, 1972.

Varones Ilustres, see Nieremberg, Juan Eusebio.

Vlam, Grace A.H. *Western Style Secular Painting in Momoyama Japan*. Ph.D. dissertation University of Michigan 1976.

Vocabulario da Lingoa de Iapam com a declaração em Portugues, feito por algvns padres, e irmãos da Companhia de Iesv. Nagasaki: Collegio de Iapam da Companhia de Iesus, 1603-04.

Von Glahn, Richard. *Fountain of Fortune. Money and Monetary Policy in China, 1000-1700*. Berkeley. Los Angeles: University of California Press, 1996.

Wang Gungwu. "Merchants Without Empire: The Hokkien Sojourning Communities" in James D. Tracy, ed. *The Rise of Merchant Empires: Long-Distance Trade in the Early Modern World, 1350-1750*. Cambridge: Cambridge University Press, 1990, pp. 400-421.

Wang Yong. "Realistic and Fantastic Images of 'Dwarf Pirates': The Evolution of Ming Dunasty Perceptions of the Japanese" in Joshua A. Fogel, ed. *Sagacious Monks and Bloodthirsty Warriors: Chinese Views of Japan in the Ming-Qing Period*. Norwalk, CT: Eastbridge, 2002, pp. 17-41.

Watanabe Kuranosuke. *Kiyō ronkō*. [Nagasaki:] Shinwa ginkō seibikai (Shinwa bunko no. 7), 1964.

Watanabe Yosuke. "Waga shiryō yori mitaru sengoku jidai tōzai kōshōshi" in Shigakkai, ed. *Tōzai kōshō-shiron*, vol. 1 Tokyo: Fuzanbō, 1939, pp. 421-72.

Watson, James L. "Standardizing the Gods: The Promotion of T'ien Hou ("Empress of Heaven") Along the South China Coast, 960-1960" in David Johnson, Andrew Nathan, Evelyn S. Rawski [eds.] *Popular Culture in Late Imperial China*. Berkeley: University of California Press, 1985, pp. 292-324.

Weiser, Francis X. *Handbook of Christian Feasts and Customs*. New York: Harcourt, Brace, 1952.

Werner, E.T.C. *A Dictionary of Chinese Mythology.* Shanghai: Kelly and Walsh, 1932.

Wicki, Joseph, ed. *Documenta Indica* IV (1557–1560). Rome: Monumenta Historica Societatis Iesu, 1956.

Wicki, Joseph. "Duas relações sobre a situação da Índia portuguesa nos anos 1568 e 1569" in *Studia,* no. 8 (1961): 133–220.

_____. "Toyotomi Hideyoshi in der "Historia de Japam" des P. Luís Fróis" in NZM vol. 40, 3 (1984): 206–20; 41, 4 (1985): 255–70.

Wieder, F.C. *De reis van Mahu en de Cordes door de straat van Magelhães naar Zuid-Amerika en Japan.* 3 vols. Werken Linschoten Vereniging XXI, XXII, XXIV. The Hague: Nijhoff, 1923–5.

Wiethoff, Bodo. *Die chinesische Seeverbotspolitik und der private Überseehandel von 1368 bis 1567.* Wiesbaden: Otto Harrassowitz, 1963.

_____. "Der staatliche Ma-tsu Kult" in *Zeitschrift der Deutschen morgenländischen Gesellschaft,* vol. 116 (1966): 311–57.

_____. *Chinas dritte Grenze. Der traditionelle chinesische Staat und der Küstennahe Seeraum.* Wiesbaden: Otto Harrassowitz, 1969.

Willeke, Bernard H. "Biographical Data on Early Franciscans in Japan (1582–1640)" in AFH, 83rd year, 1–2 (1990): 162–223.

Wills, John E. "Maritime China from Wang Chih to Shih Lang" in Jonathan D. Spence and John E. Wills, Jr. *From Ming to Ch'ing: Conquest, Region, and Continuity in Seventeenth Century China.* New Haven: Yale University Press, 1979, pp. 203–38.

Woolley, W.A. "Historical Notes on Nagasaki" in TASJ, vol. 9, pt. 2 (1881): 125–51.

Yamamoto, Hirofumi. *Sakoku to kaikin no jidai.* Tokyo: Azekura Shobō, 1995.

Yamamura Kozo, and Kamiki Tetsuo. "Silver Mines and Sung Coins—A Monetary History of Medieval and Modern Japan in International Perspective" in J.F. Richards, *Precious Metals in the Later Medieval and Early Modern Periods.* Durham, NC: Carolina Academic Press, 1983, pp. 329–62.

Yang, C.K. *Religion in Chinese Society.* Berkeley: University of California Press, 1967.

Yoshimura Kunio et al. *Deshima-machizukushi.* Nagasaki: Nagasaki bunkensha, 1986.

Yūki Ryōgo, see Pacheco Diego.

Zōho Nagasaki Ryakushi. Nagasaki shiyakusho, ed. in *Nagasaki Sōsho* vol. 3. Nagasaki: Fujiki Hakueisha, 1926.

Index

Page numbers in **bold italics** indicate pages with illustrations. When multiple notes that fall on the same page are indexed, they follow the order in which they appear on that page.